THE WORKS OF JONATHAN EDWARDS

VOLUME 10

Harry S. Stout, General Editor

A duodecimo sermon manuscript. Beinecke Rare Book and Manuscript Library, Yale University.

JONATHAN EDWARDS

Sermons and
Discourses
1720–1723

EDITED BY
WILSON H. KIMNACH

PROFESSOR OF ENGLISH
UNIVERSITY OF BRIDGEPORT

New Haven and London

YALE UNIVERSITY PRESS, 1992

Funds for editing The Works of Jonathan Edwards
*have been provided by the Pew Charitable Trusts and the
Lilly Endowment.*

*Published with assistance from the Exxon Education
Foundation. Publication of this volume was also assisted
by a grant from the Edwards Church of Northampton,
Massachusetts.*

*Printed in the United States of America by
Vail-Ballou Press, Binghamton, New York*

Library of Congress Cataloging-in-Publication Data

Edwards, Jonathan, 1703–1758.
  *Sermons and discourses, 1720–1723 / Jonathan
Edwards ; edited by Wilson H. Kimnach.*
    p.   cm. — (The works of Jonathan Edwards ; v. 10)
  Includes bibliographical references and index.
    ISBN 0–300–05136–0 (alk. paper)
    1. Congregational churches—Sermons.
*2. Sermons, American.   3. Preaching—United
States—History—18th century.   I. Kimnach,
Wilson H.   II. Title.   III. Series: Edwards, Jonathan,
1703–1758. Works. 1957 ; v. 10.*
BX7117.E3 1957 vol. 10
[BX7233.E3]
285.8 s—dc20
[252'.058]   *91–37582*
                                              CIP

*A catalogue record for this book is available from the
British Library.*

*The paper in this book meets the guidelines for permanence
and durability of the Committee on Production Guidelines
for Book Longevity of the Council on Library Resources.*

10   9   8   7   6   5   4   3   2

EDITORIAL COMMITTEE FOR
THE WORKS OF JONATHAN EDWARDS

CONTENTS

LIST OF ILLUSTRATIONS

NOTE TO THE READER

Preparation of the Text

The text of Jonathan Edwards is reproduced in this Edition as he wrote it in manuscript, or if he published it himself, as it was printed in the first edition. In order to present this text to modern readers as practically readable, several technical adjustments have been made. Those which can be addressed categorically are as follows:

1. All spelling is regularized and conformed to that of *Webster's Third New International Dictionary,* a step that does not involve much more than removing the "u" from "colour" or "k" from "publick" since Edwards was a good speller, used relatively modern spelling, and generally avoided "y" contractions. His orthographic contractions and abbreviations, such as ampersands, "call'd," and "thems." are spelled out, though pronounced contractions, such as "han't" and "ben't," are retained.

2. There is no regular punctuation in most of Edwards' manuscripts and where it does exist, as in the earliest sermons, it tends to be highly erratic. Editors take into account Edwards' example in punctuation and related matters, but all punctuation is necessarily that of the editor, including paragraph divisions (especially in some notebooks, such as the "Miscellanies") and the emphasizing devices of italics and capitalization. In reference to capitalization, it should be noted that pronouns referring to the deity are lower case except in passages where Edwards confusingly mixes "he's" referring to God and man: here capitalization of pronouns referring to the deity sorts out the references for the reader.

3. Numbered heads designate important structures of argument in Edwards' sermons, notebooks, and treatises. Numbering, including spelled-out numbers, has been regularized and corrected where necessary. Particularly in the manuscript sermon texts, numbering has been clarified by the use of systematic schemes of heads and subheads

in accordance with eighteenth-century homiletical form, a practice similar to modern analytical outline form. Thus the series of subordinated head number forms, 1, (1), *1*, a, (a), in the textual exegesis, and the series, I, *First*, 1, (1), *1*, a, (a), in Doctrine and Application divisions, make it possible to determine sermon head relationships at a glance.

4. Textual intervention to regularize Edwards' citation of Scripture includes the correction of erroneous citation, the regularizing of citation form (including the standardization of book abbreviations), and the completion of quotations which Edwards' textual markings indicate should be completed (as in preaching).

5. Omissions and lacunae in the manuscript text are filled by insertions in square brackets ([ ]); repeated phrases sometimes represented by Edwards with a long dash are inserted in curly brackets ({ }). In all cases of uncertain readings, annotation gives notice of the problem. Markings in the text designate whole word units even when only a few letters are at issue.

6. Minor slips of the pen or obvious typographical errors are corrected without annotation. Likewise, Edwards' corrections, deletions, and internal shifts of material are observed but not noted unless of substantive interest.

7. Quotations made by the editor from the Bible (AV) and other secondary sources are printed *verbatim ac literatim.* Edwards' quotations from such sources are often rather free but are not corrected and are not annotated as such unless significant omissions or distortions are involved.

Other conditions of textual preparation are related to differences of genre and factors unique to particular texts or manuscripts. For information on such matters please consult the note on the text in each volume within the Edition.

Sermons and Discourses

The General Introduction is concerned with the creative process: the activity of literary expression, its context, and its vehicles. All speakers and writers state ideas; but some express their conceptions so that generations are responsive to their expression, other authors imitate them, and in significant ways they reshape the very language they use. If they do nothing else, such persons are known as poets or literary artists; otherwise, they are known by their occupations as politicians, preachers, teachers, journalists, and so forth. But the Gettysburg Address, Martin Luther King's "I have a dream" address, and Samuel Sewall's apostrophe to Plum Island, to name three effusions of very different times, tastes, and occasions, nevertheless express their immanent principles with a power that far transcends the occasion of composition and even the originality of the principles expressed. These magnificent gestures in language do not occur merely as a result of passion, learning, or faith, or there would be many more such statements than there are. Rather, they are made by talented persons who work diligently and imaginatively at the business of expression, persons for whom the practical implementation of language is profoundly engrossing in itself, and who define themselves in the very process of expression.

Jonathan Edwards was one of these persons, and through the care of disciples and descendants we are possessed of the detailed record of his process of expression. After theology, Edwards thought most about expression: what language is, how it operates on the mind, and how its resources might be variously exploited. Like all of Christ's ambassadors, Edwards participated in a particular cultural discourse in a particular time and place. The literary culture of English protestantism and of New England in the seventeenth century dictated the context of his work, though as a seeker, literary as well as theological, he pursued innumerable leads from reading and the contemporary cultural milieu that promised means of improving his evangelizing. The one literary genre he mastered was the sermon, and his major works—excepting his personal narrative—are all sermons or amplifications of the sermon form, as in the major treatises. Thus the sermon provided the vehicle of his characteristic expression and defined its limitations.

Readers of this introduction who wish to begin with the practice of composition can turn directly to the second and third chapters, "The Making of Sermons" and "The Sermon Canon." The first chapter treats of the literary context of Edwards' work, while the concluding chapter presents the larger theoretical and practical dimensions of Edwards' homiletics. The excerpts from Edwards' manuscripts quoted in illustration of his creative process have been prepared for the reader but have not been edited as the full texts in the edition in order to preserve, as much as possible, the character of his manuscripts for this demonstration.

The period preface, sermon headnotes, and footnotes provide in this and succeeding sermon volumes the occasional and biographical contexts for the sermons. The Preface attempts a synthesis which is intended to provide a coherent biographical context for the sermons included in the volume, while headnotes permit detailed comments upon various aspects of particular sermons and related texts.

Sermon texts in this volume are not only early and thus revealing of theological and homiletical foundations hitherto concealed from the public, but they were revised and repreached by Edwards repeatedly during the years between their composition and his first year or so in Northampton. In light of these factors, the sermons have been printed as originally written while significant later modifications and additions have been published in textual footnotes and appendices to individual sermons.

Acknowledgments

In a project of several years' duration debts to persons and institutions become alarmingly extensive, and it seems inevitable that some will be inadequately acknowledged or omitted altogether. Of the eminently unforgettable debts is that owed Thomas A. Schafer of McCormick Theological Seminary whose learning and instruction shaped the entire project of sermon publication. First as my tutor in the study of Edwards' manuscripts and subsequently as partner in research over a period of years, he has inspired the highest scholarly standards and pioneered techniques of manuscript analysis. Also helpful in the early stages of the project were John Gerstner of Pittsburgh-Xenia Theological Seminary and Wallace E. Anderson of the Ohio State University who contributed to the transcription and analysis of the early Edwards manuscripts. As I assumed responsibility for the sermon publication project, I was guided and greatly aided by consultation with John E. Smith, Sydney E. Ahlstrom, and Edmund S. Morgan of Yale University, and Paul Ramsey of Princeton University.

Having conceived of a worthy project, one soon discovers that scholarship, like the army, travels on its stomach. It is therefore with deep gratitude that I acknowledge my considerable material debts to the National Endowment for the Humanities for an initiating editorial grant, and to the Lilly Endowment and the Ellis L. Phillips Foundation for crucial matching funds. More recently monies from the Pew Charitable Trust have greatly facilitated the final preparation of this first sermon volume, as the Exxon Foundation has subsidized its publication. In a similar vein is my debt to the Center of Theological Inquiry in Princeton which provided me with a nine-month residential membership during which I was able to work on the broader issues of interpretation and, at the other extreme, compile the Edition Editorial Manual. The University of Bridgeport also contributed to that year by arranging my leave with partial financial support. Money is time.

During the years of my labor on Edwards' manuscripts, most of the work has been accomplished in the Beinecke Rare Book and Manuscript Library of Yale University where the staff has been unvaryingly helpful and supportive of my work. Of early and thus crucial help were Marjorie Wynne and Suzanne Rutter; a significant contribution was also made to the Edition by Librarian Louis Martz when he provided our first permanent workroom. The Sterling Memorial Library at Yale, the Firestone Library at Princeton University, the Trask Library of Andover Theological School, and the Speer Library of Princeton Theological Seminary have also provided materials and service indispensable to the preparation of this volume.

As my work assumed final form, I was greatly aided by the incisive and yet truly appreciative readings of the text by John E. Smith, Stephen J. Stein of Indiana University, and John F. Wilson of Princeton University. In a different technical area, Teresa Cerillo and Kenneth P. Minkema expertly brought my typescript into the computer age, while Lori Fast-Minkema photographically recorded Jonathan Edwards' medium for the volume frontispiece. Finally, Judith Calvert, James Mooney, and Susan Laity of Yale University Press have guided the volume through its final stages of publication.

Throughout the years devoted to the planning and execution of an edition of Edwards' sermons and discourses, my principal editorial colleague has been Carole S. Kimnach, who has spent incalculable hours verifying transcriptions, typing proposals, editing the editor, and in fact typing this volume, most of it more than once. Meanwhile, she provided our own Jonathan and Sarah who have grown up, as children do, while their father fussed obscurely in his study. With so many helping hands and such devotion, I cannot be but hopeful that my work will prove useful.

Wilson H. Kimnach

Woodbridge, Conn.
October 1991

GENERAL INTRODUCTION TO THE SERMONS:
JONATHAN EDWARDS' ART OF PROPHESYING

CHAPTER I
EDWARDS' LITERARY MILIEU

Although the reputation of Jonathan Edwards is appropriately multi-faceted and he is deservedly recognized as a theologian, philosopher, and pioneering psychologist, the popular conception of him as a preacher is essentially correct. For in the perspective of his life and works, his career in the pulpit and the attendant body of sermons he produced constitute the hub of his diverse interests and activities. All things, like so many spokes of a wheel, met and were structured through their use in the sermons. A notebook meditation, a brief dissertation, or a lengthy treatise may constitute the fullest elaboration or best definition of one aspect of Edwards' thought, but only in the sermons are the many diverse aspects of his thought and life synthesized and artistically harmonized in works of literary art.

Edwards lived in a time when, despite all the changes that had taken place in New England since the days of the Puritans, the ministry was still the fit place for a man who wished to lead the "life of the mind," and the sermon was still the common literary vehicle for the best fruits of his thought. The sermon of Edwards' day was at the height of its formal development and combined intellectual substance, artistic form, and popular currency in a distinctive amalgam rarely equalled by a single literary form in the subsequent history of American literature. Moreover, particularly in country villages such as East Windsor, Connecticut, the sermon held the cultural field of the community, if only by default, as the minister was the voice of authority in most community affairs.

1. Early Experiences and Formal Education

As son of the village parson, the young Edwards was reared in the ecclesiastical-academic atmosphere of a home where sermons were always in the making and neighborhood youths were prepared for college.[1] His father was both the most learned and the most important man he knew, and the rhetoric of his father's preached sermons must have constituted the chief literary fare of his youth, along with the reading of the Scripture at home. His own narrative of religious experiences tells of his having played at religion in "a booth in a swamp," where he and some schoolmates retired for prayer,[2] and though there is no mention of it, one wonders if the mawkishly zealous preacher's son must not have attempted an impromptu *sermo* on at least a few occasions. At any rate, he was "abundant in duties" and early entered the "element" where he was to live out his days.

The early education of Edwards was of course first in the home, at his mother's knee and, later, at his father's tutoring school. There his education was focused, directly and indirectly, by the curriculum of Harvard College in the late seventeenth century. His mother's father, Solomon Stoddard, had been graduated from Harvard in 1662, his father in 1691, and the intellectually vital household must have been dominated by the cultural aura of the college, though removed many miles in space and more than a generation in time. And when, at the age of twelve, Edwards entered the infant Yale College, he was again placed under the tutelage of Harvard men. This suggests that Edwards was early exposed to the Latin classics, but had slight contact with modern belles lettres, that his studies in rhetoric were dominated by the philosophy of Peter Ramus, probably in the form of William Dugard's textbook, *Rhetorices Elementa*,[3] and that his formal education

1. Still the most solid and thoroughly documented study of JE's early years is John A. Stoughton's *Windsor Farmes, A Glimpse of an Old Parish* (Hartford, 1883). Stoughton focuses his study on Timothy Edwards, JE's father, and makes much use of his manuscript account-book and other personal or domestic documents, thus giving an informative picture of JE's childhood environment.

2. According to the "Personal Narrative" published by Samuel Hopkins in *The Life and Character of the Late Reverend Mr. Jonathan Edwards, President of the College at New Jersey* (Boston, 1765), p. 23.

3. I have been unable to locate, positively, the rhetoric text used in the Yale College of JE's day. Porter Gale Perrin, in his dissertation, "The Teaching of Rhetoric in the American Colleges before 1750" (Univ. of Chicago, 1936), lists Dugard and Talon's *Rhetorica* as "the two texts certainly used at Harvard and Yale" (ch. III, 77–78), though in the final analysis, he is unable to identify a "standard" or required rhetoric text at Yale in this period. Cotton Mather, writing his *Manuductio ad Ministerium* ca. 1725, refers in an off-hand way to "your Dugard . . . at School," suggesting that the Dugard reduction was as close as any text to being "standard" in the early years of the eighteenth century.

For a discussion of academic rhetoric and its relation to preaching in this period (and earlier), see Perry Miller's *The New England Mind, The Seventeenth Century* (2nd ed., Boston, Beacon Press, 1961), chs. XI and XII; and *The New England Mind, From Colony to Province*

was ultimately directed to the Ramistic high ritual of the senior thesis, a logical and rhetorical tour de force in an exceedingly formal and artificial manner in Latin.

A superior student, Edwards was selected to deliver the valedictory oration at his graduation. But what is remarkable about his undergraduate education is the lack of a distinct impression, for none of his letters home, nor his adult writings that reflect on his youth, nor even the anecdotes scraped together by his biographers suggest that Edwards was undergoing a vital educational experience in the formal course of studies. The account of his reading Locke's *Essay* and his request for the *Art of Thinking* have the color of isolated events in his private intellectual life that stand out against the uniform gray background (not necessarily unpleasant) of his collegiate program.[4] Edwards' intellectual pilgrimage seems always to have been an essentially solitary venture. The thoughts, books, and curricula of other men and institutions might be presented to him, but in the end he would educate himself; he was never desperate to rebel nor fond of innovation for its own sake, but he would unostentatiously select and reject, from the old and the new, according to some principle of personal taste.

Although it is difficult and not always rewarding to attempt tracing influences upon a writer as restless, creative, and eclectic as Edwards, there are nevertheless some authors who have been accorded great attention because of their supposed intellectual influence upon him, for instance, John Locke and Nicholas Malebranche. Perry Miller focused upon Locke a generation ago and more recently Norman Fiering has argued for the contrary influence of Malebranche, debating whether Edwards' outlook is more akin to English empiricism or Continental rationalism.[5] In matters of rhetoric as in ideas, there are elements in Edwards' vocabulary that may be identified as belonging to more than one faction or party, not to mention one person.

(Boston, Beacon Press, 1961), ch. XXV, the last selection calling attention to the changing attitude, in JE's time, toward the old Ramean formulations of rhetoric and logic.

4. The account of JE's reading Locke is given on p. 30, and the letter (1719) in which JE asks his father to send him the logic text is reprinted on pp. 31–32, in Sereno E. Dwight's *Life of President Edwards*, volume I of the ten-volume edition of *The Works of President Edwards*, edited by S. E. Dwight (New York, 1829–30). (Dwight's biography will be cited hereinafter as Dwight, *Life*, and the edition's text volumes as Dwight, ed., *Works*.)

5. Their essential discussions are presented in Miller's biography, *Jonathan Edwards* (New York, William Sloan Associates, 1949), and in Fiering's study, *Jonathan Edwards' Moral Thought and Its British Context* (Chapel Hill, Univ. of North Carolina Press, 1981).

A "divine light" or a "sense of the heart" are common property of traditional Puritans, Pietists, Cambridge Platonists, secular moralists, and others, though each faction may attach radically different significations to such terms (as in the use of "people" in modern political rhetoric). But a common rhetorical vocabulary, especially when the terms are distributed among several discrete arguments, may well be taken to represent traces of influence. In this connection, there is hardly a more interesting case than that of the possible rhetorical influence of the Cambridge Platonist, John Smith (1618–52).[6] Cited and quoted at extraordinary length by Edwards in *A Treatise Concerning Religious Affections,* Smith's expression of crucial concepts clearly appealed to Edwards.[7] Although Smith's only publication, the posthumous *Select Discourses,* is mentioned in Edwards' "Catalogue" of books, the reference is little more than a perfunctory listing in a series of books recommended by a source book and reveals nothing of Edwards, not even whether or not he was already familiar with the book. It is certain, however, that Edwards had access to the book at a crucial period in his development, for a copy of the second edition was given to Yale College by "Mr. Newton" in 1714, presumably as part of the five-hundred-volume Dummer collection, and is still there. Thus Edwards could have read the book during his senior year in New Haven or during the two succeeding years of graduate study prior to his pastorate in New York.

Any reader familiar with Edwards' idiom, and in particular with certain controlling images and metaphors from a wide variety of his writings, must be struck by the similarities of concept, terminology, and phrasing in the small volume of John Smith's printed writings. Thus the idea of God's communicating himself *ad extra* in the creation and that of his containing the creation within himself anticipate Edwards' meditations, from the early philosophical speculations to the

6. Entering Emmanuel College as a pensioner in 1636, Smith was there a student of Benjamin Whichcote, spiritual leader of the group eventually known as the Cambridge Platonists, including Henry More (1614–87) and Ralph Cudworth (1617–88) who also appealed greatly to JE. Smith was not a divine but rather a philosopher and subsequently a teacher of mathematics in Queens College. A particular friend of Henry More, Smith was known as a "walking library" who also embodied warm-hearted humanity and true Christian humility. He died of consumption at the age of thirty-five without having published or otherwise engaged the world beyond his academic close.

7. The passage differentiating "carnal Affections" from true spiritual elevation is over a page in length, but JE "cannot forbear transcribing the whole" of this "remarkable passage." See *A Treatise Concerning Religious Affections,* ed. John E. Smith, in *The Works of Jonathan Edwards* (New Haven, Yale Univ. Press, 1959), 2, 217–19n.

late *End of Creation*. And then the idea that sin weighs men down as lead, pulling them to hell "with the most swift and headlong motion" certainly encapsulates the central metaphor of *Sinners in the Hands of an Angry God*. Likewise, the spider as an emblem of the sinner appears in another Smith discourse. There are indeed seemingly endless echoes, from the need of the saint to become nothing in himself, to God's manifesting himself "in clear and lovely stamps" through the creation,[8] to the reflection that man can be truly deified through union with God in *Affections, Will,* and *End.*

But such echoes, however striking in themselves, are of considerably less significance for both Smith and Edwards than a broad range of verbal correlations pertaining to the definition of religion itself. Here, whether one identifies the language with Cambridge Platonism or with the New Light sensibility of eighteenth-century New England, the rhetorical correlations between Smith and Edwards are so suggestive, even when not so strict and literal, as to constitute an intricate structure of allusive filaments. A glance at some of Smith's dicta will indicate the outlines of this relationship.

First, Smith insists that the Gospel covenant differs from the old Law in that whereas the Law was *external,* the Gospel is *internal.*[9] The Law involved a communal ideology first; the Gospel begins in a subjective experience. Or put another way, Smith observes that the ancient Hebrews invented the concept of free will as a compensation for failed religious inspiration,[1] as moderns who preach merit are cold, illiberal, servile, slavish, and do not love God.[2] So much for Arminianism, old and new! On the other hand, the true Christian finds God through exploration of his own soul wherein he may find the divine reflected in personal perceptions of virtue.[3] This is possible because God visits saints as a "Divine Efflux running quite through our Souls," as "an inward feeling and sensation."[4] In fact, "Divine

---

8. "Stamp" is probably the most accurate English equivalent of the Greek *typos* which indicates the mark left by a blow, as a seal-ring leaves its impression on the wax seal. Smith's depth in classical philosophy is impressive throughout his writings.

9. John Smith, "A Discourse Treating of Legal Righteousness, Evangelical Righteousness . . ." in *Select Discourses,* ed. J. Worthington (1660; 2nd ed., London, 1673), p. 303.

1. Smith, "Evangelical Righteousness," p. 284.

2. Smith, "A Discovery of the Shortness and Vanity of a Pharisaick Righteousness . . . ," *Discourses,* pp. 354–58.

3. Smith, "A Discourse Demonstrating the Immortality of the Soul," *Discourses,* p. 57.

4. Smith, "A Discourse Concerning the Existence and Nature of God," *Discourses,* p. 143.

Truth is not to be discerned so much in a mans *Brain*, as in his *Heart*.
. . . There is a Divine and Spiritual sense which only is able to converse
internally with the life and soul of Divine Truth, as mixing and uniting it self with it . . ."[5] Thus, "the true Metaphysical and Contempla-
tive man . . . shooting up above his own . . . *Self-rational* life . . .
endeavours the nearest Union with the Divine Essence that may
be. . . . This Divine Knowledge . . . makes us amorous of Divine
beauty . . . and this *Divine Love and Purity* reciprocally exalts *Divine
Knowledge*. . ."[6] All of religion is then a kind of supernatural, natural
process: no artifice or construct of men, though at bottom wholly
consonant with reason which is, after all, but "a Beam of Divine
light."[7]

Smith is led to conclude that "were I indeed to define *Divinity*, I
should rather call it a *Divine life*, than a *Divine science*; it being something rather to be understood by a *Spiritual sensation*, then by any
Verbal description, as all things of Sense of Life are best known by
Sentient and Vital faculties . . ."[8] And without such a "living sense"
of the attributes of true religion, one can no more be informed of
them "by a naked Demonstration, then Colours can be perceived of
a blind man by any Definition or Description which he can hear of
them."[9] However, "when *Reason* once is raised by the mighty force of
the Divine Spirit into a converse with God, it is turned into *Sense*:
That which before was only *Faith* well built upon sure Principles, (for
such our *Science* may be) now becomes *Vision*."[1] And the result of this
spiritual transformation is nothing less than "*a new Nature* informing
the Souls of men; it is *a God-like frame of Spirit*, discovering it self most
of all *in Serene and Clear Minds, in deep Humility, Meekness, Self-denial,
Universal love of God and all true Goodness, without Partiality and without
Hypocrisie*; whereby we are taught to *know* God, and knowing him to
love him, and *conform* our selves as much as may be to all that Perfection which shines forth in him."[2]

"Being's consent to Being," the revelation of God's grandeur as
recounted in the "Personal Narrative," the early meditation upon the

5. Smith, "Evangelical Righteousness," p. 278.
6. Smith, "Of the true Way or Method of attaining to Divine Knowledge," *Discourses*,
p. 20.
7. Smith, "The Excellency and Nobleness of True Religion," *Discourses*, p. 378.
8. Smith, "Divine Knowledge," pp. 1–2.
9. Ibid., p. 15.
1. Ibid., p. 16.
2. Smith, "Pharisaick Righteousness," p. 364.

character of Sarah Pierrepont, or the late arguments relating to the nature of "true virtue": so much of Edwards' characteristic idiom, not to mention much of his overall intellectual agenda, is adumbrated in these *Discourses* by John Smith that it is impossible not to acknowledge the formative impact of the volume upon Edwards early in his career. This is not to say that Edwards did not make more "use" of other authors in his many studies; for instance, Smith's esteemed colleague, Henry More, has been shown to be one of the Cambridge Platonists most useful to Edwards, yet More's *idiom* is not generally suggestive of Edwards.[3] Edwards took intellectual building materials from various authors as he needed them and reacted to particular ideas or theories from a wide variety of sources in developing his own concepts; however, in no case is there such a broad correlation of style, particularly of metaphor and symbol, as between Smith and Edwards. This is not to say that Edwards became a stylistic disciple of Smith, for if nothing else, a gulf of culture and sensibility separated the two writers: Smith is by comparison subtle, fluid, and organically structured in thought and argument, his penchant for biological-process metaphors revelatory of the latitudinarian cast of his mind; Edwards is the more architectonic, dichotomous, and abstract in the development of his thought, his preference for physical-process metaphors involving antithetical forces being reflective of the traditional Puritan sermon form as well as Calvinist doctrine. But such differences do not preclude influence of a profound and pervasive nature; rather, they highlight both the creative receptivity of Edwards and an artistic independence which resulted from his trust in the adequacy of the Scripture to all human reflection, and his reliance upon the vital homiletic tradition of New England.

If the youthful Edwards took nothing more from the Cambridge Platonist than the notion that the operations of the mind (spirit) and the senses are wholly analogous,[4] it must have prepared him for his curiously mediatorial role between such theoretical opposites as idealism and empiricism, or rationalism and sensationalism, which has occasioned much debate among both his immediate clerical followers and later scholarly interpreters.

Against the background of seventeenth-century culture and edu-

3. Wallace E. Anderson has demonstrated the importance of Henry More for the young JE in his introduction and notes to the *Scientific and Philosophical Writings, The Works of Jonathan Edwards* (New Haven, Yale Univ. Press, 1980), 6.

4. Smith, "True Religion," p. 405.

cational forms, then, Edwards gradually awakened to his call to the ministry and the art of preaching. When he undertook preparation for the pulpit, he began by assimilating a rich tradition of English pulpit oratory and sermon literature. This tradition, deriving ultimately from the conventions of the English Puritan pulpit,[5] had been shaped by a century of development in New England and the literary productions of many eminent preachers.[6] Of course, the student preacher, if he wanted a full discussion of the theory of the Puritan sermon form, could go to one or more of the several studies of the art of preaching then in circulation: the classic, *The Arte of Prophecying* by William Perkins, or William Chappell's *The Preacher,* Richard Bernard's *The Faithful Shepheard,* or John Wilkins' *Ecclesiastes.* Since he was always a careful scholar, it is probable that Edwards did study at least one. But it would not have been necessary for him to study the art of "prophecying" abstractly, for the tradition of New England pulpit oratory was very much alive in Edwards' day; moreover, it was embodied in the very person of Timothy Edwards. The youth whose extraordinary powers of observation and analysis are illustrated in "Of Insects" would hardly have to go to a textbook in order to learn about sermon form after having sat all his life beneath his father's pulpit.

2. Two Exemplary Preachers

Perhaps the two most important influences upon Edwards' preaching style were his father and his maternal grandfather, Timothy Ed-

5. Still the best discussion of the English Puritan pulpit tradition, including full comparisons between the Puritan, Anglican, and Anglo-Catholic sermon styles (among others), is W. Fraser Mitchell's *English Pulpit Oratory from Andrewes to Tillotson* (London, 1932).

6. For an extensive discussion and analysis of the literary dimension of the New England pulpit in the seventeenth century, see Babette M. Levy's *Preaching in the First Half Century of New England History* (Hartford, American Soc. of Church History, 1945). Her work has been significantly supplemented by Robert M. Benton's "The American Puritan Sermon before 1700" (Ph.D. diss., Univ. of Colorado, 1967). Of related interest are critical editions such as A. W. Plumstead, ed., *The Wall and the Garden: Selected Massachusetts Election Sermons, 1670–1775* (Minneapolis, Univ. of Minnesota Press, 1968) and Phyllis M. and Nicholas R. Jones, ed., *Salvation in New England: Selections from the Sermons of the First Preachers* (Austin, Univ. of Texas Press, 1977). Monographs that address the larger context of the pulpit are David D. Hall, *The Faithful Shepherd: A History of the New England Ministry in the Seventeenth Century* (Chapel Hill, Univ. of North Carolina Press, 1972); Emory Elliott, *Power and the Pulpit in Puritan New England* (Princeton, Princeton Univ. Press, 1975), and Harry S. Stout, *The New England Soul: Preaching and Religious Culture in Colonial New England* (New York, Oxford Univ. Press, 1986).

wards and Solomon Stoddard, the former as a living exemplar of the preacher during his son's formative years, the latter as a master preacher to the young journeyman who shared his Northampton pulpit from 1726 to 1729. Edwards doubtless received his fundamental conception of the sermon form from his father, though Stoddard, a published critic of preaching, would certainly have suggested some master strokes to the preacher who was still developing his distinctive voice in the mid-1720s.

Timothy Edwards was a powerful and successful preacher, by all accounts,[7] although his extant sermons reveal him to have been a rather pedestrian, if intelligent and correct, writer. The form illustrated in his one published sermon[8] and in the four manuscript sermons transcribed by Stoughton in *Windsor Farmes*,[9] is a conservative form (at least, for the late seventeenth century), having the three basic divisions of Text, Doctrine, and Application, each developed through a succession of brief, numbered heads. In a sermon of moderate length on Is. 26:9,[1] Timothy Edwards employs no fewer than twenty-three numbered heads in the Doctrine and forty-four in the Application; moreover, many of these heads (averaging less than one hundred words each) contain numbered subheads within them. One does not move far without a "2dly" or a "3dly." The argument is abstract and unencumbered by imagery or metaphor; it is heavily laden with Scripture citations; the language is so "plain" as to be almost unnoticeable; the tone is forthright and serious, and the most obvious source of vitality is the frequent explicit references to men and events in the town. On the whole, it is a Puritan's Puritan form, and what it lacks in imagination and beauty in the superstructure, it makes up

7. In discussing the revivals of 1735–36, Benjamin Trumbull remarks that "No minister in the colony had been favoured with greater success than [Timothy Edwards], and now . . . his spirit was greatly refreshed by an extraordinary ingathering of souls unto Christ . . ." (*History of Connecticut* [New Haven, 1818], 2, 140).

8. *All the Living Must Surely Die, and Go to Judgment* (New London, 1732), an election sermon delivered before the General Assembly of Connecticut at Hartford, May 11, 1732.

9. They are printed together at the back of the volume, pp. 121–45. These sermons, plus several other manuscript sermons in the Edwards family collection at the Beinecke Rare Book and Manuscript Library, Yale University, would tend to qualify, if not refute, the statement of Dwight (*Life*, p. 17) that Timothy Edwards "always preached extemporaneously, and, until he was upwards of seventy, without noting down the heads of his discourse." The four sermons printed by Stoughton are dated 1694, 1709, 1712, and 1741—only the last coming from Timothy Edwards' later years—and all four appear to be about eighty percent written out. It would seem that Timothy preached *memoriter* rather than *extempore*, if Dwight is not simply in error.

1. *Windsor Farmes*, pp. 121–32.

in the solidity of its foundation. The young Edwards could have done worse than sit beneath his father's pulpit if he wanted to learn the fundamentals of the traditional sermon form, for the classic Perkinsean virtues are embodied in the sermons preached there, without adulteration through imaginative innovation.

Solomon Stoddard was probably the greatest man Edwards had ever met in his youth, and family pieties would have enhanced the vision, so that his going up to Northampton to serve in the pulpit with Stoddard must have been one of those nearly traumatic experiences that force the final posture from rapidly maturing youth. Stoddard was one of the great preachers of the latter days of the Massachusetts theocracy, and it was largely because of his efforts in pulpit and ecclesiastical politics that the atmosphere of theocracy lingered a little longer in the Connecticut valley than in the East. "Pope Stoddard," as he was only half-irreverently called, preached in the grand manner. Of course, the outward form of his sermons is the same as that employed by Timothy Edwards, the only notable difference being a reduced number of heads and subheads, allowing for fuller development within each head. Still, in comparison with the sermons of Jonathan Edwards, those of Stoddard are heavily structured and formally conservative.

Within the formal structure, however, Stoddard ranged freely with a stylistic posture of sublime confidence. He infused the "plain style" with a strong tincture of his own personality and, being gifted with a capacity for pungent, epigrammatic expression, he created, without relying extensively on the graces of imagery and metaphor, a colloquial idiom that is still vital. One of his favorite devices is the question-answer head, which he is apt to employ in any (or all) of the main divisions of the sermon. In Stoddard's hands, this conventional device, which could easily be the most dull and pedantic of strategies, becomes a potent rhetorical tool. He speaks with the magisterial abruptness of a professor before a group of admiring students, holding the spirit of inquiry within the confines of pedagogical drill. The very momentum of successive answers to the stated question carries the minds of the auditors from stage to stage of the argument, while the simple device of the rhetorical question is manipulated to yield an impressive forensic power.

> 3. Q. On what Terms doth God offer Deliverance from this Captivity?

A. 1. Not upon the Condition of their laying down the Price of their Deliverance . . .

2. Nor upon Condition of their Recompencing God for it afterwards . . .

3. But on Condition of accepting it as a free Gift through Christ . . .[2]

A substantial portion of the argument is so structured, not by logic but by the pattern of rhetoric; however, a series of assertions structured in such a question-answer pattern has some of the inevitability of logic. Very often, moreover, the conclusion or statement of thesis in a head is vigorously propounded in an aphoristic climax, corresponding in tone to the conclusion of a syllogistic demonstration:

If they were thoroughly scared, they would be more earnest in their Endeavours; Senselessness begets Slightiness.

The Pretense that they make for their Dullness, is, that they are afraid there is no Hope for them . . . but the true Reason is not that they want Hope, but they want Fears.[3]

Such expressions are not soon forgotten. Moreover, Stoddard could, and did, utilize imagery and metaphors with real art when he was so moved:

But if they were afraid of Hell, they would be afraid of Sin. When their Lusts were as Spurs to stir them up to Sin, this fear would be as a Bridle to curb them in.[4]

. . . their hearts be as hard as a stone, as hard as a piece of the nether milstone, and they will be ready to laugh at the shaking of the Spear.[5]

Men need to be terrified and have the arrows of the Almighty in them that they may be Converted.[6]

Nor is his handling of rhetorical repetition unworthy of mention.

They may have a large understanding of the Gospel, yet not be set at Liberty by it. Men may be affected with it, yet not be set at

2. Solomon Stoddard, *The Benefit of the Gospel, to those that are Wounded in Spirit* (Boston, 1713), pp. 116–17.

3. Ibid., p. 181.

4. Stoddard, *The Efficacy of the Fear of Hell to Restrain Men from Sin* (Boston, 1713), p. 5.

5. Stoddard, *The Defects of Preachers Reproved* (Boston, 1724), p. 13.

6. Ibid., p. 14.

Liberty by it. Men may be stirred up to reform their Lives, yet not be set at Liberty. There be but a few comparatively that are set at Liberty by it, therefore examine.[7]

On the whole, Solomon Stoddard was a formally orthodox, but unusually powerful and even pontifical preacher; he was a master of the controlled tone and went beyond clarity, precision, and sincerity without losing them on his way.

In addition to being an excellent example of the late Puritan preacher himself, Stoddard was a critic of preaching and a theorist in the "art of prophecying." Thus, in 1724, he published *The Defects of Preachers Reproved,* a sermon which elucidates the paradoxical doctrine, "There may be a great deal of good Preaching in a Country, and yet a great want of Good preaching." What we find in this sermon is an equation of good preaching with revival preaching, an insistence upon the minister's preaching from personal experience rather than from a mere theoretical understanding, and a fervent advocacy of "hellfire" preaching.

> When men don't Preach much about the danger of Damnation, there is want of good Preaching.
>
> Men need to be terrified and have the arrows of the Almighty in them that they may be Converted. Ministers should be Sons of Thunder. . . .[8]

He urges preachers to deal "roundly" with their congregations and "rebuke sharply" those who need reproof. Finally, he defends the sermon as he preached it from the accusations of a new faction arising in the East:

> It may be argued, that it is harder to remember Rhetorical Sermons, than meer Rational Discourses; but it may be Answered, that it is far more Profitable to Preach in the Demonstration of the Spirit, than with the enticing Words of man's wisdom.[9]

"Rational Christianity" and the essay-sermon may have been flowing with the tides into Boston harbor at the beginning of the eighteenth century, but they would not progress to the Connecticut valley if Solomon Stoddard could help it. The old Puritan sermon retained

7. *Benefit,* pp. 175–76.
8. *Defects,* pp. 13–14.
9. Ibid., pp. 24–25.

the outward form of logic, but in the hands of Stoddard and his predecessors it had become a finely tuned instrument of psychological manipulation, and Stoddard was not about to trade it for what he saw as a psychologically superficial and intellectually simplistic, though stylish, mode of discourse. For Stoddard, "rhetoric" was power.

That Solomon Stoddard, through his pedagogical presence, his writings, and his example, generally made a tremendous impression on Edwards is beyond doubt. For without really deviating from the sermon form that Timothy Edwards employed, Stoddard discovered hidden rhetorical resources in the "plain style" by insisting upon the evaluation of rhetoric in psychological terms that were more comprehensive and subtle than either the old Ramean logic or the new Reason. Certainly, Edwards grappled for most of his life with rhetorical and artistic issues—not to mention the ecclesiastical ones—that were prompted by Stoddard.

Somewhat divergent in talents and personalities, Timothy Edwards and Solomon Stoddard fortuitously complemented one another as influences upon Edwards during the years of his taking up the arts of preaching. At one significant point there was a virtual confluence of their influences:

> Let us labour in a very particular, convincing and awakening manner to dispense the Word of God; so to speak as tends most to reach and pierce the Hearts and Consciences, and humble the Souls of them that hear us . . .

Thus, in *All the Living Must Surely Die*,[1] Timothy Edwards advises ministers to preach to the end of conversion, just as Stoddard would have them preach. In urging this goal he aligns himself with a tradition that runs through the great preachers of the Connecticut valley—Hooker, Stoddard, and Jonathan Edwards—in so clear and continuous a stream that it would not seem inappropriate to speak of the Connecticut Valley School of preaching. For these preachers are distinct from most of the great Boston preachers, particularly those of the second and third generations, in that they continued to attach overwhelming importance to the experience of conversion. Indeed, the attention they gave to homiletical strategies that would promote this experience in their congregations was as keen as that of the early English Puritans to promote a more activist religion.

1. P. 25.

3. Two Significant Preaching Manuals

In addition to his formal education and the personal examples of
his father and Stoddard, there were other significant literary or rhetorical influences in Edwards' first years of preaching, such as the
two books on preaching that he certainly did read. John Edwards'
The Preacher (London, 1705)[2] and Cotton Mather's *Manuductio ad Ministerium* (Boston, 1726) are both mentioned early in Edwards' "Catalogue" of books, *The Preacher* being entered on page one (ca. 1722)
and marked with a vertical line through it, and the *Manuductio,* while
it is not entered itself, being cited no less than six times to recommend
other entries.[3] Thus, it is obvious that the *Manuductio* was repeatedly
referred to as a kind of manual, and as for *The Preacher,* there are
too many echoes of its individualistic expressions throughout Edwards' notebooks to have doubts about its importance to him.

If one can judge from the style and thought of *The Preacher,* John
Edwards was a kind of English Solomon Stoddard. He calls for a
return to true "Evangelical Preaching" and urges the themes that
became so prominent in Edwards' preaching: *"preach Christ* . . . the
true Nature of *Regeneration* . . . Christ as *Mediator* . . . the absolute
Necessity of being *Supernaturally Enlightened . . . Justification by Faith
alone,"* and so on. Moreover, he loses no time in indicating the peculiar
contemporary peril of religion: some "extol Natural Reason too high,
and give it an Ascendant over Revealed Religion. . . . there are some
Persons who have almost *reason'd* themselves and others out of *Chris-*

2. *The Preacher* was issued in three parts: London 1705, 1706, and 1709. But only
Volume I is primarily devoted to the arts and theory of preaching, the other volumes being
devoted to polemical wars with R. Lightfoot and his party. Thus, we will be concerned
with Volume I only, and so far as is known JE had only that volume.

3. This manuscript notebook, a quarto of 24 leaves and an inlaid loose letter sheet, is
bound in brown heavy paper and labelled simply "CATALOGUE." A subject of much
interest to JE scholars over the years, it is an enigmatic document. With the exception of
a few notes on the letter sheet, the "Catalogue" is a list of books that interested JE. But
the precise function of the list seems to have changed over the years, as the entries consisting of bare lists of names and titles on the letter sheet and the first two or three pages,
became concise reviews (including quotations from advertisements) in the later pages.
Moreover, the exact meaning of the markings in the notebook—entries marked with horizontal lines, vertical lines, and Xs—is still open to debate. Finally, there are some books
that JE certainly possessed or used that are not even mentioned in the "Catalogue." But
on the whole, the "Catalogue" provides the general outline of JE's reading interests, and
we may assume that those entries with markings through them were at least examined by
JE, as we may assume that he examined those books from which he took advertisements
for other books named in the "Catalogue."

tianity." Rather than offering mere human wisdom, preachers must preach so that "we should hear that many are *prickt at the Heart,* and cry out, *what shall we do to be saved.*" In order to do so, the preacher must frequently use the words "hell" and "damnation," for "as the Gospel brings with it *Great Salvation,* so it brings as *Great Damnation.*"

John Edwards is no ranter, however, and he insists that, while preaching evangelically, "the Ministers of the Gospel ought to be very Indearing and Affectionate, and to deport themselves with Love and Meekness: for in doing thus, they apply themselves most suitably to Rational Men, who are to be led, not driven; who follow the conduct of Reason rather than of Force." All in all, "a Preacher is one that must have the Gift of Perswading, and this he must do by raising the *Passions* of his Hearers." In order to preach persuasively, Edwards insists, the preacher must believe and feel intensely what he preaches; he must then communicate his personal feelings with the message so that he preaches experience, as it were. These are great demands, but John Edwards had an exalted view of the preacher in mind: "A Preacher should accommodate himself to the *Thing* he treats of, to the *Persons* he speaks to, to the *Occasion* of his Discourse, and likewise to the *Time.*" Moreover, a preacher "must be a Linguist, a Grammarian, a Critick, an Orator, a Philosopher, an Historian, a Casuist, a Disputant, and whatever speaks Skill and Knowledge in any Learned Science." Not even a young genius would feel confined by the prospect of such a career.

In addition to these opinions, John Edwards has some decided views on the art of the sermon. The "Sacred Orator" is to be stylish in utterance, or "suitable to the relish of the Age we live in," but the style is to be put in perspective by a calculated carelessness of finish and a differentiation between adequate smoothness and slickness. The address of the preacher is to be "Serious and Manly," and his doctrine is to be closely argued, sensible, and adequate in substance to the pretentions of his verbiage: anything less is "Mocking of God, and Jesting with Divinity." Ideally, sermons should be like diamonds, "Clear as well as Solid." Inasmuch as the best proofs and arguments in any sermon come from the Bible, the preacher should secure every particular head with Scripture, but more than that, he should "make use of [it] in the whole Contexture of [his] Sermons, and not . . . be ashamed of the Scripture-Phrase, as some seem to be." But perhaps most of all, the preacher must realize that his end is in the end of the sermon:

Application is the Preacher's chief Work, and it is the Hardest too: but it is the most Useful and Necessary. Wherefore he must not put off his Auditors with General Discourses, and Loose and Vain Harangues: but the Sword of the Spirit, which is the Word of God, must be set to the Breast and Heart of every particular Person. And this Close Application will be most effectual to a Holy Life, because it will stick by them, tho' the rest of the Discourse should be forgot. And in a word, the *Application* will be found to be the Best part of the Sermon.[4]

John Edwards, obviously a man of keen intelligence, wide learning, and a deep sense of the dignity of the preacher's office, had come to the conclusion—as had Solomon Stoddard—that religion was essentially an affair of the heart, and that the preacher's rhetorical strategy was therefore necessarily more closely related to the arts of psychological manipulation than to any variety of logic. Having cut loose from the security of belief in logic's efficacy, and having rejected the contemporary enthusiasm for reason, they were both forced to rely upon the subjective touchstones of the rigorously disciplined and thoroughly educated intellect, and the heart that they hoped was sanctified, as the preacher's guide and stay in the shadowy realm of the human emotions where religion seemed to live.

Cotton Mather must have represented the "Boston establishment" to Jonathan Edwards; after all, it was Cotton's father who had remonstrated with his grandfather, and there are singularly few references to Mather's many publications in Edwards' notebooks and writings—almost as if by design.[5] Yet Edwards overcame whatever qualms he might have had about the Mathers when the *Manuductio ad Ministerium* was published. Of course, by 1726 or 1728 (when he probably obtained it), Edwards was beyond the level of a student for the ministry, or even that of an apprentice preacher, but he was always ready to learn, and it seems doubtful that all of his procedures relating to the pulpit would have yet wholly solidified. At any rate, he seems to have kept the *Manuductio* at his finger tips and referred to it as an authority on matters relating to the education of a preacher.

4. Edwards, *The Preacher*, pp. 211, 217, 242–43, 248, 249, 238, 145, 146, 179, 144.

5. This dearth of references to the writings of the Mathers certainly did not result from JE's unfamiliarity with them, for manuscript inventories of Timothy Edwards' library show significant numbers of Mather publications. The inventories have been transcribed and annotated by Kenneth P. Minkema in "The Edwardses: A Ministerial Family in Eighteenth-Century New England" (Ph. D. diss., Univ. of Connecticut, 1988), pp. 646–66.

But just what impact might the *Manuductio* have had on Edwards' conception of the sermon, considering those prior influences enumerated above? Basically, it would have been that of a reinforcer and, in some instances, a qualifier of principles already held. Those areas which would have been most susceptible to qualification, or in need of clarification, centered in the relationship between rhetoric and the old logic, the new Reason, and the role of the emotions in religion. On at least two of these points, Mather is outspoken:

> Instead of Squandering away your Time, on the RHETORIC . . . the very Profession whereof usually is little more than to furnish out a *Stage-Player*; My Advice to you, is, That you observe the Flowres and Airs of such *Writings,* as are most in Reputation for their *Elegancy.*
>
> Nor can I encourage you to spend very much Time, in that which goes under the Name of LOGIC. . . . What is there usually got by the *Vulgar Logic,* but only be furnished with a Parcel of *Terms,* which instead of leading the Mind into the *Truth,* enables one rather to carry on *Altercations,* and *Logomachies,* by which the Force of *Truth* may be at Pleasure, and by some little *Trick,* evaded. The Power and Process of *Reason* is *Natural* to the Soul of Man . . .[6]

Thus peremptorily does Mather urge preachers to put away such school-boy paraphernalia as the Ramean rhetorical and logical theories. In the place of academic logic and rhetoric, Mather would put natural reason and a cultivated personal style based upon emulation of the actual practice of admired authors.

When he speaks more specifically of the art of preaching, Mather sounds even more like Stoddard and John Edwards. He places great emphasis upon the spiritual preparation of the minister as a prerequisite of effective preaching style, urging the minister to "go directly from your Knees in your *Study* to the *Pulpit.*" And when approaching the more technical aspects of rhetoric, Mather names a source as enthusiastically as if it had never been known or used before:

> But I will take this Opportunity to tell you, That there is no where to be found any *Rhetoric,* as there is in our *Sacred Scriptures.* . . . There can be nothing so *Beautiful,* or so *Affectuous* as the *Figures* every where used in them. They are *Life.* . . . For the *Pulpit-Oratory,* which is what you have in View, there can be nothing

6. Mather, *Manuductio,* pp. 34, 35.

more adviseable, than to be a Master of *Scripture-Phrases*, and employ them with an agreeable Ingenuity, on all fit Occasions. . . . [7]

Beyond this, Mather does not bother with much specific discussion but does, as usual, name a source:

I cannot set you so tedious a Task, as to Read a *Tenth Part*, of what has been offered on the *Art*, and the *Gift*, and the *Method* of PREACHING. If you Read . . . *The Preacher*, of an *Edwards*; you will do as much this Way, as I shall at present ask you to do.[8]

From these highlights, one can infer the nature of Jonathan Edwards' intellectual and psychological preparation for his career as a preacher. His childhood experiences, formal education, years with Stoddard, and private reading in the literature of the preacher's art would have combined to define certain of his ideas, predispositions, and biases with respect to the preacher's art. Thus, he was instructed to accept the traditional Puritan sermon form by the examples of his father's and Stoddard's preaching. But the freedoms that Stoddard, in particular, took with the form would have tended to encourage the use of a variant (simplified) form that would have seemed rather free in personal amplification to William Perkins and his Puritan contemporaries. In addition, the elaborate logical schemes which seemed to justify the old sermon form were either ignored or explicitly discredited by both the example of Stoddard and the most influential books on the art of preaching that Edwards read. In the place of the power of logic, Stoddard, John Edwards, and Mather put a rationally disciplined but nevertheless forthright appeal to the emotions, perhaps both because of a new awareness of the psychological complexity of the human being, and because of a reaction of conservative mentalities to the apparent threat of rational morality to religion. Finally, it would seem that all the outstanding influences, with the possible exception of Mather, combined in placing great emphasis upon preaching which would be likely to evoke the experience of conversion in the congregation: specifically, that rhetorical strategy known as "hellfire" preaching.

To identify influences—most of all in the case of Jonathan Edwards—is not, however, to identify the man. Edwards seems never to have taken in anything without turning it over in his mind and usually

7. Ibid., p. 34.
8. Ibid., p. 90.

modifying it. Thus Edwards' responses to his background must be considered, particularly his explicit statements concerning the preacher, and the use to which he put the inherited sermon form.

4. Edwards' Thoughts on Preaching

Edwards was in full agreement with his teachers respecting the exalted status of the preacher. For though his writings occasionally contain references to "earthen vessels" and sometimes emphasize the preacher's humble situation as a son of Adam, it is much more common for Edwards to see the preacher as a man exalted and even transfigured by his calling. Indeed, in some of the earliest entries in his "Miscellanies," nos. mm, qq, and 40,[9] Edwards attempts to define to his own satisfaction the nature of the call, the limits and quality of a minister's influence in society, and the power in preaching or teaching the divine Word.

> Yet it is clear that those that are in the New Testament called ministers are not every private Christian, and consequently if [any] such remain now as are there spoken of, they are distinct from other Christians. 'Tis clear they are born undistinguished; from this 'tis clear they are distinguished afterwards. 'Tis also evident that they are distinguished some way or other by Christ . . . (no. mm)

This earliest entry on the office of the preacher calls attention to the essentially aristocratic bias of Edwards, which is quite in keeping with his upbringing, while it also demonstrates his characteristic propensity to rethink every important aspect of his life "from the ground up," regardless of his background and training. He may not seriously question the assumptions of his heritage, but he will insist upon a personal formulation of that heritage in his own written words.

The preacher is, then, a "chosen one" with a distinct charisma as a result of his call to serve Christ. He is invested with a capacity and right to instruct, lead, and judge his people (no. qq); he has no pretension to civil authority, but in the all-important moral and spiritual realms he is, of all human beings, supremely authoritative. Number

9. It is to be understood that quotations from JE's writings which appear without footnote references to printed texts are taken directly from the manuscripts. In a number of instances, I have gone to the manuscripts, in the interest of accuracy, when printed texts were available.

40 contains early speculations upon the powers which would inhere
in the effective preaching of the Word, specifically:

> Without doubt, ministers are to teach men what Christ would have
> them to do, and to teach them who doth these things and who
> doth them not; that is, who are Christians and who are not . . .
>
>   Thus, if I in a right manner am become the teacher of a people,
> so far as they ought to hear what I teach them, so much power I
> have. Thus, if they are obliged to hear me only because they
> themselves have chosen me to guide them, and therein declared
> that they thought me sufficiently instructed in the mind of Christ
> to teach them, and because I have the other requisites of being
> their teacher, then I have power as other ministers have in these
> days. But if it was plain to them that I was under the infallible
> guidance of Christ, then I should have more power. And if it was
> plain to all the world of Christians that I was under the infallible
> guidance of Christ, and [that] I was sent forth to teach the world
> the will of Christ, then I should have power in all the world. I
> should have power to teach them what they ought to do, and they
> would be obliged to hear me; I should have power to teach them
> who were Christians and who not, and in this likewise they would
> be obliged to hear me.

As in a daydream, the student-preacher toys with the mystery of the
call, and at least by implication ponders the limits and possibilities of
the role of a preacher. Could he command the people, or even the
world, as a divine messenger? Obviously, there must be some immediate sign, some quality of utterance, that would in itself attest to the
supernatural ordination. In this early passage Edwards is already
pondering aspects of sermonic style, but characteristically he begins
on the most general and profound, most philosophical level. Puritan
ministers had always been urged to "preach powerfully," but in this
meditation there are new undertones, and "power" clearly relates to
a divine investiture which transcends conventional sectarian sanctions. Certainly it seems that Edwards was as well fitted to study the
art of preaching under the imperious Solomon Stoddard as any man.

Edwards did not pretend to eloquence or a fine style. Indeed, from
the first he seems to have made a point of proclaiming his lack of a
fine style.

>   . . . the practical discourses that follow . . . now appear in that very
> plain and unpolished dress in which they were first prepared and

delivered; which was mostly at a time when the circumstances of the auditory they were preached to, were enough to make a minister neglect, forget, and despise such ornaments as politeness and modishness of style and method, when coming as a messenger from God to souls deeply impressed with a sense of their danger of God's everlasting wrath, to treat with them about their eternal salvation. However unable I am to preach or write politely, if I would, yet I have this to comfort me under such a defect; that God has showed us that he don't need such talents in men to carry on his own work, and that he has been pleased to smile upon and bless a very plain, unfashionable way of preaching. And have we not reason to think that it ever has been, and ever will be, God's manner to bless the foolishness of preaching to save them that believe, let the elegance of language, and excellency of style, be carried to never so great a height, by the learning and wit of the present and future ages?

This passage, from the Preface to *Discourses on Various Important Subjects* (1738),[1] is characteristic of the tone of most of Edwards' prefaces, though the discussion is a little more explicit and fully developed. It is defensive, condemning wit and style out of hand as irrelevant to effective preaching, while also suggesting an incapacity for stylistic excellence on his own part.

Part of this may be explained by Edwards' cultural background which would have taught him to think of rhetoric or eloquence as a thing separable from the logical structure of an argument.[2] Since he

1. P. v.

2. The peculiar attitude that assumes substance and expression to be distinct and separable was quite widespread in the seventeenth century and occasioned the birth of the "plain style" among preachers and "mathematical plainness" in the Royal Society. While a detailed survey of this significant aspect of JE's cultural background is beyond the scope of this introduction, it should be stated that the crucial factor in that background seems to have been the philosophy of Peter Ramus.

With the aid of his colleague, Omer Talon, Ramus devised a new formulation of the relationship between logic and rhetoric, involving the transfer of the classical (Ciceronian) invention, disposition, and memory from the province of rhetoric to that of dialectic. This left only style, apprehended as a matter of figures and tropes, and delivery to rhetoric; rhetoric became the sideshow to thought, a crowd-pleasing (or even crowd-deluding) device. Thus, those who were intent upon the intellectual substance of their expression or were intensely earnest, such as Puritan preachers and the new scientists, tended to condemn and avoid "style" as something adventitious and frivolous. Moreover, those who cultivated rhetoric during the seventeenth century actually did tend to artificiality and ornateness, as

was consciously developing a heart-piercing manner of writing that
would be as spare and efficient as an arrow, he assumed that "style,"
being an adventitious decoration, would have to be left out. It would
not have struck Edwards that that efficacious verbal expression for
which he constantly strove and "style" might be the same thing. Thus
he really could spend much of his lifetime studying the theory and
practice of language and metaphor without "paying any attention to
style." Of course, part of the problem is also that, as in the seventeenth century, preaching styles were associated with theological positions. In Edwards' day many of the most eloquent preachers of the
East were suspect in Edwards' eyes of being rationalist, Arminian, or
just theologically jejune. He would therefore rather deny excellence
in his carefully wrought sermons than be thought—perhaps even by
himself—to be a creature of wit and style. He was too serious, too
full of thought, and too honest for *style*.

Indeed, if Edwards claimed brilliance of any kind it was the more
essential and "substantial" excellence of thought, and once again he
saw himself as being out of tune with the times:

> Our discovering the absurdity of the impertinent and abstruse
> distinctions of the School Divines, may justly give us a distaste of
> such distinctions as have a show of learning in obscure words, but
> convey no light to the mind; but I can see no reason why we should
> also discard those that are clear and rational, and can be made
> out to have their foundation in truth . . .

In the same Preface,[3] in a sustained argument of two pages, he defends the virtue of "real" fine distinctions in elaborating the "mysteries" of religion. If, as the *Manuductio* contends, reason is natural to
the soul of man, then Edwards would have him test this capacity, as
he would fully exercise the heart, in the quest of a valid apprehension
of divine truths.

Edwards may have been inspired by his father's example to use the
utmost rigor in making convicting arguments, and Stoddard undoubtedly provided the pattern for a potent, "psychological" rhetoric
for which Edwards had no name. But having a finer mind and more

---

might be expected when figures and tropes are seen more or less as ends in themselves.

For a detailed discussion of the history behind JE's attitude, and an investigation of the
long groping toward what we should today call an organic style, see Wilbur S. Howell's
Logic and Rhetoric in England, 1500–1700 (Princeton, Princeton Univ. Press, 1956).

3. *Discourses*, p. iii.

imagination than either Stoddard or Timothy Edwards, Edwards out-
performed each at his specialty while combining elements of both
their strategies. His intense interest in the mysterious power of language, however, was apparently innate.

Edwards' matured vision of the ideal preacher is most completely
delineated in his ordination sermon on John 5:35, entitled *The True
Excellency of a Minister of the Gospel* (1744).[4] There, he insists that a
minister must be "both a burning and a shining light"; that "his heart
burn with love to Christ, and fervent desires of the advancement of
his kingdom and glory," and that "his instructions [be] clear and
plain, accommodated to the capacity of his hearers, and tending to
convey light to their understandings." This peculiar combination of
head and heart, he insists, is absolutely necessary to the success of a
preacher:

> When light and heat are thus united in a minister of the gospel,
> it shows that each is genuine, and of a right kind, and that both
> are divine. Divine light is attended with heat; and so, on the other
> hand, a truly divine and holy heat and ardor is ever accompanied
> with light.[5]

That both heat and light may be acquired by the aspiring preacher,
Edwards urges him to be "diligent in [his] studies," "very conversant
with the holy Scriptures," and "much in seeking God, and conversing
with him by prayer, who is the fountain of light and love." All in all,
Edwards' ideal does not seem to be very different from that of the
traditional preacher of the time, except that in the full context of the
sermon and through the extensive use of light imagery, he suggests
a standard of transcendent dedication and nearly mystical fervor
which is rare in any age. And like Stoddard before him, Edwards
cultivated a subtle personal tone in his rhetoric which, more than any
stated principle, demonstrates the risk-taking commitment demanded
of the good preacher.

Edwards is best known for his defenses of passionate emotion, including "hellfire," in revival preaching. And, indeed, in the *Religious
Affections* he argues that "such means are to be desired, as have much

---

4. *The Works of President Edwards, in Four Volumes. A Reprint of the Worcester Edition* . . .
eighth ed. in four volumes (New York, [1843]), *3*, 580–92. This edition will hereafter be
cited as *Works,* Worcester rev. ed.

5. *Works,* Worcester rev. ed., *3*, 587.

of a tendency to move the affections."[6] Moreover, in *Thoughts on the Revival of Religion in New England,* he emphatically insists that

> Though . . . clearness of distinction and illustration, and strength of reason, and a good method, in the doctrinal handling of the truths of religion, is many ways needful and profitable, and not to be neglected . . . Our people don't so much need to have their heads stored, as to have their hearts touched; and they stand in the greatest need of that sort of preaching that has the greatest tendency to do this.[7]

As for "hellfire" preaching in particular, Edwards argues:

> Some talk of it as an unreasonable thing to think to fright persons to heaven; but I think it is a reasonable thing to endeavor to fright persons away from hell . . .'tis a reasonable thing to fright a person out of an house on fire.[8]

As for the style or manner of "hellfire" preaching, he makes this observation:

> When ministers preach of hell, and warn sinners to avoid it, in a cold manner, though they may say in words that it is infinitely terrible; yet (if we look on language as a communication of our minds to others) they contradict themselves; for actions, as I observed before, have a language to convey our minds, as well as words; and at the same time that such a preacher's words represents the sinner's state as infinitely dreadful, his behavior and manner of speaking contradict it, and shew that the preacher don't think so; so that he defeats his own purpose; for the language of his actions, in such a case, is much more effectual than the bare signification of his words.[9]

Edwards might well have extended this comment to include the "gesture of language"—specifically, images and metaphors employed in making an argument concrete—in the case of printed sermons.

In summary, it should be observed that, while Edwards placed no limits on the intensity of emotion that a preacher might attempt to

6. *Religious Affections,* ed. John E. Smith, in *Works,* 2, 121.

7. See *The Great Awakening,* ed. C. C. Goen, in *The Works of Jonathan Edwards* (New Haven, Yale Univ. Press, 1972), *4,* 387–88.

8. *The Distinguishing Marks of a Work of the Spirit of God, Works, 4,* 248.

9. Ibid., pp. 247–48.

evoke through his preaching, he insisted upon a constant balance and aesthetically pleasing harmony between emotion and thought. Indeed, he insisted that without a duly precise and comprehensive body of theological concepts in the sermon, there is no religion at all.[1]

Edwards' ideal preacher is, then, a figure of commanding intellectual rigor and overwhelming rhetorical power; he strikes a blow for religion simultaneously in the heads and hearts of his auditors, though with an emphasis upon the heart. In the performance of his duty, he shows that he is the peculiarly designated servant of his Master:

> They should imitate [Christ] in the manner of his preaching; who taught not as the Scribes, but with authority, boldly, zealously and fervently; insisting chiefly on the most important things in religion, being much in warning men of the danger of damnation, setting forth the greatness of the future misery of the ungodly; insisting not only on the outward, but also the inward and spiritual duties of religion: being much in declaring the great provocation and danger of spiritual pride, and a self-righteous disposition; yet much insisting on the necessity and importance of inherent holiness, and the practice of piety. . . . wonderfully adapting his discourse to persons, seasons and occasions.[2]

If a congregation could "hear and stand it out" under such preaching, there would probably be little hope for the English language as an instrument of salvation.

5. The Inherited Sermon Form

That Edwards accepted the traditional sermon form is undoubtedly in part due to his essentially conservative outlook. But he also had some sound practical reasons for relying upon the basic structure and general rationale of the seventeenth-century Puritan sermon. Before considering Edwards' use of the inherited sermon form, however, it is important to note briefly the sermon in its original form.

Modern scholarly studies of the seveneenth-century Puritan ser-

---

1. For an extended discussion of JE's ideas on the necessity of intellectual substance in sermons, see his sermon, "The Importance and Advantage of a Thorough Knowledge of Divine Truth," *Works,* Worcester rev. ed., *4,* 1–15.

2. "Christ the Example of Ministers," *Works,* Worcester rev. ed., *3,* 597.

mon have pointed out that the form evolved through many hands and was always subject to individual variations. Consequently, major works on sermon theory were generally efforts to codify current practices rather than to present new concepts. A few books, however, became accepted as "authorities" for generations of student-preachers, and one of the most popular among them was John Wilkins' *Ecclesiastes, Or, A Discourse Concerning the Gift of Preaching as it falls under the Rules of Art* (London, 1646). This little book had gone through six printings by 1679, and in 1705 John Edwards recommended it in *The Preacher.*

Ecclesiastes is a book to warm the heart of a Ramist, for it dichotomizes and distributes all things into their proper categories. Thus, it is not only clear in its exposition of the sermon form, but it gives a vivid impression of the mentality which gave birth to the classical Puritan sermon. The form of this sermon is, according to Wilkins, tripartite on the primary level; it consists of three "chief parts" or divisions:

> Explication.
> Confirmation.
> Application.

Wilkins subdivides each of these divisions by the Ramistic method of analysis.

First the Explication:

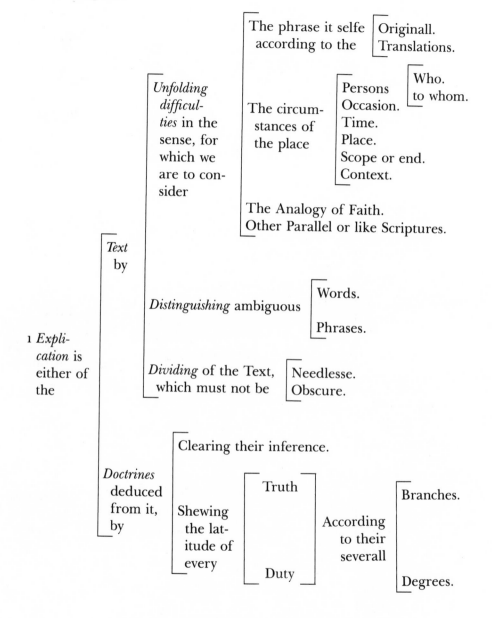

1 *Explication* is either of the

Text by

Unfolding difficulties in the sense, for which we are to consider

The phrase it selfe according to the — Originall. / Translations.

The circumstances of the place — Persons — Who. / to whom. / Occasion. / Time. / Place. / Scope or end. / Context.

The Analogy of Faith. / Other Parallel or like Scriptures.

Distinguishing ambiguous — Words. / Phrases.

Dividing of the Text, which must not be — Needlesse. / Obscure.

Doctrines deduced from it, by

Clearing their inference.

Shewing the latitude of every — Truth / Duty — According to their severall — Branches. / Degrees.

Second the Confirmation:

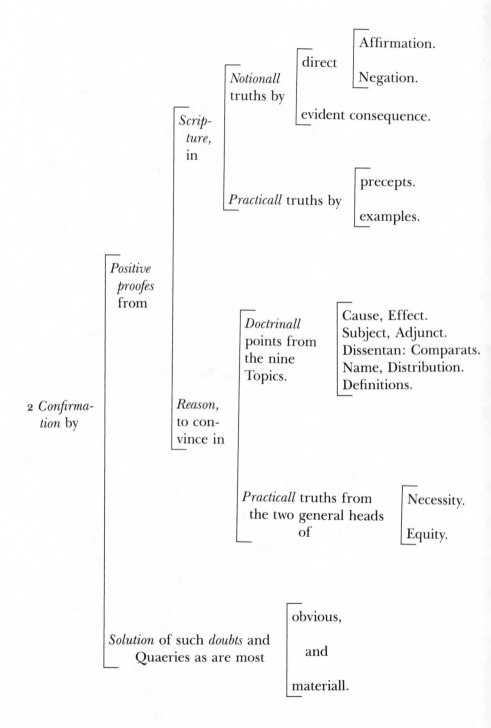

2 *Confirmation* by

Positive proofes from

Scripture, in

Notionall truths by

direct

Affirmation.

Negation.

evident consequence.

Practicall truths by

precepts.

examples.

Reason, to convince in

Doctrinall points from the nine Topics.

Cause, Effect.
Subject, Adjunct.
Dissentan: Comparats.
Name, Distribution.
Definitions.

Practicall truths from the two general heads of

Necessity.

Equity.

Solution of such *doubts* and Quaeries as are most

obvious,

and

materiall.

And finally, the Application:

3 *Appli-cation,* which is either

Doctrinall for our informa-tion

More *generall* in some truth to be acknowl-edged

Didacticall instruction.

Elencticall confutation.

More *particular* of our owne estates, to be examined by Marks, which are commonly either

Effects.

Properties.

Prac-ticall

Reproofe, which hath two parts,

Disswasive from

The aggravation of the sin.
Threats denounced.
Judgements executed.

Directive, wherein, concerning

Impediments that hinder.
Meanes to promote, more

Remote.

Immediate.

Consolation by

Promises.
Experience.
Removing of scruples.

Exhortation, to be amplified by

Motives to excite the affections from

Profit.

Danger.

Meanes to direct the actions,

Generall.

Speciall.

These schemes of the sermon's formal structure,[3] though they appear to be as involved as the work of the "school-men," do in fact provide formal outlines of the sermon structure used by Edwards. Of course,

3. From the second edition of *Ecclesiastes* (London, 1647), pp. 5–7.

it is a "loosened" structure in Edwards' sermons, for he no longer attaches much significance to the Ramistic logic which informs it, but there is more than a mere family resemblance between the form used by Edwards and that depicted by Wilkins, and a modern reader must respect the formal requirements of the sermon in much the same way as he might those of the ballad or even the sonnet if he is to appreciate what is going on in it.

In discussing the schemes, Wilkins argues that a sermon constructed on this plan not only helps the preacher to control his material, but also helps the hearers,

> who may understand and retain a Sermon with greater ease and profit, when they are before-hand acquainted with the generall heads of matter that are discoursed of. . . .
>
> An immethodicall discourse (though the materials of it may be precious) is but as a *heap*, full of confusion and deformity; the other, as a *Fabrick* or building, much more excellent both for *beauty* and *use*.[4]

Edwards would seem to agree; moreover, his congregation had listened to this style of sermon for years, and their minds moved in grooves dictated by the form. If he were to follow Christ's example and adapt his teachings to the capacities of his hearers, should not he preach in a form that they had long since grown accustomed to?

Edwards preached, therefore, in the traditional way, dividing his sermons into Text, Doctrine, and Application.[5] He also gave ample introductory and transitional statements, informing his auditory where the argument would go (at the beginning of each major head, but most comprehensively at the beginning of the Doctrine), where it was (at various points of division between heads, but especially at the start of the separate preaching units[6] of a sermon delivered over two or more services), and where it had been (at the ends of the major

---

4. Ibid., p. 4.

5. I have concluded that "Text" is the most accurate term for the first section of the sermon, since it invariably begins with the reading of a Scripture text and there is frequently *no explication* (see the bottom half of Wilkins' first scheme) if the text appears clear enough without it. When JE does refer to textual explication, he usually calls it the "Opening of the Text." "Doctrine" and "Application" are JE's customary terms for the second and third major divisions of the sermon.

6. The phrase "preaching unit" is a modern technical term used to identify the amount of material JE would normally preach during one session in the pulpit, since he often composed sermons requiring two or more preaching sessions to complete.

divisions). Indeed, an abstract of a typical Edwards sermon manuscript, preserving only the formal outline and the transitional material, sounds not a little like Wilkins. Here is a sample Doctrine:

Doctrine . . .
　Under this doctrine I would show: First, wherein this preparing of the heart consists, and secondly, give the reasons of the doctrine.
　　I. Preparedness consists.
　　　1. Ready to enjoy. 2. Ready to acknowledge.
　　　3. Ready to make good improvement.
　　　Preparedness for a mercy sought.
　　　1.
　　　2. [the above heads expanded]
　　　3.
　　In these things it is that the preparedness of the heart for mercies sought consists. Now this preparation is wrought two ways: legally and evangelically.
　　　[1.] A legal preparation.
　　　2. There is an evangelical preparation.
　　　　[It] consists chiefly in four things, viz., humility and faith, love and spiritual appetite.
　　　　　[1.] Humility.
　　　　　2. Faith.
　　　　　3. Love.
　　　　　4. Holy appetite.
　　　I proceed now:
　　II. Briefly to give the reasons of the doctrine . . . and there are two reasons . . . viz., to secure his own glory, and to promote their good . . .
　　　1. His own glory.
　　　2. Their good.

An attentive and experienced auditor should have had no difficulty following Edwards through the Doctrine of Ps. 10:17 (1735), or for that matter, through the Text and Application which are prepared with equal attention to outline and transitions.

The modern reader of Edwards' sermons may have to be reminded that, when the members of Edwards' congregation were not carried away by the emotional tides of the relatively rare awakening experience, many were busy taking sermon notes. Thus, a significant part of the appeal of the sermon form presumably lay in its facilitating the organizing of material in sermon notes. There is, in fact, a rare example of sermon notes for an extant manuscript sermon which vividly illustrates how well preacher and congregation kept together, largely because of the conventions of the sermon's form.

On September 25, 1727, Edwards preached the first section of a long (three preaching units) sermon on Is. 1:18–20. In the auditory sat a note-taker, possibly "Uncle" Joseph Hawley, with his little octavo quire of notes from several sermons by Edwards, Stoddard, and Thomas Hawley. On a blank leaf he took down the heads and some material that apparently struck him as important from within heads, as Edwards preached the sermon. Below, I have reproduced the notes in their entirety (so far as quoted), while abstracting from the full text of the sermon manuscript those parts of the sermon that correspond to the notes.

NOTES	SERMON
Is. 1:18–20, by Mr. Edwards.	Is. 1:18–20.
Doctrine is that all God's methods of dealing with man are most reasonable.	Doctrine. That all God's methods of dealing with men are most reasonable.
1. God is most reasonable in decreeing & permitting sin.	I. God is most reasonable in his decreeing and permitting sin . . .
1. God is no ways obliged to afford that grace & influence which would prevent sin in the creature.	1. God is no ways obliged to afford his creature such grace and influence as shall render it impossible for him to sin . . .
2. God may order that a thing shall be done so or that it is impossible but that it come to pass & yet not himself force the doing of it; the decrees of God have no necessity of compulsion in them.	2. God may order that a thing shall certainly be done, so that it is impossible but that the thing should come to pass, and yet not force the doing . . . [middle of head] so that God's making of it necessary that the thing should so fall out don't in the least stand in the way of our lib-

3. If it were not reasonable that God should permit sin God would not be to be feared.

4. If God were obliged never to permit sin there would be no reason to be thankful to God for preserving us from sin.

1. [Use]. Hence we learn that sinners are inexcusable in their sins they have none to blame but themselves the original of it being in their own hearts therefore acknowledge it now & cast not the blame on God.

erty; necessity may be distinguished into necessity or compulsion . . .

3. If it were not reasonable that God should permit sin, God would not be to be feared; there would be not foundation for any such thing as the fear of God . . .

4. If God were obliged never to permit sin, there would be no reason to thank God for preserving of us from sin . . .

APPLICATION
We shall make a reflection or two upon this head by way of application . . .

1. Hence we learn that sinners are inexcusable in their sins . . . [middle of head] wherefore, acknowledge your own inexcusableness now, and own that you only are to blame; don't complain of God for that for which he justly complains of you, and may justly condemn you.

Hand in hand, as it were, preacher and note-taker progress through Doctrine and Application. Only about half the sermon notes are reproduced above—there being another doctrinal proposition and the "Improvement of the Whole" to go—but the point has been demonstrated: by using the traditional sermon form, Edwards enabled his rustic congregation to assimilate and sometimes record theological arguments that might be vastly more difficult to follow or re-constitute from a "free-style" essay-sermon. In the case of this sermon, the note-taker did not miss a single numbered head in Doctrine or Application, and he took down several significant passages from within heads. (He did not record Edwards' Opening of the Text, apparently considering that preliminary matter.)

Thus, several factors may have contributed to Edwards' adherence to the traditional sermon form, but perhaps one of his strongest reasons was a purely practical inclination to use the form that worked. The rationalists, according to Solomon Stoddard, might put their thin moralizing in modish, simplified packages, but auditors of substantial theological arguments needed all the structural support they could get.

6. The Sermon in Edwards' Hands

The development and ultimate deterioration of the sermon form in Edwards' hands will be discussed shortly, but now an attempt must be made to define the formal limits of the Edwardsean sermon at the zenith of its development during the late 1720s, the 1730s, and the very early 1740s (and whenever Edwards had an important preaching occasion in subsequent years and returned to that form and style).[7] This sermon is a formal literary unit consisting of three main divisions, Text, Doctrine, and Application. There is only one significant variation in the form which is called a "lecture." The lecture is differentiated from the sermon only through the altered proportions in the Doctrine and Application. For whereas in the sermon the Application is usually a little longer than the Doctrine and often several times as long, in the lecture the Doctrine is substantially longer than the Application. Perhaps the best-known instance of the lecture variant is *A Divine and Supernatural Light* (1734) which has a doctrine of twenty-three pages and an Application of a little over three pages in the first edition.

Otherwise, so far as *form* is concerned, a sermon is a sermon—whether pastoral, imprecatory, occasional, doctrinal, or whatever.[8] Of course, this does not mean that the form was ever so fixed as to

7. The recent recovery of JE's manuscript of the *Farewell Sermon* (1750) provided confirmation that, though he employed scrap paper in all late sermons, JE returned to writing out all sermons he considered important.

8. Sermons based upon Old Testament texts tend to have longer Doctrines than those based upon New Testament texts, resulting in some lessening of emphasis upon Application in Old Testament-text sermons. This phenomenon seems to result from a necessity for relating Old Testament materials to the gospel message, which is effected in the Doctrine.

restrict variations; indeed, there were always so many variations that the very identity of the sermon as a literary form seems at times threatened. If the variations possible within the three main divisions are considered, however, it is evident that Edwards never lost sight of the paradigm.

The Text begins the sermon, invariably with the Scripture passage upon which the formal structure of the sermon rests. Indeed, it is the verse citation of the initial Scripture passage, rather than a word or phrase from the doctrine, that identifies a sermon when it is referred to in Edwards' notebooks. There is no exordium or introduction before the reading of the Scripture text, and there need not be any explication or exegesis after it, if the meaning is obvious, in order to have a complete Text. In the vast majority of sermons, however, there is a brief passage (a page, more or less) of comment and explication following the scriptural passage which Edwards designates the Opening of the Text. The Opening consists of several brief, numbered heads, frequently designated "Observation" or "Inference," in which Edwards defines difficult terms, cites other Scripture passages that parallel or complement the textual passage, and generally explains its meaning. In explication, he is never pedantic, even on those rare occasions when he introduces Hebrew or Greek words to clarify definitions; he explains carefully, but does not belabor small points. Indeed, some students of Edwards have felt the Opening of the Text to be the finest part of the sermon because of Edwards' remarkable ability to narrate the statements and events of the text as immediate experience, and in his narrations he not infrequently displays the talent of a first-rate journalist or novelist. But his narrations present concise sketches rather than murals, and the Text is never long.

Following the Text is the Doctrine, a major portion of most sermons and, structurally, often the most complex. The Doctrine usually begins with a single statement of doctrine, carefully labeled "Doc[trine]." In his inclination to formulate the entire doctrinal message of the sermon in a single statement of doctrine, Edwards was, it seems, a little unusual for his day. Most contemporary preachers tended to formulate two or more equally important statements and list them in parallel at the head of the Doctrine. Although it is Edwards' custom to draw two, three, or four Propositions or Observations from the doctrine immediately after its statement, thus dividing it for "clearing" or full discussion in the body of the Doctrine, the single statement of doctrine brings the entire sermon into a sharp thematic focus, like light rays passing through a lens, if only for a vivid moment.

But there need be no formal statement of doctrine at all. Sometimes, when the Scripture text is a clear, concise statement of thesis in itself and in need of no explication, Text and Doctrine elide and the Scripture quotation becomes the statement of doctrine, or, as Edwards puts it, the doctrine is "supplied." At other times, though rarely in Edwards' best days of preaching, there is no statement labeled "Doc[trine]," but only one or two propositions.[9] In such cases, the Proposition differs not at all from the usual statement of doctrine, unless it be a little less assertive in tone.

After the statement of doctrine and the division of the statement into Propositions, Edwards takes up the propositions, explaining the import of each and developing its implications through Inquiries, Observations, Arguments, and plain numbered heads. Each Proposition is also "proved" through Reasons. The term "reason" is actually a generic term for all "proofs" under the Doctrine, and Edwards does not frequently use it as the name for a particular head. The proofs of the doctrine are of two basic types: citations of Scripture (often attended with interpretation), and appeals to human reason and commonplace experience.

Most of the time, particularly in the shorter and middle-length sermons, the Doctrine ends with the giving of various reasons or proofs. However, each Proposition may have its own Use, Improvement, or Application, especially in the longer sermons. This occurs most often when the various propositions have quite different practical implications, and Edwards feels compelled to spell out the different duties implied by each Proposition. However, these uses are within the division of the Doctrine and are not to be confused with the third main division of the sermon. In sermons where such "doctrinal uses" are employed, Edwards often differentiates them from the third main division by calling it the "Application of the Whole."

The Application (or Improvement or Use) is the largest of the three main divisions of the sermon (except in the lecture variant), and in long sermons it may be several times as long as the Text and Doctrine together. It is usually marked by a significant alteration in tone and

---

9. A hallmark of the Stockbridge Indian sermons is that, whether written out or in bare outline, they have nothing labeled "Doc[trine]," but only Propositions or Observations, despite being virtual synopses of earlier sermons which had formal statements of doctrine.

rhetoric, and by a comparatively simple structure; for whereas the Text and Doctrine are concerned with theory, principle, and precept, the Application is concerned with experience and practice. The Application is directed to specific thoughts, attitudes, and actions of living human beings, and it gives specific advice on these attitudes and actions, in poignant language, in the light of the sermon's doctrine. But as employed by Edwards, the Application also has a subtler use, as is indicated by his own statement in this transitional passage between the Doctrine and Application of Gen. 19:14.

> The Improvement we shall make of this doctrine shall be to offer some considerations to make future punishment seem real to you.

In effect, then, the Application is a period of hypothetical experience for Edwards' auditory, a time of living imaginatively, through a "willing suspension of disbelief," a series of fictive experiences created and controlled by the preacher.

The Application or Improvement is generally structured by division into several Uses. Most of the time, the term "use" is restricted to serving as the categorical name for main heads under the division of "Application" or "Improvement," paralleling "reasons" in the Doctrine. (The two division names, incidentally, are used interchangeably, though "Application" appears to be the favored term after the first few years of preaching.) Thus, there is frequently a Use of Self-examination, or a Use of Consolation, and up to four or five such "specialized" uses, though the concluding use is most often the Use of Exhortation. Each Use is subdivided by Inquiries, Considerations, and plain numbered heads, and a list of Considerations or Directions generally concludes the Use of Exhortation.

There are several "paired" heads, such as Objection-Consideration, Enquiry-Answer, and Positive-Negative, that may appear under any one of the three major divisions of the sermon as they are needed, as may such heads as Inference, Observation, or Inquiry. In fact, it should be noted that the minor heads are generally employed in a very flexible way, and are inserted wherever they fit. Few are used only in the Text, Doctrine, or the Application.

In order to have a complete Edwardsean sermon, then, there must be an identifying passage of Scripture at the beginning and an Application (of the whole) at the end; in the middle, there must be a doctrinal discussion of the Bible text, though not necessarily an Opening of the Text or an explicitly labeled "Doc[trine]." The minimal requirements are comparatively easy to describe; the difficulties arise when one attempts to define the "outer limits" of the sermon form.

First, there is the problem of literary form versus pulpit performance. Edwards sometimes speaks of a single preaching session in the pulpit, and that portion of a long sermon which might be preached in one session, as a sermon; but he also speaks of a complex literary unit, which includes several clearly marked preaching units within it, as a sermon. Apparently he was not alone in his ambiguity, for in several eighteenth-century editions his longer sermons are printed as a series of sermons (according to preaching units) rather than as the single long sermons which, according to the form, they are. Such printing conventions preserve the root sense of the Latin *sermo* which means "talk"; moreover, they preserve the spirit of the seventeenth-century New England sermon as a speech act only incidentally preserved in print. When editing his own sermons for the press, however, Edwards scrupulously called sermons of more than one preaching unit "discourses," as in *Discourses on Various Important Subjects,* where some pieces are of one preaching unit and others of more. Modern readers especially must treat the Text-Doctrine-Application unit—however long—as a literary unit: otherwise, they will probably miss theme, logic, and form altogether.

Even when one admits that a sermon may be of any length, as long as it is carefully constructed, without losing its formal unity, there is the complication created by the "paired sermons" and the sermon series. In the case of the paired sermons, Edwards may write two sermons on the same text to be preached in series; however, they share nothing, not even the Opening of the Text, beyond the initial Scripture text. Obviously they are two sermons, though they may, if they are brief, be delivered on the same day. Then there is the variant in which Edwards announces two doctrines in two sermons, but develops only the first doctrine in the first sermon and only the second doctrine in the second sermon. Again, though the sermons are obviously meant to go together, they are formally separated. Such variations, when multiplied, led to the several sermon series which Edwards wrote and preached in the 1730s, one of them consisting of thirty preaching units.

Obviously, somewhere between the morning-and-afternoon sermon, divided between the Doctrine and the Application so that it could fill the entire Sabbath-day services, and the over-two-hundred-page, thirty-preaching-unit sermon series, the form of the sermon begins to disintegrate. Edwards became a master of his inherited sermon form, but in the 1730s, at the zenith of his mastery, he began experimenting artistically with the sermon. He apparently did everything he could do without actually abandoning the old form entirely, and the only possible conclusion one can draw from the manuscript evidence of his experiments is that he was searching, consciously or unconsciously, for a formal alternative to the sermon itself.

CHAPTER II
THE MAKING OF SERMONS

An essay, a play, a poem, indeed any work of literature, is ultimately the product of that mysterious mental activity known as the "creative process." The making of a sermon is likewise a truly artistic process, requiring of an effective preacher a degree of imaginative power and artistic discipline at least comparable to that of a poet. In order to meet the challenge of sermon-making, Jonathan Edwards gradually evolved an impressive apparatus of cross-referenced journals, notebooks, and sermons, a vast organon which, while it well may have been a means of Edwards' intellectual self-development or the mine of his treatise materials, was first of all the preacher's sermon-mill through which he attempted to meet the challenges of fresh interpretation of orthodoxy, inspirational rhetoric, and perhaps most of all, regular production.

Examining the copious extant portion of this body of writings will enable us to approach as near as is now possible to the creative process of making sermons. Before attempting analysis of the process itself, however, an inventory of the manuscript books and booklets that filled the hexagonal table and neighboring boxes and drawers in Edwards' study will help define the nature and scope of Edwards' apparatus.[1]

The remaining manuscript notebooks, alone, are of formidable bulk and diversity, but they can be divided and classified in the light of the sermon-making process. Although every line Edwards wrote

1. The lazy Susan table is now at Stockbridge but was probably in JE's possession in Northampton. It is, at any rate, a fine example of his Yankee ingenuity and practicality in solving problems of the study. The table presumably held his major notebooks, or those most relevant to an immediate project. JE's cross-reference notes occasionally refer to "the box" or "the drawer" as the repository of a particular manuscript. Most of the drawers mentioned were probably in his "scritore," as he called it, or escritoire, now in Jonathan Edwards College at Yale University, though some may have been in the "great bookcase" also mentioned in his notebooks.

may ultimately be related to the sermons, there are degrees of relevance and different functions among the notebooks. Thus, at the outset, the "Notes on Natural Philosophy" and some eleven other notebooks and booklets, most of them devoted to the elaboration of a single idea or the essential points of one of the published treatises, can be dismissed from consideration.[2] While these notes can tell us much about Edwards' mind and thought, they are not essential parts of the preacher's equipment.

1. The Notebook Resources

Those notebooks that are eminently relevant can be divided into two general groups: 1) a larger group, devoted to the recording and developing of ideas and, 2) a smaller group, devoted to the planning and regulating of Edwards' literary activities. In the first group are the "Miscellanies," "Shadows of Divine Things," "The Mind," "Notes on the Apocalypse," "Notes on the Scripture," and "Miscellaneous Observations on the Holy Scriptures." Virtually all of these notebooks (with the possible exception of "The Mind," the manuscript of which is lost) are cross-referenced to the sermon corpus, and before considering the notes on procedure a brief examination of the prime functional characteristics of each type of substantive notebook is in order.

Perhaps Samuel Hopkins' quaint observation that "Every thought, on any Subject which appear'd to him worth pursuing and preserving, he pursued, as far as he then could, with his Pen in his Hand"[3] was made with the "Miscellanies" particularly in mind. This collection of notes (many could more properly be described as essays) on Edwards' meditations and reading, filling nine manuscript volumes (seven folio, two quarto) with 1,406 entries, is the largest single repository of his theological speculations.[4] The entries have no topical

2. A fairly accurate and comprehensive list of the Edwards manuscripts now housed at the Beinecke Library, prepared by W. J. B. Edgar in 1934 and revised by Marjorie Wynne in 1964, is available at the library. This list does not include individual sermon manuscripts; they are indexed by text in a drawer of the card catalogue in the Beinecke Library reference room.

3. [Hopkins], *Life*, p. 41.

4. The accurate dating of JE's major notebooks and the early undated sermons has only recently been accomplished through the work of Thomas A. Schafer. The result of many years' study of the Edwards manuscripts, including a systematic investigation of watermarks and ink batches, his dates have been confirmed by my investigations in cross-referencing and sermon booklet stitching. Thus, this discussion relies upon Schafer's dates for sermons written before 1733 and for the following notebooks: "Miscellanies," "Notes

or thematic sequence, as is the rule in most of Edwards' notebooks; cross-references and a "table" or index prepared by Edwards unite relevant passages. Of course, there are patches of entries on one idea, reflecting the author's preoccupation with that idea at some point in time; otherwise, each new idea was added at the end of the existing list and numbered, though brief additions or revisions often could be squeezed into existing entries. There are about one hundred cross-references to sermons in the "Miscellanies" and its table. Some of these references indicate that the journal entry is itself based upon a sermon (where the entry includes a reference to a sermon), while others seem to have provided material for a sermon (where the sermon reference is added in a different ink). Some entries, especially in the index, simply refer to a sermon for its superior discussion of a point.

"Shadows of Divine Things," like "The Mind," is small and very specialized when compared with the "Miscellanies." This notebook consists of twenty-four folio leaves, plus three leaves of topical and Scripture-text tables. There are 212 numbered entries in the main section of the notebook and seven additional entries on the second leaf behind it, headed "Scriptures."[5] This last section is apparently the start of a new collection of images, specifically biblical images or types. The function of this notebook was to preserve accounts of (supposedly) natural phenomena which were, in Edwards' eyes, signs of specific aspects of God, his work, and his relationship with man. In the tradition of biblical typology, the notes record Edwards' attempt to read, not the Book of Holy Writ, but patterns in the phenomena of nature, patterns which might yield to the divinely illuminated eye messages seemingly as clear and coherent as the "messages" of the Old Testament when illuminated by the gospel.[6]

---

on the Apocalypse," "Catalogue" of books, "The Mind," "Notes on the Scripture," and "Shadows of Divine Things."

Since precise dating of most of these notebooks and many of the sermons is not essential to my argument, I will leave the more detailed discussion to the introduction of Schafer's forthcoming edition of the "Miscellanies." For my purposes, it is sufficient to point out that all of the above notebooks were begun during a burst of scholarly activity between 1722 and 1724, with the exception of "Shadows," which was not begun until 1728.

5. See below, p. 235, for the direction to make such a study of nature images from the Bible in the notebook, "Subjects of Enquiry."

6. The notebook was edited and published by Perry Miller with the title, *Images or Shadows of Divine Things* (New Haven, Yale Univ. Press, 1948), perhaps a shrewd compromise. Apparently, JE had trouble deciding what to call the book. "Images of Div[ine things]," "Shadows of Divine Things," "The Book of Nature & Common Providence," and

From a literary point of view, the notebook is at least an impressive collection of images or word-pictures designed to give key doctrinal points the utmost vividness, immediacy, and mnemonic vitality without sacrificing (as is the rule with richly suggestive images or symbols in poetry) one jot of doctrinal precision. The sermon canon offers many instances of Edwards' use of this image hoard. Indeed, the relationship between the sermon canon and the "Shadows" notebook parallels that of the "Miscellanies," and it is evident that Edwards' insight concerning an image was sometimes first recorded in a sermon manuscript. Moreover, sermon references in "Shadows" entries and its table call attention to relevant passages that Edwards never bothered to transfer to the notebook, and to particularly successful elaborations of the image in question. Whether or not Edwards had discovered the hieroglyph of the Deity in Nature, or like Newton had perceived the consistent principle within the event, he had certainly isolated, largely in the commonplaces of human experience, a suprarational confirmation of his doctrine that combined the functions of exposition and illustration, and that fixed the attention through the perception of analogy becoming symbol. The mundane and the divine, the momentary and the eternal: all are aligned through the vortex of inspired perception. Behind such an effort lay assumptions voiced by a kindred spirit many years before when he insisted that God, who "derived himself in clear and lovely stamps and impressions of Beauty and Goodness through the whole Creation, endeavors still to assimilate and unite it to himself."[7] The state of nature provides man an opportunity to complete God's creation through the spiritualization of nature, given the agents of perception and taste, as

---

"The Language & Lessons of Nature" are all on the notebook in one place or another. However, it is "Shadows of Divine Things" that appears at the head of the manuscript itself, probably the first name JE gave to the notes. Cross-references in other manuscript papers refer to the book as either "Images of Divine Things" or "Shadows of Divine Things," but never use both terms together.

It seems that the varying title may suggest more than that "Image" is a synonym for "Shadow," or vice versa (as Miller suggests in his title and in the introductory essay where he states, "The facts of experience became for Edwards, as they could not have been even for Hooker or Bunyan, the shadows, the very 'images' of divinity," p. 19). JE may, indeed, have had a point of discrimination beyond that which would separate mere tropes from types in nature (a preoccupation that Miller correctly identifies as the central purpose of the notebook), although this point of discrimination may have been problematic and a bit troublesome to the verbally meticulous scholar. For a fuller discussion of this interesting and crucial matter of "images," "shadows," and types, see Chapter IV, pp. 228–36.

7. John Smith, "A Christian's Conflicts and Conquests," in *Select Discourses* (2nd ed., Cambridge, 1673), p. 444.

offered or limited by God, re-attaching the material and spiritual in accordance with the design of the Creator.

"The Mind," as Edwards calls it in references, or his notebook for a proposed treatise entitled "The Natural History of the Mental World, or of the Internal World," was first printed from the manuscript in Dwight's *Life*.[8] Since the Dwight edition, the manuscript has been lost and we have today only the manuscript table, apparently incomplete. Although there are no sermon references in the text as published, it is obvious from a study of references to "The Mind" in other notebooks (such as the "Miscellanies" or "Shadows") that this notebook was an integral part of that corpus of notes employed by Edwards in composing sermons. Its most obvious value to the literary study of Edwards is that certain words are defined in it, such as "Excellency" and "Prejudice," which are essential to the idiom of the sermons; moreover, some of its entries, such as those on "Words," constitute the theoretical foundation of Edwards' rhetorical strategy.

The remaining notebooks in the substantive category are also the most nearly fundamental. "Notes on the Apocalypse," "Notes on the Scripture," and "Miscellaneous Observations on the Holy Scriptures" preserve Edwards' exegetical reading of, and circumambient speculations upon, the Bible. All of these notebooks are really variants of the Scripture-commentary, yet each type fulfills its special function.

The most specialized is the "Notes on the Apocalypse," a quarto notebook of some 208 numbered pages, plus eight loose leaves.[9] This work is primarily devoted to Edwards' readings of passages in the book of Revelation and their relationship to other prophetic passages in the Bible (Isaiah seems to be the most frequently mentioned). There are many cross-references within the book, and externally to the "Miscellanies," the other Scripture notebooks, and to biblical texts; there are, however, no direct references to the sermons here. Of course the sermons would be the normal depository of exegetical material from the notebook in any case, though there is evidence that

8. Sereno E. Dwight, *The Life of President Edwards* (New York, 1830). "The Mind" is printed in Appendix H, pp. 664–702. Dwight's text has been re-edited by Wallace E. Anderson and included in *The Scientific and Philosophical Writings, Works, 6,* 313–93. Anderson's discussion of the probable configuration of the manuscript is particularly informative.

9. This notebook has been meticulously edited by Stephen J. Stein in the *Apocalyptic Writings, The Works of Jonathan Edwards* (New Haven, Yale Univ. Press, 1977), 5, 97–305.

Edwards worked out material first in at least some of the many Revelation sermons.[1]

Other aspects of this remarkable notebook clearly demonstrate the extraordinary range of Edwards' "biblical" studies. Of course, there are the scholarly commentators to be excerpted and evaluated, but more remarkable are the later sections devoted to modern (contemporary) events that relate to apocalyptic or millennial historiography. The section on the "sixth vial" is composed primarily of newspaper excerpts. About half concern naval battles and piracies in which England, and sometimes Holland, triumph over France and Spain. The other half are devoted to friction between the Roman Catholic church and the governments of Roman Catholic countries. Obviously, Edwards was hoping to document the "decline and fall" of Roman Catholicism. A section on "hopefull aspects" is largely concerned with newspaper accounts of conversions (among Jews, Pagans, Mohammedans, Indians, and sundry other unregenerate folk), Roman Catholic troubles, Protestant successes (even financial), the phenomenon of Whitefield, and other "hopefull" events. Notable in these sections on contemporary events are Edwards' great factual detail (tonnages of ships taken or sunk—Roman Catholic versus Protestant—in tabular form), the focus upon financial affairs as indicators of God's Providence in the world, and the concentration upon global rather than local affairs. Here we see most vividly illustrated the truly "metaphysical" quality of Edwards' mind; Indian wars and the ancient Revelation, sinking ships and churches, money and God, eternity and the moment, or the world and Stockbridge—all were inextricably bound up, and the properly sensitized person could put his hand on the trembling web of the whole.

"Notes on the Scripture," or "SS.," as Edwards habitually designates them in cross-references, fill four manuscript volumes, two quarto and two folio, with 507 consecutively numbered entries. As in the case of the "Miscellanies," some of these are mere notes and some are essays that run on for eight or ten pages. There are also extensive quotations from secondary sources on the Scriptures, for Edwards was a diligent student of others' ideas on scriptural commentary, as in all other areas that concerned him.

Though the notebooks contain observations on many aspects of the Scriptures, a few of the topics that most interested Edwards can be

1. Ibid., p. 136.

identified. Book I in particular, though not exclusively, is devoted to the study of biblical "types." The entire book of Esther is "a shadow of gospel things and times" (no. 46); Noah's Ark is a "type of the Church in Christ" (no. 297), and "Ezekiel's Wheels" is a dynamic image worthy of pages of speculation and commentary (nos. 389, 391, 394). But the biblical accounts are not allowed to stand alone; there is a vast plan which is evident in other places and times. Consequently, Edwards notes the relation of classical and pagan myth to scriptural accounts, as in entry no. 401 ("Fables applied to Bacchus of Sacred Extract"), or more exotically in entry no. 455, where there is a discussion of "Fohi, the Chinese Noah." Lesser areas of interest are linguistic problems in translating from Hebrew and Greek, the stylistic theory of Hebrew authors, the allegory of the Song of Solomon, and the authorship of the Pentateuch.

Generally, these notebooks preserve Edwards' most direct responses to the substance of his art in preaching, the Word of God. As for sermon references, what was said of "Notes on the Apocalypse" can be applied here, for there is only one direct sermon reference in the four volumes.

In 1731, Edwards acquired from Benjamin Pierpont a large interleaved Bible,[2] which he titled "Miscellaneous Observations on the Holy Scriptures." The book, consisting of a small octavo Bible (London, 1652) interleaved with quarto pages (432 leaves, numbered [incorrectly] 1–904), is stoutly bound in full calf. The blank pages are ruled into double columns, enabling the commentator to place his annotations on the larger pages in positions proportionately apposite to the numbered verses of the double-columned, printed Bible. More-

2. The history of the exchange is somewhat dubious. The Bible bears, on its second blank page, the following inscriptions: "Benjamin Pierpont, his Book A.D., 1728" and "Jonathan Edwards, his Book, 1748." Now the third notebook on the Scriptures bears a dated item: entry 462 contains the date, January 4, 1748. The fourth (and last) notebook, moreover, is about half empty. This circumstantial evidence suggests that JE acquired the Bible in 1748 and began using it in place of the Scripture notebooks.

Internal evidence suggests another conclusion, however. First, it is obvious that much of JE's handwriting in the Bible antedates 1748 by at least fifteen years. Secondly, the Bible was rebound after JE had been using it for some time, as is indicated by stitches which pass through JE's notes near the inside margins of quite a few pages. Finally, there are records of JE's family finances at the back of the Bible (p. 904) bearing the date, September 27, 1732. After studying these bits of evidence, I have concluded that JE's dated signature was written in the Bible not when he acquired it, but when he had it rebound, probably in 1748. He most likely acquired the Bible in 1731, or at the latest, in 1732. This means that JE used the Bible and the Scripture notebooks concurrently, not consecutively.

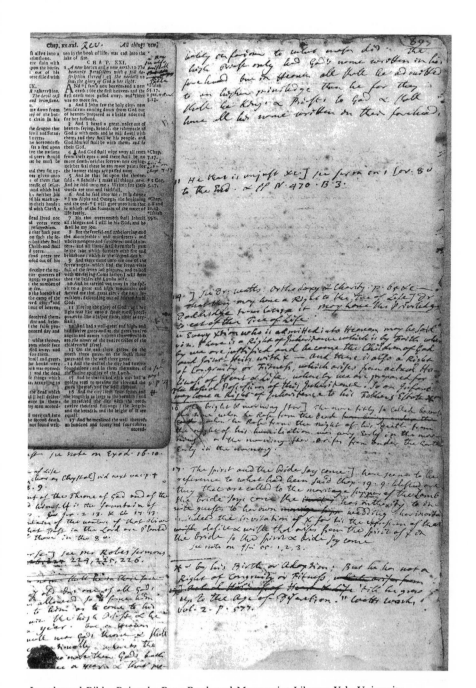

Interleaved Bible. Beinecke Rare Book and Manuscript Library, Yale University.

over, possibly as a result of measures taken when the Bible was rebound, there is frequent double-interleaving in areas where Edwards
had much to say, and there are five long "commentary chapters" (each
nine double-columned pages in length) on particular chapters of five
New Testament books. So far, it is obvious that the interleaved Bible
is an adjunct to the Scripture notebooks, primarily a depository of
the briefer, more specific remarks on biblical texts.

But perusal of the volume leads inevitably to the conclusion that
the Bible had another, perhaps equally important function in the
Edwards study. Throughout the Bible there are cross-references to
his various notebooks and to sermons, and many of these are compound:

> [Gen.] "Miscell. 702, p. 37–42; B. 5 [Miscell.] 1048; B. 3 [Notes on
>   SS.] 448; Shadows 72." (P. 8.)
> [Deut.] "See my Treatise on Justification. 95–6." (P. 148.)
> [Matt. 16:28] "SS. 484 B. 3, No 197 & 414, note on Chap 21:43,
>   Miscell. 842 B. 3, 1198 & 1199 B. 8." (P. 672.)
> [Luke 23:44] "vid. Heb. 9:12, 25–28, Heb. 7:27, Shadows of Divine
>   Things No 54." (P. 735.)
> [I Cor. 15:29] "See this text more fully spoken to in answer to a
>   question proposed to be answered before the asso-
>   ciation in one of my drawers." (P. 825.)
> [Col. 3:17] "vid. serm. on I Pet. 2:5, the three Reasons of the Doc."
>   (P. 850.)

A few representative examples, these entries do not pretend to indicate the full range of entry types. In addition to the references to
other notebooks and to the works of over forty-five authors, there are
keyed cross-references within the Bible itself, and in a few places
whole columns of related Scripture texts are listed beside a verse.
The combination of multitudinous compound references and the
comprehensive list of Edwards' interesting "keying signs" on the verso
of the title page indicates that a crucial function of the Bible in Edwards' study was that of an index; indeed, the interleaved Bible might
be designated the "Index of Indices" or "Table of Tables."[3] Although

3. The keying signs, another example of JE's Yankee ingenuity, appear at first to be a
comically inadequate jumble of variations on a few standard signs, but in practice they do
work, largely because there are so many that JE never had to repeat one within the pages
referred to. While the list may have been started to indicate cross-references within the
Bible only, it in fact became the central list of such signs, as he uses the same ones in all

each of the above-mentioned notebooks, with the exception of "Notes on the Apocalypse," has one or more tables, and though all (very probably "The Mind," too) have cross-referencing, the interleaved Bible is the place where the very cross-roads or junctions of Edwards' recorded thoughts can be found. Moreover, all of these junctions are here firmly fixed to a biblical text, and the biblical text is the ultimate point of reference in the Edwards manuscript canon. As A. V. G. Allen has observed, "Science and metaphysics do not interest him as ends in themselves, but as subordinated to a theological purpose."[4] And all theology for Edwards was ultimately founded in Scripture.

The notebooks listed above—"Miscellanies," "Shadows of Divine Things," "The Mind," "Notes on the Apocalypse," "Notes on the Scripture," and "Miscellaneous Observations on the Holy Scriptures" [the interleaved Bible]—appear to have been Preacher Edwards' essential workbooks. All but the Bible and "Shadows" were begun early in the period of Edwards' sermon-making, and all appear to have been used until very near the end of his life. Moreover, all show signs of continual reworking throughout these years ("The Mind" being included through late references to it in other notebooks), both in the sense of additional entries being made or old entries revised, and in the sense of ever-proliferating cross-references and indices that involve the above notebooks, along with many sermons, in an ever-developing body of recorded thought. Indeed, the word "corpus" might be taken in its original sense when we consider

---

his writings.

Typical of these signs are the following:

$$\text{\textasteriskcentered \ \ tt \ \ \ \ + \ \# \ \ ¶ \ \ ⋇ \ ↑ \ \ || \ \ ⋉ \ \ Ξ \ \ ⧺ \ \ ⌐ \ \ ⧧ \ \ + \ \ ⋌}$$

There are about thirty in the list, though some are merely inversions or multiples (up to three) of the same sign. A paradigm of his use of the sign would be, "See my [notebook], page [ ], at this mark in the margin *."

There are a few common signs, even in the Bible, that are not listed here, and we might note them if only to illustrate further JE's ingenuity. ⊏⧽ signifies "forward," while ⊏⧼ signifies "back." However, more common is a stylization of these figures where ↶ is the sign for "forward" and ↷ is the sign for "back." Thus, the sign, * ↶ at the end of an entry would indicate that there was an addition to it a little further on in the manuscript which would bear the sign, * ↷ at its head.

⊓ and ⊔ indicate first and second columns, respectively. They are always used when JE is making references to double-columned pages, as in the Bible itself. Thus, with a combination of words and the above signs, JE usually directed himself to the manuscript, the page, the column, and to a point in that column—all in a note no larger than many a polysyllabic word.

4. *Jonathan Edwards* (Boston, 1890), p. 6.

this group of manuscripts: the Bible is the heart from which radiate veins of cross-reference to the various specific manuscript organs which are in turn connected by less substantial veins of cross-reference to each other, as each organ (including the heart) is finely-veined within itself. There is a true circulation of references, and by following it through the manuscript corpus one can observe Edwards' ideas developing, deepening, and sometimes changing.

The above notebooks and related sermons could contribute to the nourishment and substance of any new sermon Edwards might compose, but the process of composition was regulated, directly and indirectly, by another group of notebooks, those included in the second, smaller group devoted to the planning and regulating of Edwards' literary activities. Included in this group are his "Diary" and "Resolutions" (the indirect controls), and three more specifically functional types of notebooks, the "Catalogue" of books, the sermon notebooks, and finally, "Subjects of Enquiry."

Both the diary and the "Resolutions" manuscript have been lost since S. E. Dwight edited them for publication in his *Life* of Edwards. But the texts printed in this biography can, when examined in the light of existing manuscripts, tell much about the working habits and total regimen of Edwards at the outset of his career. The dated entries of the "Diary," and the explicit references within it to the making of the "Resolutions," fix these notations primarily in the years 1722 through 1725, very near the beginning of his professional preaching career.[5] This was a time of practical preparation, a time in which the working habits of a lifetime were acquired. Both the "Diary" and the "Resolutions" are essentially handbooks, wrought out of the trials and errors of personal experience, to guide Edwards in his quest for personal salvation and the fulfillment of his spiritual and intellectual capacities in a great work. Indeed, it seems that the fulfillment and the salvation were aspects of the same thing for Edwards, so thin is the line between the self and the mission in his case.

The "Diary"[6] is the more interesting of the two documents, pri-

5. It is assumed that JE's "career" began with his appointment to the New York pastorate in August 1722. At least two or three manuscript sermons antedate this pastorate, but they are presumably either collegiate exercises or, more probably, sermons prepared as part of JE's licensing examination. Perhaps JE wrote a few sermons to have on hand when he arrived in New York. He did not date his sermons until 1733, and the date of 1720–21 for the earliest extant sermon (Is. 3:10) is a matter of supposition from the evidence of ink, paper, and handwriting.

6. Dwight, *Life*, pp. 76–94, 99–106.

marily because it is the more concrete and detailed. Scattered among the 148 dated entries are numerous statements that give specific data on Edwards' efforts in the disciplines of reading, thinking, and writing. Moreover, the "Diary" itself is an early example of Edwardsean method in notebook-making and notebook-using. The following selections are intended to exemplify the significant patterns in Edwards' hours of literary activity at this crucial point in his life:

> *Wednesday night, Aug. 28* [1723]. When I want books to read; yea, when I have not very good books, not to spend time in reading them, but in reading the Scriptures, in perusing resolutions, reflections, etc., in writing on types of the Scripture, and other things, in studying the languages . . . Remember as soon as I can, to get a piece of slate, or something, whereon I can make short memorandums while travelling.[7]

Much of Edwards' routine is summed up in this one entry. First is the reference to "books to read," hinting at the almost feverish search for new books that is so extensively documented in his "Catalogue." Second, in terms of practical priorities (for they do not have to be pursued, discovered, or even borrowed) are the Scriptures, that point of converging references in Edwards' working life which were studied continuously, often in the light of the new books mentioned first. Third, the reference to "perusing" his own writings is significant, for nearly the whole of the massive manuscript canon left at his death reveals the repeated passage of Edwards. All of the major workbooks and notebooks, and many of the minor ones and sermons, bear deletions, corrections, and additions in various shades of ink in the hands of various periods—from beginning to end and, as it were, layer upon layer. Edwards did not only develop himself through writing, but through rereading and revising his writings.[8] As early as the "Diary" period, Edwards was aware of the crucial function of these literary activities in his life: "I am apt to think it a good way, when I am indisposed to reading and study, to read of my own remarks . . . to set me agoing again."[9] Finally in this passage is the reference to "slate,

---

7. Ibid., p. 94.

8. A specific instance in this process is found in the "Diary" itself: "*Thursday morning, July 25* [1723]. Altered, and anew established the 8th Resolution . . ." (Ibid., p. 90). Also in the "Diary" are several instances of cross-referencing between the "Diary" and the "Resolutions," and within the "Diary" itself.

9. *Monday, Oct. 5* [1724]. (Ibid., p. 104.)

or something, whereon I can make short memorandums while travelling." This remark calls attention to what must have been one of Edwards' most sustained preoccupations as a scholar and writer: how to make better use of his time. Indeed, the whole of this entry is occasioned by Edwards' concern for utilizing his time with the greatest efficiency, and there are seven entries in the "Diary," plus two Resolutions, that are explicitly concerned with the challenge of time. Moreover, his entire manuscript canon testifies to his constant pursuit of efficiency and his unremitting efforts to economize mind, time, and materials. Such is the ingenuity of his numerous homely devices that, if the stories of his pinning mnemonic slips of paper to his coat, bed hangings, or to the woodwork of his study are not true, they should be.

More detailed or specific references to Edwards' working procedures come in other diary entries:

> *Monday, Jan. 14* [1723]. About 10 o'clock in the morning, made this book, and put these papers in it . . .[1]
> *Thursday morning, July 25* [1723]. . . . *Memorandum.* At a convenient time, to make an alphabet of these resolutions and remarks, that I may be able to educe them, on proper occasions, suitable to the condition I am in, and the duty I am engaged in.[2]

Here is an account of a prototypical process, according to the physical evidence of virtually all of the major notebooks (the exceptions being the notebooks prepared to outline treatises, all productions of his later years). It was Edwards' habit to make a rather tentative start (a single folio sheet or even less) in beginning each new notebook. The first jottings were usually not numbered and even the intention of the body of observations was likely to be in doubt. Soon, however, Edwards inferred the "drift" of the notes and fixed an appropriate title to the collection, thus effectively limiting its scope. As the notes began to fill additional sheets, he stitched the sheets together, forming a booklet. At about the same time, in most instances, he either paginated the booklet or gave the separate entries numbers. Having done this, he could then make a table or alphabetical index which would be kept up as the body of notes grew. These tables were usually topical, though sometimes they consisted of Scripture citations, and

1. Ibid., p. 80.
2. Ibid., p. 90.

occasionally both types of tables were made for one notebook. As the notebook gathered momentum, Edwards frequently added bunches of blank leaves, usually in the form of infolded quires. In general, the longer the notebook flourished, the thicker the added quires of new paper became. Finally, sometimes after the passage of several years, he carefully bound the notes (singly or in separately bound sections) in a heavy paper or cloth cover. The paper covers were then appropriately labelled in ink, usually in both directions (so that the title could be read if the notebook were lying upside down), and on front and back.

The "Resolutions" (most of them written in 1722)[3] add little specific information on Edwards' working methods, but they do in many instances sharply focus their author's attitudes toward his literary work. For instance, Resolution 44 establishes the complete dominion of religion in Edwards' life and work, including "scientific" or "philosophical" writings, as of January 12, 1723. Moreover, 28 establishes the Bible as the central book in Edwards' reading program, as 11 seems to establish the relationship between Bible reading and the keeping of substantive notebooks by directing Edwards to solve any question in divinity as soon as possible after it comes to mind. Finally, Resolutions 5 and 6 confirm or codify his diary's preoccupation with the saving of time. Indeed, most of these resolutions are probably codifications of attitudes and practices already nearly habitual to Edwards at the time of his making the "Resolutions." His habits of composition and notebook-making would indicate this. But the "Resolutions" were to be perused once a week, according to the headnote, presumably to insure that inclination would become practice, and the occasional virtue a habit.

The "Diary" and the "Resolutions" provide us with significant insights into Edwards' early literary activities. What is most interesting is the knowledge that habits of work established so early were to continue, virtually unchanged, throughout his lifetime. One may be surprised by the sentiment of the diary entry for "*Sabbath morning, Oct. 14* [1723]. Narrowly to observe after what manner I act, when I am in a hurry, and to act as much so, at other times, as I can, without prejudice to the business."[4] Yet this statement is seminal for Edwards' personal literary history and illuminates many of his virtues and

3. Ibid., pp. 68–73.
4. Ibid., p. 100.

faults as a prose writer, as it calls attention once again to the significant streak of Yankee practicality in this theologian, philosopher, and student of esoteric typologies.

Of all Edwards' regulatory notebooks, the most significant for his preaching are the sermon notebooks, including a portion of the "Catalogue" of books. Indeed, it is the first loose leaf of the "Catalogue" (an old letter sheet) that may be considered the earliest extant repository of sermon notes:[5]

> Texts: I beseech you, brothers,
> that ye encrease more and more
>
> ———
>
> What do ye more than others
>
> ———
>
> Not unto us, not unto us, etc.
>
> —
>
> If it be possible let this cup pass
>
> ———
>
> And his banner over me was love
> Doc. that Christ conquers believers by
> Love.
>
> ————————————
>
> Ps. 65:11 Thou crownest the
> year with thy goodness.
>   Thanksgiving

"Thanksgiving," of course, identifies the occasion of the projected sermon. Worth noting is that Edwards is here proposing a suggestive text rather than a socially relevant doctrinal idea as the foundation of the sermon. Undoubtedly the young minister, perhaps preparing to preach one of his first Northampton sermons, was composing his sermon in a kind of social vacuum, without reference to any particular group of people or to any particular situation. Later, he would nearly cease making such sermon notations. Also notable is the rhetorical quality of all but the last entry. These are suggestive rather

---

5. The left-hand column of writing on the outside of the sheet is a list of titles or brief descriptions of projects that JE was contemplating. In fact, the sheet provides documentary proof that JE conceived of his life's work at a fairly early age. The "Rational Account," the "Types of the Scriptures," and other life-works are listed here, some as early as 1723–24. The "sermon notes"—mostly scriptural excerpts—are written at the top of the column, at an angle of 90 degrees to the other entries. They were written sometime in 1726.

than explicit even as Scripture texts, as mysterious and enigmatic in themselves as "Their foot shall slide in due time."

The bulk of Edwards' extant sermon notes, however, is contained in three notebooks especially made by him for the purpose. The notebooks were not labelled, but their function is clear from the contents. Now they bear numbers in pencil on their covers (like several other notebooks) which were placed there by some past cataloguer of the Edwards' manuscripts. "14," "19," and "45" obviously have reference only to some arbitrary list of manuscripts, but the numbers still serve as convenient reference tags.[6]

Numbers 14 and 19 are thin octavos, bound in the usual heavy paper. The form of the entries alone in 19 suggests that it should be the earliest of the three notebooks.[7] It is a peculiar document, for only the first three and one-quarter leaves are taken up by Edwards' sermon notes, and the remainder of the twenty or so leaves are filled with a late eighteenth-century record of legal suits and bond payments. It seems that this notebook may have been misplaced or discarded by Edwards shortly after he started it, but remaining in the family it was resurrected for a more mundane use by a descendant.

The few leaves used by Edwards in notebook 19 provide insights into his changing techniques and interests, for they seem to mediate between the few notes in the "Catalogue" and sermon notebook 14. Most of the entries in 19 are mere notes, and many are suggestive biblical quotations, as in the "Catalogue":

Come let us walk in the light of the Lord.

Her ways are ways of pleasantness and all her paths are peace.

That follow the lamb wheresoever he goes, walk as children of light.

6. It is my supposition that the pencil markings on the JE manuscripts were made by Edwards Amasa Park (1808–1900), compiler of a notebook of materials for a biography of JE, entitled "The Edwardean" (now in the Beinecke Library). There are many other marks on the manuscripts not by JE in "black" (various shades), blue, and brown ink, and in red pencil. A. B. Grosart even signed his name here and there.

7. I have dated these three notebooks, first, by the hand and by locating copies of sermons projected in the notebooks, and second, by ink analysis where necessary. With many such tests of the entries, tentative time spans can be given to the notebooks, and finally, approximately how many sermon notes were made, on average, within a month's time can be determined. In the case of notebook 19, ink analysis alone has required that it be placed parallel to the early portion of notebook 45, in late 1741 and early 1742. This fact suggests that 19 was created specifically for itinerant preaching during the Great Awakening, as is also suggested by the use of categories of persons for topical headings.

Oh that I had the wings of a dove that I might fly away and lie
at rest.

Concerning Moses' coming from converse with God with his
face shining.

My yoke is easy and my burden light.

The above entries, taken from several places in the first three leaves
of the notebook, are representative of 19 in tone and form. They are
scriptural, suggestive, and generally pleasant or even joyful in tone.

Other entries are more specifically directed, not to problems or
occasions, but to people:

CHILDREN. Holy child Jesus.
    Concerning the infancy of Christ.
    Concerning Timothy, Samuel, etc.
    Be ye followers of God as dear children.

To YOUNG PEOPLE: Recommend the example of Shadrach,
Meshach and Abednego.
    And the example of Joseph.

OLD MEN. Those four instances of blessed missions in old age:
Moses, Isaiah, Daniel, apostle John.

The tone is still scriptural, elevated, and even impersonal, yet there
is recognition of the specific member-categories of any congregation.

Finally, there are a very few entries with a fuller formal apparatus:

These things persons ought to seek after:
    That they may live to the glory of God.
    Their own comfort.
    That they may be blessings to others.

Directions. Seek.
    With two things.
      Not with unquietness.
      Not with discouragement.

Ps. 103:1 Bless the Lord oh my soul and all that is within me bless
his holy name.
    We ought to love and praise God with all that is within us.

Matt. 6:31–32 For after all those things do the gentiles seek.
    Doc. A worldly man is in the light of God like a heathen.

Here, more explicitly in each succeeding example, are the emerging outlines of the sermon form. The last example, occurring on the last page used for sermon notes, is as formal as any entry in number 19. Moreover, a note of warning is evident in this last doctrine, as in a few entries not recorded here, definitely a very minor note in this sermon notebook. The examples given above (and taken out of their true order to emphasize the various types of entries) were all written ca. 1741–42, a tentative dating since, though thirty-one entries in sermon notebook 19 are marked as having been used,[8] only one corresponding sermon manuscript has been located.

Sermon notebook 14, extending from 1736 through 1738, contains the most fully developed material of the three sermon notebooks. Moreover, it bears the most obvious signs of handling and wear. Paginated by Edwards, it contains sixty pages in all, although six leaves (twelve pages) have been torn from the volume (no more than two leaves from any one point, however). The fact of the torn-out pages, plus the presence of several passages keyed to passages on other pages, indicates that number 14 was a true sermon "workbook" as well as a list of subjects.

Entries in this notebook are more frequently complete in that they contain both a stated text and its correlative doctrine, and many bear occasional labels as well as the auditory classifications cited in the case of number 19. Thus, there are entries reserved for "Fast," "Thanksgiving," "Contribution," "Sacrament," "Lecture," and "Ordination." Edwards appears to be working in a more systematic way in number 14, and the entries are, even when brief, a little further along the road to the completed sermon.

The most significant innovation in number 14, however, is the inclusion of actual outlines of sermons:

> Heb. 5:12 For wherefore 'tis time ye ought to be teachers ye have need that one teach you again which be the first principles of the oracles of God.
> DOC. Every Christian should make a business of endeavoring to grow in knowledge in divinity.

What we mean by divinity.

8. In all three sermon notebooks (as in other notebooks and even in some sermons), JE marked passages "used" by placing a single vertical line through the middle of the entry. JE seems to have been wholly consistent in this usage. Deletions are made in two ways: simple lining out (like this) in the case of a few words, and crossing out of longer passages with a large "X" that extends from the first to the last lines of the deleted entry.

Sermon Notebook 14. Beinecke Rare Book and Manuscript Library, Yale University.

How many kinds of knowledge or divinity there are.
Two-fold: speculative, spiritual.

Should grow in both.
The former is necessary to the latter.

Our business should doubtless consist much in the improvement of those faculties whereby we are distinguished from beasts. We have faculties above beasts because of a higher business.

This is reasonable; therefore, to obtain knowledge and surely especially knowledge of those things for which we especially received our faculties to know.

The main business of the life of a Christian is to live to God, and everyone should gain knowledge about those things that appertain to his main work so men in their several trades should strive to get knowledge in them.

Those things most worthy to be known.

In these things our main happiness consists. (pp. 58–59.)[9]

The sermon of which this example is the epitome is printed in the *Works*, Worcester rev. ed., *4*, 1–15; however, there is no extant manuscript of the fully developed sermon. There must have been one, though, for this outline is much too brief, at this period in Edwards' career, for pulpit delivery.[1] Apparently it is a rare instance of a first rough sketch of a sermon. Quite probably, the pages removed from number 14 contained other such drafts, since Edwards did not remove pages where all the entries were marked "used" in any one of the three sermon notebooks. Nor, on the other hand, did he remove long-unused entries. Perhaps he sometimes removed outlines

9. In this introduction, page references to manuscripts paginated by JE will be given parenthetically following quoted material. Unless noted otherwise, the manuscripts are part of the Beinecke Library collections.

1. In this passage, and in many of the following sermon excerpts, the lines correspond to lines of division that JE drew between heads and between units of thought within heads. These lines vary in length according to the significance of the divisions, and the lines above reproduce this characteristic. JE apparently began using the lines (undoubtedly an aid to reading in the pulpit, and perhaps a tool of organization in composition) in his third extant sermon (Heb. 9:27), though they have been added to all of the sermons.

such as this to facilitate the copying and elaborating necessary for a complete draft.[2]

At least two kinds of material are evident in this outline: heads, as one would expect, and what can best be described as the "essential phrasing of ideas," comparatively lengthy passages that appear, more or less verbatim, in the midst of longer passages in the printed sermon. This indicates that Edwards was interested not only in getting the formally structured intellectual burden of the sermon into his notes, but apt phrases, similes, and illustrations as well. In the case of this entry, both argument and illustration are incomplete, and some significant portions of the printed sermon are hardly hinted at.

Unlike numbers 19 and 14, sermon notebook 45 is a fairly substantial octavo, containing 198 numbered pages (pp. 168–98 blank). It is obviously a continuation of the previous notebooks, and was probably begun in late 1738 or early 1739. This largest sermon notebook provides a fascinating "sermonic chronicle" of Edwards' final years at Northampton, the period of transition, and the years at Stockbridge. The last verifiable entry was made sometime in 1755 or 1756.

In character, this notebook is different from the previous notebooks, particularly in that many of the entries are really notes on preaching duties rather than textual or thematic briefs for sermons:

> Preach a sermon wherein I would direct souls in seeking salvation from the hints given in the story of Joseph. (P. 9.)
>
> To preach a sermon against robbing fruit trees and gardens, etc. before next fruit time if I should live. (P. 13.)
>
> Preach a sermon to children the sabbath after next to stir 'em up to love the Lord Jesus Christ. (P. 29.)
>
> To choose some subject on purpose to show how unreasonable it is that persons should strive less in religion after conversion than before. (P. 41.)
>
> Reprove others for telling their judgments when they think others are converted. (P. 53.)
>
> Show under some text what will make a happy people. How

---

2. A note in the *Works,* Worcester rev. ed., *4,* 1, identifies the sermon as "Dated November, 1739," the date apparently being that of first preaching. This does not disprove my hypothetical terminal date for notebook 14, however, as the sermon in question is one of the last entries in it, and I have supposed that JE might have drawn upon unused entries for months after making them.

religion would proceed in the right channel among them, and how happy and beautiful that would be. (P. 85.)

Show very particularly how common people are led into a false, imaginary religion through the mistake of the terms that ministers use such as having the eyes opened, seeing, etc. (P. 115.)

Here, in addition to the normal cares of the pastor, are Edwards' attempts to stabilize his congregation during the turbulence of the Great Awakening (the several entries following p. 50 having been made in the early 1740s); indeed, one can observe in entries such as these a significant shift from the theological to the psychological in Edwards' thinking about sermons. The sermon is not merely the prepared word of God, nor even the preacher's inspiration on some aspect of religion or life, but a response to a specific social situation in the town. Of course, such entries represent only one aspect of notebook 45, but it would seem to be a significant one. Otherwise, the last sermon notebook continues many of the themes of the previous notebooks, with perhaps greater emphasis upon the admonitory than is evident in number 14.

In form the entries tend more and more to be mere statements of thesis or identifications of issues that must be considered before the congregation. The sermon's text seems quite adventitious in most cases:

Preach a sermon about the spirit of God in directing us into the way of duty. (P. 10.)

To preach on the subject of the darkness that is in the mind of man. (P. 19.)

Doc. from some text; God's manner is first to give grace, then to try it, then to crown it. (P. 64.)

Concerning the labors and fatigues that husbandmen endure for temporal good: to urge this as an argument why they should labor for spiritual good. (P. 88.)

Doc. from some text, there is but one way to heaven and all other ways are ways to hell.

Prov. 15:24 . . . [added later.] (P. 94.)

In this same category of entries is one made sometime in early June 1741:

Doc. from some text, that there is nothing that keeps wicked men every moment out of hell but God's sovereign pleasure. (P. 52.)

As scholars have observed, Edwards wrote two sermons on the text of Deut. 32:35 before he composed his most famous sermon, but a perusal of the sermon manuscripts reveals that it was not the text but the above thematic inspiration that produced the thought, the peculiar tone, and the power of *Sinners in the Hands of an Angry God.* Likewise, the language of many entries in sermon notebook 45 indicates an increasing tendency to a direct personal response to the question of what to proclaim from the pulpit.

For this reason, the series of entries in number 45 constitutes a kind of sketch or outline of the events in Edwards' life, particularly those crucial events during the late 1740s and early 1750s.

> Hos. 4:4 Let no man strive nor reprove another, for thy people are as they that strive with the priest.
>
> Doc. For a people to contend with their minister tends to make their case as to their spiritual good past all remedy.
>
> I choose this time to treat on this subject because now there is no contention between me and my people. (pp. 132–33.)

This entry, made in March or April of 1749, may well indicate a leader's gambit, particularly when one recalls Edwards' remark to his friend in Boston, Thomas Foxcroft, in a letter dated May 24, 1749. He speaks of his relationship with the Northampton congregation during the catastrophic qualifications controversy: "I seem, as it were, to be casting myself off from a precipice; and have no other way, but to go on, as it were blindfold, i.e. shutting my eyes to everything else but the evidence of the mind and will of God, and the path of duty . . ." Apparently, he never prepared the sermon for delivery.

A few months later, there is another unused entry:

> In Moses' Blessing of Levi.
> ORDINATION. Deut. 33:11 Smite through the loins of them that rise against Him, and of them that hate Him, that they rise not again.
> Subject: The danger of injuring the ministers of Christ. (P. 136.)

And yet another entry, made nearly a year after the first in this series:

> Prov. 11:8 The righteous is delivered out of trouble and the wicked cometh in his stead.
>
> Doc. There is approaching a great change in the state of things wherein things will be turned upside down with regard to the state of the righteous and the wicked. (P. 143.)

Soon after the above entry, perhaps in January of 1750, a yet more specific entry:

> FAREWELL SERMON Jer. 25:3 From the thirteenth year of Josiah the son of Amon King of Judah even unto this day (that is the three and twentieth year). The word of the Lord came unto me and I have spoken unto you but ye have not hearkened. (P. 143.)

And still later, perhaps in late May or June of 1750, there is the entry for the farewell sermon that was actually preached on July 1:

> FAREWELL SERMON.
> Doc. ministers and the people that have been under their care must meet one another before Christ's tribunal at the Day of Judgment. II Cor. 1:14 (P. 146.)

Edwards did not cease to preach in Northampton with the farewell sermon, and there is a section of number 45 where entries are marked, often alternately, "Northampton" and "Indians." Typical of the former category in tone is the following entry:

> AT NORTHAMPTON. These words, The blackness of darkness forever.
> Subject: The everlasting dismal darkness of the pit of Hell. (P. 154.)

After this section is a page with the word "Indians" inscribed in large letters at its head, and the following brief list beneath:

> Backsliding when the unclean spirit is gone out of a man, etc.
> Christ hast redeemed us to God by his blood. Blood of a mere man could not have done it.
> Concerning the importance of knowing the holy Scripture.
> Doc. the gospel is good news.
> II Thess. 1:7, 8, 9, 10. In flaming fire.
> Concerning the duty of parents and children.
> They that be whole need not the physician, but they that are sick. I come not to call the righteous but sinners to repentance. (P. 167.)

Thus, the process begins all over again; the notes for the teaching of the Indians are, in retrospect, a fair synopsis of the notes for the teaching of Northamptonites. Perhaps at this stage of his career, Edwards could see little difference between his "savage" and "civilized" congregations. The bulk of the Indian outline sermons written at Stockbridge confirms this, as a matter of fact, in that they are not original but outlines of Northampton sermons, mostly from the 1730s with now and then a deft change of illustration or occasional reference.

Whether or not the note was actually developed into a sermon, the very making of such sermon notes as those in this last series indicates the significance of the sermon in the life of the renowned writer of metaphysical treatises. The sermon bodies forth the contours of life, marks the point at which theology becomes a part of it, the point at which the learned theologian must step forth as a witness and grapple with life. For even in the case of the Calvinist-Idealist, there is the truth of the paradox that transfigures all of Edwards' thought: "'Tis as much men's duty to be converted as 'tis to perform any act that is in their own power."[3]

The leaf from the "Catalogue" of books and the succeeding three sermon notebooks[4] provide a documentary record of the first stage of the sermon-writing process which, with the exception of the hiatus between 1726 and 1736, spans most of Edwards' preaching career. A few conclusions about Edwards' changing attitudes toward the sermon and sermon-making implicit in these entries over thirty years would seem to be in order. For Edwards' attitude toward the strategy of the sermon appears to have undergone a few significant changes, and though it must be acknowledged that he is one of the most consistent of writers in both technique and theme, certain undeniable changes in emphasis over the years of sermon notebook entries can nevertheless be recognized.

First, the primary function of the sermon notebook itself seems to alter over the years. At the beginning, it is a storehouse of inspirational material, for the most part scriptural phrases and references

3. Sermon notebook 45, p. 104.

4. Yet another booklet might be added: a coverless bundle of seven leaves, mostly octavo, bearing the title "Subjects" on the first leaf and "Mohawks" on the third. For the most part, it contains Scripture excerpts and doctrinal statements comparable to those found in the other sermon notebooks. The hand and the references to the Indians indicate that this booklet belongs to the early Stockbridge period. I suppose that this booklet was made during JE's trial visit to Stockbridge during the winter of 1751, when JE's regular sermon notebook was probably left behind in Northampton. The booklet contains no sermonic ideas beyond those in the "Indians" list above. The ms. is now in the library of the Andover Newton Theological School.

to specific episodes in the Bible. Gradually the notebook becomes a workbook, perhaps indicating an increasing devotion to the art of making sermons, but more likely indicating an effort to eliminate the need for a full first draft, separate from the pulpit draft of the sermon. Finally, the business of pulpit strategy seems to take precedence over the matters of material and homiletical technique, and it is for this reason that the last pages of Northampton entries do give us a suggestive sketch of pastor and congregation in conflict.

Another significant change occurs in the focus of the entries, that is, in the implicit or explicit context in which they were written. The earliest entries, those bits of Scripture, seem to have been selected for their mere rhetorical suggestiveness. In the early sermon notebooks as well, the entries are frequently indicative of a mind completely absorbed in Scripture and relatively indifferent to any practical application thereof. But as the preacher became more intent upon his role as pastor, the isolated bits of Scripture give way to entries preoccupied with auditory: "Old Men," "Virgins," "Natural Persons," and "Children." Soon, not only auditors but occasions— "Fast," "Thanksgiving," "Sacrament," "Lecture," and even "Expedition to Canada"—were dutifully noted and prepared for. Finally, Edwards begins making specific references to particular problems and (probably) to individuals in his congregation. The overall movement is obviously from the private to the public context, from the general theme to the specific issue, and from the eternal (or at least, the temporally general) to the immediate moment. It should be remembered that these entries do not necessarily mirror changes in the end product, the sermon, but they do indicate changes in the process of sermon composition and, ultimately, in Edwards' conception of the bases and primary function of sermons.

Lastly, the changes in the quality of utterance, or the "tone of voice" in the thirty years' entries should be noted. Again, there is a development which parallels the changes that have been discussed above. The earliest entries are positive, even joyful, and a few are virtually ecstatic. Moreover, they tend to be impersonal; the subject, a meaningful passage of Scripture, is set down with minimal commentary or recorded response, as if the passage itself radiated meaning and needed no clarification or even a context to make it sermonic material. These earliest entries are suggestive, allusive, and even a little enigmatic. Before long, however, more explicit principles were set down.

The Scripture is still very much in evidence, but the voice of the commentator and interpreter becomes more and more dominant. Gradually, the elaboration of an ethical or doctrinal principle becomes the true subject of the entries, and the "voice" necessarily becomes less meditative and more didactic. In the last fifteen years, the didactic tone is wholly dominant; the entries are generally specific answers to practical pastoral problems, and the tone is not infrequently admonitory (a notable swell in jeremiads occurs in the late 1740s and in 1750). On the whole, then, the tone of the sermon notebook entries becomes more personal over the years, as the focus of attention shifts from the supposed origin of the message to the recipient(s), and even to the messenger.

Perhaps the most interesting aspect of these developments is this relationship between the impersonal and the personal, and the "private" and "public" entries. Surprisingly, the earliest scriptural citations are the most impersonal in tone, while the later notes referring to "external" events are the most personal. Inevitably, perhaps, public involvement heightens the sense of self and brings out the fullest variegation of even the meditative scholar's colors.

Like all of the other major notebooks and workbooks examined here, the sermon notebooks that were kept for any length of time, numbers 14 and 45, are cross-referenced to other notebooks in the manuscript canon. Moreover, there is notable internal cross-referencing in number 14 (befitting its workbook character), and there are several references in number 45 to published works by authors other than Edwards.

The last of the regulatory notebooks to be treated is "Subjects of Enquiry," a brief notebook with a slightly deceptive title. This notebook is constructed entirely of fan paper,[5] with the exception of one leaf which is a bid prayer,[6] and it is bound in heavy paper covers (such

5. The fan paper is referred to by Dwight, (*Life,* p. 487) as a by-product of the Edwards ladies' domestic industry, undertaken at Stockbridge to relieve the family of the heavy expenses of moving. Hence, it would seem that this notebook was made circa 1751. The hand would confirm this approximate date. Dwight's testimony notwithstanding, fan papers appear in sermon manuscripts as early as 1745; moreover, one entry in the notebook directs JE to make a "dictionary showing the force of terms and phrases [of the Scripture] both in English and Hebrew" (p. 19), and the dictionary was begun in 1747. Thus it would seem that JE began this notebook sometime in 1746, perhaps continuing it through his move to Stockbridge for five years or so.

6. A "bid prayer," as JE called it, or a "bidden prayer," as its various avatars have been called over the centuries, was in JE's day a written request for a congregational prayer. Some private grief, usually, though occasionally a family celebration, motivated members

covers being absolutely necessary in order to keep under control the butterfly-wing-shaped fan paper remnants). There are forty-four numbered pages in it, twenty-seven of which were used during what appears to have been a brief period of a few years. The whole character of the notebook, physical and intellectual, suggests that it is a document of a "period" in Edwards' life, perhaps a period of reassessment and redirection.

To a certain extent, it is a collection of "Things to be particularly enquired into and written upon," as the motto or sub-title states, and there are quite a few entries like the following:

> Upon what accounts the sense and relish of the mind is called light, knowledge, understanding, etc. (P. 9.)
> Concerning the means God makes use of for the confirmation of the saints in Heaven. (P. 9.)

Such a random collection of more or less theological topics constitutes a part of the notebook. However, it soon becomes evident to the reader of the notebook that there is a central preoccupation which links most of the entries. Certain topics and themes—Christ's powers and deeds, the accuracy of the prophets, the process and conditions of redemption, the historical truth and typological unity of the Scriptures—recur in entry after entry. Moreover, especially as one progresses through the latter half of the notebook, the matters of style and literary technique appear with some frequency:

> Concerning the mischief that is done through improper distinctions by reason of difference of words and names, supposing there be an answerable, proper, real and thorough distinction in things.
> Show this in particular concerning the divine attributes, and

---

of the congregation to request the preacher to lead the people in an appropriate prayer during the sabbath service. A typical example is the following:

> Reuben Cors and his wife desire the prayers of this church that God would sanctifie his holy hand to them in taking away of their child by death; their parents desire the same.

Such requests were written on small pieces of paper, and during the 1740s, in particular, JE used the blank versos of these notes in making sermon booklets and the smaller notebooks. A social chronicle of Northampton is preserved on the versos of JE's manuscripts. (There are also letters, marriage bans, deeds, proclamations, bills of sale, and so forth.) For a unique exploration of the cultural legacy contained in these scraps of paper, see Stephen J. Stein, "'For Their Spiritual Good': The Northampton, Massachusetts, Prayer Bids of the 1730s and 1740s," *William and Mary Quarterly*, 3rd Ser., 37 (1980), 261–85.

concerning the graces and virtues, the faculties and affections of the soul. (P. 1.)

In reading the Epistles observe the references to the history of Christ. Facts needed by the evangelists. (P. 16.)

Read the Book of Psalms, comparing them with Dr. Watts' and Tate and Brady's versions and the sense they give of 'em. (P. 18.)

Particularly to enquire concerning the things which make a history of past ages to be credible in a present age. (P. 21.)

Read the Bible through and observe the images of divine things—how there used. (P. 24.)

There are numerous other passages, scattered here and there in entries on various subjects, which indicate a preoccupation with the problems of effective verbal communication, and more particularly with the communication of history, and most of all, with the communication of the history of events related in the Bible. Indeed, the "Subjects of Enquiry" seems, on the whole, to be as much the nature and method of effective expression as it is any particular topic or doctrine.

But this is not all. In many respects this notebook is primarily a procedural checklist. It is the device by which Edwards regulated all the business of his study but the writing of sermons (sermon notebook 45 being in use at this time), and when one observes the regimen he wonders how much time was left for sermons. It is, perhaps, these most perfunctory jottings on the work of the study that reveal most clearly what was going on at this period:

See the papers in my drawers containing the minutes of arguments to prove the truth of the Christian religion. (P. 1.)

Write on the two dispensations and take the hints from Mr. Glass' notes on the Scripture texts, num. 3, pp. 15, 16, 18, 19, and 27. (P. 12.)

To be writing my treatise concerning the human nature. (P. 15.)

Make a table of names of authors we have an account of in history. (P. 15.)

Draw up a more perfect table of the "Miscellanies." (P. 15.)

Read the Scriptures in the originals. (P. 19.)

Read the Scriptures, at least such parts as are most likely, in order to observe how the visible things of the creation are made use of as representations and types of spiritual things, that I may note them in my book about images of divine things. (P. 19.)

Read the Scriptures in order to make a dictionary showing the force of terms and phrases both in English and Hebrew. (P. 19.)

Add another leaf at the beginning of my papers on faith and then complete the heads of things implied in faith with references. (P. 20.)

Make a table to papers concerning History of the Work of Redemption. (P. 20.)

Make tables of what I have written on several subjects, especially of such as I have written more largely upon—at least tables of the texts of Scripture. (P. 22.)

Make a table of what I have written concerning the evidences of the truth of the Christian religion. (P. 23.)

Table to traditions of the Heathen concerning divine matters. (P. 24.)

Besides these entries, there are many others directing Edwards to read and reread the Bible (usually to observe the record on some specific issue) and his favorite commentaries on the Scriptures. What was going on during this period is evident; Edwards was drawing things together on both practical and theoretical levels. On the practical level, he was attempting to systematize and thus make immediately available the voluminous corpus of notes and writings in which he had, over the years, developed his thought. On the theoretical level, he seems to have been engaged in a final "searching out" of the Scriptures to facilitate a definitive formulation of the more abstruse but essential points in his theology. Finally, on the artistic level, he was apparently groping for the secret of persuasive historical narrative.

What was the occasion of this turn of events? Edwards himself has made the record clear, with what seems to be characteristic openness, in his letter to the trustees of the College at Princeton, written on October 19, 1757:

My method of study, from my first beginning the work of the ministry, has been very much by writing; applying myself, in this way, to improve every important hint; pursuing the clue to my utmost, when any thing in reading, meditation, or conversation, has been suggested to my mind, that seemed to promise light, in any weighty point; thus penning what appeared to me my best thoughts on innumerable subjects for my own benefit. The longer I prosecuted my studies in this method, the more habitual it became, and the more pleasant and profitable I found it. The farther I travelled in this way, the more and wider the field opened, which has occasioned my laying out many things in my mind, to do in this manner, if God should spare my life, which my heart hath been much upon . . . I have already published something on one of the main points in dispute between the Arminians and Calvinists: and have it in view, God willing (as I have already signified to the public), in like manner to consider all the other controverted points, and have done much towards a preparation for it. But beside these, I have had on my mind and heart (which I long ago began, not with any view to publication) a great work, which I call a *History of the Work of Redemption,* a body of divinity in an entire new method, being thrown into the form of a history; considering the affair of Christian theology, as the whole of it, in each part, stands in reference to the great work of redemption by Jesus Christ; which I suppose to be, of all others, the grand design of God, and the *summum* and *ultimum* of all the divine operations and decrees; particularly considering all parts of the grand scheme, in their historical order . . .

I have also, for my own profit and entertainment, done much towards another great work, which I call the *Harmony of the Old and New Testament,* in three parts. The first, considering the prophecies of the Messiah, his redemption and kingdom; the evidences of their references to the Messiah, etc. comparing them all one with another, demonstrating their agreement, true scope, and sense; also considering all the various particulars wherein those prophecies have their exact fulfillment; showing the universal, precise, and admirable correspondence between predictions and events. The second part, considering the types of the Old Testament, showing the evidence of their being intended as representations of the great things of the gospel of Christ; and the agreement of the type with the antitype. The third and great part, considering the harmony of the Old and New Testament, as to doctrine and precept. In the course of this work, I find there will be occasion for an explanation of a very great part of the holy Scriptures; which may, in such a view, be explained in a method, which to me seems the most entertaining and profitable, best tending to lead the mind to a view of the true spirit, design, life and soul of the Scriptures, as well as their proper use and improvement. I have also many other things in hand, in some of which I have made great progress, which I will not trouble you with an account of. Some of these things, if divine providence favor, I should be willing to attempt a publication of. So far as I myself am able to judge of what talents I have, for benefitting my fellow creatures by word, I think I can write better than I can speak . . .[7]

If the notes in the latter half of "Subjects of Enquiry" were made after July 1750, one could argue that Edwards was simply pulling things together after the agony of his dismissal, perhaps during that awkward period when he had no official pastorate. However, both the above letter and the evidence of the manuscript remains indicate that the great effort toward a final synthesis was no mere accident of circumstances[8] and that the turn of events in Northampton at most expedited a process that was already in progress. Whatever the ecclesiastical politics may have been, it is certain that Edwards was operating, as a scholar, thinker, and writer, in the midst of a vast but ever more systematic network of notebooks and manuscript sermons by the period of his removal to Stockbridge. "Subjects of Enquiry" and sermon notebook 45 are the prime regulatory notebooks of this period of transitions.

I have now surveyed that structure of writings which served as the vehicle and guide of Edwards' intellectual life. Inasmuch as sermon writing was the central activity of that life, at least until the distractions of Great Awakening controversy and the appeal of the "final synthesis" resulted in the notable decline in sermon composition in the 1740s and 1750s, I have also in effect surveyed the apparatus which engendered the long succession of sermons that established

7. Dwight, *Life*, pp. 569–70.
8. That JE may have pursued a "grand design" in his life is suggested by a peculiar list on the letter sheet of his "Catalogue" of books:
Natural Philosophy
the Mind
the Rational account
Lovely Christianity
the State of controversies
Satan defeated
Apocalypse
types of the Scripture
This list, made about 1723–24, is a most extraordinary prophecy when viewed in the perspective of the author's life. One does not need to read anything into the entry to perceive that JE had a clear knowledge of his interests and some anticipation of his life's work at a very early period. Undoubtedly, his manuscripts did "grow upon his hands," but as they grew he was ready with an appropriate "improvement" of them.

Edwards' initial reputation as one of the outstanding preachers of his time.

2. *The Apparatus of Sermon Production*

In order to understand the actual process of sermon composition, it is necessary to examine the operation of this apparatus. Although Edwards certainly did not mark even a large minority of his sources in notebooks and sermon manuscripts when he borrowed materials to make a new sermon, there are enough cross-references to give an accurate impression of the operation. The following excerpts illustrate three typical relationships between the individual sermon and the notebook corpus: 1) the origin of a sermon or part of a sermon in the notebooks, 2) the sermon as a stylistic refiner of doctrinal ideas in the notebooks, and 3) the sermon as a part of the "reference cycle" of notebook entries.

After having had his initial inspiration for a sermon—an inspiration which might be defined, in the light of the sermon notebooks, as either scriptural, doctrinal, or occasional—Edwards searched his "tables" and ultimately some of his notebook entries to see what materials he had on hand. Then, if for some reason he did not immediately set about the composition of the sermon, he made a note such as the following, found in sermon notebook 45:

> LECTURE. John 10:37. If I do not the works of my Father, believe me not.
> Doc. That the miracles that Christ wrought were divine works or were the works of God. See Miscell. No. 512. (P. 7.)

A few months later, he finally prepared a lecture on the text, John 10:37–38, which has the doctrine, "The miracles that Christ wrought when he was here upon earth were divine works" (preached in two installments at the public lectures on January 30 and March 12, 1740). If the manuscript of this sermon is compared with "Miscellanies" entry no. 512, it becomes obvious that the latter served as a storehouse of data for one of the most important doctrinal subheads of the sermon, as well as being the source of the sermon's text and general rationale. The "Miscellanies" entry is as follows:

> 1   512. Christian Religion. Christ's miracles
> were such as were properly divine works and are

often spoken of as such in the Old Testament.
Particularly his walking on the water when in a
5   storm and the waves were raised; Job 9:8, which alone
spreadeth out the heavens and treadeth on the waves
of the sea. His stilling the tempest and raging of
the sea: Ps. 65:7, which stilleth the noise of the
seas, the noise of their waves. Ps. 107:29, he
10   maketh the storm a calm so that the waves thereof
are still. Ps. 89:8–9, O Lord God of hosts who is
a strong Lord, like unto thee or to thy faithfulness
round about thee, thou rulest the raging of the
sea; when the waves thereof arise thou stillest them.
15   Ps. 93:4, The Lord on high is mightier than the
noise of many waters, yea than the mighty waves of
the sea. Job 38:8–11, or who shut up the sea
with doors . . . and said hitherto shalt thou come
and no further, and here shall thy proud waves be
20   stayed.
    Casting out devils. Job 41, with Ps.
74:13–14. Is. 51:9.
    Feeding a multitude in the wilderness. Deut.
8:15–16, who brought thee forth water out of the
25   rock of flint, who fed thee in the wilderness.
Christ did that which the Children of Israel questioned
whether God could do. Ps. 78:19–20, 23–25,
Can God furnish a table in the wilderness, and
Ps. 146:7, which giveth food to the hungry.
30   Telling men's thoughts. Amos 4:13, That declareth
unto man what is his thought.
    Raising the dead. Ezek. 38; Is. 26:19, Thy
dead men shall live; together with my dead body
shall they arise. Awake and sing ye that dwell in
35   the dust, for thy dew is as the dew of herbs and
the earth shall cast out the dead. Ps. 68:20, He
that is our God is the God of salvation and unto
God the Lord belong the issues from death. I Sam.
2:6, The Lord kills and he makes alive; he bringeth
40   down to the grave and bringeth up; so Deut. 32:39,
See now that even I am he and there is no God with
me; I kill and I make alive. See II Kings 5:7.

Opening the eyes of the blind: Ps. 146:8,
the Lord openeth the eyes of the blind. Is. 29:18,
45   35:5 and 42:7.
Healing the leprosy. II Kings 5:6–7, compared
with Deut. 32:39.
Unstopping the ears of the deaf. Is. 29:18
and 35:5.
50   Healing grievous sores or wounds or issues.
Job 5:17–18.
Christ healed such diseases as of old were
appointed to be types of our soul's diseases, or the corruption
of our nature, such as the plague of leprosy
55   and issues of blood.
Loosing the tongue of the dumb. Is. 35:6.
Causing him that hath an impediment in his
speech to speak plain, Is. 32:4.
Lifting up her that was bowed and bound together
60   by a spirit of infirmity. Ps. 146:7–9,
the Lord looseth the prisoners, the Lord raiseth
them that are bowed down.
Restoring the lame. Is. 35:6.
Healing the sick: Ps. 103:3, who forgiveth
65   all thine iniquities and who healeth all thy diseases.
Remarkable is that place, Ex. 15:26.
Christ joined pardoning sins with his healing the
sick. When one came to be healed, he first told him
that his sins were forgiven; and when the Jews were
70   stumbled at it, and found fault that he should
pretend to forgive sins, then immediately upon
it he healed the person's disease, that they might
believe that he had power to forgive sins; and
tells 'em that he does it for this end, Matt. 9:2,
75   Mark 2:3, Luke 5:18. Now if Christ were an impostor,
can it be believed that God would so countenance
such horrid blasphemy as this would be, as to
enable him to cure the disease by a word's speaking,
a work which God appropriates to himself as his own
80   work, and joins it to forgiving iniquities; and
mentions them as both alike his peculiar works?
Would God give an impostor this attestation to his

blasphemous lie when he pretended to do it as an
attestation to his divine mission?

85   Christ urges this argument with the Jews when
they found fault with his calling himself the son
of God. John 10:37, if I do not the works of my
Father, believe me not.

     There are three other things that is to be

90   remarked of Christ's miracles, viz. 1. that they
were such as it was prophecied he would work. 2.
they were works of mercy and love. No needless
miracles; and 3. they were lively types of
the great spiritual works of God and the Redeemer.

This *omnium gatherum* of "Scripture proofs" related, at least through
typological analogy, to Christ's miracles (which are in turn presented
as proof of Christ's divinity) presents a list of thirteen categories of
miracles and three general observations on the subject. There is no
very apparent logic to the order of the list, and hand and ink show
that one or more entries were squeezed into the list at times subsequent to the writing of the main body of material. But for Edwards,
such a mass of material could be the very stuff of a sermon, particularly if it were delivered as a "lecture" to substantiate some important doctrinal point.

Thus, in the sermon on Christ's miracles (the text of which is recorded in the "Miscellanies" entry, lines 87–88), Edwards masses
Scripture proofs in the third subhead under the first Consideration
of the Doctrine, an Observation which corresponds to the third "remarkable thing" listed at the end of the above entry (lines 93–94).

> 3. 'Tis worthy to be further observed that most of Christ's works
> were those very works that had been from age to age spoken of
> as the proper and peculiar works of God among the only people
> that worshipped the true God.
>
> So was his walking on the sea in the time of a storm when the
> waves were raised. Job 9:8, "which alone spreadeth out the heav-
> ens and standeth upon the waves of the sea." ⌒ His stilling the
> tempest and raging of the sea, saying, "Peace, be still," as we have
> account, Mark 4:39.
>
> This also is spoken of from time to time in the Old Testament
> as the peculiar work of God. Ps. 65:7, "He stilleth the noise of
> the seas, the noise of their waves." Ps. 107:29, "He maketh the

storm a calm so that the waves thereof are still," and Ps. 89:8–9, "O Lord God of Hosts, who is a strong Lord like unto thee, or to thy faithfulness round about thee? Thou rulest the raging of the sea; when the waves thereof arise, thou stillest them," and Job 38:8–11, "Or who shut up the sea with doors, and said, hitherto shalt thou come and no further: and here shall thy proud waves be stayed?"

So Christ often cast out devils which is an instance of delivering the people of God from the Spiritual Leviathan which is spoken of as a peculiar work of God in the Old Testament.

Ps. 74:14, "Thou breakest the heads of the dragons in the wilderness." Is. 51:9, "Awake, awake, put on thy strength, O arm of the Lord; awake, as in the ancient days, in the times of old; art not thou it that hath cut Rahab, and wounded the dragon?"

So Christ fed a multitude in a wilderness and herein did what was spoken of old as a peculiar work of God. Deut. 8:15–16, "who brought thee forth water out of the rock of flint; who fed thee in the wilderness." ⌒ Christ herein did that which the Children of Israel questioned whether God could do. Ps. 78:19–20, "Yea, they spoke against God; they said, Can God furnish a table in the wilderness? Behold, he smote the rock, that the water gushed out. Can he give bread also, can he provide flesh for his people?"

We have often an account of Christ's telling men what their thoughts were. Matt. 9:4, "Jesus knowing their thoughts: Wherefore think ye evil in your hearts?" Luke 5:22, But when Jesus perceived their thoughts, he answering said unto them, What reason you in your hearts? And chapter 6:8, "and he knew their thoughts and said unto the man," etc.

And chapter 9:47, "and Jesus, perceiving the thought of their hearts, took a child," etc. and 11:17, and Matt. 31:34 . . .

This also is spoken of {as the proper and peculiar work of God}.

Amos 4:13, "For, lo, he that formeth the mountains and createth the winds, and declareth unto man what is his thought."

Christ several times raised the dead; this also . . . as Ps. 68:20, "He that is our God is the God of salvation; and unto God the Lord belong the issues from death." I. Sam. 2:6, "The Lord kills and he makes alive; he bringeth down to the grave and bringeth up." Deut. 32:39, "See now that I, even I am he, and there is no God with me; I kill and I make alive."*] ⁄ #II Kings

5:7, "And it came to pass when the king of Israel had read the letter, that he rent his clothes and said, am I God, to kill and make alive, that this man doth send unto me to recover a man of his leprosy?† next p.

---

*Christ often opened the eyes of the blind: Ps. 146:8, "The Lord openeth the eyes of the blind."

We have an account of Christ's healing persons of issues and grievous sores and wounds. This also is spoken of as the peculiar {work of God}. Job 5:18, "For he maketh sore and bindeth up; he woundeth and his hands make whole."

We read of Christ's healing one that was bowed by a spirit of infirmity and was bowed together so that {she in no wise could lift herself up} (Luke 13:11–13, 16).

Ps. 146:8–9, "The Lord looseth the prisoners; the Lord raiseth up them that are bowed down."

Christ often healed the sick.

This also is spoken of {as the peculiar work of God}, and remarkable is that place, Ex. 15:26, "I am the Lord that healeth thee."

Ps. 103:3 "who healeth all thy diseases, who forgiveth all thine iniquities." So Christ joined pardoning sins with his healing the sick like God. When one came to be healed, he first told him that his sins were forgiven him, and when the Jews were stumbled at it and found fault that he should pretend to forgive sins, then immediately upon it Christ healed the person's disease. ⌐Leprosy in particular. Matt. 8:2–3, Matt. 11:5, Luke 17:12# last p.

---

† 4. And lastly, here, they were such works . . .

Perhaps one's initial response, upon comparing the two passages, is surprise at how little the "list" is altered as it is converted into a sermon. Only three particular cures (lines 48–49, 56–58, 63) are omitted from the sermon; some fifteen specific references to Scripture texts are altered, either through insertion or deletion, and the three general observations (lines 52–55, 72–94) are absorbed into the overall argument of the sermon. There was obviously no great reworking of the notebook materials.

Still, there are a few notable changes in the structure and wording of the material that account for some positive changes in the sermonic version. Most obvious, perhaps, is the development of the citation from II Kings 5:7 and its removal (by following the pairs of keying signs), along with the reference to curing leprosy (lines 46–47), to the end of the subhead. By this revision, Edwards focuses the attention of his auditory on two crucial points at the climax of the third Observation: 1) the duality (moral and physical) of man's affliction as typified by the image of the leper, and 2) the inability of any earthly power to remedy this affliction. Only God, operating through Christ, can work the necessary cure. The passage quoted from II Kings is, moreover, both concise and vivid with the rhetoric of the Old Testament.

The wording of the sermon passage is obviously more coherent, less discursive and, in effect, simplified. One addition, however, stands out above the other alterations: the introduction of a characteristic Edwardsean "tonic phrase."[9] "Peculiar work of God" repeatedly calls our attention to the unique powers of God and God-in-Christ, and that is, after all, the point of the sermon.

Thus Edwards converted a "Miscellanies" entry into a sermon (or part of one) with a minimum of fuss and bother. Indeed, there are many instances in his writings of passages transferred from notebooks to sermons with even less modification than in this example. The few changes made in this material, however, prove Edwards to have been sensitive to aesthetic and rhetorical considerations as well as efficient. He provides an overwhelming mass of Scripture evidence for his point, maintains a clear line of argument, and achieves a rhetorical climax. He not only made few changes; he made only those that were necessary and correct.

Sometimes Edwards did make substantial revisions in his notebook

9. See the discussion of this device in Chapter IV, pp. 241–43.

materials when incorporating them in a sermon. Such stylistic improvements were recognized and duly noted, in at least a few instances, for future reference. The sermon containing the improved material thus became a part of the notebook apparatus. An instance of this process can be found in "Miscellanies" entry no. 614:

614. Wisdom of God in the Work of Redemption. That our Mediator should be neither the Father nor the Holy Spirit,[1] but the middle person between them, was fit and necessary upon a like account as it was necessary that he should be neither God the Father nor one of fallen men, but a middle person between them. It was not meet that the Mediator should be the Father, because he sustained the rights of Godhead and was the Person offended and to be appeased by a Mediator. It was not fit that he should be one of fallen men because they were those whose Mediator he was to be, or that he was to mediate for. It was not fit that he should be either God the Father nor a fallen man because he was to be Mediator between the Father and fallen man. Upon the same account, 'tis not fit that he should be either the Father or the Spirit, for he is to be Mediator between the Father and the Spirit. In being Mediator between the Father and the saints he is Mediator between the Father and the Spirit. The saints, as saints, act only by the Spirit in all their transactings wherein they act by a Mediator; i.e. in all their transactings with God they act by the Spirit, or it is the Spirit of God that acts in them; they are the temples of the Holy Ghost; the Holy Spirit dwelling in them is their principle of life and action. There is need of a Mediator between God and the Spirit, as the Spirit is a principle of action in a fallen creature. For even those holy exercises that are the actings of the Spirit in the fallen creature can't be acceptable nor avail any thing with God, as from the fallen creature, unless it be by a Mediator. The Spirit in the saints is it that seeks blessings of God through a Mediator, that looks to him by faith and depends on him for it. 'Tis not suitable that the same person that seeks should be Mediator for itself, for the obtaining the things that it seeks. See this better expressed in sermon on Eph. 3:10, in the 8th and 9th pages of the sermon.

It is obvious that Edwards has been wholly absorbed in working his

---

1. MS: "Son."

reductio in this entry and, though it bears the marks of a copied piece, he has not taken time to refine the expression of his ideas.

Turning to the sermon on Eph. 3:10 (dated March 1733), a work proclaiming "the wisdom appearing in the way of salvation by Jesus Christ," one finds a significant recasting of the materials from no. 614. The passage indicated by Edwards' note constitutes most of the second half of the second Reason of the first Consideration under the first Proposition of the Doctrine:

> . . . ╱ There are three increated persons, the Father, Son, and Holy Ghost, and Christ alone of these was a suitable person for a redeemer. It was not meet that the Mediator should be God the Father, because he, in the divine economy of the persons of the Trinity, was the person that holds the rights of the Godhead and so was the person offended, whose justice required satisfaction and was to be appeased by a Mediator.

> It was not meet that it should be the Holy Spirit, for he in being Mediator between the Father and the saints, he is so, in some sense, between the Father and the Spirit. For the saints in all their spiritual transactions with God act by the Spirit; or rather, it is the Spirit of God that acts in them; they are the temples of the Holy Ghost. The Holy Spirit dwelling in them is their principle of action in all their transactings with God.

> But in these their spiritual transactings with God, they act by a Mediator. These spiritual and holy exercises can't be acceptable or avail anything with God, as from a fallen creature, but by a Mediator. Therefore Christ, in being Mediator between the Father and the saints, may be said to be Mediator between the Father and the Holy Spirit that acts in the saints. ╱ And therefore, it was meet that the Mediator should not be either the Father or the Spirit, but a middle person between them both.

> 'Tis the Spirit in the saints that seeks the blessing of God by faith and prayer; and, as the Apostle says, with groanings that cannot be uttered, Rom. 8:26. Likewise, the Spirit also helpeth our infirmities. For we know not what we should pray for as we ought, but the Spirit itself maketh intercession for us with groanings that cannot be uttered. The Spirit in the saints seeks divine

blessings of God by and through a Mediator; and therefore, that Mediator must not be the Spirit, but another person.

Still perhaps a complicated notion, but this revision is considerably improved by a general syntactical and organizational tightening. Moreover, the public statement has a more explicit contextual introduction, a more direct or focused utterance, and a more memorable conclusion, the last largely the result of introducing the apt and vividly worded scriptural passage.

Thus, a representative of this type of revision demonstrates how Edwards used the sermon to clarify and form thoughts previously expressed in the notebooks. It might be noted in passing that Edwards does not here or elsewhere talk "down" or evasively to his congregation, as has been suggested in the past. His preparing of the milk for babes seems to have consisted primarily in clarifying his thought, though not over-simplifying, and in making fundamental stylistic improvements.

A sermon such as this one thus became an integral part of Edwards' "working papers" and an essential vehicle for the articulation of his thought. The extent to which a sermon was involved in the cycle of cross-references that united Edwards' notebook corpus of course varied. Some sermons are referred to only once, while others are cited many times in various notes, tables, and indices. An example of a "significant" sermon is one written in 1738, on the text of Gen. 3:11, stating in its Doctrine that "the act of our first father in eating the forbidden fruit was a very heinous act." This sermon participates in two separate cycles of reference, one involving the interleaved Bible and the Scripture notebooks, and the other the "Miscellanies." An examination of the passages participating in these exegetical and doctrinal cycles will give some sense of the operation of the cycles and the importance the sermon manuscript could assume in them.

In order to take up the cycle, it is wise to go to the great terminus of reference cycles, the interleaved Bible. A perusal of the first pages turns up the following entry on page nine under the text, Gen. 2:17:

> 17. vid. no. 47 & 320 & 325. See sermon on Gen. 3:11, second [section], p. 8, 9, 10, 11. In the day that thou eatest). It don't seem to me necessary that we should understand this that death should be executed upon him in that day when he eat. But that it may be understood in the same manner as Solomon's words to Shimei, I Kings 2:37 . . . The thing that God would signify to Adam by

this expression seems to me to be that if he but once presumed to taste that fruit, he should die. You shall not be waited upon to see whether you will do it again, but as soon as ever you have eaten, that very day shall death be made sure to you. You shall be bound to die, given over to death without any more waiting upon you . . . Those words signify that perfect obedience was the condition of God's covenant that was made with Adam, as they signify that for one act of disobedience he should die.

Following the references first to the Scripture notebooks, one discovers more textual exegesis:

> 77. [The original number 47, renumbered by an early editor after he broke up Edwards' original quire.] Gen. 2:17. In the day that thou eatest thereof, dying thou shalt die. This expression denotes not only the certainty of death but the extremity . . . and so it properly extends to the second death, that death of the soul, for damnation is nothing but extreme death. And I am ready to think that God, by mentioning dying twice over, that he had respect to two deaths, the first and the second. And that to those words the Apostle John refers in the 20 of Revelation and 14, when he says this is the second death. . . . See notes on Rev. 20:14. See further concerning this no. 325.

If the first reference is followed back to the interleaved Bible, related thoughts and citations are again encountered:

> [Rev. 20:] 14. This is the Second Death.) In calling this the Second Death, there seems to be respect had to the repetition . . . dying thou shalt die, as signifying two deaths; or the repetition of the word "wo" in this book, chapt. 8:13, implies so many distinct woes. See Scripture notes no. 47. See the second [section of] sermon on Gen. 3:11, p. 8, 9, 10, of that sermon.

The cross-referencing between Scripture notebook no. "47" and the Bible entry under Rev. 20:14 is representative of a common, though by no means invariable, practice.

Returning to the original list of references under Gen. 2:17, one finds the next reference is to the second Scripture notebook, no. 320. This time, there is no problem of renumbering.

> 320. In the day that thou eatest thereof, thou shalt surely die.) This in addition to notes in Blank Bible. And besides Adam died

that day for he was ruined and undone that day. His nature was ruined, the nature of his soul, which ruin is called death in Scripture. . . . The nature of his body was ruined that day and became mortal, began to die . . . he was guilty of death. And yet that all was not executed that day was a token of his deliverance, and his not dying that day a natural death is no more difficult to reconcile with truth than his never suffering at all that death that was principally intended, viz. eternal damnation. . . .

Edwards sometimes designates the interleaved Bible the "Blank Bible," though it is now the opposite of blank. The last Scripture notebook entry mentioned in the Gen. 2:17 entry is also in the second Scripture notebook:

325. This is addition to num. 47. Gen. 2:17. Dying thou shalt die). If we sometimes find such kind of doubled expressions and also this very expression, dying thou shalt die, as in Solomon's threatening to Shimei, when no more is intended than only the certainty of the event, yet this is no argument that this don't signify more than the certainty, even the extremity as well as certainty of it. Because such a repetition or doubling of a word according to the idiom of the Hebrew tongue is as much as our speaking a word once with a very extraordinary emphasis. But such a great emphasis, as we use it, signifies variously; it sometimes signifies certainty, at other times extremity, and sometimes both.

It is now appropriate to examine that portion of the sermon on Gen. 3:11 that is cited in both of the Bible entries and which is, through those entries, connected with all the Scripture notebook entries quoted above. The passages cited are in the fifth Particular under the Doctrine:

5. The command was enforced with a very terrible threatening, denounced in a most awful, peremptory manner. God said to Adam, "You shall not eat thereof; in the day that thou eatest thereof, thou shalt surely die." In the original it is, "dying thou shalt die." As you may see, in the original there is a repetition of the word which don't seem to be fully expressed in our translation, for the expression, "dying thou shalt die," according to the idiom of the Hebrew tongue, denotes both the certainty and also the extremity of the death that should be inflicted. . . .

And the repetition of the expression may intimate more deaths than one. God thereby threatens two deaths, even the temporal death of the body and the eternal death of the soul. So that when God says, "dying thou shalt die," so much may be understood, as if he had said, "in dying or in the death of your body, you shall die in soul; one death shall be an entrance into another. Your bodies' dying shall be but the beginning of your souls' eternal dying. . . ."

Which I humbly conceive the apostle John alludes to when he calls eternal death the Second Death. Rev. 20:14, "And death and hell were cast into the lake of fire. This is the Second Death. . . ."

The apostle John seems to suppose that the repetition of the expression "dying" implies two distinct deaths, of the same manner as the repetition of the word "wo" in this same book. 8:13, "wo, wo, wo" signifies three distinct woes . . .

God would not wait any longer to see whether he would transgress again a second [time], but that day that he eat, this day death should be made certain as the consequence. In the same manner as Solomon's words to Shimei are to be understood, I Kings 2:37 . . .

. . . it is reported that the condition of the covenant was perfect obedience, and that for but one transgression death should ensue.

And accordingly, Adam did in a sense die that very day that he sinned. He was ruined and undone that day; his nature was ruined, the nature of his soul, which ruin is called death in Scripture . . . and the nature of his body also was ruined that day and became mortal, began to die, and his whole man became subject to condemnation as guilty of death. . . .
. . . our first parents presumed to eat and . . . [cast] contempt upon God's awful threatenings, and [ran] as it were on the thick bosses of God's buckler, as if they would dare God to do his worst.

Although these excerpts from the fifth Particular do not include much of the sermon's development and exclude most of the best rhetoric, they do give a sense of the interrelationship between the sermon and the notes in the interleaved Bible and the Scripture notebooks.

The second cycle of references—or, the second half of the Gen. 3:11 sermon cycle—links the sermon to several "Miscellanies" entries. As the interleaved Bible was the natural place to look for the nexus of exegetical writings, so, in the quest for speculation on a particular theological theme, one goes to the table of the "Miscellanies." Here, under the topic of "Adam's first sin," is the following reference:

> Adam's first sin, how far imputed to his posterity, sermon on Gen. 3:11; why only imputed, 717.

Entry no. 717, in the second book of the "Miscellanies," contains these thoughts:

> 717. First Covenant, The Fall. Why only Adam's first transgression is imputed to us. . . . Sentence of condemnation was already immediately passed upon Adam and on his posterity with him, when he had broken the covenant, agreeable to the threatening contained in the covenant. . . . The voice of that covenant still is directed to us in that if we sin in ourselves or in our surety we shall die, but if we obey in ourselves or in our surety without sin, we shall live, and though it be impossible for us to obtain life by obeying ourselves, as obedience is the price of life, yet there is still encouragement for our obedience, as obedience may be otherwise a means or occasion of life to us, and that no less than before in those that live under the gospel. So that the sins of such don't only expose 'em to punishment, but to a punishment no less aggravated than if we could obtain life by obedience as its price, and on other accounts much more aggravated. See this matter much more clearly set forth in Answer to the Enquiry in the beginning of [the third section of] my . . . sermon from Gen. 3:11. . . .

The sermon's version of the statement is as follows:

> Answer. . . . the time of Adam's trial as the covenant head of his posterity was over as soon as that act was completed. . . . That covenant that God made with Adam, or that constitution of God which appointed him to stand as covenant head of mankind, did not appoint him to act as the head of mankind forever or to all eternity, but only during the time of his probation, which was to

continue either till he had persevered in obedience, till God was pleased to confirm him and reward him, or else till he fell, but either of these was to put an end to his probation. If he had stood till God had been pleased to admit him to eat of the tree of life, and so to confirm him, then his time of probation would have ceased, and he would no more have acted as the public head of mankind after that. . . .

In addition to the above cluster of passages, there are three other "Miscellanies" entries that refer to the Gen. 3:11 sermon:

> 374. Original Sin. . . .
> Imputed. Adam's eating the forbidden [fruit] might have some peculiar aggravations, as he did it, that are imputed only to him. . . . The peculiar personal aggravations of the act are not imputed to us, and his sin concerns his posterity only as it was a direct breach of God's covenant and an act of rebellion against God's express law. . . . See this more particularly explained and reasons given in sermon on Gen. 3:11.
> 788. Imputation of Adam's Sin. How the whole of the style or language used in the three first chapters of Genesis proves that these words, "in the day that thou eatest thereof, thou shalt surely die". . . had respect not only to Adam but his posterity. See my . . . sermon from Gen. 3:11, the first Use, and also from the nature of all covenant transactions in Scripture.

Again, Edwards has pinpointed the passage:

> Application
> I. Hence we learn how guilty we all come into the world . . .
> 1. This is manifest from the Scripture both of the Old and New Testaments. It is manifest first by the whole account that is given us there of this affair in the first chapter of Genesis. . . . I say it is manifest those words had not respect to Adam alone, but to mankind in general. God spake to Adam as the head of the human race. The style that is used throughout those chapters shows it. . . . The grant that is herein given of the earth was not only to our first parent, but to his posterity, and we still possess the earth by virtue of that grant. . . .

> 2. We have no account of any covenant transaction in the whole

Bible with any of mankind where the seed or posterity are not included. . . .

---

3. . . . The New Testament is very particular in this matter, in the latter part of the fifth chapter of Romans. "Therefore, as by the offense of one, judgment came upon all men to condemnation; even so by the righteousness of one, the free gift came upon all men to justification of life. For as by one man's disobedience many were made sinners, so by the obedience of one shall many be made righteous, etc. . . ."

The last "Miscellanies" entry was made late in Edwards' career.

1221. Christ's Righteousness. How Christ has the first and chief benefit of it. [JE here quotes a long passage from a discourse on justification by another author and concludes the entry with the following note.] Remember, if I have opportunity, more fully to consider this matter and carefully consider what is mentioned of aggravating circumstances of Adam's sin, not imputed to his posterity, in my sermon on Gen. 3:11, and consider what circumstances in Christ's obedience answering them are not imputable to believers.

Thus the cycle of Gen. 3:11 is completed, at least in so far as explicit references are concerned. But what has just been presented is, in reality, the "inner circle." The quotations above omit Scripture text references, some of which would undoubtedly lead to new cycles if they were checked in the interleaved Bible; also omitted are references to published works that Edwards consulted. In other words, any cycle such as that presented above may well be like the first ring in a pool of water: other rings flow out from it until the entire pool is encompassed, so thoroughly did Edwards cross-reference his material. (See diagram below.)

But the immediate intent of this third and last demonstration is to show how completely sermons were apt to be absorbed into the apparatus of Edwards' "working papers." He seems rarely to have forgotten a good sermon, or even a good passage in a sermon, and as other parts of this study will show, he frequently re-used his sermons. But whether the sermon is viewed as an extension of the notebooks, a tour de force on a theological point, or merely another segment of Edwards' vast system of recorded theological thought, one fact cannot

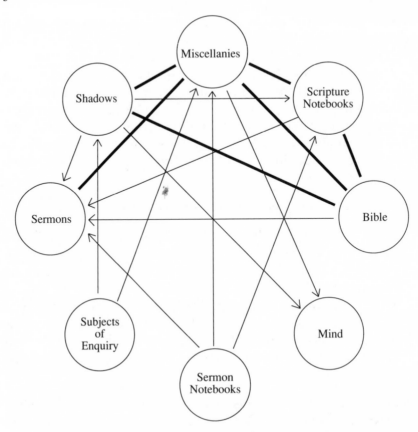

This figure represents the functional relationships among the major notebooks and the sermon corpus in the reference cycles. Only explicit cross-references are depicted here. Heavy lines indicate two-way cross-references, while arrows indicate single-direction references. The "Notes on the Apocalypse" are included in "Scripture Notebooks."

be escaped: the sermon is, in the hands of Edwards, a seminal literary form. All the evidence points to "the great Pains he took in composing his Sermons, especially in the first Part of his Life."[2] If the evidence seems to indicate changes in his habits of composition as the years passed, a change in form and, for better or worse, new functions of the form must be anticipated.

3. Changing Techniques of Sermon Production

When the making of a sermon is considered, even in the most general terms, it is virtually impossible to speak once for all times in

2. Hopkins, *Life,* p. 46.

Edwards' life. Rather, consideration must be given to at least three phases in his development as a writer of sermons, during each of which he worked in significantly different ways. These three periods are determined more by alterations in Edwards' methods of sermon composition than by "outward" events in his life, though there is naturally a general correlation between the two. The first period, 1722–27, can be described as a period of apprenticeship, since the most important event within these years, both for the man and his art, is the brief first pastorate in New York, from August 1722 to May 1723. The second period, 1727–42, is that in which Edwards achieved mastery of the sermon; it was during this time that he attempted to fill the shoes of the charismatic Stoddard, whipped his congregation through a crescendo of revivals (the last of which was probably the greatest event in human affairs they had witnessed), and won international attention as a preacher. The final period, 1742–58, a truly multifaceted period, is best described as a time of permutation, in both Edwards' public life and his literary pursuits.

For the story of the preacher in his study, the periods are best defined by changes in the sermon manuscripts themselves.

In the beginning, Edwards made an octavo sermon booklet prior to writing out the sermon. It consists of four infolded sheets and is stitched up the fold to form a neat quire. If he was to preach only in the morning or at an evening lecture, one quire would suffice, and several of the sermons written during the years 1722–27 fill just one quire. If he had to preach both in the morning and afternoon, or if his subject could not be expounded in one pulpit session, Edwards prepared a second booklet, in which case the Text and Doctrine usually fill the first booklet and the Application the second. In such instances, the second booklet often begins with an outline of the points that have been made in the first booklet. These outlines are most elaborate in the earlier sermons, such as that on Heb. 9:27 (1722):

> Heb. 9:27 Doc. All men must certainly die, and after that their everlasting state will be determined.
> 1. all must die.
> 2. after death their everlasting state, etc.
> 1. there is a future state.
> 1. the light of natural reason.
> 1. because the natural conscience.
> 2. rewards and punishments not in this life.

3. because this can answer the end of creation.
4. because of the natural strong desire.
5. soul distinct from body.
6. consent of all nations.
2. Revelation.
1. God expressly declared it.
2. sent his son.
3. Christ died.
4. rose again and ascended.
5. confirmed by the wonderful powers of the Holy Ghost.
2. a fit judgment.
1. particulars.
2. general.
1. because the nature of things requires it.
2. the Scriptures reveal it.

We are come in the third place to show that judgment will determine the state forever . . .

With a little attention and imagination, the numbers unscramble
themselves and a staggered outline, with letters and Roman numerals,
emerges quite clearly.

The assets of such a system are obvious. It is neat, and there is a
complete correlation between the literary unit and the oratorical unit,
between the length of the manuscript and the length of time in the
pulpit. On the other hand, there are some equally obvious drawbacks
in this practice.

First, the infolded leaves of the octavo quire provide a rather arbitrary unit. Perhaps this is just what the novice preacher wanted,
but as he gained a "feel" for the sermon form, he must have wanted
to write a little more or a little less. The manuscripts indicate that
this was the case, for quite a few of these early sermons have a leaf
or two (most commonly a two-leaf unit, stitched to the back of the
quire) added to the original unit. Some of these additions result from
revisions before repreachings at later times, but many were apparently made at the time the sermon was composed. Moreover, the
infolded sheets of the quire gave the writer lock-step limitations in
the development of his material. Upon review of what he had written,
if he wished to add to or alter his material, there was little he could
do but cut and stitch (or pin, as Edwards sometimes did).

He must, it seems, have had the sermon pretty well in hand before he ever committed it to the quire. That Edwards did, in the first years, have the sermon more or less written out before he attempted to record it in the sermon booklet is clearly indicated by the nature of the comparatively few revisions that appear in these sermons. They are, for the most part, revisions or corrections of scribal errors: omitted words, botched phrases that need only a word or two shifted about to stand correct, and the like. Moreover, these sermons frequently display that common error of the copyist, the doubled article, conjunction, or preposition. There are no extant notes or first drafts of sermons from this period, but it seems likely that Edwards wrote the sermons out entirely in a first draft before he filled in the booklet.

That a writer so concerned with efficiency and even the conservation of paper as Edwards obviously was could long be happy with such a procedure, especially when under the pressure of serving as pastor while attempting to develop himself through study and journal-writing, is doubtful. It is not surprising, therefore, to see evidence of experiments with new forms of sermon booklets within the third dozen extant sermons. A sermon on I Cor. 2:14 (1723) is written in two quires of smaller leaves, having twelve rather than eight leaves in each quire. Such a booklet—similar to those used by his father—would waste less paper if a page had to be added or subtracted, but otherwise it is little better than the full-sized octavo quire. There is only one such sermon.

There is no radical alteration in Edwards' procedure, however, until 1726–27, the year in which he undoubtedly experienced greater pressure than ever before, as the newly appointed colleague of Solomon Stoddard. Preaching a few of the week-day lectures and half of each Sabbath, the younger minister saved some time by repreaching most of the sermons he had written in earlier years[3] while he labored to produce new ones of equal or better quality. It is at this time that he wrote a sermon on Job 14:5, a sermon which differs from previous sermons in that its sheets are not infolded in a quire, but stacked one upon another in units of the two leaves produced by the final octavo fold, with the exception of one sheet which acts as a kind of wrapper for all but the last two leaves. Moreover, it is evident that the booklet was stitched after the sermon was written. Thus, if

---

3. They were marked with a shorthand symbol (‾ʀ̣‾). He also applied this symbol to sermons written at Northampton for at least two years.

the need to add or drop a paragraph or more became evident to Edwards in the course of preparing the sermon, he could have made the change without disturbing, in most instances, more than a two-leaf unit.

Another experiment in booklet fabrication is represented by Hos. 13:9 (1727). This sermon booklet was apparently made as a normal quire, but before writing the sermon in the booklet Edwards folded the leaves away from the center stitching in opposite directions, making two units of four leaves stitched back to back. Then, folding the two units together, he produced a booklet composed of signatures. As if struck by the idea of signature units, Edwards began making up sewn signatures, of just four leaves each, within a few months of the Hos. 13:9 experiment. The individual signatures could be written upon one at a time, for as many units as the sermon required, and the signatures then sewn into a single sermon booklet upon completion of the writing. On the face of it, such a procedure would seem to combine much of the neatness of the quire with the flexibility of the stacked folded sheets.

In this same year, yet another variation occurs, and in retrospect it is the most notable innovation of all. One sermon on Ps. 102:25–26 appears, on the surface, to be written up in the old way, that is, in two octavo quires. Upon leafing through the sermon, however, one finds that only the second booklet is a standard octavo quire. The first booklet actually incorporates only two octavo leaves, the remaining ten leaves being duodecimo. Perhaps the smaller leaf appealed because it allowed even greater flexibility than the octavo folds, less paper being added or subtracted in the event of a major alteration. Perhaps, too, the sermon constructed wholly of duodecimo leaves would be easier to "palm" in the pulpit.[4] Whatever his reasons, Edwards began using duodecimo leaves in 1727, and after a brief period when there are a few booklets of mixed leaves—such as Ps. 102:25–26—and an apparent vacillation between octavo and duodecimo booklets, he finally settled upon the duodecimo booklet, composed

4. Hopkins asserts that JE "carried his Notes into the Desk with him, and read the most that he had wrote . . ." (*Life*, p. 48), and other accounts of JE's preaching confirm him. However, it must have been a rather tense situation if the young preacher preached in this manner in 1727, while Stoddard was still about. For Stoddard had preached and published, only three years before, *The Defects of Preachers Reproved*, in which he comments upon the "late Practice of some Ministers, in Reading their Sermons . . ." With characteristic finality, he states that "There be some Cases wherein it may be tolerable . . . but ordinarily it is not to be allowed." (P. 23.)

Sermon Booklets. Beinecke Rare Book and Manuscript Library, Yale University.

of four-leaf signatures, and averaging twelve leaves per preaching unit. Apparently, he had found the best sermon booklet for his purposes: neat, compact, flexible, and economical of paper. It had emerged from a period of trial and experiment, and embodied features that first appeared separately. But having settled upon it in 1727, Edwards was to continue using this form of the duodecimo booklet throughout the period of his greatest preaching in Northampton.

During his first years as a preacher, Edwards seems to have made fewer significant experiments with the form of the sermon than he did with the sermon booklet. The basic form of the sermon was, as I have indicated, inherited, traditional, and even ingrained. It did not occasion many thoughtful pauses, apparently, on Edwards' part. Of course, if Edwards did write most of the early sermons out in full before committing them to the booklets, one could not expect to find much evidence of thoughtful pauses anyway. But there are a few interesting formal experiments in these early sermons, and a few peculiar traits of the holograph that deserve attention.

For instance, in the earliest sermons of 1722 there are evident attempts to provide a few aids to pulpit delivery:

/Strong\
. . . strong, hale and healthy men . . . then they
/Forsake\
must leave all these things . . . (Heb. 9:27.)

At first, one might suppose these added words to be insertions or corrections, but they are not, and Edwards makes insertions and corrections in his normal manner (with carets and lining out) in the same pages. Apparently, such superscript words were intended to warn him of the drift of the argument as his eye scanned the page. Such devices would indicate that Edwards preached from a booklet from the start. This particular device apparently did not work well, however, for it does not appear in more than one or two sermons. Another similar device did catch on, and Edwards used it, albeit sparingly, for years:

But all other men must die in the ordinary way of separation of their souls from their bodies, men of all Ranks, Degree, and Orders must die:

strong	Kings and Princes	Rich	Good	
weak	beggars	Poor	Bad	(Heb. 9:27.)

He seems always to have liked juxtaposition of opposites and other varieties of parallelism, and was inclined to render the pattern of juxtaposition in such an outline form. This example also calls attention to an additional fact of importance, that Edwards used some outline in his sermons from the very beginning, though at first outlining was restricted to a running line in place of a biblical passage or the kind of syntactical compression represented in the above example. Another type of compression used in these first years is simple abbreviation of individual words. For a few years, there are a number of the seventeenth-century abbreviations: "y^e, y^t, y^m, y^y." There are also, and for the remainder of Edwards' life, his own abbreviations of many common words: "Chh." for "church," "thems." for "themselves," and so forth. Finally, he seems virtually to have ignored systematic punctuation and capitalization in his sermons (but not in his sent letters), and though a few of the earliest sermons contain commalike marks, they bear no apparent relation to the sense of the sentences. With these exceptions, it can be said that the earliest sermons are fully written out.

Aside from making the sermon as compact and efficient for pulpit use as he could, Edwards was always very careful in elaborating the full structure of his sermons, if only for the people who were taking notes. A representative example of the early sermon is Ezek. 7:16 (Edwards' first Fast Day sermon), a sermon filling two of the octavo quires, one for the morning and one for the afternoon. Throughout the sermon, Edwards makes explicit statements about the relationships between the various major heads of the argument, and each head is carefully fitted into its proper place. An outline gives his sense of the formal structure:

BOOKLET I

Ezek. 7:16 [Text read and commented upon exegetically.]
    Observations:
      1st
      2nd
      3rd
Doctrine. That at a time when a people are called to a general humiliation, it becomes each one to mourn for his own iniquity. [Follows a brief recognition of the occasion.]

Explaining of the Doctrine:
    I. What is intended in the Doctrine by mourning for our iniquity.
    II. Why it becomes each particular person in times of public humiliation to mourn for their own iniquity.
I. What is intended in the Doctrine . . .
    1. Negative side.
        1
        2
    2. Positive side.
        1
        2
II. Why it becomes each particular person . . .
    1st Reason
    2nd   "
    3rd   "
    4th   "
        1
        2
        3

BOOKLET II

Ezek. 7:16 [Text reread and reviewed.]
Doctrine. [Doctrine restated and outline of the argument of Booklet I presented.]
Improvement.
    I. Use of Instruction.
        1st Inference
        2nd   "
    II. Use of Examination.
    III. Use of Exhortation.
        1st Consideration
        2nd   "
        3rd   "
        4th   "
        5th   "
            1 "special case"
        1st Direction
        2nd   "
        3rd   "
        4th   "

In the outline, those subheads not given names are not given special names by Edwards; he simply refers to them, from time to time, as "particulars."

It is evident from the above example and others like it that Edwards was intent upon a mastery of the intricate traditional sermon form in his early sermons, and perhaps struggled to keep his own head clear as he "cleared the heads." Whatever the case, the sermons of the 1722–27 period are frequently explorations of the formal sermon structure and are as fully written out, as a group, as any he wrote. By 1727, Edwards seems to have possessed a comfortable mastery of his chosen form.

As has already been observed, Edwards left comparatively few traces of revision in the early sermons, save those occasioned by scribal errors. There are, however, enough creative revisions to make a faint pattern of literary significance when the evidence of all the sermons is collated. First, it seems that Edwards had a tendency to use language that was a little too colloquial, or even coarse, for the decorum of the pulpit. Thus we find him changing "stick by him forever" to "remain with him forever," and the like. It is not that Edwards was squeamish, as his nineteenth-century editors were, for when he wished the pungency of colloquial expression to enliven an analogy, he would use it freely:

> [Contrasting the saint and the unregenerate.] In short, the one in the whole of his life has his soul chiefly set upon heaven and on the glories of Christ there, having his mind tossed above the ground by faith. The other spends his days in grovelling in the dirt, makes his mind much like a mole or muck worm, feeding on dirt and dung, and seldom lifts his mind any higher than the surface of the earth he treads on . . . (Phil. 1:21).

Edwards clearly possessed a very keen sense of the flavor of words, and these early revisions indicate that he wished the general tenor of his language in sermons be only a little removed from what must have been normal in serious conversation; he wished a decorum of language befitting the pulpit but would not hesitate to utilize the vigor of a vulgar idiom when the situation favored it, and he was certainly aware of the effect to be had when the pulpit decorum was interrupted.

Other revisions indicate attempts to ease the elaborate and even painful syntax of the philosopher, sometimes sacrificing minor qualifications of points for the sake of simplicity. Also, there is a noticeable attempt to avoid certain rather strong rhetorical devices, such as alliteration and rhythmic repetition, which apparently came quite naturally during the heat of creation. He did use these devices, but as with colloquialisms, he apparently wished to keep them in reserve for emphasis and the final perorations. Another interesting pattern in Edwards' revisions draws attention to the words, "profit" and "pleasure." Many of these early sermons tell of the joys of religion and the appeal of Christ, and in revision Edwards often shifts, when attempting to arouse the congregation, from the analogy of the "profit motive" to a direct appeal to the "pleasure principle." In doing this, he seems to be moving away from a conventional trope and developing a more original appeal. It is obvious that the word "profit" came to him first, but he changed it to "pleasure," stressing the immediacy of the saint's reward through the metaphor of the senses.

One of the more interesting of Edwards' devices for revision is his technique of "keying" passages. This technique was developed during the days of the octavo quires when it was most difficult to manipulate the leaves of his sermon booklets, although having acquired the knack he never quite left off using it. Basically, it is a simple enough device, and it is interesting in Edwards primarily because of the lengths to which he went in using it. One instance of it has already been presented (above, p. 79), but in the earlier "octavo days" it could be a performance. Perhaps it would be best to represent the operation of this restructuring device diagrammatically:

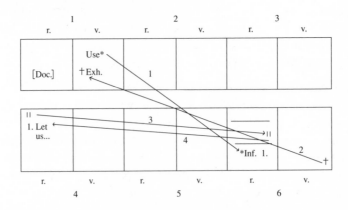

In the above representation of twelve actual pages in one of the earliest sermons (Matt. 16:26), I have indicated leaf and page divisions and supplemented Edwards' symbols with numbered arrows to indicate the path of the reader's eye when shifting from section to section in accordance with the keying signs. Where there is no keying, and within each keyed passage, one proceeds from leaf to leaf, recto to verso, top to bottom of each column. Could one possibly do this in the pulpit? Apparently, if he were used to it, and especially if he got the warning of the list of key signs, in order, at the top of the first page of the sermon (as is often done in early sermons). Indeed, if one spends long periods of time with Edwards' manuscripts—sermons or notebooks—he must get used to working with keyed structures of much greater complexity than this. For better or worse, Edwards used these pairs of signs for shifting the order of lines and paragraphs, and for "keying in" paragraphs that had to be added at the end of the quire or section (as represented above). Sometimes, he supplemented the keying symbols by simply pinning slips of paper with the added paragraphs (and key signs) to the proper page of the sermon.[5] It is easy to see how inefficient and awkward these devices were, and Edwards greatly facilitated sermon modification when he shifted from the octavo quire to the duodecimo signatures—not to mention paper shuffling in the pulpit.

With his arrival at the duodecimo sermon booklet in 1727, Edwards entered upon the second, and greatest, period of his preaching career. During the years between 1727 and 1742, he continued to develop his homiletical technique, experimenting with variations on the standard sermon form and, perhaps more significantly, experimenting with new rhetorical strategies. It was during this period that he assumed full control of the Northampton pulpit (in 1729) and rose to eminence as a preacher, leader of revivals, and interpreter of religious experience.

In this second period, the basic process of sermon-making continued along the lines established by the end of the first period. However, certain changes were taking place in Edwards' study that were to have a significant impact on his working methods. Perhaps the most notable development was that his notebooks now "grew much faster on his hands." The major notebooks, described above in terms of their participation in the reference cycle, were now developing to the point

5. It is possible that these slips of paper with their straight pins attached gave rise to the legend of JE's pinning notes to his clothing, since until recently a number of them floated unattached among his mss. and nineteenth-century investigators may have interpreted the evidence imaginatively.

that they could be increasingly relied on as sourcebooks for sermon materials. The function of the interleaved Bible as a comprehensive index after Edwards acquired it in 1731 indicates how great was the growth of his dependence upon these notebooks. Each type of substantive notebook was "on tap," as it were, to yield its peculiar kind of material to the Text, Doctrine, Application, or even to the whole of any sermon in the works. Moreover, as the years passed there were more and more sermons to draw upon, and Edwards drew upon them in a variety of ways. What these developments most contributed to was an increased emphasis on flexibility in the sermon manuscript. After deciding upon a sermon text or topic (perhaps taking it from a sermon notebook entry), Edwards had to rough out a sermon in such a way that he could incorporate appropriate ideas, arguments, images, and Scripture passages from his notebooks or from other sermons cited in the notebooks. Thus, it is not surprising to see in his sermon manuscripts of the years 1729–30 signs of "blocked out" structure.

There are suspicious blanks in Edwards' generally tightly crowded sermon manuscripts as early as 1722 or 1723 (in Job 1:21, for instance), but in themselves they do not count for much, being so few and far apart. As Edwards gained mastery of the pulpit, however, and as his time was increasingly taken up by study and pastoral duties, he gradually began outlining sections of his sermons. Now some of this outlining is apt to be found in any part of a sermon, and Edwards presumably outlined those parts that were simplest or easiest for him to remember. But by 1729 a pattern begins to emerge: the conclusions of the Doctrine and Application divisions of the sermon are most apt to be left in outline. Moreover, these outlines are not "pure" outlines, that is, the outline itself does not fill up the page. Rather, a series of heads is scattered over several pages where they might be expected to come in a fully developed text. Some of them have additional material beneath them and some do not; in these passages there is every degree of development or non-development. The conclusion is inescapable that by 1729 Edwards was not writing out his sermons in first drafts, but rather blocking them out, perhaps with the aid of outlines (such as that reproduced above, pp. 97–98), and developing them as the difficulty of the subject required and time permitted. Of course, with such a system, it would be comparatively simple to rough out the sermon and then fill in the skeletal structure with flesh from the notebooks.

As the notes proliferated and the sermon booklet became more and more flexible, the inevitable happened. In the 1730s and early 1740s, the sermons become longer and more complex in structure, and since the time in the pulpit remained the same, Edwards carefully divided these longer sermons into preaching units which are marked in the sermon booklets by little summaries and restatements of the text and doctrine. Generally, there is, in the 1730s, a preaching-unit division every ten leaves. But since any number of four-leaf signatures could be stitched together, and since as there was more and more in the notebook reservoir to draw upon, it is not unusual to see single sermons of thirty or forty leaves in this period. Of course, such sermons might take two or more weeks to deliver.

The increased complexity of these sermons is not unanticipated in the first period, for there are various compounds of Doctrines and Uses in some of the 1722–27 sermons; moreover, there are a few pairs of sermons, if not true sermon series (the term "series" being reserved for three or more related sermons), but in the decade from 1729 to 1739 there is a marked tendency to write more complex sermons and, finally, sermon series. An early example of the new formal complexity is Matt. 13:23 (1729), a thirty-four-leaf sermon, comprising three preaching units or "sections," and having three doctrines. An outline of the major divisions gives some sense of the sermon's complexity:

SECTION I

Matt. 13:23
>Text read and explained or "opened."
>". . . from the words I observe three doctrines:"

Doctrine 1. That which distinguishes the profitable hearers of God's Word from all others is that they understand it and bring forth the fruit of it.

Doctrine 2. That men's knowledge is the root and foundation of their fruitfulness.

Doctrine 3. That there is a great difference in the degrees of grace and fruitfulness among the truly godly.

>Doctrine 1. is then divided into two propositions:
>>Prop. a. is developed here.
>>>Use for Doctrine 1 a.

SECTION II

Matt. 13:23

          Prop. b. of Doctrine 1. is expounded here.
              Use for Doctrine 1 b.
      Doctrine 2. is developed here.
              Use for Doctrine 2.

SECTION III

Matt. 13:23

Here there is a summary of the above development, undoubtedly because sections I and II were preached in the morning and afternoon of the same day, while section III was preached the following week.

Doctrine 3. is developed here.
Application.

The Application improves *all three doctrines* in a final synthesis.

Note that Edwards here formally differentiates between "Use" and "Application," the latter term being reserved for the major division of the sermon, while "Use" is the term for a particular head within the larger division. This practice is his rule, though he is not wholly consistent. Note, also, that Edwards no longer takes pains to make the formal divisions of the sermon correspond exactly with the preaching units.

Such complexity, in many formal variations and combinations, along with the tendency to write longer and longer multi-unit sermons, apparently had some impact on Edwards' practice in making up his sermon booklets. Starting in 1733, there is a tendency to make the single folded sheet the basic unit of the duodecimo booklet. And instead of the four-leaf signatures, there are bunches of two-leaf folds which are gathered together and stitched through the side, close to the folds. This is a quite intermittent phenomenon in the early and mid-thirties, but by 1736 it is becoming standard practice, and by 1740 a booklet of signatures is hard to find. Of course, the two-leaf unit allows even greater flexibility than the four, but Edwards did not stop there.

One characteristic of the "gathering," as I term the sewn two-leaf folds stitched into booklets with a single side stitch, is that it facilitates the inclusion of single leaves, because the stitching is through the side rather than on the fold. Perhaps this appealed to Edwards, for around 1735 he began the practice of including torn up letters, bid prayers, bans, proclamations, bills of sale, and the like in his sermons. Very often, of course, one side of the leaf was covered with writing, but this gave Edwards his smallest booklet unit, the single page, and consequently the greatest possible flexibility in sermon booklets.

In the thirties and early forties there are many short sermons, prime examples being the manuscripts of *A Divine and Supernatural Light* (13 leaves) and *Sinners in the Hands of an Angry God* (11 leaves), but a most notable development in this period is the inevitable break-ing up of long and complex sermons into true series. Thus, there is the series of three sermons on John 16:8 (1730), the series of five sermons on II Cor. 13:5 (1735), the series of sixteen sermons (1738) later published as *Charity and its Fruits*, the series of thirty sermons (1739) later published as *A History of the Work of Redemption*, the series of six sermons on the parable of the sower, Matt. 13:3–7 (1740), and finally the series which was, as Dwight puts it, "preached from his own desk" in 1742 and 1743.[6] This series was later made into *A Treatise Concerning Religious Affections* (1746). Indeed, it seems obvious that, at least from 1735, there is an increased tendency to preach treatises from the pulpit. Study of the "History of Redemption" sermon series manuscripts reveals that much of the series was written in the manner of a treatise (though in duodecimo booklets), many preaching unit divisions being added with a thick-stubbed pen only after large sec-tions of the work had been written. Perhaps the booklets and the sermon form were becoming so flexible that the sermon was dissolv-ing under the pressure of the long, long thoughts.

During the years 1727–42, the amount of revision in the sermons quite naturally increases. However, the amount of revisions involved in the first writing (as opposed to revisions for repreachings, fre-quently made years later) is not often as great as one might expect, supposing that Edwards was blocking out his sermons during this period, rather than writing a complete first draft. There are a few interesting evidences of creative struggle, as in Ps. 82:6–7 (1729) and Job 11:12 (1731), where we find abortive attempts at sermons on other texts. Apparently Edwards started the sermon, progressed through a few lines of the Opening of the Text, gave up, then turned the paper upside down and started a new sermon, one of those cited

---

6. Dwight, *Life*, p. 223. Dwight does not say that he saw the sermon manuscripts, and he probably did not. At any rate, they are not now extant.

above. There is also evidence of the drawback of blocking out material: inevitably, the author's prediction of how much he has to say under any particular head will not always be accurate, and there are many instances of heads so packed, so filled with lines and lines-between-the-lines, that it is impossible to decipher them without a magnifying glass. At the same time, of course, the next head may be half empty, and in many instances this is the occasion for keyed passages.

On the whole, the 1727–42 period does not present revisions of a kind markedly different from those described above for the period, 1722–27. There is the same occasional vacillation between synonyms, the rephrasing of lines here and there, but few if any truly substantive innovations or alterations. Although Edwards was now doing more of his creating in the sermon booklet, he still undoubtedly used a preliminary outline in which he roughed out not only structure but images and tropes (most of the outlines in the sermon notebooks are from the thirties). Moreover, he was frequently using materials that he had already worked up in notebooks or other sermons. Finally, he seems not to have worried about the well-wrought phrase or the delicate balance of syntactic structure in much of his sermon writing. Rather, he seems to have desired to dramatize spiritual questing in the very gesture of his language. Many of his sermons thus have a sprawling, surging power that is comparable to the imaginative exhaustiveness of Whitman in the nineteenth century or the obsessiveness of Faulkner in the twentieth. His people—those connoisseurs of sermons and preachers—averred that "although Mr. *Edwards* was perhaps the more learned man, and more animated in his manner, yet Mr. *Jonathan* was the deeper preacher."[7] This assessment was a clear-eyed and penetrating stylistic evaluation, particularly in its juxtaposition of *learning* and *depth*. The knowledge of Scripture, classical philology, and systematic doctrine possessed by Timothy Edwards was all that the Puritans had demanded of a preacher intellectually, and the animated manner suggests the rhetorical and oratorical qualities corresponding to the "lively," "nervous," or "heart-piercing" affective dimension of preaching which was also considered to be essential. However, the concept of depth suggests in this context a level of authenticity and psychological realism beyond the reach of the most ardent ideologue.

7. Dwight, *Life*, p. 17.

One true innovation of the period, though an oratorical rather than a literary one, might be mentioned since evidence of it has already appeared (see pp. 77–79, 82), and it is suggestive of the function of the sermon manuscript at this time. What I have named the "pick up line" [╱] first appears in the late twenties, but around 1731 it suddenly becomes very common (often between four and seven per page) and continues to be prevalent until 1742. At first, one might think that it had something to do with revision or with the making of paragraphs. It is not involved with either operation, however, and its function can only be explained in terms of pulpit delivery. Apparently, Edwards desired to make his delivery more dynamic and flexible, and the "pick up line" was his compromise, for the time, between reading and *memoriter* delivery.[8] Placed before each sentence or phrase containing a major thought or illustration, the lines enabled Edwards to do at least two things. First, he could look up from the manuscript more easily without losing his place, or without as much careful review of the sermon just before preaching. Second, the lines would make his delivery more flexible in a formal sense. If he desired to speak extemporaneously within the context of the written sermon, or if he desired to leave out certain sections for some reason, the lines would provide so many "handles" subdividing the text of the written sermon by which he could adjust the relationship between the sermon as written and the sermon as spoken.

Thus, once again, the literary keynote of this period is "flexibility." Whether in the makeup of the sermon booklets, the process of composition, or the delivery in the pulpit, Edwards seems to have been doing everything possible to increase his efficiency and permit the maximum number of variations and alternatives. Obviously, he was a very busy man.[9]

Of all the innovations in sermon composition during 1727–42, cer-

8. Hopkins reports that JE considered his reading of sermons in the pulpit "a Deficiency and Infirmity." *Life*, p. 48.

9. Though JE himself left no statement on his customary schedule of sermon composition, it is evident that he frequently worked on more than one sermon at one time, a practice common enough among his contemporaries (see John Barnard's description of his habitual methods of sermon composition in his "autobiography," published in *Mass. Hist. Soc. Coll.*, 3rd ser., Vol. 5, 187–88). Though he "lived by rule," JE was no automaton, and he worked at his notebooks and his sermons with varying degrees of intensity. Sometimes he must have completed more sermons than he needed, while at other times he would inevitably be in need of sermonic materials. Thus, he apparently stored some of his output in fruitful times against times of dearth, as is suggested by a note at the end of a manuscript on Cant. 2:16; the note states simply that this is a "Put by lecture."

tainly the most notable is the new activity of preparing sermons for publication. This is the period during which Edwards prepared for the press the first ten of the eventual twenty-two sermons that he published.[1] Moreover, with the exception of his *Farewell Sermon*, the most famous sermons were all printed during these years, and it was these sermons, first as orations and then as printed literature, that established his reputation in New England and elsewhere. Of his several publications during this period, perhaps *God Glorified in the Work of Redemption* (1731), *A Divine and Supernatural Light* (1734), and *Sinners in the Hands of an Angry God* (1741) have won the greatest reputation as sermons. And because they are all short, one-preaching-unit sermons, they are representative of Edwards' prototypical sermon form.

In preparing these sermons, Edwards first composed fully written-out duodecimo sermon manuscripts in the fashion described above as characteristic of this period. He then preached the sermons in Northampton, revised the first and third for notable presentations in Boston and Enfield, respectively, and then prepared "fair copies" for the printers when his auditories requested it.[2] All three of the original manuscripts bear reasonably close likenesses to the printed texts, for Edwards was not one of those preachers who preached and then wrote a literary version, but they also prove, when collated with the printed texts, that Edwards took considerable pains to send forth his sermons to the printers in their best stylistic dress.

Of these three sermons, *God Glorified* seems to have undergone the most extensive stylistic revisions. There are three shades of ink in the sermon manuscript: one for the original Northampton sermon, one for the additions and revisions for Boston, and one for revisions before printing. However, the result of these layered revisions bears only a general resemblance to the printed text. Edwards must have

1. I have not included in this count a sermon on Judg. 5:33, which Dwight lists as a probable publication, because I have found no evidence of it. It may have been preached and parts of it used in one of the publications on the revivals, resulting in a myth of its publication. Also, I have not included *Religious Affections*, though it was worked up from sermons. On the other hand, I have included *Distinguishing Marks*, though it was considerably reworked before publication.

2. In this context *Sinners* is an anomaly. JE is usually explicit about who requested a sermon for publication and/or paid for it. However, there is no such note on the extant copies of *Sinners*, an omission which is significant in the context of the sermon's having caused no stir when delivered in Northampton prior to the Enfield visit. If no one from Enfield requested publication, it seems that JE must have taken the initiative, apparently for the first time.

prepared another working draft of the sermon, no longer extant, before he prepared the fair copy for the printer, a meticulousness one would expect of a man like Edwards when preparing his first published sermon. Of the many stylistic revisions that were made, perhaps the most interesting is his "phrase polishing," a technique observable whenever one of his manuscripts is prepared for the press, but particularly in evidence in *God Glorified*. Though the sermon was virtually written out in manuscript, there are few sentences that appear in print exactly as they appear in the manuscript. Comparing the conclusion of the sermon as it is written in the manuscript (and as it was preached in both Northampton and Boston) with the corresponding last paragraph of the printed sermon gives a fair representation of this kind of revision. First, the manuscript version:

> This doctrine should teach us to live by faith. And then we should exalt God alone by praise: he that glories should glory in the Lord, or ascribing to God alone all blessing and praise, giving him the glory of all he enjoys.

> Hath any man hope that his sins are pardoned and that his iniquities are redeemed and that he is justified and received into God's favor? Let him give all the glory of it to God. Is any man converted and sanctified and his mind endowed with true excellencies and divine ornaments of the grace of God's spirit? Let him give all the glory of it to God, who alone has distinguished him from others and made him to differ from the worst of men. Let not man be lifted up as though it were from him or through him.

> Is any man exalted to that honor of being a child of God? Let him give all {the glory of it to God}. Is any man exalted to that blessedness of having a title to eternal life? Let him give {the glory of it to God} and let his hope humble [him] and cause [him] to reflect on his exceeding unworthiness of such {a favor} and not exalt him. ╱ Has any man much spiritual comfort and strong hope? Let it not exalt him. Let him ascribe {the glory of it to God}. Is any man eminent for holiness? Doth any man abound in good works? Let him take nothing of it to himself, but to Him [through] whose workmanship we are created in Christ Jesus to good works.

And then the printed version:

And this doctrine should teach us to exalt God alone as by trust and reliance, so by praise. *Let him that glories glory in the Lord.* Hath any man hope that he is converted, and sanctified, and that his mind is endowed with true excellency and spiritual beauty, and his sins forgiven, and he received into God's favor, and exalted to the honor and blessedness of being his child, and an heir of eternal life: let him give God all the glory; who alone makes him to differ from the worst of men in this world, or the miserablest of the damned in Hell. Hath any man much comfort and strong hope of eternal life, let not his hope lift him up, but dispose him the more to abase himself, and reflect on his own exceeding unworthiness of such a favor, and to exalt God alone. Is any man eminent in holiness, and abundant in good works, let him take nothing of the glory of it to himself, but ascribe it to him whose *workmanship we are, created in Christ Jesus unto good works.*[3]

Essentially, these two passages are the same, and yet they have markedly different impacts. At first, perhaps, one notices that three paragraphs in the manuscript have been compressed into one paragraph in the printed version, as approximately twenty-seven lines have been reduced to nineteen lines. The compression results largely from revisions dictated by Edwards' sensing that the rhetorical device of question-and-answer, so effective in oratory, often produces little more than redundancy and fragmentation in print. The structure of the printed passage, moreover, is not only uncluttered by rhetorical questions, but it has been recast to permit a more continuous development of the dominant theme. On the level of the polished phrase, there is the fine economy of the recast first sentence, the introduction of the perspective-sharpening "miserablest of the damned in hell," and the substitution of "spiritual beauty" for "divine ornaments" (though one might lament the loss of the colorful and concrete "ornaments"). Finally, the obvious repetition of the manuscript passage is exchanged for a subtler repetition ("Hath any man . . .") in the printed version.

While the amount of revision varies greatly from passage to passage in *God Glorified,* the above revisions probably represent the median. At least they are indicative of Edwards' real sensitivity to the fine points of tone, rhythm, and structure, and they prove that he was

---

3. *God Glorified in the Work of Redemption, By the Greatness of Man's Dependence upon Him, in the Whole of it* (Boston, 1731), pp. 24–25.

not at all reluctant to labor over his writing in the manner of a literary artist until his style was properly polished for publication. Certainly, the Edwards of the early and middle periods manifests a continued interest in style, whether he is preparing a sermon for publication or for the Northampton pulpit, and traditions concerning his indifference to style are to be doubted.

In *A Divine and Supernatural Light*, where all revisions subsequent to the first-draft revisions were presumably made for the printed version of the sermon, there are "revisions" that go far beyond polishing or even "reworking" in the usual sense. There is polishing of the sort described above, and as in *God Glorified* some passages are condensed while others are expanded, but it is in the structure that one first encounters striking discrepancies between the sermon as preached (the manuscript) and as printed. Though many sentences are transferred from the manuscript to the printed text verbatim (more, perhaps, than in *God Glorified*), collation reveals that this sermon has been heavily reworked.

Edwards preserved the over-all proportions and structure of his sermon (or lecture, according to its proportions), but within the larger divisions structural changes too numerous to be described in detail here were made. A characteristic structural change is the inversion of the components of a unit, whether they be the beginning and end of a paragraph, or several related paragraphs. In the manuscript, for instance, the third Consideration under the Use of Exhortation begins with the idea of submission to Christ and concludes with the allusion to II Cor. 3:18 and the idea of the soul as an image of the Lord's glory. In the printed text, however, many of the same words and all the same ideas are presented in the reverse order. A comparable instance occurs in the positive demonstration of the first Proposition of the Doctrine, under the second Inference from the definition of "this spiritual and divine Light," where the same process is in evidence, this time involving several paragraphs. The manuscript presents the "conviction of the truth and reality," first "directly" and second "indirectly." Examination of the printed sermon reveals that the order of these blocks of material has been reversed. Between the extremes of these examples, there are several other instances of this type of restructuring.

What was Edwards' purpose in such shifting about of his materials? The pattern indicates that he was trying to place first in each unit the less exciting, the less conclusive, and the secondary, while he saved the best arguments and most important points for last. As a result, the printed version of the sermon has more of a rhetorical and thematic crescendo than the manuscript version, where there are several slight anticlimaxes.

At the climax of the sermon's crescendo, and in this sermon it is at the end of the Doctrine, there is a long passage concerning "reason" and "the sense of the heart." Perry Miller makes much of it and quotes a portion of it in his biography, *Jonathan Edwards*,[4] remarking that "Edwards threw out to the townsmen, and by publishing it to all New England . . . this crucial passage." The manuscript indicates, however, that the townsmen may have had to wait the nine-month gestation period, along with the rest of New England, before they were first confronted with this particular phase of the argument in print. For during the time that Edwards held the manuscript, he made revisions of yet another kind; he inserted significant materials in the version to be published that were probably never preached at all.

There are obvious signs of the process of insertion in the duodecimo sermon booklet, including both keying letters and a sheet of passages-to-be-added that is now stitched into the booklet. The keying letters, carefully inscribed capitals—"A," "B," "C," "E," and "F"—are scattered throughout the manuscript, four in the Doctrine and one in the Improvement. They seem to be unique in Edwards' sermon revision procedures, and may indicate a desire to work in a more systematic way for a longer period of time than was his custom. Four of the letters do not, however, mark major additions to the sermon, the average length of additions in their passages being only a sentence or two. But the letter "E" marks an addition in the first Inference under the positive demonstration of the first Proposition of the Doctrine (beginning, "There is a twofold understanding or knowledge of good . . .") that has both bulk and significance.[5] It establishes the juxtaposition between mere speculative understanding and the sense of the heart that prepares the way for the peroration at the end of the Doctrine. The climactic passage itself was added to the printer's copy without so much as an asterisk in the sermon booklet.

4. New York, World Publishing Co., 1963, p. 64.

5. This paragraph is a slightly revised transcription of "Miscellanies" entry no. 489. The borrowing was first pointed out to me by Thomas A. Schafer. One other passage draws upon "Miscellanies" entry no. 187, though not as extensively as in the case of 489. The sermon may contain still other as yet unidentified borrowings.

The sheet of passages-to-be-inserted contains seven paragraphs of Scripture citation and commentary that were probably drawn from the interleaved Bible or the "Notes on the Scriptures" notebooks. Each paragraph has a line drawn through it to indicate, in Edwards' customary way, that it has been used. These passages have been inserted in the sermon at various points, not always corresponding to the order in which they appear on the note sheet. There are no signs to key these passages, and they were undoubtedly inserted directly in the printer's draft as Edwards developed it. There are also several other passages, like the final statement in the Doctrine, that have no insertion marks or keying signs in the sermon booklet, but the sheets upon which they were worked up have been lost—unless Edwards copied them from notebooks, as seems likely.

A Divine and Supernatural Light thus provides an instance of a sermon so heavily revised or "worked up" that it has a considerably heightened tone, and a notably altered profile, in print. It is very much the same sermon that Edwards preached in 1733, but the revisions, particularly the insertions of new material, have made the difference between a good and a great sermon.

Sinners in the Hands of an Angry God was preached and printed late in the period, and the revisions for printing were more radical than in either case discussed above. But it is a paradoxical case, and *Sinners* is both the least and the most revised of the three sermons. It is the least revised in that the printed sermon and the original manuscript are almost identical up to the beginning of the four Considerations concerning "that wrath that you are in such danger of." But this last three-sevenths of the sermon is probably quite different from any version of the sermon that was preached. Comparison of the printed text with the original Northampton manuscript, the later outline,[6] and all manuscript revisions reveals that all the devices of revising, inserting, and restructuring were used to such an extent that the printed version is both a compound of all previous versions and unlike anything before it. Moreover, if the last two-thirds of the Application, in a sermon where the Application is the most important major division, are virtually new and different, then the sermon is virtually different.

The manuscript variants of the sermon can be characterized as having a much larger proportion of encouraging, mild-toned pastoral

---

6. The matter of repreachings will be discussed in Chapter III, pp. 140–63.

advice than is anywhere to be found in the printed version of *Sinners,* and the original Northampton draft seems to have the greatest percentage of such comparatively mild language, particularly in the last two-thirds of the Application. This is not at all unusual, for even in the most fiery of "hellfire" sermons—and several manuscript sermons contain passages considerably more lurid than anything in *Sinners*— Edwards generally preserves a nice balance between the carrot and the stick. In fact, when *Sinners* is considered in the light of the other sermons that Edwards wrote, it seems to be not only his most striking (if not "best") sermon, but seems a bit of a performance, something of a hothouse plant among the daisies. The precise genus of this plant will be addressed in the next chapter.

The final preparation of this sermon for the press may be viewed most profitably in the historical context of the Great Awakening, the triumphs of Whitefield's dramatic oratory, the surprising success of Edwards at Enfield, and finally, in the wider context of Edwards' growing reputation—a reputation that rested, even as early as 1741, largely upon the written word.

Edwards, the undramatic preacher with the unimpressive voice, had established himself as a spiritual leader of some note during the thirties when his sermons, later published in *Discourses on Various Important Subjects* (1738), had precipitated an awakening in a rather crusty congregation and he had written so vividly about the event in *A Faithful Narrative* (1737). During the Great Awakening it was Whitefield who held the field (literally and figuratively) at the height of the excitement. Although Edwards seemed to admire the work of Whitefield, he had questions concerning various aspects of the revivalist's principles,[7] and, being human, he could not have helped comparing himself, as a leader of awakenings, with the British visitor. There was little doubt that Whitefield was the greatest revivalist that anyone had seen, but a man of such perspicacity as Edwards might have noted, upon reading printed sermons of Whitefield, the relative blandness of the revivalist's arguments when compared with those of his own contrivance.

When a sermon of his own did ignite a reputedly hardened congregation just as completely as any of Whitefield's might have been expected to, and yet at the same time adumbrated one of his most cherished doctrines, might not this man, who had already seen the

7. For a few of the questions, see Dwight, *Life,* p. 147.

real difference between the preached and the printed sermon, have wished to establish in the permanence of print what had proven to be not only an excellent revival sermon, but one that verbally dramatized the essential theological point? As in the case of *God Glorified* and *A Divine and Supernatural Light,* however, the most perfect sermon in print might not be the sermon that a good pastor would deliver in person to his congregation. In the realm of print there is room for that which might seem overwrought in oral delivery, particularly when the speaker is addressing people who have an intimate pastoral relationship with him. Perhaps Edwards, with his voice and habitual manner in mind, wondered how a Whitefieldian performance could be achieved gracefully and convincingly.

Unlike Whitefield, Edwards had always lived with a pen in hand, and he was more apt to be at his best when he had a paper, rather than a room, to fill with words. Perhaps it occurred to Edwards that if Whitefield had been called to lead the battle in the field, he himself was best suited to carrying it on in the closet—both in the present and in future times, both at home and throughout the world. Knowing what doctrine most needed to be asserted, and feeling that he had proved his mastery of the revival sermon as well as his understanding of the process of religious experience in a revival, Edwards set about the composition of the ideal revival sermon, one so immediate and powerful as to be a model for the present and future, and a memorial to, and justification of, his own work and that of his cohorts in the neighboring towns during that momentous season. Certainly, the sermon was not delivered as it stands in print, nor is it probable that Edwards would have wanted to deliver such a sermon if he could have; rather, Edwards attempted a literary coup that utilized techniques and rested upon precedents already established in preparing for the press *God Glorified, A Divine and Supernatural Light,* and *Discourses on Various Important Subjects.* The product of his efforts is undoubtedly the most "literary" performance of his career. Not long after *Sinners* came the controversies, the treatises, and the virtual end of sustained effort in the composition of sermons.

If the great development in Edwards' career as a maker of sermons during the period, 1727–42, was the preparation of sermons for the press or the conversion of oratory into literature, one might wonder what Edwards' relation with the press was, and how much he was involved in, or had control over, the printing of his sermons. There is, however, all too little evidence concerning the specifically literary aspects of his transactions with his publishers, the printers S. Knee-land and T. Green. There are, for instance, no extant copies of the manuscript drafts of sermons that Edwards sent to the printers, but the existing evidence indicates that the printers followed Edwards' directions very closely, although they reserved decision for themselves in the use of capital letters and italics. There is also some evidence that Edwards was involved, directly or through an agent, in the actual process of preparing the printed work.

For instance, there are letters to the Rev. Thomas Foxcroft of Boston. In these letters, Edwards gives directions for the insertion of new material in works then in the press. These letters happen to concern the preparation of such works as Edwards' self-defense in the qualifications controversy and his treatise on the *Freedom of the Will*, but one remark indicates that the working relationship between Edwards and Foxcroft may have extended back beyond this late period:

> I am indeed concerned . . . and ashamed to ask it of you to continue that assistance with respect to this piece which you have afforded in times past, with respect to former publications. (April 13, 1753.)

What were these services? Other excerpts give some idea of their range:

> N.B. I desire that what is written on the opposite leaf may be inserted in the body of the discourse (not in the margin) in that section of the second part entitled, *Of Liberty of Will Consisting in Indifference,* near the beginning, after these words or words like these, "But in as much as this opinion has been of such long standing in the world . . ." (No date; a letter fragment.)
>
> If I did say so, I desire (if it ben't too late) it may be altered thus: "*The people offered sacrifices* . . . as is evident by Ex. 8:25–26," or words to that purpose, if they can be added with good connection. (June 5, 1749.)

Reading this last letter enables one to understand more fully the context of a note at the end of the errata list on page vi of *Discourses on Various Important Subjects* (1738):

> N.B. The reader is desired to observe that by means of the wrong placing of something sent to be added, after the copy of these discourses was gone to the press, the two last paragraphs . . .

It seems that publishing was sometimes a rather rickety operation for Edwards, and yet there was great concern and some effective intervention. Another letter to Foxcroft tells of further participation of the author himself in the business of editing:

> I have sent an account of errata to Mr. Kneeland and would now acknowledge my great obligations to you [for] the care you have taken about the impression. (December 20, 1754.)

Thus, Edwards was apparently able to correct proof, at least some of the time.[8] Despite all the difficulties attendant upon geographical distance in the eighteenth century, Edwards certainly managed to keep closely involved in the process of publication, though this sometimes meant entrusting some of the literary work to an agent.[9] Thus, his obvious respect for and trust in his agent notwithstanding, he sometimes agonized like the fond author:

> With respect to any alterations that you may think needful to be made, it becomes me much to prefer your judgment to my own: but it is very difficult, and almost impossible for another to enter into all the views of a writer or to know everything he has in view in all that he says. And therefore, a little variation of sentiment may much thwart and disappoint his design insensibly to another. (June 30, 1752.)

The letters to Foxcroft indicate, in fact, that Edwards took a most lively interest in all phases of the production of his works:

> With respect to the character, I should be glad the book might be printed in the best character Mr. Kneeland has, and that it should be done every way in as handsome a manner as may be. . . .

8. One of the few bits of concrete data I have been able to locate is a two-leaf unit of scrap paper in a sermon, Luke 12:35–36 (1742); it is a bit of page proof (p. 206) from *Discourses on Various Important Subjects* which bears a correction—the deletion of a comma—in JE's hand. Inspection of the first edition of the work showed that the correction was made.

9. Whether or not JE chose Foxcroft as his agent because he had read the latter's *A Practical Discourse* (1718), or because of his reputation as one of the best preachers in Boston, is doubtful. Some of JE's letters, in which he sympathizes with the ailing and aged man, indicate that there was no one else in Boston who could be trusted to treat his writings with due consideration. Whatever the reasons for his choice, though, JE could not have found a better literary agent in Boston than the colleague of his antagonist, Charles Chauncy.

Mr. Hawley tells me that Mr. Kneeland has sent for new types; perhaps they will be better than any he now has. (May 24, 1753.)

I should be glad that you would endeavor that this book may be printed in a pretty good paper and character and may be printed correctly, and that particular care may be taken that the printer don't skip over a whole line as they sometimes do . . . (June 30, 1752.)

. . . but yet I should insist on good white paper and the printer's best types . . . (March 6, 1754.)

He bound the books poorly. The covers are so apt to warp that they will warp as they lie upon the table. I wish that he would take care that the books sent to Scotland may be handsomely bound . . . (December 20, 1754).

This concern with materials and the aesthetic aspects of book production is not really surprising, if one has examined Edwards' manuscripts, for most of his manuscripts are written on high-quality paper, and the multileaved manuscripts are generally meticulously bound.[1]

Finally, there is much evidence in the letters to Foxcroft of Edwards' hot pursuit of subscribers, a necessary function of the author and his friends or sponsors in those days. But what is interesting is the zest and ingenuity of Edwards in the pursuit. In this letter, he is asking Foxcroft to see about drumming up some business in an advantageous season:

I have had thoughts of writing to some gentlemen your way to take some of the proposals, and endeavoring to promote subscription, but I did not know but I should be thought too troublesome. I should be glad if I knew anybody that I could be so free with

---

1. An interesting illustration of the care given to all details of notebook-making is in a note found on the inside of the back cover of Book II, "Notes on the Scripture":

> If I live to make another book of this sort, to observe to cut the gashes for the stitching in deeper and not so near to the joinings of the stitch that the book may open more freely and fully. And let the sheets be divided into twice so small divisions and starch no paper in a paper cover, for that makes it crack. And if that don't do, try next stitching the backs of all the divisions of sheets to a slip of leather, and sew the cover over the leather.

This passage is transcribed (with some errors) on p. 374 of Ola E. Winslow's *Jonathan Edwards* (New York, 1940). Questionable is Winslow's transcription of "starch" as "stitch," for the very page on which the note is written is an illustration of JE's problem. He had starched [glued] the end leaves of the notebook to the paper cover, and it cracked and broke off at the hinge. Subsequent notebooks were stitched, but not "starched," into heavy paper covers.

as to desire 'em a little to exert themselves in the time of the Commencement at Cambridge . . . with respect to the other two colleges, New Haven and Newark, I have no difficulty. I know who to improve. (May 24, 1753.)

These letters[2] and other bits of related information give some idea of Edwards' involvement with the publication of his works. While the letters, in particular, come from a later period than that being discussed here, one in which publishing was for several reasons of more importance to Edwards than it would have been in the 1727–42 period, nevertheless they are indicative of attitudes that were well formed by the end of the thirties, and perhaps by the mid-thirties. Edwards' increasing desire to publish—sermons, reports, and other materials—and his increasing tendency to preach long, treatise-like sermon series in Northampton are hallmarks of the period. It is obvious that Edwards was developing ever larger and more complex bodies of thought at this time, and it is also clear that the sermon, whether in the pulpit or in print, was beginning to seem a rather limited vehicle. Perhaps, after all, one could not hope to develop more than a single "clear and distinct" idea in one sermon, a mere grain of an idea in the shadow of the "Rational Account."

From the very first years of his preaching career, Edwards had used some abbreviations and occasional compression of syntax in his sermon manuscripts, but as the years passed he increased the use of these devices until portions of his sermon manuscripts became outlines. Around 1740, at the time of the heat and bustle of the Great Awakening, however, more and more sermons appear with such a great percentage of their pages in outline that it becomes questionable whether a sermon is written-out with much outlining in it, or a heavily developed outline. Soon, by 1741 anyway, there is no question that many sermons are in outline, with only an occasional block at all developed. Then one day in January 1742, after having written out a few lines of the Text of a sermon on Dan. 5:25, Edwards drew a vertical line down the center of the little duodecimo page, dividing it into double columns. After that, nearly all of Edwards' Northampton sermons are so divided. This alteration marks the commencement of the third and last period, 1742–58.

2. The letters are now in the Beinecke Library, filed under Foxcroft's name. This is the result of Foxcroft's having reused the MSS for his own writing by turning them ninety degrees and writing over JE's fine pen with a pen of much greater width.

The period breaks down into at least two phases, from the point of view of a student of Edwards' literary activities as well as from that of the biographer: the years at Northampton, and the years at Stockbridge.

It is the sermon booklets, themselves, that set the tone of these years in Northampton. If one merely examines the physical character of the booklets, he immediately notices that something has happened. The booklets are now virtually all gathered: wads of leaves with rather perfunctory stitching through the sides (and some of the words) near the fold. Moreover, they have a new raggedness or shoddiness of appearance, for the irregularly cut slips of used paper, first seen here and there in the mid-thirties, now become a staple in sermon booklet make-up (often making a sermon manuscript much bulkier than the length of the sermon text would require it to be). Because Edwards sometimes used the margins of old letters for his notes, the remainder of a head is often hidden among an alien scrawl. Even this is not the worst: in 1745 comes the "fan paper."[3] In these days of ecclesiastical conflict and publishing enterprise, as Edwards was using his best paper for letters (ever more frequent), printers' drafts of treatises, and the all-important notebooks of folio and quarto dimensions, he resorted to improving the very remnants of fashion to the cause of the pulpit. Consequently, swatches of this flimsy, nearly transparent stuff, always smaller than a duodecimo leaf and having at least one curved edge, are found filling out substantial sections of sermon booklets in the late forties. The careful, practical Edwards always found some good paper for the first and last leaves of the sermon booklets, however, so that words committed to fan paper would have a better chance of survival.

The mere physical properties of a manuscript may not always mean very much, but they are significant in Edwards' case because his manuscripts were obviously given great consideration and care over many years, and there are numerous indications (as in his letters to Foxcroft) that he was quite appreciative of fine paper and the few luxuries of the study. Indeed, the physical qualities of the manuscripts are all too indicative of internal developments.

The division of the duodecimo page into two columns was a truly decisive step for Edwards because it effectively prevented anything

---

3. A very thin rice paper having many of the properties of onionskin, though less dense, was stamped with floral designs. Ladies apparently cut the paper into semicircular sections, fitted it to fan sticks, and then painted the decorative stamped designs.

like a written-out sermon, or anything but the slightest textual development. Since his earliest days, Edwards had drawn a horizontal
line across the page after the development of each major unit of
thought within the head, and as his tendency to abbreviate and outline
grew, the lines moved closer together. Now, by adding the vertical
line in the center of the page, he divided the roughly four-inch-square
duodecimo page into four, or more often six and sometimes eight,
little squares—each square presenting a writing area the size of a
postage stamp. And, as one might expect, as the years pass the writing
tends to recede from all four margins of the box, until, in many
sermons of the late forties there are only a few words huddled at the
center of each box. Moreover, these alterations signal still further
alterations, for during this period the sermon itself becomes less and
less of a literary structure.

The sermon form inherited by New England preachers from the
seventeenth century had a built-in tension, a tension between the
single theme established by the text and/or doctrine, and the parti-
cularization and tendency to fragmentation caused by the elaborate
system of heads. In the eighteenth century, when the "old logic," as
Edwards called it, was losing its hold over the minds of preachers
and congregations alike, the old sermon form began breaking up.
Now, the old tensions emerged and triumphed. In Boston and in
"liberal" pulpits, the trend seems to have been in the direction of the
single theme, a literary essay delivered from the pulpit. Edwards, who
sustained the old sermon form longer than many of the eastern
preachers, seems to have taken the other road in the forties, the road
to fragmentation and the list. For as he developed his sermons less
and less, and gradually gave over to the outline, so he seems to have
placed less and less emphasis upon the old intricate relationships
between the parts of the sermon. The major divisions—Text, Doctrine, Application—remain, even though the statement of doctrine
tends to dissolve into a mere proposition or "three things I shall here
discuss," but the hierarchy of heads and subheads nearly vanishes,
and the form becomes not an essay but a mere list of ideas on the
subject. Significantly, Edwards tends to mark the "heads" of these
outlines with large Roman numerals—much larger than the numerals
of the written-out sermons—as if only the arbitrary march of numerals gave order to the sermon.

Thus, the outline sermon of the forties is often much less of a
sermon than an earlier sermon would be if it were reduced to an

outline. It just does not have as many essential parts. The shift to outline sermons has been explained in the past in several ways, but the most frequent explanation is that Edwards "had mastered the pulpit." This is an improbable analysis. Edwards had surely mastered the pulpit by 1735 when he led the first widely publicized awakening among his own people and preached some of his finest sermons, and he had gained all the mastery he was ever to have over the sermon form by 1727. More plausible is the notion that Whitefield, whom Edwards met and heard preach in October 1740, impressed Edwards with his "spontaneous" delivery and caused Edwards to emulate him as best he could. But even this notion is open to serious question, for Edwards was always his own man, and though he laboriously copied pages of other men's books into his own notebooks, he invariably picked just those ideas that passed his own rigorous tests for a place in his system of thought and rejected their less sound neighbors out of hand. So, it seems, he (who had experimented with extensive outlining before he saw Whitefield) would have taken the measure of Whitefield's delivery and used what he could use, and rejected the rest. But what could he have used? Hopkins, who knew him, reports:

> Tho' . . . he was wont to read so considerable a part of what he delivered; yet he was far from thinking this the best way of preaching in general; and look'd upon his using his Notes . . . [as] a Deficiency and Infirmity. And in the latter part of his Life was inclined to think it had been better, if he had never accustomed himself to use his Notes at all.[4]

But he *had* accustomed himself to using them. Also, one might recall the remarks in Edwards' letter to the trustees of Nassau Hall:

> I have a constitution, in many respects peculiarly unhappy . . . often occasioning a kind of childish weakness and contemptibleness of speech, presence, and demeanor, with a disagreeable dullness and stiffness, much unfitting me for conversation . . . [5]

And perhaps qualify them in the light of further reports by Edwards' devoted disciple and admirer, Hopkins:

> He possessed but a comparative small stock of animal Life: his animal Spirits were low, and he had not Strength of Lungs to

4. *Life*, p. 48.
5. Dwight, *Life*, p. 568.

spare, that would be necessary in order to make him what would be called, an affable, facecious Gentleman, in all Companies.[6]

He had not a strong, loud Voice; but appear'd with such gravity and solemnity, and spake with such distinctness, clearness and precision; his Words were so full of Ideas, set in such a plain and striking Light, that few Speakers have been so able to demand the Attention of an Audience as he.[7]

What appears in the above testimonies, positively and negatively, is that there is little ground for supposing that Edwards had one jot of that dynamic, histrionic, improvisatorial quality that would be absolutely required if he were to turn one of these late Northampton outlines into a sermon even remotely resembling the sermons of the twenties and thirties. Even on the purely intellectual level, the record preserved in notebooks and sermon manuscripts of the play of Edwards' mind during the processes of revision and the working-up of material gives little precedence for the kind of on-the-spot intellectual improvising that would be required to transform such lists into unified wholes with even a little of that old ideational richness.

In 1744 there was the infamous "obscene book" episode, and that embarrassing debacle, Hopkins informs us, "seemed in a great Measure to put an end to Mr. Edwards's Usefulness at *Northampton* . . ."[8] It was a poignant trial for all. But did Edwards push his people so much harder than he had before, or were the social changes of the time solely responsible for this congregational rebellion? Or had Edwards, by 1744, lost some of his power over that congregation of sermon connoisseurs through having become, particularly in the light of just-past Great Awakening sermonizing, a dull or at least perfunctory preacher?

The evidence of the sermon manuscripts of the forties indicates that, even before 1744, Edwards was giving several things priority over the sermons, whether in materials or effort in production. As the decade wears on, not only do the sermon booklets look more like bundles of waste paper and the outlines grow more and more like bare lists, but the very nature of the notation in the booklets changes. Whereas Edwards had always written in his booklets the words that he expected to speak to the congregation, and even in the outline

6. Hopkins, *Life*, p. 42.
7. Ibid., p. 48.
8. Ibid., p. 55.

form preserved the decorum of the oration, he now began to write notes *on* sermons. Beside the brief notes for heads, or in place of a head, one is likely to encounter such statements as "Conclude with some consideration to enforce the whole" (Luke 12:35–36), and often there is no hint of what that consideration might be. Perhaps the most persuasive proof of the matter is established through the few exceptions to the rule. When Edwards had an extraordinary preaching occasion during the forties, such as an ordination sermon, a guest lecture, or a difficult case to put across at home, he seems to have returned to his earlier practice, and there are a few single-columned, largely written-out sermons in the forties that can be traced to such special occasions. The recently discovered manuscript of Edwards' farewell sermon is a fine example, for it is a single-columned, fully written-out manuscript which apparently leaves no room for improvisation, though Edwards certainly knew what he wished to say and certainly had sufficient inspiration upon that momentous occasion to preach *extempore*.

Many factors were involved in Edwards' dismissal from Northampton; they have been analyzed and speculated upon by biographers and scholars from Samuel Hopkins to Patricia Tracy, and they will be re-examined in the future.[9] The only point to be insisted upon in the context of the sermon manuscripts is that Edwards' attitude toward pastoral preaching during the forties must be considered as an important factor in such evaluations. Moreover, the manuscript evidence suggests that this attitude, in comparison with past attitudes, was one of indifference. Edwards had achieved his triumph as a preacher and author of literary sermons by the first years of the forties (as he had developed his fundamental ideas and theological positions), and by the mid-forties he was busy converting one of those treatise-like sermon series into a published treatise, preparing materials for new treatises, seeking out the significant controversial points of the day and recording them in one of his bulkiest single notebooks,[1] writing numerous letters to friends and colleagues on

9. See Patricia J. Tracy, *Jonathan Edwards, Pastor* (New York, Hill and Wang, 1980), for the most searching and richly speculative social analysis of JE's troubled Northampton pastorate. Virtually every serious biographer has devoted considerable attention to JE's dismissal, though the issue of his adequacy in the pulpit during the last few years has not been discussed.

1. "Controversy/Book C," also "Sundries," is a 300-page folio which JE kept in his last Northampton and Stockbridge years. In it he gathered notes on his extensive reading, but also wrote voluminously under such headings as Original Sin, Perseverance, Regeneration,

both sides of the Atlantic, and, at least in the late forties, he was preparing, with the aid of "Subjects of Enquiry," the vast synthesis of notebook materials that would be necessary if he were to write the Rational Account of Christianity. Gradually, subtly, and perhaps even subconsciously, but nevertheless unquestionably, Edwards was withdrawing from Northampton. His congregation sometimes grumbled that he was making too many guest preaching appearances for his own good, but they could only have sensed that he was launched upon a voyage that rendered his horseback peregrinations insignificant, a voyage from the world of the village pastor to that of the international community of thinkers and intellectual leaders in religious affairs. When the climax came in the Northampton qualification controversy and Edwards was ejected from the pulpit, one wonders if, except for worries about his "most chargeable" family, he was not greatly relieved.

However, if he had hoped that the days of struggle would end with his departure from Northampton, he was wrong, for the years at Stockbridge brought new conflicts around the Indian mission, continuations of the old one for at least a while, and an ever-increasing effort to keep up with his self-imposed obligations of defending Calvinist doctrine and the New Light psychology throughout Western civilization. Indeed, in many ways the years at Stockbridge were tremendously productive, and the student of Edwards' thought in treatise form might see them as a grand climax, but these years encompass the virtual cessation of sermon composition.

During Edwards' first weeks in Stockbridge, when he left family and undoubtedly most of his beloved notebooks back in Northampton,[2] there is a strange Indian Summer of the sermon for three brief weeks. Perhaps it was just that Edwards had little to do, or maybe the indomitable pastor decided to give the Indians his best at the start of his mission. Whatever the reason, there are a few sermons, all written in January of 1751, that look like ghosts from the past. Here, again, are written-out sermons on the octavo leaves of the first period,

---

Universal and Particular Redemption, Justification, Saving and Common Grace, Foreknowledge of God, Efficacious Grace, Nature of True Virtue, Importance of Doctrines and Mysteries in Religion, Future Punishment, Tests of Orthodoxy. Significant use of the notebook has been made by Paul Ramsey in his edition of the *Ethical Writings, Works of Jonathan Edwards, 8* (New Haven, Yale Univ. Press, 1989).

2. It was during this winter and early spring of 1751 that JE apparently made and used the little supplement to his sermon notebook 45, entitled "Subjects."

single columns, and pick-up lines. It is true that the structures of these sermons are less elaborate than those of the early sermons, having in fact a little of the late Northampton "list" in them, but might not this result from Edwards' consideration of the Indians' intellectual limitations? Slowly, painfully, he plowed new ground with the old steady hand:

Matt. 13:47–50. Again, the Kingdom of Heaven is like unto a net.

By the Kingdom of Heaven sometimes is meant Heaven and the state of happiness in another world; here is meant the Christian Church, or the whole company of Christians all over the world.

The people of Christ are the Kingdom of Christ because they are that part of the world that belongs to Christ and that have Christ for their King.

As King George's people are his kingdom, they being that part of the world that he rules over, or that have him for their king.

'Tis called the Kingdom of Heaven because Christ the King is from Heaven and the laws of his kingdom are all from Heaven. And the new heart and new nature that his people have given them is holy and heavenly. And the country they are to live in forever, with Christ their king, is Heaven.

'Tis said that this Kingdom of Heaven is like a net that was cast into the sea. The sea is the whole world of mankind. As a net that is cast into the sea don't take all the fish in the sea, but only goes round and fences in a few, so the Kingdom of Christ don't take all the world, but only a part.

And he is off once again, into the theological thickets of election, damnation, and salvation. It is, indeed, familiar territory, and the only really strange aspect of these sermon manuscripts is that they are not stitched. In fact, none of the Stockbridge Indian sermons is stitched, indicating that Edwards obviously did not intend to draw upon them or integrate them in the sermon files of his reference cycle. He seems to have preached each one only once or twice and then buried it in a drawer.

By the end of January, Edwards was probably beginning to realize that the Indians could not take much doctrine, and that a little went further than a lot; or perhaps some of his books and notebooks arrived, enabling him to spend more time in study. At any rate, before the end of January there is a final return to the outline form, and the sermons are hereafter written on folded pages torn from an old ledger (the leaves being octavo in shape, but a little smaller than foolscap octavo). By 1753 the average Indian sermon is a single fold (two leaves) in length, and a few fill only one page—Text, Doctrine, Application, and all.

As for the white congregation at Stockbridge, for the most part they heard the written-out sermons from the early Northampton days, usually in somewhat abbreviated form. On a few rare occasions Edwards seems to have written a sermon for the white congregation, and when he did so he used the late Northampton form: double columns, outline-box notation, and duodecimo booklet (still the palmed booklet in the white church). But such sermons (Job 5:17, 1753) are exceedingly rare—as rare, almost, as the "special occasion" written-out sermons—and one can generalize that Edwards did not regularly compose sermons for the whites at Stockbridge.

Thus in his last years Edwards seems to have continued to concern himself primarily with his studies, his publications, his role in the international clerical and intellectual community, and with such important practical matters as preserving his mission and defending his hapless Indians against the vicious depredations of frontier entrepreneurs. As a result, his career as a creative preacher faded away into a few scrawled lines on old notebook leaves.

If his last group of sermons, the Indian sermons, have any real value it is probably as a documentary record of Edwards' relationship with, and attitude toward, the Indians. After having read many of these last outline sermons, along with the published materials relating to Edwards' struggles to save the Indians and their mission, one might conclude that his tears[3] upon hearing the advice of his colleagues to accept the presidency of Nassau Hall were occasioned not by his having to leave the white congregation at Stockbridge, nor by the prospect of moving his household once again, nor by fears concerning his

3. Hopkins, *Life*, p. 79.

possible inadequacy in the role of college president, nor by fears for his work (especially as he would undoubtedly have a better environment for study and writing in Princeton), but by that Puritan conscience that told him he was, perhaps for a second time, sacrificing a congregation to the advancement of his own career—even if his career was that of a leading spokesman for Christ. This time, he knew, the sheep in the fold were particularly helpless, and he also knew the wolves who would charge upon the fold as soon as he left the gate untended.

Edwards nevertheless bade farewell to a group of his Indians on January 15, 1758. The sermon he delivered is one of his last, and a good example of a late outline. Though it is so brief that it can be printed here in its entirety, it has vestiges of power and real poignancy that are not wholly dependent upon historical perspective. At the bottom of the first page of the sermon is a list of five Indian names, perhaps the names of those faithful followers who deserved special recognition on parting. The choice of the text, alone, was a masterstroke:

> Luke 21:36. Watch ye, and pray always.
> I. Many dreadful things are coming upon this wicked world.
> II. The righteous, and they only, shall be thought fit to escape those things that shall come.
> III. All at last must be called to appear before Christ.
> > Christ will come.
> > All must see him.
> > All must be brought before him.
> IV. The righteous shall be thought worthy to stand before Christ and no others.
> > 1. The righteous worthy.
> > 2. Wicked not worthy.
> V. We should watch and pray always that we may be thought worthy {to stand before Christ}.
> > 1. Watch
> > 2. Pray
> > 3. Always
> > > Application
> What must watch against.
> How watch.
> What need of watching.

Always.
Prayer.
> What pray for.
> How pray.

In elaborating the Doctrine of this sermon, Edwards certainly heard echoes of his first farewell sermon, though present circumstances may have rendered them profoundly ironic.

CHAPTER III
THE SERMON CANON

Edwards wrote a great number of sermons during his career and he apparently saved almost all of them, stored in a file according to text, where he could draw upon them for repreachings or for information and statement in his reference-cycles. The extant sermon manuscripts, probably at least four-fifths of the original sermon corpus, number roughly 1200.[1]

From the earliest (Is. 3:10, 1721) to the latest (Luke 21:36, 1758), the nearly continuous stream of manuscript and printed sermons provides a record of Edwards' literary, theological, and general intellectual life throughout thirty-seven of his prime years, although there is a tapering off, particularly in the literary dimension, during the last sixteen years. These sermons preserve the moments at which Edwards appeared fully engaged: applying abstract theological and philosophical principles to concrete situations in a rural community or a mission outpost; attempting to place the urgent affairs of men in the context of eternity and, in so doing, evaluate the projects and deals of the colonial bourgeoisie within the eternal plan of the Deity.

1. The first systematic attempt to sort and catalogue the sermons was made by Glenn R. Pratt in 1958, as part of a dissertation, "Jonathan Edwards as a Preacher of Doctrine" (Temple University). The Pratt index lists 1352 sermons. This number is erroneous, however, primarily because Pratt tended to confuse sections of a sermon with whole sermons, and vice versa. He did not realize that JE frequently wrote one sermon in two booklets in the early years, or that the later years would present such "flexibility" in sermon booklet form.

The card file index of the sermons in the reference room of the Beinecke Library, based upon the Pratt index but much reworked and improved by Thomas A. Schafer, contains 1164 card entries. This index is significantly more accurate than the original Pratt index, but too often the card index is apt to list as one sermon a single manuscript bundle which contains material preached on one text. Upon reading the material, however, it is evident that the bundle is not one sermon, even in several sections, but a sermon series on one text. (There is much evidence that JE tended to stitch completed sermon entries in fat bundles, probably to simplify filing.) Hence, it would seem that the figure 1164 is conservative.

They show him pressing through the redundant veils of current events, through the great conflicts of the world, through western civilization and world history, to the Word becoming Light; they show him striving to create a sense of the relationship between "now" and "forever," and between a sublime God and man. Here is Edwards utilizing pre-Freudian psychoanalysis in the service of evangelical Calvinism, and speaking in the farmers' idiom while employing the pre-Jungian archetypes of the most esoteric of languages, biblical and natural typology, in order to infuse an old sermonic form with a new intellectual reality and emotional vitality. The message, the style and context, together, reveal a complex man behind the words: hotly engaged yet cool-headed, speculative and experimental yet dogmatic in essentials; learned and metaphysical yet most practical; mystical and yet shrewd; plain-speaking yet artful. But Edwards' ideas are never palpably confused and he was no hypocrite; rather, both man and ideas are subtle, and his style is simple only when articulating a simple point. The focus of these complexities, moving in the dynamic of time, is preserved in the sermon canon, and while the "Miscellanies" might rival the sermons as intellectual and spiritual documents, the sermons remain unrivaled as a reflection of the man and his art in the midst of life.

This mass of sermons can be roughly divided among the three chronological periods of Chapter II: 1722–27, 1727–42, 1742–58. In the first period, there are about 65 sermons, all fully written out. The second period comprises about 645 sermons, the vast majority of which are fully written out, although significant outlining appears here and there in the last 140 or so. The final period, 1742–58, includes about 510 sermons, the majority of which are more or less in outline. Moreover, within this last period, the "Indian sermons," most of which are the barest outlines, represent all but a handful of the 200 sermons written after the move to Stockbridge.

1. Manuscript versus Printed Sermons

When this total body of extant sermons is compared with the number so far printed, it is evident that only a tiny portion of even the written-out sermons has been printed: 72 sermons plus the two sermon series published as *Charity and its Fruits* (16 sermons) and *A History of the Work of Redemption* (30 sermons). Moreover, although the editors' selections (after the first 22 published by Edwards) confirm

the most general proportions of the total canon in indicating a pre-
ponderance of New Testament texts over Old Testament texts, there
is little that is representative beyond that, save in the two sermon
series. Although Edwards' favorite sermon texts were, in descending
order, Matthew, Luke, Isaiah, Psalms, John, I Corinthians, Proverbs,
and Romans, the proportions of the list of printed sermons are Isaiah,
I Corinthians, Psalms, Romans, Matthew, John, Luke, and Proverbs.
Moreover, both Ezekiel and Hebrews are better represented in print
than Proverbs.

Such quantitative inventories, while they do indicate the general
nature of the problem, are of very limited significance. A sermon's
Scripture text, as a matter of fact, tells little about its contents. As
Ola Winslow has observed, "This young man had a genius for finding
Scripture to his purpose, and finding it in unexplored and scriptural
corners."[2] The text thus gives no indication of whether or not the
sermon will contain "hellfire," a celebration of Christ's beauty, or any
number of other possibilities. Indeed, there sometimes seems to be
an impish perversity in the selection of texts, and it is as common to
have minatory sermons preached from a Gospel text as it is to have
a sermon about Christ preached from the Old Testament. Two of
Edwards' most sulfurous sermons are Luke 16:24 ("That the torments of Hell are exceeding great") and Rom. 9:22 ("God has no
other use to put finally impenitent sinners to, but to suffer his wrath"),
while some of his brightest sermons are Zech. 4:7 ("The gospel dispensation is finished wholly and entirely in free and glorious grace"),
Cant. 1:3 ("Christ Jesus is a person transcendently excellent and desirable"), and Jer. 17:7–8 ("They that trust in God have a full fountain
of good to live upon, that won't fail in evil and calamitous times"). If
you want a jeremiad, look under Luke as well as Jeremiah. The justification for this seeming capriciousness or perversity is, of course,
the serious commitment to the concept of the "harmony of the Scriptures" and to the discipline of typological interpretation, both aspects
of the view that the Bible is a unified account having a single theme,
the working of man's redemption through the second Person of the
Trinity.

Even beyond the level of Text and Doctrine, there is plenty of
unpredictable innovation and seeming digression, for as has been
observed in connection with *Sinners*, it was Edwards' habit in preach-

2. Winslow, *Jonathan Edwards*, p. 140.

ing to mix threats and allurements. Thus, passages of dehortation and images of hell may be found in sermons that are nominally and generally celebrations of the more pleasant aspects of religion, and, on the contrary, many "hellfire" sermons contain passages of poetic beauty to counterbalance the horrific element, especially in conclusion. The reader of Edwards' funeral sermon for his "own dear child," Jerusha, may be astounded to read, after a lengthy and moving tribute to a beautiful person who "cometh forth like a flower and is cut down," a long and detailed inventory of the follies of Northampton youth, culminating in bitter recriminations and an indictment of "that shameful, lascivious custom of handling women's breasts, and the different sexes lying on beds together [bundling]." Yet, by the end of the sermon, Edwards has returned to the subject of Jerusha's personal qualities and to a fine eulogy which was delivered, according to Edwards, solely to inspire and awaken the listeners. The extremes of thought and emotion in this sermon make the concept of decorum practically irrelevant, though the sermon must have left the congregation deeply impressed and is undoubtedly efficacious.

Likewise, in a sermon bearing the doctrine, "It is a strange punishment that God has assigned to the workers of iniquity," one finds a lengthy paean to the beauties of the universe, asserting that "the God of nature has put all things in excellent and beautiful order and made things mutually subservient, and directed them to excellent ends such as the glory of God and the good and happiness of mankind." The same sermon speaks at length of the surprising joys of heaven as well as of the "strange" [monstrous] punishment of the wicked. Moreover, even in a sermon bearing the doctrine, "Men as they are by nature are perfect slaves to corruption, or they are entirely under the dominion of sin," one reads that "the human nature is an excellent nature; far more excellent than that of the brute creatures. Reason is a noble faculty; it is the candle of the Lord, Prov. 20:27. 'Tis that wherein chiefly consists of the natural image of God." There are no contradictions in these sermons, nor any truly irrelevant digressions; rather, there is a characteristic Edwardsean richness and amplitude of conception that results from Edwards' refusal to over-simplify or to address a point wholly out of context. Only the lecture or the eccentric tour de force, such as the published version of *Sinners,* is in danger of being narrowly focused or intellectually and emotionally monotonic. Nor was Edwards ever apparently unaware of the matter of balancing antitheses and maintaining a sane perspective, and in the late sermons, when he tended to write notes to himself on sermons rather than sermon notes, one sometimes finds such a note as "to make a hopefull conclusion."[3]

Such diversity or richness of subject matter and stylistic treatment would be difficult to represent adequately in even three hundred sermons, let alone seventy-two and two sermon series. That is, it would be difficult even if the sermons in print represented the full range of Edwards' sermons. However, when the types of sermons previously printed are compared with those in manuscript, it is evident that several categories of sermons are represented only peripherally or not at all. For instance, in the category of "occasional sermons," only the ordination sermons, all of which were printed in Edwards' lifetime, are well represented. Other significant types of occasional sermons, such as earthquake sermons, drought sermons, war sermons, Fast Day sermons, New Year's sermons, and Thanksgiving sermons are either poorly represented or not represented at all. Moreover, a few general categories of sermons are not in print: sacrament sermons, Indian sermons, children's sermons, sermons on church polity and ecclesiastical affairs (excluding ordinations), and perhaps most noteworthy, a whole facet of Edwards' sermon canon that might be designated "mystical," a large number of sermons treating of the ecstasies of religious experience and couched in the language and types of the Song of Songs. Certainly, in numbers and in the intensity of individual performances, these sermons would go far toward counterbalancing and complementing the better-known legal and awakening sermons.

Moreover, there is one category which is, unhappily, adequately represented: bad sermons. Edwards was, like all preachers and literary artists, capable of producing inferior work. The "bad" sermons do not disgrace him as a preacher, particularly when it is remembered that the preacher, like the editorialist, must perform as best he can, and within sometimes severe thematic limits, at frequent stated in-

---

3. Not only did JE try to balance the tones and arguments within sermons, but, according to the Preface to [Five] *Discourses* (1738), he saw the necessity of balancing successive sermons:

What is published at the end, concerning the excellency of Christ, is added on my own motion; thinking that a discourse on such an evangelical subject, would properly follow others that were chiefly legal and awakening, and that something of the excellency of the *Savior*, was proper to succeed those things that were to show the necessity of *Salvation*. . . . (P. v.)

tervals.[4] Perhaps they are not very bad, but they are comparatively perfunctory exercises that get the doctrine stated and detail an appropriate response, but little else. And what is worse, some of them are not brief. Of course, these are not sermons prepared for the press by Edwards himself, but pieces culled from his sermon hoard by editors (including his son) after his death. It seems that these editors not only picked a limited range of sermons, those embodying certain evangelical themes, but printed the first sermons they found dealing with the desired topic. The result is that inferior sermons were sometimes printed while superior sermons making the same theological points remained in manuscript. Finally, the great nineteenth-century collections of Edwards' sermons seem to have printed sermons primarily because they were already in print.

All in all, then, it can hardly be expected that students of Edwards' sermons who have been dependent upon hitherto printed sources would have had more than fragmentary impressions of the preacher. Past editors have had good intentions, but too often their goals have been severely limited and their selection procedures unscholarly. The result is that, except for the sermons he published himself, Edwards' printed sermons might as well have been selected by enemies as by friends, and if nothing else, they make Edwards-the-preacher a smaller, narrower man than he was, according to the ample evidence of his sermon manuscript canon.

2. *The Varieties of Sermons*

When the canon itself is confronted, one immediately seeks ways of assessing it that are more meaningful than mere chronological groupings or attempted winnowings of the written-out from the outlinish sermons. In this exercise, some notable precedents have been established. For instance, Faust and Johnson have classified Edwards' sermons as "disciplinary, pastoral, doctrinal, and occasional,"[5] a sound enough set of categories, though a rather coarse sieve. Such categories give the reader more peace of mind than help in isolating significant kinds of sermonic material. A much more elaborate (and theological)

4. Benjamin Franklin's observation that itinerant preachers such as George Whitefield had the advantage of *rehearsing* their delivery could have included that the itinerant has to compose sermons only occasionally as well. *The Autobiography of Benjamin Franklin*, ed. Leonard W. Labaree et al. (New Haven, Yale Univ. Press, 1964), p. 180.

5. *Jonathan Edwards, Representative Selections* (New York, 1935), p. cx.

structuring of Edwards' canon is supplied in the index prepared by Glenn R. Pratt.[6] Pratt attempts to place each of the identified manuscript and printed sermons under one of the following headings: "Anthropology," "Christology," "Ecclesiology," "Eschatology," "Ethics," "Soteriology," and "Theology Proper." In addition, each of these headings has five or more subdivisions or "subjects" within it, constituting a very fine sieve overall. And yet, when one reads the sermons under these various headings, he may well discover that one of the best passages on the character of Christ comes in a sermon under the rubric of "Eschatology," or that the most valuable portion of a sermon, to his way of thinking, is contained in a digression from the nominal topic of the sermon and hence is not noted in the sermon's category label. Again, the very richness of Edwards' sermons, all his logical rigor and single-mindedness notwithstanding, makes them rather slippery creatures when one attempts a categorical inventory.

Perhaps Edwards himself could help in this matter, since he was a student of his own sermons and a frequenter of his manuscript library. This library was undoubtedly filed by biblical text, as all of Edwards' references to sermons contain at least the sermon's text. In addition to the text, there is often a reference to some specific subdivision of the sermon, such as "the third Inference," and sometimes, especially when more than one sermon exists on a single text, an identifying phrase from the sermon's doctrine. The references themselves are usually part of a notebook entry, listed under a topical heading in a notebook table or placed under a biblical text in the interleaved Bible. Of course such references are citations of specific sermons and parts of sermons, not means for cataloguing the sermon corpus as a whole. It seems unlikely that Edwards himself could have very readily put his hands on every passage dealing with a particular idea, image, theme, or occasion, and by and large his notebook references to sermons are highly selective. But he did preach large numbers of his sermons two or more times, frequently after the passage of several years, and because of his need to preach certain types of sermons at certain times, he must have had a way of making a more precise selection than a mere textual citation would allow. The evidence suggests that his first check-point in the search for a certain kind of sermon may well have been the sermon notebooks.

The sermon notebooks have already been considered as store-

---

6. See note on p. 130.

houses of sermonic ideas (see Chapter II, pp. 56–68), but the careful crossing out of used entries with a single vertical line (clearly marking, but not obliterating the entry) and the addition of chosen texts to entries that lacked texts when first made indicate that Edwards referred back to the sermon notebooks to see with comparative ease just what kinds of sermons he had on hand. Moreover, to facilitate this search he used yet another device, the sermon label, written in large letters (twice or thrice the normal notebook hand), usually at the head of the entry. The character of these labels indicates the manner in which Edwards himself thought of the sermon, and the proportion of instances of the various labels gives some indication of Edwards' preaching needs as he saw them. The following list results from a canvass of sermon notebook 45, the largest collection of sermon notes made during Edwards' years at Northampton and Stockbridge:

Sacrament	37	sermons
Fast	30	"
Ordination	22	"
Lecture	11	"
Young People	10	"
Thanksgiving	9	"
Rulers	5	"
Civil Authority	4	"
Education	3	"
Justice	3	"
Contribution	2	"
Covenant	2	"
Farewell Sermon	2	"
Moral Honesty	2	"
Private Meeting	2	"
War	2	"
Church Government	1	"
Contention	1	"
Darkness	1	"
Expedition to Canada	1	"
Funeral	1	"
Little Children	1	"
Peace	1	"
Preparation to Sacrament	1	"
Relative Duties	1	"

There are many unmarked sermons in the notebook aside from those listed above; there are also unlabeled sermons that might have been given one of the above labels, and there are groups of sermons (such as awakening sermons) that might have been given labels and yet have none. But this labeling was only semi-systematic—some titles being clearly redundant—and was obviously not intended to be exhaustive. Perhaps Edwards did not bother to label his most memorable sermons.

The list, however, certainly does indicate the way in which Edwards considered the output of his labors. Though some of the labels might be termed "occasional" while others are "thematic" or "topical," the inescapable impression given by the whole body of sermon labels in the three extant sermon notebooks and the "Catalogue" letter sheet is that Edwards considered every sermon to be, in a very literal sense, "occasional."[7] That is, every sermon, despite the abstract tone resulting from the conventions of the traditional sermon form, is a response to a specific situation in society. Even the revisions of sermons for guest appearances in Boston and elsewhere show Edwards' efforts to tailor a sermon to a particular audience. When all the evidence is considered, the Edwardsean sermon seems to stand between the ephemeral oration and the homily as an occasional piece: eternal verities are presented, but just those verities that have eminent relevance to the moment and the people. And the printed sermon, no matter how much it is reworked for the reading public, necessarily bears the stamp of its occasion, though knowledge of the original context is necessary to appreciating it.

Thus, it seems wise for even those whose interest in Edwards' ser-

---

7. Of course the occasional nature of the sermon is fundamental, the word *sermo* signifying a talk—inevitably occasional as is any act or public gesture. The great seventeenth-century preachers, such as John Cotton, Thomas Hooker, and Thomas Shepard, seem to have taken this for granted, as is suggested by the fact that many of their sermons were first printed from auditors' notes, the notes constituting a kind of report on a specific public act (see Larzer Ziff's *The Career of John Cotton* [Princeton Univ. Press, 1962], pp. 158–59). By JE's time, however, the widespread printing of sermons seems to have encouraged the notion of sermon-as-literature. Numerous prefaces to eighteenth-century sermons indicate that, when the preacher had good reason to anticipate publication, he wrote a discourse that could not be delivered in its entirety from the pulpit because of time limitations, necessitating the preaching of abstracts from the written work. The preacher thus wrote in the spirit of the treatise as much as that of the sermon, and created literature for the press as much as the scenario of an occasional oratorical performance (for instance, see the "Advertisement" to Peter Clark's sermon before the Annual Convention of Ministers in Boston [Boston, 1745].

mons is theological, literary, or philosophical to consider the occasional social context[8] of every sermon as an unavoidable and essential aspect of its significance. Likewise, the division of the sermon canon into categories should hardly be attempted without giving consideration to the evident occasional aspects of the sermons being classified. Once this important aspect of the sermons is given due attention, however, there are many ways of cataloguing the sermons and both coarse and fine sieves have their valid uses. But beyond the level of rough classification by text and/or stated doctrine, any attempt at comprehensive, descriptive cataloguing is an arduous business, productive of dubious fruits.

In his own use of the sermons Edwards seems to have relied on several devices of reference and classification: the simple ordering of the mass of sermons by biblical text, the citation of outstanding sermons and parts of sermons in the notebooks and their tables, the "occasional" listing of sermons in the sermon notebooks (which also provided a simple list of texts and doctrines for many sermons), and finally, the various data recorded in the individual sermon booklets. This last aid-to-selection, recorded largely in shorthand, is primarily concerned with important practical information on a particular sermon's pulpit history, such as date and place of delivery, and would undoubtedly have been of great use to Edwards in the selection of one sermon from among a handful of possibilities.[9] Inasmuch as Ed-

8. In "Jonathan Edwards' Sociology of the Great Awakening," *New England Quarterly*, 21 (March 1948), 50–77, Perry Miller edited passages from three unpublished sermons which illustrate JE's capacity for addressing himself explicitly to a situation and to particular types of people in his congregation. Passages such as these are not unusual in JE's sermons; indeed, some passages quoted in this study are more explicit than any quoted by Miller. Miller's passages represent a kind of "norm of explicitness" for JE when speaking to his congregation (or certain parts of it) on current events.

What Miller does not stress in his interpretation is JE's insistence upon the underlying principles rather than the surface details in even his more explicit statements, such as those quoted in Miller's article. JE does not mention names or describe events that his congregation would have known before he started to speak. For instance, he preached a sermon on the recent earthquake in 1727, but the word "earthquake" is not even mentioned until the mid-point of the sermon, and then it intrudes almost casually: "God sometimes threatens and warns a people by extraordinary things in providence, sometimes by strange sights in the heavens and sometimes by earthquakes . . ." (Jonah 3:10).

9. William P. Upham decoded JE's shorthand and published a key for it in "On the Shorthand Notes of Jonathan Edwards," *Mass. Hist. Soc. Proc.*, 2nd ser., *15* (1902), 514–21. Upham's discussion and key provide a very helpful start, but it is one thing to know the individual letter-symbols and another to read the shorthand words composed of these symbols. Moreover, JE is not consistent in his shorthand usage. I have illustrated some of the more important shorthand words at appropriate points in this discussion.

wards obviously "farmed" his sermon hoard in order to provide sermons for future use, aside from maintaining it as a supplement to his various specialized notebooks, he was necessarily concerned with the "production record" of each sermon.

3. Edwards' Reworking of the Sermons

By studying these notes on preaching and related markings in the sermon booklets, one can approach and contemplate, at least in imagination, one of the most interesting activities in Edwards' study: the use of the sermon collection in satisfying the demands of the pulpit. Although the sermons demonstrably contributed much to Edwards' recorded system of thought, they were primarily the initial outlet of that thought, and within the sermon collection itself, the primary direction of development is toward new sermons through the careful and frequently ingenious reuse of old sermonic materials. Of the twelve hundred or so sermons extant, about four hundred are marked as having been repreached, at least in part, between one and three times. In several cases, sermons are marked as having been repreached five, six, or seven times.[1] Such numerous repreachings involved deliveries in several towns, but many of those repreached only once or twice were repreached only in Northampton, usually after several years' interval and frequently with some kind of alteration. The greatest number of repreached sermons were delivered in Stockbridge to the white congregation who seem to have heard only old Northampton sermons (except for about ten) during the six years Edwards preached to them, though they were thus permitted to hear some of the most carefully wrought sermons of the early thirties.

The preparation of sermons for repreaching can best be considered in the light of the three basic procedures involved in preparation: revision, recasting, and cannibalism. Of course, Edwards preached some sermons a second time without making any significant alterations in the original (though there is hardly one where there is no evidence of a "once over lightly," affecting a few words and phrases

---

1. Of some sixteen sermons clearly marked as having been preached between three and seven times that I have examined, only two were chosen for publication by JE's early editors. Perhaps they did not print sermons merely because they had obviously appealed to JE and/or his audiences. This is just one of several seemingly sensible criteria for selecting sermons that the editors apparently ignored.

Sermon Revisions. Beinecke Rare Book and Manuscript Library, Yale University.

here and there), and these sermons can be covered by noting the interesting variety of signs by which Edwards kept track of them:

+ is always found in the upper left-hand corner of the front of the sermon booklet, sometimes alone and sometimes with a date. It seems to indicate at least one repreaching, though sometimes more. In the latter case, there is often additional information somewhere in the sermon booklet. [Ps. 73:25; I Kings 18:21 (with date).]

-ᴋ. is the shorthand symbol for "Northampton," placed on sermon booklets (in various places) during a period of a little more than a year subsequent to Edwards' arrival there. It indicates repreaching only when it appears on a sermon written before his call to Northampton in 1726. [Phil. 1:21.]

..,∴ apparently constitute an effort to indicate the number of times a sermon has been repreached. They usually appear in the upper left portion of the booklet's first page. [I John 4:16.]

◖ also apparently indicates the number of times the sermon was preached (or repreached). The number of dark sections is apparently the indicator. The sign usually appears in the left margin of the sermon's first page. [Is. 32:2.]

⅏, ⅏ signify "the second time" and "the third time," respectively. One of them is found most frequently at the head of a sermon, or between the Doctrine and Application. Quite often, the symbol is part of a shorthand entry such as that below. [Gen. 25:29–34.]

⁓₃ᴵᴸ⁻ᴵˋ is "preached the second time" and is often followed by ⸍, "at," and the name of the place, whether a town or a "private meeting." Such entries may be entirely in shorthand or involve a mixture of longhand. ⼔⼂ is "third." Such statements usually occur in the same places as the symbols immediately above. [II Sam. 23:5.]

Most of the above signs may occur in combination with their fellows, and many have further explanatory material accompanying them somewhere in the sermon booklet. Sometimes, Edwards does not use a symbol at all but simply writes, "Preached the second time at . . ." Edwards thus noted instances of repreaching in his sermon booklets, as well as first preachings outside his regular pulpit (though it seems that these performances were, in fact, repreachings). The same signs also appear on the booklets of sermons that have been revised, recast, or cannibalized, but in these cases there are usually additional, more detailed technical notations which indicate what has been done in the way of modifying the sermon.

When Edwards revised a sermon for the purpose of repreaching (as opposed to revisions made to improve the initial sermon, discussed in Chapter II), he frequently attempted to effect a change in the facade of the sermon without actually reworking it. Thus, it is not uncommon to find a note such as the following: "The second time from Prov. 3:14, Aug. 1748." (Luke 11:27–28; 1729–30.) Both texts, it turns out, can be used to introduce the same doctrine: "The hearing and keeping the word of God renders a person more blessed than any other privilege that God ever bestowed on any of the children of men." In the same manner, a second doctrine is sometimes written in. The doctrine of Matt. 6:33 (1727) is "Religion should be the main business of our lives"; however, included at the foot of the same page is an alternate doctrine: "God expects of us that we should subject all our other concerns to our spiritual concerns." Again, the remainder of the sermon could easily support either version of the doctrine. For obvious reasons, it was more difficult to invent interchangeable doctrines, and there are fewer sermons with alternate doctrines than with alternate texts.

Another device, often found in conjunction with one of the above changes, is the marking of portions of a sermon for repreaching. Generally, Edwards marked them either with brackets[2] or with lines in the left-hand margins of the pages. The bracket is sometimes used in the conventional fashion, in pairs, and in this case it usually marks off a fairly small unit such as a paragraph or a head per pair of brackets. More common than this type of marking, however, is the single, double bracket (ב). It is used to mark the end of a section to be repreached and is frequently found one-half or two-thirds of the way through the Doctrine or Application, and sometimes in both divisions. In such cases there is always a shorthand note, saying, "From the doctrine to the mark the second time, ב" (Eccles. 9:10; 1728), or giving some similar direction.

The left-hand margin lines represent an advance in the degree of revision, in most cases, in that they are more selective than the double bracket. Rather than merely demarcating less than the whole of a Doctrine or Application, the lines indicate heads, paragraphs, sen-

2. Sometimes, though rarely, JE used pairs of brackets to indicate deletion, or to mark a passage as a kind of pastoral aside to the congregation. But such passages are usually quite brief and rarely have an explanatory note, the context being sufficient indication of what is intended. Most of these usages occur in early sermons, and it was JE's usual practice to indicate the deletion of paragraphs by large Xs through them.

tences, and in many instances, single lines to be preached. Thus, the revised sermon is a synopsis of the entire original sermon, or a complete stratum that runs the full length of the original, rather than a sequence of truncated subdivisions. Job 34:21 provides a fine example of the technique and is also representative in that the note on re-preaching does not mention the margin lines in particular. Apparently, Edwards often felt that the lines needed no explanatory note.

Perhaps the most radical and interesting of Edwards' many synoptic revisions of this type is the revision of his famous sermon on Deut. 32:35.

1. Always exposed to fall.
2. Suddenly fall.
3. By their own weight.
4. Nothing but that 'tis God that holds 'em up.

---

1. No want of power in God.
2. They deserve it.
3. They are condemned to it.
   'Tis the place they belong to.
4. God is angry enough with them.
5. The devil, if not restrained, would immediately fly upon them and seize them as his own.
6. They have those hellish principles in them that if God should take off his restraints.
7. 'Tis no security that there are no visible means of death at hand.
8. Their own care and prudence to preserve their own lives.
9. The schemes they lay out for escaping damnation.
10. There is no promise.

Application

Use of awakening.
This is the case with you.
You are, as it were, heavy with sin and those things are as spiders' webs.
The black clouds of wrath hang over you.
The bow is bent.
The wrath of God is like a rapid stream that is dammed up.
Your damnation don't slumber.

You hang over the pit by a slender thread and the flames of wrath flashing about it.

God holds the thread in his hand.

You are held over just as one holds a spider or some hateful insect over a furnace.

There is no other reason to be given why you did not go to hell last night.

---

1. Whose wrath this is.

2. 'Tis misery that shall be inflicted to that end: to show what the wrath of Jehovah is.

---

3. 'Tis the fierceness of his wrath, especially on gospel sinners.

---

4. 'Tis certain unavoidable wrath.
5. 'Tis speed of wrath. You know not how soon.
6. 'Tis everlasting wrath.
7. 'Tis certain unavoidable wrath, Job 21:19–20.

Here, the entire sermon has been excerpted on a single folded duo-decimo sheet (clipped to two-thirds its ordinary height), probably for delivery to the white congregation at Stockbridge.[3] The outline does

3. The identity of this piece is interesting and somewhat problematic. Upon first seeing it, bound to the back of the *Sinners* sermon manuscript, as if it constituted the last two leaves of the sermon, one immediately supposes that it is the original outline for the sermon (though it is rather clean for such a worksheet). Upon collating it with the Northampton draft of the sermon and the printed version, however, it immediately becomes clear that the outline follows the printed version much more closely in the crucial second section of the Application (See Chapter II, pp. 113–14). It seems certain that it was written after, or at the same time as, the special draft for the printer. The thought arises that JE, under the influence of Whitefield, might have made an outline of his Northampton sermon for the Enfield performance. With the outline, his preaching would necessarily have been more "spontaneous"; moreover, if this were the Enfield outline, it would be a logical bridge between the first and printed versions. But close examination of the ink of the outline reveals that this ink (obviously lighter than the ink of the first draft) has a vehicle quite different from that of any ink used during the summer of 1741. The hand also looks later than 1741, though it is unusually neat for a very late hand.

If one persists in examining JE's dated or datable manuscripts, he eventually comes upon this very ink (an ink with an uncommonly thin vehicle) in sermon notebook 45, p. 154, and in the Indian sermons, Jude 13 and Phil. 2:7, of July-August, 1756. Thus it seems that JE, used to preaching from outlines at that time, chose an outline of the printed version, with its significantly harsher tone, over the original Northampton-Enfield version when he prepared to preach in Stockbridge. It is probable that the sermon was delivered to the white congregation because it is not marked "St. Ind.," the invariable label on the sermons preached to the Indians.

not contain statements of text and doctrine, but Edwards stitched it to the original sermon manuscript to avoid confusion about its identity. At the time of delivering the sermon, he doubtless had little difficulty recalling the main heads of his most famous sermon. Indeed, certain discrepancies between the outline and the original sermon (such as the reversing of the "bent bow" and "dammed stream" passages) suggest that Edwards may have made up the outline from memory.

What would Edwards gain from this last type of synoptic revision? Presumably he gained in the greatest possible degree what must have been one consideration whenever he chose to repreach less than the whole of a written-out sermon: flexibility, an opportunity to garnish the well-known sermonic structure with the inspirations of the moment. Another consideration, particularly in cases where brackets or margin lines are used, appears to have been the reduction of sermon length from two or more preaching units to one. Most of Edwards' Northampton sermons were written to be preached in at least two units, morning and afternoon, but when he preached out of town, and many of his notes indicate repreachings out of town, he probably preached only during one session much of the time.

Thus far only those revisions involving no major additions to the sermon text, and in many instances the reduction of the text, have been discussed. A step beyond such revision is that which involves the insertion of new material in old sermons. Edwards frequently added new material to an old sermon when he prepared it for repreaching, even when reducing its overall length. Many of these revisions and additions are of a very minor sort, involving the correction of syntactical problems, the sharpening of definitions, the insertion of "pick up lines," and the addition or deletion of minor points with a minimal use of ink and paper. Such revisions are not recognized in notes, and the only basis for identifying them as corrections for repreaching, rather than corrections made during the composition of the sermon, is the disparity in ink and/or hand.

Sometimes, however, these minor additions do contribute enough to alter significantly the course of the sermon's argument, or at least change the tone of the argument. In such cases, note or no note, the sermon is truly "revised." Many of these significant revisions are quite brief, however, and like the following example, they are inserted in the small blank spaces between heads or at the tops and bottoms of pages. In this sermon, Edwards is telling his congregation how sinners are abused by the very master they serve, and he apparently discovered his most apt illustration after the sermon was written, quite possibly at the time he prepared it for a repreaching, for the passage is squeezed in at the bottom of a completed page:

> . . . [Satan and his cohorts] do by you as I have heard they do in Guinea, when at their great feasts they eat men's flesh. They set the poor, ignorant child, who knows nothing of the matter, to make a fire, and while it stoops down to blow the fire one comes behind and strikes off his head, and then he is roasted by that same fire that he kindled, and made a feast of and the skull is made use of as a cup, out of which they make merry with their liquor.
>
> Inf. So Satan, who has a mind [to] make merry with you.

John 8:34 ("Wicked Men's Slavery to Sin.") is considerably enhanced by this, its most memorable illustration.[4] The insertion, like several other such exotic bits that turn up in Edwards' sermons, has been scavenged from some travel book or sailor's yarn, but Edwards does not settle, here or elsewhere, for a mere vivid picture or entertaining anecdote as sauce for his theological fare. Rather, it is the most poignant and concise of exempla, and within a few lines the sinner is revealed in all his weakness, blindness, and self-deception, as personified Evil is presented in all its deadly viciousness, grossness, and—in the long view—self-destructiveness. Here is a single compound image comparable to those that Edwards began collecting in his notebook, "Shadows of Divine Things." Before leaving this scene, due acknowledgement should be given to the humor tincturing the whole passage, though most obvious in the last line. It is the humor of Dante in the "Inferno" and of Milton when he describes the decline of Satan

4. Most revisions of this sort are not easily quoted because they consist of a new strand of thought (or image) that is applied to the sermon in small bits and pieces; a word here, a phrase there. In most instances, it is impossible to illustrate such revisions without reproducing a large part of the sermon.

One instance of such revision may be readily observed by the reader if he will turn to *Sinners in the Hands of an Angry God*. There, under the second and fourth Considerations under the Doctrine, he will find two references to the "sword of divine Justice," each concluding the head in which it appears. Now, in all essentials, the language of these two heads is unchanged between the manuscript and the printed sermons; that is, except for the image of the sword. There is no hint of a sword in the manuscript. Obviously, these two insertions constitute a "serial revision" undertaken to enhance the development of the Doctrine in the printed version. Such additions, often much more extensive and elaborate, are not infrequently made to sermon manuscripts as a part of the revision for repreaching.

in *Paradise Lost,* a humor of the "divine eye" which may elude soft-hearted modern readers, though they are well acquainted with its worldly relative, "gallows" or "black" humor. Such humor flickers through many of Edwards' sermons.[5]

Thus, Edwards frequently improved his sermons with the greatest deftness and artistic economy, altering or adding only a few passages here and there, yet effecting substantial changes in the sermon's rhetorical impact. In many instances, the material to be added could not be inserted so readily in blank spaces contiguous to the text and in these cases Edwards' first resort was "keying." This technique, discussed and illustrated in Chapter II (pp. 100–01), was a favorite device, employed by Edwards in all his writings, in both first-draft revisions and in revisions made long after the original draft. In preparing an old sermon for repreaching, he often concluded that paper, ink, and time could be significantly conserved through the use of keyed additions (the additions being written either in blanks anywhere in the original booklet or on a leaf or two affixed to the end of the sermon booklet), even after the advent of the flexible duodecimo gatherings.

Major revisions through such insertion of new material are typified by that carried out in the preparation of *God Glorified* for the notable repreaching in Boston. In this instance, as in many similar cases, the new material is substituted for old in some passages, thus combining the techniques of incremental and synoptic revision. Three passages, filling three and one-half leaves, are added to the back of the sermon. Although they are not actually keyed to the points of insertion in the original draft, the brackets marking the deletion of the original material to make room for the additions (see below) mark the points of insertion adequately, since only three large units are involved in this operation. The substitutions occur in two places in the Doctrine and one in the Application. The first of the passages of the Northampton version involved in the revision is as follows:

> III. And lastly, we have all in him. We have not only all our good of him and through him, but our own good consists in him: he is that good.
>
> [God is the highest good and the only true good of the creature,

---

5. No less an authority on preaching than William Perkins gives full sanction to this form of irony. In *The Arte of Prophecying* (*The Workes* [London, 1617] 2, 643–73), he maintains that "An Ironie signifieth a just reprehension of sinne" (p. 659).

an all-sufficient good, infinite river of good. God himself is that good which we are brought to the possession and enjoyment of by the purchase and redemption of Jesus Christ. This is that good which God bestows on the redeemed: he bestows himself upon [them]; himself is the portion of their souls. Believers have all their spiritual good in this world by God's communicating himself to them. 'Tis by their dwelling in God, and God in them, and he will be that portion in which they will be eternally blessed in another world.

Believers have all their good by the communication and indwelling of the Holy Ghost. All spiritual good consists in the communion of the Holy Ghost. 'Tis thus that believers come to have holiness and that they come to have true joy and happiness, both in this and in the other world.]

The form of what Christ purchased for us is that well of water, as spoken of [in] John 4:10, and those rivers of living water; John 7:38, He that believeth on me, out of his belly shall flow rivers of living waters. But this spoke he of the Spirit which they that believe on him should receive.

This is also that river of living water that proceeds from the throne of God and the Lamb; Rev. 22:1, This is the river of God's pleasures.

Christ laid down his life that we might obtain this; Gal. 3:13–14, He was made a curse for us that we might receive the promise of the Spirit through faith. The Holy Ghost is the sum of all the spiritual blessings which God hath promised. Therefore, 'tis called the Spirit of Promise, Eph. 1:13. This is the great promise of the Father; Luke 4:49, and behold I send the promise of the Father upon you. This promised thing Christ received; it was given into his hand as soon as he had finished the work of our redemption, to bestow on all that he had redeemed: Acts 2:33, Therefore, being by the right hand of God exalted, and having received of the Father the promise of the Holy Ghost, [he] hath shed {forth this, which ye now see and hear}.

'Tis by partaking of the Holy Ghost that believers [have] communion with Christ. God hath given the Spirit not by measure unto him, and they do receive of his fullness and grace, grace.

This is the inheritance of the saints, and therefore that life of the Holy Ghost which believers have in this world is called once and again the earnest of the inheritance and purchased possession, Eph. 1:14, II Cor. 1:22 and 5:5. 'Tis a part of that, an earnest of that which shall be given in great fullness hereafter as their purchased possession.

The Holy Spirit and good things are spoken of in Scripture as the same: as if the Spirit of God comprised all good things. Math. 7:11, How much more shall your heavenly Father give good things to them that ask him. In Luke, it is Luke 11:13, How much more shall your heavenly Father give the Holy Spirit to them that {ask him}?

Thus, 'tis God that has given us the Redeemer and of him the purchase is made, so 'tis God that is the redeemer and the price, and 'tis God that is the good purchased. 'Tis so that all that we have is of God and through him and in him: Rom. 11:36, For of him and through him and to him, or in him, are all things, to whom be glory forever and ever. The same in the Greek, that is here rendered "to him," is rendered "in him" (I Cor. 8:6).

We have all of God the Father through the Son and in the Holy Ghost, so that God is the Alpha and the Omega in this affair of redemption.

This is the original third reason under the Doctrine [Proposition I]. Comparison of this head with the corresponding head in the printed version (*Works*, Worcester rev. ed., *4*, 174–75) shows that the first two paragraphs after the introduction have been deleted by brackets (the only brackets by Edwards in this passage) in order to permit the insertion of the material differentiating the "objective" from the "inherent" good. Having added this theological subtlety, the first of the three passages added at the end of the sermon booklet, Edwards returns to the original material for the remainder of the head.[6]

The second addition, the entire Proposition II, "God's glory is ad-

---

6. The rearrangement of this material on p. 175 of the printed text indicates that there must have been another draft of the sermon between the extant manuscript and the printer's copy. Because certain emendations, made after the Boston additions in a third ink, alter the manuscript in the direction of the printed text, it seems that the Boston text was in some respects closer to the above text than to that printed.

vanced in redemption by this means, viz. by there appearing in it so great and universal a dependence of the redeemed on God" (*Works,* Worcester rev. ed., *4,* 176–77), has no antecedent in the original Northampton draft. The only related alteration of any consequence in the first draft is the division of the original Doctrine into two Propositions in order to provide the customary formal anticipation of the added major head.

The third and last addition is inserted in the Application in place of the last half of the original Inference I (*Works,* Worcester rev. ed., *4,* 177–78). The addition is numbered "Inference 2," and the original second and third Inferences are renumbered "3" and "4," respectively. The material deleted from Inference I is as follows:

> God's having ordered it thus, that the creature should in all respects have so great a dependence upon him in the affair of redemption, tends to the glory of God, as we are thereby more directly led thereby to the acknowledgement of God's all-sufficiency and have the greater reason to behold and contemplate him as the infinite and only good. He is so much the more directly set in our view as such; which way soever we turn our eyes, we have so much the greater occasion given us to have respect to him and to his. There is reason that we should love him of whom we have all that is: the author of all our good. And again, we have reason to have respect to that which is the medium of all our good—through which we receive it—and we have surely reason to love that which is all our good.
>
> God should have our whole souls; our hearts should not be divided. If we had one good only from God, and through another that was not God, and in another distinct from [him], our hearts would be divided between the good itself and him from whom we received it. But now there is no occasion for their being divided, seeing all these are God. God is our all in all. God also is exalted according to ancient prophecies, Is. 2:17.

Thus, if the original sermon, incorporating the material and structure presented above, is compared with the revised version delivered in Boston, represented by the printed text, a famous sermon illustrates what Edwards commonly did when he revised an old sermon by means of the insertion of new materials through keyed passages. The revised sermon is essentially the same as the original, but the three major additions emphasize a particular aspect of the sermon's thesis—the exact degree of man's dependence on God—that is much less emphasized in the original version. Thus, the first addition introduces the categories "objective" and "inherent" into the exposition of God's gifts to Man, making the "all" in "all our good" specifically universal and unqualified. The second and largest addition focuses the auditory's attention on the notion of the work of redemption as the mere glorification of God, where the redeemed are no more than adjuncts to the process of divine self-fulfillment. Again, nothing new is added to the original idea, but points that are only suggested in the first draft are now, because of the addition of Proposition II, made explicit and emphatic. The third addition, significantly placed in that division of the sermon devoted to practice, whether in action or thought, immediately calls attention to "those doctrines and schemes of divinity that are in any respect opposite to such an absolute and universal dependence on God."

Taken together, the additions constitute a significant revision of the Northampton draft of *God Glorified,* yet the revision is properly described as "stylistic" rather than "substantive." Perhaps the best description of it would be "an occasional revision," for here, as in most other cases, Edwards is intent upon fitting his sermon to the character of the audience and the nature of the occasion. Certainly the fine distinctions of the first addition are most appropriate to the learned Boston audience,[7] and the arguments of the second and third additions are progressively obvious and explicit challenges to the Arminian or "liberal" tendencies then current among the Boston clergy. It might also be noted that those passages deleted to make room for the additions are generally pastoral in tone, the advice of a minister to his flock. The revised sermon, as a whole, is more erudite and speculative, and thus more suited to a public lecture before other ministers.

Through a variety of maneuvers Edwards could, then, revise an old sermon for repreaching with a minimum of ink, paper, and time—and a maximum of effect, all things considered. It was possible to repreach the same sermon in formal disguise, or alter it to fit a new occasion. Sometimes, indeed, Edwards simply tried to make an old sermon more effective from a literary point of view. Less frequently, though in a significant number of instances, Edwards revised

---

7. The atmosphere and circumstances attending the delivery of this sermon at the Boston Public Lecture in July 1731 are discussed at length in the first chapter of Miller's *Jonathan Edwards.*

a sermon until it became, in reality, a different sermon. Such sermons are "recast."

In many instances, the classification of a sermon as either "recast" or "heavily revised" is a matter of arbitrary judgment, since the categories are contiguous. However, it is certain that in more than a few instances Edwards so reworked a sermon that the end product is essentially different from the original sermon, though the text and doctrine remain the same. In many cases, one cannot tell just what the original sermon manuscript was like because many of its leaves have been discarded. A few sermons, however, exist in two forms, and by collating them the process of "recasting" can be understood.

One of the most interesting examples of this technique is Cant. 1:3. The sermon exists in two forms and in two separate booklets, the first written in 1728 and the second in 1733. The sermon was first delivered in Northampton and the second version was prepared, according to a note at the head of the booklet, for delivery in Boston.[8] Comparison of the different versions of the same material in these two sermons yields significant insights into Edwards' literary sensibility. In the first version he is preparing a message for his own congregation; in the second version he is preparing the same message for a more sophisticated auditory in Boston, where he would speak as a peer lecturer rather than a pastor. As usual, Edwards fits the sermon to the audience and the occasion with the greatest care. For instance, though the text is the same in both versions, the Opening of the Text is, in each case, fitted to the occasion. The Northampton version is as follows:

> Cant. 1:3. Thy name is as ointment poured forth.
>
> It was a custom among the Jews to anoint themselves with oil, whereby they made their faces shine, which used to be esteemed a considerable adornment. We read [in] Ps. 104:15 that the use of oil was to make the face to shine. There was also another end of it: they were want to perfume their oil and make it very odoriferous, and anoint themselves with it so that wherever they went

---

8. The Boston version suggests a whole story just in its physical details. It is, first of all, an unusually neat sermon. Secondly, it was written in an octavo booklet (unlike the first version) several years after JE stopped using that form of sermon booklet. The larger booklet, plus the extraordinary neatness of the hand, make the Boston version practically a printer's "fair copy" as it stands. Did JE, having made a conquest of the Boston auditory just two years previously, go to Boston "primed for the press"? If he did, he was disappointed.

they might be encompassed with a fragrancy. They used a great deal of art in perfuming their ointments. But of all ointments that were amongst them, the holy anointing oil was the sweetest and had the most excellent fragrancy. This was compounded by God's art, and not man's. 'Tis to this oil that the grace of charity is compared in the 133 Psalm; with this oil there was none to be anointed but sacred officers that were eminent types of Jesus Christ. We read of the composition of it [in] Ex. 30:23–25: Take unto thee principal spices, of pure myrrh five hundred shekels, of sweet cinnamon half so much, even two hundred and fifty shekels, of sweet calamus two hundred and fifty shekels, of cassia five hundred shekels, after the shekel of the sanctuary, and of oil olive an hin; and thou shalt make it an oil of holy ointment, an ointment compound after the art of the apothecary. It shall be an holy anointing oil.

This holy anointing oil signified the Holy Ghost. The priests were anointed with this oil to signify Christ's being anointed with the Holy Ghost, and the spices and fragrancy of the ointment signified the graces of the spirit of God. Therefore, when it is said in this verse, "because of the savor of thy good ointments thy name is as ointment poured forth," it intends "because of thy graces and excellencies." Spiritual grace and excellency is often compared in this song to the same spices that the holy anointing oil was compounded [of], especially in the thirteenth and fourteenth verses of the fourth chapter.

'Tis because of those, that is, because of his excellency, that his name is as ointment poured forth. That is, he was so excellent a person that the very mentioning of his name, or the knowledge of his attributes, beholding the beauties he maketh of himself, filled the heart with delight as the pouring out of a sweet ointment. Especially the holy anointing oil caused a sweet fragrancy, [and] the ointment, when pouring out, was under the best advantages to send forth its savor.

In comparison with this detailed exegesis, the Boston version is fluent, elegant, and discursive:

Sol. Song 1:3 Thy name is as ointment poured forth.

The name or title that is given to this song, viz. the Song of Songs, confirms it to be more than a mere human song, and that these things that are the subject of it are above [the] terrene or temporal. We read [in] I Kings 4:32 that Solomon's songs were a thousand and five, but this one song of his which is inserted in the canon of the Scripture is distinguished from all the rest by the name of the Song of Songs, or the most excellent of his songs, or more than all his other songs: as the subject of it is transcendently of a more sublime and excellent nature than the rest, treating of the divine love, union, and communion of the most glorious lovers, Christ and his spiritual spouse, of which a marriage union and conjugal love (which, perhaps, many of the rest of his songs treated of) is but a shadow.

The song begins with the spouse's expressing her sense of the excellency of Christ, her longing desires after him and delight in him. His excellency and her compliance in him is beautifully and livelily set forth in that expression that I have chosen now to insist on: Thy name is as ointment poured forth. Such was her sense of his loveliness, and so great was her delight in him, that she loved his very name. It was precious to her; the very mentioning of it was to her like the pouring forth of some fragrant ointment.

Perfumed ointment was a thing very much used among the Israelites of old, both to common and sacred purposes. It was made use of by divine direction as a suitable type of the graces of the holy spirit. There was an holy anointing oil, appointed of God for this purpose, that was of an extraordinary fragrancy, being compounded by divine art, that any were forbidden to imitate upon pain of being cut off from among his people.

Possibly, special respect may be had to this holy ointment in the text. The excellencies of Jesus Christ are often in that song compared to the very same spices with which that holy oil was perfumed, and the name of Christ may most fitly [be] compared to this most precious and holy ointment that was appointed on purpose to represent that grace that he is full of and is the fountain of.

The name of Christ is compared to ointment poured forth because then it is under the greatest advantage to send forth its odors. The name of Christ filled the soul of the spouse with delight as the holy anointing oil, when poured forth, filled the sanctuary with its fragrancy.

The broader frame of reference, encompassing the entire song rather than a single image from it; the more discursive speculation on the relationship between Christ and the redeemed, and the more sustained exposition—after the manner of an essayist as much as that of an expositor—all contribute to make the Boston version a more effective literary performance. The thesis is essentially the same, and the thematic essentials of the Northampton sermon have been worked into the mold of the second sermon, but the materials obviously have been recast and shaped to new ends. As the sermons develop to their respective conclusions, the differences between them increase until the true differentiation of ends becomes evident in the subheads of the two Applications. Whereas the Northampton version is one long, passionate Exhortation in the Application, the Boston version's Use is more like an "aid to reflection": "The use that I would make of what has been said is to move and persuade to an acceptance of the gracious offer that Christ makes of himself to us." In Northampton, Edwards preached as an evangelical pastor, herding his flock to heaven; in Boston, he preached as a collegial instructor presenting his understanding of a portion of the Word for the consideration of fellow-inquirers. A subtle alteration in the Doctrine of the Boston version points up the difference.

> Northampton version: "That Christ Jesus is a person transcendently excellent and *desirable*."
>
> Boston version: "That Jesus Christ is a person transcendently excellent and *lovely*." [Ed. italics.]

The very inflexibility of the (then) old-fashioned octavo quire which was used for the Boston version has proven a boon, for it caused exposure of the very process of recasting. Normally, after his shift to duodecimo signatures, Edwards would not have allowed an entire deleted head to remain in the sermon booklet; it was simple to pull out a four-leaf signature or cut away a two-leaf unit. However, the quire, with its infolded leaves, commits the writer to what he has written, unless he wishes to take extraordinary pains. Thus, when Edwards was recasting the fourth Proposition under the Doctrine and suddenly decided that the recast version was not working out, he did not discard the unsatisfactory version. He simply drew a long, vertical line-of-deletion through it and wrote another version immediately after it. Consequently, in the two versions of the sermon, there are three versions of this fourth Proposition. Since Edwards was attempting to make essentially the same point in all three versions, a collation of the three gives considerable insight into the kinds of changes Edwards would consider when making substantial stylistic revisions.

First, there is the Northampton draft:

4. These divine excellencies are set forth to our view to very great advantage in the person of Jesus Christ; the constitution of his person is such that the divine excellency appears in him with very great advantage. The great and terrible God is infinitely exalted above us, and his majesty did, as it were, forbid that we approach to himself and intimate acquaintance with him. But Jesus, god-man, is near to [us]; he is one of us, so that we may come to him boldly and behold all those glorious excellencies united to our own nature. We behold the divine glory under great advantage in Christ because in him it is with us, is come to dwell amongst us. The divine beauty is given to us in Christ so that we may see and enjoy, be familiarly conversant with it. That, that was at a great distance, is now come near to us, and as we hereby can behold it under greater advantage, so it should appear more lovely and amiable to us.

'Tis an endearing consideration that all this divine excellency is in our nature, is united to humanity. We should love him now, not only because he is thus glorious and excellent in himself, but because he is one of our brethren, as he calls his disciples his brethren. It likewise adds honor and luster to the human excellencies of Christ that they are in a divine person. What can be a greater honor to man, himself?

And then the first, rejected, Boston draft:

4. The states and conditions that Christ has been in do set forth his glory in the stronger light. If we consider the low condition that he was in in this world, if we consider him as born of an obscure virgin or brought forth in a stable and nursed in the arms of his humble mother, and then consider this child as a person that is the great and mighty God, the King of Glory, by whom and for whom all things are made, his divine glory will the more powerfully strike our minds. His outward meanness, though it was a veil to his glory and seemed to hide and obscure it, yet in the issue does but illustrate it: the two extremes of his infinite

majesty and excellency, and such external meanness, tends the more intensely to fix the mind on each other.

If we had such a view of him as the shepherds had who first heard the multitude of the heavenly hosts honoring the occasion of his birth with their heavenly songs and telling 'em that this day was born unto them a savior, even Christ the Lord, and then come and find him an infant lying in a manger, should we not be the more affected and surprised by the consideration of the greatness and dignity of his person?

Having deleted this attempt (probably before it was fully developed), Edwards began to write another version immediately below it.

4. The character that Christ sustains, and his relation to us recommend his excellencies to our esteem and love. He is our redeemer and savior. The very end of his being as god-man, or in such a constitution of his person, is that he might be our redeemer. The consideration of this tends to endear the excellencies both of his divine and human nature to us. ⌒ He is lovely as an infinitely wise, holy, and gracious person, but he is more lovely to us considered as an infinitely wise, holy and gracious redeemer. ⌒ When we consider these glorious and amiable perfections as in one who is ours and we his, it may surely well render them the more dear to us. ⌒ There is no person in the world that stands in so endearing a relation to Christians as Christ; he is our friend and our nearest friend, Job 15:15. I call you not servants but I have called you friends. He is our brother, Heb. 2:11. He is not ashamed to call them brethren. He is our father, Heb. 2:13. But that relation which our spiritual union with Christ is most frequently compared [to] is of an husband or spouse. ⌒ There is no relation that implies nearness and dearness but what is made use of in Scripture to represent our relation to Christ, and the nearest earthly relations are but shadows of it and fall vastly short of fully representing the intimacy and excellency of it. ⌒ We may well have the more complacence in his glory and beauty on this account.

Here are three "castings" of the notion that Christ is peculiarly attractive because of his unique character and his special relationship with Man. The second version of Proposition 4 seems to have been something of an adventure in sentiment, but Edwards was obviously ill at ease with the "obscure virgin" and her "externally mean" infant; here, as elsewhere, he was virtually incapable of writing in a "sentimental" vein, and he apparently sensed that it was another Christ, the Redeemer, that was the true inspiration of his sermon.

In the third version, Edwards returns to the form of the Northampton version, but recasts it in a more fully elaborated passage in which there is less emphasis upon approaching Christ and more on contemplating Him, as would be consonant with the shift from "desirable" to "lovely" in the statement of the doctrine. The first and third versions are quite obviously closely related, but Edwards would insist upon those subtle changes dictated by the new occasion and the markedly different audience. Though his syntax may seem rough or careless, his rhetorical strategy is always carefully calculated and subtly modulated.

These three versions of one head give a glimpse of that process of recasting sermons that seems to have occupied Edwards on many occasions. The evidence shows him to have been interested in innovation and imaginative in the reuse of his materials, but cautious rather than exuberant as a craftsman even when preparing a showpiece for Boston. The example of the two Cant. 1:3 sermons is also indicative of the important function of his sermon collection as a source of sermonic materials for recasting into new sermons. That such recasting of sermons, in part or in whole, was a common practice for Edwards, particularly after his first few years at Northampton, is seemingly beyond doubt, though the fact that he did not mark the sources of such borrowings makes a precise assessment of the activity difficult. There are many instances of two or more sermons on one text, but collation of the sermons frequently fails to reveal any internal similarities, at least such as would suggest recasting or significant borrowing of materials. On the other hand, the browser among Edwards' sermon manuscripts occasionally encounters passages that have a very familiar sound, though he has read no sermon with the same text or a very similar doctrine previously.

The third and last technique employed by Edwards in the preparation of sermons for repreaching I have designated "cannibalism." The term may be sensational, but it does accurately describe Edwards' practice of fleshing out sermons with the physical components of other sermons, though in the case of sermon booklets the process could sometimes be reversed after preaching needs were met.

Perhaps the simplest variety of cannibalism is that in which parts of sermons were only borrowed, perhaps without any tampering with the sermon booklets. This type of cannibalism would be unknown today were it not for Edwards' shorthand notes in the sermon manuscripts, but these notes tell the story quite plainly:

[Num. 14:22–23] Doctrinal part the second time.
[Mark 9:44] Preached the Application a second time.

These and many similar instances indicate that it was occasionally Edwards' practice to carry two sermons into the pulpit so that he might preach the Doctrine from one and the Application from the other. The resulting sermon would, of course, be a fleeting phenomenon, vanishing as soon as the two original sermons were returned to their places in the sermon file. Moreover, in most instances, the note on the sermon does not give the identity of the accompanying sermon. A slight variation in this practice is indicated by tell-tale stitching holes in such sermons. Apparently, Edwards sometimes took the trouble to detach the portions to be preached, stitched them into a booklet for the preaching, and then reversed the process when the performance was over. At least once, it seems, he did not reverse the process. A sermon on Rom. 5:7–8 has a full Text and Doctrine but no Application; the Application does exist, however, and is now stitched to the end of a sermon on II Cor. 9:15.

Slightly more complex than this procedure is a technique illustrated in the manuscript of a sermon on Neh. 2:20—or rather sermon*s* on Neh. 2:20. Originally, the manuscript booklet contained two sermons on the same text designed to be preached in series. The first sermon's Doctrine asserts, "It becomes those that are the servants of God earnestly to apply themselves to the building of the city of God," while the second states, "Those that are not God's true servants and don't join in building up his church and kingdom have no portion, nor right, nor memorial in God's Jerusalem." Each of the sermons is complete, with full Text, Doctrine, and Application, and the two sermons do not even share the opening Scripture quotations, since Edwards employs the first part of the verse for the first sermon and the latter part for the second sermon. Still, the two sermons are obviously a pair and they have been stitched into one booklet.

A third sermon is hidden in the booklet, however, and it emerges when, following the directions of a shorthand note, one reads just those parts of both sermons marked by vertical lines in the margins.

When the marked passages are brought together, they comprise about six pages from the Doctrine of the first sermon and about seven pages from the Application of the second, though they do not include all passages in either division. Obviously, such selective blending of parts would take more effort in the study than the type of cannibalism described in the first example, but then it enabled Edwards to weld parts from two sermons having virtually opposite (or obverse) theses into a single, rather effective sermon. The end product of all these maneuvers is a fairly small sermon booklet containing either a choice of three sermons for delivery in a single pulpit session, or a pair of sermons for delivery in the morning-afternoon Sabbath service.

So far, only "temporary" cannibalism (which does not necessarily prevent reuse of the original sermon) has been considered. There is another, more literal variety of cannibalism, however, in which the original sermon's identity is virtually destroyed as it is incorporated in a new sermon. One of the most vivid examples of this technique is a sermon on Matt. 21:5, written in 1727 when Edwards was shifting from octavo to duodecimo booklets. The discrepancy in size between the original sermon booklet and the additions makes the process of cannibalizing quite obvious in this case, though it is difficult to trace in other instances.

Edwards apparently began writing a sermon on Matt. 21:5 in duodecimo booklet leaves. He wrote the Text and Doctrine sections but, when he came to the Application, turned to the sermon file for a "ready-made."[9] He took an earlier (1722–23) sermon, cut off those pages that contained the Text and Doctrine, and then placed this remnant of the octavo quire after the new Text and Doctrine. Finally, he wrote a new concluding section for the Application on a duodecimo leaf, placed the leaves in order and stitched the whole together. Thus, the Matt. 21:5 sermon booklet is a sandwich: duodecimo-octavo-duodecimo, or new-old-new. A whole new sermon that reads quite fluently over all its joints was created, but the process occasioned the death of an old sermon in order to make the new one.

Such true cannibalism is difficult to detect, particularly if all the sermons involved were written at about the same time, and especially if they were written while Edwards was using the duodecimo gatherings. In such cases, well-integrated bits of cannibalized sermons

---

9. He may, of course, have had the Application in mind first and written the new parts to accompany the old part.

could hardly be differentiated from the new sections, particularly if the leftovers were thrown away. Edwards did not, incidentally, always throw away the remnants of cannibalized sermons, probably because he hoped to find a use for them in other sermons. As a result, there are now a few forlorn Applications, Doctrines, and assorted subheads stored with the sermons in the sermon file. At least some of the apparent gaps in Edwards' sermon writing are probably the result of his having cannibalized the sermons written at those times.

One peculiar variant of cannibalism is extant in only one or two instances, but deserves attention because of the light it sheds upon Edwards' capacities as an ingenious manipulator of sermonic materials. This technique involves a combination of cannibalism and recasting, the end product of which is a rather strange "siamese sermon."

Rev. 21:18, an example of the type, can be described as a two-booklet sermon of the early octavo quires with the normal development of a single sermon through two booklets, plus inserted leaves from a second sermon, two in the first booklet (containing the Text and statement of doctrine) and one in the Application in the second booklet (containing the remainder of the Doctrine and the Application). It seems likely that Edwards took two sermons, cut up one, and inserted the necessary parts in the body of the other. The result is a single sermon that could be preached from one of two beginnings. He might have started with the "main" sermon and preached a sermon on Rev. 21:18 with the doctrine, "There is nothing upon earth that will suffice to represent to us the glories of heaven." Or, he might have started with the grafted-on "head and shoulders" of the second sermon and preached from I John 3:2, "That the Godly are designed for unknown and inconceivable happiness." In either case, he would have delivered most of the Rev. 21:18 Confirmation and Application, though when he preached from Rev. 21:18 he probably omitted most or all of the exposition of the inserted I John excerpts.

What would have been the value of such a strategy? It would have enabled Edwards to carry two sermons in the booklets normally accorded to one. Moreover, the fact that the two sermons share many passages would have made it fairly easy to preach the sermons alternately, with a minimum of preparation before entering the pulpit on any particular occasion. And when would such considerations have been of significance to Edwards? When he was on the road, preaching in several towns in comparatively quick succession, with fatiguing days on horseback in between the preaching sessions. Indeed, the back of the first booklet bears confirmation in a mixture of shorthand and longhand: "Preached at Scantick, at New Haven, at Fairfield, [at] New York, at Bolton and Glastonbury." All the notes seem to have been made at the same time, at least within a few weeks.

With such practical ingenuity, the Yankee preacher made many a sermon go the last mile. Revision, recasting, cannibalism, and all the specific techniques comprised within these broader categories, constitute the essential technical means by which Edwards strove to make his collected sermons more than just a vast repository of recorded thought. He intended, it seems, to make the collection a carefully inventoried store of sermons and sermonic materials—a warehouse of parts and wholes to be visited whenever the demands of the pulpit strained his creative energies or, in later years, threatened other projects dear to his heart. But even more than a storehouse, the sermon collection seems to have become a generator of sermons, old sermons producing, or at least facilitating the production of, new sermons. In the final analysis, it was undoubtedly through the study and reworking of his own sermons that Edwards developed his style and the character of his public utterance.

4. From Sermon to Treatise

The sermons in Edwards' file were intended for yet another public function, even after they had been used the last time in the pulpit. The manuscript evidence indicates that it was to the sermons that Edwards intended to go when, and if, he succeeded in articulating the "Rational Account of Christianity" or, what seems to have been more on his mind in later years, the "History of the Work of Redemption."[1]

The intimate relation between sermon and treatise first becomes apparent in 1738 with Edwards' publication of *Discourses on Various Important Subjects,* for in addition to more conventional sermons the volume contains the lengthy and erudite discourse, *Justification by Faith Alone.* Constituting nearly half the volume, the printed discourse is

1. The sermon series (or treatise disguised as a sermon series) ultimately published as the *History of the Work of Redemption* was not the history JE had in mind when he wrote to the college trustees. More probably, it was intended to be a kind of outline for the fully developed history, the latter undoubtedly being conceived as a massive, multi-volumed work. (See Chapter IV, pp. 255–58.)

several preaching units in length. It begins with the conventional textual exegesis and formal statement of doctrine, but the formal Application is virtually invisible as the brief fifth major head under the Doctrine. Here the lecture format has been greatly expanded for the printed version and the normally brief Application has been formally suppressed. The result is what could be called Edwards' earliest published treatise.[2]

A similar operation may be observed in 1741 with the publication of *The Distinguishing Marks of a Work of the Spirit of God.* This work, first preached as a sermon in New Haven, September 10, 1741, was printed that year "with great Enlargements" by the author. Edwards not only amplified the work, but wrote additions that must have tripled the length of the original, perhaps surprising those "Ministers and other Gentlemen" who had earnestly desired that Edwards print the sermon.[3] The result is a brief treatise having many of the formal characteristics of the sermon: a Text (including a proper opening or exegesis), the numerous numbered heads and subheads of the Doctrine, and finally, a clearly labeled Application. The most notable formal difference between *The Distinguishing Marks* and a printed sermon is that there is no clearly labeled or italicized doctrinal statement, though the statement, "My design therefore at this time is to show what are the true, certain, and distinguishing evidences of a work of the Spirit of God, by which we may safely proceed in judging of any operation we find in ourselves, or see in others," provides the same kind of thematic focus. As in the case of *Justification by Faith Alone,* it could be argued that the sheer length of the single literary unit would automatically disqualify it as a sermon and place it in the treatise category. In any case, the work seems suspended in a formal limbo, somewhere between a sermon and a treatise.

Some Thoughts Concerning the Present Revival of Religion (1742) is much more of a treatise in form, although it, too, bears some of the

2. Examination of the sermon manuscript reveals only two formal preaching units but enough material for four or five. However, closer examination shows much of the material to be keyed additions to the basic sermon. In the Preface to the *Discourses* JE states that the *Justification* discourse was delivered "at two public lectures" (p. ii) but that it "is printed much larger than it was preached" (p. v.), confirming the manuscript evidence.

3. The manuscript of the sermon preached in New Haven is no longer extant, but the time limitations imposed by the occasion of the delivery would have prevented the sermon's being much longer than *A Divine and Supernatural Light* or *Sinners in the Hands of an Angry God.*

formal features of the sermon. It is, for instance, prefaced by a scriptural text, and throughout the body of the treatise there is the elaborate division of the argument into many subheads within, and in some respects independently of, the five main divisions. Even the little outlines of heads-to-come, originally part of the sermonic apparatus and apparently first intended as an aid to congregational notetakers, appear regularly in the body of the treatise, though they are superfluous in a printed work. Such signs point to the form and decorum of the Edwardsean sermon.

Turning to the major treatises, one first encounters *A Treatise Concerning Religious Affections* (1746), a work reputed to have been preached as a sermon series in its first version, and one which presents familiar signs of the sermonic form, particularly in Part I where there is even a formal "Doctrine." The evidence of Edwards' working manuscripts suggests that any or all of his treatises may have been built up, more or less, from sermons in the file. Of course it is always difficult to trace borrowings from the sermons in the treatises because, as with the purely verbal cannibalism (or self-plagiarism) in the sermons, Edwards in most cases did not bother to mark borrowings. He simply copied out the needed material and returned the source-sermon to the file. There are, however, sufficient tracks in the extant workbooks to suggest the general practice.

Sometimes, because of a lack of time or paper, Edwards did not bother to copy out relevant materials from his sermons but simply left a note in the apposite place upon the workbook page, presumably with the intent of at least consulting the sermon before writing the treatise. Thus, there are four explicit references to sermons in "Christ's Example" (2 leaves), four in "Miscellaneous Observations Concerning Faith" (51 pages), five in "Signs of Godliness" (20 pages), and two in "Of Free Will" (4 leaves). In addition to such special citations, other sermons would of course be drawn upon as part of the reference cycles which link the main notebooks.

Thus, when Edwards made his "Subjects of Enquiry" and began drawing together both his accumulated learning and theories of rhetoric for the great, climactic effort of the "History of the Work of Redemption," it was inevitable that he would attempt to utilize the sermon file's full potential. There was one problem, however; the sermons had no table as did most of the major notebooks and there was probably little hope of making one for such a mass of material in a reasonable time. Only some rough screening device would be plausible in ideal circumstances, let alone in those that engulfed Edwards during the last decade of his life.

At his death, the "History of the Work of Redemption" was apparently only tentatively roughed out. Only three small notebooks (one of them consisting of the margins of part of a printed book) were especially devoted to the plan and format of the work, and to the marshalling of historical data. In these notebooks there are references to three particular sermons, and a check of these sermons reveals that two of the three are marked with a peculiar sign: נ. This sign is not rare in the sermon manuscripts; indeed, more than two hundred sermons are marked with it, always in the upper left-hand corner of the first page (or as near as other writings on the manuscript permit). It is usually isolated by a line, thus, נ); or when it must be placed more in the middle of a page, by two lines, (נ). The sign seems to have been added to most of the sermons in an ink other than that in which they are written, and the little isolating line suggests that the sign is to be differentiated from those shorthand notations that relate to preaching.[4]

The character of this sign and the frequency of its incidence suggest that it represents a large-scale screening effort, an attempt to cull from the sermon file a large group of sermons on various texts and with diverse doctrines. Certainly, there is little obvious similarity

4. There are other comparable signs that appear on numbers of sermons. Most common is ל, a sign of dubious meaning. It very frequently occurs in groupings: ל ל ל ל ל. There are instances of up to ten on one sermon. It can be found in combination with a mysterious "No. 10" or "No. 20." It is sometimes found near the נ sign, apparently in the same ink. However, in a good many instances, perhaps the majority, this sign is in an ink that seems to be different from any ink positively identified as JE's. Were it not for the few instances that do seem to be in his ink, I would attribute it to someone else. But the character of the notation, knowledge of JE's methods, and the instances wherein the ink does seem to be his: all conduce to the conclusion that the sign was originated by JE, though someone with knowledge of its meaning (undoubtedly JE, Jr., whose markings are common in the manuscripts) continued to use it after JE's death.

Though the meaning of the sign is obscure—it often resembles the shorthand for "L S D" or "L S T," or possibly "L T D T"—there is no doubt that it, with seemingly allied signs, represents other efforts to organize the sermons according to a particular criterion of reference. In the case of the ל sign, there does seem to be an evident pattern: the sermons having several of the signs in a row tend to be "hellfire" sermons, and the greater the number of signs, the more intense the heat of the sermon. Thus it seems that the ל may be a kind of "decibel rating" for imprecatory sermons. If it is, the signs were probably applied in an effort to segregate likely revival sermons from the general run. But whatever the precise meaning of these various cryptic signs, it seems clear that they represent an effort on the part of JE to organize the sermon canon for special uses.

between the sermons except for the marking sign, but this sign does appear to be made up of two letters from Edwards' standard shorthand alphabet: r(R) and ɔ(D). It seems most probable that the sign is a kind of shorthand abbreviation for the word, "ReDemption." Moreover, a knowledge of Edwards' habitual procedures in the study confirms the likelihood of such a screening practice.

Thus it is probable that Edwards' sermon archive was not only a part of his vast system of theological thought, a hoard of sermons and sermonic materials for pulpit use and a source of materials for the polemic treatises, but also one of the prime sources of materials for the great synthesis or great system—whatever its eventual title— that was to have been the capstone to a life of the most intense intellectual effort and sustained theological speculation.

5. The Question of Literary Development

It has been usual for modern students of Edwards' sermons to observe, sometimes rather petulantly, that there is no literary "development" in the sermons over the years. Most of these students have not, it seems, made this evaluation in the light of the manuscript sermons but only after having read, at most, the comparatively few sermons in print. Still, if they did read a significant portion of the manuscript canon, they might make the same judgment, and perhaps add that the sermons not only fail to develop, but actually disintegrate during the years after the Great Awakening. They would be right, of course. For whether consciously or not, they are judging Edwards by a post-Romantic notion of development, by a criterion which acknowledges development only when the author significantly modifies the form of his expression, presumably in order to accommodate, and thus attest to the presence of, the uncompromising demands of novel ideational elements or unique personal experiences.

But Edwards belonged to a culture which admired "What oft was thought, but ne'er so well expressed," or normative literature. The sermon in particular had strict formal limitations, being designed to convey (theoretically) unchanging dogmatic essentials through a verbal structure which was eminently public, conventional, and fixed, so that the listeners might never be lost through a lack of familiar signs. Edwards, moreover, had a reputation even among his contemporaries for being opposed to formal innovation. But within the generally fixed form of the sermon, and despite a strict consistency in doctrine, Edwards *did* experiment and innovate.

A writer who professed indifference to "modishness" and "politeness," Edwards has been mistaken occasionally for an American primitive who was oblivious to the subtleties of literary style and the traditions of genre. However, though his style was not contrived to become a focus of attention in itself, and though he adhered to a conception of the sermon form that had been under attack even during his grandfather Stoddard's prime, Edwards frequently manifests great sensitivity to the merest turn of phrase or to the penumbra of convention, and hence expectation, surrounding a recognized literary form or genre.[5] If one examines his practice carefully, evidence can be found that he consciously exploited the "listener-response factor" in his sermons, and even extended such efforts in print through various modifications of homiletical convention. Consideration of Edwards' response to literary tradition and popular convention in the sermon at the peak of his preaching career leads inevitably to *Sinners in the Hands of an Angry God,* his most famous sermon among contemporaries and the consensus certification of his "artistry" among modern critical readers.

Sinners is usually identified as the best of Edwards' "hellfire" sermons; however, comparison with other examples of that genre among Edwards' sermons reveals that *Sinners* is not even a proper "hellfire" sermon, let alone the best. Sermons such as *The Eternity of Hell Torments* and *The Future Punishment of the Wicked Unavoidable and Intolerable* serve to mark the distinction between a true hellfire sermon and the proto-eschatological formulation of *Sinners,* focused as it is upon the here and now. Perhaps Edwards himself supplied the proper category when, subsequent to the Enfield preaching, he gave it a titular identity as a "hands" sermon. It is, after all, neither the slipping foot image of the text nor the keen implication of the statement of doctrine's "mere pleasure" that so "fixes the mind." Moreover, in establishing the sermon's identity through this particular image, Edwards probably touched his contemporaries more deeply than if he had made the fires of God's wrath his keynote, for "hands" sermons appear to

---

5. JE's sensitivity and his audacity in wielding the editorial pen are dramatically illustrated in his revisions of David Brainerd's manuscript diary, where he virtually remade Brainerd to fit his own taste in theology and literary style. See *The Life of David Brainerd,* ed. Norman Pettit, in *Works,* 7, 79–84, 100–53.

have been part of a significant tradition, both more poignant and less routine than "hellfire" sermons.

The central image is explicated in a sermon preached by one of Edwards' most esteemed colleagues and published in Boston only days before Edwards joined his Grandfather Stoddard in Northampton:

> This agency and activity [of God] is plainly intimated of in my text, which speaks of the hands of the living God, and of falling into them. The hand is for working, and for striking if need be; for expedite and lively working, and for terrible striking. In both respects it intimates a life the most active imaginable.[6]

Thus Benjamin Colman presents the image of the hand as an emblem of the full range of God's activity among men: his Providence, his vengeance, his immanent power generally, and particularly his *immediacy*. Indeed, Colman specifies the metaphor of the hand as the way of defining God in life.

But Edwards' familiarity with the metaphor certainly antedated his possible reading of Colman's sermon. His father had employed it in preaching, though not by the evidence with particular emphasis.[7] However, as a student in Yale College Edwards seems to have read in the folio edition of the *Works* of Ezekiel Hopkins which had been given to the college a couple of years prior to his arrival.[8] Here could be found a level of rhetoric quite beyond that cultivated in East Windsor parish, as Hopkins evokes God's hands in a characteristic meditation:

> "Can thine heart endure, or can thine hands be strong," says God, "in the day that I shall deal with thee?" The very weakness of

6. Benjamin Colman, *It is a Fearful Thing to Fall into the Hands of the Living God. A Sermon Preached to Some Miserable Pirates, July 10, 1726, on the Lord's Day, before their Execution.* (Boston, 1726), p. 5.

7. Timothy Edwards utilizes some of the *Sinners* imagery in a similar context in an unpublished ms. sermon on Acts 16:29–30, now part of the collection of his manuscripts at Washington University Library, though the hands are more implied than explicit.

8. A copy of a folio edition of the *Works* of Bishop Ezekiel Hopkins was given to Yale College in 1714 by a Mr. Love. (The title page is now missing, but it appears to be that printed in London in 1701.) The book would thus have been in the Yale Library before JE's arrival in 1716. That he read the book at least by his graduate years is likely, and a hint that it may have made a favorable impression is given in his ms. "Catalogue" of books where he notes Hopkins' book, *Death Disarmed of its Sting* (London, 1712), on p. 2. This latter title is identified on its title page as a "supplement" to the *Works* and thus a book JE might have wished to read after being excited by the *Works*.

God is stronger than men; God can look a man to death. The
breath of God's nostrils can blast the soul, and burn it to a very
cinder: Oh! then tremble to think what wrath his heavy hand can
inflict upon thee; that hand that "spreads out the heavens, and
in the hollow of which he holds the great waters of the sea"; that
hand of God in which his great strength lies; oh! what wrath will
it inflict upon thee, when it falls upon thee in the full power of
his might?[9]

Here is a passage comparable in color and vivacity to anything Edwards achieved in the hortatory vein, yet it is merely the introduction
to an even more intense and arresting passage. Clearly, this is not
language that would have been lost upon one who instinctively appreciated the power of imagery to invest speculation with the reality
of experience. Hopkins, moreover, exploits the "hands" metaphor in
many contexts in the same volume, and one of his major sermons was
preached from the Heb. 10:30–31 text which is the biblical source
of the metaphor. Entitled "The Dreadfulness of God's Wrath, Explained," the sermon is devoted to interpreting the twin propositions
of the text that vengeance belongs to God, and that God is terrible
in the exercise of his wrath.[1] In order to focus this compound theme
of authority and capacity Hopkins uses the metaphor of direct involvement through the manual implementation of justice, deploying
in a series of passages the most poignant images of pain and anxiety.
In all cases, Hopkins insists, he wishes to provide "some *demonstrations*
of the dreadfulness of the wrath and vengeance of God . . ."[2] Such
vivid rhetoric is required, insists Hopkins, "because men are not persuaded that these dreadful terrors of the Lord . . . are anything but
an honest artifice. They look upon them as things only invented to
scare the world into good order, and to awe men into some compass
of civility and honesty . . ."[3] However, "If He only withdraw His power
by which He upholds all things in their beings, we should quickly fall
all abroad into nothing . . ."[4] Clearly Hopkins is insisting that imaginative rhetoric is not only a tool of expression but an agent of understanding where the realm of ultimate truth, or supra-reality, is concerned. Not to excite the imaginative powers deeply enough is to

9. "Of Serving God, with Reverence and Godly Fear," *Works*, p. 725.
1. *Works*, pp. 404–18.
2. "The Dreadfulness of God's Wrath," p. 417.
3. Ibid.
4. Ibid.

strand the flock upon the dead-level ideology of ordinary religion, far short of an ideal apprehension of the divine reality which can only be approached in human terms upon the wings of metaphor. Not to mount upon such wings is to lose all hope of appreciating anything of that incomprehensible reality which is nevertheless the literal foundation of mundane reality. The upholding hands (or in Edwards' favorite image, the sustaining thought) which comprehend all things should be *recognized* even if they cannot be grasped, for God is as close as the atoms which compose and sustain our being, and as remote.

In such language, then, the power, authority, and immediacy of God were communicated by those preachers who felt that hardened sinners needed to have their complacency penetrated by the armor-piercing device of sensational imagery. The hand image had been fully sanctioned by the Bible and was clearly associated with the power of God to act *in this life,* particularly in terrible, retributive acts. Such brutal language is suited to extreme situations, as addresses to condemned convicts, though Hopkins insists that "Those commonly prove the most stable and stayed Christians, that have been most harassed by legal terrors before they enjoy the sense of comfort; for the structure of grace in the heart is quite contrary to other buildings; it stands firmest when it is laid upon a shaking and trembling foundation. It is a seed that never thrives so well as where the heart is most broken up, and where the wrath of God hath made long and deep furrows in it."[5] Perhaps Hopkins believed that unawakened persons actually would be better informed if they were to feel as convicts awaiting execution.

Having been exposed to one of the master preachers of "hands" sermons at an impressionable age, and having some acquaintance with the convention in any case, Edwards seems to have experimented with the peculiar sermon format over the years so that he was prepared, in the spring of 1741 when his own congregation no longer responded adequately to his exhortations, to unleash the power of this traditional, but highly specialized variant of the awakening sermon. In order to appreciate the nature of its tradition, one should consider a few of the elements of *Sinners in the Hands of an Angry God* that have been most remarked in comparison with passages from other sermons in the tradition of "hands" sermons. Perhaps most

5. "Of Serving God," p. 727.

noted are Edwards' use of imagery involving physical suspension and pressure, the insistence upon temporal pressure from passing time, both through mere assertion and through metaphor, and finally the intensity resulting from repetition of various sorts.[6] The notion of the unawakened sinner's being upheld by God's hand implies both the sinking weight of the sinner and the lowering, virtually depressive presence of a disapproving Deity, tenuously counterbalanced by mere mercy. In sermons Edwards was familiar with, these conditions were conventionally treated as interrelated. Here again, one might look to the earlier inspiration, Ezekiel Hopkins:

> Believe it, as long as you continue in a sinful state you are wrapt about with ten thousand curses, the wrath of God is continually making its approaches unto you, and there is only a thin mud wall of flesh to fence it out, which is still mouldring and falling away, and whether it will be able to hold out one day longer you know not; you hang over the bottomless pit only by the weak thread of a frail life, which is ready to be snapt asunder every moment; and if some consuming sickness should fret this thread, or some for-unseen casualty should break it off suddenly; if death work a change upon you before grace works a change in you, of all God's creation you are the most miserable; better that you had been the most loathsome creature that crawls upon God's earth, yea, better that you had never been, than that you should forget and neglect this great work of renovation one moment too long; therefore use no delay; every moment that is not this present is too long a delay; while you are dreaming of repentance and converting some months, or possibly some years hence, God may snatch you away before the next sand is run in time's glass, and where are you then? "Now is the accepted time, now is the day of salvation"; whatever is not now may be too late, and e're that time comes that you have prefixed to your selves, God may set up your

6. These points were highlighted most effectively by Edwin H. Cady in "The Artistry of Jonathan Edwards," *The New England Quarterly*, 22 (March 1949), pp. 61–72, and by Willis J. Buckingham in "Stylistic Artistry in the Sermons of Jonathan Edwards," *Papers on Language and Literature*, 6 (Spring 1970), pp. 136–51, though many others have also noted them. Cady emphasizes the imagery while Buckingham stresses the rhetorical figures, including repetition. Cady's article is something of a classic now, though his discrimination between fresh and stale images seems to miss the point of JE's use of biblical imagery. It was the congregation's *familiarity* with certain images through earlier preaching and reading that enhanced their terror during the shock of recognition.

souls as flaming monuments of his displeasure, and severity, in hell forever.[7]

The vision of progressive precariousness in both physical and temporal dimensions is presented here with much of the keen sense of timing, vivid imagery, and exploitation of the figural structures of incremental repetition to be found in Edwards.

Sometime during his early ministry at Northampton, Edwards may well have read a sermon by the English dissenter, Jeremiah Burroughs, which had been reprinted in Boston, for one of his parishioners later professed to have been converted by a reading of it, and such a powerful work may well have been recommended to the pastor.[8] Upon reading it, Edwards would have heard Hopkins confirmed in all rhetorical essentials by passages like the following:

> They are guilty of desperate folly that squander away their precious time, seeing all depends upon it. . . . Death is called there [Job 18:14] the "King of Terrors": and well may it be so; for indeed it is the most dreadful thing in the world, to those that understand the meaning of their own sinful state and condition . . . Certainly (except thou hast good assurance of the work done between God and thy soul) the sight of the infinite ocean [of eternity] thou art launching into immediately after death, cannot but make thee give a dreadful shriek, when thou seest thou art now like to miscarry eternally. Death taking an ungodly man, it is no other but the cutting asunder of the thread upon which he hung over the pit of eternal misery: it is the pulling up of the flood-gates of God's eternal wrath. Here when afflictions are upon men and women, God's wrath is but only like the little droppings of water through the flood-gates: as you see in flood-gates, there will be some leakings forth of some drops of water only, but there is a vast difference between those drops, and when the flood-gates are pulled up, then the streams gush out abundantly. Just so it is with God's dealings here in the world with ungodly men: it may be God's hand is upon them in many afflictions; but these are but

7. "The Nature and Necessity of Regeneration: or, the New Birth," *Works*, pp. 566–67.

8. *A Preparation for Judgment: A Sermon Preached in London*, 2nd ed. (Boston, 1713). This sermon evidently stimulated the conversion of one John Ingerson when he lived in Northampton before the Great Awakening, according to his "relation" in the Westfield, Massachusetts, church records (p. 138) made when he later joined that church. (The Westfield entry was first called to my attention by Thomas M. Davis.)

as some few drops of his wrath: But when death comes and finds them unprepared, then God pulls up the flood-gates and then the streams of the wrath of the almighty overflow them. Death to them will be no other than *the sergeant of the Lord of Hosts, to hale them to prison*:[9] it will be a taking up of the draw-bridge: it will be to them a dismal and dreadful sunset, that brings with it a night of eternal darkness; and that will be a most dreadful sunset, that shall never have day more. . . . The time is short: the word is, the time is wrapt up, it is folded up. It is a metaphor taken from cloth, that is folded even to the very fag end. The time is all folded up . . . therefore let your hearts be taken off from the creature. . . . those that understand themselves aright, would not venture to be in an unconverted state one hour, for ten thousand worlds.[1]

Not quite so sustained and sonorous as Hopkins' oratory, this passage by Burroughs nevertheless contains the vivid images of suspension and depression, the incremental repetition, and the insistence upon time: the virtual matrix of *Sinners* rhetoric. One prominent additional note, however, is that of the condemned prisoner. With that in mind, let us return to the first of the "hands" sermons mentioned, Benjamin Colman's *Hands of the Living God*.

The secure fool says in his heart, "The living God is not present, nor sees nor knows, nor will bring me into judgment." When at the same time the foolish sinner is within the dreadful hand of that God, whom he is denying and daring by his security. He therefore is above all men in danger of God's taking him presently and tearing him to pieces. . . .

How fearful will the hands of the living God be in the hour of death and in the day of judgment? When the king of terrors advances with his mortal dart in his hand, and pointed at thy guilty heart; then fear and the pit and the snare will together present themselves before thee. Thy heart will be then sore pained within thee, and the horrors of death will fall upon thee; . . .

How soon, how suddenly they may fall into His hands. . . . When they lie down to sleep, their eyes may be closed in eternal death. . . .

You can never, never get out of those living hands, when you

9. Ed. italics.
1. Burroughs, pp. 39–62.

are fallen into them. No: while God lives he will hold you fast (in everlasting chains) and "none shall pluck you out of his righteous hands."[2] When God judges sinners in his righteous and terrible providence, or when his wrath falls upon their consciences, or when death arrests them to carry them in their impenitence to the judgment seat of Christ, and to the place of everlasting torments; then, then do they fall into the hands of the living God. . . . It is as when one falls into the hand of a powerful enemy; or rather as when a criminal falls into the hand of justice, and it is arrested, arraigned, convicted, condemned to die and executed. All impenitent sinners are always in the hand of God's justice, under his wrath and curse, under the sentence of eternal death. And not seldom they fall into the hand of his judgments here in this life, both as to soul and body. But it is especially at death and in the day of judgment, that they fall into the hand of the living God. Then it is laid upon them, lays hold of them, holds them fast, and falls upon them. This is the second death.[3]

Thus, in a sermon preached in conjunction with an actual execution of condemned pirates, Benjamin Colman establishes most explicitly the true identity of the "hands" sermon: it is a mode traditionally associated with *addresses to the condemned*—in the most literal sense. The rhetoric characteristic of the mode is of course peculiarly poignant when the auditory contains actual condemned criminals.[4]

Just as Edwards relied mainly upon the traditional language and imagery of the Bible for his most successful effects in *Sinners*—the importance of the spider image has been greatly exaggerated—so he exploited the specialized sub-genre of the execution sermon for this address to the unconverted: than whom, in Edwards' eyes, no type of human could be more completely or surely condemned. The tradition in which he preached is subtly yet openly acknowledged by Edwards in several ways. There is the imminent confrontation with death and eternity, then the many variations upon the theme of

2. Colman, pp. 19–21.
3. Colman, pp. 9–10.
4. There are a number of printed eighteenth-century sermons that were preached before convicts condemned to execution, and most have a rhetorical family resemblance as "hands" sermons, though comparison shows how rare is a sustained intensity comparable even to Colman's. Noteworthy are Cotton Mather's sermon in *Pillars of Salt* (Boston, 1699); Increase Mather's *The Folly of Sinning* (Boston, 1699), especially the second sermon, and his sermon on an accident (rather than an execution), *The Times of Men are in the Hand of God* (Boston, 1675).

suspense-suspension-hanging, and inevitably the there-but-for-the-grace-of-God-go-you motif common to the type.

But the most significant conventional element, one that Edwards not only acknowledges but intensifies and exalts in his reification of the format, is the insistence upon the union of power and authority in the governing entity. From the statement of doctrine, with its phrase "mere pleasure" suggesting the formulaic identification of sovereign right but elevating "his majesty's" to the supreme "mere," to the prominent thread of references throughout the sermon contrasting the relative impotence of earthly princes with the omnipotence of God in dealing with rebels and otherwise condemned persons, Edwards displays considerable artistry in ringing new changes upon this central element of the execution sermon.[5] Not only does God have a personified Justice threatening death, but the earth, the elements, indeed all the creation, including devils, hell, death, and invisible fields of Newtonian force: all are contrived within the closed system of God's sovereignty to the end of destroying the condemned. The unregenerate sinner has no further court of appeal, no alternative system of values with an objective foundation; the sole escape is through the door where Christ beckons (in contrast to the trap in the floor).

Certain contrasts between the Puritan awakening sermon and the sub-genre of the execution sermon are readily apparent, despite the underlying similarity of tone. The traditional awakening or "hellfire" sermon stresses the predicament of the unregenerate who are caught between the ancient strictures of the Bible and a future settling of accounts. Their predicament is absolute, but the actual judgment is indeterminate in time and place. As the preacher interprets the Scripture, formulates abstract principles or doctrines derived from it and finally applies them to the unregenerate, the emphasis tends to be upon the ultimate order of divine justice in all of its sometimes remote aspects. The threat of hell is undisputed, but it is not present in time or place; the authority of God to punish evil and the present culpability of the unregenerate suffice at most to promise torment in a

---

5. In the text of the first edition of *Sinners* (Boston, 1741), the juxtaposition of God and earthly princes is made explicit immediately after the statement of doctrine on p. 5, enhanced by the play upon law and justice on p. 6, reflected in the phrase "service of God's enemies" on p. 13, brought to the sharpest focus on pp. 16–17, highlighted again on pp. 19–20, and reinforced throughout the sermon by a web of terms, allusions, and suggestions too intricate to be discussed here.

dimension of being quite beyond "real life." Finally, the very identity of the unregenerate is often in question.

The execution sermon is, on the other hand, immediate in time and place. The condemned criminal is in the hands of the civil law and he personifies realized doom in a very human context. His ultimate fate as a sinner may be undecided, but his fate as a mortal is certain and immediate. However, though the emotion is powerful, it is also complex: there is always the possibility that he *is* one whom God will save, and the civil powers cannot rejoice in the execution of a fellow sinner as the perfect Deity might, and so forth. All in all, ministers appear to have seen executions as a nasty business, however necessary, and few execution sermons seem to represent the best efforts of their authors.

But in *Sinners in the Hands of an Angry God,* Edwards finally achieved an absolutely sustained tone, a sharply delimited range of imagery, and a syntactical structure tightly integrated through both small and large patterns of repetition. The sheer centripetal force of meditation upon the governing idea of the sermon, although a quality apparent in many of Edwards' writings, is unequalled in intensity elsewhere. In a series of parallel rhetorical maneuvers spanning the entire sermon, Edwards removes the psychological supports of virtually all involved witnesses, and suddenly the entire community finds itself suspended over the pit of mortality, wholly vulnerable within and without, while a new sense of the eternal moment of God's real time dispels the last illusions of progression (escape) in life or discourse. As the final paragraphs warn, even while indicating the concomitant of hope found in all depictions of divine wrath, there is only a moment in which to awake and turn to Christ before being turned off the scaffold.

If Edwards displays awareness of the traditional "hands" sermon in his use of the conventional biblical imagery that we have just seen employed similarly by authors he probably in some sense drew upon, and if he paid the customary tribute of genius by discovering new potentialities within the old form, then it is through telescoping the conventions of the Puritan awakening sermon and the execution sermon that he discovers the most significant dimension of his innovation in *Sinners.*

Considered in the context of homiletical tradition and the background of Edwards' own reading, *Sinners in the Hands of an Angry God* provides ample illustration of the peculiar mixture of literary or cultural conservativism and imaginative innovation which characterizes so much of Edwards' writing. In this case, he takes up the traditional vehicle of communal ostracism, the execution sermon, and turns it back upon the crowd, exploiting the suppressed tendency of each individual to identify with the condemned in his heart and thus to assess himself by that act of comparison. Since the condemned in this case is every "natural" human being, the argument easily could have become an exercise in theological abstraction, but emulation of Ezekiel Hopkins' evocative rhetoric and Colman's personal address to those literally condemned helped Edwards achieve the authentic sense of urgency which distinguishes the sermon. Of course such syntheses of tradition and innovation evolved slowly in Edwards' literary practice, and years intervened between Edwards' initial response to Hopkins' sensational rhetoric and the final version of his adaptation of it preached in 1741.

In certain general ways, then, the sermon canon does document Edwards' literary development, especially if one demands of "development" only a continuous process undergoing marked changes in time. In the first year, he was seen struggling with wooden transitions and inflexible sermon booklets. Subsequently, his style became less self-conscious if not always more graceful, and the sermon booklet grew more flexible. In the 1730s there was ample evidence of a literary power in the sermons which anticipated the virtuoso performance of *Sinners in the Hands of an Angry God*. At the same time, however, there was an increasing tendency to preach longer sermons, sermon series, and finally, sermon-treatises. By the early 1740s, what had been only hinted at in the late 1730s was becoming obvious: Edwards was growing impatient with the limitations of the sermon form. His ideas were becoming more comprehensive and more complex in articulation, and the sermon was being stretched beyond its formal limits. Finally, there was the ultimate triumph of the treatise as the prime vehicle of Edwards' public utterance, and the concomitant decline of the preached sermon.

The evidence of the sermon canon does suggest, in the final analysis, that it may be most accurate to describe Edwards' progress in terms of "deepening" rather than "developing." In thought and in literary form, he remained moored to certain fixed points. His ideas in the sermons do not alter radically over the years: there are the early sermons celebrating the joys of religion, but there are also some late ones, and in addition to the imprecatory sermons of the 1740s there are some from the mid-1720s. In the form of his expression Edwards displayed his conservative temperament as much as in his theology, adhering to the Ramean structures of argument and "accurate distinction and close application of thought" in exposition, however much others turned to alternative methods and modes of suasion. Having one method and one process (always excepting the simple narrative of experience), Edwards pursued the larger implications of his doctrines and amplified his analyses until sermon became treatise.

J onathan Edwards was very much concerned with literary theory, particularly with those aspects of it that related directly to the writing of his sermons and treatises. Moreover, without actually abandoning either the traditional sermon form or the manner of the plain style, he experimented and innovated to a surprising degree, considering the limitations imposed by such conservative allegiances. It is appropriate to examine with some care Edwards' general literary theories, but even more his practices, particularly those specific stylistic techniques that made possible a highly individual voice in spite of superficial stylistic self-effacement.

1. Seminal Thoughts on Writing

In his writing, Edwards seems always to have been more interested in persuasion than mere expression, and the bulk of the writings he published are clearly propagandistic or polemical. Even his earliest notes on style and literary strategy, the list of rules on the "cover" (an ordinary folio leaf that may have been an end sheet) of the notebook, "Notes on Natural Philosophy," are the thoughts of one who viewed writing as a utilitarian engine of psychological power. These notes were apparently written for the specific purpose of preparing a scientific treatise, but they nevertheless constitute a general theory of writing which provided a foundation for Edwards' later writings, including sermons. A review of these early principles is necessary to an understanding of what was, at least in a chronological sense, the starting-point of Edwards' recorded literary theory.[1]

---

1. These rules have been transcribed and edited by Wallace E. Anderson in *Works, 6*, 192–95, along with other rules on the same leaf pertaining more specifically to a scientific treatise. Since the rules are more material to literary than to scientific matters, they have been reproduced here for the reader's convenience, along with the rules from *The Ladies' Library* which Anderson does not reproduce. In certain particulars this text varies from

[1. Try] not only to silence [opposition] but to gain *readers*.[2]

[2. To give but] few prefatorial admonitions about the style and method. It doth an author much hurt to show his concern for these things.

[3. What is] prefatorial, not to write in a distinct preface or introduction, but in the body of the treatise. Then I shall be sure to have it read by everyone.

[4. Let much] modesty be seen in the style.

[5.] Not to insert any disputable things, or that I will be likely to be disputed by learned men, for I may depend upon it they will receive nothing but what is undeniable from me, that is, in things exceedingly beside the ordinary way of thinking.

6. *The world will expect more modesty because of my circumstances—in America, young, etc. Let there then be a superabundance of modesty, and though perhaps 'twill otherwise be needless, it will wonderfully make way for its reception in the world. Mankind are by nature proud and exceeding envious, and ever jealous of such upstarts; and it exceedingly irritates and affronts 'em to see 'em appear in print. Yet the modesty ought not to be affected and foolish, but decent and natural.*

7. When I would prove anything, to take special care that the matter be so stated that it shall be seen most clearly and distinctly by everyone just how much I would prove; and to extricate all questions from the least confusion or ambiguity of words, so that the ideas shall be left naked.

---

the Anderson text, usually because of editorial intervention (annotated).

The rules were written at different times, the first six in 1723, the next eight in 1724, and the remainder by 1726. A number of the rules are in JE's shorthand, indicated in the text by italics. Both the Anderson transcription and that above are based upon the work of William P. Upham, presented in "On the Shorthand Notes of Jonathan Edwards," *Mass. Hist. Soc. Proc.*, 2nd ser., *15* [1902], 514–21.

2. This first rule, previously somewhat enigmatic, is here rendered complete for the first time. In the manuscript, the word "readers" is in shorthand, unlike the remainder of the rule, and Dwight could not read JE's shorthand. But why did Upham miss it? The only plausible explanation is provided by certain letters and documents in the Beinecke Library relating to the Upham transcription. These letters indicate that Upham did not work alone on the transcription; rather, Franklin B. Dexter transcribed the longhand portions of the rules, while Upham transcribed the shorthand. Thus, there are two separate manuscript transcriptions, one by Dexter and one by Upham, each numbered to correlate with the other. It would seem that Upham glanced at number one, saw that it was in longhand (except for the overlooked last word), and left it for Dexter. But Dexter, like Dwight before him, could not read the full entry, and simply copied out the longhand.

8. In the course of reasoning, not to pretend to be more certain than everyone will plainly see it is, by such expressions as "it's certain," "it's undeniable," etc.

9. To be very moderate in the use of terms of art. Let it not look as if I was much read, or conversant with books or the learned world.

10. In the method, in placing things first, respect is to be had to the easiness and intelligibleness, the clearness and certainty, the generality, and according to the dependence of other things upon them.

[11.] Never to dispute for things after that I cannot handsomely retreat upon conviction of the contrary.

[12.] In writing, let there be much compliance with the *reader's* weakness, and according to the rules in The Ladies' Library, Vol. 1, p. 340 and seq.[3]

In order to present the "entirety" of number 12, including that which is only referred to in Edwards' note, the full list of six rules from *The Ladies' Library* is inserted here:

> Rule I. *Acquaint your selves thoroughly with the state of the Question; have a distinct Notion of your Object, whatever it be, and of the Terms you make use of, knowing precisely what it is you drive at.*
>
> Rule II. *Cut off all needless Ideas, and whatever has not a necessary Connection to the Matter under Consideration*; which serve only to fill up the Capacity of the Mind, and to divide and distract the Attention. From the Neglect of this come those causeless Digressions, tedious Parentheses, and impertinent Remarks, which we meet with in some Authors: For, as when our Sight is diffus'd and

3. This reference has been the source of some confusion. C. H. Faust and T. H. Johnson (*Representative Selections*, rev. ed., New York, Hill and Wang, 1962, p. cii.) state that "The reference is to modesty in writing." If one turns to Volume I, p. 340, of the first edition of *The Ladies' Library* ("Written by a Lady [probably Mary Wray]"; published by Sir Richard Steele, London, 1714, 3 vols.), he finds a statement urging the reader to "care not to oppress the modesty of the humble. . . ." But this is no advice to a writer; rather, it is a statement about proper social conduct, and it occurs in a chapter entitled "Charity." Moreover, the statement is not part of any list of rules. Only one such set of rules occurs in the three volumes of the *Ladies' Library*, and they are printed in Vol. I, pp. 490–93.

Why JE wrote "p. 340" instead of "p. 490" is problematic. Perhaps he used the second edition of the work and the rules were on p. 340 in that edition; they have moved to p. 311 in the seventh edition.

extended to many Objects at once, we see none of them distinctly; so when the Mind grasps at every Idea that presents it self, or rambles after such as relate not to its present Business, it loses its Hold, and retains a very feeble Apprehension of that which it shou'd attend. Some have added another Rule, *That we reason only on those things of which we have clear Ideas.* But that is a Consequence of the first; for we can by no means understand our Subject, or be well acquainted with the State of the Question, unless we have a clear Idea of all its Terms.

Rule III. *Conduct your Thoughts by Order; beginning with the most simple and easy Objects, and ascending, as by Degrees, to the Knowledge of the more compos'd.* Order makes every thing easy, strong, and beautiful. That Superstructure whose Foundation is not duly laid, is not like to last or please: Nor are they likely to solve the difficult, who have neglected, or slightly past over the easy Questions.

Rule IV. *Leave no part of your Subject unexamin'd*: It being as necessary to consider all that can let in Light, as to shut out all that is foreign to it. We may stop short of Truth, as well as overrun it; and tho' we look never so attentively on our proper Object, if we read but half of it, we may be as much mistaken, as if we extended our Sight beyond it. Some Objects agree very well when observ'd on one side, which upon turning the other shew a great Disparity. Thus the right Angle of a Triangle may be like to one part of a Square, but compare the whole, and you will find them very different Figures. A moral Action may in some Circumstances, be not only fit but necessary, which in others, where Time, Place, and the like, have made an Alteration, wou'd be most improper; and if we venture to act on the former Judgment, we may easily do amiss; if we wou'd act as we ought, we must view its new Face, and see with what Aspect that looks on us.

To this Rule belongs that of *dividing the Subject of our Meditations into as many parts as we can, and as shall be necessary to understand it perfectly.* This indeed is most necessary in difficult Questions, which will scarce be unravell'd, but in this manner by pieces: And let us take care to make exact Reviews, and to sum up our Evidence justly, before we pass Sentence and fix our Judgment.

Rule V. *Always keep your Subject directly in your Eye, and closely pursue it thro' all your Progress*; there being no better sign of a good Understanding, than thinking closely and pertinently, and reasoning dependently, so as to make the former part of our Discourse support the latter; and *this* an Illustration of *that,* carrying Light and Evidence in every Step we take. The Neglect of this Rule, is the Cause why our Discoveries of Truth are seldom exact, that so much is often said to so little purpose, and many intelligent and industrious Readers, when they have read over a Book, are very little wiser than when they began it. That the two last Rules may be the better observ'd, 'twill be fit very often to look over our Process, so far as we have gone, that so, by rendring our Subject familiar, we may the sooner arrive to an exact Knowledge of it.

Rule VI. *Judge no farther than you perceive, and take not any thing for Truth, which you do not evidently know to be so.* Indeed in some Cases we are forc'd to content our selves with Probability, but 'twere well if we did so only, where 'tis plainly necessary; that is, when the Subject of our Meditation is such, as we cannot possibly have a certain Knowledge of it, because we are not furnish'd with Proofs, which have a constant and immutable Connexion with the Ideas we apply them to; or because we cannot perceive it, which is our Case in such Exigencies, as oblige us to act presently on a cursory View of the Arguments propos'd to us, where we want time to trace them to the bottom, and to make use of such Means as wou'd discover Truth.

Obviously, this set of rules is intended to help the writer (or speaker) become master of his thought and thus a formidable, though perspicuous, advocate in any inquiry or debate. A compend of thought popular in the early eighteenth century, the rules are reminiscent of Arnauld and Nicole's *The Art of Thinking,* Descartes' *Discourse on Method* or *Rules for the Direction of the Mind,* and Locke's *Essay* (particularly Book IV). But to continue Edwards' own list of rules:

[13.] Let there always be laid down as many lemmata or preparatory propositions as are necessary to make the consequent propositions clear and perspicuous.

[14.] When the proposition allows it, let there be confirming corollaries, inferences for the confirmation of what had been before said and proved.

[15.] Oftentimes it suits the subject and reasoning best to explain by way of objection and answer, after the manner of dialogue, like the Earl of Shaftesbury.[4]

4. This is apparently a reference to Shaftesbury's *Characteristicks of Men, Manners, Opin-*

16. Always, when I have occasion to make use of mathematical proof, to acknowledge my ignorance in mathematics, *and only propose it to 'em that are skilled in that science whether or no that is not a mathematical proof.*

17. *Before I venture to publish in London, to make some experiment in my own country; to play at small games first, that I may gain some experience in writing. First to write letters to some in England, and to try my [hand at] lesser matters before I venture in great.*

18. If I publish these propositions *that are so metaphysical that 'tis probable [they] will be very strange to many learned divines and philosophers, to propound 'em only by way of question, as modestly as possible, and the reasons for 'em; not as if I thought them anything well demonstrated, but only as worthy to bring the matter into consideration. Entirely submit 'em to the learned in nature and . . .[5] and if it be possible, to conceal my determination.*

19. *Lest I may mention a great many things, and places of Scripture, that the world will judge but frivolous reasons for the proof of what I drive at, not to mention such as I fear it of as what I depend on for proof, but to bring 'em in so that the force of the reasons will naturally and unavoidably be brought to the mind of the reader.*

20. *To bring in those things that are very much out of the way of the world's thinking as little as possible in the beginning of a treatise. It won't do, for mayhap it will give an ill prejudice and tincture to the readers' mind in reading the treatise. Let them be given a good opinion of the others first, and then they will more easily receive strange things from me. If I tell it at first, it will look something like affectation of telling something strange to the world. They must be pleased with seeing what they believed before cleared up before they will bear to see their opinions contradicted. Let the way be so paved that they may be unavoidably confirmed . . .[6] a belief.*

21. Use as few terms of art as I can conveniently.

---

ions, Times (London, 1711), and perhaps to *The Moralists,* one of the pieces collected in the *Characteristicks,* which exemplifies the dialogue technique. JE may also have been impressed by Shaftesbury's theories on dialogue in *Soliloquy, or Advice to an Author,* or in *Miscellaneous Reflections* (both in the *Characteristicks*). What else he took from the Deistic moralist—confirmation of his own tendency to repetition, or ideas on the apprehension of goodness—is a debatable point. JE's casual, non-committal reference seems almost guarded, but illustrates his interest in the latest, most popular literary forms.

5. Illegible shorthand symbol.
6. Lacuna in text, the result of a tear in the MS.

In this apparently random compilation of twenty-one numbered reminders, maxims, and rules for writing, certain preoccupations and
attitudes that were to endure in Edwards' thought and writings are
revealed through patterns of repetition. Thus, Edwards' preoccupation with clarity and precision in his style appears in six entries,
while number 7, in particular, embodies Edwards' youthful optimism
concerning the possibilities of verbal precision, and states his high
aim of writing so that "the ideas shall be left naked." Number 12
refers him to those six rules or elaborate directions in *The Ladies'
Library* that would help him to discipline his thought and writing so
that his expression might have such precision and stark clarity or
realism as would be required to evoke the shock of recognition implied in the word "naked."

Another stylistic preoccupation that looms very large in these rules
is the reiterated insistence upon modesty. Again and again, in at least
nine entries, Edwards admonishes himself in one way or another to
be modest. Before one makes any observations on Puritan neuroses
or virtues, however, it should be noted that number 6 clearly identifies
this particular variety of literary modesty as a stylistic strategy; moreover, it shows Edwards to have been conscious of the subtlety requisite
to the success of such a ploy.[7] Other numbers detail particular tactics
to be employed in this generally defensive strategy.

The very frequency of these reminders suggests that perhaps Edwards was concerned with self-control, as well as with stylistic effect.
Of the various attitudes, or casts of mind, evident in these entries,
one notices more than a hint of sheer personal ambition. Indeed, the
very first rule states that it is not enough to defeat the opposition
with polemic or proof, but that it is equally important to win a following of readers. Thus, at this early stage of his career, Edwards was
planning to stake out a claim in the world of letters; he had not yet
published anything, but he was thinking of the conditions necessary
for the favorable acceptance of successive future writings. The extent
of his ambition and the tenor of his self-confidence are further adumbrated in number 17, where he identifies London as the center of

---

7. Here and elsewhere in his style notes JE reflects the literary ambience he shared with
contemporaries such as Benjamin Franklin, who discovered that nothing worked so well
as to "put on the humble Enquirer" (*Autobiography,* ed. Leonard W. Labaree et al., New
Haven, Yale Univ. Press, 1964, p. 64). The immediate source of influence in this particular
instance seems to have been James Greenwood's *An Essay towards a Practical English Grammar*
(London, 1711), a work used and cited by both Franklin and JE.

his cultural world and lays plans for a methodical, prudent siege. Even Boston was no more than a playground for this unknown backwoods upstart! Well might he caution himself about allowing immodesty to show; these entries prove him to have been supremely ambitious and coolly, though not foolishly, self-confident.

Of course, there is more than the mere absence of foolishness in this list; rather, there is a canny worldliness which tinctures many of the entries as the aspiring author identifies his intended audience, notes the peculiarities of his personal relationship to it, analyzes the literary problems arising from these peculiarities of situation, and makes precociously sage notes toward a plan for overcoming such problems as can be overcome by a rhetorical strategy. Some of these entries are so worldly-wise, so sure in their diagnoses of the problems, that it seems more than probable that Edwards was not their origi- nator. In at least two entries (12 and 15) Edwards makes explicit his dependence upon the precepts or example of printed works, and other entries may well have been so derived. Several of these entries, however, sound like "tips" that an older person might have given to a young author seeking advice. Certainly, throughout his life, Ed- wards appears to have been always ready to learn from every book, conversation, and experience that might be in any way useful to his purposes.

But whether original or borrowed, all of these precepts are valuable indicators of Edwards' early thought on his literary career. His selec- tion of just these points, rather than many others that must have been in one way or another available to him, and the values exhibited through his choices, provide material sufficient for a sketch of the author as a young man. The emergent character study derived from the implications of literary theory is not entirely unfamiliar. In fact, it seems to be the young man described in the first pages of Benjamin Franklin's *Autobiography*: the ambition to excel in writing, the willing- ness to learn from literary precedents (even from the same works, apparently) and the advice of others, the assumption of a guise of modesty, the preoccupation with clarity and precision in thought and word, and the precocious pragmatism or worldliness. Certainly these young men were cut from the same cloth. If anything, Edwards' notes suggest the more soaring ambition, directing him to a conquest of the London "world," while the young Franklin seems to have been satisfied when he triumphed before his provincial fellows.

How deeply Edwards sympathized with the mainstream of the Enlightenment at the time of writing these notes is difficult to say, but it does seem evident that he was willing to challenge the likes of the Royal Society in their kind of game and, ultimately, on their home court. Of course, to succeed in such an enterprise he would have to master their literary strategies. There is little evidence that Edwards did not take the *Ladies' Library* rules seriously at this time, however, and his phrase, "the ideas shall be left naked," suggests more optimism about the efficacy of rational communication than even Thomas Sprat evinces in his advocacy of "a close, naked, natural way of speaking."[8] To speak (or write) nakedly is only a step in the direction of a naked idea, but here again Edwards shows his talent for pursuing the implications of ideas to a logical, but often radical conclusion.

However, the treatise anticipated in these notes was not to be written, and the Augustan establishment was not to be put "clean out of conceit with [its] imagination" by the "very rational philosophical truths" of the young man from Connecticut. Rather, Edwards would turn his attention to an analysis of the fundamental factors that condition all verbal communication, the nature of the human mind and the nature of words.

Perhaps, after having meditated upon Locke's *Essay* or some attacks upon it, those very biases of perception that are indicted in "Of the Prejudices of Imagination"[9] (originally intended to serve as a preface or "lemma" to the scientific treatise on the mind) seemed to loom ever larger as impediments to mere rational arguments. Particularly after the commencement of his personal conversion in 1721, he must have been increasingly aware of the role of the senses in realizing those very nearly ineffable experiences of the "religious affections" which became the new center of his life. Certainly, the "Personal Narrative" emphasizes a wide variety of sensory experiences and nebulous "imaginings" as at least concomitants of the true religious sensibility, and as the yet-aspiring author turned to this new area of study, he found himself necessarily less concerned with the externals of the world scene and more concerned with the "inscape" of the mind.

The notebook entitled "The Mind" seems to represent, in part, an attempt to ascertain the limits of verbal argument in a world of public dogmas and private sensibilities.[1] It was one thing for a philosopher

---

8. *The History of the Royal Society of London*, 2nd ed., London, 1702, p. 113.
9. Printed in Anderson, ed., *Scientific and Philosophical Writings, Works, 6*, 196–201.
1. Such an approach was hardly unprecedented, and the popular rhetoric text of Ber-

to appeal to the Augustan world's ostensibly solid foundation of reason in the course of demonstrating a few "rational philosophical truths." It was something else to write persuasively about the evidences of religious experience for a learned world that increasingly looked askance upon "eccentric enthusiasms." How could one convince the most sophisticated audience that he had identified a functioning spiritual system as surely as Newton had identified the true physical system? Indeed, how could one discuss the spiritual—patently irrational or suprarational in itself—at all in a world that increasingly urged conformity to a dead level of rational consensus?

Poised between the rhetoric of Locke's *Essay* and the Cartesian approach of *The Art of Thinking*, Edwards first sought for a viable alternative to the "old logic"[2] which would enable him to discuss the most subtle and exalted experiences in a way that would meet the most rigorous philosophical standards of the age, while yet permitting due recognition of the all-important spiritual dimension. Ultimately, the result might be a systematic exposition of "reality," but as it is experienced rather than as scientific calculations objectify it, and with the human sensibility as the efficient measure of reality when informed by the Divine Mind.

But knowledge, apprehended by the mere natural mind was a dubious thing, and the communication of knowledge a perilous enterprise, particularly when the knowledge to be communicated was of a spiritual or complexly intellectual sort. Thus the notes in "The Mind" dwell frequently upon such problems as the limitations of the mind, the elusiveness of knowledge, and the perils of words.

> [22]. PREJUDICE. Those ideas which do not pertain to the prime essence of things, such as all colors . . . and all our sensations, exceedingly clog the mind in searching into the innermost nature of things, and cast such a mist over things . . . For these will be continually in the mind and associated with other ideas, . . . and it is a continual care and pains to keep clear of their entanglements . . . The world seems so differently to our eyes, to

---

nard Lamy, *The Art of Speaking* (London, 1676), insists that study of the mind is prerequisite to eloquence (p. 110). Lamy in fact anticipates several emphases in "The Mind," such as the analogy between the operations of the senses and the mind, the power of imagery in language, the idea as the object of perception, and the power of beauty.

2. The complex influences of the "old" logic of Ramus and Burgersdijck, radically modified by the "new" of Arnauld and Locke, are discussed in the introduction and annotation of the *Scientific and Philosophical Writings* by editor Wallace E. Anderson.

our ears and other senses, from the idea we have of it by reason, that we can hardly realize the latter.[3]

[18]. WORDS. We are used to apply the same words a hundred different ways; and ideas being so much tied and associated with words, they lead us into a thousand real mistakes. For where we find that the words may be connected, the ideas being by custom tied with them, we think that the ideas may be connected likewise, and applied everywhere, and in every way as the words.[4]

These two entries, alone, suggest some of the great obstacles that Edwards saw in the way of effective rational argument, for they assert that both minds (of listeners or readers) and words are encrusted with associations that would obscure or even destroy the fine pattern of a rational discourse, especially when it is concerned with the eva-nescences of subjective experience. How could one hope to clear the heads of his audience, or having done that, keep from introducing new confusions through the very words of his argument?

Even if one could make a clearing in the mental overgrowth and introduce terms that were precisely and truly defined,[5] he would still have to contend with the very slipperiness of concepts in time.

[5]. CERTAINTY. . . . We have not such a strength of mind that we can perfectly conceive of but very few things; and some little of the strength of an idea is lost in a moment of time as we, in the mind, look successively on the train of ideas in a demon-stration.[6]

[57]. DURATION. "Pastness," if I may make such a word, is nothing but a mode of ideas. . . . When it is, as we say, "Past," the idea after a particular manner fades and grows old. . . .[7]

[65(a)]. . . . But there is a sort of veterascence of ideas that have been a longer time in the mind. When we look upon them they do not look just as those that are much nearer. This veterascence

3. Jonathan Edwards, "The Mind," ed. Wallace E. Anderson, in *Works, 6,* 348–49.
4. Ibid., p. 345–46.
5. Entry no. 48 of "The Mind" gives JE's notion of "a true definition": "that, which would give anyone the clearest notion of the meaning of the word, if he had never been in any way acquainted with the thing signified by that word." (Ibid., p. 367.)

He then follows this statement with a model definition (of "Motion") in which he defines the term by enumerating the particulars which it comprises. This kind of descriptive def-inition obviously appealed to JE, for he uses it throughout his writings.
6. "The Mind," p. 339–40.
7. Ibid., p. 372.

consists, I think, in blotting out the little distinctions, the minute parts and fine strokes of it. . . .[8]

As an idea is apt to fade in the mind during the course of a lengthy argument, it seemed almost inevitable that the "prejudices" of the listeners or readers would combine with the vagaries of verbal associations to threaten all true precision and the ideational coherence of an argument; that is, unless the argument were set back on the straight and narrow track from time to time with some kind of redefinition. But the very descriptive definition Edwards is inclined to employ in his argument involves just that lengthy process cited in entry 5 as a source of the weakening of true conceptions of ideas. Indeed, after studying some of Edwards' meditations in "The Mind," one might wonder if Edwards believed in a wholly efficacious rational argument at all.

In all this morass of confused significations, decaying meanings, and mental mists, there was apparently at least one bright spot of certainty for Edwards. In entry 66, he asserts that there are "All sorts of ideas of things [that] are but the repetitions of those very things over again . . ."[9] That is, there is a whole category of human experience in which there seems to be a direct and exact correlation between the experienced reality, the idea or concept of it, and the word for it. Thus, one's argument might be clear and efficacious if only he could talk in such authentic terms continually. But this category is restricted, according to entry 66, to the most simple and immediate of subjective experiences, "the ideas of colors," and such. Obviously, one who restricted himself to a vocabulary of such severely limited concepts would be able to discuss only literally superficial topical areas. Indeed, at least once, Edwards suggests that perhaps humans—philosophers included—are inadequately equipped to discuss, in any profound, precise, and effective way, the very things that were, in the eyes of a zealous young minister and student of theology, the most important:

> [35]. . . . But we have got so far beyond those things for which language was chiefly contrived, that unless we use extreme caution we cannot speak, except we speak exceedingly unintelligibly, without literally contradicting ourselves.

8. Ibid., p. 382.
9. Ibid., p. 383.

> *Corol.* No wonder, therefore, that the high and abstract myster-
> ies of the Deity, the prime and most abstract of all beings, imply
> so many seeming contradictions.[1]

In the course of his studies in the Scriptures, however, Edwards
discovered at least the hint of a solution to his predicament, and this
hint is most vividly expressed in "The Mind" through two successive
entries which seem to be intentionally juxtaposed:

> [19]. SENSATION. SELF-EVIDENCE. Things that we know
> by immediate sensation, we know intuitively, and they are properly
> self-evident truths: as, grass is green . . .[2]
>
> [20]. INSPIRATION. The evidence of immediate inspiration
> that the prophets had when they were immediately inspired by
> the Spirit of God with any truth is an absolute sort of certainty;
> and the knowledge is in a sense intuitive . . . Such bright ideas are
> raised . . . All the Deity appears in the thing . . . The prophet . . .
> sees as immediately that God is there as we perceive one another's
> presence when we are talking together face to face.[3]

Despite all the limitations of the human mind and the terrible difficulties posed by the spiritual realm, it seemed that the ancient prophets had received communications about spiritual things that were as
clear, as true, and as memorable as the simplest sensory experiences.
Moreover, they had succeeded in conveying their notions in a most
effective way, for they had preserved the simplicity and immediacy
of the truths while directing the minds of their audience to the very
heart of the "abstract mysteries." What method had they employed?
The very language of modern philosophers seemed to preserve the
secret:

> [23]. The reason why the names of spiritual things are all, or
> most of them, derived from the names of sensible or corporeal
> ones, as "imagination," "conception," "apprehend," etc., is be-
> cause there was no other way of making others readily understand
> men's meaning when they first signified these things by sounds,
> than by giving of them the names of things sensible to which they

---

1. Ibid., p. 355.
2. Ibid., p. 346.
3. Ibid., p. 346. This passage is virtually a paraphrase of the sentiments expressed by
John Smith in his *Select Discourses* (See above, p. 8).

had an analogy. They could thus point it out with the finger, and so explain themselves as in sensible things.[4]

"They could thus point it out with the finger" is a characteristically Edwardsean statement; he not only understands the way of the ancient prophets (and of modern poets), but employs their device himself when he would identify it. He achieves simultaneous definition and illustration; he gives the *sense* of the thing.[5] In a lifetime of sermon writing, Edwards continued to employ the power of imagery, not as decoration for an abstract argument nor even as illustration—though these functions were incidentally fulfilled—but rather as a source of stability and certitude, of freshness and immediacy, of meaning. Imagery, fused metaphorically to abstract concepts, would touch the mind of the auditor as surely as an "immediate sensation"; moreover, the simple image had a way of sticking in the mind as an indivisible unit. A well-chosen image could transform thought into experience and neatly fix the most paradoxical of concepts.

All this may seem to leave the whole matter of rational argument—let alone an old or new logic—far behind, and in a way it does. Edwards shows signs of becoming increasingly indifferent to the mere logical proof, or pure rational argument, as he becomes more involved with pastoral teaching. At least one entry in "The Mind" shows a healthy awareness of the very real limits of human reason:

> [68]. REASON. A person may have a strong reason, and yet not a good reason. He may have a strength of mind to drive an argument, and yet not have even balances. . . .
>
> Persons of mean capacities may see the reason of that which requires a nice and exact attention and a long discourse to explain—as the reason why thunder should be so much feared, and many other things that might be mentioned.[6]

One immediately thinks of entry 28 in "Shadows of Divine Things," which identifies thunder with God's majesty, or of Edwards' com-

---

4. Ibid., p. 349.

5. JE's inclination to employ this type of metaphorical definition when he approaches "abstract mysteries" is now well known. Notable examples are his definition of "absolute nothing" as "that the sleeping rocks dream of " ("Of Being," ed. Anderson, in *Works*, 6, 206), and his conclusion to the discussion of God's role in maintaining the universe in time: "And, if it were not for our imaginations, which hinder us, we might see that wonderful work performed continually, which was seen by the morning stars when they sang together" ("Things to be Considered and Written fully about," ibid., 241–42).

6. "The Mind," p. 384.

ments on thunder in the "Personal Narrative."[7] Perhaps with the "religious affections" particularly in mind, he insists that reasoning is not the sole guide to the truth, and that other ways of knowing and communicating essential truths are practically superior to reasoning.

Certainly, an argument which relied upon imagery and metaphor as prime vehicles of thought had several types of justification in Edwards' eyes. First, the precedent of the ancient prophets and the Scripture: how frequently they "pointed it out with the finger," and with what efficacy! Then the sensational psychology of Locke gave epistemological precedence to the senses and sense [intuitive] experience, a "modern" theory which yet seemed to correlate with the mode of ancient prophecy, particularly as interpreted by John Smith and the Cambridge Platonists. Edwards was familiar with the long-standing Puritan interest in the historical symbolism of typology, and the practice of "improving" the commonplaces of life after the manner of Thomas Manton and John Flavel.[8] These last preachers argued that common objects (aspects of the natural scene, domestic and farm implements, and so forth) "may be improved two wayes; viz., In an argumentative, and in a Representative way; by reasoning from them, and by viewing the resemblance that is betwixt them and spiritual matters."[9] Such an approach—particularly that of the second way—is a favored strategy in Edwards' sermons.

Thus it is not surprising to see Edwards, in the early and middle years of his preaching career, attempting to improve upon, and extend the limits of, rational argument and learning in religious writing.

---

7. One of the stranger passages in JE's writings is his illustration of changed perceptions of thunder storms following his awakening, in which he does not suggest any change in the storm itself or in its threat to himself, but rather views it from the divine perspective as mere high spirits or play. Of course, no rationalization is given of the change, nor could there be without introducing the idea of being killed for the sport of God. In the context of the "Personal Narrative" the change in attitude toward thunder exactly parallels the changed estimate of the doctrine of election. See the passage in Samuel Hopkins, *Life*, p. 27.

8. John Flavel's *Husbandry Spiritualized* (London, 1669) was very popular in JE's time and JE quotes Flavel, even naming him, in his sermon on Num. 23:9. Thomas Manton's theories on "improving common objects," briefly summarized in the Epistle Dedicatory of *Husbandry Spiritualized*, are propounded in *A Practical Commentary, or an Exposition with Notes on the Epistle of James* (London, 1651)—a book owned by JE and cited in the interleaved Bible (p. 875).

9. Thomas Manton, *A Practical Commentary*, p. 545. Manton appears to have been esteemed by JE, and there are a number of references to his works in JE's notebooks. Undoubtedly Manton's theories confirmed JE's general tendency to perceive common phenomena in symbolic terms.

It is only fair, however, first to acknowledge the place he consistently gives to the intellectual content of religion:

> . . .'tis in this way only that God gives grace to the world, by instructing of them in the principles of religion. If knowledge were not a necessary means of grace, there would [be] no need of the Bible. . . . There are some are so ignorant that they are scarcely capable in an ordinary way of having grace. (Sermon on Prov. 8:34; 1732.)

He asserts, moreover, that reason is a very important guide in the pursuit of religious truths:

> . . . Reason . . . is the natural image of God in man . . .
> [Reason] is the highest faculty in man and is designed by our maker to ever rule and exalt sense, imagination, and passion, which were made to be servants. (Sermon on Job 31:3; 1729.)

Edwards adhered to this seemingly rationalist position throughout his life; on the other hand, he frequently "put reason in its place," as if his listeners might mistake the true center of balance in his position. For instance, one early sermon contains two separate arguments in proof of the doctrine, and joining the arguments is the following transitional statement:

> Thus I have proved a future state and another world from the light of natural reason. The reason why I have spoken so much on this head is because many men are more easily convinced by such kind of arguments than those that are drawn from Scripture. I shall now, in the second place, prove it from the clearer light of Revelation, or the Word of God. (Sermon on Heb. 9:27; 1722.)

Perhaps even in the pulpit, at least in the first years, Edwards wanted to demonstrate that he knew the way the world was going and that he could keep up with the best of the avant-garde if he so desired. But he also wished to declare his true position and, as it were, stand above the current intellectual fads. There are several other early sermons that give proofs from "natural reason" while suggesting that these arguments are "only for those who are impressed with such proofs."

As the years passed and the time of the Great Awakening drew near, Edwards appears to have placed even less emphasis upon the rational argument, and sometimes, as in one ordination sermon, he is openly contemptuous of man's "natural" understanding:

> Divine Revelation in these things don't go a begging for credit and validity by approbation and applause of our understandings . . . (Sermon on I Cor. 2:11–13; 1740.)

On the whole, then, there is in Edwards a nice balance between reason and faith. He suggests that religious truths are all, at bottom, reasonable, but that human reason frequently falls short of an adequate comprehension of them. The fault would seem to be in the very cumbrousness of the reasoning process itself in the imperfect world of men. When salvation or damnation is the issue—or when thunder cracks in the sky overhead—the process of reasoning may seem ludicrously inadequate, particularly if other means of ascertaining the truth are available.

It is obvious that Edwards was fascinated by the possibilities of his reasoning powers and by the vistas opened through the newer approaches in William Brattle's compend of logic, the *Essay* of Locke, and *The Art of Thinking*. The refinements made the Ramist approach seem like an old toy, and it is almost a note of embarrassment that one hears in the entry on Logic in "The Mind":

> [17]. LOGIC. One reason why at first, before I knew other logic, I used to be mightily pleased with the study of the old logic, was because it was very pleasant to see my thoughts, that before lay in my mind jumbled without any distinction, ranged into order and distributed into classes and subdivisions, that I could tell where they all belonged, and run them up to their general heads. For this logic consisted much in distributions and definitions; and their maxims gave occasion to observe new and strange dependencies of ideas, and a seeming agreement of multitudes of them in the same thing, that I never observed before.[1]

But when the evidence of hundreds of Edwards' sermons is considered, the question of the precise role of the "new logic" becomes more than a little dubious. It is true that many of Edwards' writings contain superb rational arguments, and that Edwards is a competent and confident logician. It is also a truism to refer to Edwards' "pitiless logic" in his polemical treatises and admonitory sermons. But when

---

1. "The Mind," p. 345.

one asks what, precisely, is the contribution of logic to the literary effectiveness of any of these works, he is very likely to find himself uttering phrases such as "very pleasant to see . . . thoughts . . . ranged into order and distributed into classes and subdivisions . . ."

Indeed, it is probable that Edwards relied on logic and rational exposition in great part for what might best be termed aesthetic effects. A symmetrical structure, clarity of focus, pleasingly neat distribution of parts and wholes, and the sense of a progressive movement through the stages of a developing argument: all are noteworthy aspects of Edwards' mastery of rational discourse and logical argument. But the actual proof hardly depends upon either sweet reasonableness or iron syllogisms; ultimately, proof is the simple proclamation of the revealed Word of God. Truth is in the Scripture, and after the Word has been made known there is only the matter of deducing a logically ordered list of particular implications and relating these to the common experiences of life.

If the proof comes from authority, whence the power? Again, it seems that the logical structure is peripheral to the source of literary power in Edwards' sermons. Though the subtle persuasion which results from a carefully structured argument is important, the prime source of power lies in Edwards' use of certain literary devices such as imagery, metaphor, repetition, and allusion. As the justification is essentially authoritarian, so the appeal is directed as much to the emotions as to the intellect, specifically, as imagined experience. That this preoccupation with the human heart or emotional apprehension did become intensified through years of preaching experience, resulting in even less reliance upon mere rational arguments and logical proofs, is attested in several of Edwards' papers, particularly in "The Mind."

The bulk of "The Mind" notebook is a metaphysical inquiry and its language is theoretical if not always abstract. At the end of the manuscript, however, is a list of some fifty-six *Subjects to be handled in the Treatise on the Mind*. This list, written in two series, seems to have been compiled some time after the bulk of the entries in "The Mind" were made in the mid-1720s; in fact, internal evidence suggests that the first series may have been written at the time of the Great Awakening (though perhaps in the late 1730s), while the second series was probably written as late as 1747.[2] In any case, the whole list shows a

2. The manuscript no longer exists, but Dwight, who saw it, says that there were two

reorientation in Edwards' approach to the subject matter of "The Mind." He has turned from metaphysical theorizing to the practical implications of many of the earlier speculations. In brief, he has moved from philosophy to psychology, and from the realm of the student/thinker to that of the thinking pastor. Edwards may have had in mind a more modern, psychologically oriented sequel to Stoddard's *A Treatise Concerning Conversion,* with special emphasis on preaching and the ministerial office in the context of the revivals.[3] The "mind" in question is now less an ideal "Mind of Man" and more the perverse and mysterious "minds of men" which a preacher must address. Likewise, the focus of the projected treatise would seem to be less directed to the internal world of Edwards himself and more inclusive of the mental society he saw roiling about his pulpit. This change clearly parallels the development of the sermon notebooks discussed in Chapter II.

The issues that now loom large are not merely metaphysical problems involving "old" and "new" logics, but such practical issues as the popular resistance, through social forces and cultural conditioning, to particular ideas or pastoral leadership in general; the weakness and instability of the human mind "in the flesh"; the very important and yet mysterious "laws" governing the religious affections, and finally, the secrets behind success or failure in the pulpit. Answers to the problems posed here could hardly be discussed adequately in the technical vocabulary of eighteenth-century rationalism.

Many of the basic terms and issues remain constant throughout "The Mind" and its topical lists; however, as the center of Edwards' attention moved from the study to the pulpit, the focus of his inquiry became ever more intently centered in that area of the human mind he at first sought to master or overcome, the emotions. For his primary concern became the religious experience, and this experience

---

series of entries, the point of division coming after entry 26 (*Life*, p. 668). The list is printed in Anderson, ed., *Works, 6,* 387–93.

3. This unwritten treatise, entitled "The Natural History of the Mental World," is identified as a "great synthetic book in moral philosophy" by Norman Fiering in *Jonathan Edwards's Moral Thought and Its British Context* (Chapel Hill, Univ. of North Carolina Press, 1981), p. 72n. However, the scientific-sounding title notwithstanding, the work outlined was clearly directed to the professional conduct of preachers and pastors, as is indicated by references to preaching style (no. 6), differences between enthusiasm and grace (no. 9), the sense of the heart (no. 14), and the practical nature and limitations of language (nos. 35 and 54). The thrust of the work as a whole is directed to the larger issues of communication and leadership.

seemed to be hidden away below the rational surface of the mind in a welter of feelings, impulses, and dark forms. The story implicit in the document, "The Mind," is Edwards' gradual acceptance of his calling to work with human minds in all their messiness as the theater in which he, as spokesman of the Savior, must operate.

2. Light and the Heart

Edwards redefined two conventional concepts during his prime preaching years which imposed a kind of order upon the area of his operations, at least in his own mind. These concepts are "a divine and supernatural light" and "the sense of the heart." With these two notions and certain supportive concepts, he could justify in rational language the very enterprise of his ministry despite all the barriers and pitfalls adumbrated in "The Mind." He could hope to touch the souls of his people and effectively guide his congregation despite the inadequacies of language and the evident mental labyrinths which presented an apparently impenetrable barrier to the best of mere rational arguments.

"Divine and supernatural light," defined most successfully in the sermon of 1734, is the name Edwards gives to the experience of "A true sense of the divine excellency of the things revealed in the word of God, and a conviction of the truth and reality of them, thence arising."[4] "A true sense" means "an accurate knowing *and* feeling" of these spiritual [supernatural] truths, a total apprehension of the "naked" ideas—in all of their complexity and subtlety—despite the limitations of the words used to represent them. Such a stupendous feat of cognition could only occur, Edwards maintains, if there were a sudden infusion of "light" [awareness] from a superhuman source. Thus, he seizes upon the visual image of a burst of light from the sky, suddenly flooding a landscape that has been identified but hitherto largely hidden in shadows. The moment of realization is a moment of the most intense emotion, a shock of recognition so great that the "distinct image" which replaces the old shadows is never erased, and thus the subject of the experience is never again the same.

Although the actual illumination of the religious truths might come immediately from God and thus be utterly beyond the control of the minister, the mapping of the territory, or the presentation of struc-

4. *Works*, Worcester rev. ed., *4*, 441.

tured concepts, is very much his duty. The landscape of shadows must be presented to the mind or there is nothing to illuminate. In "Miscellanies" entry 782, probably written late in the 1730s, Edwards recorded his speculations on the mysterious process of cognition. In this meditation, variously entitled by Edwards, "Ideas, Sense of the Heart, Spiritual Knowledge or Conviction, Faith," he traces the levels of meaning from the minimal level of "signs" (mere words or concepts known only "by sound") through to the highest level of affective perception. The preacher, he maintains, is inevitably a purveyor of signs, since the necessity of discussing many abstract and complex issues in a short time requires his merely mentioning ideas that would have to be described in all their parts before one had even a complete speculative understanding of them. The listener, however, suffused by a "divine light," might hope to perceive instantaneously the full depth and subtlety of the message.

Edwards divides the ways of knowing into three main divisions: (1) "only some sign that the mind habitually substitutes in the room of the idea"; (2) "*apprehension,* wherein the mind has a direct *ideal view* or *contemplation* of the thing thought of "; (3) "the SENSE OF THE HEART . . . all that understanding of things that does consist in or involve such a sense or feeling is not merely speculative but sensible knowledge." The "sense of the heart" necessarily involves the will; it predicates choice, affirmation or rejection. For Edwards, this involvement of the will (the affections) is the essence of religion.[5] Only when one feels, as well as knows or apprehends, an idea has he arrived at full cognition, the stage that is designated by the term "spiritual."[6]

There were, then, some significant changes in Edwards' attitude toward the interrelationship of reason and emotion in human nature, the nature of knowledge, and the function of language. At first, when an inexperienced (and seemingly unawakened) but ambitious young

---

5. As Perry Miller puts it, "Edwards' 'sense of the heart' was precisely the mind filled with the idea and with all its associates, and then consenting to it. . . . The rational conviction becomes transformed into the spiritual." ("Jonathan Edwards on the Sense of the Heart," *Harvard Theological Review, 41,* April 1948, 128.) The source of JE's terminology is probably his favorite rhetorician, John Smith, who wrote "Divine Truth is not to be discerned so much in a mans *Brain,* as in his *Heart.* . . . There is a Divine and Spiritual sense which only is able to converse internally with the life and soul of Divine Truth, as mixing and uniting it self with it . . ." (*Select Discourses,* 2nd. ed., Cambridge, 1673, p. 278.)

6. JE notes in "The Mind" that, if it is to be located in any particular part of the body, "The soul may also be said to be in the heart or the affections, for its immediate operations are there also." ("The Mind," p. 352.)

man, he apparently believed that he could effectively control people's minds and opinions by the sheer power of his arguments. He saw himself as a kind of Christian Philosopher before the citadel of the Enlightenment, ready to turn its lauded powers of reason and scientific inquiry back upon the worldly establishment in the cause of Christianity. But the treatise on Natural Philosophy was never written, and soon signs of grave doubts about the omnipotence of reason and the nature of the human mind appear. Perhaps Edwards' personal religious experiences (later described in the *Personal Narrative*) suggested how little the speculative intellect is involved in some of the most important of human experiences, and his growing appreciation of the beauties of the girl across the New Haven churchyard may have made him more aware of significant experiences that were exceedingly difficult to "rationalize."[7] Finally, the mental dialogue with Locke, Norris, and others must eventually have caused grave doubts about the adequacy of words and "rational discourse" in general, particularly when the task was mediating a subject as vast or exalted as those with which Edwards seems always to have been concerned.

At any rate, a second phase in Edwards' development is signalled by the writing of "The Mind." Around 1723, after having had the experience of some kind of conversion, the call to the ministry, and a period of preaching activity in New York, Edwards began a thorough re-evaluation of the mind. It is not that he ever questioned reason as the "candle of the Lord," or that he for a moment abandoned the notion that logical discourse is the most effective mode of communication, but rather he realized that after reason and logical discourse have exerted their full influence over the human mind, there are vast areas that may be left untouched; specifically, those areas conventionally designated "the heart," "the affections," or "the will."

> Doc. That the reason why men no more regard warnings of future punishment, is because it don't seem real to them. (Gen. 19:14)

Thus, in a sermon preached in 1727, Edwards seizes upon the crucial point: though reason and logical arguments may make theological dogmas seem *true*, do they make them seem *real?* Is there a due sense

---

7. Dwight assigns the date of 1723 to the "tribute" to Sarah Pierrepont, and the tone of the piece suggests that JE's love for Sarah was in full bloom by that time. (*Life*, p. 114.)

of the message as well as a mere understanding of it as an abstract principle? The amazing complexity of the mind itself and the subtlety of experience preoccupied Edwards during the period in which he worked on the main body of notes in "The Mind," and though this notebook seems abstract and rationalistic in its language, it is significantly concerned with the knowledge and experience of beauty (Excellence),[8] the most exalted and significant, yet subtle, supra-rational, and even mysterious of common human experiences.

The third phase of Edwards' development corresponds roughly with the flowering of his career as a preacher. It is characterized by the tone of the lists of topics at the end of "The Mind," by the revival tracts, and by many sermons preached during the period. During this third phase Edwards is fully aware of the complexities of the human psyche and the limitations of the English language when one is dealing with the religious affections. But he is beyond the period of inquiry and discovery so far as the basic principles are concerned; rather, he is a professional preacher and pastor, concerned mostly with the effective application of his knowledge of men and words.

Considering the acknowledged limitations of language and the problems inherent in discussing the "high and abstract mysteries" of religion—compounded by the notion that mere natural men could not possibly see the truths and beauties of religion without a supernatural infusion of light—one might suppose that Edwards would have quailed at the challenge of the pulpit. Of course, he did not quail, nor did he show the slightest reluctance to bring a great arsenal of mind- and sense-disturbing rhetorical devices into most of his sermons. Indeed, the sermon notebook entry which laconically directs Edwards to "Preach a sermon . . . to stir 'em up to love the Lord Jesus Christ" indicates that, in practice, Edwards operated pretty much in the spirit of his advice to his congregation when he told them to prepare themselves for the infusion of saving grace: "'Tis as much men's duty to be converted as 'tis to perform any act that is in their own power." One acts as if preaching, in itself, could bring down grace, as if salvation could be won by an effort of free will. Is this open hypocrisy, or some kind of psychological game?

8. There are fifteen entries in "The Mind" explicitly devoted to excellence or excellency—the sum of ethical and aesthetic beauties. The next most often cited topic has a mere six entries. For a full discussion of excellence, a central concept in JE's thought, see R. A. Delattre, *Beauty and Sensibility in the Thought of Jonathan Edwards* (New Haven, Yale Univ. Press, 1968).

The principle that permits this kind of thought is designated in Edwards' writings by the word "fit."⁹ The term, as he uses it, is an ethical-aesthetic description of the relationship between the inherent and external means of an operation, between the two discernible aspects of the same operation which occur simultaneously and are thus not themselves causally related. In the case of conversion, the faith and the converting ordinance are simultaneous, paired aspects of God's single gift. Likewise, preaching, when it is a converting ordinance, is necessarily accompanied by an infusion of supernatural light. If a would-be saint struggles mightily for saving faith, he does not actually "earn" the saving grace, though it would be "fit" that he receive it; likewise, a great and powerful preaching performance (or written sermon) does not, of itself, engender conversion, though it may be so good as to become a "fit" vehicle for the transmission of saving grace. God supplies the Word immediately through the Scripture and the preaching; he has also provided each person with a faculty of understanding and a sense of the heart. It is the task of the preacher to fill the understanding by clearly expounding the Scripture and to "stir up" the heart by introducing the idea of self into the context of the Word. Then, if God wills, the words of the preacher become God's Word and the auditor's heart is filled with a "divine light" which permits an immediate recognition of the truth and reality of the Word. If the logic and rhetoric of the preacher are very effective, and if the auditor is attentive and earnest, it is fitting that God give his Spirit simultaneously to the words, thus making them His Word, and to the heart of the auditor, causing a gracious infusion of faith. But God's acts are never commanded or conditioned by either preachers or auditors, and the most brilliantly apt sermon may leave the most earnest auditor sitting cold and hopeless, though intellectually informed.¹

If the secular mind finds all of this to be yet a little improbable or abstrusely theological, one might consider the parallels with a common phenomenon in aesthetic experiences. It is that experience

---

9. JE's occasionalist doctrine of fitness is traditional, having been shared by seventeenth-century Puritans, Cartesian philosophers, and Neoplatonists. However, the concept of fitness must have been most apparent and palpable to JE in the context of his own preaching and rhetoric, and especially in the context of the awakening sermon.

1. The relationship between preaching and conversion is discussed at length in the third chapter of Conrad Cherry's *The Theology of Jonathan Edwards: A Reappraisal* (New York, Doubleday, 1966), aptly entitled, "Word and Spirit."

which underlies the platitude, "Beauty is in the eye of the beholder," and which sometimes occurs when one contemplates an esteemed work of art, such as the majestic "David" of Michelangelo, in a conscious effort of appreciation.

Assuming cultural background has conditioned one to expect the experience of beauty when viewing this statue, his first act is to study it. One takes stock of the overall proportions, then of the details; he walks back and forth or stands and meditates, attempting to gain possession of all the aesthetic "facts" of the statue. Then, having seen all that the eye can see, and having thought of all the relevant ideas and arguments he can summon up, he must sooner or later become aware of a response. Is it beautiful? Do I really *feel* the beauty, or do I just *know* that "it is beautiful" because I have been instructed to hold that opinion, or because the statue fulfills a set of academic aesthetic criteria? Or perhaps it is more complicated than that. Perhaps the statue is beautiful on some days and not on others, not because either the statue or the lighting has changed, but obviously because of the viewer's state of mind. Sometimes, when personal anguish or bitterness is great, things that usually seem most beautiful are empty forms.

For Edwards, the preacher's role in the abstract medium of language is analogous to that of the sculptor. As Michelangelo attempts to embody in stone the fact of masculine beauty, making immediate and concrete at least one version of an ideal beauty, so Edwards attempts to set forth, as clearly, precisely, and poignantly as possible, the reality of the Word. In order to produce effective works, both sculptor and preacher must be inspired, and a large part of this inspiration is experienced as a submission of the artist to the informing ideal he labors under. Thus, sculptors sometimes speak of "freeing the form from the stone," while Puritan preachers spoke of "earthen vessels" which contain "shining light."

But once the piece is completed and every last detail has been articulated, the work is not truly fulfilled. Someone must view the sculpture or listen to the sermon. And when all the surfaces and details of the sculpture are revealed to the viewer's eye, or the several heads of the sermon are digested and the doctrine understood, the work is not fulfilled. Indeed, not until the sense of the work's power and beauty suffuses the viewer's consciousness; not until, in an instant, the viewer suddenly perceives the principle investing the whole aggregate of surfaces and details, and he joyfully consents to the aesthetic validity of the work, is that work really fulfilled. The work has then become an experience, involving the whole person, and the quality of that experience is beauty. In the case of the sermon, of course, the sudden realization of the informing principle is the confrontation with God's Word, and the consent is to the beauty of holiness rather than to the holiness of beauty.

In both cases, the final stage of fulfillment is strange, unpredictable, and hence exciting and wonderful. No one can be made to see beauty through the greatest art; least of all can one make oneself see it. One can only prepare oneself for the confrontation, yield to the work's presence, and hope. Beauty must be in the eye of the beholder, for in the final analysis all he ever possesses is a subjective impression—an image—of the statue. In the chronology of fulfillment of the "David," from the gleam in the artist's eye to the experience of beauty, the last formative blow is struck by the viewer's eye.

Sermon and carved marble provide the essential objective focus for the experience of beauty. Doctrine and surfaces must be created first so that the experience of beauty is "responsible." For Edwards, to experience holy beauty without the controlling Word in one's mind is to be an enthusiast, to suffer from "vain imaginings." On the other hand, to possess only the "facts" of the work and not sense its true beauty is to be damned.

This analogy between preacher and artist calls attention to the perspective of Edwards' thought on the working of the divine Spirit. Just as he contends in "The Mind" that the essential quality of God is excellency or beauty, so his conception of the working of the Spirit through the preached word has the same basic structure as generally held theories of the experience of art.

Having thus identified the real psychological limitations of the sermon, Edwards set out to do all that the peculiarities of the English language and the human mind would allow him to do. He strove with all his might, it seems, in the weekly sermons and lectures to create images of the Word so perfect and powerful that the experience of saving faith would be wholly fitting in his auditory. He conceived of the operation of the sermon upon the hearers dually. Because he considered the "mind" to comprise an intellect or understanding and a heart or will, he attempted to appeal to both, for the saving image must have its substance in order to have its form. In his sermon on Hebrews 5:12 (1739), Edwards asserts flatly that

No speech can be any means of grace, but by conveying knowledge. Otherwise the speech is as much lost as if there had been no man there, and he that spoke, had spoken only into the air . . . He that doth not understand, can receive no faith, nor any other grace; for God deals with man as with a rational creature; and when faith is in exercise, it is not about something he knows not what.[2]

And concomitantly, according to his personally definitive *Treatise Concerning Religious Affections,*

Such books, and such a way of preaching the Word . . . is much to be desired, as has a tendency deeply to affect the hearts of those who attend these means.

. . . if the things of religion, in the means used, are treated according to their nature, and exhibited truly, so as tends to convey just apprehensions, and a right judgment of them; *the more they have a tendency to move the affections, the better.*[3]

Both the understanding and the affections must be brought into play; indeed, as Perry Miller has observed,

. . . when the word is apprehended emotionally as well as intellectually, then the idea can be more readily and more accurately conceived. When the word sets in train a sequence of passions, out of it—not invariably, but frequently—there emerges, like Venus from the foam, a "sensible" concept.[4]

The "sensible concept" of the preached word finally emerges, however, only when there is an infusion of "divine light" from God: an experience more wonderful, though less inexplicable to Edwards, than the realization of the statue's beauty in the viewing of it. Because of the supernatural infusion, concepts and tropes, logic and rhetoric, rational discourse and poetical evocation are fused in the vivid experience of faith:

A mind not spiritually enlightened beholds spiritual things faintly, like fainting, fading shadows that make no lively impression on his mind; like a man that beholds the trees and things abroad in the night. . . . that goes in the dark into a garden full of the most

2. *Works,* Worcester rev. ed., *4,* 4–5.
3. *Works, 2,* 121–22. Ed. italics.
4. "The Rhetoric of Sensation," reprinted in *Errand into the Wilderness* (New York, 1964), p. 181.

beautiful plants, and most artfully ordered, and compares things together by going from one thing to another to feel of them and to measure the distance: but he that sees by divine light is like a man that views the garden when the sun shines upon it. There is, as it were, a light cast upon the ideas of spiritual things . . . which makes them appear clear and real which before were but faint, obscure representations. ("Miscellanies," no. 408.)

Edwards labored to create sermons so effective that an infusion of light and grace would be as fitting in their presence as would be the final realization of beauty in the presence of the most painfully wrought work of art. Of course Edwards, like any literary artist, relied upon certain devices in developing his sermons, some virtually required by his genre and some the product of stylistic innovation. Consideration of the most important of these devices and those aspects of style that give Edwards' sermons their "Edwardsean" character is essential to an appreciation of the conscious artistry investing Edwards' productions.

3. Stylistic Techniques

. . . he studied the Bible more than all other Books, and more than most other Divines do. His uncommon acquaintance with the Bible appears in his Sermons . . . He took his religious Principles from the Bible, and not from any human System or Body of Divinity. Tho' his Principles were *Calvinistic,* yet he called no Man, Father.[5]

As usual, the precise and veracious Samuel Hopkins is closer to the truth than many more pretentious students of Edwards. His sermons, alone, prove Edwards to have been a "textuary among textuaries," one of the most imaginative and profound students of the Bible's style and substance in colonial America. Not that he was ever a fountain of scripture texts, as some preachers of an earlier day, but the aptitude and penetration displayed in his use of scriptural passages are truly extraordinary. Any consideration of Edwards' literary qualities must give priority to his use of the Scripture.

Although each of Edwards' sermons begins with a scripture passage and seems to be derived immediately from that passage, it is

5. Hopkins, *Life,* pp. 40–41.

now clear, through the examination of the sermon notebooks, that the sermon frequently originated in an occasion or personal inspiration of Edwards himself and that he subsequently located a biblical text to match the preconceived doctrine. So thorough was his knowledge of the Bible that he could always find a text—often in an out-of-the-way corner—that seems the certain source of his doctrine, and it is virtually impossible to differentiate those sermons that began with biblical texts from those that began with doctrines or occasions by merely examining the finished work. So close is the fit in all instances, that Edwards has been accused of drawing "the baldest, most obvious doctrine"[6] from his scripture texts; but the very obviousness seems an accomplishment when one considers that in many cases the text was actually preceded by the doctrine.

But are his doctrines really so obvious? Surely, they are clear, explicit, declarative statements that usually translate the poetic or suggestive passages of the Bible into abstract propositions, and in this Edwards seems to be a traditional Puritan preacher. However, is the doctrine, "There is nothing that keeps wicked men at any one moment out of hell, but the mere pleasure of God," a bald or obvious recapitulation of the independent clause, "their foot shall slide in due time"—or even of the whole verse? The doctrine goes beyond baldness or obviousness as a flash of lightning enhances a dark cloud. The very explicitness, concreteness, and thoroughgoing particularity have a poetic potency all their own, and what was before ominous is now awful and immediate. Such pungency in doctrinal statements is not rare in Edwards' sermons and many of his doctrines must have given an edifying shock to his sermon-wise congregation. Here are a few examples of his art in drawing doctrines:

> Prov. 24:13–14 My son, eat thou honey, because it is good; and the honeycomb, which is sweet to thy taste: /So shall the knowledge of wisdom be unto thy soul: when thou hast found it, then there shall be a reward, and thy expectation shall not be cut off.
>
> Doctrine: It would be worth the while to be religious; if it were only for the pleasantness of it.
>
> Cant. 1:3 Because of the savour of thy good ointments thy name is as ointment poured forth, therefore do the virgins love thee.

6. Perry Miller, *Jonathan Edwards* (New York, World, 1963), p. 48.

Doctrine: Christ Jesus is a person transcendently excellent and desirable.

Matt. 12:30 He that is not with me is against me; and he that gathereth not with me scattereth abroad.
Doctrine: There are no neuters in religion.

These examples are not atypical in any way, nor are they even the best of their kind; rather, they represent the quality of statement that Edwards was apt to make on any ordinary sabbath in Northampton. They show Edwards at work within the tradition of the plain style, each doctrine clear, simple, and logically apposite to the text. Indeed, they are so "plain," so colloquially forthright in tone, that the declarative simplicity becomes noteworthy in its own right. A kind of humility is implicit in such statements; the stated doctrine abstracts an essence from the biblical passage without pretending to rival the original in rhetorical beauty, making the Word immediate without seeming to emulate or improve upon it. On the other hand, there is such a confident sweep in these doctrines, such uncompromising clarity and particularity, that they abstract and concentrate the essence of authority which inheres in the Scripture.

Authority is, of course, the primary quality of the Scripture, and the sermon's text is the formal root and foundation of the entire sermon. In the light of the opened text which precedes it the preacher's argument is authoritative, a link of communication between God and man. However, Edwards, like Puritan preachers before him, was not content merely to found his sermon upon the Scripture. He braced his argument at various points with "scripture proofs," citations of passages that confirmed or paralleled his argument, and virtually every sermon has its sprinkling of biblical citations, like so many pins securing the joints of the logical structure.

Sometimes, as in the Opening of the Text in "Wicked Men Useful in their Destruction Only" or throughout much of "The Perpetuity and Change of the Sabbath,"[7] biblical citations cluster thickly about a point, and in some of the manuscript outline sermons, such as Deut. 32:23 or Is. 8:9–10, a main division of the sermon may consist of little more than an extensive catalogue of biblical citations. Of course, such citations function as scripture proofs, and they would have been appreciated by Edwards' note-taking congregation as references for

7. *Works*, Worcester rev. ed., *4*, 300, and 615–37, respectively.

Bible studies, but when the density of biblical passages reaches a certain point one feels the presence of a new type of rhetorical argument, incantation.

Incantation, or the ritual invocation of the Word through the quotation of Scripture passages at crucial points in the sermon, is one of the most ancient and even primitive of the preacher's rhetorical devices, yet in Edwards' day Holy Writ still had much of its divine aura, its mystery and subliminal powers. There are numerous instances in his sermons where the sheer accumulation of Scripture passages obviously surpasses the requirements of scripture proof or even elucidation, though these needs may be met along the way. In such passages, Edwards is employing the raw quantitative power of massed Scripture citations to substantiate his argument and make his auditory see him as one "who would *Speak as the Oracles of GOD.*"[8] Often, Edwards achieves a subtly impressive presence even in print through incantation, though he is sparing in the use of the device in comparison with some of his seventeenth-century forebears. Whatever its relative importance, incantation always strengthens the impression that the preacher is in command of his subject, or in touch with the Word.

But Edwards' most impressive use of the Scripture is in the very fabric or verbal contexture of his sermons. The average Edwards sermon contains many images, metaphors, aphorisms, and seemingly prosaic phrases from the Bible, very often from the immediate context of the sermon's identifying text. It has been remarked that, in the imagery of *Sinners*, "for the most part [Edwards] fails when he depends upon [biblical images] rather than upon the careful, artistic elaboration of the symbols of his own imagination."[9] It is true that the spider image—a non-biblical image as developed by Edwards—is very effective, as are some of the other innovative tropes; however, Edwin Cady is nearer to relevant standards of evaluation when he speaks of "the organic oneness of theme, image, and 'application,'"[1] for it is neither the biblical nor the private images that are remarkable, but the fusion of both in an artful unity. Probably it was the striking amalgam of colloquial immediacy and archetypal authority

---

8. Cotton Mather, *Manuductio ad Ministerium* (Boston, 1726), p. 103. Mather heartily endorses "scriptural preaching."

9. Edwin H. Cady, "The Artistry of Jonathan Edwards," *New England Quarterly*, 22 (March 1949), 65.

1. Ibid., p. 71.

in the organic texture of *Sinners,* rather than a single category of tropes, that "burned into the minds" of the people at Enfield. By his peculiar blend, Edwards brought life into the word and the Word into the realm of immediate experience for his listeners.

This synthetic idiom, involving the utilization of the full gamut of scripture language, constitutes one of the major evidences of Edwards' true creative genius as a writer of sermons. He was not merely "saturated in Scripture" and therefore tended to sound like it when he wrote, as seems to have been the case with more typical conservative preachers of his day, but he consciously insinuated key words, tropes, and figures from the Bible into the seemingly "natural" or colloquial idiom of his sermons, modifying his materials when necessary so that a true fusion of idioms results.

To see this process in action in its most obvious form, consider one biblical text Edwards selected:

> Job 31:3. Is not destruction to the wicked? and a strange punishment to the workers of iniquity?

No notable images, tropes, or figures appear in this text, and one might expect Edwards to formulate a doctrine stating simply that wicked men shall be punished. However, the textuary seized upon the most "workable" word in the text and formulated his doctrine thus:

> It is a strange punishment that God has assigned to the workers of iniquity.

The word "strange"—a common enough word in Edwards' day as now—is then worked into the fabric of the discourse, subtly at first, but with increasing emphasis. As the sermon develops, the vivid images of hellfire preaching are brought forth in abundance: "billows of the mighty deep rolling over the soul . . . killed with thunder . . . those perpetual streams of brimstone . . ." and so forth. A reader (or listener) has become engrossed in the variety of images and metaphors by the time he encounters the clause, "they will have a strange and wonderful sensation of misery under God's wrath," and "strange" takes one almost by surprise, like a half-forgotten memory. But it returns again and again: "The bodies of the wicked, after the resurrection, will be strange, hideous kinds of bodies; there will be a strange crew at the left hand of Christ at the Day of Judgment. . . . such a strange punishment as being suitable to such a strange and

monstrous evil . . . the torments being principally spiritual and consisting in the horrors of the mind makes it appear like some strange
fable or dream," and so on to the peroration at the sermon's conclusion, "and if you continue in this state that you are now in, as you
are a strange sort of sinner so your punishment will be distinguish-
ingly strange." Throughout the sermon, there is an ebb and flow of
the word as Edwards builds to crescendoes of repetition followed by
extended hiatuses where there is no mention of "strange." As a nice
twist, the concluding direction of the sermon demands that people
must be "singular" in this world, and avoid popular forms of sin and
corruption, if they are to be saved at last.

That is the essence of the technique, though this example is the
simplest possible form of it. More often, Edwards employs several
words, images, tropes, or figures from the Scripture (though not all
from the sermon's text) in developing his argument. The resultant
pattern of biblical language forms an allusive linkage between the
Scripture and the argument of the sermon that need never be broken,
even when Edwards is making occasional references or introducing
innovations of his own. Moreover, many of the borrowed words are
so commonplace—like "strange"—that even a seasoned Bible reader
may not be sure whether a particular term or image is from the Bible
or from "life." Of course, that is what the technique is all about.

Sometimes, indeed, Edwards displays an uncanny virtuosity in
matching his scriptural borrowings to the occasional context of the
sermon. For instance, in a day of border raids and Indian attacks
along the wooded frontiers of New England, Edwards describes the
church, when come upon evil days, as "a woman in a wilderness."
The immediate occasion of the sermon (Eccles. 11:2) was an earthquake (December 7, 1737), and the sermon is filled with references
to local natural phenomena—quakes, northern lights, strange distem-
pers—which are both frightening in themselves and symbolic "shadows" of future turmoil in "the world of mankind." In this context of
darkness and strange threatenings in the New England countryside,
the brief phrase, "a woman in a wilderness," has a haunting suggestiveness and seems to be just one more aspect of the frightening local
situation. The citizens of Northampton knew well the threat of the
great woods at night; they knew of the not-so-remote Indian captiv-
ities, of wolves and similar perils of the forest. What, then, could be
more appropriate or more tinged with local color, when describing a

confused and troubled church, than the image of a lost woman, alone in the dismal forests of western Massachusetts?

Besides being a brilliant touch of realism, however, the image is a quotation from the twelfth chapter of Revelation. Many in Edwards' congregation would surely have caught the simultaneous impact of ancient biblical prophecy and the immediate local ethos, confirming their sense of the Bible's relevance to their lives and the living tradition of prophesying. The phrase is, as usual, only one of several instances of "scriptural echo" in the sermon. Whatever the character of the auditory, whatever the occasion or theme of the sermon, Edwards could find some outstandingly appropriate words or phrases from the Scripture to insinuate into the course of his argument as mediatorial threads securing an apparently seamless whole.

Thus, in several ways—selecting and matching texts and doctrines, choosing apt scripture illustrations and proofs, furnishing incantatory catalogues, and synthesizing a powerful scriptural idiom—Edwards demonstrates his mastery of the Bible's text and his brilliant artistry in its use. One must therefore be cautious about claiming originality for Edwards in any particular usage, for those effects that sometimes seem most original are likely to be derived, directly or indirectly, from the Bible. Of course Edwards himself would have been more pleased by recognition of his imaginative use of the Scripture to define contemporary experience than by claims for his "originality."

Of all the materials Edwards borrowed from the Bible or from life, he seems to have done more with imagery in composing his discourses than with any other device. Possessed of an intensely concrete and particularistic imagination, Edwards' abstract logic and his metaphors are alike vivified by simple but poignant (usually visual) images. The vividly delineated image appealed to Edwards from his earliest days, according to the evidence of works such as "Of Insects" which is remarkable for the vividness and particularity of its visual images; but Edwards consciously espoused the use of imagery in his sermons and more mature writings in accordance with his theory of language:

> 'Tis something external or sensible that we are wont to make use [of] for signs of the ideas of the things themselves. For they are much more ready at hand and more easily excited than ideas of spiritual or mental things which, for the most part, can't be

[fully realized] without attentive reflection . . . ("Miscellanies," no.
782.)

All his sermons are filled with images, nearly every significant idea
being linked to, and thus apprehended in terms of, one or more
images. Images contribute much to the apparent density of thought
and experiential immediacy that characterizes the sermons. The
power of specification, most often achieved through the use of carefully selected images, is surely the source of much of Edwards' total
rhetorical power.

But the merely rhetorical images are comparatively few. The vast
majority of the images in Edwards' sermons are directed at a higher
goal than making the abstract or complex concrete; they are, in conjunction with similes and metaphors, analogical vehicles for divine
truths.[2] Whether from the Bible or from "life" (the difference rarely
being notable when the images were taken from agricultural pursuits
in eighteenth-century New England), images of natural phenomena
and the most commonplace human activities and experiences are
pressed into service as bearers of the mysteries of religion. Of course,
the practice is as ancient as Christ's parables, and Flavel, Manton, and
numerous New England preachers relied on it, but Edwards brought
his own techniques to this resource as he did to all the conventions
he took up. Generally, Edwards' imagery is notable for the degree of
progressive elaboration in the case of a single image, and for the
centripetal focusing, in the case of several images, upon the central
idea of the passage.

A simple example of the elaborated image occurs in a sermon prepared for the Stockbridge Indians. Here (Ps. 1:3), Edwards begins
by declaring in the doctrine that "Christ is to the heart of a true saint

---

2. JE felt justified in taking images of nature and society for this end since he felt the
world about him was essentially symbolic. Entries from "Shadows of Divine Things" define
his attitude:

> There is a great and remarkable analogy in God's works . . . God does purposely
> make and order one thing to be in agreeableness and harmony with another . . .
> why is it not reasonable to suppose He makes the whole as a shadow of the spiritual
> world? (no. 8)

> One thing seems to be made in imitation of another, and especially the less
> perfect to be made in imitation of the more perfect . . . Why is it not rational to
> suppose that the corporeal and visible world should be designedly made and
> constituted in analogy to the more spiritual, noble, and real world? (no. 59)

> The works of God are but a kind of voice or language of God to instruct
> intelligent beings in things pertaining to Himself. (no. 57)

like a river to the roots of a tree that is planted by it." He then develops his argument, all the while bringing out new implications of the central image of a tree by a river:

> His blood was freely shed—blood flows as freely from his wounds as water from a spring. . . . Christ is like a river in the great plenty and abundance of his love and grace. . . . The tree that spreads out its roots by a river has water enough: no need of rain or any other water. . . . as the water enters into the roots, so Christ enters the heart and soul of a godly man and dwell[s] there. . . . a tree planted [by a river] is green in time of great drought when other trees wither.

A more elaborate development of an even simpler image occurs in a Northampton sermon on Job 18:15. Here, Edwards takes the image from the text and proceeds to "open" it:

> Brimstone shall be scattered upon his habitation. The wrath of God is very often in Scripture represented by fire and brimstone.
>
> Here brimstone is said to be scattered or strewed upon a wicked man's habitation: not yet kindled, but there lying to break out into a flame in due time, to consume him and his habitation together. By their habitation, we may understand all their enjoyment or their outward affairs and concerns in general. A wicked man's house and everything that is his has brimstone scattered upon it and there is the curse of God attending [it]. There is the wrath of God [that] goes along with all; the fire of wrath, or hellfire, as it were lying hid in its principles—in it already—to breach out into a flame at the appointed time. The reprobate's enjoyments have a seed of hell as it were in them, which seed will certainly bring forth its fruit.
>
> The brimstone of hell is scattered upon his habitation, out of which the flames of hell will by and by arise.

The sheer repose of the concluding sentence in this passage's envelope pattern gives the same sensation of threat as the phrase, "the mere pleasure of God," in *Sinners*, the impact of the sentence resulting from its position as the culminator of the fully elaborated brimstone time-bomb image.

More extended elaborations than these may be found in a number of Edwards' sermons. One outstanding example is Jer. 6:29–30 (1729), a sermon preached shortly after the death of Solomon Stoddard. The doctrine announces the theme of the sermon: "It argues great danger of being finally left of God, when sinners have lived long unconverted under eminent means of conversion." But the central, sustained image of the sermon is introduced in the Opening of the Text:

> The prophets had been blowing the fire so long that the bellows were burnt out, and yet they could extract no good silver: it all proved to be lead. The lead is consumed of the fire.

The burnt-out bellows are none other than the deceased titan of the Connecticut Valley, Solomon Stoddard, and the lead is those who remained unconverted under his ministry, now the responsibility of Edwards himself, while the fire is that of hell which awaits the damned. After a powerful elaboration of the image in the Opening of the Text, Edwards begins the Doctrine, arguing abstractly for the most part, but from time to time recurring to the bellows image:

> 'Tis always the effect of God's Word either to harden or to soften . . . and the better and more powerful the means are, the more effectually do they harden if they don't soften. There can be no more effectual way to harden a man than for him to go and live in sin under some eminent minister.

As the bellows heat up the soul-testing fire, the members of the congregation are tried and spiritually separated. Upon reaching the Application, Edwards returns to a more overt use of the image in his "Use of awakening to the unconverted of this town":

> . . . you have stood it out until the bellows are burnt. You had the preaching, the calls and warnings of your eminent deceased minister 'till he was worn out . . . but the founder melted in vain as to you; he did not cease blowing 'till the bellows were worn out, as it were burnt out in vain trying if he could not extract some true silver from amongst the lead.

Other examples of the extended elaboration of an image are the vine image in "Wicked Men Useful in their Destruction Only" and the image of the traveler in "The True Christian's Life, A Journey Towards Heaven."[3] Though neither image dominates its sermon as brilliantly as the bellows image does Jer. 6:29–30, both are well developed over substantial portions of the sermons.

3. Both sermons are printed in the *Works*, Worcester rev. ed., *4*, 300–12, and 573–84, respectively.

Much more common than the progressive elaboration of a single dominant image is the massing of several different images about a thematic point. Many a New England preacher scoured Bible, home, fields, and sea for poignant images to illustrate his doctrines, and too often the diverse images were piled upon the doctrine in such profusion that either there was some conflict or discontinuity in imagery, dissipating the force of the doctrine, or the images themselves tended to absorb the attention of the auditory, leaving the doctrine in the background. But Edwards was able to achieve a fine unity-in-diversity in his massed images, so that as he adds more and more images the thematic center of the sermon is more intensely and clearly illuminated. As he elaborates each of several images, often in an interlocking pattern, the dynamic of the argument assumes a centripetal character wherein the complementary conjunctions of the several images coincide precisely with the connotations of the theme that the images are intended to vivify. Thus, the more images added, the sharper the sense of theme or doctrine, and the greater the diversity of images the more intense the light at the central point of fusion. *Sinners* is the renowned exemplar of this technique and certainly the purest example.

On the simplest level, the technique consists of little more than a listing or cataloguing of related images. In the imprecatory sermon, Edwards resorts to such forthright statements quite frequently:

> [The sinner's] heart . . . is a sink of all manner of filthiness and abomination . . . a rendezvous of devils . . . a grave full of dead men's bones and crawling worms, and all manner of nauseous putrafaction . . . a jacques of filthiness and abominable stench. (Ps. 24:7–10.)

After that, Edwards' congregation must have had a "sensible apprehension" of his point, perhaps sufficiently memorable to evoke an instant response to a sermon (Ex. 16:20) preached a little later which asserts that unregenerate sinners "stink" in God's nostrils. The above list, while exhibiting some variety of imagery, is obviously focused upon the repulsiveness of sin and the concept is not so much elaborated by the accumulated images as it is colored. But colored it is, and the very gesture of listing has the familiar incantatory quality of good invective.

Beyond the accretive force of the above example is a kind of synthetic massing of images wherein the images not only accumulate but fuse in new compound images:

> But as the Scripture represents the matter [of hellfire], this fire is not only fire of an ordinary degree of heat. But it is a furnace of fire: Matt. 13:42, "and shall cast them into a furnace of fire." Furnaces are made for the dissolving and refining of metals and such like uses that require an excessive degree of heat. How miserable would a little, venomous worm be, lying forever in such a furnace and yet full of quick sense?
>
> Hell is also called a lake of fire: Rev. 20:15, "and whatsoever was not found written in the book of life was cast into the lake of fire." A lake of liquid fire, like burning brimstone or melted metal; what an expression of misery is this! to be like to be plunged into such a burning lake and there to lie forever! (Luke 16:24.)

In this simple but representative example, Edwards efficiently synthesizes the hearts of two images to make a new and more poignant image. By the insertion of "melted metal" in the second paragraph, he fuses the concreteness and "nearness" of the image of melted metal (most of his congregation having surely seen melted lead) from the furnace image with the sense of vastness and depth suggested by the lake image. By such deft moves Edwards often weaves several images, sometimes quite disparate in themselves, into a single compound image.

One of the most exuberantly imaginative instances of this synthetic massing of images occurs in Ps. 24:7–10, a sermon having the doctrine, "Jesus Christ entering into his glory after his suffering was a sight worthy to be beheld with great admiration." Here, Edwards displays his ability to integrate secular learning with biblical and natural materials in artful imagery.

> When Christ ascended into heaven, after his sore battle or conflict with his enemies in his death and suffering, and his glorious victory over them in his resurrection wherein he appeared to be the Lord strong and mighty, the Lord mighty in battle, the word was proclaimed to the gates of that Eternal City and [to the] door of that everlasting temple, that house not made with hands, eternal in the heavens, that they should be cast up that the King of Glory might come in.
>
> Signifying with what joy and welcome Christ was received in

heaven by his Father and all the heavenly inhabitants when he returned thither after his victory over sin and Satan in his death, when Christ ascended to heaven, the Son led in triumph in a most joyful manner, as the Roman guards when they had been forth on any expedition and had obtained any remarkable victory, when they returned to the city of Rome whence they were sent forth by the supreme authority of that city, used to enter the gates of the city in triumph. The authority of the Roman state gladly opening the gates to 'em and all the Roman people receiving them with shouting and the sound of the trumpet and such like manifestations of joy, with many attendants and their enemies that they had conquered led in triumph at their chariot wheels: so the Psalmist, in Ps. 47:5, speaking of Christ's ascension, says, "God is gone up with a shout, the Lord with [the sound of a trumpet]."

And 'tis probable that the day of Christ's ascension into heaven was the most joyful day that ever was, for there when he ascended, as it were, leading principalities and powers in triumph at his chariot wheels, attended with a glorious retinue of angels and many saints that rose and ascended with their bodies into heaven with him, when Christ thus joyfully ascended, this sight was beheld by the angels and those holy ones. They saw it with great joy and admiration, and therefore, when that word was proclaimed, "Lift up [your heads, O ye gates; and be ye lift up, ye everlasting doors; and the King of Glory shall come in]," they upon it inquire, "Who is this King of Glory?" which is a note of their great admiration at the sight which they beheld.

The devil had been the instrument of Christ's being put to death. He put it into the heart of Judas to [betray Christ], and he stirred up anger and malice in the chief priests and leaders and elders of the people to offer cruelty to him, so that their cruelty and the cross they used as the instrument of his death was, as it were, the devil's sword he used in battle against Christ. And when Christ rose, he got the victory over him and slew Satan, as it were, with his own sword, as David cut off Goliath's head with his own sword. And Christ ascended into heaven in triumph, as it were with the head of Satan in his hand, as David, after he had slain Goliath, went up to Jerusalem with the head of this Philistine in his hand.

"Heathen" triumphal processions and Old Testament episodes (types) are here fused to create a vision as learnedly elaborate and vivid as a passage from *Paradise Lost*. Caesar, the young David, and the resurrected Christ seem upon first consideration to be rather incompatible images—certainly diverse colors for a single portrait. And yet Edwards finds, as he so often does, just those facets in each image that can be successfully wedded, making a new configuration both possible and artistically plausible. Moreover, the tension of metaphorical unity in literal diversity serves to enhance this vision of Christ's triumphant entry into heaven, and the passage lacks only the scope of sustained thematic development to show Edwards at his best.

Though *Sinners* remains Edwards' virtuoso piece, there are a few other sermons in which the handling of imagery is comparably inspired. One sermon worthy of comparison with *Sinners,* and complementary to it in theme, is the concluding sermon of that series (I Cor. 13:1–10) published as *Charity and its Fruits.*[4] "Heaven is a World of Love," as it is entitled in the printed text, is a sermon of Dantean simplicity, scope, and grandeur. In it Edwards depicts the heaven that awaits those who do not slip into hell. Perhaps for the same reasons that many who have read Dante's "Inferno" have not read his "Paradiso," this sermon has not received the attention given *Sinners,* and yet its vision of heaven is perhaps the supreme example of Edwards' systematic massing of images about a theme. The structure of his vision makes it comparable to Dante's *rosa sempiterna*, and in addition to making an exemplary sermon, Edwards has provided in this work a catalogue of his essential divine images:

> Heaven is a part of the creation which God has built for this end, to be the place of his glorious presence. And it is his abode forever. . . . And this renders heaven a world of love; for God is the fountain of love, as the sun is the fountain of light. And therefore the glorious presence of God in heaven fills heaven with love, as the sun placed in the midst of the hemisphere in a clear day fills the world with light. . . . Seeing he is an all-sufficient Being, it follows that he is a full and overflowing and an inexhaustible fountain of love. Seeing he is an unchangeable and eternal Being, he

4. The sermon series was first published by Tryon Edwards in a volume he entitled *Charity and its Fruits; Or, Christian Love as Manifested in Heart and Life* (New York, Robert Carter & Brothers, 1852). As editor, Tryon Edwards significantly modified and amplified JE's text, a practice which has been corrected in the following excerpts.

is an unchangeable and eternal source of love.[5] All the persons who belong to that blessed society are lovely. The Father of the family is so, and so are all his children. The Head of the body is so, and so are all the members.[6]

That world is perfectly bright without any darkness, perfectly clear without spot. There shall be no string out of tune to cause any jar in the harmony of that world, no unpleasant note to cause any discord.

That God who so fully manifests himself there is perfect with an absolute and infinite perfection. That Son of God who is the brightness of his Father's glory appears there in his glory, without that veil of outward meanness in which he appeared in this world, as a root out of dry ground destitute of outward glory. There the Holy Spirit shall be poured forth with perfect sweetness, as a pure river of water of life, clear as crystal . . .[7]

Love is in God as light is in the sun, which does not shine by a reflected light as the moon and planets do; but by his own light, and as the fountain of light. And love flows out from him towards all the inhabitants of heaven. . . . The infinite essential love of God is, as it were, an infinite and eternal mutual holy energy between the Father and the Son, a pure, holy act whereby the Deity becomes nothing but an infinite and unchangeable act of love, which proceeds from both the Father and the Son.

. . . And the saints and angels are secondarily the subjects of holy love, not as in whom love is as in an original seat, as light is in the sun which shines by its own light, but as it is in the planets which shine by reflecting the light of the sun. And this light is reflected in the first place and chiefly back to the sun itself.[8]

The soul which only had a little spark of divine love in it in this world shall be, as it were, wholly turned into love; and be like the sun, not having a spot in it, but being wholly a bright, ardent flame.[9]

---

5. Jonathan Edwards, *Charity and Its Fruits,* ed. Paul Ramsey, in *The Works of Jonathan Edwards* (New Haven, Yale Univ. Press, 1989), *8,* 369. See Ramsey's extensive discussion and exhibits relating to the recovery of JE's original text.
6. Ibid., p. 370.
7. Ibid., p. 371.
8. Ibid., p. 373–74.
9. Ibid., p. 374–75.

All things shall flourish there in an eternal youth. Age will not diminish anyone's beauty or vigor, and there love shall flourish in everyone's breast, as a living spring perpetually springing, or as a flame which never decays. And the holy pleasure shall be as a river which ever runs, and is always clear and full.[1]

And all this in a garden of love, the Paradise of God, where everything has a cast of holy love, and everything conspires to promote and stir up love, and nothing to interrupt its exercises; where everything is fitted by an all-wise God for the enjoyment of love under the greatest advantages. And all this shall be without any fading of the beauty of the objects beloved, or any decaying of love in the lover, and any satiety in the faculty which enjoys love.[2]

All shall stand about the God of glory, the fountain of love, as it were opening their bosoms to be filled with those effusions of love which are poured forth from thence, as the flowers on the earth in a pleasant spring day open their bosoms to the sun to be filled with his warmth and light, and to flourish in beauty and fragrancy by his rays. Every saint is as a flower in the garden of God, and holy love is the fragrancy and sweet odor which they all send forth, and with which they fill that paradise. Every saint there is as a note in a concert of music which sweetly harmonizes with every other note, and all together employed wholly in praising God and the Lamb; and so all helping one another to their utmost to express their love of the whole society to the glorious Father and Head of it, and [[to pour back]] love into the fountain of love, whence they are supplied and filled with love and with glory.[3]

Though they give no adequate view of the sermon's structure or argument, these excerpts do represent the heart of Edwards' imagery—in this and most other sermons presenting the ecstatic dimension of religion.

The diverse images that are here fused and interfused, coalescing about the central image of the Deity as a bright aureole signifying refulgent love, constitute a compendium of such crucial image groups in Edwards' thought that a cursory survey of them would seem most appropriate.

1. Ibid., p. 383.
2. Ibid., p. 385.
3. Ibid., p. 386. Double brackets indicate text from Tryon Edwards' edition.

First there is the absolutely essential light imagery, the stuff of Edwards' various symbols for the spiritual world. Logically enough the sun, the seemingly eternal and inexhaustible source of light and life, is the pervasive symbol for God. The image is divided into its facets to symbolize the Trinity:

> The Father is as the substance of the sun. The Son is as the brightness and glory of the disk of the sun, or that bright and glorious form under which it appears to our eyes. The Holy Ghost is as the heat and powerful influence which acts upon the sun itself, and being diffusive, enlightens, warms, enlivens, and comforts the world. ("Miscellanies," no. 370.)

The sun's most obvious effects upon the world provide the basic symbols for the direct influence of God in human affairs. Thus, "the various sorts of rays and their beautiful colors do well represent the various beautiful graces and virtues of the spirit, and I believe were designed on purpose, and therefore the rainbow is a sign of the Covenant" ("Miscellanies," no. 362). Stars, moon (as reflector), flames, lamps, and candles are some of the other more prominent light images.

The sky, the metaphor of heaven, is one of the less prominent of Edwards' images, but its various aspects play a significant role in his symbolism. The sky and its blue color suggest the future state of the saints ("Shadows," nos. 21 and 114), and such phenomena as clouds, winds, thunder, and lightning are invested with divine significations.

From the earth comes the image of the garden, including images related to farming, and images of plants, trees, vines, and flowers. This family of images is perhaps second only to light imagery in its prevalence throughout Edwards' sermons. One of the most important and interesting clusters of images in this family relates to the practice of grafting ("Shadows," no. 166), used by Edwards to symbolize the mysterious union between Christ and the church and individual saints.

The river (-stream-ocean) image, in its various avatars, is almost as important as the garden image. Moreover, Edwards' speculations on the river images ("Shadows," nos. 15, 22, 71, 77, 78) and his use of them in sermons indicate a very important symbolic function of the group: presenting his crucial (and sometimes ambiguous) speculations on time, and the relationship between God's works and time.

From man's immediate being and province, Edwards takes images relating to the human body, the home, the family, and the church society. All of these are presented in one way or another as microcosms, and the more concrete images such as the body are frequently used to develop the more abstract, such as the church society ("Shadows," nos. 130 and 193), though all ultimately relate to the universe as a God-invested cosmos. Edwards often delights in dwelling upon the harmonious relationships between the parts that compose one of these images, though he is also ready to utilize the "dark underside" when appropriate.

Also from the human province, though not in practice often directly related to it, are images of musical sounds. For Edwards, who displays some musical culture, music represents harmony, and harmony is taken to be the primary factor in all beauty.[4] The beauties of musical harmony are usually attributed to the heavenly sphere (as in the sermon excerpts above) and symbolize the perfection of all relationships there.

So far, this list of images and image groups has presented essentially static images; but there is one image in the sermon excerpts above that is eminently dynamic: the fountain. A "supportive image" usually fused with another, the fountain is nevertheless one of Edwards' most important images, signifying a creative process or dramatic outpouring. Almost as prevalent as light imagery, the fountain usually appears as one aspect of the following central images: the sun, the river (a kind of horizontal fountain into the sea), the vine or tree (slow-motion fountains because of the life-giving sap systems), and the heart. In a few instances the image is used alone to indicate a spring of water, but most often it is Edwards' device for calling attention to the dynamic quality in other images, and thence to the underlying dynamism of the powers and principles of the creation.

The centripetal focusing of massed images, each of which is rich with associated meanings for those familiar with Edwards' writings, is thus responsible for much of the success of "Heaven is a World of Love." All the main images discussed above are represented in the sermon, but despite the fact that they constitute a veritable survey of Edwards' "positive" images, the sermon is unified and economical in

4. JE, who received some formal training in music during his childhood, defended the singing of hymns in his Northampton congregation, and when writing to Sir William Pepperell about education, insisted that "music, especially sacred music, has a powerful efficacy to soften the heart into tenderness, to harmonize the affections, and to give the mind a relish for objects of a superior character." (Dwight, *Life*, p. 478.)

its development. Edwards often displays the truly integrative imagination of the finest metaphysical poets, and this quality is probably most evident in his handling of imagery.

From these illustrations of Edwards' handling of imagery, it is evident that most of his images, including biblical images, are presented through tropes. There are some metaphors but far more similes, and the reader sometimes becomes aware of insistent qualifiers: "as if," "as it were," and so forth. As he tends to use the more obvious device of the simile, foregoing the dramatic metaphor, so Edwards tempers all of his symbolic images and tropes. He not only insists that each trope be relevant to the doctrine it illustrates, but he insists that it be subservient at all times, never seducing the reader's mind from what should be engaging his attention. In essence, Edwards' is a chaste rhetoric. He gave much thought to developing a theory of tropes, and as usual the Bible was consulted as his first authority. In a sermon (Rev. 21:18; 1723–24) which presents the glories of heaven in the imagery of the vision of Revelation, Edwards states that

> We are not to imagine that this description is a literal description, as if the place of the abode of the blessed should be such a city, so wide, having the walls just so high, having the gates made of such precious stones as are here upon earth, or that the streets of the city are made of literal gold. But we must consider that the thing was represented to John in a vision and, as other visions used to be, by similitudes: by such similitudes as we are capable of receiving, taken from such things as are found upon earth.
>
> Although all things upon earth are insufficient to represent to us these glories, nor are we capable of conceiving of it, yet God condescends, when he speaks of these things, to our way of apprehension. And because we are most apt to [be] affected by those things which we have seen with our eyes and heard with our ears and had experience of, therefore, God has taken his similitudes by which he would shadow forth heaven to us from those things which, although they are but faint shadows, have yet an analogy, and in those things wherein they are compared, a likeness. And the thing resembled differs no otherwise from the similitudes, in no more degrees, than as they are more excellent and glorious.
>
> Amongst the many men that are in the world, some are of one disposition and some of another; some have an inclination to one thing as the chief of all their earthly goods and some to another.

Therefore, eternal life is represented by various similitudes, so as
to suit to the disposition of everyone. There is nothing that is
esteemed highly by men, that is not sinful, but what the glories
of heaven are likened to.

All biblical imagery that purports to describe the unseen or the spiritual realm is a form of accommodation to man's imaginative limitations, and a certain amount of suggestiveness or richness of appeal
is required of the similitudes in order that they may touch all the
members of a diverse auditory; in general, the spiritual is literally
sensationalized.

Scriptural metaphor is suggestive rather than precise, but Edwards
insists it is true to meaning in terms of human experience:

> . . . the Scripture representations of the misery of the damned
> are not hyperbolical. They are not to be looked upon as false and
> incredible, nor to be taken in any sense below their proper sig-
> nification.

> But these things that are used as similitudes, instead of exceeding
> the reality, are only faint images and shadows of the torments of
> hell. And therefore we find everything that gives an idea of an
> extreme misery is used to set forth hell's torments, because no
> one is sufficient to express it. (Rom. 9:22; 1730.)

In a sermon on Luke 16:24, he presses the point even further:

> But when metaphors are used in Scripture about spiritual
> things, the things of another world, they fall short of the literal
> truth, for those things are the ultimate, the very highest things
> that are aimed at by all metaphors and similitudes.

> God's aim, when he tells us about hell, is not to set it out with
> uncertain metaphors and similitudes, but really to let us know
> what hell is. 'Tis unreasonable to think any otherwise.

> So that we may very rationally conclude that the similitudes that
> are used in Scripture about hell don't go beyond the truth. That
> metaphor of fire will probably be no metaphor after the resur-
> rection.

Thus, while admitting that the images and tropes of the Bible are
"aids to reflection," Edwards argues that they are more true, in a
literal sense, than false, and that the use of them in preaching would
be no error so long as the preacher did not *understate* them.

Finally, in his second sermon on Rom. 9:22 (1741), Edwards sanctions, at least by implication, the free play of the preacher's imagination in his attempts to suggest the nature of the spiritual world:

> . . . in hell the wicked will be the subjects of every kind of suffering that their nature dreads, [or] that which is equivalent to it.
> . . . every kind of fear or dread that human nature is the subject of is an affection that the creator and disposer of the world has implanted in human nature, and no affection that God has put into human nature shall be in vain or without some use.
> And so whatever else you can think [of] that you find seems very horrible to you, and that your nature shrinks at the thought of, if you continue unrepentant and live and die unconverted, it will come upon you, either that very thing or that which is fully answerable to it.

The principle would apply likewise to virtuous yearnings and the joys of heaven. Thus Edwards defends the right of the preacher to stretch his imagination in depicting the spiritual realm through metaphors and similes. For even non-scriptural tropes and symbolic images, such as those fabricated from personal experience and the power of the imagination, are ultimately under the control of God.

However liberal or experimental Edwards seems in such statements, in his study he strove to determine the limitations of a responsible and realistic rhetoric. In his "Notes on the Scripture," "Miscellaneous Observations on the Holy Scriptures," "Notes on the Apocalypse," "Miscellanies," "Shadows of Divine Things," and "Types" he devotes much attention to speculation on matters that are as literary and rhetorical as they are theological. Likewise, many of his sermons are preoccupied with the specifically literary dimension of passages from the Bible. All this was not unusual for a minister of the English Puritan tradition, of course, but the scope, depth, and imaginative vitality of his work set it apart. At the heart of these literary-theological studies was an attempt to define a vocabulary that would bridge the apparent gap between the eternal world of spiritual reality and the Lockean world of sensational experience in which men lived. Though the existence of the world as an idea in the mind of God might be demonstrably "true" ("The Mind," no. 13), the observant and practical minister knew that as far as the members of his flock were concerned, the world of concrete phenomena perceived through the senses was "real" ("The Mind," no. 34). In order to bridge that crucial gap—as Newton had bridged the gap between physical phenomena and the abstract principle of gravity—and, in doing so, give his flock a greater chance of recognizing the "supernatural light," Edwards had to find both an authoritative sanction for the undertaking and a way of relating his vocabulary to those orthodox religious principles that he wished, ultimately, to uphold and substantiate. Finally, inasmuch as his intended auditory would have a higher percentage of New England farmers than members of the Royal Society, the "new vocabulary" had to have currency with the commonalty or nothing at all would be accomplished.

Up against seemingly insuperable odds, Edwards turned once again to his basic text for all studies, the Bible. There, in the New Testament, he found the luminous paradigm:

> The scope of the chapter [Heb. 9]: to show how the things of the law and first covenant were types, shadows of things under the gospel state, and how much more excellent the antitypes.
>
> There is a parallel run between the tabernacle and heaven, between the sacrifices of bulls, goats, and calves, and the sacrifice of Christ.

He had long been aware of the practice of typological interpretation; in fact, the passage quoted above comes from a sermon (Heb. 9:27; 1722) written at the very beginning of his career before he began making his notebooks of scripture commentary. And "the types" should have been familiar to his congregation, as typology in one form or another had had currency since the days of the Fathers in the Christian church and was increasingly popular among theologically conservative preachers in the New England of Edwards' day.[5] The first two volumes of his "Notes on the Scripture" show Edwards himself to have been not only aware of the practice of interpreting types but an ardent practitioner. Moreover, he saw the great value of the types as artistic vehicles of communication:

5. For discussion of the history of typology including JE's milieu, see the introduction to Perry Miller's *Images or Shadows of Divine Things* (New Haven, Yale Univ. Press, 1948), the essays by G. W. H. Lampe and K. J. Woollcombe in *Essays on Typology* (Naperville, Studies in Biblical Theology, No. 22, 1957), the special typology issue of *Early American Literature*, 5 (Spring 1970), which includes an extensive checklist of works on the subject (separately bound as Part 2), *Literary Uses of Typology: From the Late Middle Ages to the Present*, ed. Earl Miner (Princeton, Princeton Univ. Press, 1977), and Mason I. Lowance, Jr., *The Language of Canaan: Metaphor and Symbol in New England from the Puritans to the Transcendentalists* (Cambridge, Harvard Univ. Press, 1980).

The principles of human nature render types a fit method of instruction. It tends to enlighten and illustrate, and to convey instruction with impression, conviction and pleasure, and to help the memory. These things are confirmed by man's natural delight in the imitative arts, in painting, poetry, fables, metaphorical language, and dramatic performances. This disposition appears early in children.[6]

Thus, as the years passed and his notebooks proliferated, he kept typology always in the foreground of his meditations. Perhaps his final statement on conventional typology is that written at the head of his notebook entitled "Types":[7]

TYPES: texts of Scripture that seem to justify our supposing the Old Testament state of things was a typical state of things and that, not only the canons of the law were typical, but that their history and state and constitution of the nation, and their state and circumstances, were typical. It was, as it were, a typical world.

So far, one might call Edwards an avid typologist, but not notably different from the more conventional typologists of the late seventeenth century.

However, since the publication of Perry Miller's edition of *Images or Shadows of Divine Things* in 1948, it has been evident that Edwards did not stop with conventional typology in his search for a new rhetoric. After all, conventional typology was preoccupied with linking the Old Testament to the New; what Edwards wanted was a "vertical typology,"[8] something to link the "true" and the "real" worlds in a

6. Dwight, *Works*, 9, 110.

7. The small (ten leaves, octavo, bound in gray paper), half-filled notebook entitled simply "Types" is apparently one of the later notebooks, ca. 1747–50. All of its entries appear to have been made within a few years at most. Though it contains some lists of types or images with Scripture references, it is primarily devoted to the theory of typology as ultimately interpreted by JE. Thus, it is a kind of theoretical companion volume to "Shadows." Apparently, Miller did not know of "Types," perhaps because it is in the Andover Collection.

8. The term "vertical typology" attempts to define JE's peculiar innovations in typological interpretation; it suggests his conception of functioning hierarchy within a monistic cosmos. Although his application of typological methodology to nature and non-biblical history makes his thought comparable to that of allegorists or Platonic exegetes, JE is to be differentiated from them because of his apparent insistence upon the actual organic unity, temporal and spatial, of the cosmos. Obviously influenced by the new science in his youth, and familiar with the work of Newton, JE envisioned a single cosmos, the ideal aspect of which was eternal, and hence "true," and the subjective sense of which was "real."

simple, "sensible idea." Early in his speculations, he is obviously testing the boundaries between "types," "images," "shadows," and "similitudes." He finally began to move steadily in the direction of "vertical typology":

> For indeed, the whole outward creation, which is but the shadows of beings, is so made as to represent spiritual things. It might be demonstrated by the wonderful agreement in thousands of things, much of the same kind as is between the types of the Old Testament and their antitypes, and by there being spiritual things being so often and continually compared with them in the Word of God. And it's agreeable to God's wisdom that it should be so, that the inferior and shadowy parts of his works should be made to represent those things that are more real and excellent, spiritual and divine, to represent the things that immediately concern himself and the highest parts of his work. Spiritual things are the crown and glory, the head and soul, the very end, and alpha and omega of all other works. What, therefore, can be more agreeable to wisdom than that they should be so made as to shadow them forth? ("Miscellanies," no. 362.)

His "early idealism," his sentimentalist psychology, and his Newtonian search for the underlying principles of force in the spiritual cosmos: all could be reconciled in this new typology. Moreover, the true "natural" types, if they could be positively identified, would furnish the preacher with a vocabulary that synthesized instruction, illustration, and proof. The type is, in literary terms, fundamentally an image; thus, such a device could be both true (according to the analogy of the world) and real (according to the evidence of the senses). Consequently, there might not need to be a distinction between a new way of thinking and the old way of talking; one might really do both simultaneously. If natural phenomena were invested with spiritual principles, to apprehend the image would be to apprehend the principle, and to apprehend the principle is to see the truth:

To the mathematically "deficient" JE, Newton's language of mathematics was a truly esoteric, mysterious language, yet it had precisely defined the unity of the "true" and the "real" in the "lower" physical universe or shadow world. Thus, using modern physical science as a suggestive model and biblical typology as a guide and precedent, JE sought for the language that would permit efficient definition of the unity of the "true" and the "real" on the highest (spiritual) level. The eternal act of God's will and the fleeting subjective sensations in men might be successfully discovered as one, just as Newton had perceived an eternal principle in a falling apple.

There is no other properly spiritual image but idea, although there may be another spiritual thing that is exactly like [it]. Yet one thing's being exactly like another don't make it the proper image of that thing. If there be one distinct spiritual substance exactly like another, yet [it] is not the proper image of the other; though one be made after the other, yet it is not any more an image of the first than the first is of the last. . . . Seeing the perfect idea of a thing is, to all intents and purposes, the same as seeing the thing; it is not only equivalent to seeing of it, but it is seeing of it, for there is no other seeing but having an idea. Now by seeing a perfect idea, so far as we see it, we have it; but it can't be said of anything else that, in seeing of it, we see another, speaking strictly, except it be the very idea of the other. ("Miscellanies," no. 260.)

As he wrote in entry no. 67 of "The Mind," "An idea is only a perception, wherein the mind is passive or rather subjective."

The preacher, by providing his congregation with verbal archetypes of the spiritual world through evoking images from the sensuous world, might place them face to face with a spiritual truth that seemed as near and real as nature and history. As Perry Miller has observed,

As against the degraded plain style, with its irresponsible tropes, its reliance on argumentation and meditation, he set up the idea of a pure style. In his art, the rhetorical figures would once more be subjected to the rule of the idea, and the supreme figures would no longer be ingenious compounds of one thing with another but perceptions of the actual identity of those things which are truly united in the eternal system of things.[9]

What right did Edwards think he had to undertake such a task, and what were his anticipations of success? He was no New England Philo Judaeus; he was cautious and precise enough in all his inquiries to seem a very scientist. Perhaps he even had to talk himself into it despite misgivings, as he appears to be doing in these passages from "Types":

To say that we must not say that such things are types of these and those things unless the Scripture has expressly taught us that

9. *Images or Shadows*, p. 23.

they are so is as unreasonable as to say that we are not to interpret any prophecies of Scripture, or apply them to these and those events, except we find them interpreted to our hand . . . for by the Scripture it is plain that innumerable other things are types that are not interpreted in Scripture.

If we may use our own understanding and imagination not at all in interpreting types, and must not conclude anything at all to be types but what is expressly said to be and [is] explained in Scripture, then the church is under the old [Dispensation]. . . .

If, indeed, there was such a thing as a work of redemption progressing in time, it would be only reasonable to expect God and the spiritual world to be drawing ever nearer and becoming more "visible." As for the nature of the problem posed by typology,

> Types are a certain sort of language, as it were, in which God is wont to speak to us, and there is as it were a certain idiom in that language which is to be learnt the same that the idiom of any language is; viz. by good acquaintance with the language, either by being naturally raised up in it or having it by education. But this is not the way in which corrupt man first learnt divine language, as by much use and acquaintance, together with a good taste or judgment, [but] by comparing one thing with another and having our senses, as it were, exercised to discern it, which is the way that adult persons must come to speak any language, and in its true idiom, that is not their native tongue. ("Types.")

There are, of course, dangers in such an undertaking:

> Great care should be used, and we should endeavor to be well and thoroughly acquainted, or we shall never understand [or] have a right notion of the idiom of the language. If we go to interpret divine types without this, we shall be just like one that pretends to speak any language that ben't thoroughly learnt. If we shall use many [incorrect] expressions that fail entirely of the proper beauty of the language, they are very harsh in the ears of those that are well versed in the language.
>
> First, to lay down that persons ought to be exceeding careful in interpreting of types, that they don't give way to a wild fancy. [Second,] not to fix [on] an interpretation unless warranted by some hint in the New Testament of its being the true interpretation, or a lively figure and representation contained or warranted

by an analogy to other types that we interpret on sure grounds. ("Types.")

But all things considered, though "God han't expressly explained all the types of Scripture, [he] has done so much as is sufficient to teach us the language" ("Types"). On the basis of such a conclusion, Edwards began a collection of the "divine idiom" he saw in the world about him.

"Shadows of Divine Things" is one of Edwards' major specialized notebooks, and compiling its 212 entries occupied him, on and off, for thirty years. Containing primarily "vertical types" from nature and history, the notebook (like his other long-term notebooks) manifests phases in its development. In the early entries, Edwards is evidently enthralled with the learning of God's language and the entries have an aura of wonder and enthusiasm about them; it is enough just to record the wonderful idiom. As the years pass, however, the entries seem to become more perfunctory in tone and, at the same time, more completely analyzed and elaborated. Edwards also manifests an increasing tendency to return to previously recorded images as if worrying them. Finally, in the late entries, he resorts more and more to quoting from other authors. It is as if over the years he became a little troubled by his enterprise, as if he needed more and more confirmation and enrichment of his earlier efforts.

There are signs, however, that this project may have been something of a problem from the very beginning. For "Shadows" is his only notebook with so many alternate titles, and some of them have quite different implications from others (see Chapter II, pp. 44–45 n.). Moreover, one might wonder why Edwards did not use the word "type" in one of them. Meticulous, cautious, and judicious by nature, he seems to have been dubious about the precise nature of his collection of verbal specimens.

He apparently found adequate sanction for the words "image" and "shadow" in Heb. 10:1; at least, by the time he attempted formulating the theory of his enterprise in "Types," he made a point of copying in the passage,

> Chapter 10:1 For the law having a shadow of good things to come and not the very image of the things, etc.

The passage distinguishes between "image" and "shadow" very pointedly, and despite the fact that he could suggest both terms in alternate titles and referred to the notebook in cross-references by either term, Edwards himself carefully differentiated "image" from "shadow." Thus, in a notebook meditation on the types of the Old Testament before the coming of Christ, he observes that

> On several accounts, the shadow of a thing is an exceeding imperfect representation of it, and yet has such a resemblance that it has a most evident relation to the thing of which it is the shadow. Again, shadows are dark resemblances; though there be a resemblance, yet the image is accompanied with darkness or hiding of the light: the light is beyond the substance so that it is hid. . . . the shadow [is] ever accompanied with darkness and obscurity . . . ("Notes on the Scripture," no. 288.)

On the other hand, in a comment on Heb. 1:3 in the interleaved Bible (p. 798), Edwards speculates on the meaning of the words "express image" in this manner:

> It seems to be well translated "express image," meaning an image that exactly answers the original as the impression does the seal. But it may be observed that whatsoever is the express or exact image of a thing, is in the Apostle's sense equivalent or of equal value with that thing, it having a full answerableness.

These passages reveal the connotations Edwards saw in the traditional terms "image" and "shadow." For him, they were not synonymous, and thus the apparent confusion of them in naming and referring to this collection of notes indicates a real apprehensiveness, or at least a tentativeness, in his personal evaluation of the new "language."

Within the collection itself, there are signs of problems. As early as entry no. 25, Edwards notes that there are things in the world which are "not properly shadows and images of divine things that yet are significations of them, as children's being born crying is a significance of their being born to sorrow," and by entry no. 169, there is an almost wistful quality in the observation that "some [images] are very bright, some you can scarcely determine . . . as there is the light of twilight, signifying the approaching sun." The more extensive the quest became, the more likely it appeared that the efficient spiritual image or "vertical type" might turn out to be nothing more than a fusty trope, or a mere Flavelian meditation upon local scenes and manners. Edwards had set his sights very high and he was too diligent in his studies to risk losing what ground he had gained in a rhetorical swamp. Within the book of "Shadows" itself he had left a reminder of where to look for standards when the going got rough:

> The book of Scripture is the interpreter of the book of nature two ways, viz. by declaring to us those spiritual mysteries that are indeed signified and typified in the constitution of the natural world; and secondly, in actually making application of the signs and types in the book of nature as representations of those spiritual mysteries in many instances. (No. 156.)

Taking heed of this reminder, Edwards made a note to himself, sometime around 1750, in his "Subjects of Enquiry":

> Read the Scriptures, at least such parts as are most likely, in order to observe how the visible things of the creation are made use of as representations and types of spiritual things, that I may note them in my book about images of divine things. (P. 19.)

Perhaps after more than twenty years' work on "Shadows," Edwards made this note with a sigh. But if he had to return at last to the grammar school of the Scriptures, he would—anything to put the rigor into his studies necessary to avoid fatal solecisms. At the back of "Shadows," on a blank leaf, there is a single column of seven entries written in a late hand under the heading, "Scriptures." It is a list of images or "natural" types from the Bible (flies, rivers, valleys, and so on), several of them having textual references.[1] There is also a loose, two-leaf folio sheet, written in the same hand as "Scriptures," which contains some thirty-eight additional entries of the same character, frequently with extensive textual listings.

From this evidence, it is obvious that Edwards worked hard in his last years to establish scripturally authoritative standards for assessing the contents of "Shadows." Did he ever achieve the precision and certainty he craved? A partial answer must be that, according to his own statements in the letter to the college trustees and the circumstantial evidence of his extant manuscript notebooks, he was still very much in the midst of his investigation at the time of his sudden death in 1758. A more satisfying answer, perhaps, is that provided by Edwards in a late entry in "Types":

> I expect, by very ridicule and contempt, to be called a man of

---

1. This list was not acknowledged in Miller's *Images or Shadows*.

a very fruitful brain and copious fancy, but they are welcome to it. I am not ashamed to own that I believe that the whole universe—heaven, earth, air, and seas—and the divine compilations and history of the Holy Scriptures be full of images of divine things—as full as a language is of words—and that the multitude of these things that I have mentioned are but a very small part of what is really intended to be signified and typified by those things; but that there is reason for persons to be learning more and more of this language, and seeing more of that which is declared in it, to the end of the world without discerning all.

This curious passage, with its combination of self-conscious defensiveness and passionate affirmation, seems to reflect Edwards' final doubt about the probability of his mastering the divine idiom while never once doubting the reality of its existence. Moreover, it suggests that Edwards may have finally decided to cease attempting identification of particular divine images while continuing the search for the larger patterns—the "divine syntax," as it were—in nature and history.

Whatever one may think of the philosophical and theological qualities of "Shadows of Divine Things" and related writings, he must recognize their literary significance. In his life-long study of images, types, metaphors, and symbols, Edwards went far toward mastering the poetic archetypes of his community and systematizing a mythos of his civilization. He also developed a personal style that is both concrete and suggestive, seemingly colloquial and yet richly allusive. Living at the end of one literary era, he drew upon the best in his theological heritage, combined it with some of the most advanced literary practice of his day, and thus produced several of the most memorable works of the American Puritan culture.

Although the development of Edwards' mastery over imagery and metaphor—from the youthful productions characterized by vivid imagery and a naturally particularistic imagination, to the mature triumphs of systematic imagery and symbolism in the greatest sermons—may provide the most important and engrossing chapter in the history of his sustained literary efforts, there are other aspects of Edwards' art that must be considered, both because of their intrinsic importance and because of their being inextricably bound up in the progress of his tropes and imagery. These techniques relate to figurative language and the internal structuring of his sermons: rhythmic devices, logical structures, and the manipulation of perspective.

Most obvious and simple, yet frequently most important and effective, are the rhythmic devices of repetition and parallelism. Indeed, it has been remarked that "repetition of words and constructions is the essence of his style."[2] His earlier sermon manuscripts indicate that a tendency to repetition was as innate in Edwards as his love of concrete images and details.[3] But genius and toil turned what might well have been a rhetorically fatal vice into a source of formidable literary power. The use of simple repetition in the Scripture attracted Edwards' attention, and in "Notes on the Scripture," no. 325, he observes that "such a repetition or doubling of a word, according to the idiom of the Hebrew tongue, is as much as our speaking a word once with a very extraordinary emphasis. . . . it sometimes signifies certainty, at other times extremity, and sometimes both." The notably soft-spoken and undemonstrative preacher could put such an aid to good use.

Even the simplest repetition is carefully calculated to call attention to essential points, and to take advantage of the variegated rhythms of English prose. There is, for instance, the statement of doctrine in a sermon on Eccles. 6:4,

> There are some persons that are born miserable and live in darkness, and die in darkness, and when they are dead go into eternal darkness.

In the course of the sermon, Edwards picks up the verbal lead and discusses "a positive darkness . . . a darkness that can be felt . . . blackness of darkness." A comparable use of repetition occurs in the statement of doctrine in "Glorious Grace."

> The gospel dispensation is finished wholly and entirely in free and glorious grace; there is glorious grace [which] shines in every part of the great work of redemption. The foundation is laid in

2. Faust and Johnson, *Selections*, p. cxii. In this trait JE is identified with a rich tradition of English homiletics, as is suggested by the fact that Dudley Fenner's *The Artes of Logike and Rethorike* (Middleburg, 1584) devotes no fewer than three chapters to the repetition of word forms and three to repetition of syntactical structures.

3. For instance, in Matt. 16:17, JE originally wrote, "He is the author of the knowledge of all moral prudence; he is the author of all knowledge and skill . . . ," but revised it to read, "He is the author of all moral prudence, and of all knowledge and skill . . . ," thus eliminating the redundant "knowledge" and the needless parallel construction. There are enough such revisions in his sermons—most notably in the 1720s and early 1730s—to indicate that he tended to lapse into pointless repetition of words and constructions.

grace; the superstructure is reared in grace, and the whole is finished in glorious grace.

"Glorious Grace" is one of Edwards' earliest sermons, but he is already an artist, making the repetition of "glorious" and "grace" evocative of the ringing of festive bells.

Many times, of course, Edwards uses repetition in sermon passages simply to emphasize the importance of a point local to that passage, as in this example from "Wicked Men's Slavery to Sin,"

> So that these discourses were delivered in the most public manner, at the most public time, and in the most public place that could be: before the whole nation of the Jews, and many of other nations who went up to Jerusalem to worship.

From the last two examples, it is clear that Edwards employed alliteration and risked unconventional usage in order to give greater emphasis to the repeated words and, sometimes, to build a crescendo within the passage.

A more elaborate and extensive incremental repetition is also evident in the earliest sermons. Sometimes, a head within a sermon may involve the exploitation of a word from the text or doctrine that has not been emphasized previously in the development of the sermon; such is the case in the second proposition under the Doctrine of Dan. 4:35, a sermon having the doctrine that "God doth whatever he pleases."

> II. The sovereignty of God in doing whatever he pleases . . .
>
> He created the earth as he pleased; he made a place for the sea where he pleased; he raised the mountains where he pleased, and sunk the valleys where he pleased. He created what sort of creatures to inhabit the earth and waters he pleased, and when he pleased he brought a flood of waters and covered the whole earth, and destroyed all its inhabitants.
>
> And when he pleases, he'll dissolve this curious frame of the world and break all to pieces and set it on fire, when the earth and all the works that are therein shall be burnt up and the heavens shall be dissolved and rolled together as a scroll; when God pleases, he'll roll all together as when a man takes down a tent. In such things as these relating to the material world does God manifest his sovereignty.

Sometimes, apropos of nothing earlier in the sermon but rather a disposition in his congregation that he wished to toy with, Edwards seizes a word or phrase and plays with its connotations through incremental repetition. Here is an instance from a sermon on Prov. 9:12.

> 1. Such is the nature of things that there is a necessary connection in point of justice between those ways [of sin] and utter ruin. Such is the nature of those wicked ways, and such is the nature of justice, and such is the holy and righteous nature of God, and such is the nature of moral government, and such is the nature of the constitution of the world, that a connection between ways of sin, if continued in, and the utter ruin of the sinner is requisite and unavoidable. God is not to blame that justice is of such a nature as it is, and he is not to blame for being himself of a just and righteous nature. And therefore, that misery and ruin that is the consequence of sin may be looked upon as necessary, and not merely arbitrary.

The play upon "nature" and "necessary," enhanced by the insistent repetition of "such is the nature," give the passage a lively and righteously mischievous quality that is by no means unprecedented in Edwards' sermons.[4] It may be assumed that the congregation had a new sense of the nature of things after that passage.

These samples have demonstrated simple and incremental patterns of repetition in single passages, but much of Edwards' best repetition is of a larger pattern; indeed, in many cases a single pattern dominates a whole Doctrine, Application, or even an entire sermon. Edwards' earliest extant sermon, "Christian Happiness," is dominated by repeated variants of the doctrinal statement. Below are concentrated the main segments of the pattern.

> Doctrine. A good man is a happy man, whatever his outward condition is.
>
> . . . and we are now to show that the state of a good man is such, whatever his outward circumstances are, but we shall first observe . . .

4. A comparably witty passage involving similar incremental repetition is to be found in "Great Guilt No Obstacle to the Pardon of the Returning Sinner," *Works*, Worcester rev. ed., *4*, 426, 3rd paragraph (head I.).

Secondly, the good man is happy in whatsoever condition he is in, and that [is] because . . .

How happy, then, must the condition of such a man be. Let any man now ask himself . . .

Secondly, the godly man is happy in whatever circumstances he is placed because . . .

. . . but the time would fail to stay to enumerate all the happinesses of a good man, even in this life. . . .

And now I hope I have sufficiently cleared it up: the godly man is happy in whatsoever worldly circumstances he is placed.

Use

Inference 1. Then we may infer that the godly man need not be anxious about his worldly condition whatsoever. This no man in the world can deny that grants what has been asserted. For surely, if none of those worldly afflictions are able to do him any hurt, and if he is a happy man in the midst of them all . . .

Inference 2. Hence we may see the excellent and desireable nature of true godliness, that which will cause that a man be a happy man in whatsoever condition he is in.

But such is the state of the good man, and however troublesome those afflictions may seem to a good man at present, yet . . .

But you are now exhorted to . . . embrace that which will make you happy men in whatever condition you are in, and whatsoever your outward circumstances are.

You are happy men in whatsoever condition you are; you, for your parts, have got into those ways which are ways of pleasantness and those paths which are paths of peace. You are happy, and you will be happy, in spite of all the world, men and devils.

Eleven separate passages, distributed throughout the Doctrine and Application, reiterate the essential parts of the doctrine statement— "good man," "happy man," and "what(so)ever-outward-condition"— with sufficient emphasis and regularity to dominate the sixteen-page sermon. In the course of the sermon's argument, the "good man" is fully identified, his happiness defined, and the conditions under which he might have to live are delineated; thus, in accordance with the definition of incremental repetition, the repeated terms grow rich with associated meaning as the sermon progresses, and since the terms are themselves interrelated, a vivid notion of Edwards' doctrine gradually emerges. From the passages quoted above, it is obvious that the repeated elements neither prove nor illustrate in themselves; rather, they constitute a dynamic point of reference for both argument and illustration which moves through the sermon relating its various elements to the central idea. In the context of the sermon, the pattern of repetition is never clumsily obtrusive, but rather quietly insistent.

This technique, illustrated above in a very early and unrefined state, was later developed by Edwards into one of his most effective rhetorical devices. In fact, the matured device is so important and unusual that it deserves to be differentiated from "incremental repetition," and I have thus identified it as the "tonic word (or phrase)."[5] Like the tonic chord in music, the tonic word serves as a constant point of reference and foundation for the elaborations and variations which surround it. The somewhat cumbersome series of terms employed in Is. 3:10 is reduced, in the matured device, to a single word, or occasionally a phrase. One instance of a tonic word has already occurred in this chapter in the illustration of another point. "Strange" functions as a tonic word in the sermon on Job 31:3 (above, pp. 211–12).

Another fine example of the tonic word occurs in Eccles. 11:2, a sermon delivered after an earthquake (December 11, 1737). The sermon's doctrine is that "We ought to prepare for whatever changes may come to pass in the world." The sermon is very long (46 leaves) and was delivered in four preaching sessions—a challenge to any real aesthetic unity. But in the first section of the sermon, Edwards begins striking the tonic word introduced in the doctrine:

> Great changes will come. We live in a world of change; the state of mankind is subject to continual changes.

> [The image of the wheels in Ezekiel is] indeed a lively emblem of God's providence towards the world of mankind; such sort of changes do mankind constantly undergo.

5. Originally conceived during studies leading to my Ph.D. dissertation, "The Literary Techniques of Jonathan Edwards" (Univ. of Pennsylvania, 1971), the concept of the tonic as a subliminal reinforcer and thematic point of reference within JE's arguments has only been amplified by subsequent study. Within the form of the sermon presented here, the tonic structure of echoes provides the most comprehensive literary structure uniting the multiple subdivisions of the text.

> There are great changes . . . yet in the womb of providence. . . .

> The time that we live in seems especially to be a time wherein we are called upon to prepare for approaching changes.

In the second and third sections, however, there is little direct use of the word as Edwards discusses specific instances, such as strange natural phenomena, new diseases, the wars of religious factions, and the earthquake at hand—all instances of threatening changes. Only infrequently is there a statement such as, "the first thing that warns us of great approaching change, viz. the prophecy of [the] Scripture." But in the fourth section of the sermon, as he nears his end, Edwards picks up the tonic word with greater frequency:

> . . . we can't be prepared for changes any other way than by getting an interest in things that ben't liable to changes.

> They have that hope that is sure and steadfast, and as an anchor keeps a ship steadfast in a storm, so does the hope of a Christian keep his soul steadfast through the storms and changes of the world.

With a final juxtaposition of "steadfast" and "change," Edwards returns to the tonic word in his conclusion.

So far, only examples of tonic words that continue throughout whole sermons have been represented, and such are certainly the most dramatic. But Edwards often uses a tonic word only within a head, and thus each of several heads may have its own tonic word, as so many separate movements in a musical composition. Usually, a tonic word tends to dominate one of the main divisions of the sermon—Text, Doctrine, or Application—though there are a great many instances, such as the following example from Job 18:15, where a minor head coalesces about its own tonic word. This head concludes the sermon.

> 2. Use of warning to beware of those things that will bring you into danger of its proving [that you are cursed by God] at last.
> 1. Beware of continuing long under gospel calls in rejection of the Lord Jesus Christ.
> 2. Beware of going on in repeated acts of sin against clear light.
> You have lived under the enjoyment of great light. . . . Beware, therefore, of every vicious [act].

You have often had warnings in the word and in providence. Beware of known and allowed wickedness against such warnings.

3. If you would not be followed with God's curse in all your concerns, beware of going on in sin under great mercies. . . .

Beware of going on in sin under such.

And beware of {going on in sin} under special mercies, remarkable deliverances, and answers of prayer for you: have you been healed when dangerously sick? brought back from [the grave]? Rescued when greatly exposed by accident, or whatever other special service you have received? Beware.

Thus, after a gradual increase in the frequency of repetition, the head (and the sermon) ends on the tonic word.

On the whole, the words selected by Edwards to serve as tonic words are remarkable for their plainness. They are common words which have no great suggestiveness or particular vividness. Indeed, some of them—such as "unmixed" in Luke 16:24—seem rhetorically useless. But that is the whole point: to select a word that was so commonplace to every member of the congregation that it would be almost beneath notice. The average tonic word has a clear, because minimal, meaning; it neither suggests much beyond a "simple idea" nor possesses the weighty concreteness of an image. Therefore, it has a kind of "negative capability" which enables it to become the nexus of diverse images, tropes, and ideas, as it "moves" through a passage or sermon via the device of repetition. In its passage, this "naked" term acquires associations from the context of the sermon, and in turn forms that context in such a way that the relationship between the tonic word and its context is analogous to that between the cherry's stone and its fruit. With such a device, Edwards strove to create the conditions in his auditory which predicated "the mind filled with the idea and with all its associates, and then consenting to it."[6]

Parallelism—the repetition of syntactical patterns and structures of thought—is also a major device in Edwards' rhetorical repertory. In the case of parallelism, as in so many other instances, one need not look far for precedents and influences: ". . . the versification of the Bible is of a kind totally unlike that which prevails in English literature. . . . Its underlying principle is found to be the symmetry of clauses in a verse, which has come to be called 'Parallelism.'"[7] Inas-

---

6. Miller, "Sense of the Heart," p. 128.
7. R. G. Moulton, *The Literary Study of the Bible* (New York, 1899), p. 46.

much as Edwards' Bible's verse was printed as prose, and he seems not to have differentiated between the prose and verse in the Bible, I suppose that he took the apparent form of the verse as a model for his own highly rhythmical prose, for Edwards' sermons display a remarkable number of variations on parallelism, several of which are recognized as conventional forms in biblical verse.

Coordination, the simplest form of parallelism, is the dominant structure in Edwardsean syntax. In the unpunctuated sermon manuscripts, the exposition characteristically evolves through a succession of declarative statements and ampersands. Unedited excerpts from a sermon on Ps. 108:4 give the flavor:

> This metaphor [God's mercy is great above the heavens] very naturally signifies in the general a superlative inexpressible & Incomprehensible Greatness & Excellency of the mercy of G. the Expanse of the Heavens is the Greatest & most Extensive thing that we have in view or that we have any notice of by our senses & the height thereof is Immeasurable & Inconceivable

> In G. Infinite Greatness & Infinite Goodness & mercy are joined together the mercy of G. is like a sea or like a deluge noahs flood was so great that it was above the tops of the mountains but the mercy that is in the Heart of G. is greater it is above the heavens and overtops our sins that are like great mountains that are grown up to Heaven

The remarkable thing is that it is as clear as it is, and it is that clear because of the inexorable forward movement of the agglutinative syntax. The formula is essentially that of the ancient storyteller: "and then, and then, and then," although other elements make the total impression far from simple. In this manner of expression, the listeners are given the impression of being led, ever outward and onward, from the point of departure to some unrevealed destination. Or, if one thinks of the auditory as receiving facts, ideas, and experiences, the impression of weight and massiveness is enhanced by the sustained sequence of coordinated units of thought. It is a most simple, yet forceful syntax.

Beyond the fundamental level of coordination, Edwards employs parallelism for various rhetorical effects. One of the more effective devices is the doublet, a pair of words, roughly synonymous, which connotatively supplement each other and, together, enhance a point with the emphasis of concise parallelism. A fine example of the technique occurs in "The Nakedness of Job":

> We have an instance in this chapter of one of the greatest men in the world, in the most prosperous worldly estate and condition, brought to be externally one of the meanest of men . . . a most remarkable instance of the vanity of worldly honors, riches and prosperity. How soon is it gone and lost; how many hundred, yea, thousands of accidents may deprive the most prosperous of all in a little time, and make him most miserable and forlorn?

In addition to emphasizing the point indicated by each doublet, the pairs of words parallel the other pairs, of course, and thus call attention to a pattern of thought: worldly condition-riches-loss-misery.

Edwards frequently employs a more insistent, reduplicative parallelism when he wishes to emphasize a major point, the simple structure enabling him to put forward the maximum number of ideas per word. In Luke 17:9, he insists that God is under no obligation to man, and that "obedience and labors and prayers and tears" do not compromise God's essential freedom:

> This [that God is under no obligation] is certainly plain reason, and if it be, then God don't owe salvation, nor pity, nor pardon, nor the answer of prayers, nor the mitigation of punishment, nor converting, nor assisting grace for any thing that we do in religion, because as we have showed already, he owes us nothing at all, not the least benefit anyway.

With incantatory power, the succession of negations represents so many slamming doors to those who are looking for an easy way out. A comparable use of parallelism occurs in "A Warning to Professors," involving a long series of similarly structured queries, though here the effect is that of a probing surgeon's knife.[8] In both examples, however, the essential effect of the parallelism is to advance the argument at such a rate that the auditor is fully occupied in taking it in, and has little pause to rationalize or reply. It is a rhetoric of brute power.

There is, in all the examples cited above, a kind of rhythmic progression, and all of Edwards' parallel constructions give some sense of crescendo—if only through the impression of rapidly increasing

---

8. *Works*, Worcester rev. ed., *4*, 535.

mass. Some of his most dramatic perorations, however, are achieved through the combination of parallelism and the periodic sentence structure, as in II Kings 7:3–4.

> If you are so wicked that you are like a dead man; yea, if you are so wicked that you are not only dead, but rotten; yea, if you have been dead so long that your bones are dried, yet God can bring you up out of your grave and bring you into the land of Israel.

The gradually altered idea, plus the repeated construction, make this a kind of "incremental parallelism." Such magniloquence is generally reserved for the conclusion of a head or sermon, though less emphatic variants of the pattern, often involving several sentences, may be found whenever Edwards is making a summary within his argument.

Other complex forms of parallelism are employed by Edwards to facilitate juxtaposition, antithesis, and contrast of ideas. Among these is the sustained juxtaposition of two antithetical alternatives, as illustrated in "The Unreasonableness of Indetermination in Religion."[9]

> And there are but two states in this world, a state of sin, and a state of holiness, a natural state, and a converted state. . . . There are but two masters, to one of which we must be reputed the servants, Baal and Jehovah, God and mammon. There are but two competitors for the possession of us, Christ and the devil. There are but two paths, in one of which you are to travel, either in the strait and narrow way which leadeth unto life, or the broad way which leadeth unto destruction.

The sheer weight of the rhetoric and the vivid simplicity of statement make a passage such as this much more powerful than one with a more varied structure. Edwards frequently employs this formula, particularly when concluding a phase of his argument. An expanded version of this juxtaposition through parallelism appears in the "dialogue" passages, the traditional Objection-Answer formula as improved through Edwards' keen sense of verisimilitude and his dramatic flair. One of the better instances of this technique occurs in "Great Guilt No Obstacle to the Pardon of the Returning Sinner," where the minister appears carrying on a realistic debate with an imaginary sinner.[1]

9. *Works*, Worcester rev. ed., *4*, 342.
1. *Works*, Worcester rev. ed., *4*, 426–28.

Whether in the briefer or more expanded form, the movement of this type of parallelism strongly suggests the "characteristically Hebrew" Pendulum Figure that is found throughout the Bible.[2] The figure in Edwards' sermons sets up the same rhythms of thought and emotion as are found in the Bible. Moreover, one can easily see in the sustained or expanded parallelism a significant source of structure. Already, in passages from Job 18:15 (p. 215), Dan. 4:35 (p. 238), and Eccles. 11:2 (pp. 241–42), statements have been presented that reiterate the opening idea more or less in parallel form at the conclusion, making an envelope figure which structures the passage as a unit.[3] Between the sustained parallelism and envelope figures, a prime source of internal structure in Edwards' prose is defined.

Syntactical parallelism, whether simple or complex, brief or sustained, is simply the outward form of a parallelism of ideas, for Edwards, again following the tradition of the Bible, thought in terms of parallels: God and man, heaven and hell, salvation and damnation, conversion and reprobation, and on and on. For every concept, there is its parallel: God the king of the universe, man the king of the world; heaven the city of light, hell the city of darkness; salvation the end of the true saints, damnation the end of the unregenerate, and so forth. Moreover, between the extremes cited here, there are hierarchies of parallels between the Scripture and life, the divine and the mundane, Christ and the church, and so on to men and worms, or possibly spiders. Thus the structures of parallelism in Edwards' sermons are more than rhetorical structures for his theological arguments; the rhetorical gesture of parallelism is itself a theological argument. "Christ, the Light of the World" presents a veritable symphony of parallelism—simple and complex, brief and sustained—as well as a synthesis of most of the techniques and devices that have been discussed thus far in this chapter. In his lyrical celebration of Christ, Edwards harmonizes the idiom of the Scripture, images, similes, metaphors, types, repetition, and parallelism in an exuberant style characteristic of the sermons of the twenties. The doctrine of this sermon is, "Jesus Christ is the light of the world;" I quote from the third Observation under the second Proposition of the Doctrine.

2. For a discussion of the Pendulum Figure and its importance as a mode of Hebrew thought and expression, see Moulton, pp. 58–59, et passim.

3. The significance of the Envelope Figure in the Bible is discussed in Moulton, pp. 56–58, 543.

Third. And lastly, light is of a quickening, reviving, and refreshing nature. It revives one that hath been long in darkness again to behold the light; so Christ Jesus revives the souls that come unto him by faith. Here you may run a parallel between the sun and Jesus Christ, the Sun of Righteousness.

1. As the sun, when it rises, all things are thereby revived and awakened out of sleep and silence, so when Jesus Christ shines into the souls of men, they are revived out of their deep and dead sleep of sin. When the sun arises, the world that before was all still and silent, and seemed to be dead, now is revived and raised up by the light thereof, and all things begin to stir and move: things seem to have new life put into them; man rises out of his sleep and sets about his business; the husbandman goeth forth to his labor, the beasts come out of their dens, the birds begin to sing and chant forth their notes, and the world is again put into motion. So it is in spiritual matters with respect to Christ. Before he shines into men's souls, they are dead and dull in a deep sleep, are not diligent at their work, but lie still and sleep and do nothing respecting their souls. All their affections are dead, dull and lifeless; their understandings are darkened with the dark shades of spiritual night, and there is nothing but spiritual sleep and death in their souls.

But when Christ arises upon them, then all things begin to revive, the will and affections begin to move, and they set about the work they have to do. They are now awakened out of their sleep: whereas they were still before, now they begin to be diligent and industrious; whereas they were silent before, now they begin to sing forth God's praises. Their graces now begin to be put into exercise, as flowers send forth a fragrancy when the sun shines upon them.

2. As the sun by his returning influences causes clouds and storms and cold to fly before it, so doth Jesus Christ, the cold, tempests, and clouds of the soul. In the winter season, the heavens are frequently overcast with clouds that hide the pleasing light of the sun; the air is disturbed with winds, storms and tempests, and all things are chilled with frost and cold. The rivers and streams are shut up with ice, the earth is covered with snow, and all things look dreadful, but when the sun returns with its warming influences, the heavens are cleared of dark clouds and the air stilled from tempests, the ice and snow and cold are fled. So the souls

of men in their natural state are like winter, perpetually disturbed with the storms of lust and vice, and a raging conscience; their souls are all beclouded with sin and spiritual darkness. But when Christ comes with his warming influences, things are far otherwise: their minds are calm and serene, warmed with holiness and religion, and the clear sunshine of spiritual comfort.

3. As when the sun returns in the spring, the frozen earth is opened, mollified and softened, so by the beams of the Sun of Righteousness the stony, rocky, adamantine hearts of men are thawed, mellowed, and softened, and made fit to receive the seeds of grace. In the winter, the face of the earth is closed and shut up as a stone, unfit for any thing to be sown in it, but is loosened in the spring by the warm beams of the sun; so [is] the heart in its natural state frozen and like the stony ground, so that the seeds of God's Word take no rooting in it, but it is as if we should cast seed upon the bare rock. But when Christ melts the heart by shining upon it, the seed then sinks into it and takes root and begins to germinate and spring forth.

4. As the sun revives the plants and trees and fruits of the earth, so Christ Jesus by his spiritual light revives the soul and causes it to bring forth fruit. In the winter, the trees are stripped of their leaves and fruit, and stand naked, cease growing, and seem to be dead; the grass and herbs are killed, and all things have the appearance of death upon them. But when the sun returns, then all things have the appearance of a resurrection: things revive again, the trees and fields put on their green livery and begin to bud forth, anew, and flourish and grow. The grass and herbs begin to peep forth out of the ground, and all things look green and flourishing: the fields, meadows, and woods seem to rejoice, and the birds sing a welcome to the returning spring. The fields and trees are adorned with beautiful and fragrant flowers.

Just such an alteration is made in the soul at conversion by Jesus Christ, only far more glorious:

> My beloved spake, and said unto me, Rise up, my love, my fair one, and come away. For, lo, the winter is past, the rain is over and gone; the flowers appear on the earth; the time of the singing of birds is come, and the voice of the turtle is heard in our land; the fig tree putteth forth her green figs, and the vines with the tender grape give a good smell. Arise, my love, my fair one, and come away (Cant. 2:10–13).

In conversion, graces do spring forth in the soul which are like the sweet flowers that adorn the face of the earth in the spring, and like the sweet melody of singing birds. The soul of one upon whom Christ has shined differs as much from the souls of the wicked as the earth, beautified with the vernal sunbeams, and, when covered with ice and snow, and vexed with storms in the dead of winter.

To chronicle the varieties of parallelism, alone, in this excerpt—leaving out the synthetic scriptural idiom; the nature imagery from the Connecticut Valley; the similes, metaphors, and symbols; the puns, alliteration, and assonance—would constitute a kind of academic parlor game. Nevertheless, taken as a total impression, the passage offers the prepared reader an authentic representation of the mind and rhetorical manner of the young preacher. Here is his great theme, his central imagery, and his characteristic diction—before the "chastisement of the trope," the years of refining and disciplining metaphors in "Shadows," and the acquisition of that cool self-possession and incisive precision which mark the years of his stylistic mastery. Lacking the focus of an adequate tonic word, or the centripetal cohesion of philosophically systematized imagery, the passage seems to explode in all directions, the constraints of the sermon's numbered divisions and the power of the central metaphor notwithstanding. But it is a joyous, effervescent explosion, and in its final configuration depicts a mind reveling in the very plenitude of parallels (analogies) between the Word and life, the Deity and nature, and finally, its own ideas and its sensations. This is the mind and the style that underlay all the homiletical experiments and developments in Edwards' subsequent career.

In concluding this study of the primary rhetorical and literary resources of Edwards' sermons, it is necessary to consider three techniques which, while not of such importance as those already discussed, are nevertheless worthy of consideration: Edwards' use of the *a fortiori* construction, his "rhetoric of logic," and his manipulation of point of view.

The *a fortiori* or "all the more reason" construction—originally indicating increasing necessity in a logical proof—is employed by Edwards as his primary supplement to simile and metaphor in developing analogical bridges between the seen and the unseen, or in suggesting the plausible route between the present state of sensation and a different state at some point in the future. The apparent reason for Edwards' wanting to supplement metaphors and similitudes is that they have a certain static or self-contained quality that might prevent the less imaginative members of his congregation from having a truly sensible impression of them. To say that God in heaven is "like the sun" supplies a vivid image, but it leaves a considerable amount of the imaginative responsibility of interpretation to the auditory, and some might not be able to meet the challenge. Moreover, because of his adherence to Scripture precedent and the use of familiar images in forming his metaphors, there was always the danger that a similitude would lose its impact through overuse.

Thus, in an effort to "open up" the metaphor and give it freshness, Edwards dramatizes the process of the mind's apprehension and interpretation of it through the "what is more" formula.

> If the natural sun of this lower world be so bright and glorious, how glorious is the sun of the heavenly world, in comparison of which this world is but a dark dungeon? And if the very inhabitants that are enlightened there by the rays of Christ's glory do themselves shine as the sun, how brightly then does he shine who is a sun to them, and does as much exceed them in glory as the sun exceeds our bodies? (Ps. 24:7–10.)

In the same way, Edwards labored to bring new life into the notoriously dead metaphors related to the brevity of life and the nature of eternal punishment.

> Consider that if you do go to hell, hell is certainly near. How near, you can't tell, but in the general that it is near you may be certain. If you should live fifty years longer, how soon will they be gone! How soon is the revolution of the year finished, and how soon are fifty of them numbered! It would terrify you if you knew you was to burn at the stake, or [be] roasted to death by the Indians fifty years hence. It would appear near to you; you would be ready to count the months and the days. But what is that to the being cast into hell, into that place of extreme torment that we have been telling you of, at the end of fifty years?
>
> Consider how dreadful it will be to suffer such an extremity forever. It is dreadful beyond expression to suffer it half an hour—the misery, the tribulation, and anguish that is endured. Do therefore but consider what it would be to suffer day after

day, to have no rest day nor night for thousands, for millions, of years; yea, forever and ever. They will despair of ever being delivered; that despair will double their torment, yea, more than double it. If a person had the headache or toothache, or any other such pain, and knew he was to have it all his lifetime, and not have a moment's rest, it would more than double the affliction; it would magnify it exceedingly. How much more are pains increased when the subject of them knows he shall endure them to all eternity. If a person knew they were to endure a pain all his lifetime, that would not be despair because there is an end, but there is utter despair accompanies the torments of the damned. (Luke 16:24.)

Filling the mind with particulars, and controlling the process of imagined sensation, Edwards guides his audience inexorably along the narrow way from the "reality of here" to the "reality of there." Though tropes and symbolism might indicate the way and illumine the goal, only the painstaking and reiterative *a fortiori* could drive a lazy or reluctant imagination to the goal, dramatizing the mind's quest for a sensible knowledge of spiritual truth and reality in the process.

Indeed, when one considers many of Edwards' series of parallel constructions, and particularly his "lists," there is often more than a suggestion of the upward (or downward) movement of the *a fortiori* construction: "the meanest object of their lusts is set higher than [God]. He has less respect shown him than a few shillings, or than a morsel of meat, or a draught of strong drink, or a little brutish pleasure with a harlot" (Mal. 1:8). In this way, Edwards intensifies the rhetorical and ideational rhythms of his prose, keeping a highly reiterative style free of dull, dead levels. Obvious and subtle by turns, this theoretically simple device fulfills a variety of essential tasks in Edwards' writings.[4]

The "rhetoric of logic" sounds self-contradictory since rhetoric and logic are conventionally differentiated as disciplines.[5] Nor do I contend that logic is anything but logic. What I would insist, however, is that Edwards' mastery of deductive logic, and his various uses of it

4. For a fine example of variations on *a fortiori*, see the sermon on Luke 22:44 printed in Dwight, *Works, 8*, 159–94 (particularly the concluding two or three pages).

5. It should be observed, however, that classic homiletical manuals such as William Chappell's *The Preacher, or the Art and Method of Preaching* (London, 1656) effectively conflate rhetoric and logic in presenting student preachers with strategies of argument.

in the sermons, have quite notable rhetorical consequences. Edwards himself was never immune to the aesthetic qualities of logic:

> One reason why at first, before I knew other logic, I used to be mightily pleased with the study of the old logic, was because it was very pleasant to see my thoughts, that before lay in my mind jumbled without any distinction, ranged into order . . .[6]

And there is no evidence that this aesthetic appreciation of logic, or the old joy in playing with it, departed when Edwards switched to the newer, more "useful" logic.[7] Indeed, most of his sermons, including the imprecatory ones, contain at least a few passages of fine logical argumentation, and many sermons contain displays of logical brilliance that do not always seem to be mere utilitarian tools.

From the rhetorical point of view, Edwards' logical mastery is that which enabled him to give adequate form to passages of massed images and heavily particularized sensations, perceptions, and conceptions. Moreover, it enabled him to keep his rhetorical balance when weaving a network of parallels and juxtapositions between the divine and mundane worlds. All in all, Edwards' peculiar density of style would be little more than a massing of particulars were it not for the remarkable logical discipline of his analytic imagination.

In the final analysis, "logic is logic," and perhaps Edwards' logic is rhetorically most impressive when it is presented as logic, specifically, in the "rational proof " of the Doctrine where he argues not only a positive proof, but first eliminates alternatives in a negative proof. In many such negative-to-positive proofs, Edwards moves grandly through the whole range of evident possibilities until the espoused principle is left standing alone and dominant.[8] The dramatic gesture of such logic—suggesting a metaphysical plow that moves slowly and methodically, yet inexorably and effortlessly to the goal, clearing away all obstacles in its passage—establishes a most commanding "presence" for the preacher, however humble his professions or general tone. Edwards, as a connoisseur of logic, would not be the last to appreciate the power and beauty, or the purely aesthetic qualities, of the grand syllogistic gesture.

6. "The Mind," *Works*, 6, 345.

7. For that matter, JE's near obsession with parallels, juxtapositions, images and shadows, types and antitypes, and so forth, suggests that his mind always bore an impression of the early Ramean stamp.

8. A representative example would be the first proposition of the Doctrine in *A Divine and Supernatural Light, Works*, Worcester rev. ed., *4*, 439–43.

With so much of every sermon being formal, symmetrical, and systematic, it seems that Edwards felt the need for a maverick element, an implement of shock and surprise. He found such a device in the manipulation of the point of view. As indicated by the personal pronouns used, the point of view in the "average" Edwards sermon has certain basic patterns. Thus, in the Opening of the Text, the unity of the minister and congregation is emphasized by references to the first person plural: "we are told"; "in this passage the apostle says (to us)," and so forth. In the Doctrine, and sometimes in the Application, references to the saved and the damned are usually in the third person, emphasizing their status as objects of contemplation by the group comprising the preacher and congregation: "they glorify God," or "they writhe in pain," as the case may be. In the Application, however, and particularly in the uses of exhortation, the point of view is radically altered by shifting to the second person. The preacher separates himself from the congregation, as if leaving them to stand alone under the light of the Word: "if you do not, you will surely suffer"; "[you] come to the waiting arms," and so on.

Sometimes, Edwards not only isolates the congregation before God, but calls attention to their standing in the world—suggesting that he knew well which was probably the more immediate concern of a Yankee congregation. For instance, in a sermon (Neh. 2:20; 1738) preached not long before the publication of *A Faithful Narrative* in Boston, he suddenly turns the klieg light of public opinion upon his people in the Use of Self-examination:

> . . . There has a great deal been done among us at one time or other since the like remarkable pouring out of the Spirit of God upon us to pull down the city of God. God has set us high as a city set upon an hill and very great has been the fame of us throughout this land, and also in the other England. Great notice has been taken of the great work that was here wrought and the profession we make; the account that was sent over to London of it has already had two impressions there. The first impression was soon dispensed and it has been printed there a second time, and they have lately sent over to enquire how things are amongst us now. And this work has often been spoken of in pulpits abroad; it has been twice mentioned in election sermons in Boston that were, as it were, preached before the whole country.

There are congregations I have been informed of where the

whole account as printed in London has been read at length, and you know persons from time to time have come hither to see what remaining fruits there are of this work. And the narrative that has been twice printed in London is now printing again in Boston. Was there ever a town in New England so much set up to public view in religious aspects—as a city that can't be hid—and was there ever a town in the country on whose holy and Christian conversation, honor and influence of religion did so much depend, and whose good behavior would tend so much to build up the city of God, and that ill behavior tend so much to pull it down? But have there not been many things amongst us that have tended to pull it down?

Suddenly, his congregation is thrust before the tribunal of the world and history. One can imagine the turning of heads.

Particularly in imprecatory sermons, Edwards may at any moment alter the point of view, giving the shock of a sudden new perspective. Thus, he may develop an image, say, of a "muck worm," crawling and slithering through the barnyard, apt to be trodden under foot at any moment—all in all a contemptible object—in a third person (objective) narration. Just as the congregation has become fascinated in contemplating the despicable object from the point of view of an attentive human observer, Edwards is likely to assert, "you are that miserable worm!" and then continue the development of the image, but from the worm's point of view, enumerating in detail the heat and stench of the worm's surroundings, the threatening hooves overhead, and so forth. In the same way, Edwards is fond of first delineating experiences and ideas from the human point of view, and then—with little or no transition—suddenly re-envisioning them from a divine point of view. The combinations and permutations of the manipulated point of view yield effects ranging from the thrill of Miltonic cosmic perspectives to vertiginous transits in time and space, from the sense of liberation to the sense of unbearable confinement and oppression. Certainly, as it is sometimes employed, the manipulated point of view seems to constitute the necessary element of madness in Edwards' method.

4. The Historical Mode

The final segment of this discussion of Edwards' literary theory and practice is hardly more than a footnote, though Edwards would have wished that there might be reason for more. In his last years, apparently, he entered a fourth phase as a theorist, though this phase was never brought to fruition in practice. The letter to the trustees at Princeton speaks of his work on "a body of divinity in an entire new method, being thrown into the form of a history." On the basis of this letter and several extant manuscripts, I have concluded that Edwards consciously redirected his efforts, in his last years, away from the essentially expository forms of the sermon and polemic treatise, to the mythic narrative he called history.

From his early notes and lists of titles for treatises, Edwards manifested throughout his life an inclination to undertake the most ambitious writing projects. The only question seemed to be what subject to undertake or what form to give the work. He seems always to have wanted to write a vast work that would systematically expound the ultimate unity of the spiritual and material, the divine and human spheres. But in what form? Should it be a "scientific" treatise that proved all of nature to be nothing more than an idea in God's mind, or a psychological study that analyzed the relationship between the human experience and God, or a "rational account" that would presumably outline, in the abstract vocabulary of philosophical theology, the whole system of God's operations—or perhaps a typological account that would indicate the divine thread running through all history?

In 1739, at the peak of his preaching career, Edwards preached a series of thirty sermons on Is. 51:8 which was published after his death as *A History of the Work of Redemption*.[9] In the series, Edwards proposes to delineate "the work of redemption . . . that God carries on from the fall of man to the end of the world." Of course, the title proposed for the "body of divinity in an entire new method" is a *History of the Work of Redemption,* and thus one might suppose that Edwards thought more and more of the historical form, in his last twenty years, as the most desirable form for his systematic theological work.

His extant manuscripts testify to the probability of this supposition. Of course, any or all of Edwards' sermons and basic notebooks might have been put into service as sources for his history, but he also left three notebooks devoted specifically to the "Work of Redemption." The first of these (123 pp., octavo) is devoted to significant historical

9. See *A History of the Work of Redemption,* ed. John F. Wilson, *Works,* 9.

events, the second (30 pp., octavo) to the format of the history, and the third (21 pp., quarto) to the history of the church in particular. The first two notebooks contain explicit references to Edwards' sermons, and the first and third seem to contain much material from secondary sources. They are all late notebooks and provide indisputable circumstantial evidence that Edwards was very much engaged in his history at the end of his life.

In the area of style and form, there is also very interesting evidence. Edwards' regulatory notebook, "Subjects of Enquiry," contains the following notes and directions, written in the 1750s, which appear to indicate his interest in acquiring the essentials of the historical mode of writing:

> Particularly to enquire concerning the things which make a history of past ages to be credible in a present age.

> Show how parallel, in many instances, historical evidence of a past age, by the testimony handed down to us, is to the evidence we have of what is presently of the existence and estate of a distant country or nation that we have never seen.

> And consider what may be argued from this, that we see, ourselves, to what degree truth is maintained in narration of things past, in our age, and so may argue how it will be through many such ages. For the ages are all continuing. The last half of our age is the first half of another, and so all are interlaced as it were.

> We argue in the same manner as that concerning the truth of narrations concerning distant places; so far as we travel, we have opportunity to see with our own eyes how far truth is kept in its carriage through such a distance, etc.

Several other notes direct him to make tables which would provide working indices for nearly all of his major notebooks, including a "table to papers concerning History of the Work of Redemption." Finally, in numerous late entries related to various biblical and historical studies, the word "fact" occurs with remarkable frequency for Edwards.

That Edwards had finally settled upon the historical mode as the only one suited to the expression of his vast accumulation of theological thought seems obvious. Perhaps only the historical approach appeared sufficiently persuasive in an era which emphasized authenticity more than logic or authority. At any rate, the master preacher and controversialist clearly set out at the end of his life to master the art of historical narrative.[1] Had he lived, he might have produced one of the most interesting works in American literature, for he had the intellect and literary talent, the materials and the will. But just as he was getting all his tables in order and thinking out the historical strategy, all efforts ceased.

Although Edwards did not live to write his systematic explication of Christ's great works in historical metaphor, he left the vast bulk of material from which he would have developed his narrative. Distributed among the various specialized notebooks and sermons discussed in this introduction, and partially revealed in finely finished fragments through the several major treatises which Edwards composed, the detailed vision can no more be recaptured than an egg reassembled. What is available in the sermon canon now being published in chronological series is Edwards' thought in its own historical context, the thirty-five-year evolution of his theological expression in the only format which enabled him to test its aesthetic validity and spiritual efficacy in the context of life. The present history is the literary history of a homiletical artist whose work decisively transcended New England Puritanism in response to the challenges of a diverse new society.

1. These speculations should be qualified by the detailed investigation of John F. Wilson into the documents and evident theory of the project in his introduction to the *Work of Redemption, Works*, 9, 11–13, 63–72, and in his Appendix B to the same volume, 543–56.

SERMONS AND DISCOURSES, 1720–1723

PREFACE TO THE
NEW YORK PERIOD

My heart seemed to sink within me, at leaving the family and city,
where I had enjoyed so many sweet and pleasant days. . . . As I sail'd
away, I kept sight of the city as long as I could; and when I was out
of sight of it, it would affect me much to look that way, with a kind of
melancholy mixed with sweetness.[1]

Y EARS later, while writing his "Personal Narrative," Jonathan Edwards recalled that day in April 1723 when he concluded his first pastorate. In retrospect, the New York pastorate had been a brief golden age in the springtime of his career: an eight-month sojourn during which he left Yale College, the Connecticut Valley, and even New England to become minister to a Presbyterian congregation in a community where he was no one's son, grandson, or nephew.[2] The pastoral call had come when his own awakening was in its second year of fervid bloom, and the months in New York provided some of his most stimulating moments of meditation and spiritual fellowship. Particular events of the ministry in New York between August 10, 1722, and Edwards' departure on April 26, 1723, are obscure in the standard biographies, though the previous two years of graduate study at Yale College and the succeeding year prior to his assuming the position of tutor at Yale in June of 1724 are even less adequately documented.

The New York City entered by Jonathan Edwards must have impressed him with its vitality and cultural diversity much as it had Madame Knight some eighteen years earlier. If there were only seven to ten thousand inhabitants in a city occupying a mile or so of the

1. [Samuel Hopkins] *The Life and Character of the Late Reverend Mr. Jonathan Edwards, President of the College at New Jersey* (Boston, 1765), p. 31.

2. Particularly in the context of his later appointments, the New York ministry to a small group of English Presbyterians who had split off from their original church stands out as a striking diversion from family and region. The post was hardly promising but JE was clearly as stimulated by it as his parents were worried. An offer from a newly formed congregation in Bolton, Connecticut, elicited a polite but cool response from JE, so his father supplied a warm cover letter before passing it on. The letters are printed in John A. Stoughton, *Windsor Farmes: A Glimpse of an Old Parish* (Hartford, 1883), pp. 83–85.

southern tip of Manhattan island, it was still more urban in every sense than any community Edwards had inhabited. Ecclesiastically, the port city hosted large numbers of Dutch Calvinists and French Huguenots, smaller congregations of Dutch Lutherans, Scottish Presbyterians, and Jews. The English inhabitants most closely connected with financial and political power in the colony were affiliated with the Church of England. The English Presbyterians who had come to New York from New England constituted a minority among the Scottish Presbyterians, and the disaffected separating group who employed the eighteen-year-old Edwards as an unordained supply preacher were probably more like an extended family than an institutional church, worshipping in houses or a rented room.[3] Such a tenuous social and ecclesiastical position would have been isolating for even a gregarious personality, and the young man who was as shy and introspective as all evidence indicates that Edwards was at this time must have been particularly isolated. Certainly there is no evidence of his attempting professional fraternization with the other ministers of New York, nor is he known to have met or conversed with James Anderson, the Scottish pastor of the congregation from which his employers had separated. On the other hand, the evidence of Edwards' memoirs suggests that his Presbyterian "family" provided a wonderful sanctuary for the cultivation of his sense of divine things and the trial of his art as a preacher. Moreover, the congregation may have provided a precedent of fervent Christian fellowship which remained to shape Edwards' taste in congregational decorum for years to come. Although the complicated spiritual events attendant upon Edwards' formative years of thought and reflection, and his first steps in defining a professional life, have continued to remain obscure, some of the most commonly known of his writings stem from this period. Before turning to the New York sermons, an attentive consideration of some aspects of these published writings is necessary to help establish the full context of the months in New York as intellectually and spiritually continuous with the relatively private graduate years and the years of increased public and professional involvement which succeeded.

One of the most significant documents of the New York period is

3. The ecclesiastical context of the separation leading to JE's New York appointment is discussed in Charles A. Briggs, *American Presbyterianism* (New York, 1885), pp. 176–84, and documented in *Minutes of the Presbyterian Church in America, 1706–1788*, ed. Guy S. Klett (Philadelphia, Presbyterian Hist. Soc., 1976), pp. 32–57.

the "Diary," accompanied by the symbiotic "Resolutions," the manuscript of which is now lost, its text having been transmitted through the edition of Sereno Dwight which omits shorthand notations and may modify other expressions.[4] The "Diary" and "Resolutions" may antedate the actual removal to New York, although Dwight was convinced that the December 18, 1722, entry which begins his text was in fact the first entry.[5] The identification of the "Diary" with New York is sound, in any case, for it flowered there and in the months of 1723 immediately after Edwards' return home to East Windsor. The "Diary" focuses attention on Edwards the person as no other document he left, probably not even the "Personal Narrative," although the narrative is a superior expression of his spiritual history and prepared for eyes other than his own. But the "Diary" is the mirror of self-consciousness held close, and as such it directs our attention to the great effort of the New York months. Before, as a graduate studying at college, Edwards had explored theological literature, experienced a troublingly unconventional conversion and accepted his vocation. In New York, however, he was confronted with the task of becoming a professional in the highest sense: of integrating personal yearnings, quantities of old and new theology, a family ministerial tradition, and the new practical demands of the moment in a way of life which would, in the Puritan tradition he was heir to, demonstrate the value of the sacred in a secular world. That the "Diary" gives so much evidence of struggle and intense self-examination is hardly an indication of morbidity or neurosis, as has sometimes been suggested, but rather testifies to Edwards' unusually realistic grasp of his challenging situation in the light of his high ambition. As one of "Christ's ambassadors," of course, he was literally in the business of holiness, and there is little or no margin in the business for one who would lay claim to a puritanical aegis. He was either ultimately earnest or ultimately a fraud. Thus the "Diary" not sur-

---

4. *The Works of President Edwards: With a Memoir of His Life* (10 vols., New York, 1828–30), *1*. Samuel Hopkins, a more accurate transcriber of JE than Dwight, gives only excerpts from the "Diary" and "Resolutions" in his *Life*. Dwight prints all of the "Resolutions" (pp. 68–73 and the "Diary," though he intersperses it among other biographical materials in the seventh and eighth chapters, pp. 76–94, 99–106.

5. That JE is well into the thirties in his numbered "Resolutions" at this time, viewed in the light of the fact that the resolutions seem to spring from meditations within the "Diary" as much as they are guides for the life recorded and examined in it, suggests that an undetermined number of loose leaves may have been lost or discarded before the "Diary" booklet was made.

prisingly dwells upon what Edwards perceived to be the crux of the
Christian life, the experience of holiness, and the practical consequences of the unremitting pursuit of this existential identification.[6]

> *Dec.* 22, *Saturday.* This day, revived by God's Holy Spirit; af-
> fected with the sense of the excellency of holiness; felt more
> exercise of love to Christ, than usual. Have, also, felt sensible
> repentance for sin, because it was committed against so merciful
> and good a God.[7]

Related entries in both the "Diary" and "Resolutions" show Edwards
attempting to assess his progress in personal holiness in the most
rigorous, systematic way, involving a spiritual accounting at the end
of each day, week, month, and year.[8] Of course, he soon concluded,

> I find, by experience, that, let me make Resolutions, and do
> what I will, with never so many inventions, it is all nothing, and
> to no purpose at all, without the motions of the Spirit of God; for
> if the Spirit of God should be as much withdrawn from me always,
> as for the week past, notwithstanding all I do, I should not grow,
> but should languish, and miserably fade away. I perceive, if God
> should withdraw his Spirit a little more, I should not hesitate to
> break my Resolutions, and should soon arrive at my old state.
> There is no dependence on myself.[9]

With the absolute necessity of attaining the proper savour of holiness
before him and the realization of his personal unreliability, Edwards
defines the experiential nexus of his Calvinist theology. In the years
ahead he would not only strive to educate himself thoroughly in all
learning, both sacred and secular, which might bring a more adequate
understanding of this insight into the human predicament, but he

6. In comparison with other renewal movements, English Puritans stressed the subjective experience of the individual in determining his status within the religious community,
and Timothy Edwards clearly fostered this dimension of Puritanism in East Windsor. But
it should be understood that, from JE's point of view, the appeal to experience encompassed
figures as diverse as the Cambridge Platonists, John Locke, and Anthony Ashley Cooper,
third Earl of Shaftesbury.

7. Dwight, *Life,* p. 76.

8. Although like his Puritan forebears JE was no observer of the liturgical calendar—
not even Christmas or Easter—he was very calendrical in regulating both his private and
public affairs; thus, New Year's Day was the most emphatic moment for self-evaluation and
practical reformation, as the New Year's sermon was a major one for his church. For various
purposes JE also observed quarters, months, weeks, and days in cycle.

9. Dwight, *Life,* p. 77.

would continue to pursue through the most rigorous self-analysis the exact nature of his own experience. Even his sermons would serve as tools of self-analysis,[1] and the self would serve as the primary testbed of religion at least until the mid-1730s when he undertook the analysis of religious experience in a communal setting.

Simultaneously, the "Diary" reveals Edwards' continuing struggles involving a much more mundane dimension of professionalism. Most evident, though more often implicit than explicit, is the struggle of an intensely ambitious and competitive young careerist to overcome the selfish responses that are virtually inseparable from such a nature. Thus, there are several warnings which indicate Edwards' awareness of a tendency to belittle those who are evidently his inferiors while resenting those who have apparently gained the advantage in the race for worldly success.

> *Saturday night, May* 4. Although I have, in some measure, subdued a disposition to chide and fret, yet I find a certain inclination, which is not agreeable to christian sweetness of temper and conversation: either too much dogmaticalness or too much egotism, a disposition to manifest my own dislike and scorn, and my own freedom from those which are innocent, sinless, yea common infirmities of men . . .[2]

On the other hand, as he wrote a little earlier, he could not allow enviousness to become customary, either, however ineradicable it might be: "I will not murmur nor be grieved, whatever prosperity upon any account I see others enjoy, and I am denied. To this I have lately acted contrary."[3] Just what the occasion was is not recorded, but in this note the give and take of competitive professional life seems directly reflected.

Such realistic self-appraisals occur on a variety of themes in the "Diary," scattered among Edwards' more conventional pieties and asceticisms. Like the style and strategy notes for a young writer on the cover of the "Natural Philosophy" notebook which were begun a few months later, these observations reveal Edwards to have been

1. Ibid., p. 91.
2. Ibid., pp. 84–85.
3. Ibid., p. 82. In another much longer meditation entered under January 10, 1723 (p. 78), JE proposes a kind of systematic asceticism as a defense against material want and worldly failure.

purposefully professional in orientation and indeed quite ambitious in a wholly conventional sense.[4]

In the retrospective view of his "Personal Narrative" written nearly twenty years after these events, however, his spiritual struggles in New York were best understood as the efforts of a rather naive youth to master his personal religious life.

> I felt in me a burning desire to be in every thing a complete Christian . . . I had an eager thirsting after progress in these things. My longings after it, put me upon pursuing and pressing after them . . . I sought an increase of grace and holiness, and that I might live an holy life, with vastly more earnestness, than ever I sought grace, before I had it. . . . My experience had not then taught me, as it has done since, my extreme feebleness and impotence, every manner of way; and the innumerable and bottomless depths of secret corruption and deceit, that there was in my heart.[5]

Subsequent passages strengthen the note of retrospective qualification: "But I have reason to be infinitely humbled, when I consider, how much I have failed, of answering my obligation."[6] His vulnerability was further evident during the months following the New York pastorate and a similar period of nearly a year in the Bolton, Connecticut, pulpit when, according to his narrative, "I was again greatly diverted in my mind with some temporal concerns . . . greatly to the wounding of my soul; and went on through various exercises, that it would be tedious to relate, that gave me much more experience of my own heart, than ever I had before."[7] Just what these affairs were, occurring between September 1725 and Edwards' arrival in Northampton in the fall of 1726, may best be suggested by consideration of his public role during the period: the serving of one more year at Yale College in the onerous tutorship, a brief period of preaching in

4. Although the style and method notes are directed to a particular project, they inevitably reveal basic attitudes and a general methodology as well. They reveal the young JE to have been as self-aware and as calculating in the literary marketplace as the young Benjamin Franklin was, albeit with a different market segment in mind. See my analysis of the rules above, pp. 180–88.

5. Hopkins, *Life,* pp. 28–29.

6. Ibid., p. 30.

7. Ibid., p. 33. The research of Thomas A. Schafer has considerably enlarged our awareness of JE's involvement with the Bolton pastorate between May 1723 and May 1724. A discussion of the episode will appear later in this series.

Glastonbury (probably as a candidate), negotiations with the church in Northampton, and, yes, even the engagement to Sarah Pierrepont. Considering the emphasis Edwards places upon virtual isolation from the world and its affairs, pleasing as well as trying, when describing moments of spiritual growth in the "Personal Narrative," this period must have been distracting in the extreme, both in its aggravations and temptations. In the remainder of his narrative, Edwards refers to a deepening sense of his earlier inadequacies: "It is affecting to me to think, how ignorant I was, when I was a young Christian, of the bottomless, infinite depths of wickedness, pride, hypocrisy and deceit left in my heart."[8] By 1739 or 1740 when the "Personal Narrative" was most likely composed, Edwards had learned much about himself, as well as about the short-lived effects of a widely publicized revival and the fickleness of human nature, so there is no reason to take these self-assessments as less than literal.[9]

At the mid-point of his career, then, Edwards was able to look back to its beginnings in New York and observe that "I was a far better Christian, for two or three years after my first conversion, than I am now; and lived in a more constant delight and pleasure . . ."[1] Later years brought a greater appreciation of God's sovereignty and Christ's glory, as well as his own directly proportionate deficiency and need, but the years of innocence—more precisely designated "ignorance" by Edwards—were themselves more glorious experientially. He was then more *constantly* aware of the delightful presence of the spirit even while attempting to pursue the sometimes conflicting though inter-related ends of evangelical ministry, personal seeking, and professional advancement.

Most of all, according to the "Diary," the period centering in the New York pastorate was one of the verification of Edwards' religious identity. Between the first consequential conversion experience in the spring of 1721 and September 1723, when he received his M.A. at the Yale College commencement, was the period of Edwards' greatest Christian fervor, whether viewed from the perspective of three years

8. Ibid., p. 38.

9. In the perspective of history, the 1734–35 conversions are sometimes nearly tele-scoped with the Great Awakening, obscuring the fact that the revival had virtually collapsed in Northampton by 1736. Manuscript sermons yet to be published from the years 1736–38 reveal JE in the agony of seeing his people inexorably backsliding just as world attention, responding to his own promotional exertions, was being focused upon them. An excerpt from a sermon in which he speaks directly to the issue is printed above, pp. 254–55.

1. Hopkins, *Life,* p. 38.

in the "Diary" or seventeen years in the "Personal Narrative."[2] His spiritual life during the period is thus characterized in the "Personal Narrative":

> My mind was greatly fixed on divine things; I was almost perpetually in the contemplation of them. Spent most of my time in thinking of divine things, year after year. And used to spend abundance of my time, in often walking alone in the woods, and solitary places, for meditation, soliloquy, and prayer, and converse with God. And it was always my manner, at such times, to sing forth my contemplations. And was almost constantly in ejaculatory prayer, wherever I was.[3]

Moreover, "my sense of divine things seemed gradually to increase, till I went to preach at New-York . . . While I was there I felt them very sensibly, in a much higher degree, than I had done before."[4] The New York period was, by his own account, the time of Edwards' greatest religious intensity. He might subsequently have become more learned, wiser, and deeper, but he was never again to have such "inward burnings" in his own heart. To some extent, perhaps, he was conscious of having approached the summit, or that last height of ecstatic experience that was to be allowed him, for the "Diary" records his struggles to inch just a little closer to his goal as his foot slips repeatedly. His constitution cracks and mental focus blurs; he is disappointed and frustrated, but only renews his efforts. Finally a friend, or perhaps his parents, suggested sensible restraint or a little Calvinistic resignation, but Edwards would have none of it: "It is suggested to me, that too constant a mortification, and too vigorous application to religion, may be prejudicial to health; but nevertheless, I will *plainly feel it and experience it,* before I cease, on this account."[5]

The great craving for authenticity is hardly an indication of psychological maladjustment in Edwards' case, nor is it necessarily evi-

2. The "Diary" entry is that for Sept. 26, 1726 (Dwight, *Life*, p. 106), the passage from the "Personal Narrative" that was quoted in the preceding paragraph.

3. Hopkins, *Life*, pp. 27–28.

4. Ibid., p. 28.

5. Dwight, *Life*, p. 80. Ed. italics. JE's sentiments here are very close to those of John Smith in "Of the True Way or Method of Attaining to Divine Knowledge": "Were I indeed to define *Divinity*, I should rather call it a *Divine life*, than a *Divine science*; it being something rather to be understood by a *Spiritual sensation*, than by any *Verbal description*, as all things of Sense and Life are best known by Sentient and Vital faculties . . ." *Select Discourses* (2nd ed., Cambridge, 1673), pp. 1–2.

dence of spiritual heroism of Romantic proportions, for it seems that Edwards had a real spiritual problem at this time which would have disturbed any intelligent and scrupulous person in his circumstances. The problem is clearly alluded to in the "Personal Narrative" and is explicitly stated in the "Diary." Indeed, the extant text of the "Diary" suggests that Edwards may have actually begun his diary in order to deal with the problem:

> *Dec.* 18. . . . The reason why I, in the least, question my interest in God's love and favor, is,—
> 1. Because I cannot speak so fully to my experience of that preparatory work, of which divines speak:—
> 2. I do not remember that I experienced regeneration, exactly in those steps, in which divines say it is generally wrought. . . .[6]

The concerns stated here would have been very real to most of Edwards' contemporaries and certainly to his mentors. As the "Diary" unfolds, Edwards' preoccupation with this apparent deficiency in his spiritual qualifications becomes clear. Significantly, though, it does not become explicit until after his return home from New York on the first of May 1723.

> *Thursday morning, July* 4. The last night, in bed, when thinking of death, I thought, if I was then to die, that, which would make me die, in the least degree fearfully, would be, the want of a trusting and relying on Jesus Christ, *so distinctly and plainly as has been described by divines*; my not having experienced *so particular* a venturing, and entirely trusting my soul on Christ, *after* the fears of hell, and terrors of the Lord, encouraged by the mercy, faithfulness and promises, of God, and the gracious invitations of Christ.[7]

And the following month:

> *Monday morning, Aug.* 12. The chief thing, that now makes me in any measure to question my good estate, is my not having experienced conversion *in those particular steps,* wherein the people of New England, and anciently the Dissenters of Old England,

---

6. Ibid., p. 76. Two further concerns enumerated in the entry, respecting faith and conduct in broad terms, seem to arise from the lack of confidence predicated by the first two.

7. Ibid., p. 88. Ed. italics.

used to experience it. Wherefore, now resolved, never to leave searching, till I have satisfyingly found out the very bottom and foundation, the real reason, why they used to be converted in those steps.[8]

A final reflection occurs nearly two years later, not far in time from his engagement to Sarah Pierrepont and during the spiritually difficult period of the tutorship:

> *Friday, May* 28. It seems to me, that whether I am now converted or not, I am so settled in the state I am in, that I shall go on in it all my life. But, however settled I may be, yet I will continue to pray to God, not to suffer me to be deceived about it, nor to sleep in an unsafe condition; and ever and anon, will call all into question and try myself, *using for helps, some of our old divines,* that God may have opportunities to answer my prayers, and the Spirit of God to show me my error, if I am in one.[9]

Even in the more structured and subtle "Personal Narrative," Edwards is quite above board in indicating that the pattern of his awakening was unorthodox and that what proved in retrospect to have been his first real step in conversion was unaccompanied by terror, was essentially unidentifiable in conventional terms and for that very reason gave him no thought "that there was any thing spiritual, or of a saving nature" in it.[1] On the contrary, it was a series of sudden and mysterious reversals in his outlook, ranging from his attitude toward the principle of God's sovereignty (as manifested in the doctrine of election) to his reaction to the phenomena of thunder storms, that gave him "great satisfaction as to my good estate"[2] and ultimately justified his apparently confident reference to "my conversion" near the end of the "Narrative."[3] No wonder that, as early as 1725 when he appeared upon the verge of a permanent pastoral settlement, Edwards reminded himself in the "Diary":

> *Friday, Feb.* 12, 1725. The very thing I now want, to give me a clearer and more immediate view of the perfections and glory of God, is as clear a knowledge of the manner of God's exerting

8. Ibid., p. 93. Ed. italics.
9. Ibid., p. 105. Ed. italics.
1. Hopkins, *Life,* p. 25.
2. Ibid., p. 27.
3. Ibid., p. 36.

himself, with respect to Spirits and Mind, as I have, of his operations concerning Matter and Bodies.[4]

Such a problem at the outset of his adult life and professional career might well have caused secret agonies. Edwards might have wondered if he were not really a fraud in his high religious vocation or have doubted his ability to guide others through the perilous steps to conversion in his future career. However, it is apparent that not only did he wrestle with this problem in the relative comfort of his private self, but actually had it discovered to some part of the world as well.

It has been shown that although the problem was on his mind when he went to New York in the fall of 1722, it apparently became much more vexing after his return to East Windsor the following spring. The discriminating factor, it seems, was the presence in Windsor of his chief mentor, his father. The Reverend Timothy Edwards had prepared his son for college, had inevitably given him his practical introduction to the ministry, and was continuing to direct the progress of his career, including the decision that he leave New York and enter into an agreement with a congregation at Bolton, Connecticut.[5] Timothy Edwards was undoubtedly proud of this only son who seemed to promise so much, but Timothy was not one to gloss over anything, not to mention matters of importance. Indeed, he was renowned for a certain intransigence, an indominatibleness in matters that he cared about, whether he appeared to be carrying the day or not. Thus he struggled for years with his patient but apparently stubborn flock over his salary, ministerial prerogative, and the implementation of the Saybrook Platform: he was not loath to berate them in sermon after sermon over matters large and small with undifferentiated vehemence. On the issue of the proper morphology of conversion he seems to have been a liberal traditionalist, adhering to a simplified step theory while admitting the possibility of unpredictable personal variations from the norm. Perhaps his distinguishing trait, however, was an intense desire for personal oversight and control of his awak-

---

4. Dwight, *Life*, p. 105.

5. In a letter of December 10, 1722, to the Bolton search committee, JE shows little inclination to leave New York; however, "considering the circumstances of the [New York] Society and my Father's inclination to the contrary, it seems most probable I shall not settle here . . ." (Stoughton, *Windsor Farmes*, p. 84). The Bolton post was hardly more promising than that in New York, as events proved, but it did put JE back within his father's ecclesiastical territory.

ened parishioners' spiritual struggles, and in his frequent counselling sessions he probably tended to dominance, if not manipulation. The conversion relations he sedulously preserved reveal a conventional structure, stressing the preparatory struggles and treating the joys of the new birth only briefly.[6] Thus, however intense his son's "inward burnings" may have been, it is unlikely that Timothy Edwards readily accepted them as constituting an authentic conversion if they did not have the prevailing *structure*. And nothing is more obvious from the evidence of the "Diary" and the "Personal Narrative" than that they did not have the conventional structure.

Both the "Diary" and the "Personal Narrative" stress Edwards' unhappiness at leaving New York, especially noting the "most bitter parting with Madam Smith and her son."[7] In stark contrast, neither document breathes a hint of filial joy upon the return of the young minister to the bosom of his family. And during the succeeding months at home, the only references to his family are in self-admonitions. Most obvious are two references in the "Diary" and one of the "Resolutions." First in apparent chronological order, Resolution 46 was composed sometime in the spring of 1723:

> 46. *Resolved,* Never to allow the least measure of any fretting or uneasiness at my father or mother. *Resolved,* To suffer no effects of it, so much as in the least alteration of speech, or motion of my eye; and to be especially careful of it with respect to any of our family.[8]

Taken by itself, the resolution seems little more than a general admonition to Christian behavior in the family; however, the specificity

6. Timothy Edwards' interest in the conversion process and his empirical approach to it in practice clearly anticipate JE's career in many respects. That he may have shaped his son's spiritual and professional development hardly mitigates the likelihood of sharp disagreements, particularly in the early years of JE's career, since the most poignant disagreements are those between fellow-travelers, particularly teacher-fathers and earnest pupil-sons. The pattern of conversion narrative cultivated in the East Windsor congregation is analyzed and illustrated by several examples in Kenneth P. Minkema's "The East Windsor Conversion Relations: 1700–1725," *The Conn. Hist. Soc. Bulletin,* 51 (Winter 1986), 9–63. For the most penetrating analysis of Timothy Edwards' pastorate, including his preaching and theory of conversion, see also Minkema's "The Edwardses: A Ministerial Family in Eighteenth-Century New England" (Ph.D. diss., Univ. of Connecticut, 1988), chs. 1–3.

7. Dwight, *Life*, p. 66.

8. Ibid., p. 71.

of the second portion suggests tension at the very least. Moving on to the "Diary" entries of the following summer, the first links the notion of filial obedience with the endurance of unjust persecution:

> *Friday afternoon, July* 19. 1 Peter, ii.18. Servants, be subject to your masters, with all fear; not only to the good and gentle, but also to the froward: How then, ought children to honor their parents.—This verse, together with the two following, viz. "For this is thank-worthy, if a man, for conscience toward God, endure grief, suffering wrongfully; for what glory is it, if, when ye be buffeted for your faults, ye shall take it patiently; but if, when ye do well and suffer for it, ye take it patiently, this is acceptable with God."[9]

The entire passage is scripture quotation *except* "How then, ought children to honor their parents," which is Edwards' interpolation. While the first passage from scripture presents the idea of enduring injustice, it is noteworthy that the second adds the idea of suffering religious persecution: a remarkable context for his first diary reference to his parents. The second citation occurs the following month:

> *Tuesday morning, Aug.* 13. Have sinned, in not being careful enough to please my parents. *Afternoon.*—I find it would be very much to my advantage, to be thoroughly acquainted with the Scriptures. When I am reading doctrinal books, or books of controversy, I can proceed with abundantly more confidence: can see on what footing and foundation I stand.[1]

What had he done to displease his parents, and why would he then be led to thoughts of polemic divinity and the bedrock of scripture proofs? Taking the three passages together, it appears that there was considerable family tension and that this tension involved a disagreement about religion or the interpretation of the Scriptures. The circumstantial evidence of the "Diary" offers a clear indication at this point, for the August 13 entry quoted above follows directly upon Edwards' August 12 meditation on the morphology of conversion quoted earlier (pp. 269–70). This conjunction strongly suggests that the specific religious issue over which Edwards and his parents differed was the validity of conversion which did not follow in "those steps"

9. Ibid., p. 89.
1. Ibid., p. 93.

of "the Dissenters of Old England." Looking further back in the "Diary," it now makes more sense that the July 4 entry, the first part of which was quoted above (p. 269) and which contains an explicit reference to the old morphology "described by divines," concludes with the resolution: "for the future, to observe rather more of meekness, moderation and temper, in disputes."[2]

A real diary does not usually spell out contexts or interpret situations for readers beyond the author and neither does Edwards', but it is not exactly secretive, either, on the subject that undoubtedly caused him great personal anguish and possibly threatened to become a public embarrassment to his career. The ongoing debate with his father over the morphology of conversion seems to have been kept within the family, although there are hints in the "Diary" that Edwards may even have argued the issue publicly. How long the debate continued or when it actually began are difficult to determine since the "Diary" clearly begins in medias res and soon peters out as Edwards turned from self-analysis to the affairs of his professional life.[3] Some perspective on the situation of the New York period is available, however, in one passage of the "Personal Narrative." Otherwise silent on the debate, the narrative offers one scene involving father and son which may well represent the actual beginning of the disagreement:

> Not long after I first began to experience these things, I gave an account to my father, of some things that had passed in my mind. I was pretty much affected by the discourse we had together. And when the discourse was ended, I walked abroad alone, in a solitary place in my father's pasture, for contemplation. And as I was walking there, and looked up on the sky and clouds; there came into my mind, so sweet a sense of the glorious majesty and grace of God, that I know not how to express. I seemed to see them both in a sweet conjunction: majesty and meekness joined together: it was a sweet and gentle, and holy majesty; and

2. Ibid., p. 88.

3. Although the "Diary" runs from December 1722 to June 1735, the vast bulk of it (over two-thirds) is concentrated in 1723. Allowing for missing early leaves that may have reached back as far as 1721, the proportions as well as the substance of the record point to the year of 1723 as the period of JE's most sustained self-examination. It is also the year of his most significant intellectual flowering as his independent biblical and theological studies rapidly gained momentum.

also a majestic meekness; an awful sweetness; a high, and great, and holy gentleness.[4]

It was apparently in the spring of 1721, while home from graduate study at college during the vacation, that Edwards had this conversation with his father. It is clear from the context of the narrative that "some things that had passed in my mind" refers to nothing less than Edwards' recent awakening, that which the narrative identifies in retrospect as the true conversion. More than the obscuring perspective of time in the narrative seems to be involved in neutralizing Edwards' idiom here: it is as if he were writing so that the account would be literally true and hence honest, but fully significant only to someone who knew his story intimately beforehand. He continues to describe this most intimate and crucial interview in even more opaque language: "I was pretty much affected by the discourse we had together." "Pretty much affected." How much the master of specification leaves unspecified! Did he then stroll out to the pasture filled with warmth and good feeling, there to find an anthropomorphic correlative in nature for his mood, or did he flee an essentially incomprehending and distressed mentor to gaze skyward with tear-streaked face, projecting into the heavens the vision of a parent who could be both a wise mentor and a maternal comforter; one who could be strong without being stiff, loving without being weak, and accepting without being unjust?

The evidence presented heretofore suggests that the second construction is the more plausible: there is little to support the notion of Timothy Edwards' being either very tolerant of the unconventional or particularly responsive to idiosyncratic approaches to spirituality, especially in the case of his own dear son whom he was carefully molding to fill the expectations of family and the profession of the Puritan ministry. Thus it is probable that by the time he arrived in New York Edwards had been embroiled for nearly eighteen months

4. Hopkins, *Life*, p. 26. JE's conversion, which he admittedly could not adequately describe, had taken place in early 1721 (Ibid., p. 25). An interesting factor in the background of this interview between father and son is a certain manuscript sermon by Timothy Edwards now in the Beinecke Library which was preached in the spring of 1721. The sermon, on the text of Cant. 4:16, cites two sections of Solomon Stoddard's *A Treatise Concerning Conversion* (Boston, 1719). One of the passages cited stresses that "the difference between saving and common Grace don't lie in the *degree,* but in the *nature* of them" (p. 7). As a whole, the treatise is innovative, incisive, and places a premium upon subjective experience as opposed to normative behavior. Thus there may have been three approaches to conversion in play during the interview: those of son, father, and grandfather.

in an absolutely fundamental argument with his father (and by implication his mother) involving nothing less than his spiritual identity
and his fitness for the ministry. Possessing more than a little of his
father's sense of integrity and even his stiffness (according to his own
assertions in the "Diary"), the brilliant youth who had already exercised a genius for observation and speculative analysis in his scientific
notebook and who in the contemporary "Prejudices of the Imagination" essay inveighed not against the imagination per se but against
conventional preconceptions,[5] now undertook a resolution of his crucial theoretical problem. While he clearly did not cease to be troubled
by his unconventional spirituality, his response was to begin a study
of the roots of spirituality which would preoccupy him on various
levels for much of the remainder of his life.

The New York period is thus best understood as one of great pres-
sures and tensions: of temporary autonomy but merely suspended
conflicts with parental expectations, of high hopes for a great career
but an untenable or at least unpromising current position, and of the
most exalted spirituality complicated by important self-doubts and
uncertainties. Because of his character or genius, Edwards responded
with vigor, personally and professionally, making the period one of
rapid intellectual and spiritual unfolding. Given his age, his relative
isolation in a strange city, and most of all the very spiritual conflicts
just explored, Edwards was inevitably self-absorbed. Despite his role
of pastor, he was hardly drawn out of himself as he was to be in the
tutorship, not to mention the years at Northampton, but even as a
professional he worked with his own thoughts and experiences.[6] Thus
he took as his point of departure a radically subjective definition of
graciousness or holiness. In noting this preoccupation with holiness
in his "Diary," developing a definition of it in the first entry of his
new "Miscellanies" notes, and devoting at least one sermon exclusively
to it, Edwards began the quest which the "Personal Narrative" would
eventually celebrate as the most direct fruit of his conversion.[7] The

5. *Works, 6,* 196–201. It is clear from the essay that JE understands "imagination" to
be mere image-combining and thus restricted to conventional sense impressions. According
to our post-Coleridgean usage, he is really calling for *more* imagination if anything.

6. A few weeks after his arrival home from New York, JE resolved in his diary to
discover his motivations, in this case relating to the failure to perform certain duties. His
method is noteworthy: "searching and tracing back . . . all the subtle subterfuges of my
thoughts . . . that I may know what are the very first originals . . . to do this sometimes in
sermons." Dwight, *Life,* p. 91.

7. See "The Way of Holiness," pp. 468–79 below.

concept was thus not only important doctrine to Edwards, but it provided a key to the resolution of the puzzling issues of his own experience. Holiness is presented in his meditations of the day as an abstract, a priori concept *and* an experience; an *experienced idea,* in effect. As such, it is the dynamic mediator between divine Being and earthly being, or between truth and reality. Only the holy are conformed to the supreme spirit of God to such an extent that their perceptions and their (Scripture-based) knowledge of truth are finally consonant. They are children of Adam and sinners, but they are imbued with a principle which transfigures both nature and spiritual reality, revealing an ultimate harmony between the spheres of faith and experience.[8]

Edwards' preoccupation with the perception of the highest good as the true inception of the new life is everywhere evident in the sermons of the New York period. The mood is thus optimistic despite the conventional cautions of the Calvinistic preacher: the plight of all men as sinners may be serious and action may have to be taken immediately, but Edwards gives no hint that his auditory is unlikely to heed his word once they are simply informed. Moreover, although these sermons stress the need for a kind of heroic effort, there is little sense that many of the listeners are unlikely to respond adequately. The joy of intense piety unites with the resilience of youth, infusing the sermons with Edwards' personal ardor, idealism, and hope. It is likely that the action recommended in "The Way of Holiness" is at least an extrapolation of the struggles behind the "Diary" entries treating of his sustained efforts to experience holiness:

> Meditate on the holiness of God, and see if you cannot see a conformity, a *likeness* in your mind. There is no likeness or comparison in degree . . . but yet there is a likeness in *nature* between God and the soul of the believer.[9]

And in "The Duty of Self-Examination" Edwards continues his emphasis upon the *underlying principle* of actions as the key to one's spiritual state. In "True Repentance Required" he insists that "True

---

8. A more traditionally theological description of this process would emphasize the operations of the Holy Spirit, but JE usually emphasizes the subjective or experiential and thus the psychological dimensions in his definitions.

9. P. 477 below. Note also that the phrasing here is virtually identical with that of Solomon Stoddard in his differentiation of saving from common grace quoted above (p. 275n.).

contrition may be known by the principle it arises from, and that is love to God and the Lord Jesus Christ."[1] In his analysis, Edwards observes: "I do not say that a true penitent's thoughts always run exactly in this *order,* but I say that they are of this nature, and do arise from this principle."[2] Mysteriously, the "principle of life" comes to dominate the soul and the soul streams out or blossoms in the rays of divine love. As expressed in "Living to Christ," "he lives in Christ and Christ lives in him, yea, not only lives in him but is his life. He is invigorated with him, with his Holy Spirit which is diffused as new life all over his soul."[3]

Edwards' organic model of conversion, focused upon a certain taste for holiness—not yet refined to a "new simple idea"—rather than being constructed of a series of activities or even a very structured pattern of experience, may have appeared somehow insubstantial even to Edwards. Caught as he was between modes of discourse, that embodying the traditional sanctions of the "Dissenters of Old England" on the one hand and the "new logick" of the Continental Rationalists which impressed him by its more subtle and rigorous structures of thought on the other, it is no wonder that during the New York period there is ample evidence of his efforts to formulate basic theoretical positions in his sermons and notebooks. To make the sanctified life of the saint more concrete than a vague aspiration yet more richly personal than traditional Puritan models as they had ossified through years of usage was one of Edwards' chief preoccupations.[4] He wrote meditations upon the saint's life, divine attributes, Christian love, and many other essential concepts in these New York sermons, working over traditional ideas, exploring and analyzing the archetypes always with zeal and perhaps with delight in the agility and power of his penetrating intellect.

At some point in 1723, whether during his final weeks in the city or during the rather melancholy period following his return to East Windsor is not certain, Edwards tried his hand at a new form with memorable results.[5]

1. Pp. 513–14 below.
2. P. 514 below.
3. P. 570 below.
4. While both his metaphysics and his rhetoric document various foreign influences, from the Cambridge Platonists to the Malebranchean John Norris, which JE absorbed in his college reading, it should be kept in mind that both Timothy Edwards and Solomon Stoddard were stimulating JE to search for new formulations of religious experience as well.
5. There is no extant manuscript of the meditation alleged to be of Sarah Pierrepont,

They say there is a young lady in New Haven[6] who is beloved by[7] that Great Being who made and rules the world, and that there are certain seasons in which this Great Being in some way or other invisibly[8] comes to her and fills her mind with exceeding sweet delight,[9] and that she hardly cares for anything except to meditate on him. That she expects after a while to be received up where he is,[1] to be raised up out of the world and caught up into heaven, being assured that he loves her too well to let her remain at a distance from him always. There she is to dwell with him, and to be ravished with his love and delight forever.[2] Therefore, if you present all the world before her with the richest of its treasures she disregards it and cares nothing[3] for it and is unmindful of any pain or affliction. She has a strange sweetness in her mind and singular purity in her affections, is most just and conscientious in all her conduct,[4] and you could not persuade her to do anything wrong or sinful if you would give her all the world, lest she should offend this Great Being.[5] She is of a[6] wonderful sweetness, calmness and universal benevolence of mind, especially after this Great Being[7] has manifested himself to her mind. She will sometimes go about from place to place singing sweetly and seems to be always full of joy and pleasure, and no one knows for what. She loves to be alone walking in the fields and groves and seems to have someone invisible always conversing with her.

One of the most remarkable works in early American literature, this meditation has been variously described as a "tribute" or an "apostrophe," but it is probably best described as a meditative poem—

---

and there are two variant texts with claim to have been transcribed from the autograph manuscript, the first in Dwight's *Life,* pp. 114–15, and the second in Stoughton's *Windsor Farmes,* pp. 82–83. Dwight states that the piece was "written on a blank leaf " (p. 114) while Stoughton explains that it was "upon a blank leaf of a book, which is still preserved" (p. 82). Below, substantive variants of the two published texts are noted.

6. Stoughton: blank.
7. Dwight: "of."
8. Dwight: "invisible."
9. Stoughton: "delights."
1. Stoughton: "to be where he is."
2. Stoughton: "dwell with him. Therefore . . ."
3. Dwight: "not."
4. Stoughton: "in her conduct."
5. Stoughton: "the Great Being."
6. Stoughton: "She is for wonderful."
7. Dwight: "Great God."

perhaps "ode" would be most appropriate—by one who refers in his "Diary" to "singing forth the meditations of my heart in prose."[8] (We, in an age of free verse, need not cavil at calling "singing prose" po- etry.) This song is evidently a tribute to Sarah Pierrepont, as the two editors of the manuscript text state independently, perhaps even con- stituting a kind of marriage proposal to the thirteen-year-old girl if, as alleged, it was presented to her as an inscription on the fly-leaf of a gift book.[9]

But our concern in this context is more properly with the poem itself. It begins with a distinctively American equivalent of the "once upon a time" motif in "they say" and sustains the tone and diction of the fairytale or world of wonder throughout. The simplicity and clar- ity of statement contribute to the creation of an image of doric ab- straction and timelessness, such an image as invests Keats' "Ode on a Grecian Urn." The meditation is certainly not consciously archaic, yet the "young lady" is curiously abstract in delineation, like the pro- tagonists of Greek myth rather than those more sensuous images characteristic of the Bible and of modern Western literature. The "Great Being" likewise might have a variety of names since he is hardly pinned down as the distinctive deity of the Judeo-Christian ethos: he is simply the "Great Being who made and rules the world." Clearly, the realm of the poem is that of the spiritual ideal, as abstract also as a New England gravestone carving. And in this realm the essentials are as evident as details in Aegean sunlight or points in Calvinistic exegesis: the consciousness of the divine presence, the in- spiration of "divine light," the joy of liberation from "the world," the value of salvation realized, the exotic free spirit or inspired *isolato*. The analysis could be phrased in various ways and some of the ser- mon titles from the New York period would be quite appropriate in the naming of parts; what is important is that the poem defines an archetype, and when all is considered the image may refer plausibly enough to Sarah Pierrepont, but it is more certainly an ideal type of the young Jonathan Edwards as revealed in his sermons and private notes of the period. From having an ecstatic sense of communication with God to separating oneself from the world through wandering in "fields and groves," the traits may well have been those of Sarah

    8. Dwight, *Life*, p. 94.
    9. Stoughton's description certainly suggests that JE wrote the meditation on the free endpaper of a book, perhaps a collection of devotional writings, for presentation. The recipient could hardly have been other than the meditation's subject.

Pierrepont, but the terms more certainly reflect the literary currency of Edwards' rhetoric during the New York period.

Young men in love tend to perceive what they will in their mistresses, and Edwards, as passionate and idealistic a youth as can be found in any age or culture, was far from exceptional in this respect. What is more, Sarah seems to have accepted the challenge of his vision as well as his hand if accounts of their later lives together are to be believed, including his own in *Some Thoughts Concerning the Present Revival of Religion in New England* (1742).[1] But to understand this poem in such a limited biographical or occasional context alone is to neglect a dimension of its significance that is essential to any consideration of Edwards' spiritual and intellectual growth during the New York period. For it is clear from consideration of this mirroring of his own image in the piece that one of the chief achievements of Edwards in his poem is the realization of the Christian life as he then was striving to conceive of it. In homiletical exposition he had replaced the concept of a distinctive *structure* of experience with the notion of a *principle* of experience, as has been noted above, but for Edwards at this time that indwelling principle was itself perhaps somewhat too abstract and impersonal a conception to be wholly satisfying, especially when contrasted with the human drama of the traditional conversion narratives. Thus the poem is a *humanizing* of the abstract notion of God's supernatural presence in the lives of converted persons, reflecting through an emblematic human figure the essential values and relationships respecting conversion and the new life as Edwards then apprehended them.[2] The economy and elegance of the piece put it on an artistic footing with anything he wrote.

1. See the text in *The Great Awakening*, ed. C. C. Goen, *Works, 4*, 331–41.

2. Although there is nothing in this formulation by JE that would be offensive to either his father or Solomon Stoddard, neither does it embody the language in which they defined the operations of saving grace. Most noticeable, perhaps, is the absence of the element of negation in tandem with affirmation. But both the concepts and phrasing of the Cambridge Platonist John Smith are again prominent as JE attempts to address the real state of holiness. For instance, the following passages from "Of the Excellency and Nobleness of True Religion" prefigure the quiet exaltation of JE's meditation: "*one that is informed by True Religion, lives above himself, and is raised to an intimate Converse with the Divinity*" (p. 378); "Religion is Life and Spirit, which flowing out from God . . . returns to him again as into its own Original, carrying the Souls of Good men up with it" (p. 380); ". . . a flight of the Soul alone to God alone" (p. 412); "Holy and religious Souls being once toucht, with an inward sense of Divine Beauty and Goodness, by a strong impress upon them are moved swiftly after God" (p. 430 in *Select Discourses*).

Unconventional, socially isolated, yet wholly orthodox and morally unexceptionable; a chosen one, esoteric, mystical, yet wholly amiable and attractive: the complex spiritual aspirations of Jonathan Edwards during the first phase of his professional life are expressed here, as the "Diary" expresses the turbulence attending his efforts to clarify his personal spiritual goals. But the actual life of his ministry, through which he established an ongoing relationship with the world, including his most meaningful human relationships such as that with the Smith family, can best be inferred through the medium of the sermons. The sermon is, after all, the primary document of the pastorate as practiced by Jonathan Edwards in any period of his life, but especially so at a time when other aspects of the pastoral round were minimal and he was obviously in the process of working out the essential public stance of his ministry, including theological emphases and homiletical or rhetorical strategies.

When he went to New York, Edwards probably carried fewer than a dozen sermons with him, although he would have had to supply nearly forty preaching occasions during his stay there. Inevitably, he must have spent much of his time simply meeting the demands of the pulpit. With such a high sense of spiritual seriousness and intellectual rigor, though still relatively inexperienced in developing sermon arguments, he must have lavished hours on his early sermons, including time expended attempting to memorize them.[3] Significantly, it was under the practical pressure of developing his ideas for sermons, rather than in hours of exalted private speculation during his graduate studies, that Edwards began those notebook meditations which eventually became the vast "Miscellanies" of his systematic theological thought. Identifying essential concepts through the insights of his personal quest, Edwards gave depth and power to the standard messages of the pulpit while serving in a pastorate which could easily have been the most perfunctory of professional relationships. Of the sermons that he must have prepared before or during the New York pastorate, twenty-four (three of them fragments) re-

3. Given the preference of JE's father and grandfather Stoddard for *extempore* or *memoriter* preaching, one must assume that JE made an initial effort to preach without relying upon his manuscript, at least for some months. There are in fact a number of formal or stylistic devices in these early sermons (discussed in the appropriate places) which might have functioned as mnemonic aids also. On the other hand, there is no record that JE ever preached without his manuscript.

main in the Edwards manuscript archive at the Beinecke Library.[4] Neither dated nor marked with signs identifying them as New York sermons, they have been identified through form and content, and especially through physical characteristics. Never before published, these sermons contain Edwards' earliest extensive writings in any category and are preceded only by some of the scientific notebook speculations and "Of Insects" from his three final years at New Haven, besides a very few letters. Thus both the foundations of his theological thought and the inception of his career as one of the greatest preachers our nation has produced may be given consideration for the first time in these sermons. Indeed, among the earliest five sermons which were apparently written over a period of several months before his going to New York is that on the text, Is. 3:10, a sermon which may well be the one he prepared for his licensing as a preacher and may even be his first formal effort in the sermon genre.

This earliest extant sermon, "Christian Happiness" is indeed a tentative exploration of the form, for it contains only fourteen heads, of which a mere three are subheads. Despite the simplicity of his sermon's structure, Edwards employs elaborately careful transitions such as "But we shall first observe, which is our first proposition . . ." and so forth. In a few weeks, however, he tackled longer sermons (to be delivered in two installments, morning and afternoon) containing over fifty heads. He occasionally had trouble keeping track of head numbers, and these first sermons have a decidedly mechanical quality, largely because each head is begun with a short topical statement, as in an outline, which is immediately repeated in the ensuing sentence as the argument begins in earnest. By the time of his departure for New York, he had achieved a little self-confidence in the form, having composed eight or ten sermons,[5] and during the course of his stay there he succeeded in composing sermons that clearly anticipate the great productions of the 1730s.

Upon first reading these sermons, one may be struck by the naiveté and rustic vitality of the style. Although there is nothing trivial or

4. The third of the fragments will be published later in this series since it constitutes less than half of the later sermon in which it has been incorporated.

5. I am assuming that at least a few of the sermons have been destroyed or lost, perhaps as many as forty percent. It is difficult to assess how much writing or preaching JE was doing during those weeks before his departure for New York, and it could be that he wrote no more than a half-dozen sermons.

facetious, the pulpit decorum is slightly strained by expressions such as "the tip of happiness" to describe a saint's glorification, "[God] thanks no one for his being" to indicate God's autonomy, and "have your ease and sleep quietly in a whole skin" to describe sinful sloth. Similar are "can you suck eternal life out of [worldly prosperity]?"; "Christ Jesus in regeneration gives the body of sin . . . such a blow on the head as he never recovers"; and "The pleasures of religion raise one clear above laughter, and rather tend to make the face shine than screw it into a grimace."[6] Such statements, complemented by numerous colloquial turns of phrase and Anglo-Saxon monosyllables, give an earthy twang to the style, a tone that would go nicely with the homely similitudes of Thomas Hooker. Edwards, however, has hardly any references to domestic life. On the contrary, the similitudes in these sermons are more apt to involve figures such as Alexander the Great, debauched Roman emperors, and African headhunters, while scenes are commonly drawn from the Old Testament, the "dream" of John Bunyan, or Foxe's *Martyrs*. There are images and metaphors drawn from nature, but most of these involve universals such as the sun, moon, and stars, rather than anything suggestive of locale.

These apparent incongruities are aggravated by the presence, particularly in the earlier sermons, of rather academic tropes and figures amid the plain talk. One cannot predict when an elaborate homoeoteleuton, pleonasm, or other device—usually a variety of repetition or parallelism—will suddenly arise.

> Should we not think him a prince of extraordinary clemency, he a master of extraordinary goodness, he a father of great tenderness, who never [commanded] anything of his subjects, his servants, or his children but what was for their good and advantage? But God is such a king, such a lord, such a father to us.

Coming at the end of a head as a peroration, this triadic passage from "Christian Happiness" is comparatively successful and brief; however, such rhetoric too often seems precious or grandiloquent when it appears suddenly in a context of notably less elegant sentences. Another device, one that Edwards continued to use long after

6. The last two of these expressions seem to owe something to John Smith's *Select Discourses*, as Smith writes that "the whole business of Christ is *the greatest Blow to Sin* that may be . . ." (p. 338), or that religion is not melancholy but gives "vigorous masculine joy" (p. 406).

he abandoned the merely decorative, is the *a fortiori* formula, though in its first appearance in the same sermon it is also a little heavy-handed:

> And is there any man here present that would be at all afraid of the pain of the prick of a pin for a minute if he knew that after it he should enjoy a life of—suppose—seventy years of the greatest prosperity imaginable without the least molestation? No more reason to fear a short life of [seventy] years filled up with trouble and affliction when he knows that, at [the] end of it, he shall enjoy an eternity of the highest happiness. For there is infinitely more difference between an eternity and seventy years, than between seventy years and a minute, and vastly a greater difference between heavenly happiness and the greatest torments of this world, than between the greatest worldly prosperity and the pain of the prick of a pin.

Obviously, Edwards was exploring and testing the conventional rhetoric of the sermon form in these first sermons, simplifying the structure of statement of his immediate mentor, his father, while enriching and complicating the idiom in the spirit of the Cambridge Platonists and English metaphysicals whom he had been reading in his graduate studies, and sometimes straining more than a little in the execution. With a few exceptions, his performances are all too reminiscent of many a college freshman's efforts in the essay: paragraphs are either too long or too short; ideas are sometimes developed, but when this fails they are dutifully pounded instead, and despite passages of fine exposition, there is too little sense of the whole in each of the parts. Edwards was more fortunate than the modern essayist, however, because of the design of the sermon form he inherited provides a kind of literary corset that enforces a minimal symmetry upon expository ripples and bulges. But this merely "external" or formal unity aside, there are only a few sermons that suggest their author's capacity to exploit the tremendous dynamic potential of the form. Only in later years would Edwards develop a sure sense of the movement from Text to Doctrine to Application which is a grand descent from the Mountain: from Holy Writ to abstract principles to personal values and actions; from the realm of God to the realm of human understanding to the sensibility of the human heart; from the eternal to the temporal to the existential moment. Eventually, he would not only recognize the nature of the form, but would exploit its dynamic potential more artfully than any other American preacher—but not in his earliest sermons.

When the literary dimension of these early sermons is assessed as a whole, perhaps the outstanding achievement is a certain concreteness through specificity, including the subtle handling of visual imagery. Of course, Edwards has long been noted for his imagery, but in later works it is simply one aspect of a carefully orchestrated style. Here, however, it is outstanding both for its quality and its density. This is all the more remarkable because the subject matter of these sermons is more abstract than is common in the later sermons. The phenomenon reminds us that rarely has a man, commonly designated an abstract thinker, had such a concrete imagination as Jonathan Edwards, nor has one who was not a professed poet often been as obsessed with rendering essentially abstract ideas so concretely. His visual imagery hardly needs to be illustrated here, for it is everywhere in passages used to illustrate other points.

Turning from the form and style of the sermons to matters of theme and intent, the impressions of naiveté and vitality are confirmed. The sermons are naive primarily in that so much is attempted in them. At the beginning of the Application of "God's Excellencies," Edwards insists that "the whole of Christianity follows as an improvement from this doctrine." His topical range within sermons is also impressive and since most of the sermons deal with basic conceptions such as grace, redemption, the Christian life, and the experience of holiness, he manages in these twenty-three sermons to touch upon most of the issues and themes of his later writings. A reader acquainted with the major sermons and treatises of Edwards will frequently recognize familiar echoes in turning over the pages of these early sermons. A case in point is this passage from "Glorious Grace":

> We are dependent on free grace even for ability to lay hold on Christ already offered, so entirely is the gospel dispensation of mere grace . . . they dishonor God and the gospel who depend on anything else but mere grace. . . . they take away the praise, glory, and honor that is due to God . . . and set up themselves as the objects of it, as if their salvation at least partly was owing to what they have done. . . .
>
> [Some] hold that they are able to prepare and fit themselves for salvation already merited, or at least are able to do something towards it of themselves. And it is to be feared that many that

don't openly profess either their own righteousness or their own strength do very much depend upon both.

Here Edwards' maiden publication, *God Glorified in the Work of Redemption* (1731), is clearly prefigured nearly a decade earlier, indicating that Edwards was already on the trail of the Arminians in New York.[7]

In much the same way, *A Divine and Supernatural Light* (1734) is anticipated in "Christ, the Light of the World"; indeed, the whole sermon is an Ur–*Divine Light,* but in this passage Edwards states the essence of his argument:

> Christ enlightens the soul by his Holy Spirit. Although the Word be quick and powerful, yet it is nothing; it is but a dead letter without the application of the Holy Spirit. . . . but Jesus Christ, when he enlightens the mind, sends forth the Holy Spirit to dwell in the soul, to be as a continual eternal light, to manifest and make known spiritual things to the believer.

Coming perilously close to the "inner light" of his Quaker contemporary, John Woolman, Edwards here makes his initial public commitment to immediate divine illumination as an indispensable dimension of religious knowledge.[8]

The subjects of true religious affections and the morphology of conversion—personal issues in New York and the subject of so much critical attention in the Northampton years—are hardly given the sustained examination in these early sermons that was to be accorded

7. There can be little doubt that JE's early focus upon Arminianism was in part a response to the very recent debacle at Yale College when Rector Timothy Cutler and tutors Johnson and Browne espoused the Church of England and were dismissed by the Yale trustees for their heresy on Oct. 16, 1722. Like Cutler, Johnson, and Browne, JE had been a great reader of the new books from England and was deeply impressed with both new ideas and new rhetoric, but JE was determined to stand for the New England Way, and anti-Arminianism seems to have become his banner.

8. Neither here nor elsewhere is there evidence of Quaker influence upon JE's rhetoric. Certainly Newton's *Optics* influenced him as a scientific thinker (see Anderson, ed., *Works,* 6, 41–45), and the preoccupation with perception stimulated by that work in England and reflected in literary works such as James Thompson's *The Seasons* (1726–30) may be likewise observed in JE. But the more immediate influence upon his rhetoric is a much older work: again, John Smith's *Select Discourses.* Thus Smith identifies God as "Eternal Father of Lights" (p. 151), speaks of "a Light that descends from Heaven which is only able to guide and conduct the souls of men to Heaven" (p. 279) and which is perceived by "a Divine and Spiritual sense" (p. 278) in men, for God enlightens the faculty more than the object (p. 373).

them subsequently; however, a few of the crucial issues are broached, sometimes in passages tantalizingly slight. Thus, in "True Repentance Required," after describing the heart-cleaving humiliation of true repentance and the new apprehension of sin resulting from it, Edwards insists that the process of conversion cannot be easily codified: "I do not say that a true penitent's thoughts always run exactly in this order, but I say that they are of this nature and do arise from this principle." Similarly, he insists, "This humiliation, which is the effect of godly contrition, is not always to the same degree, but it is always of the same nature . . ." In other sermons, he declares that neither profession nor church membership is a guarantor—"neither circumcision availeth anything nor uncircumcision, but a new creature"—and professes that "true converts themselves need to be converted."[9] Though he is much concerned with the conversion experience in these sermons, Edwards is far from attempting that new delimitation and codification of religious experience that the events of the 1730s and 1740s were to force upon him; on the contrary, as in his most mature writings, he seems to oppose anything that smacks of a foolish consistency in matters of religion.

One more motif that has considerable interest in retrospect appears in a remarkable number of the New York sermons:

> [Sin causes his servant to] do his work upon the very edge of a dreadful precipice, where . . . he is in imminent danger every moment of slipping and falling into a bottomless pit of liquid fire . . . we know not how near we may be to the end of our lives and to the brink of an endless eternity, and if we han't our eyes about us we are in danger of dropping into the bottomless pit every moment. [In their attempts to gain worldly things, sinners] come so near to the pit that their feet are every moment ready to slip. [God] preserves us from annihilation. We should immediately drop into nothing if he did not uphold us. . . . [but] God has declared that he will not be mocked, and those that will not hear [his call] . . . God will make such know that it is a terrible thing to fall into the hands of the living God.[1]

Although there were no metaphorical spiders in New York, this is

---

9. See "The Way of Holiness" and "Living to Christ."

1. In order of quotation, these excerpts are from "Wicked Men's Slavery to Sin," "The Importance of a Future State," "The Nakedness of Job," "Dedication to God," "The Duty of Hearkening to God's Voice."

clearly the "Newtonian" aspect of the rhetoric of *Sinners in the Hands of an Angry God* (1741). These passages are only a few of the anticipations of *Sinners* evident in the New York sermons, suggesting the depth of theological and artistic significance in that notorious climax of Edwards' preaching career in 1741.

Other themes anticipating major works are evident in the New York sermons; one who looks for hints toward the *History of Redemption*, the *Freedom of the Will*, or for that matter nearly any one of Edwards' major works of his later years, is almost certain to find more than a hint of his subject in this topical mélange. Of course, Edwards was hardly appreciative of the hints we perceive in retrospect, and we would be mistaken to value these early sermons only for their anticipation of later works, for most of all the New York sermons represent a distinctive phase of Edwards' preaching career that was not to be repeated.

Despite the heterogeneity and even the incongruities of these sermons, both rhetorically and thematically, there is a clearly defined intent that links virtually all of them: the definition of the Christian life in experiential terms. It is significant that the first sermon has the doctrine, "A good man is a happy man, whatever his outward circumstances are," for it is an evocation of Christian happiness and an exposition of the ground of it that constitute the central preoccupation of these sermons. Perhaps another collage of passages from several sermons can best adumbrate the locus of Edwards' exalted view of the Christian experience as he presents it, characteristically aspect by aspect, through sustained meditations in many of the New York sermons.

> A life of love, if it be from rational principles, is the most pleasant life in the world. . . . But especially must a life of love to Christ be very pleasant, above all other kinds of living, because as Christ is of all things most excellent, so is the love of him a more excellent kind of love than any other, and the more excellent and refined the love is, the greater and purer is the pleasure of it. . . . the pleasures that result from it must be solid, real, substantial, and never-fading.
>
> Those that have a vehement love to any person can with pleasure spend their time in thinking of that person and of his perfections and actions, so with what great delight may those that love Christ with an [active] love spend their thoughts . . . [they]

may make new discoveries to all eternity and yet not have discovered all.

The union between Christ and those that love him is more close, and communion more intimate than between any other lovers. . . . there is no such near or intimate conversation between any other lovers, as between Christ and the Christian.[2]

Predominant in this picture are the "life of love" and the sensible pleasure that accrues from it: a fusion of the affectional and rational dimensions of the self through communion with the supreme principle of life, excellence, personified in Christ.[3] Concomitant with such a life is a new perception of reality, including fundamental self-awareness, and an immediate apprehension of the paradox of the "fortunate fall":

> When a man is enlightened savingly by Christ, he is, as it were, brought into a new world. . . . he is like one that was born and brought up in a cave, where [there] is nothing but darkness, but now [he] is brought out into the lightsome world enlightened by the beams of the sun . . . [he] looks and gazes with sweet astonishment . . . he now sees things in their true shapes and colors . . . he sees his own vileness and filthiness, which he had often heard of before, but never believed. . . . he had often before heard many discourses about religion, about God and Jesus Christ, heaven and hell, free grace and mercy, the excellency of religion and the glorious mysteries of the gospel, but it all seemed as a strange thing to him before, but now . . . he sees with his own eyes and admires and is astonished, as being really sensible of the truth of these things.
>
> . . . we should frequently be reflecting on our old sins and lamenting of them before God. This frequent lamenting of sin

2. From the "Application on Love to Christ."

3. This aspect of JE's thought, central throughout his life and just coalescing during the New York period, has been given sustained analysis by Roland A. Delattre in *Beauty and Sensibility in the Thought of Jonathan Edwards: An Essay in Aesthetics and Theological Ethics* (New Haven, Yale Univ. Press, 1968). Although he notes intellectual and rhetorical traditions involving the Puritans and the Cambridge Platonists (p. 120), Delattre seems unaware of possible direct influences such as that of John Smith. See also the discussions of Excellency in Anderson, ed., *Works, 6,* and of Beauty, Benevolence, and Love in Paul Ramsey, ed., *Ethical Writings, The Works of Jonathan Edwards* (New Haven, Yale Univ. Press, 1989), *8.* Another important discussion of these concepts is in Norman Fiering, *Jonathan Edwards's Moral Thought and Its British Context* (Chapel Hill, Univ. of North Carolina Press, 1981).

will not decrease, but increase our comfort. For daily lamentation, contrition, and humiliation, we shall be largely repaid by the Holy Ghost, even in this world, by spiritual joys and delights.

He will [give] you liberty to recreate and delight yourself in the best, the purest, and most exquisite pleasures as much as you please, without restraint.[4]

Ultimately, the holiness of sanctification is bestowed, the self is transfigured and suffused with divine joy, and life through love transcends death. In such passages, the nineteen-year-old preacher is obviously writing at the limits of his rhetorical competence and effects range from mawkishly sentimental vignettes to visions hauntingly suggestive of the illuminations of William Blake.

Holiness is a most beautiful, lovely thing. . . . 'Tis almost too high a beauty for any creature to be adorned with; it makes the soul a little, amiable, and delightful image of the blessed Jehovah. How may angels stand with pleased, delighted, and charmed eyes and look and look with smiles of pleasure upon that soul that is holy! . . . What a sweet calmness, what a calm ecstacy doth it bring to the soul! Of what a meek and humble nature is true holiness, how peaceful and quiet.

Grace and holiness is the same in this world as in the next, but only in this life it is like a spark, but there shall be like a flame. . . . There shall be no darkness or dullness, which the best complain of in this world. They shall be active as angels; their souls shall be full and overflowing with an active, sprightly holiness, love and joy.

At death the believer . . . is adorned with a perfect and glorious holiness; the work of sanctification is then completed and the beautiful image of God has then its finishing strokes by the pencil of God, and begins to shine forth with a heavenly beauty like a seraphim: then that grace which was so suppressed and kept under by the devil and the remainders of corruption, begins to find itself at liberty, breaks out and flames forth in pure flames, and the soul begins to shine like the brightness of the firmament.[5]

---

4. From "Christ, the Light of the World," "True Repentance Required," and "Christian Liberty," respectively.

5. From "The Way of Holiness," "Life through Christ Alone," and "Dying to Gain," respectively.

Many a sabbath, the New York congregation was thus courted to seek holiness as Edwards presented them with a remarkable vision of happiness, at once intense and abstract, through an appeal both simple and exalted.

The meditations of these sermons are frequently constructed upon a single image or metaphor, but sustained elaboration through hundreds of words often produces a visionary, self-absorbed statement that threatens to overwhelm even the stout-ribbed sermon form. Driven as one enamored of love itself, and perhaps less constrained by the sense of pastoral routine than he would be in later years, Edwards only once or twice achieves a completely harmonious integration of the formal requirements of the sermon and the internal logic of a major meditation. Perhaps "Christ, the Light of the World" is his most successful New York sermon in this respect, as well as in most others.

Such an intense preoccupation with the invisible world may have startled Edwards' congregation, but he insisted that "if there be no future state of rewards and punishments in the other world, then the whole of religion is immediately thrown up and destroyed."[6] Thus he strove with all his might to make the "other world" itself real; more than that, he tried to establish its relation to this world clearly, sensibly, and memorably. He warns in his first sermon that to attempt to describe heaven by "talk of raptures and ecstasies, joy and singing, is but to set [it] forth by very low shadows of the reality, and all we can say by our best rhetoric is really and truly vastly below what is but the bare and naked truth"; likewise, "if we had a clear and full apprehension of [hell], only barely an idea of it without any fear of our bearing it, that it would overcome human nature and kill us immediately." Yet he insists that "it is impossible we should love, fear, and obey God as we ought except we know what he is, and have right ideas of his perfections . . . wherefore . . . I . . . speak of these things comparatively . . . because comparisons are a great help to our weakened, dull minds to conceive of things that are far out of the ken of our imaginations, and the outmost verge of our most outstretched thoughts."[7]

When Edwards left New York on that bittersweet day in spring, he was a preacher. If his mastery of the sermon form was incomplete,

6. "The Importance of a Future State."

7. From "Christian Happiness," "The Value of Salvation," and "God's Excellencies," respectively.

he had at least established himself in it and, in the process, had begun to exploit its potential as a means of inquiry into aspects of his own religious experience. It is noteworthy that these sermons are intended more to lure people into heaven than to frighten them out of hell, for the hortatory dimension is overshadowed by the poetically evocative in most of them, and the auditor is less the subject of instruction or the object of attack than he is witness to an expression of faith. As a discovery of Edwards' own intensely imaginative apprehension of a religious orthodoxy and a rhetorical tradition, these sermons have a doctrinal and formal conventionality that seems essentially staid in intent, although an internal or spiritual energy constantly threatens to breach conventional decorum both theologically and rhetorically. The pursuit of seminal Christian myths, metaphors, and images in passages of incantatory intensity suggests that these sermons may provide the best analogue to Edwards' meditations by the Hudson.

THE nearly calligraphic hand of the Is. 3:10 manuscript suggests that this is a special sermon. No other sermon is so meticulously indited, and that in conjunction with the apparent date of composition in late 1720 or early 1721 leads to the supposition that this piece is not only the earliest extant sermon but perhaps Edwards' first formal sermon, composed for his licensure or delivered as an academic exercise.

The academic note is basic to the sermon in its classical *bonum hominem* theme. Although the convention may have been utilized primarily for the purpose of a foil to the radical Christian asceticism of the argument, the fact that many biblical citations were added only for a subsequent repreaching indicates that the original auditory may well have been an academic one. Supporting this assumption is the repeated emphasis upon man as a "reasonable being" and the emphasis upon the mental world and its relationship to a transcendent reality. Although the sermon advocates a traditional Christian piety as the key to true happiness, the overall character of the argument is that of an address to putatively intellectual or sophisticated persons.

The literary devices deployed in the sermon are some that in later years would constitute Edwards' essential rhetorical arsenal: vivid imagery, vigorous statement, repetition, parallelism, and analogy *a fortiori*. Here, however, they are sometimes less subtly employed; indeed, they too have something of the academic exercise about them in that they tend to stand above the plane of discourse as discrete entities, betraying the hand of the artificer. Much of the time, however, the argument evolves with considerable power and clarity of focus, each stage being clearly articulated in the larger structure.

The external form of the sermon is simple, involving only three tertiary subheads. It is that form which Edwards would continue to employ throughout his career, but now in a version markedly free of logical or formal bifurcation. This seems to parallel the notably spare argument from Scripture "proofs," that is, explicated Scripture passages offered as authoritative evidence. Again, the literary evidence indicates a learned if not a secular auditory, one that might not take notes by heads and perhaps one that would appreciate sustained elaborations of points.

Perhaps the most remarkable passage in the sermon is the beginning, "Reasonable beings . . ." here clearly intended as the authentic title for human beings. This note is sustained throughout a sermon preached specifically to "men" who are characterized primarily by their rational capacity. Even the limits of the discourse, as in references to heaven, are defined by the limits of human mind. Edwards' first sermon appears to be that of a conscious rationalist who would stress the fact while at the same time acknowledging the limits of reason before the mysteries of Christian orthodoxy. The sermon defines the truly good life for the reasonable Christian.

* * *

The sermon manuscript is an octavo quire of eight infolded leaves. A small slip containing some brief additions for a later repreaching of the sermon was originally pinned at the center fold of the booklet between the first and second leaves, though it is now loosely inserted. Not only is the hand neat and formally elaborate, but Edwards avoided most abbreviations that he employed in later sermons. There are some neat deletions of passages and various division lines which were added later in connection with at least two repreachings. On the whole, this manuscript is an unusually attractive example of a single preaching unit sermon, written in the first instance without regard to time-saving or eye-catching devices that were to become routine in later sermon manuscripts. One device employed in this manuscript and rarely if ever used again is the parenthetical aside to the auditory, carefully marked with bracket-shaped parentheses. Edwards apparently soon decided this device was a distraction or a quaint gesture born of self-conscious unease.

CHRISTIAN HAPPINESS

ISAIAH 3:10

*Say unto the righteous, it shall be well with him: for they shall eat the
fruit of their doings.*

R EASONABLE beings, while they act as such, naturally choose those
things which they are convinced are best for them, and will certainly
do those things which they know they had better do than leave undone. (And, indeed, who in the world could imagine that there were
such unreasonable creatures in the world, as that at the very same
time that they themselves know a thing to be much to their advantage,
yet will not choose or do it?) God always deals with men as reasonable
creatures, and every [word] in the Scriptures speaks to us as such.
Whether it be in instructing and teaching of us, he [gives us] no
commands to believe those things which are directly contrary to reason, and in commanding of us he desires us to do nothing but what
will be for our own advantage, our own profit and benefit, and frequently uses this argument with us to persuade us to obey his commands. For, "can a man be profitable to God as he that is wise may
be profitable unto himself; is it any pleasure to the Almighty, that we
are righteous, or is it gain to him, that we make our ways perfect?"
(Job 22:2–3). But God has told [us] that if we be wise, we shall be
wise for ourselves, and God, in our text, gives it as a special charge
to assure the godly from Him that his godliness shall be of great
advantage to him. (And that we may the better understand it and see
how it is brought in, let us look back on the foregoing words.) God,
in the beginning of this chapter, denounced great and terrible judgments against the children of Judah, as in the first [and succeeding]
verses:

> For, behold, the Lord, the Lord of hosts, doth take away from
> Jerusalem and from Judah the stay and the staff, the whole stay

of bread, and the whole stay of water . . . and babes shall rule over them. And the people shall be oppressed, everyone by another, and everyone by his neighbor: the child shall behave himself proudly against the ancient, and the base against the honorable. . . . For Jerusalem is ruined and Judah is fallen . . . Woe unto their soul! for they have rewarded evil unto themselves [Is. 3:1,4–5,8–9].

But yet in the midst of all this, however dreadful the judgments may be upon the generality of the people, however woeful the case of the rest of them may be; yet say unto the righteous, assure him and cause him to know, "that it shall be well with him." And here we may observe what a particular care and concern the Almighty seems to have about [the righteous]; he suddenly stops and, as it were, breaks off abruptly the thread of the foregoing prophecy, and gives the strictest charge: go and tell the righteous that, however the people should be oppressed, however Jerusalem should be ruined and Judah should be fallen; yet, that he need not fear, for it should be well with him. Wherefore, what we shall insist upon shall be this:

DOCTRINE.

A good man is a happy man, whatever his outward circumstances are.

By "happy" in the Doctrine is not meant what in the most strict sense it is taken for, the actual enjoyment of the highest pleasure and perfection without the least mixture of the contrary, for that is reserved for every godly [person] to be enjoyed only after this life; but it is sufficient in our sense to make a man happy [if] his condition be very excellent, desirable and joyful; and we are now to show that the state of a good man is such, whatever his outward circumstances are. But we shall first observe, which is our first proposition, that

Prop. I. The outward or worldly circumstances of a good man are sometimes very afflictive. God often sees cause to afflict his children for their good, and we see no distinction made in this world, in the administration of worldly good things, between the good and [the] bad; God causes his sun to shine and his rain to fall alike on the just and on the unjust. Indeed, in some respects the good man is most liable to worldly evils; there are many godly men that enter into heaven through much tribulation, and Christ tells those who are his disciples that they must expect no other than tribulation here, and gives them the reason of it: John 15:18–19, 'tis because they are not of this world. If they were of this world, the world would love them, but because they are not of this world they are exalted clear above the world, and this spiteful and invidious world always hates and envies all that are above it; so that as things sometimes stand, the godly man may say that if there be no resurrection, he is of all men the most miserable. But,

Prop. II. The good man is happy in whatsoever condition he is in; and that,

First, because no worldly evils can do him any real hurt; secondly, because of those advantages, spiritual joys and satisfactions, he enjoys while here; and thirdly, more especially from the joyful hope and certain expectation, of the enjoyment of the perfection of happiness, eternally, hereafter. But,

First. Because no worldly evils can do him any real hurt. The good [man] is exalted out of the reach of all worldly evils; they cannot send forth their baneful influences so high as to touch him, and all the hurt they can do him is but as a sharp medicine. Although it be bitter, yet [it] takes away those diseases that would in the end, if they were let alone, be a thousand times more painful and troublesome to him. A good man may look down upon all the whole army of worldly afflictions under his feet with a slight and disregard (that is, *as evils,* for he ought to have the greatest regard to them as they are for his good), and consider with himself and joy therein that, however great they are and however numerous, let them all join their forces together against him and put on their most rueful and dreadful habits, forms and appearances, and spend all their strength, vigor and violence with endeavors to do him any real hurt or mischief, and it is all in vain. He may triumph over them all knowing this: light afflictions, which are but for a moment, shall only work out for him a far more exceeding and eternal weight of glory, and, that although sorrow continue for a night, yet joy cometh in the morning: remembering God's promise that all things shall surely work together for his good, and nothing shall offend. If he loses all the worldly good things he has, his estate, friends and relations, or if his body is put to the greatest tortures and pains imaginable, he may consider that it is all best for him that it should be, and that all the hurt they can do him is only to his body. And our Savior has commanded us not to fear them that even kill the body, and after that have no more that they can do; and whatever the world does against him, he has that to comfort him, that Christ has overcome the world.

How happy, then, must the condition of such a man be! Let any man now ask himself whether he should not think himself happy if he were delivered so from all those evils, that he was assured they would never trouble him more: if he were sure that he should never feel any more pain in his body, never have any want of any good things the world can afford, and never have any care and trouble [about] them; well then, is it not all one as if they never happened to him, if when they do happen to him they do him no hurt? Yea, is it not more than equivalent, if when they happen they not only do him hurt, but good? But this is the condition of a good man, and although good men are often grieved and troubled by worldly afflictions, and indeed they ought to be grieved for their sins, for the purging away of which their[1] afflictions come, yet the godly has no occasion to be troubled any further about them (Matt. 5:3–4,10–12).[2]

Second. The godly man is happy in whatever circumstances he is placed because of the spiritual privileges and advantages, joys and satisfactions, he actually enjoys while in this life. How great a happiness must needs [it] be to a man to have all his sins pardoned and to stand guilty of nothing in God's presence: to be washed clean from all his pollutions; to have the great and eternal and almighty Jehovah, who rules and governs the whole universe, and doth whatsoever he pleases in the armies of heaven and amongst the inhabitants of the earth, reconciled to him and perfectly at peace with him. How great a pleasure and satisfaction must it be to him to think of it, and not only that God is reconciled to him or has nothing against [him], inasmuch as all is pardoned; but also that this same almighty being who created him, who keeps him in being and who disposes of him and all other things every moment, loves him, and that with a great and transcendent love; and that He has adopted him and taken him to be His child, and given Himself to him to be his father and his portion, and that takes care of him as one that is very dear to Him, continually guides and directs him, and will lead him to the fountain of living waters. And how joyful and gladsome must the thoughts of Jesus Christ be to him, to think with how great a love Christ has loved

1. MS: "his."
2. JE added the verse citations later.

him, even to lay down His life and suffer the most bitter torments
for his sake, Who also now continually intercedes for him at the
throne of grace; to consider that so great a person as the eternal Son
of God, who also made the worlds, is his lord and master, and is not
ashamed to call us brethren, Who will come in and sup with him,
and He with him, and to see His arms expanded to embrace him and
offering Himself to be embraced by him. And beside, what a satisfaction and pleasure must it give to his mind to think that he is now
sanctified and made holy, adorned and beautified with those lovely
graces that make him lovely in the sight of God and excellent in the
sight of saints and angels; to reflect on himself and consider that he
acts rationally and doth that which the best of beings has commanded,
that he in some measure acts worthy of the nature of a man, in some
measure answers the end of his coming into the world in glorifying
God and doing good to his fellow creatures, and that he has not lived
altogether in vain: not as it is with many; they live in the world and
burthen the same, and had better be dead than alive for all the good
they do in it, or any they do towards manifesting the glory of him
that made them. The reflection on these things affords such a peace
and pleasantness to the mind, as far exceeds and is immensely above
all outward delights. What there is no wicked man doth know, neither; neither hath it entered into their hearts to conceive how great
are the comforts and pleasures of the godly, and how great [the]
things God hath prepared for all those that love [him], even in this
life; their pleasures are of vastly a more refined, higher and more
noble kind than those of the wicked, besides the many other advantages that this has above that, but especially that taken notice of in
the *Doctrine*: that no worldly afflictions in the world are able to deprive
them of them, but they, as rightly improved, do only serve to give
them a quicker and more lively sense of spiritual enjoyments. But the
time would fail to stay to enumerate all the happinesses of a good
man, even in this life; I shall therefore pass to the next particular.

Third. And lastly, from the joyful hope and assured expectation of
the enjoyment of the completion of happiness eternally hereafter, to
pretend to describe the excellence, the greatness, or duration of the
happiness of heaven, by the most artful composition of words, would
be but to darken and cloud it. To talk of raptures and ecstasies, joy
and singing, is but to set forth by very low shadows of the reality, and
all we can say by our best rhetoric is really and truly vastly below what
is but the bare and naked truth, and if St. Paul, who had seen them,

thought it but in vain to endeavor to utter it, much less shall we pretend to do it, and the Scriptures have gone as high in the descriptions of it as we are able to keep pace with in our imaginations and conception. We shall only say this, that the good man has the assurance and certainty of this: that he shall at last surely enjoy such a happiness as the Scripture describes to us. He has the best testimony, and the strongest security of it; he has a well-grounded hope that what he loves now above all things he shall then enjoy to the full of his desires, and whatsoever little beginnings of pleasure he feels now, he is assured, shall bestow[3] the highest perfection without the least mixture of the contrary. And now I leave it to every particular man's consideration, how great the happiness is in the actual enjoyment, and how great in the expectation of it, and with this consideration, the grounds of the hope of this happiness can't be in the least lessened by the greatest worldly afflictions. And now I hope I have sufficiently cleared it up: the godly man is happy in whatsoever worldly circumstances he is placed.

USE.

Inf. I. Then we may infer that the godly man need not be afraid of any temporal afflictions whatsoever. This, no man in the world can deny that grants what has been asserted, for surely if none of these worldly afflictions are able to do him any hurt, and if he is a happy man in the midst of them all, then he has no cause to be afraid of them.[4] His God has promised to defend him from the baneful influence of them all, and what need a man be afraid of storms and tempests without, that has so good a shelter? The Lord Jesus Christ is the captain of his salvation—to fight against them for us, to defend us from them and overcome them—and why should a man fear his enemies when the captain who undertakes for his defense is so potent as certainly to be able to overcome them, and besides what, he knows his afflictions in a few moments will have an end, and that after that he shall enjoy an eternity of the greatest bliss and happiness? And is there any man here present that would be at all afraid of the pain of the prick of a pin for a minute, if he knew that after it he should

3. Doubtful reading.

4. JE at first continued at this point to contrast the good man with the wicked, "who are of so low and weak and helpless minds that any of these light afflictions have power over them," but deleted the passage at the time of composition.

enjoy a life of—suppose—seventy years of the greatest prosperity imaginable, without the least molestation? No more reason to fear a short life of seventy years filled up with trouble and affliction, when he knows that, at [the] end of it, he shall enjoy an eternity of the highest happiness. For there is infinitely more difference between an eternity and seventy years, than between seventy years and a minute; and vastly a greater difference between heavenly happiness and the greatest torments of this world, than between the greatest worldly prosperity and the pain of the prick of a pin.

Inf. II. Hence we may see the excellent and desirable nature of true godliness. That which will cause that a man be a happy man in whatsoever condition he is in, and carrieth immutable happiness along with it, and such a happiness as by nothing in the world can be taken from him, that secures against all worldly evils so far as that they shall not be able to hurt him, must be of a very excellent and desirable nature. But this godliness doth, and hath a tendency to keep a man's mind bright, serene and calm, and that in the midst of the most raging and impetuous worldly storms to keep it always joyful and cheerful, and maintain always a clear sunshine of joy and comfort in it. Indeed, Christianity is now so low in the world, and there is such a want of the lively and vigorous actings of grace, even in those that are godly, that one, upon a cursory view, would think there was no such a tendency in religion as we talk of; but howe'er the case is now in this degenerate age, yet there has been a time in the first ages of the church when the Christian religion had so great an influence on the minds of almost all that professed the name of Christ, that they did not regard all the worst the world could do to them. They slighted and despised all the tortures and pains that could be invented against them, and even the very women and children disregarded them and triumphed over them, and showed themselves to be happy, and were joyful in the midst of flames or on a gridiron, and enjoyed much more pleasure and satisfaction there than the wicked man does in the greatest affluence of the highest sensual delights: so that we see this certainly is the nature and tendency of Christianity. However, for want of due exercise it fails, and it is always either for want of a sufficiency of it, for[5] want of the exercise of it, or from the natural imbecility and weakness of human nature, that it doth not always produce those effects.

5. MS: "of."

Inf. III. We may hence learn that to walk according [to] the rules of religion and godliness is the greatest wisdom. It is surely a great point of wisdom for any man to shun and avoid, if he can, troubles and afflictions, and it [is] also certain that it is as great a part of wisdom for a man, if he can, to get into such a state as that, if troubles and afflictions do come, they can do him no real hurt, or be sure that[6] they not only do him no hurt but good: but such is the state of the good man, and however troublesome those afflictions may seem to a good man at present, yet if they do him but good, it is really and truly as good for him—yea, better—than if they did not befall him. Although this may be a hard lesson to receive, yet it is as certain as that God is true, and however some may endeavor to dissuade to the contrary, every man's reason will give testimony to it, and surely 'tis the part of a wise man to choose what his reason tells him is best for him. They certainly are the wisest men that do those things that make most for their happiness, and this in effect is acknowledged by all men in the world, for there is no man upon earth but what is earnestly seeking after happiness, and it appears abundantly by their so vigorously trying all manner of ways; they will twist and turn every way, ply all instruments, to make themselves happy men; some will wander all over the face of the earth to find [it]: they will seek it in the waters and dry land, under the waters and in the bowels of the earth, and although the true way to happiness lies right before 'em and they might easily step into it and walk in it and be brought in it to as great happiness as they desire, and greater than they can conceive of, yet they will not enter into it. They try all the false paths; they will spend and be spent, labor all their lives' time, endanger their lives, will pass over mountains and valleys, go through fire and water, seeking for happiness amongst vanities, and are always disappointed, never find what they seek for; but yet like fools and madmen they violently rush forward, still in the same ways. But the righteous are not so; these only, have the wisdom to find the right paths to happiness.

Inf. IV. Hence learn the great goodness of God in joining so great happiness to our duty. God seems to have contrived all methods to encourage us in our duty; he has not only told us that by our faith and obedience we should escape eternal torments, although indeed, if it were only that it would be enough, one would think, to persuade any man that had the least spark of reason in him, that was not stark

6. MS: "if."

mad and had a mind to be always as miserable as he could be; but he has done more than this, but has told us that by it we should gain eternal happiness, and he has given us not only encouragement that we shall enjoy happiness after this life, but we shall have God to be our director, our guide while here, and even in this life [he] will be a tender father to us and will keep off all evils that may do us any real harm, and provide for us whatever we stand in need of; and yet not only so, but the thing required of us shall not only be easy but a pleasure and delight, even in the very doing of it. How much the goodness of God shines forth even in his commands! What could the most merciful being have done more for our encouragement? All that he desires of us is that we would not be miserable, that we would [not] follow those courses which of themselves would end in misery, and that we would be happy; and God, having a great desire to speak after the manner of man, that we should not be miserable but happy, has the mercy and goodness that he forwards us to it, to command us to do those things that will make us so. Should we not think him a prince of extraordinary clemency, he a master of extraordinary goodness, he a father of great tenderness, who never [commanded] anything of his subjects, his servants, or his children, but what was for their good and advantage? But God is such a king, such a lord, such a father to us.

Inf. V. We hence learn [what] we are to do for a remedy when we are under affliction: even embrace religion and godliness. All men in trouble and affliction are ready to embrace any remedy that will help them out of it. Here has been now set before [you] that which is a sovereign remedy, which doth as good as perfectly free a man from all manner of worldly troubles and afflictions, and is proof against the greatest, worst, most terrible of afflictions in this world, and this is the only remedy that will in all cases help a man against [them], so that if we are in affliction, or when we are—as we all, first or last, must be—without hope, we know our remedy.[7] We know what we are to do, and any man [who] is in affliction and knows what is the only help he can have, and will not embrace it, he must e'en sit down and

---

7. MS: "Here has been now set before that which is a sovereign remedy, which doth as good as perfectly free a man from all manner of worldly troubles and afflictions, and is proof against, the greatest worst most terrible and the greatest of afflictions in this world and this is the only remedy that will in all cases help a man against so that if we are in affliction. or when we are as we all without first or last must be. hope we know our remedy." JE later deleted "as we all without first or last must be."

bear his remediless afflictions; so that the wicked man has no pretense to any comfort under afflictions that does not resolve to reform,
for he is one that knows the help of his affliction and yet won't take
it, and therefore, without any manner of comfort, must e'en bear to
be afflicted still.

Exh. I. To the ungodly: to forsake his wickedness and to walk in
the ways of religion. You have now heard of the happiness of the
religious man, and it [is] such a happiness as you never yet experienced; you never yet have had experience of the spiritual comforts
of the noble, exalted, and pure pleasures of the godly. You, for your
part, have had experience of no other sort of pleasure but those of
sense and fancy; you have taken up, contented hitherto, with such a
sort of pleasure as the beasts enjoy as well as you. You now are invited
to the excellent and noble satisfactions of religion; you are invited to
such a happiness as is the happiness of angels, and happiness that
will be able to satisfy your desires. Be persuaded, then, to taste and
see how good it is; keep no longer grovelling in the dirt and feeding
on husks with hogs. Don't exercise yourself any longer in such things
as are beneath the nature of a man in serving the devil. One would
think that a man that had any spark of reason and was so noble a
creature as a man, would never bring himself down to be always at
the devil's beck, and to be led about just like blind fools, through
ditches and sloughs and all the worst and most filthy places, to make
sport for the devil. Don't follow him any [longer]: he is leading of
you directly to hell. Assert your own liberty, and don't suffer yourselves to be such mean and abject slaves. Don't exercise yourselves
any longer in acting below yourselves, in pleasing and tickling yourselves any longer, and thinking yourselves happy in wallowing and
rolling yourselves in the mire. You perhaps think yourselves mighty
happy in enjoying your hateful and abominable lusts, and so are the
beasts ten times as happy as you are in the same things: those be not
the pleasures of a man. The pleasures of loving and obeying, loving
and adoring, blessing and praising the Infinite Being, the Best of
Beings, the Eternal Jehovah; the pleasures of trusting in Jesus Christ,
in contemplating his beauties, excellencies, and glories; in contemplating his love to mankind and to us, in contemplating his infinite
goodness and astonishing loving-kindness; the pleasures of [the] communion of the Holy Ghost in conversing with God, the maker and
governor of the world; the pleasure that results from the doing of
our duty, in acting worthily and excellently: these, these are the plea-

sures that are worthy of so noble a creature as a man is. And those that take up, satisfied, with other sort of satisfactions as don't answer the end for which a man was made, and as they degrade themselves below the nature of a man and divest themselves of their manhood and seem rather to choose the nature of beasts, and as they invert[8] the order of nature, for the God of Nature hath set man above the beasts and made him ruler over them, but make themselves even with them, or rather below them: so it is [a] pity they be not allowed to be beasts, and are not thought unworthy of the name of a man. But you are now exhorted to leave off your beneath practices and embrace that which will make you happy men in whatever condition you are in, and whatsoever your outward circumstances are.

Exh. II. Is to the godly to go on and persevere and make progress in the ways of religion and godliness. Go on in those excellent ways in which you have begun; let nothing in the world discourage you. You are happy men in whatsoever condition you are; you, for your parts, have got into those ways which are ways of pleasantness and those paths which are paths of peace; you are happy and you will be happy in spite of all the world, men and devils. Do not be discouraged by any evils that you meet with while here, neither be overmuch concerned about any troubles that you may expect. It is said of the good man, Ps. 112:7–8, "He shall not be afraid of evil's tidings: his heart is fixed, trusting in God. His heart is established, he shall not be afraid." And indeed, when God is a man's refuge, what need he fear what man can do unto him? And remember that all the afflictions are just at an end, and then you shall enjoy the greatest happiness without any interruption. The greater your goodness, the greater your comfort will be whilst here; the firmer your faith is, the stronger your hope; the more live and vigorous your grace, the more ardent your love, the more comfort, pleasure and satisfaction will you enjoy in this life.

Go on, therefore, and forgetting the things which are behind, be pressing forward towards those which are before, even towards the mark for the prize of the high calling of God; and those afflictions will seem less and less to you, and your path will shine brighter and brighter, even till at length the night of this life shall be turned into

---

8. MS: "divests himself of his manhood and seems rather to choose the nature of beasts, and as he inverts . . ."

perfect day, when God shall wipe away all tears from your eyes and there shall be no more death; neither sorrow nor crying, neither shall there be any more pain, for the former things will then be passed away.

THE VALUE OF SALVATION

THIS and the following four sermons are from the earliest period of the New York pastorate, though it is possible that one or two antedate it, composed in anticipation of New York or as "candidating sermons" for trial appearances elsewhere during the spring and early summer of 1722. In this case, the reference to "this city" in the first exhortation under the Use suggests that Matt. 16:26 is one of those composed after Edwards' arrival in New York.

Thematically, there are many similarities between this sermon and the preceding one on Is. 3:10. The broad juxtaposition of Christian and secular values, the insistence upon the preeminence of the individual soul and of personal spiritual considerations, even within a cosmic context, and the call for spiritual renewal in the idiom of a quasi-academic rationality are common to both. The very comprehensiveness of the sermons, treating of the good life ontologically and ethically, identifies them as efforts in definition, as if Edwards were establishing the practical bases of the Christian religion upon which he would predicate his pastoral career. The virtuous person, capable of rationally pursuing his own greatest interest with rigorous realism and great determination, is the necessary positive sine qua non of Edwards' preaching at the outset. To this potentially heroic spirit Edwards presents those conceptions that were to remain essential to his homiletics: man's tragic predicament, his total dependence upon the mercy of a sovereign deity, the necessity of saving faith and the realistic hope of achieving it.

The early artistry of Edwards is likewise much in evidence, prefiguring his later career in its essential resources. Perhaps most notable is the attempt to discuss with some specificity the unseen and the practically unknowable: the true predicament of the body and soul in this world, the eternal life in heaven or hell after death, and the relative values of the terrestrial and supernal conditions. His powers of specification, patience in argument, and audacity in pursuit of the implications of his doctrine impress, even when the overall development is less sustained than that which he would eventually achieve as a mature preacher. Edwards' youthful vigor also emerges in the occasionally exuberant or colloquial vocabulary which ripples the surface of his solemn discourse—language which was for the most part rendered more decorous through his revisions for a repreaching in Northampton several years later.

Formally, the sermon is significant in two respects. First, it is one of two sermons from this earliest period which comprise two preaching units. Perhaps more significant is the lecture format of the piece. The Doctrine is approximately three times as long as the Application, making the sermon clearly a lecture. The tone of the piece is perhaps less "lecturely" than that of "Christian Happiness," but in most respects it does reflect the more intellectual mode. Even small touches, such as precisely identifying the soul as "that thinking being that is contained in the body of every living man," contribute to the aura of the lecture format. Subsequent additions to the sermon for a Northampton repreaching (see Appendix), though they enlarge the Application, do not modify the proportions in a way that would suggest it to be other than a lecture. The occasion for this substantial discourse is not known, but the combination of theme and form strongly suggests that it was an early effort to establish in New York the lines along which his ministry would proceed. Even in 1722, New York City was a center in the world of trade, and Edwards may have seen this doctrine as particularly appropriate to his pastoral situation, or perhaps just what an ardent splinter group such as the one which had engaged him might approve.

* * *

The manuscript sermon fills two octavo booklets, the first now of nine leaves and the second of ten. At the time of the New York preaching, each consisted of eight leaves, the infolded quire which was the "standard" booklet unit during Edwards' first years of preaching. For a repreaching several years later in Northampton, Edwards revised the idiom of the sermon fairly heavily, wrote a revised opening for the textual exegesis of about three-quarters of a page on a leaf which he stitched to the outside of the first booklet, and wrote a substantial addition of about three and two-thirds pages on a double leaf which he stitched into the second booklet just before the last leaf. These additions had to be keyed to the text since the infolded booklets could not easily be opened for the insertion of new material at the points where it would be used. Since the revision of the opening varies mainly in that the text of Christ's promise to Peter is quoted at length (Matt. 16:17–19), it has not been reproduced here. The additions to the Application are substantive, however, not only in length but in the new emphasis upon the potential of laymen in working the awakening and conversion of their fellows and in promoting religion generally. Since this new conclusion, perhaps reflecting the influence of Solomon Stoddard, is important and contrasts interestingly with the original sermon, it is reproduced in an appendix to the sermon.

THE VALUE OF SALVATION

MATTHEW 16:26.

*For what is a man profited, if he gain the whole world, and lose his
own soul, or what shall a man give in exchange for his soul?*

THESE words are occasioned by the pride, ignorance and unbelief
of Peter, one of the chief—if not the very chief—of the disciples,
whom Christ honored by making of him the rock upon which he
would build his church, and making of him a chief defense of the
same—that is, the chief amongst men, for although the church was
built on the foundation of the prophets and apostles, yet Christ himself is the chief cornerstone—whom Christ had also honored by giving him the keys of the kingdom of heaven in a more especial
manner.[1] The way wherein St. Peter manifested that corruption which
dwelt in him was this: our Lord, as it is said in the twenty-first verse,
told his disciples, perhaps more plainly than ever before, how he must
go to Jerusalem and suffer many things of the elders, chief priests
and scribes, and at last be killed, which was very surprising to Peter
who, it seems, had been carried away hitherto with that common
error of the Jews that expected when the Messiah came, that he would
reign in abundance of worldly pomp and glory. And therefore, the
news of [the] sufferings and death of him who he believed to be the
Messiah and the Son of God, as in the sixteenth verse, was very
unexpected, and very much contradicted the notion he had received
and his ambitious expectation of being the chief man next to Christ
himself in his earthly kingdom, because Christ had told him he
should be the rock on which he would build his church and that he
would give him the keys of his kingdom. Wherefore, Peter, being so
much moved by the vain desire of earthly prosperity, ignorance of
the nature of Christ's kingdom, and the great unbelief of what his

---

1. JE at first continued here, "so that from this we may see that there are remainders
of corruption in the best," but deleted it at the time of composition.

311

Lord had told him, rebukes him and says, "Be it far from thee, Lord: this thing shall not be unto thee"; which brought a very severe reproof from Christ, as in the twenty-third verse: "Get thee behind me, Satan: thou art an offense unto me, for thou savorest not of those things that be of God, but those that be of men." That is as much as if he had said, "Thy heart is not set enough on heavenly and spiritual happiness, honor and glory, which is of God, but too much on worldly honor, pomp and applause, which is of men," and took occasion to tell his disciples plainly that if they would be of his kingdom, they must not expect worldly good things, but they must deny themselves and take up their cross and bear that; and if they expected to live in his kingdom, they must be ready to lay down their lives for his sake, as in the twenty-fourth and twenty-fifth verses: "Then said Jesus unto his disciples, If any man will come after me, let him deny himself, and take up his cross, and follow me. For whosoever will save his life shall lose it: and whosoever will lose his life for my sake shall find it." And to explain the matter a little more to them, and that this news might not be damping and discouraging to them, he tells them in the verse of our text that the salvation of the soul was far more to be valued than all those worldly pomps and glories which they expected; yea if it were the whole world, it would be nothing in comparison of the life of the soul, neither would it profit a man if the soul was lost, "for what is a man profited if he gain the whole world and lose his own soul, and what shall a man give in exchange for his soul?"

In the words may be observed, first, the things that are compared, and they are the whole world and the soul of man. The comparison is between the whole world and the soul of one man: all the riches, all the silver and gold, all the honors and glories, pomp and pleasures of the same, and that thinking being that is contained in the body of every living man. Secondly, there is the third thing[2] they are compared in, and that is profit, value, or worth. Thirdly, the determination or result of the comparison very strongly implied in those two interrogations: what shall it profit a man, and what shall he give in exchange? The determination is made on the side of the soul, insomuch that the whole world is looked upon as good for nothing in

2. This awkward locution is no accident since JE rewrote part of a line in order to make room for inserting the word "third"; however, during later revision for a Northampton repreaching he deleted "third" for obvious reasons. Apparently his original intention was to suggest an equation in which "profit" is the third term, following "world" and "soul."

comparison of it, a determination of it[3] quite contrary to the general opinion of the men of this world, which they abundantly manifest by their taking so much more care for but a very little part of the world than they do for the salvation of their own souls; wherefore, the

DOCTRINE.

The salvation of the soul is of vastly more worth and value than the whole world.

And this we shall endeavor to make out by these following particulars:

I. Because all worldly good things shall have an end. First, the world in general shall one day have an end: the very earth itself, with all the works of it, shall be burnt up; the very elements shall melt with fervent heat, and the heavens, too, shall pass away (II Pet. 3:10, Matt. 24:35 and Rev. 20:11). All the hosts of heaven shall be dissolved and the heavens shall be rolled together as a scroll, and their host shall fall down as a leaf falleth off from the vine and a falling fig from the figtree; then everything shall be devoured in the flames together, and then where will be all the fine cities of the world, with which the earth now prides herself? Where will be all the silver and gold which is so hugged, and made so much a god of in the world? What then will become of the kingdoms and great monarchies of the earth? Where will be the proud palaces of potentates and emperors, and whatsoever else the proud men of the world do glory in and swell themselves with the thoughts of? They shall all be burnt up together in the same fire in which the men themselves, who so set their hearts upon those things as to make them their happiness, shall be burnt up.

II. The whole world shall have an end with respect to every particular person at death. When a man dies, the world has an end with respect to him: all worldly pleasure, profits and honors, with him are come to an end. To what advantage, then, will be bags of gold and silver? If he hugs them never so close, he must leave them forever and ever when once he leaves the world. What great comfort will it be to him then to think that[4] while he lived, he lived in great pomp: that he had all things at command, was arrayed in gorgeous and

3. MS: "very seldom made amongst" follows, before "quite contrary to," apparently a phrase JE rejected but failed to delete.
4. MS: "of."

shining apparel, was lifted up in point of riches and honor above others of his fellow men, insomuch that he used to look upon [them] as worms under his feet? To what pleasure will it be to him to see men come bowing and cringing to him when he is dying? What pleasure will it be to him to think he has[5] great affluence of sensual pleasure and delight? What good will it do him then that he used to rule with uncontrolled dominion over [a] great part of the earth, or if he could grasp the whole world when he is dying? What good did it do Alexander Magnus when he was dying to think that [he] had conquered the whole world? He must leave his conquered world to him upon whom God in his providence pleases to bestow [it]: though he conquered the world, yet death must have a conquest over him at last, and he whom the whole could not contain must at last be confined to only a narrow grave. A few feet square of ground is large enough for him now, whom the earth was not broad enough for before. The rich man, who fared sumptuously every day and shone in gorgeous apparel, at last begs that he may receive a drop of water of him whom he used to look upon as his dog in his lifetime. See Luke 16:19 and onward: see there what became of the rich man who was so rich that he had no room where to bestow his riches. He talks of pulling down his barns and building greater, and there he would bestow all his goods, and says to his soul, "Thou hast much goods laid up for many years. Take thine ease; eat, drink and be merry." But God says unto him, "Thou fool, this night thy soul shall be required of thee: then whose shall those things be, which thou has provided?"

III. Worldly good things are very uncertain, and oftentimes come to an end before death. There is no certainty of anything here below; if we were sure we should live always, it is quite uncertain and precarious whether or no we should[6] enjoy worldly goods. There are many accidents may deprive us of them, and when we think we hold them fastest, they oftentimes slip out of our hands soonest; when we think there is least danger, there is oftentimes—yea, most commonly—the greatest danger of losing of them. A man may be so deprived of worldly good things whilst alive that he had better be dead than alive, for matter of any temporal good he enjoys. There have been such instances in the world before now and many such

---

5. MS: "is."
6. MS: "shall."

happen without doubt every day, but one alone shall suffice at this time; namely, that of Job. He without doubt enjoyed as many worldly good things as almost any man in the world. See Job 1:3–4: "His substance was also seven thousand sheep, and three thousand camels, and five hundred yoke of oxen, and five hundred she asses, and a very great household; so that this man was the greatest of all the men of the east. And his sons went and feasted in their houses, every one his day; and sent and called for their three sisters to eat and to drink with them." And there is no reason to think but that he held them with as little danger of losing of them, but see what becomes of all those things, from the thirteenth verse to the end of the nineteenth:

> And there was a day when his sons and his daughters were eating and drinking wine in their eldest brother's house: and there came a messenger unto Job, and said, The oxen were plowing, and the asses feeding beside them: and the Sabeans fell upon them, and took them away; yea, they have slain the servants with the edge of the sword; and I only am escaped alone to tell thee. While he was yet speaking, there came also another, and said, The fire of God is fallen from heaven, and hath burned up the sheep, and the servants, and consumed them; and I only am escaped alone to tell thee. While he was yet speaking, there came also another, and said, The Chaldeans made out three bands, and fell upon the camels, and have carried them away, yea, and slain the servants with the edge of the sword; and I only am escaped alone to tell thee. While he was yet speaking, there came also another, and said, Thy sons and thy daughters were eating and drinking wine in their eldest brother's house: and, behold, there came a great wind from the wilderness, and smote the four corners of the house, and it fell upon the young men, and they are dead; and I only am escaped alone to tell thee.

But yet this is not all: see the second chapter, the seventh and eighth verses. How easily may a man be deprived of his substance,[7] either by fire or water, or the wind or the earth—obnoxious, to be destroyed by all the elements. And then, how easily is a man deprived of his honor and reputation in the world; how many men have been brought

---

7. For the Northampton repreaching, JE deleted the remainder of this sentence, substituting the following: "through his own mistakes or shortsightedness or imprudence, or the ill-will or injustice of other men, or an adverse providence. Prov. 23:5, 'Riches certainly make to themselves wings . . .'"

down from the highest worldly glory to the meanest and most shameful state and condition. How uncertain are friends and relatives; their being dear to us won't keep them from being taken from us. When death's time comes, all the world can't hinder them from parting. How many diseases are there which deprive many men of a capacity of enjoying any of the comforts or pleasures of life, and there are innumerable unforeseen accidents which may deprive us of them.

And what if a man doth live to grow old and none of those accidents happen? Yet there is but a little part of this life that man is capable of tasting worldly pleasures. Old age will certainly come on in a little time and the days wherein we shall say we have no pleasure in them: when the sun and the light, the moon and the stars shall be darkened, and the clouds return after the rain; when the keepers of the house shall tremble and the strong men shall bow themselves, and the grinders cease because they are few, and those that look out at the windows shall be darkened and the doors shall be shut in the streets; when the sound of the grinding is low and we shall rise up at the voice of the bird, and all the daughters of music shall be brought low; and when we shall be afraid of that which is high and fears shall be in the way, and the almond tree shall flourish and the grasshopper shall be a burden, and desire shall end because at last man must go to our long home and the mourners go about the street. And then the silver cord must be loosed, and the golden bowl broken, the pitcher broken at the fountain and the wheel at the cistern, and the dust must return to the earth as it was, and the spirit return to God who gave it. Justly, then, may we cry out, "Vanity of vanities, all is vanity!" as in the twelfth chapter of Ecclesiastes.[8]

But on the other hand,

IV. The soul is immortal and shall certainly endure forever and ever. We have heard that all worldly things shall certainly be destroyed at the end of the world, and besides that, they will certainly be at an end with respect to every particular man at death, and oftentimes come to an end before death; and there [is] not the least certainty of their enduring till that time. And if man live to old age, the enjoyment

---

8. While most of the foregoing paragraph is a virtual quotation of Eccles. 12:5–8, quotation marks have not been deemed appropriate since JE is neither quite citing nor quoting but, characteristically, leading his auditory into a realm where incantatory language fuses the essential data of experience with the revealed Word, resulting in a "discovery" of the reality of life in Scripture, and thus demonstrating in turn the authority of Scripture in defining life. A similar passage occurs on pp. 320–21 below.

of them will certainly be at an end before death; and if he don't live to old age, then they will certainly be at an end before that time comes. But none of these things are so with respect to the soul: when heaven and earth shall be destroyed, when everything upon the face of the earth shall be burnt up, when the sea shall [be] dried up (Rev. 21:1, "And there was no more sea."), when the sun, moon and stars shall come to an end, the soul shall endure still. When the body shall die and return to dust, the soul shall remain; when worldly good things shall have an end by accidents, by diseases or old age, the soul will remain. The world shall continue but a few moments, but the soul shall remain throughout all eternity; the world shall last no longer than the conflagration, but the soul shall last through an eternity that has no end. Worldly profits and pleasures shall last no longer than the body, and many times not half so long, but the soul shall last as long as God lasts. Surely that which lasts forever, if it be worth anything, if it lasts always, must be worth vastly more than that which lasts but a little while: that good which lasts millions of ages must be worth more than that which lasts but a minute, but eternity is infinitely more longer than the life of man, than a thousand years is than a minute.

V. All the world, if it could be enjoyed forever, would be little worth. Solomon, who knew better the value of the world than any man in the world because of his great wisdom, and had more experience and better opportunities to know than any man ever had, yet cries out, "All is vanity and vexation of spirit!" He is so full of it that he breaks out upon it: his very first words, as soon as he begins to write his book of Ecclesiastes, are "vanity of vanities," that is the greatest vanity of all vanities; "vanity of vanities" repeated over again, "all is vanity," and so in the third verse, "What profit hath a man of all his labor under the sun?" He tells us that he had seen them all, that is, enjoyed them all; and behold, all was "vanity and vexation of spirit," as in the fourteenth verse. He tells us that he got himself wisdom, that is, worldly wisdom, that he set himself to try mirth and pleasure. He tells us he got himself houses and vineyards, gardens, orchards, trees and all kinds of fruits, and servants and maidens, and great possessions and cattle, above all that were in Jerusalem before. He got him silver and gold, men singers and women singers, and all sorts of instruments of music and whatsoever his eyes desired; he kept not from them, neither did he withhold his heart from any joy. And then [he] tells us that all was vanity and vexation of spirit, and there was no profit under the sun; and is any man so vain and foolish as to think he knows better than Solomon, or if he thinks he doth, does he know better than God, by whose spirit he speaks?

There is so much disappointment, so much vexation, so little solid pleasure in the enjoyment of any of these things that render them all truly such as Solomon describes them to be: nothing but vanity and vexation of spirit. And a very great plenty of them [are] more of a burden than a comfort, and but a very poor enjoyment for eternity, and such as a wise man would never be contented to take up with; and indeed, it is the goodness of God that he has not appointed these things for our portion. But we shall speak of each of the good things of this world in particular.

First. Riches are in themselves [of] little worth. If a man were to enjoy as much silver and gold as he could wish for, he would find but very little satisfaction. And what rich man has there ever been whom riches have made happy? Kings and great men of the world are generally as unhappy as poor men, and have generally as much trouble and affliction with worldly good things as poor men have for want of them. Riches are given to men only for them to carry, to support them through the wilderness of this world in the way to heaven; and generally, the more riches the greater [the] burden, and that is but poor provision, generally to live upon through one's life, that one is forced to take up with in a journey through a desolate wilderness. Neither would one be willing to carry that burthen all one's life that they may be willing to bear on a journey; and besides, worldly riches are so far from bringing satisfaction with them, the more one has of them the more we want. That is but a poor sort of drink which, instead of quenching thirst, the more one drinks the more thirsty they are.[9]

Second. It is so with respect to honor and worldly pomp. Honor may at first mightily please men and puff them up very full with a mean and unworthy sort of pleasure, but that is soon over and men generally, except they are very foolish and vain indeed, grow more into a distaste of it; all the happiness that is enjoyed in it is only because other men think them happy, and not from any solid or substantial happiness that is found therein. A wise man, if it were not that he desired it for the public good, would be glad to be deliv-

9. This and the preceding sentence illustrate JE's frequent neglect of grammatical agreement and parallel construction, especially where pronouns are involved. However, here and elsewhere his meaning is usually clear and editorial intervention is not required.

ered from the burthen of it and enjoy the happiness of a more refined life with only the enjoyment of some select friends, than be entangled and hampered with great and honorable posts and places.

Third. Worldly pleasure is in itself but a worthless thing. Men generally have very great expectations from sensual pleasure before their enjoyment, but they almost vanish in the enjoyment, and men that have great expectations from them are always disappointed. They are like shadows and phantoms which vanish as we endeavor to embrace them, and if one doth enjoy them to the full, their nature will allow them to last but a very short time, and after one is a little used to them they are loathed and hated.

Fourth. 'Tis so with respect to friends. Indeed, the pleasures of friendship have the preference to all worldly [things], but these also, if we view them narrowly, we shall find unworthy of setting our hearts much upon. First, because our temporal or earthly friends are unable to keep off evils and distresses from us, let them be never so near and entire friends; all that they can do for us for the most part, is but to wish and desire our welfare. They are unable to keep off misfortunes from happening unto us, and let them lay out themselves never so[1] much, they cannot secure us against troubles and afflictions; there never was an earthly friend yet, let [him] be never so friendly, let him be never so rich, powerful and great, that could secure from crosses, trouble and afflictions. Secondly, the best of them are uncertain; there is no certainty of the best friends' not separating and falling. Human nature, even in the best, is so full of infirmities and inconstancies that there is no depending nor trusting the best of them all.

So that we see that if this world and the good things of the same could be enjoyed forever, it would be but of small value. We have seen that riches are so, inasmuch as they afford no solid satisfaction to the mind and generally bring more vexation than comfort, and when they are in abundance are more of a burthen than [a] delight. We have seen that worldly honor and pomp is so, and that the pleasure that is enjoyed therein is but a mere shadow and vanity; we have seen that worldly pleasures are so, inasmuch as they always bring disappointment and always cheat and deceive those who pursue them, and because they are naturally incapable of enduring long and generally bring distaste and loathing after them; we have seen that

1. MS: "for."

friends are also so, inasmuch as their love is not very profitable to us, they being unable to save us from misfortunes, and besides, they are uncertain and inconstant. And in short, that all this world, with all its riches, glories, pleasures and delights, is but the greatest of vanities, and a mere vexation of spirit. But,

VI. The life and salvation of the soul is of inestimable worth and value. Though the whole world is good for nothing in comparison, yet the life of the soul is of inestimable worth and value, insomuch that the value of the same cannot be conceived of nor imagined, and that appears:

First, because the salvation of it is the deliverance of it from so great misery, and secondly, because so great happiness is to be enjoyed in the salvation of the soul.

First. Because the salvation of the soul is its deliverance from so great misery. This misery which the soul is saved from is very dreadful.

1. Because in it they shall [be] deprived of all manner of good forever:

[(1)] They shall be deprived of all the pleasures they used to enjoy in this world. They shall no more enjoy the pleasures of eating and drinking, no more enjoy the pleasures of seeing and hearing; they shall no more enjoy their lusts: there shall be nothing in hell for men to satisfy their lust upon. They will have taken their leave, then, of all the riches, honors and pleasure of the world, which they used so to hug and make a god of; their dear lusts, which were so dear to them that they would not part with them for heaven, that they would not let go [of] for God himself, and all the happiness which God could bestow upon them: they must part with them for nothing now, never to enjoy anything like them again. If they have been used to please themselves by handling of their silver and gold, with the shining of precious stones and jewels, they shall enjoy no more of them forever; if they have been used to gorgeous apparel and to deck themselves with shining and glistening robes, they shall never more be clothed with any other sort of garments but scorching and tormenting flames which will wrap themselves about their otherwise naked bodies forever; if they have been used to dwell in proud and stately palaces upon earth, they will have nothing for their habitation then but the bottomless pit and the dismal and doleful dungeon of outer darkness; instead of lying at ease in beds of down, they shall have nothing but a sea of liquid fire for their bed, flames instead of

[the] wine and strong drink with which they used to intoxicate themselves: they shall have nothing but the cup of God's wrath and fiery indignation which they shall be compelled forever to drink. Instead of that wicked company which they used so much to delight in, they shall have nothing [but] damned sprights for their company in hell; instead of their cursing and swearing, lewd and debauched conversation, they shall yell and roar out forever and ever under God's dreadful wrath.

(2) They shall be deprived of spiritual pleasures and communion with God. They shall see many come from the east and from the west and sit down with Abraham, Isaac and Jacob, and they themselves cast out to weep and gnash their teeth (Matt. 8:11–12). They may knock at the door forever and never receive any other answer but, "Depart from me; I know you not, ye workers of iniquity." They will be bound hand and foot and cast into outer darkness, and shall never be admitted to the wedding. Their beholding the happiness of others who shall be with God in heaven, and to think that they might have enjoyed the same had not they been fools, will be an inexpressible aggravation of their misery: they will see then that nothing in the world is so valuable as the favor of God which they have lost and which they so much despised while here on earth; they will see then how excellent heaven and the happiness thereof is, which they used so to laugh at and scorn when they might have obtained [it] if they would; they shall see how wise those persons were which they used so to despise and have in derision.

2. This misery from which the soul that is saved is saved from is dreadful because of the positive torments which shall be endured. How much doth a single spark of fire, if it remain upon any part of the flesh, torment one. How much must the body be tormented that is plunged all over in a sea of fire! When only some one part of the body is in pain by the toothache or headache, how troublesome is it, and such as one would not endure always, without ceasing, upon any consideration: how dreadful must it be to have every part of the body in most exquisite torment, both within and without, and not only [the] body but the soul, too!

3. The misery from which the soul is saved is dreadful because it is eternal and mixed with despair. After the soul and body have roasted millions of ages in hellfire, it will not be at all nearer the end of its misery, and this the soul shall know and be assured of, and shall not in the least doubt of it. If a man were sure that he must

bear the pain he feels only from a drop of scalding water throughout eternity without intermission, the thoughts of it would fill the mind with dreadful horror and amazement: with what horror, then, must it fill the mind at the same [instant] that it feels hell-torments, to know and be assured that it must feel those same torments forever and ever!

Thus we have represented to you something of the misery which the soul that is saved is saved from; which without doubt is so dreadful in itself that if we had a clear and full apprehension of it, only barely an idea of it without any fear of our bearing of it, that it would overcome human nature and kill us immediately. Of how much value, then, must the salvation of the soul be which is salvation from so great [a] misery! Deliverances are reckoned great or small according to the greatness of the evil which we are delivered from; wherefore, without doubt, the deliverance of the soul from hell is of more value than all the world.[2]

Second. The salvation of the soul is of inestimable worth and value because the happiness that will be enjoyed by every saved soul will be inestimable: first, because the saved soul shall be delivered from all evil; secondly, shall be brought to the enjoyment of all good; thirdly, this happiness shall be eternal.

1. Shall be delivered from all evil. There shall be nothing to interrupt the happiness of believers: there shall no evil approach the gates of heaven.

---

2. Here ends the first preaching unit. At the head of the second unit is a brief summary which was read at the start of the sermon, a necessary part of an oral sermon of more than one preaching unit though irrelevant to a literary sermon not delimited by pulpit time blocks:

Doctrine: That the salvation of the soul is of vastly more worth and value than the whole world. 1st, by showing the world in general should come to an end at the conflagration of the world; and 2d, that it should come to an end with respect to every particular person at death. 3dly, by showing the uncertainty, fodeyness and vanity of the world, whereby it is liable to come to an end before death. 4thly, by showing that the soul was immortal. 5thly, that if all the world could be enjoyed forever, it would be little worth. 1stly, we showed that riches were little worth; 2dly, that honors were little worth; 3rdly, that worldly pleasure is so likewise; 4thly, that earthly [friends] are in comparison but little worth. 6thly, we showed in the sixth place that the salvation of the soul was more worth than all the world because it is of inestimable worth and value. And that, 1st, because it is deliverance from so great misery, and we showed that the misery from which a saved soul was delivered was very great because in it the soul was deprived of all good. 2dly, all evil was brought upon it. [3dly], this misery would be eternal and mixed with despair. We shall now proceed to show that,

(1) They shall be perfectly delivered from sin and temptation. The saved soul leaves all its sin with the body; when it puts off the body of the man, it puts off the body of sin with it. When the body is buried, all sin is buried forever, and though the soul shall be joined to the body again, yet sin shall never return more: it is sown in corruption but shall be raised in incorruption, sown in dishonor but shall be raised in glory, sown in weakness but raised in power, sown a natural body but raised a spiritual body; and this corruptible must put on incorruption, and this mortal immortality, when death—not only natural death, but spiritual death—shall be swallowed up in victory. Sin is always a great trouble and affliction to the godly in this life. They have frequent combats fought between the body of death and the spirit of life, between the law of the members and the law of the mind, but after death there shall be no more such strifes; there shall [be] no more assaults of lusts to be resisted; there they shall not be afflicted with the temptations of Satan; he shall never come near heaven to lay snares and practice his wiles. They shall no more be tempted by the shining vanities; they shall then live in a world which, as it will be infinitely above this for gloriousness and excellency, so the glory of [it] will not draw them from God, but only excite and stir them up to praises of him, and give them to see what a mere vanity this world is in comparison of it. This life is a warfare to believers against these adversaries, and they must sometimes even agonize against them in order to overcome them, but there they shall be perfectly free from all these things; that life will be a sort of a perpetual triumph over these enemies, instead of a warfare with them.

The saved soul shall be unspotted: without "spot, or wrinkle, or any such thing" (Eph. 5:27). They shall be holy, unblamable and unreprovable in the sight of God: they shall be pure as the light itself.

(2) It shall be delivered from all manner of affliction. Good men in this world oftentimes meet with abundance of affliction: many travel so as it were through a sea of blood. This is a very troublesome world, full of crosses and disappointments, full of cares and solicitudes, and full of fears and anxieties. Good men in this world are hated by this world, scorned, despised and often persecuted by them (Heb. 11:35–38). And others were tortured, not accepting deliverance that they might obtain a better resurrection, and others had trial of cruel mockings and scourgings; yea, moreover, of bonds and imprisonments. They were stoned, they were sawn asunder, were slain

with the sword; they wandered about in sheepskins and goatskins, being destitute, afflicted, tormented: of whom the world was not worthy. They wandered in deserts and mountains, and in fens and caves of the earth; but when they get to heaven there will be no more of this: they will never more be afflicted, either by misfortunes and evil accidents, sickness, shame, disgrace, fears and cares, but they shall rest from their labors. They shall wash their robes which were stained with their own blood; they shall have all tears wiped away from their eyes, and there shall be no more death, neither sorrow nor crying.

2. They shall be brought to the enjoyment of all good. In heaven all the faculties of the soul shall be completely satisfied. The understanding shall there be satisfied; the understanding, as it enters into heaven, shall as it were come out of a dark and gloomy place into a place that is full of heavenly light. A great deal of pleasure it is that wise men have by that little understanding which they have here: what then will the saints enjoy in heaven, where their knowledge and understanding will be so enlarged? The will also will be completely satisfied there; whatsoever they desire shall be bestowed upon them. The affections also will be satisfied; their love will [be] very much enlarged and yet satisfied. They shall live in a most glorious place, the heaven of heavens, God's throne and the palace of his glory. If the palaces of earthly princes are so glorious, how glorious must that be which is the palace of Jehovah! If the temple at Jerusalem, a temple of men's building, was so splendid and glorious as to cause the Queen of Sheba even to swoon at the very sight of it, how glorious must that temple be which the Almighty has built for himself with his own hands!

But the dwelling in such a glorious place is but the least part of the happiness of heaven. There is the conversation with saints: with holy men of old, Moses, Job, David, Elijah, etc., with the prophets [and] apostles, and besides that, with the man Christ Jesus who was crucified for mankind at Jerusalem. Neither is that the chief thing, the Beatifical Vision of God: *that* is the tip of happiness! To see a God of infinite glory and majesty face to face, to see him as he is, and to know him as we are known; there to be admitted into the most intimate acquaintance with him, to be embraced as in his arms: this is such a privilege as Moses himself could not be admitted to while on earth. The vision and fruition of God will be so intimate and clear as to transform the soul into the likeness of God: "We shall be like him, for we shall see him as he is," says the Apostle (I John 3:2).

3. This happiness shall be eternal. This crowns [it]: however great the happiness of heaven were in itself, yet it would detract from it if it were not to be eternal. If the saints in heaven were sure they should enjoy heaven some thousands of years, and after that it should be at an end, it would cast a great damp upon their joys and delights; it would much grieve them to think that they should lose so great [a] happiness, and at last it would be a cloud in their light, a bitter in the midst of their sweet. But it is not so; they are sure that they shall enjoy it forever, and this redoubles the joy: Rev. 22:5, "And they shall reign forever and ever." So great is the happiness of the saved soul. They shall be delivered from all manner of sin, temptation, trouble and affliction, and shall live in the palace which God has built and where he himself doth dwell, and there shall enjoy everything they wish for. They shall enjoy the company of prophets, apostles, martyrs, angels and archangels; they shall see the man Christ Jesus, and even Jehovah himself, the Eternal Three in One, and shall be intimately united to him, and this happiness of theirs shall endure as long as God endures. How precious, then, must the salvation of that soul be in whose salvation is so much happiness.

VII. The salvation of the soul is more worth than all the world because the world can be of no advantage at all if the soul is lost.

First. Because there can be no enjoyment of the world in that misery into which the lost soul will be plunged, and this is that which is most immediately implied in our text, "What would it profit a man if he should gain the whole world and lose his own soul?" That is, what would all this world profit a man, that he had all the world in his possession while on earth, if he loses his soul at last? What will it profit him then if he lives all his lifetime drowned in pleasure and honors? What will it profit him that he was arrayed in silver and gold once, that he wore a crown on his head and held a scepter in his hand? All his riches and honors won't cool his tongue, but rather increase the flame by which he is tormented. If he could have his gold and silver all in hell with him, what good would it do him? Every time he looked upon it, it would only fill him with the greater torment that he did not improve the same to better purposes upon earth. It will nothing but add twinges to his torment to think in how great prosperity he lived while on earth, and in what misery he is now plunged into; every thought of it will be as a drop of scalding brimstone falling upon him, which will cause him to roar out forever and ever.

Second. The world can be of no profit if the soul is lost, inasmuch as the soul is in effect the man. The soul is in effect the man, and the body without it is no more than a stick or a stone. 'Tis the soul that thinks, that perceives pleasure, that enjoys good, and the body without the soul enjoys nothing. Nay, there is not so much as external sense without the soul; the body cannot enjoy any of its worldly pleasures and good things without it; none of the senses can be gratified without it: the eyes can behold no pleasant sights, the ear can hear no music, the palate can taste no sweetness, nor any of the senses be gratified. Well then, and what is all the world worth to a man if he himself be lost; what is the world good for if there be no man to enjoy it, or in the words of our text as they may be interpreted, what will it profit a man if he gain the whole world and lose *himself* ("Soul" in the Scriptures is often put for "self")?

VIII. It appears that the salvation of the soul is more worth than all the world because God himself has set such an high value upon it. Without doubt, if God values the soul above all the world, then the salvation of it is more worth than all the world. For God is a God of infinite knowledge and wisdom, and certainly knows the value of the soul and the value of the world also, but God has prized the soul above all the world.

First. Inasmuch as he has made all the world—that is, all this world—for the sake of the soul, nothing is plainer than that the soul must be more worth than all the world. If the world is made for the soul, it is always a maxim: *finis est prestantior mediis,* the end is more excellent than the mean; but that the world was made for the sake of the soul the very make of things evidences, and it might easily be discovered had we no revelation of it. Nothing is plainer to reason [than] that the earth, the sea, the air, cattle, trees, and all were made for man and fitted to his use, but besides reason, the Scriptures also plainly tell us as much. God created the world first as an habitation and afterward created man as the inhabitant and gave him rule over all things, which plainly evidences that all things were made for him; and therefore, God, by making the world for man, has set a higher value upon him than the world. The world is but a tabernacle or house, and surely the inhabitants are more than the house. If the inhabitants are lost, what is the house worth to those inhabitants?

Second. Inasmuch as he has sent so many of his servants, the prophets, to the end that the souls of men might be saved. God in his Word makes mention of this as a great instance of his care for the salvation of men: II Chron. 36:15, "And the Lord God of their fathers sent to them by his messengers, rising up betimes, and sending them because he had compassion on his people, and on his dwelling place"; and, Jer. 7:25, "Since the day that your fathers came out of Egypt to this, I have even sent unto you all the prophets, daily rising up early and sending them," and so in the twenty-fifth chapter at the fourth verse. And it certainly is a great and astonishing instance of God's care and concern for the salvation of men's souls to condescend to inspire some particular men for their sake, to condescend to speak to men face to face and have an immediate intercourse with them; surely, it is a thing very astonishing that the Almighty Jehovah should speak to men and converse with men, but God has done this very frequently, and almost continually from the creation of the world into the captivity into Babylon, and not only to inspire them but to work many wonderful miracles by them. How often has even the very course of nature been altered, and the laws of nature been made to stand by for the sake of the welfare of men's souls! Before the flood, doubtless, God had very frequent intercourse with good men, as we know he had with Adam, with Abel, with Enoch and with Noah, and after the flood God for some time used to do likewise, as with Abraham, Isaac, Jacob, Joseph, etc., and it was all to this end, even the salvation of the soul. To this end did God work all those wonders in the land of Egypt; to this end, ultimately, it was that [he] divided the Red Sea and caused the Children of Israel to pass over dry-shod; to this end did God descend upon Mount Sinai in such a wonderful and awful manner, and there speak to Moses as a man speaketh with his friend; to this end was Jordan divided and the Canaanites driven out from before the Children of Israel, and to this end was all that intercourse that God had with the Children of Israel throughout the times of the Old Testament.

Third. Inasmuch as he has sent his own son into the world to die for the sake of the salvation of the soul of man, how highly he's prized the salvation of the soul! That he should send his own and only son from the highest heavens, from his own bosom, down to earth to die for the sake thereof; that God, who had no need of us, whom the salvation of our souls will not profit in anywise, should as it were give up one that was the very same in substance with himself, one who was infinitely nearer and dearer to him than the nearest and dearest relations amongst men; that he should deliver up such an one to be cruelly killed and tormented for the salvation of the soul: surely, the salvation of the soul must be very precious, or else God would never value it so much as to give his son for it. What a price is here set upon salvation of the soul—the blood of the Son of God! Would any man give up his only son that was very dear to him, into the hands of wicked and cruel men to be dreadfully tormented, for anything but what was very precious? The same, with infinitely more reason, may we conclude that God would never give up his son to be cruelly tormented and killed for anything but what was very precious and valuable, but this hath God done for the sake of the salvation of the soul. Certainly, then, the salvation of the soul must be more worth than all the world. Can any man be so mad as to think that God would [be] giving his son to die that men might have gold and silver, or that they might live in worldly pleasure and honor? Surely, no. Wherefore, God has set a higher price on the soul than on the whole world.

Thus we have endeavored to show that the salvation of the soul is more worth [than] the whole world, and I suppose it is by this time so plain that it is impossible for a man to doubt of it.

USE.

Inf. I.[3] Our miserable and lost estate by nature. Is the soul so precious, and is the salvation of the soul more worth than all the world, and the loss of the soul more than the loss of all the world? Then how dreadful is our lost condition by nature, for our souls naturally are all lost souls, naturally in a lost estate and condition, bound over unto the eternal wrath of God, and to suffer his indignation forever. We are all "by nature children of wrath" (Eph. 2:3); we are naturally condemned to everlasting misery; we are naturally unbelieving, and "he that believeth not is condemned already" (John 3:18). What a dreadful thing is it to be a condemned person. A person that is condemned to a bodily death is looked [upon] as a miserable creature: how much more miserable are those which are condemned to spiritual and eternal death, but so we are all by nature.

3. This and the following inference were originally written at the end of the manuscript; however, when preparing the sermon for the Northampton repreaching JE keyed them to be moved into this position. Both the conventional sermon form and the substance of the inferences confirm that, though they were apparently added to the manuscript as an after-thought, they belong in the present location and were probably in that position during the first oral delivery of the sermon.

Inf. II. The great folly of the greatest part of the world. [They] neglect their souls and do nothing, pursue violently after the pleasure and vain profits of the world. They are laboring for those vanities of vanities as if they were the most precious things imaginable, and neglect that which is really so; they spend themselves for the world as if they were to live in the same forever and ever, whereas it will fade and vanish like [a] phantom in a few moments, and they must be parted from it forever, and see it no more at all. Thus foolish and sottish are the greatest part of the world: they take care for the world but take no care for themselves; they love the world but hate their own souls.

Well, is it so? Then,

[*Exh.*] I. Let us take utmost care that we don't lose our souls. For what will it profit us if we gain the whole world and lose our own soul, and what will we give in exchange for our souls? We have now heard the most powerful arguments in the world to persuade us [to] take care of our souls. We have first heard Christ Jesus with his own mouth declaring that if we gain the whole world and lose our own souls, it will not profit [us]. Where is a man that don't take care to get the world, that is not willing to spend much labor and strength rather than not get the world, rather than have none of the world? How are men continually busied in getting the world! If we look out into this city[4] at any time, we may behold men of all kinds, earnest in pursuit of the world: and why should not men take as much care of that which is so much more valuable and precious, even the salvation of the soul, without which the world is good for nothing? Why should [we] labor and spend ourselves for that which will shortly be at an end, and all the while neglect that which will endure forever and ever; why should we take so much care for that which we must leave and take an everlasting farewell of in a very short time, and be careless of that which, if we obtain [it], shall never be separated from us? Why should [we] be anxious for that which is changeable, fading and vanishing, and liable to be destroyed by innumerable accidents, which the very moth and rust can despoil us of, and take no thought for such a treasure as neither moth nor rust can conquer, nor thieves break through and steal?

What folly is it to be so very careful for that which, if it could be

---

4. "This city" is apparently a specific reference to New York. When JE revised the sermon for the Northampton preaching, he substituted "the world" for "this city."

enjoyed forever, would be very little worth, and yet be careless of that which is of such inestimable value and worth. How unreasonable is it for us to labor so earnestly for a worthless world and not regard our deliverance from most dreadful torments which shall endure forever, and not take care to secure to ourselves complete and eternal happiness: to be unconcerned about that misery which we shall unavoidably fall into if we do not take much care, and which all careless persons are going with a swift career into, and yet be so much concerned about the world which we cannot enjoy there. How ridiculous is it for a man to moil and toil, spend and be spent for the world and for worldly enjoyment, and all the while care not what becomes of himself; to be concerned for a world to enjoy and not to be at all concerned for himself that enjoys it; to be anxious about his habitation and take no care for himself that inhabits it! Let us not, therefore, act so exceeding foolishly, ridiculously and unreasonably; let us take no thought for this present any otherwise than as the means of the good of our souls, and let us take utmost care of our precious and immortal souls and not neglect them.

And that we may be stirred up thereunto, let us consider these two things: first, the danger of neglecting our souls; secondly, the inexcusableness [of it].

First. The danger. If we neglect our souls, they will most certainly presently be lost—as certainly as a stone will roll down a hill if it be not held up. If we neglect our souls, they will in a very short time be in hell-flames, and the longer we neglect them the worse it will be and the more difficult to stop them in their career. The soul in its fallen estate naturally tends to hell and destruction as much as a stone tends to the center of the earth, and the farther it goes the faster, the swifter and more impetuous is its course; wherefore, we must take utmost care.

Second. Consider the inexcusableness of neglecting the salvation of our souls:

1. We cannot plead impotency. We cannot plead that we are not able to take care of our souls, for we certainly can if we will. There never was a man yet that endeavored to take care for the salvation of his soul and found that he could not.

2. Nor, we cannot plead the difficulty of it. We find that taking care for other things is not so difficult but that we conquer the difficulty: no man lies still and starves and pleads that there is a great deal of difficulty in laboring and taking care for food. How would

such an excuse be laughed at by everyone, and it is a thousand times as ridiculous for a man to lie down in everlasting burnings and then plead that it was [a] difficult and troublesome thing for [him] to take care to shun and avoid it. No, this will not do; let no man feed himself up with thoughts of making this excuse on the great day of accounts. Let every man take as much care for the salvation of his immortal soul as the generality of men do to get the world,⁵ and without doubt he will have life everlasting, will be saved from hell, and will be brought to everlasting happiness [and] the enjoyments of heaven, [including] the society of saints and angels there, the sight of the man Christ Jesus, and the Beatifical Vision of Jehovah himself, the Eternal Three in One God, blessed forevermore.

3. We cannot plead ignorance. We cannot plead that we did not know that we had souls to save; we cannot plead that we did not know that there was such need of caring for our souls in order to their salvation; we cannot plead that we did not know that our souls were worthy of taking care for. How fully have we been instructed in those matters in God's Word, and how frequently are we there commanded to take care of our souls: how frequently are we told that if we do not we shall certainly be damned forever! We live in a land where there are Bibles enough for us to read, and where we are not prohibited from reading of them, and if [we] do not read it is our own fault, and if we are ignorant when we have such opportunities to know, what excuse will that be to us? And besides, none of us here present can after this time plead any such excuse, for if we never knew before, we know how we have now heard sufficiently both of the worth of the salvation of the soul and the danger of neglecting [it].

*Third.*⁶ We shall give some directions that we may know aright to care for our souls:

1. We must take care not to walk in those ways in which, if we walk, we shall be certainly lost. If we would not be lost, we must not take wrong paths; if we continue to walk in those ways which lead to destruction, without doubt we shall come to destruction at last. We

---

5. When revising the sermon for Northampton JE deleted a portion of this sentence, beginning here and extending through "everlasting happiness." He then interlineated the following amplification: "be as careful, as steady and as laborious in it, as persevering and unwearied—and there is a greater probability of his obtaining life everlasting than of the careful, laborious man's obtaining the world—and that he will be brought to [. . .]"

6. MS: "2dly."

all know that the ways of sin and iniquity are wrong paths; everyone knows [that] all the paths that are contrary to God's commands are paths that lead to destruction and that they all meet together in hell; wherefore, let us take care that we do not walk in those paths.

2. We must seek unto God that he would save our [souls]; we are weak and unable to save ourselves. We cannot do it without God's help; except he put forth his hand and help, we shall not be able [to] escape destruction and misery. We are like persons that are falling from a precipice into some dreadful pit and cannot possibly stop ourselves from falling still further. We must look and pray to God for help, or else we are inevitably lost.

3. We must in these things strive with all our might. If we think to have our souls saved, we must strive and labor for it; some little care and concern will not do. We must not think that barely seeking will do, but we must strive also; nothing that is great and excellent is attained unto without difficulty: riches are not to be gotten without difficulty; earthly honor and reputation and renown is not to be attained without much difficulty; learning and wisdom requires a steady labor and industry before it can be obtained, and can any man think that such things as these require the greatest diligence, and that heaven and the salvation of the soul may be had without pains and industry? The Christian life, for that reason, because of the diligence and labor that is required in it, is called a race and a warfare, because in running and fighting generally the utmost of the powers are laid out. Let us therefore not spare any pains and labors in these things: let us deny ourselves of those things which are most dear to us when they stand in the way of our duty; let us deny ourselves of all our lusts and fight valiantly and vigorously against our spiritual adversaries; let us resist them with all our might and not give an inch of ground to them. Let us call in all our powers and lay them out against whatsoever opposes us in this way of God's commands. Let us press forward in the way to heaven violently, for many there are that seek that shall not be able: Matt. 11:12, "The kingdom of heaven suffers violence, and the violent take it by force." Let us therefore so run as not uncertainly, so fight not as one that beateth the air, for they that run in a race run all, but one receiveth the prize. Let us therefore keep under our bodies and bring them into subjection.

4. Let us strive thus constantly and steadily. Let us keep our minds steadily and constantly upon heaven, the prize of our high calling, and let us be continually meditating on heavenly things. Let us run

in the way of God's commands without flagging or fainting; we must not think that our striving will do if it be only by fits and starts, but we must strive constantly and unweariedly: men don't use [to] stop sometime and run sometime when they were upon a race; men, when they are engaged immediately in a battle, don't use to stand still now and then to rest when their enemies are about them, for if they so do they are in danger every minute of being killed.

[*Exh.*] II. Let us do our utmost to forward the salvation of other men: their souls are as precious as our own. Is it not [a] great pity that things which are so precious as souls are, should be lost? Should we not, if we saw any man in distress of body and in great danger of dying, be willing to lend him a hand to save his life? Why, let us look about us and we shall see thousands of men in a sorrowful condition, and in danger of dying every moment. Should we see a man a-drowning, should not we be willing to afford him some assistance to help him out of the water? If we look about us we may see thousands of poor souls drowning in sin and iniquity, and in danger of being drowned in the lake of fire and brimstone. Let us therefore do what we can for them; perhaps we may be instrumental of saving several souls from everlasting ruin and destruction. If each one here present should do what he could towards it, there is no doubt to be made but that many souls might be saved by their means. Let us therefore do our utmost; don't let us be so inhuman as to see men sick and not help them.[7]

Appendix to Matthew 16:26

First. Let us take all opportunities to persuade men less to mind earthly things and more to regard the affairs of their souls. There is scarcely any man, high nor low, but what, if prudence be used in observing the proper time and manner, may have an opportunity of doing a great deal of good this way.

Persons generally excuse themselves from this and say, "To what purpose would it be for me to concern myself to go to persuade and exhort them, or to reprove them for their wickedness, for their ill language, their rude and debauched conversation? They'll regard it

7. At this point, in preparing the Northampton revision, JE appended a substantial addition of nearly four pages which completed the sermon by supplying the second exhortation with three subheads and adding a third new exhortation. These additions stress the necessity of aiding the conversion of others, and, since they constitute an enlargement of the sermon's Application by one half, the shift in emphasis is necessarily significant. This material is printed in the Appendix to the sermon.

no more than a puff of wind; they'll nothing but make a laugh and a ridicule of it. I shall be reproached by them and they'll be never the better, will no way alter their behavior." But nevertheless there are opportunities [through] which, if they were diligently observed, we might speak to good purpose, and we should not be likely to be reproached for it. And whether 'twas much regarded in the time of it or no, yet if it were done prudently and with understanding, would be likely to be called over in his mind and perhaps make some impression on his heart.

God's providence is very variable toward all persons. Sometimes they are in prosperity and sometimes they are brought to sorrow and mourning by this variety. God by turns is striving with men's hearts, and these changes give opportunities of speaking for the salvation of the soul of our fellow creatures, wherein a prudent person might reasonably speak to good effect, and, it may be, redeem the soul of his brother from the hand of the Adversary: Prov. 25:11–12, "A word fitly spoken is like apples of gold in pictures of silver, as an earring of gold, and an ornament of fine gold, so is a wise reprover upon an obedient ear."

Prudence is likewise to be used in choosing the persons that we would persuade, as well as the opportunity. If there are some persons that are like swine, that will trample pearls under their feet and turn again and rent us, yet all are not so; some have more morality and civility in them, and some are of a more kindly natural temper, and if we could do good upon no other, yet surely we might upon our near friends and familiar acquaintances. All men have some that they are more especially acquainted with; our interest in such might be improved for God's sake, and for their souls' sake.

Second. Another way wherein we ought to seek the salvation of others' souls is by our example. No objections can lie against this way of recommending religion and spiritual-mindedness: we may let others see our minds and know our thoughts of things as well and better by our behavior than by our words.

Let all that see our lives see that we, for our parts, are very much concerned for the good of our souls, and that we think that eternal salvation is a matter of the greatest importance. This will be a likely way to make others think so far, or at least, to put them upon thinking whether it is so or no, and so bring them to consideration, which is a good step. Matt: 5:16, "Let your light so shine before men, that they may see your good works, and glorify your Father which is in heaven." This way, we may silently reprove, and manifest our dislike of, vicious conversation and debauched practices by carefully abstaining from them and absenting ourselves from such company, and by using ourselves to a conversation that is contrary and savors of other things. Hereby, it may be we may save souls from death and hide a multitude of sins.

Third. Another way of promoting the salvation of the souls of others is by doing our part to the promoting and encouraging [of] the means of grace: by endeavoring what in us lies that they shall be dispensed, enjoyed and encouraged; by showing all respect and reverence to holy things, to the sabbath, to the word preached and to [the] sacraments, [and by watching] that we do nothing to hinder them or their efficacy on men's souls.

Exh.[1] III. If the salvation of men's souls is so precious, let us be exhorted earnestly to pray for the accomplishment of those times wherein there will be such plentiful effusions of God's spirit to the conversion of men's souls. If the soul of every man is worth more than all the world, surely 'tis lamentable and even dreadful to think that there are but few souls that are saved, that far the greatest part are in a state of damnation and going to hell, that men are so thinly traveling in the way to heaven, and that the way to destruction, though so broad, is so thronged and crowded.

There is a time coming that there will be very great change in the world: those nations which now are covered with the darkness of heathenism and idolatry, or other false religions, shall be enlightened with the truth, and there shall be a more extraordinary appearance of the power of godliness amongst those that profess it, when God's spirit shall be poured out on old and young, and the knowledge of God shall cover the earth "as the waters cover the seas" (Is. 11:9); "When they shall teach no more every man his neighbor, and every man his brother, saying, Know the Lord; for they shall all know him, from the least to the greatest" [Jer. 31:34];[2] "When the fullness of the Gentiles shall come in and all Israel shall be saved" (Rom. 11:25–

---

1. MS: "Use." The specific heading "Exhortation" has been employed here and above in the two previous main heads since the categorical term "Use" was appropriated by JE for the heading of the third major division of the sermon. To avoid such confusion, JE soon began using the terms "Application" and "Improvement" for the division heading, leaving "Use" for major subheads not more specifically identified.

2. This citation was not made by JE although a blank space was left for it, probably indicating that he was undecided between the citation supplied and Heb. 8:11, the source of some of his phrasing here.

26). These, and suchlike expressions, signify that all nations shall be Christianized and be visibly holy, and that multitudes—great multitudes all over the face of the earth—shall be brought to the saving knowledge of God. All those that are truly sensible of the worth of souls will think these very glorious times and will long for them. They are generally thought to be very near, which is a consideration that ought to stir up all Christians earnestly to pray for them, for though God has appointed the time of these things in his own counsels, yet he will be enquired of for them by his people before he accomplishes them: Ezek. 36:37–38, "Thus saith the Lord God, I will yet for this be enquired of by the house of Israel, to do it for them; I will increase them with men like a flock. As the holy flock, as the flock of Jerusalem in her solemn feasts; so shall the waste cities be filled with flocks of men: and they shall know that I am the Lord."

WICKED MEN'S SLAVERY TO SIN

Wɪᴛʜ purposeful vigor, Edwards rings changes on the theme of servitude in this striking sermon: complacency, blindness, obsession, enslavement, torment, and death. He insists that the bizarre notion of sacrificing soul and body for the purpose of gaining pain and death is actually a common activity among those conscious sinners who seek the world and the self—literal dead ends—despite the offer of life, liberation, and true happiness through Christ, a choice which the sermon implies is always a real alternative for all living persons. Though the theme of self-destructive enslavement to evil is implacably pursued throughout the sermon, tension is somewhat dissipated by a succession of diverse similitudes gathered from Scripture, history, and myth, as when one rummages the pages of an old chronicle or martyrology, illustrating and enlivening the subject with brief glimpses of emblematic scenes.

Although a lack of development prevents most of these similitudes from being more than broad thematic hints, there is a thread of imagery running through the sermon, structured by repetitions and echoes, which progressively focuses the reader's attention upon the notion of ironic entrapment, followed by torment and execution. Thus, with considerable subtlety, Edwards at first evokes the iron maiden of the Spanish Inquisition (p. 344), followed more obviously by the brazen bull of Perilaus (p. 346), and finally most forcefully by the brief but vivid scene of entrapment and death at the hands of cannibals (p. 349). This climactic scene, suggestive of a black mass, encapsulates the plight of the paradoxically child-like sinner who seeks a feast only to become one. Having perversely rejected communion with the self-sacrificing Savior, the natural man is himself sacrificed to infernal powers he would "make merry with," the full weight of irony bearing upon *with* and the relationship implied therein. So man blindly courts death in life.

But for all the traditional pessimism in this sermon concerning the nature of "natural" man, the essential optimism seen in others of the early sermons emerges in Edwards' linking innate reason and religion

337

(p. 343); and his insistence that sin is somehow beneath man, or a kind of morbidity, clearly indicates his exalted conception of man's potential for real virtue. Likewise, the insistence upon the continuity of the visible and invisible worlds in a disarmingly offhand comment—"consider . . . how small a part of the world of intelligent beings are the inhabitants of the earth" (p. 347)—provides a glimpse of that light of faith which ultimately illuminates the horizon of his meditation upon man's capacity for self-betrayal.

* * *

The booklet containing this sermon is neatly written and is nearly a model of the sixteen-page octavo quire unit. Although the sermon, unlike many others of this group, seems not to have been selected for repreaching later in Northampton, the first draft was rather carefully revised at or near the time of composition. Indeed, the physical details of the manuscript confirm the character of the text as one that is, if somewhat underdeveloped, a product of considerable artistic and intellectual effort.

The most interesting single detail of the manuscript also correlates with the text in that the extended simile of the Guinea cannibals, the rhetorical climax of the sermon, is the only major passage to have been inserted after the sermon was completed. Whether Edwards had simply heard the story after the completion of the sermon and felt it was too apt to be left out, or whether upon reading the sermon he concluded that he must have at least one developed analogy to add weight and color, the whole passage of nine lines is squeezed into a space that ordinarily would have held four or five lines at the bottom of the penultimate page. The passage seems appropriate where it is, but it is curious that this blank space was the only one in the whole booklet of such size, suggesting that Edwards knew of the story but needed to consult a source, or that he realized the need of a resounding example during composition and left the space for a yet unknown one. If the latter situation was the case, the metaphor he found proved to be longer and more elaborate than he had planned, but too good to discard or condense more than it is.

WICKED MEN'S SLAVERY TO SIN

JOHN 8:34.

Jesus answered them, Verily, verily, I say unto you, Whosoever committeth sin is the servant of sin.

THIS whole chapter is composed of nothing but excellent speeches and discourses of Christ to Jews in the temple on the Feast of Tabernacles, one of the great feasts wherein all the males were to appear before the Lord at Jerusalem, the city which he had chosen to put his name there. So that these discourses were delivered in the most public manner, at the most public time, and in the most public place that could be: before the whole nation of the Jews, and many of other nations, who went up to Jerusalem to worship.

In these discourses are contained many glorious and mysterious truths of the gospel, by the divine light of which many were convinced and believed on him, as in the thirtieth verse.

Which, Christ, who knew what was in man, perceiving, directs his discourse to them in particular, and tells them plainly, as he was always wont to do, that if they intended to be his disciples, they must be so rooted and established in their belief, and to persevere therein in spite of all opposition; "If ye continue in my word, then are ye my disciples indeed."

And [he] tells them for their encouragement, if they were established in the truth they should be made free by it, having respect to the bondage they were in to the Romans, as much as if he had said, "Although you are under the heavy yoke of the Romans, yet if you heartily embrace my doctrine, you shall be made free, and shall enjoy a better and more glorious liberty than [if] you were perfectly delivered from their servitude and enjoyed freedom under your own kings and rulers, under your own vines and your own fig trees" (which was but a type of this gospel liberty; see Zech. 3:10).

To which the Jews, agreeably to their pride and self-righteousness, make answer, signifying that they did not want to be made free, being naturally free by the nobleness of their birth and excellency of descent: being the children of Abraham, not acknowledging that it was possible for them to be bound.

This same national pride has continued amongst the Jews ever since, even to this day, for they claim to themselves a natural right of being masters of the whole world, and expect actually to be made such when their messiah comes.

But Christ assures them, in our text, that whatever they might think of themselves as to the Romans, yet that they are under a base servitude unto sin; for, "Verily, verily, I say unto you, he that committeth sin is a servant of sin."

1. Observe in the words who are the persons of whom Christ speaks, and that is "whosoever committeth sin." That is, whosoever allowedly doth it, for that must be the sense of the words: whosoever accustoms himself to sin, and is habituated to it.

Let him be who he will that so doth, he is a servant of sin: let him be a child of Abraham, in their sense, or not a child of Abraham; let him be a Jew or a heathen; let him be bond or free in other respects; let him be a prince or monarch, that holds all the world in servitude and slavery, or the meanest subject.

2. What is affirmed of them, to wit, that they are servants; however great rule they may bear in the world, yet if they commit sin they themselves are servants and slaves to this master.

DOCTRINE.

Wicked men are servants and slaves to sin.

We shall explain and clear up this doctrine by answering these two queries: first, how does it appear that wicked men are slaves to sin, and second, in what respects are they so? But,

[*Query*] I. How does it appear that wicked men are servants and slaves to sin? Perhaps you may think with yourself, "I don't see but that wicked men are happy, and live as free as the best men in the world." Or it may be you may object in your mind that you are very wicked yourself, and take yourself to be as free, and no more of a slave, than the best saint upon earth. But, however though you can't see that you are under slavery now because of your blindness, which is one effect of your servitude, yet you will plainly see it when you get into the other world, and will be made sensible of it before that time if ever you are set at liberty. And 'tis to be hoped that you will see it now, if you duly attend to the following particulars.

First. Wicked men labor hard and undergo many difficulties in the service of sin. Wicked men generally think that the way of holiness and religion is much the hardest, and theirs to be much the easiest. They wonder that men will be such fools as to tie themselves up to such strictness, so that they can't have the liberty to enjoy their pleasure but must be forced to live by rule, and must live a sober, strict and mortified life, must be forced to be tied up to the rules of religion. They don't like this way of living; they love to have more liberty, and therefore think that a wicked life is a great deal most eligible.

But they are very much mistaken, for godly men have a great deal the best of it, even in this world. 'Tis true a strict religious life is most contrary to corrupt nature, but yet, after all, the service of God is a great deal easier than the service of sin. The yoke of Christ is abundantly lighter than the iron yoke of Satan.

What infinite pains and labors do men take to satisfy their insatiable lusts which enlarge their desires as hell, like the horseleach which says, "Give, give," and the fire which saith, "It is not enough" [Prov. 30:15–16].[1] The lusts of men are very fitly compared to the fire, for the more fuel you throw on, the more furiously will they burn and rage.

What infinite pains will wicked men take to get riches, who know of nothing better. They keep seeking, pulling and drawing, and are never satisfied. The covetous man, if he should get the whole world in his possession, would be no more satisfied than when he has nothing. Alexander, after he conquered the world, was so far from being satisfied that he sat down and wept that there were no more worlds to conquer; found more grief that there never [would be] another world than joy and comfort that he had conquered this.

What pains do men take, what anxieties do they undergo, in the service of pride, in pursuit after honors and great places, and what an infinite number of disappointments and discontents do they meet with!

How many accusations of conscience do wicked men sin under! Job 15:20–21, "The wicked man travails in pain all his days . . . a dreadful

---

1. These brief phrases illustrate nicely JE's frequent disregard of verbal exactitude when quoting scripture.

sound is in his ears." He trembles for fear that he shall die, but yet sin, his master, makes him go on in his service notwithstanding.

He undergoes the fear of hell and the great judgment in his service, and at the same time hastens these things upon him which he fears; for sin and lust greatly shorten the life of man, as well because it provokes God to cut him off in the midst of his days—"Be not wicked overmuch . . . for why should you die before thy time," says Solomon [Eccles. 7:17]—and then because it naturally tends to drink up the animal spirits, [and] eat up the principle of life in men. Lust is like a worm that continually gnaws at the root of life.

And there are multitudes of other ways whereby sin destroys the comfort, happiness and good things of this life, which might be mentioned if the time would allow, so much labor and so many difficulties do men undergo in the bondage of sin. How truly then may it be said, "He that commits sin is a servant of sin."

Second. The wicked man is devoted to the commands of sin, and therefore may be said to be under slavery to it. Wicked men are very obedient servants to sin. All things in the world must give way to the commands thereof: the commands of God must not stand in competition with them, but must all bow down and be trampled upon by sin. His own interest and happiness must also give place when sin requires it, and so devoted are wicked men to their lord and master, sin, that they will rather burn in hell forever than disobey him and rebel against him. They stand ready to be sent on any errand that sin requires them to go [on]; they wait at sin's gates, and watch at the posts of his doors, like an obedient lackey, to hear what commands he has for them to do. Thus, if sin requires them to steal, swear, defraud, or commit fornication, it is done; if sin commands them to do that which tends to their own ruin and destruction, it is done; if sin commands them to run and jump into the bottomless pit, the sinner immediately obeys, and runs with all his might towards this pit of fire and brimstone. And whatever fears and dreadful apprehensions he may have on his mind, yet he is such a devoted servant to sin that it shall be performed. Thus he is entirely given up to obey this tyrant, sin.

Third. It appears that a wicked man is under slavery to sin because he himself receives no manner of advantage by sinning. He undergoes all this hard service, attended with so many intolerable difficulties, all for nothing. The poor sinner will moil and toil, night and day, all his life-long for sin, and he himself not at all the better for it. He has nothing from sin but his labors for his pains; there is no happiness that he is to receive after he has done his work, but he labors for nothing but to please sin and the devil, and because sin commands him so to do.

Sin serves them worse than any poor slave upon earth is served. There are many servants that are dealt cruelly by, but none so hardly dealt with as the servants of sin. Many servants are allowed [recompense] for their service, but just so much as to keep them alive; but sin don't do that, but instead of that, nothing but destroys their life continually.

There is never any advantage accrues to men from any sin. They never are the happier for pride, malice, revenge, drunkenness, lasciviousness, swearing, cursing and damning: these things do a man no manner of good, neither in this world or the world to come. All the good they do is to lay up great stores of wrath in the other world for them. Every oath and every curse makes hellfire a great deal hotter for 'em, against they come into it, and that is all the profit they get by it.

Neither is there any good got by those sins which seem, at first sight, as if they had a tendency at least to increase his outward good things, such as theft, fraud and deceit, covetousness, etc. If their money or lands are increased by these means, yet a curse goes along with them, and such kind of goods are cankers that eat out a man's substance. And besides, they are never enjoyed with any pleasure or comfort, but are like spectres and apparitions that continually affright the conscience. Prov. 16:8, "Better is a little with righteousness than great revenues without right." Thus the sinner doth the hard service and drudgery of sin for nothing in the world.

Query II. In what respects is a wicked man servant to sin?

First Ans. The wicked man serves sin with his soul. The sinner serves this master with his whole heart and soul, and all that is within him. His understanding is given up to the obedience of sin; [he] won't see the truth of the plainest thing in the world because sin bids him shut his eyes. [He] won't be made to understand any spiritual truth because sin won't allow of it. The eye of his reason must be open only to those things that sin allows him to see; he must keep his eyes fast shut, only when sin gives him leave to open them. Sin will not suffer the understanding of a sinner to see the gloriousness of God and the excellency of Christ, what is his own happiness, and the great danger he is in of misery. No, but sin makes him serve him blindfold and with his eyes shut.

So, likewise, the will and affections are given up to sin. The sinner wills those things which are agreeable to sin, and avoids everything that is contrary thereto. It will not allow him to choose that which will make him happy and blessed forevermore, but causes him to choose death and misery rather than life.

It will not suffer him to love that which is truly lovely and amiable, such as a most excellent and glorious God, a most lovely Jesus, holiness, amiable Christianity, the saints and the like, but only those things which are most loathsome and hateful. [It] causes him to hug devilish and filthy lusts and sins, which are more filthy than a toad, and will stab him to the heart while he is embracing of them. Thus sin maintains a tyranny over our very hearts and souls: never was poor slave so tyrannized over as sinners are by sin. Other masters have only the outward man in their service, can rule only their outward actions and have no dominion over their thoughts and wills, but sin enslaves the very soul, so that he believes, wills, loves, nor thinks nothing but what sin allows of and commands. When sin commands him not to think about a future state of happiness, or misery and an eternal judgment, forbids him to consider of the great things of the gospel—the hatefulness of sin, the excellency of Christ, the necessity of faith, repentance and the like—the wicked man obeys sin in all this. Sin commands him to think of the pleasantness, of the enjoyments, of his lusts, the sweetness of sensual pleasure, of worldly riches, prosperity and ease, and herein the sinner obeys this tyrannical master. There is no man in the world has so absolute a command over his servant as to command his thoughts; every servant [can think what he] will, for all his master [can do], but sin has dominion over the very thoughts of a sinner.

Second [*Ans.*] The body of a wicked man is also enslaved to sin. Whenever the wicked man exercises his body, it is in the service of sin. Prov. 21:4, "And the plowing of the wicked is sin." The hands, feet, tongue, eyes, ears and all are about the devil's work. Rom. 6:19, "For as ye have yielded your members servants to uncleanness, to iniquity unto iniquity . . ." Thus sin governs the[2] whole man, both soul and body, and all the actions of both.

---

2. MS: "their."

Third [*Ans.*] The substance of a wicked man is devoted to the service of sin—neither to the service of God, nor of his fellow-creatures, nor his own service, but the service of sin—to be fuel to his lusts, to pamper his pride, to nourish his luxury, to strengthen him to sin and fat him for the slaughter: such a slave as this, is the wicked person to sin.

APPLICATION.

I. Hence, learn that we are all by nature servants and slaves to sin. We are all sinners by nature, and all sinners, by the assertion of Christ, are servants or slaves to sin (Eph. 2:3), so that we see what state and condition we are born into the world in, even bondage and servitude. We are all born slaves; our souls and our bodies, with every power of both, come into the world bound to sin. We are born not only with the livery, but also with the fetters and chains of sin upon us. And as soon as ever we come to the use of our reason, as soon as we can speak or go, sin is such a hard master to us that he sets us to his drudgery, and makes us labor in his service as soon as we are able to stand on our feet by our own strength. And in this condition are all mankind, but only those that are redeemed by Christ: they are all born under bondage to sin.

II. Hence, learn how much all wicked men are to be pitied. When we see a servant that is cruelly dealt with by his master, made to labor hard perpetually and without ceasing, night and day; to go through fire and water, cold and heat, amongst briers and thorns, in perpetual danger of his life; and all this for nothing; his master will neither allow him food nor clothing, nor anything else for his service, we pity and have compassion on such an one.

But wicked men that are under the service of sin are much more to [be] pitied. Their master is more barbarous, their labor more difficult, and all for nothing, but only to please sin, their master. The servant of sin is in a more pitiable condition than ever a poor caitive[3] slave that is condemned to labor in the mines, or forced to work himself to death in chains, and moil and toil himself till he rots in the prison of his servitude.

What heart is so hard, and who is so inhuman, as not to pity and compassionate the poor sinner who is in such dreadful bondage to

---

3. A variant form of "caitiff."

sin, who won't allow him to have his eyes open, but causes him to labor blindfold, least if he should see, he should find out a way to escape from his captivity? Who won't allow [him] to take care of his own welfare, but makes him do his work upon the very edge of a dreadful precipice where the ground is slippery, and upon a hillside,[4] and he is [in] imminent danger every moment of slipping and falling into a bottomless pit of liquid fire; [or] makes him labor in a wilderness, full of wild beasts—lions, tigers, dragons, and fiery serpents—where those that come are generally tore to pieces? What heart cannot pity those that are under such a tyranny?

What objects of pity are those kings and princes that serve sin at this rate; what objects of pity are all rich men that put confidence in riches and are slaves to the sin of covetousness; what objects of pity and compassion are men that are in great worldly honor and glory, and are under the dominion of pride! How ought the Christian to weep as if his head were waters and his eyes fountains of tears over these, though perhaps they have multitudes of slaves under them. Alas, the servitude of their negroes is better than theirs, a thousand times better than theirs.

But especially how ought we to pity, and be moved with compassion, for those poor creatures, those miserable, undone men who are given to swearing, rioting, luxury, drunkenness and lasciviousness. There is never a poor creature that is burnt in a brazen bull or is roasted alive, that is in such a miserable, lamentable and pitiable condition as they are, although they may swim in sensual, sinful and devilish pleasures and delights.

III. *Exh.* To leave off the service of sin and assert your own liberty. You that are in such a miserable and lamentable condition, and are laboring in sin's mines, are now invited to leave off his service and become free. Why will you be a slave to sin? Do you love to be a servant? Is it not much better to be free and at liberty? There is no need that you should be a servant; wherefore, let all poor servants of sin come out of their bondage, and resolve that they will serve sin no more. Come, be bold and courageous, and don't be afraid to disobey sin; if you so do, you will not be hurt for it; the devil can't hurt you for rebelling against sin. You have no more need to serve sin than to cut your own throat, which indeed you are doing as long as you serve

4. MS: "side hill."

sin; wherefore, continue no longer in his services. Consider for motive:

First. How base a master you serve. You have the most base, hateful and shameful master in the world. If the master that you serve were honorable, you would have some excuse for continuing in his service, but instead of that you serve the most dishonorable and mean master in the world. You serve that base, hateful and detestable thing, even sin. If you search all over the creation, from end of it to the other, you will not find another such an ignominious master.

You, to your shame and disgrace, are servant to the filth of the creation, which is too filthy to be allowed in it, and therefore at last shall be cast out of it and burnt in unquenchable fire. You serve that master who is the very loathing and stink of the universe; if this master is so vile, how vile is the servant?

'Tis a thousand times as dishonorable a thing to be a servant of sin as it is to be [a] servant of the meanest beggar. You would be ashamed to be servant to a loathsome and filthy vagabond, clothed in rags and all over defiled with filth and pollution; and why are you not ashamed to be a servant of that which [is] infinitely more vile and contemptible?

Sin is a thing vastly beneath man's nature. When you serve sin, you serve a master that is vastly beneath yourself, and make yourself a slave to that which is not worthy of anything but loathing and detestation. You admit him not only into your house, and the best room of it, but into your very hearts, into the inward closet of your soul; and there place him in the throne of your affections where reason, your most excellent [faculty], and religion, which vastly exalts reason, ought to sit, and subject your reason and all those excellent faculties which your Maker has given you to him: strip yourself of all manner of wisdom, prudence, and innocency to prepare yourself to serve him, and then like an abject slave, bow down before him and suffer him as it were to set his foot upon your neck, and entirely give yourself up to his commands. How mean and vile do you make yourself, and how do you expose yourself to the scorn and derision of the whole creation!

But perhaps you may say to yourselves, "However mean and base a thing it may be to serve sin, yet it is so common in this world that it is no disgrace to me here; I am not the less respected for it amongst my fellow-men, and therefore I will continue in my wicked course." But consider in answer to that, how small a part of the world of intelligent beings are the inhabitants of the earth; although you don't get disgrace by serving sin in the world of wicked men, yet what dishonor and shame do you get in the invisible world. What open shame will you be put to before the whole world, visible and invisible, before long, when God himself will laugh at your calamity and mock when your soul comes before the whole universe: when you will be exposed to the derision of saints and angels, when your own conscience will upbraid you and call you a fool a thousand and a thousand times, when the devil himself, who now speaks so fair to entice you, will mock and deride you!

Second. Consider how mean is the service you do. The master whom you serve not only is mean, but also the service you serve under him is above all things vile and contemptible: to serve sin is to become a fool and divest one's self of reason and understanding, and act more filthily than the brute beasts. Sinners often in Scripture are called fools, fools because their transgressions are afflicted, says the psalmist, and indeed they [are] eminently and enormously foolish, so foolish as to run into hellfire. They are also in Scripture called beasts: "I fought with beasts at Ephesus" [I Cor. 15:32], says the apostle Paul; and again, "Beware of dogs" [Phil. 3:2]. So that the service of sin is to act the fool, the madman, the beast, and further than that, the devil. Wicked men very often are called the children of the devil, and sometimes the devil. Christ tells his disciples that one of them was a devil; that is, a wicked [man].

The service of sin is to wallow in the mire of our lusts like swine, to swallow down loathsome iniquity like water. How wonderful and astonishing is it that ever a man that was born into the world with the faculty of understanding, and endowed with an immortal soul, should debase himself and bring himself down, as to such mean and base servitude. Wherefore, resolve no longer, like a man of a mean and low spirit, thus to submit yourself to such filthy drudgery.

Third. Consider how cruelly and tyrannically you are dealt with by sin. If you were but sensible how cruelly you are handled by sin, you would immediately resolve to cast off his iron yoke and serve him no longer. The service of sin is a most tyrannical service; men therein lose their reason and understanding. Sin makes all his servants labor till they are blind and mad, till they are not able to see whereabouts they are, and then leads [them] away towards their own destruction.

In the service of sin man becomes sick and weak. Wicked men are spiritually sick, and this sickness is occasioned by the cruel service of sin. The wicked man labors in the fire of his own conscience, which is the flashes of hell-flames, till at last he kills himself in his service if he continues in the same. Thus cruelly are you dealt with by your master; the work he sets you about is to whet a knife whereby your own throat is to be cut, to sharpen and poison arrows that are to be thrust into your own hearts, to make a fire for yourself to be burnt in. For every sin a wicked man commits is a laying up wrath against the day of wrath, is a whetting the sword of vengeance, a poisoning the arrows of wrath that are to be wet in your own heart's blood, and a throwing fuel into hellfire. They do by you as I have heard they do in Guinea, where at their great feasts they eat men's flesh. They set the poor ignorant child who knows nothing of the matter, to make a fire, and while it stoops down to blow the fire, one comes behind and strikes off his head, and then he is roasted by that same fire that he kindled, and made a feast of, and the skull is made use of as a cup, out of which they make merry with their liquor. Just so Satan, who has a mind to make merry with you.[5]

Fourth. Consider what poor wages you will have for your services. Death, eternal death, is all the wages that ever you will receive for your service: Rom. 6:23, "For the wages of sin is death"—after all your pains to please the devil, after all your hard labor, after all those difficulties you undergo in obeying sin's commands; after you have given up your reason, understanding and innocency, and made yourself a beast and a fool that you may serve this, your abject master.

After you have spent your life and your soul in this slavery, after you have been vexed by the fears of death and been scorched by your conscience, and have rotted in sin's prison and Satan's chains, all the wages you shall have for your pains is nothing but one of the chiefest—that is, one of the deepest and hottest—places in the lake of fire and brimstone.

This is the wages due to you for your hard service and cruel servitude. Satan is willing enough you should have it—he'll not begrutch it you—nor God is not so unjust as not to pay it: the harder you labor, and the more work you do for sin, the greater will be your wages. You shall have a larger cup of vengeance and a hotter place than

5. This extraordinary illustration may have come to hand in some collection of emblems or even in a travel narrative, though no source has been discovered in books to which JE is known to have had access. Of course it is possible that he means just what he says in "I have heard," and that the tale came from conversation with sailors or travelers in the port city of New York.

others who have sinned but little in comparison of you. God will deal justly with everyone, will do with all according to their works, and they that do most work for sin will have a reward accordingly, and a proportionable retribution.

THE IMPORTANCE OF A FUTURE STATE

With a forthrightness rare even in a young preacher, Edwards makes brutally explicit the underlying issue of this sermon and of Christian ethics: "If there be no future state of rewards and punishments in the other world, then the whole of religion is immediately thrown up and destroyed" (p. 362). Moreover, he pursues the issue on the most practical pastoral level, as stated in the first few paragraphs of the Use: "There are a great many that live under the gospel [who] . . . if one could look into the closet of their hearts, he would there plainly discern that they questioned the truth of these great truths of Christianity; that they neither believed the Scriptures to be the Word of God, nor Christ to be the Son, nor the truths of a future state and eternal judgment" (p. 368). Without this essential foundation of belief, he argues, there is little point in considering the moral and philosophical aspects of religion.

But such faith should not be all that difficult if one stops to reflect, he insists, for both the evidence of human reason and divine revelation mutually support it; indeed, even ancient heathens and contemporary American Indians have always supported it! And the sermon attempts, primarily through challenging the listener's ability to draw reasonable inferences from the religion he professes and from his personal sense of reality, to establish the conviction of a future judgment and an awareness of one's probable relation to it. Intense, condensed, nearly a précis of an argument and yet two preaching units long, the sermon evolves from a rather theoretical exposition in the Doctrine to a psychological prodding in the Use anticipatory of later awakening sermons. Indeed, the sermon is both fundamental and holistic in spirit, suggesting an attempt to cover its declared ground with exemplary thoroughness, forcing a yea or nay on a series of issues more often dismissed through tactful silence or an evasive salute.

The spirit of this piece is further illustrated in the formal dimension of the sermon. Nowhere in the canon of Edwards' sermons is there a sermon with such explicitly articulated parts. Although this is not his first sermon, and may be a sixth or tenth (assuming some to be lost), Edwards seems to be concentrating on the articulation of formal structure in this sermon with the same intense dedication to fundamentals. Thus the sermon is almost a model—perhaps "skeleton" would not be inappropriate—of the sermon as he understood it to be and would continue to pursue it. Heavily doctrinal, though not sufficiently so to be identified as a lecture, the sermon is remarkably self-conscious in its argument and form.

Although coincidental, it is fitting that this sermon is linked bibliographically with the "Diary" and "Resolutions" manuscript(s) (see p. 367n.). Through the "Diary," Edwards scrutinized his personal performance in the light of his code of Resolutions, and that spirit of rigor, of assessing fundamentally, and that formal preoccupation with the real structural relationship between parts and the whole can be seen as unifying his private and public writings during his pastorate in New York. It is likely that Edwards worked by turns and with equal intensity of concern upon these superficially unrelated documents.

* * *

The manuscript of this sermon is one of Edwards' most interesting, for it contains a program of experimental procedures that is not repeated. The text itself is divided between two octavo booklets of eight and nine leaves, respectively, the second beginning with an outline summary of the first, indicating that it was preached at a later hour or day. The sermon was evidently repreached at least once, as indicated by some small revisions in a later ink as well as a shorthand symbol probably indicating that it was preached at Bolton, Connecticut. Most of the evidence of experiment and revision is connected with the initial draft and preaching, however, and pertains to pulpit efficiency.

First, there are various abbreviations, including "y" contractions and ampersands, that are employed on the opening page or two of both booklets, though Edwards seems to have returned to spelled out words in each booklet as he became engrossed in the argument. More unusual is a device he seems to have used only this once, throughout the first booklet and in the first pages of the second: superscript topical words or "catchwords" of a new sort, each enclosed in a half-balloon above the line in order to identify the subject of the phrase below it. At first glance these words (sometimes brief phrases) appear to be insertions, but the context makes clear that they were intended only to catch Edwards' eye during pulpit delivery. A similarly schematic device, though used only once in the sermon, is the arranging of several contrasted terms in vertical pairs, separated by vertical lines, so that they appear as a kind of chart. Less dramatic, but of the same ilk are the extraordinarily neat summary outline in the second booklet, the placing of certain passages in boxes or rectilinear balloons, and the use of larger script for some headings and key words.

Since these devices pertain exclusively to the oral publication of the sermon and are essentially irrelevant to the literary text, they have not been reproduced here; however, the exaggerated formal structure and insistent paragraphing are inevitably part of the literary text and reflect the same preoccupation with clarity of form and efficiency of operation. The manuscript is that of one who is laboring, if not struggling, to achieve an efficient pulpit instrument.

Finally, it should be noted that the manuscript reveals evidence of struggle in the composition of the sermon, in that two leaves in the first booklet have been shorn of their mates in the quire after all four were apparently written upon, and in the second booklet the final leaf is separate and is actually stitched inside the penultimate leaf.

THE IMPORTANCE OF A FUTURE STATE

HEBREWS 9:27.

And as it is appointed unto men once to die, and after that the judgment.

T HE scope of the chapter: to show how the things of the law and first covenant were types [and] shadows of things under the gospel state, and how much more excellent the antitypes.

There is a parallel run between the tabernacle and heaven: between the sacrifices of bulls, goats and calves, and the sacrifice of Christ, between their blood and his blood; between the high priests and Christ, between their entering into the Holy of Holies and his entering into heaven. But only, there is this difference: the high priests entered often into the holy place, but Christ the antitype of them entered but once into heaven, as in the two verses foregoing our text: "Nor yet that he should offer himself often, as the high priest entereth into the holy place every year with blood of others; for then must he often have suffered since the foundation of the world: but now once in the end of the world hath he appeared to put away sin by the sacrifice of himself." And this is illustrated by the verse of our text, "As it is appointed unto men once to die, and after that the judgment." That is, as man, for whom Christ died and was offered for, is to die but once, so Christ that died was offered but once to save him from death, from spiritual and eternal death, and from the sting and power of natural death.

As man dies but once, and after that the judgment, after that his everlasting state is decided; so Christ suffered but once to deliver from everlasting misery and procure everlasting happiness after death, and shall appear a second time to determine openly and publicly the everlasting state of every man, as in the next verse.

The verse of our text imports these things:

1. That all men must die. It is spoken of men in general, "It is appointed to men." It is so appointed and ordained of God and

354

therefore must certainly be, in that there is no reversing or avoiding the decree and appointment of God.

2. That after death the eternal state of men shall be everlastingly decided.

(1) Implied in the words, "And after that the judgment." Judgment is spoken of here as "by way of eminency"[1]: not *a* judgment [or] some particular judgment that was to be in force awhile and after that to be reversed; but *the* judgment, the Final Judgment, that judgment that will be in force forever and shall determine the state of men to eternity.

(2) Inasmuch as 'tis compared to Christ's dying but once. As it is appointed to men once to die and after that the judgment, so Christ once suffered, which implies that men shall never have another opportunity to live in this world and to die; according as they die that once, so it must be. They shall never die again that they may have an opportunity of dying better than they did before. They shall never have the benefits of the death of Christ offered to 'em again; after they are once dead, Christ will never die again to save 'em. If they have not procured to themselves the benefits of the death that Christ has died already, they shall never have the opportunity of another death of Christ.

DOCTRINE.

All men must certainly die, and after death their everlasting state will be determined.

I. All men must die.

By death, in a theological sense, is meant the destruction of those earthly tabernacles, and an everlasting forsaking of this world and going into the next. Agreeably to this description, it may be said that every man that ever was, is, or will be dies; thus, in some sense died Enoch and Elias: their earthly tabernacles were in some sense destroyed, they were so transformed. No more earth and animal, but spiritual: their corruption was destroyed and they put on incorruption; their mortality was destroyed and they put on immortality. They also left this world and went into the other.

---

1. JE originally included the Greek phrase, κατ’ ἐ ξοχην, but deleted it at the time of composition. He apparently had difficulty finding an English equivalent, first writing "by way of emphasis." Actually, English has no equivalent so exact as the French *par excellence*, but JE had no French and rarely employed foreign loan-words or idioms in any case.

In this sense also, those who shall be found alive at our Lord's second coming shall in some sense die; their earthly tabernacles shall be destroyed and made quite of another nature. They shall also leave this world. This world itself indeed then will be destroyed, so that it will be just all one to them, as if they died in the common acceptation of the word, and in the way wherein the rest of men do die.

But all other men must die in the ordinary way of separation of their souls from their bodies. Men of all ranks, degrees, and orders must die: strong [and] weak; kings, princes [and] beggars; rich [and] poor; good [and] bad.[2]

However strong, hale and healthy men may be, there is none strong enough to resist death; death will conquer them as easily as other men. However great they may be in the world, they must die: kings and emperors, czars and sultans must bow down before death, must give place to the king of terrors. Such men as Nebuchadnezzar, Xerxes, Alexander and Julius Caesar must die as well as other men, and then they are no better than the meanest of their subjects.

The rich must become as poor as the poorest when death calls 'em away from their riches; [see] Job 3:18–19.

The bad must die as well as the good. Let 'em be never so unfit and unprepared to die, they must come to it; let 'em be never so unwilling to go where death would carry 'em, they must go; let 'em hang back never so much, be never so dreadfully afraid, let them cry out never so much with their fearful apprehensions, death will hear none of their cries. He will have no pity nor compassion on them, but will hale them along into eternity whether they will or no.

And then they must leave all these things: they must leave all their money, all their honor; their pleasures and friends, their houses and lands, and whatever else they had upon earth.

And this must most certainly and surely be. If they are never so wise, they are not cunning enough for death; however powerful they are, they are not powerful enough for death. If all the world, from end of it to the other, should be called together, they could not save a man from dying. Amongst all the curious arts and inventions that have been found out since the beginning of the world, there is no invention to keep a man from dying.

2. In the MS this sentence is schematized as follows: "Men of all ranks, degrees, and orders must die:

strong	kings and princes	rich	good."
weak	beggars	poor	bad

This is one of the more radical of the devices JE experimented with in this sermon, all of them apparently designed to facilitate oral delivery.

II. After death, the final and everlasting death finds them. So judgment will leave 'em, and as judgment leaves ['em], so it will be with them to all eternity.[3]

Under this head we shall show: first, a future and eternal state; second, a future judgment, [and] third, that that judgment will be final and everlasting.

First. There is a future and eternal state and condition. We shall prove this, first, by the light of natural reason; secondly, from the clearer light of revelation.

1. By the light of natural reason.

(1) It appears from that natural conscience that God has placed in the mind of every man.

There is certainly such a thing as a conscience in the mind of every man; there never was a man yet but what has experienced it: man brings it into the world with him. Heathens and atheists have it as well as other men; see what the Apostle saith of the heathen, Rom. 2:14–15: "For when the Gentiles, which have not the law, do by nature the things contained in the law, these, having not the law, are a law unto themselves: which show the work of the law written in their hearts, their conscience also bearing witness, and their thoughts the meanwhile accusing or else excusing one another." Little children show that they have a conscience in them before ever they [hear] anything of the Word of God.

Now this conscience that God has implanted in us naturally makes men afraid when they have committed any secret sins. Though no man in the world sees them, yet if they are not very much hardened they [are] naturally apprehensive of punishment, and I believe every one here present has experienced this first or last.

So also when we have done any virtuous act, any good action, we naturally expect that it will be the better with us for it.

Now God has implanted in us this natural disposition of expecting a reward or punishment, according as we do well or ill, for this disposition is natural to us: 'tis in our very nature; God had made it with us. And to what purpose should God make in us a disposition to expect rewards and punishments if there are none? God don't create in us an expectation of that which is not true, but this will be much illustrated by the following particulars.

3. There followed here a sentence which was deleted at the time of composition: "If they are good when they die, they shall be good forever; and if they are bad when they die, they shall be bad forever."

(2) Rewards and punishments according to men's works are not dispensed in this life. The natural conscience tells us that rewards and punishments will be dispensed somewhere, and at some time or other, but we plainly see that they are not in this life. Wherefore, there must be a future state.

The nature of God makes it impossible but that men must be dealt with according to their works, for he is a most just God and the governor of the world: Gen. 18:25, "Shall not the judge of all the earth do right?"

But as things stand in this world, the most wicked men in the world prosper and flourish, and are in far greater prosperity than the righteous. See Ps. 73, from [the first] verse to the eighteenth, where the Psalmist says the wicked were in far greater prosperity than the righteous, and can any man think that it will be so always? Can any man think that God will suffer sin and iniquity, which he hates, always to have the upper hand of holiness, which he loves? But if there be no life after this, it will be so oftentimes.

Can it be thought that God will let a Nero, who was guilty of the murder of so many thousand souls: who murdered his own nearest relations, his best friends and benefactors, the best and most honorable men in the city, without any manner of occasion; who burnt the city of Rome only to make sport, who was guilty of so many horrid cruelties that the sun hid his face from the sight of them: can it be thought that God would suffer him to live swimming in sensual pleasure all his lifetime, and at last go unpunished?

When many hundreds of thousands of those who were the best and holiest men upon earth went through all manner of troubles and difficulties in their life, and at last have been tortured and tormented to death with the worst torments all the world can think of, can it possibly be so when a most holy, just and merciful God looks on it?

Who can believe that God suffers pirates, who make it the business of their life to murder and destroy men, to live a jovial and merry life and go unpunished at last? But they will go unpunished, many of them, except there is a future state; wherefore, we see it cannot possibly be that there is no world to come wherein a distinction is made by God between the good and bad.

(3) Because, if there is no future state, man cannot answer the end of his creation.

Man must be made for some higher end than barely to enjoy this world, because if that were the end of his creation, God has [not] made him higher than the beasts that perish in vain. He has given him the power of reason and understanding in vain, for he could enjoy this world as well without reason, or anything but that sense that the beasts have, as well as with. If that be the end of making man, man is made in vain, for there is no need of making man to enjoy, because beasts can enjoy the world as well as man.

The end of making man, therefore, must be the glorifying of God and the enjoyment of him, which ends are not to any effect obtained if men's souls are turned to nothing at death.

Who can suppose that God made man to glorify Him so miserably as we are capable of in this life, and enjoy some little communion with Him for about sixty or seventy years, and then the man is annihilated, and the glory of God and the enjoyment of him is at an end forever? Who can think thus?

Therefore, we must necessarily conclude that man was made to glorify God forever, and to enjoy him to all eternity, and consequently that there is another world.

(4) It appears that there will be a future and eternal state because God has created in man a strong desire of enduring always.

Now, it is a thing that is quite inconsistent with God to create in man a strong desire of enduring forever, and at the same time make him of such a nature as is uncapable of enduring above about seventy years. Wherefore, we may conclude that God implanted in him such a desire that it might stir him up to do good and eschew evil, that his eternal state might be happy and not miserable, and therefore, that the soul will undoubtedly endure forever.

God has undoubtedly created man with such a desire and made it natural to us. For every man finds in himself a natural horror of being turned to nothing when he dies.

The beasts who are not to endure forever have no desire of it. They think nothing of it. God has not made them capable of conceiving of a future state because he has not made them capable of it; therefore, we may justly conclude that those whom he has made capable of conceiving of it, he has also made capable of it.

(5) God has made the soul of a nature quite distinct from the body, and therefore it will not die with the body.

That the soul is of a nature quite distinct from the body appears because the soul is immaterial and the body material: the soul can think and understand, which no matter or body can do.

It is observed of some persons, that when their bodies are very sick, decayed, and almost destroyed by some disease, the soul will be as whole as ever, which plainly shows it to be something distinct from the body. It is observed of some persons when they are dying, that their understanding and the faculties of the soul are higher and better than ever, and sometimes hold good to the last breath, when the soul doth as it were sit upon the lips of the dying body, just ready to take its flight, which is a clear evidence the soul don't die when the body doth.

(6) It appears that the light of natural reason tells us that the soul will endure forever because all the nations of the earth agree in it.

It is not only Christians that own it, but Jews, Mahometans and heathens do all believe it. Amongst the different nations of the heathen there is in the world, that are of different opinions in other things, worship different gods, live in distant countries—perhaps some on one side of the earth and others on the other—yet all believe [in] another life after this, which plainly and evidently shows that the bare light of nature teaches them. How else should they all agree in it?

Even the barbarously ignorant Indians here in America have light enough to believe *that,* for they do all believe it, and did before ever they heard of Christians.[4]

Thus I have proved a future state and another world from the light of natural reason. The reason why I have spoken so much on this head is because many men are more easily convinced by such kinds of arguments than those that are drawn from Scripture.

2. I shall now, in the second place, prove it from the clearer light of revelation, or the Word of God.

(1) Inasmuch as God has expressly declared [it] in his Word.

I need not go to multiply instances of this kind: the whole Bible, especially the New Testament, is one continued declaration thereof, either implicit or express.

Now what greater confirmation could be desired than to have God himself declare it to us over and over again? Who can desire a greater confirmation of anything than the word of an all-seeing, omniscient

---

4. JE is here reflecting a notion that fascinated the English colonists from the earliest days. Whether a Puritan such as John Eliot (as reported in the third book of Cotton Mather's *Magnalia Christi Americana*) or a worldly Virginian such as William Byrd (as reported in his *History of the Dividing Line*), the English seem to have relished confirmations of the broad outlines of their religion by American Indians, as if Indian culture represented "natural" thinking, somewhere between innate ideas and animal instinct.

God? But God in his Word has often declared to us, that there is certainly another world.

The light of nature told us so before, so that there was all reason in the world to believe it, but God has put the matter past all doubt, and has told, himself, expressly that it is certainly so. And therefore, everyone must believe it that don't think the Almighty Jehovah lies.

(2) He has abundantly confirmed it by sending his Son into the world.

Who can believe that God would send his Son into the world from the highest heavens, down to earth to take upon him our natures, to appear in the form of a servant, when he knew at the same time that the soul which he came to save should have an end at death? Especially considering,

(3) That for this Christ died, viz. that the soul might be saved in the other world.

Now who can think that Christ would die to save men in the other world if there is no other world? Who can be so prodigiously unreasonable as to think that Christ would be crucified between two thieves to procure eternal life to men, when he at the same time knew that the souls of all men should be turned to nothing at the end of this life?

(4) Another world is abundantly proved from Christ's resurrection unto life again, and ascension into heaven.

By Christ's resurrection from the dead, the world has actually seen the other world, for they have seen a man after this life in another life; so that the world has seen the future state in Christ accomplished by his resurrection from the dead, for his resurrection was his beginning of a future state. The light of reason convinces the world that it is so: the Word of God puts it past doubt. Christ's incarnation is a certain proof of the truth of it; by his death we have a repeated demonstration of it, but by his resurrection and ascension we have seen it all accomplished already in one instance. He has been seen not only to begin the life that is after this by his resurrection, but actually to enter into the place of the other world by his ascension.

We have thereby a certain proof that all men shall rise from the dead, because one man is risen already, even the man Christ Jesus, who has declared that he will raise all the rest. I Cor. 15:20: "But now Christ is risen, and become the first fruits of them that slept."

Christ has shown that the resurrection is a thing possible, because [he] is risen: he has shown that he is able to raise men from the dead because he has raised himself. Christ says, John 10:18, that he has power to lay down his life, and power to take it again, and Christ has shown that he intends to raise men from the dead; for to this end Christ both died, and rose and revived, that he might be lord both of the dead and [the] living.

(5) All this is sealed by the power of the Holy Ghost.

All those wondrous miracles [which] have been wrought from the beginning of the world, have been wrought for the confirmation of the truth of a world to come.

Particularly the miracles wrought by Christ and his apostles were more directly a proof of it. What an innumerable multitude of miracles have been wrought to prove this! For this end were so many devils cast out, so many sick healed, the blind saw, the deaf heard, the lame walked; thousands were fed and filled by a few loaves and fishes; the waters were hardened, the wind and storms stilled, and even the dead raised. One true miracle is a demonstration of the truth of that for the proof of which it is wrought: what, then, are so many?

Thus we have proved the truth of another world, first by natural reason, in that every man's conscience gives testimony to it; and because if there be none, men are not dealt with by God according to their deserts; nor is the end of man's creation obtained; and God has implanted the natural desire of enduring forever [only to be] frustrated; and the sense of all nations upon earth contradicted.

And then we proved it by Revelation, in that God has expressly and positively declared it over and over, and has sent his Son into the world to die, which would be wholly in vain if it were otherwise; and besides, we have seen it already accomplished in one instance, even Jesus Christ, by his rising from the dead and ascending into heaven, and all this confirmed by multitudes of great and wondrous miracles.

Thus we see what ample proof God has given us of this great and important truth of another world; so that if we don't believe it from so great, so many and clear demonstrations of it, there is no more to be said to us, but we shall be left inexcusable.

The reason why I have so particularly insisted upon this point is because it is a matter of the greatest importance and concern. The whole of religion depends upon it. If there be no future state of rewards and punishments in the other world, then the whole of religion is immediately thrown up and destroyed.

And then because it is to be feared that there are many that profess the Christian religion who don't firmly believe it; and therefore it is of much importance that it be irrefragably proved, to convince all men of how much concern it is to prepare for the other world.

If men were but fully established in this, that they must certainly be rewarded with an everlasting reward or punished with everlasting punishment in the other world, it would certainly have a great influence into their hearts and lives. And therefore, that every one of us may be fully established in this truth, let us well digest the foregoing arguments and retain them in our minds.

Second. We have shown that there is a world to come; we come now in the second place to show that there is a future judgment.

The future state will not be just as it happens, as this state is; but there will be a judgment. In the first place, how it shall be.

1. Every particular man will be judged as soon as dead.

Although we are ignorant of the particular manner of that particular judgment which will be given upon every man at death, yet there certainly is a particular judgment. They shall either be condemned or acquitted as soon as dead, and there is no condemnation nor acquittal without previous judgment; to receive a sentence according to their actions is to be judged, but this every man shall at death [experience].

2. All men shall be judged publicly, at the end of the world, according to their works. In this world men are distinguished from one another according to their riches, worldly power, and high descent, but then all such distinctions shall cease forever, and men shall be higher and more honorable than others are as they are more religious and godly. That there shall be a public judgment of all men at the end of the world appears:

(1) Because the nature of things requires it. Men are wicked and base openly, and it is fit they should be judged and condemned openly also. They break God's laws before God, angels, and men and devils, and it is very fit that they should be condemned to everlasting punishment for it before God, angels, and men and devils. The righteous, many of them, suffer openly for righteousness' sake before the world, and it is fit that they should be rewarded for it, also openly and before the world. They are put to open shame and disgrace upon the account of religion, and what can be more fit than that they should openly be honored upon the same account?

(2) The Scriptures abundantly declare it. Everybody that has read the Bible knows this, because the New Testament is full of it, from one end to the other. Jesus Christ very often declared it with his own

mouth; the angels from heaven declared it, and the holy, by the Holy Spirit, gave abundant testimony to it. Wherefore, I shall not mention the particular places.[5]

Third. We are come in the third place to show [that] the judgment will determine the state forever.

It will not only determine the state for some millions of millions of years, but an infinite, endless number of millions of years. When once the last awful words have proceeded out of the mouth of the Judge, the eternal condition is at once determined forevermore, according to these last words: "So it must be. So it must most certainly and unavoidably be."

It will not be as it is in human judgments. Human judges, do what they will, can't determine the estate of men but a few moments. All that they can do is to condemn them to die, and after they are dead they can have nothing at all to do with 'em. If they would never so feign, they can't make his sentence reach beyond death. When once a man is dead, he is out of his reach.

5. Here ends the first preaching unit. At the head of the second unit is the following outline, noticeably more schematic than that employed in Matt. 16:24, in which JE reminds the congregation of what they had heard in the morning:

Heb. 9:27. Doc. All men must certainly die, and after that their everlasting state will be determined.
1. All must die.
2. After death their everlasting state, etc.
1. There is a future state.
1. The light of natural reason.
1. Because the natural conscience.
2. Rewards and punishments not in this life.
3. Because that can answer the end of creation.
4. Because of the natural strong desire.
5. Soul distinct from body.
6. Consent of all nations.
2. Revelation.
1. God expressly declared it.
2. Sent his son.
3. Christ died.
4. Rose again and ascended.
5. Confirmed by the wonderful powers of the Holy Ghost.
2. A future judgment.
1. Particulars.
2. General.
1. Because the nature of things requires it.
2. The Scriptures reveal it.
We are come in the 3rd place to show the judgment will determine the state forever . . .

But when the great Judge in the other world condemns a man, the condemnation reaches to the end of eternity, which hath no end; they shall more than die every minute, but yet they will be in the Judge's hands. They must undergo such deaths forever without ceasing.

When an earthly judge rewards a man for any action, he can't make his reward remain after the man is once dead. But the heavenly Judge, when he rewards in the other world, his reward will never be at an end.

Men often may appeal from an earthly judgment to another, or perhaps may have their case reviewed, but there is no such thing in the other world. When once the judgment is past, it's past forever: there is no reversing of it. There will be no persuading the Judge to alter his judgment. There [will] be no such thing as a reviewing of the case. The Judge is omniscient and it is impossible that he should make a wrong judgment; therefore, there can be no occasion for a second judgment.

Neither is there any appeal from his judgment to the judgment of some [other]. He is the highest judge in the world: all other judgments must be tried at his judgment, but his judgment will never be tried by any other.

How solemn and awful a thing is it to receive an eternal doom and sentence. It is accounted an awful thing to receive sentence of an earthly judge; it is what has made the stoutest hearts to tremble. What, then, must it needs be to receive an everlasting sentence from the great God which will determine our condition without end?

1. The sentence of the Judge in the other world will determine to the everlasting happiness of the godly.

The godly in this world are oftentimes judged by temporal judges to pain and torment. Millions of godly men have been adjudged to tormenting deaths. But after the Judge of heaven and earth has past that blessed sentence upon them, Matt. 25:34, "Come, ye blessed of my Father, inherit the kingdom prepared for you from the foundation of the world," they will be happy and inherit that kingdom, that glorious kingdom, in spite of all the regions of darkness, which will then be put everlastingly out of a capacity of molesting of them, and the godly will be exalted clear out of the reach of their molestations.

2. The sentence of the great Judge will determine the misery of the wicked to eternity.

O how dreadful and amazing will every word and syllable of that sentence be: Matt. 25:41, "Depart, ye cursed, into everlasting fire, prepared for the devil and his angels." And for that reason, because it carries eternity along with [it], although now, perhaps, as it stands before their eyes in the Book of God, it don't fright them at all. They can read it without being moved at it or terrified in the leastwise; but however they slight it now, every syllable of it then will be a clap of thunder that strikes to their very souls, for that reason: because they are big with eternity, and [the sentence] determines and dooms them to misery without any end, or hopes of an end. This judgment will determine them to everlasting misery because:

(1) They will never have a pardon. Pardon was offered to 'em here over and over again; God would feign have pardoned them in this life, but they would not accept of it. He waited upon 'em with abundance of patience and long-suffering; he used [to] invite them, woo them, and even entreat them to accept of pardon. God used then to speak to them in this style: "How shall I give thee up, Ephraim; how shall I deliver thee, Israel? How shall I make thee as Admah; how shall I set thee as Zeboim? Mine heart is turned within me; my repentings are kindled together" (Hos. 11:8). And, "O that they were wise, that they would consider their latter end!" [Deut. 32:29]. Thus God used to entreat them in this life, but then they did not like the way wherein God offered pardon to them. They found fault with the way, and would not accept of pardon because God did not offer them pardon in their way. Although the way was [given] freely, without money and without price; although it was by the death of God himself, in the human nature of the Second Person in the Trinity, yet they did not like the way.

Although they were miserable and wretched condemned criminals, yet they must have the choosing of the way wherein they will be pardoned and saved, or else they would not be saved nor pardoned at all.

But when they come to be judged in the other world, they shall have no more pardons offered to them. They shall not be pardoned then if they would. If they would not be pardoned when God would, they shall not be pardoned when they would; if they would not answer when God called, God will not answer when they call, but will laugh at their calamity and mock when their fear cometh.

After the sentence is once passed, they may beg and plead forever for pardon, but they will never have it granted them: their Judge will be inexorable to all their cries and prayers. They were like the deaf adder in this world that would not hear the voice of [the] charmer, charming never so wisely. In the other world, God will be as deaf as they were; he'll not hear their cries and prayers, though they pray never so earnestly.

(2) They will never have another trial or probation. God will never try them again; he has tried them once, and he'll not try them a second time.

They shall never have Christ offered to them more. They will see then what fools they were that they did not accept of him when he was offered; but however they repent, they shall never have the offer again. God will never offer to clothe them with the glorious robes of Christ's righteousness. God will offer them no more the merits of the sufferings of Christ and his blood, to purge and wash them from their sin.

They shall never more have the Bible in their hands: that precious book which they so abused and despised upon earth. They shall never more hear the joyful sound of the gospel, the precious calls of the gospel which sounded so thick in their ears upon earth. They shall never more enjoy ordinances and those precious vessels in which God is wont to convey grace to the soul.

They will have no more invitations by ministers. They will no more enjoy sabbaths which they so neglected, although they would give ten thousand worlds for one sabbath more. Thus they will be deprived, forever, of all means of grace and salvation. And so we have finished the explicatory handling of the Doctrine.

USE.

Inq. What can be the thoughts of wicked men, when they happen to think of death and [the] world to come?[6]

6. This inquiry, and some expressions relating to the awareness of a future life in subhead (3) under the exhortation to the first answer, below, are paralleled and probably anticipated by manuscript notes on a sheet of paper from which JE made a cover for his manuscript diary. The notes, numbered 1 through 6 and ranging from a single sentence to over two hundred words per entry, apparently constitute sermon notes or a magazine of sermon ideas of some sort, though the correlation with this sermon is so limited as hardly to justify the term "draft." This passage correlates with note 2, while the passage below correlates with note 1. Most of the notes, all but two of which have been crossed out as if used, correlate generally with the Use of this sermon. The "Diary" cover reminds us that most of the sermons composed in the early years were probably developed from notes or earlier drafts.

They know that they must die. Wicked men can't but know that they must die, as well as other men. They see that everybody dies after a little while; they must needs expect to die sometime or other. Though most of 'em are so foolish as to think they shall live a long time first, yet they know they must certainly die at last. And furthermore, they know that they can't carry their sensual pleasures into the other world with 'em; they know, as well as the godly, that [they] can't carry away any of their money, or any of their wicked companions with them.

They hear also, over and over again, that if they go on in their wickedness, they must certainly be damned forever. They hear it from the mouth of God himself; they hear it often declared by the ministers of Christ; they hear it irrefragably proved, and yet they go on in their wickedness. One would think that the thoughts of it should so affright them that they should not dare to stir an inch further in their cursed ways, but yet they go on as if they had never heard anything at all about it. Now what can be the thoughts of such men?

I answer:

First. Some that live under the gospel don't really believe [in] a world to come.

There are a great many that live under the gospel and say nothing about these matters. They appear outwardly as if they did really believe 'em: if anyone says it is so, they will give their assent to it as true; but all the while, if one could look into the closet of their hearts, he[7] would there plainly discern that they questioned the truth of these great truths of Christianity; that they neither believed the Scriptures to be the Word of God, nor Christ to be the Son, nor the truths of a future state and eternal judgment.

There are a great many in Christian countries who go along all their lifetime toward an eternity, and never believe that they are going to eternity before they come to die and see hell-flames before their eyes, and actually begin to feel them.

And that is the reason that a great many are so debauched. That is the reason that many will swear profanely almost as often as they open their mouths. That is the reason that many men make no more of cheating and defrauding, of drunkenness and other scandalous crimes: they do not really believe [in] any heaven or hell, or any such thing. The reason why they dare to play and be so bold upon the

7. MS: "they."

very brink and edge of the bottomless pit, is because they are blind and don't see it.

Exh. Let this sort of persons be exhorted [as] an help against their unbelief:

(1) To ask themselves the question, whether or no they ever seriously considered to see whether these things were so or no.

If they never considered of it, never examined the arguments that were brought to prove it nor compared them with the objections that arise in their own hearts against it: what folly to take it upon trust that it is not so, without ever examining the case. When all nations believe it, when all the wise men upon earth have believed it, what folly is it for a man to say it is not so without ever trying the matter, and so to venture his everlasting happiness or misery upon a mere peradventure and nothing else. What folly is it for a blind man to run into a pit of fire and brimstone, and say it may be there is none there.

Let them not depend upon that before they have thoroughly pondered and impartially weighed the matter. Don't let them excuse themselves by their unbelief if they have never canvassed the reasons that are brought to prove it; and therefore,

(2) Let them well consider the reasons that were brought to prove a world to come.

If they can believe that God has made every man's natural conscience (which tells him that rewards and punishments must be dispensed) to lie to us; if they can believe that God will never deal with men according to their deserts, that he will always suffer virtue and holiness of life to be undermost, and wickedness and vice to be uppermost; if they can believe that God will suffer such cruel and barbarous men as Nero, and the pirates who make [it] their business to kill and rob men, to go unpunished, and holy men who are put to tormenting deaths for righteousness' sake to go unrewarded; if they can believe that the end of man's creation in glorifying God can be obtained in seventy years, and sometimes in two or three minutes' time; if they can think that God made man with a strong desire of enduring forever on purpose to be frustrated, and that the sense and natural reason of all nations upon earth is wrong; if they can think that Jehovah lies, and that he sent his only Son into the world to die, rise again and ascend into heaven, for nothing; if they can think that all the wondrous miracles that ever were wrought prove nothing: I say, if they can think all this, then they can think that there is no world to come, and not else; and if they can think so, there is no more to be said to 'em, and [they] are out of hopes of being made to believe the plainest thing in the world in these matters.

Wherefore, if any don't fully believe [in] a future state, let him thoroughly weigh these arguments.

(3) Let such persons consider, what would be their thoughts of another world if they were upon their deathbeds and just ready to fetch their last breath.

Men generally han't the same thoughts of things when they come to die as when they were in health; especially wicked men's opinions of the things of another world differ, as far as the East is from the West.

Therefore, consider what will be your dying thoughts of these things. You now perhaps look upon death as at a great distance, and that you shall live a long time in the world, and that blinds your eyes; therefore, think with yourself: what if you were now dying? Do you think that it would seem so to you then, as it doth now?

The most atheistical men in the world, some of them, when they have come to lie on a deathbed, have been quite of another mind from what they were in their health. In their health they have thought that there was no world to come, no such thing as hell, have thought that it was nothing but a mere fiction invented to fright folks; but when they lay a-dying, they have been as fully convinced of a hell as if they were actually in it, and some of them have actually felt it before they have been dead. Therefore, represent to yourselves, as if you were leaving the world, how would it seem to you should you have [had] no suspicion at all that you was going into another world? And if so, believe it now and live accordingly.

Second. Some scarcely ever think anything about it, Ps. 10:4, "God is not in all his thoughts": though they live under the gospel—under the glorious gospel—where the Sun of Righteousness shines right in his eyes, yet they shut their eyes against the light. Though God should be more in their thoughts than anything else whatsoever; though religion should be the great business of their lives; though they were made for that very end, to think and meditate upon God; though all their thoughts, words and actions should be directed to God through Jesus Christ, and Christianity should be the great spring of everything they do: yet instead of that, they care nothing at all about [God]. They'll allow God no share in their thoughts, words, nor actions, and though one would wonder how they do to avoid it, yet they hardly ever think anything about religion.

Though nothing in the world is of so great importance, though their eternal condition depends upon it, though they must burn in hell forever if they don't take utmost care to keep themselves out of it, yet they think little more of God, heaven, or hell than the heathen. They will speak of God in a profane way; they'll take his name in vain, though they never think of him. They will damn persons to hell, though they never think of their own danger of being damned. Thus surprisingly thoughtless are some persons.

In opposition to these, I would give this exhortation, viz.,

Exh. Let all persons be frequently thinking and considering of things of the other world.

Let not any of us go to hell thoughtless, not considering where we are going. What folly is it not to be wary and careful to avoid so great danger! We are, in this world, in a very dangerous place; we know not whereabouts we are; we know not how near we may be to the end of our lives, and to the brink of an endless eternity, and if we han't our eyes about us, we are in danger of dropping into the bottomless pit every moment.

Men generally, when they walk in a dangerous place where there are pits and gins and traps, have[8] to have their eyes open and not to go blindfold. Let it be considered that this world is such a dangerous place, and as full of such dreadful pits and snares as it can hold; and more by half are caught in them than escape them, and everyone that don't take special care is taken in them.

Let us therefore at least look about us and consider which way we are travailing:[9] there surely can be no harm in taking care of ourselves. If any man is travailing in the road that leads to destruction, let him at least think which way he is going, that he may not have hell-flames about him before he thinks of it.

8. MS: "Love." Although "L" and "h" can closely resemble one another in JE's hand, "Love" seems clearly written and apparently represents a slip of the mind rather than of the hand, if it is a slip at all.

9. JE is apparently employing this spelling in conscious word-play, since he ordinarily spelled "travel" in the modern way. By returning to archaic spelling (or simply punning), he combines the notions of laboriousness and suffering (as in childbirth) with the metaphor of the journey of life. Such devices are rare in the sermons and become rarer as he grows older.

Third. Some men are so stupid that the thoughts of another world make no impression upon them.

The hardness of the hearts of some of the children of men is truly very astonishing: they seem to be harder than a rock, a flint, or an adamant. The powerful words of the Most High make no impression upon them; the fire and hammer of God's Word will not break their rocky hearts; the swift thunder-bolts of God's threatenings won't split them. All the powerful strokes that are made upon them rebound as a ball from a marble wall.

They can bear to hear about hell-flames and eternal torments without being at all frightened or moved by it, although they at the same time know that they are going to this same place of torment.

They can hear of Christ's dying love all the days of their life and not mind that. They can hear about heaven and everlasting happiness, and that it [is] offered and may be obtained, and not be half so much moved as if they heard that there was an opportunity to get sixpence. And in truth, all the great things of eternity make no more impression upon their minds than upon the stones of the street.

[*Exh.*] Now it will be proper for all such persons, for their awakening, to ask themselves what they intend to do in this case: whether they intend to do something, or whether they intend to do nothing and let it be as it will. If they do nothing, they certainly and most unavoidably will be destroyed and undone forever.

Death hastens on towards us and we hasten towards that, and it cannot be long before we shall meet: every breath we draw and every step we take, brings us nearer to eternity; we are carried towards eternity irresistably, and cannot stop one moment if [we] never so much desire it. We cannot cause the glass of time to stop, do whatever we can, but it will continue to run.

And when we die, there is but two places to go to: heaven or hell, and to one or the other of them we must all go. We cannot, when we die, slide away privately to some by-place and not be taken notice of, but we must come before our Judge and be judged to either happiness or misery. We cannot annihilate or turn ourselves to nothing. Now let all stupid and senseless persons, who take no care for another world, think within themselves what they intend to do. Consider that text, Is. 10:3, "What will ye do in the day of visitation, and in the desolation which shall come from far? To whom will ye flee for help, and where will ye leave your glory?"

Fourth. Some think to put it off till they come to die, and so depend upon their last prayers.

They think that God is a very merciful God, and won't refuse to hear a poor creature upon his deathbed that must be damned if God don't hear them. They think that they will pray very earnestly then, will pray with all their might, and intend to tell God that they trust in his mercy and goodness in Christ, and if they perish, they perish trusting upon God and his mercy.

They think, when they come to die, to repent and be sorry that they did not seek God before. They think that they will tell God so, that they are heartily sorry that they did not seek his face before, and to beg pardon for it, and they think that God won't refuse, being a very merciful God. Let such sort of persons consider:

1. That God is jealous of his honor, as well as gracious and merciful. You know the second commandment, where it is said, "I the Lord your God am a jealous God." God never did, nor ever will, do anything that tends to his own dishonor, and therefore those who live all their lives' time in breaking God's commands before his face, may justly fear and expect that God will magnify his justice in turning a deaf ear to all their most earnest and piteous cries upon their deathbeds. Doth not God expressly say, Prov. 1:24–31,

> Because I have called, and ye refused; I have stretched out my hand, and no man regarded; but ye have set at nought all my counsel, and would none of my reproof: I also will laugh at your calamity; I will mock when your fear cometh; when your fear cometh as desolation, and your destruction cometh as a whirlwind; when distress and anguish cometh upon you. Then shall they call upon me, but I will not answer; they shall seek me early, but they shall not find me: for that they hated knowledge, and did not choose the fear of the Lord. They would none of my counsel: they despised all my reproof. Therefore, shall they eat of the fruit of their own way, and be filled with their own devices.

2. Let it be considered that God knows that they disobey him with that expectation of depending on his pity when they die, and therefore may justly expect that he will frustrate them.

God sees that you intend to disobey him as long as you live, with hopes that you shall obtain pardon when they die by their earnest cries to him, and therefore they may justly expect that God will frustrate that which they make use of to encourage them in sin.[1]

---

1. The wrenching shifts from third to second person and back within this head con-

3. Let it be considered by them that there is very few in a thousand that put off this soul work till a deathbed, that pray as earnestly as they think they will, that find mercy.

There are very few that think just as you do: that have depended upon their last prayers and thought they would pray earnestly then, and thought they would repent as you think you will, and thought that God would certainly pity them and pardon 'em, that have found mercy at last.

4. Let it be considered that an ordinary deathbed faith and repentance will signify nothing, barely a sorrow for sin because it has brought them to the very mouth of hell, because they are afraid they shall [be] damned for it, [and] will be nothing to the purpose at a dying hour.

A mere forced trust in the mercy of God in Christ, because he sees that he shall be damned in two or three hours else: such a sort of dependence will not serve him then, nor keep him out of hell.

5. Let it be considered that a true faith and repentance will not be in your power when you come to die. You think you will trust in God's mercy and repent of your sins when you come to die, and so you hope you shall be saved. Alas, truly so to do will be out of your power—clear out of your power.

6. Consider that the circumstances of your death may put you past a capacity of praying to God and seeking his mercy.

You may die suddenly, in a moment by some accident, and not have the least time for it. How many thousands have died so, and perhaps those that trusted to their last prayers as you do? Or if you die in sickbed, perhaps you may be deprived of your reason—such things doubtless often happen as a judgment [upon] such sort of presumption as yours—or you may lie all the time in tormenting pain, so as to be uncapable of settling your thoughts upon anything. Such instances have very frequently happened.

Fifth. Some intend to take care of their souls before they come to die, but put it off to a more convenient opportunity. Some that are young put it off till they are old: they think it will be a better time then; they have a mind to have the pleasure of youth out first. Others put it off till they are settled in the world; others till such a particular

---

stitute an unusually blatant form of JE's tendency to shift to direct address as the hortatory intensity increases. Although he would have regularized the usage in preparing the sermon for the press, I have let his idiom stand here and elsewhere where the reader is not likely to be confused as to the referent of the pronoun.

occasion or business is over; others intend to do it sometime or other, but fix upon no time.

[1.] Let it be considered that those who put it off are like never to do it [at] all, and it most commonly happens so. They, it may be, take up a resolution that they will begin at such a time; when that time comes, they break their resolution and put it off till another time, and so they commonly do till they are out of the world and enveloped in hell-flames.

2. The longer it is omitted, the harder it is; like a stone that rolls down an hill, the farther it rolls the harder stopped.

3. Consider that you may die before that time comes; it very commonly happens so. It is not only possible that it may be so, but probable that it will be so.

Wherefore, let nobody put off their great work to a further opportunity, but set about it this minute, and go on in it with all our might and vigor till we perpetrate the same. Let us look continually unto God for his help and assistance: pray earnestly in all prayers and supplications, without ceasing. Let us not only seek, but strive in the great work, knowing that there are many that seek that shall not be able.

Sixth. Some think there is no need of such strictness in order to get to heaven.

They think if they are but baptized and go to church, and attend the public worship and ordinances of God, and do but keep to the outward forms, they shall undoubtedly go to heaven, without any scruple. They love to have an easy, smooth way to heaven. They hate this strictness; they say there is no need to be so strict: they make the way [to] heaven so broad that there is no need of crowding at all, but instead of that, one may rove about on one side and t'other as much as they please.

They think that one may go to heaven swearing and breaking the sabbath all the way.

But to these I make answer: doth not the Scripture frequently say directly the contrary? If they will look into the Bible, they will find quite contrary to this.[2] Doth not Christ expressly say that strait is the

2. Following at this point are ten lines JE deleted at the time of composition:
How often doth the Scripture represent the Christian course to a warfare! Surely, when men are actually engaged in a battle with the enemy men must be very careful, watchful, [and] earnest in the work they are about, especially when we

gate, and narrow is the way that leads to life, and few there be that find it? Don't Christ expressly say that those that intend to go to heaven must strive, because many seek and are not able? Don't Christ expressly say that those that would be his disciples must take up their cross and follow him, and that we must even cut off our right hands and pluck out our right eyes that offend? Doth not the Scripture compare the Christian course to a race wherein those that run, run all, but one alone receiveth the prize; don't the Scripture expressly say that without holiness, no man can see God? Surely these expressions hold forth a considerable degree of strictness.[3]

How often doth the Scripture represent the Christian course to a warfare or fight! Surely, fighting is not such easy, smooth work as they make the work of a Christian. It cannot be: either the Scripture is false, or else the way to heaven is not so wide as they would make it; either God speaks false, or else the obtaining [of] salvation and [the] escaping of hell requires strict holiness of heart and life.

---

have such potent adversaries to fight with as devils, the wicked, and our own lusts.

If we ever intend to get to heaven in spite of so many and so strong adversaries,

we had need to stand having our loins girt and our lamps burning.

JE apparently felt this amplification too much diverged from the rhetorical tone of Christ's injunctions which provide the final "proofs" in the sermon, though he briefly returns to the similitude of warfare in the final paragraph of the sermon.

3. The biblical passages referred to are, in order of reference: Matt. 7:14; Luke 13:24; Matt. 16:24, 5:29–30; I Cor. 9:24, and Matt. 5:8 or John 3:3.

FRAGMENT: FROM AN APPLICATION ON SEEKING GOD

AMONG Edwards' manuscripts are a number of fragments of sermons, sometimes incorporated in later manuscripts and sometimes, as in this case, standing alone. They result primarily from Edwards' habit of occasionally plundering his store of manuscripts in order to facilitate the production of new sermons. Generally, when a sermon was so exploited the most useful portions were used and the less valuable discarded. In a few cases, however, Edwards seems to have found the unused portions too good to discard and so saved them, sometimes preaching them in conjunction with parts of other sermons, sometimes writing new material to complete them, or some combination of both. In this case, the fragment appears to be most of an Application, and when Edwards arrived in Northampton he composed an additional head to shape it to the occasion at hand, presumably preaching it with the Text and Doctrine from another sermon. The resulting sermon was an oratorical event for which there is no correlative literary text.

The existing text, though only about half of a sermon and devoid of the initial biblical text and statement of doctrine which give complete sermons their primary identity, is a focused and reasonably coherent statement concerning those practical strategies which inevitably come under consideration when the process of seeking salvation is discussed. Of the original Application, only two of at least five uses remain and they are addressed to the general congregation and to a sub-group of the unawakened, respectively. Thus there is some discontinuity between the major heads as the fragment stands, and we may presume the likelihood of an original first exhortation to the previously awakened members of the congregation which would have preceded the extant exhortation. On the whole, the Application is conservative intellectually and emotionally, stressing a more sincere employment of conventional exercises rather than a new spiritual regimen.

In the Appendix to this fragment is a first exhortation which was prepared for the repreaching of the Application in Northampton. It probably occupied the place of the original exhortation to the awakened and was apparently directed to a specific ceremonial event having to do with the Northampton ministry or meetinghouse. The occasion is obscure, but the most probable historical context is that of Edwards' ordination and installation in the Northampton congregation as assistant to Solomon Stoddard.

*   *   *

As the above comments imply, the manuscript of this sermon is fragmentary. It is a stitched bundle of seven octavo leaves, neatly written but containing significant lacunae where leaves have been cut from the original manuscript. As now folded, the booklet consists of a two-leaf unit followed by two single leaves (with stubs of cut-off pages protruding), another double leaf, and the single leaf of the Northampton addition. Read in this order, the text appears to begin with the Use of Exhortation, II., continue through the Use of Instruction, III., and conclude with the Use of Exhortation, I. This makes little sense in several respects, and the peculiar stitching of the booklet—it has two centerfold stitchings rather than the usual one of the octavo quire—suggests physical irregularities in the manuscript. If one folds the manuscript inside out at the beginning of the Use of Instruction, however, the text falls into the logical sequence of its presentation below: Use of Instruction, III., Use of Exhortation, I., and Use of Exhortation, II. The booklet folds rather easily in this manner, as if it had been done before, though the stubs of the cut-off pages protrude into the center of the booklet causing it to unfold.

Even when the booklet is put in what appears to be the original order, there are lacunae both immediately before the beginning and at the end of the Use of Instruction, and the one at the end suggests that the original Use of Instruction continued on further than it now does. However, a crossout at the end of the use in Northampton ink indicates that Edwards was aware of these "loose ends" and simply avoided them at the Northampton preaching. Thus, though it is not crossed out in the manuscript, the fragmentary statement opening the Application as it is printed here was certainly not preached in Northampton. Finally, it might be noted that the second Use of Exhortation was abbreviated through several separate deletions when repreached in Northampton, though such late deletions are not noted in this original version of the text.

FRAGMENT: FROM AN APPLICATION ON SEEKING GOD

[. . .] too bright and precious to lie in this filthy and muddy world, into the empyrean heavens, those regions of pure light, to the enjoyment of Jehovah.[1]

III. [*Use of Instr.*] By what means is God to be sought? Perhaps there may be some that, having heard that in seeking God we seek his reconciliation, love, communion, and eternal enjoyment, may be ready to hear with a listening ear how God is to be sought. I answer,

First. The first thing to be done, is the clearing ourselves of all hindrances and impediments in all works to be performed. The first thing is to remove impediments.

Now we have many things which, if they are not removed, will forever effectually hinder our finding of God. We are tied down; we are fast bound; we cannot go out upon the search after God till we are loosened. Now, what are these hindrances, what are these bonds and chains, but our sins? Therefore, he that would seek God must resolve to forsake all his sins, and resolve to forsake 'em forever, and must forsake 'em, or else it is to no purpose to pretend to seek God. God will never be reconciled to love, commune with, and be enjoyed by, one that keeps his dear sins to enjoy at the same time.

God and sin are the most irreconcilable things in the world; God will not be entreated to dwell with sin; 'tis in vain to seek for it: if God enters, sin must be turned out of doors. The praying, the seeking, the solemn meeting, and everything of that nature which he doth that don't forsake his sin and lusts, is no better accounted of by God than mockery, and an abomination:

> The sacrifice of the wicked is an abomination [to] the Lord (Prov. 15:8). Bring no more vain oblations; incense is an abomination unto me; the new moons and sabbaths, the calling of assemblies,

1. These lines represent the conclusion of the second use of the original Application. Apparently this use was one of information, and possibly the first was of self-examination; in any case, the argument seems to be moving from an assertion of the value of the human soul to consideration of means for its salvation and the inevitable call for practical efforts to that end.

I cannot away with; it is iniquity, even the solemn meeting. Your
new moons and your appointed feasts my soul hateth: they are a
trouble unto me; I am weary to bear them. And when ye spread
forth your hands, I will hide mine eyes from you: yea, when ye
make many prayers, I will not hear: your hands are full of blood.
Wash you, make you clean; put away the evil of your doings from
before mine eyes; cease to do evil; learn to do well; seek judgment,
relieve the oppressed, judge the fatherless, plead for the widow.
Come now, and let us reason together, saith the Lord: though
your sins be as scarlet, they shall be as white as snow; though they
be red like crimson, they shall be as wool. If ye be willing and
obedient, ye shall eat the good of the land: but if ye refuse and
rebel, ye shall be devoured with the sword: for the mouth of the
Lord hath spoken it (Is. 1:13–20).

Wherefore, he that would seek and find God must, as the first thing
in order to it, forsake every known sin, and spit this sweet morsel out
of his mouth, and not retain one least, but take his leave of that which
he wickedly made his darling. Not only commission, but also omission. Do our duty in all things to our utmost.

Second. The second step is to [make] inquiry after God. When we
have taken our leave of our sinful courses, and parted with all our
lusts, then we are to set out on our search after God by inquiring
after him; and say, "What shall I do to be saved? How, where, and
by what means may God be found?" That is, we ought to get well
instructed in the revealed will of God, to know what are his commands that we may obey them: what are those things he requires of
us, that we may obtain his love and favor, that we may perform them;
what is the most likely ways to go, that we may find God, that we may
walk and run in them. We are naturally full of darkness, and there
is a mist or cloud which overshadows us, and except it be removed,
we shall stumble and fall, shall wander and be lost.

If men did but make due inquiry, they would not be at a loss to
know which way they should get to work in seeking of God. We must
apply ourselves for this end to the Scriptures, and must get acquainted with the Word of God, and must meditate therein. If a man
were condemned to death, and it was told him he might obtain a
pardon, if he would; would he be slack, do you think, in inquiring
which way, and what he must do that this pardon may be obtained?
Neither should we be slack—if we did but know, and were sensible

[of] what a miserable, dreadful state of condemnation we are in by nature—in inquiring after reconciliation.

Third. By calling after him in prayer: "Ask and receive, knock and it shall be opened unto you, for he that asketh receiveth." Having parted with our sins according to the first particular, and informed ourselves of the will of God according to the second, we must pray without ceasing, with all prayer and supplication, that God would manifest himself to us, and be found of us.

There must not only be public and family prayer, but secret prayer; this is what is particularly commanded and urged in the gospel. He that would find God must frequently retire from all the world, and secretly make his application to Him who seeth and heareth in secret, and earnestly cry after that God whom we have lost, and wait for an answer from him, that we may find him and enjoy him.

Fourth. God is to be sought in those ways where he used to be found, and where he often discovers himself. And what are those ways wherein God used to be found? They are his ordinances: the very end for which God has instituted ordinances, is that in them the children of men may meet with him and find him.

God is wont to be found in these ways; God is wont to command life forevermore upon the mountains of Zion; Christ walks in the midst of his golden candlesticks, and there you may find him. These are the golden pipes by which grace, as precious oil, is conveyed into the soul; these are the breasts of holy and heavenly consolation. See Cant. 1:7–8, "Tell me, O thou whom my soul loveth, where thou feedest, where thou makest thy flock to rest at noon; for why should I be as one that turneth aside by the flocks of thy companions? If thou know not, O thou fairest among women, go thy way forth by the footsteps of the flock, and feed thy kids beside the shepherds' tents."

You see that Christ commands us to go by the footsteps of the flock, in the common path, wherein believers have gone before us and found him, in the way where Christ used to be found. And where is that? Beside the shepherds' tents; that is, in the way of God's ordinances. This is a way which God himself has marked out, and which has been found successful by thousands. We need not wander in the wilderness, where there is no way, but we have a track; yea, a plain path to be a direction to us, and what we have to do is to run on with all our might in this path.[2]

2. At this point the new first Use of Exhortation was inserted for the Northampton

* * *

II. *Use of Exh.* In the second place, is to those who have never yet found God: to those destitute, desolate creatures, who are lost, have no God they can claim any interest in, who are without God in the world, who are poor, who are blind, who are naked, who are undone, yea, who are dead (may the voice of God in his Word raise them). To those who have nothing to depend upon, have nothing to live upon, or that they pretend to live upon, above seventy years; who have no defense they can betake themselves to in time of danger and distress, who have no stable happiness they can fly to in time of trouble and affliction: let them set their very hearts and souls to seek the Lord; they have need enough of it.

You have already heard how God is to be sought, and therefore there is no need of your being at a loss; wherefore, now hearken, to some motives to persuade you to act according to those directions. The motives are of three kinds, drawn first, from the consideration of what you will find, if you find God; second, from the consideration of what you will lose, if you never find him; and third, from the consideration of what you will get, by seeking of other things and neglecting him.

First. Consider what you will find, if you find God.

1. You will find a Savior, and an everlasting sure defense from all evil; certainly that is worthy the most diligent seeking, which when obtained, will effectually deliver one, and when delivered will eternally preserve and defend one, from all manner of evil.

He that finds God finds an eternal deliverance from all manner of affliction, and even all fear of affliction, in a little while; and they shall never more feel the least pain, the least disappointment, the least fear or trouble, but shall be forever freer from it than the unborn child. There is nobody that loves to feel pain and affliction, but would gladly be delivered from it. Why, then, should they need any arguments to persuade them, to seek an universal and sovereign remedy that may be found? What would not one give for a medicine, that would certainly forever preserve the body from all diseases? What

---

repreaching. It is to be found in the Appendix to the sermon. When he inserted the new material, JE apparently cut out some of the concluding portion of the original Use of Instruction since the page includes part of a sentence following this one, deleted at the time of the Northampton revision. The Northampton Use of Exhortation also replaces an original first Use of Exhortation.

would not a warrior give for something that would effectually preserve from the force of martial weapons? What would not the mariner give for something effectually to preserve him from shipwreck and all dangers of the sea? What would not many give [for something] that would certainly always preserve from death, and prolong the life forever?

But who would not be willing to be at a great deal of pains to find that, that will, surely in a very short time, not only deliver one from all those evils, but eternally free [him] from all manner of evil, great and small? Is not this enough to persuade you to seek after God? Won't telling of you that it is your duty, and showing the mighty obligations by which you are bound in reason, justice, and gratitude? Yet one won't think [but] that, that which has so much at interest in it, should surely have its effect.

2. But second, if you find God, beside that you will find all good; you will not only be freed from all evil, but be brought to the possession of all good.

You are saying, among the rest, "Who will show me any good?" You mean worldly, sublunary good, which is not worthy the name; but then and then only, do you inquire after real, solid good, when you say, "Lord, lift thou up the light of thy countenance upon me."

God is an infinite, self-sufficient, all-sufficient, essential, overflowing good: he is the source of all good. There is no truly and properly good thing but what is a communication from this original good; he that finds God shall eternally possess all the good he will, or can, desire.

3. If you find God, you will find complete and everlasting happiness, resulting from this deliverance from all evil, and the perfect enjoyment of this good. You are certainly seeking after happiness; everything you do, it is that you may be happy. What do you follow business of your particular calling for, but that you may be a happy man? Or if you spend your life in idleness, it is for happiness. If you spend your life in sin, it is because you foolishly think to be happy therein. Wherefore, seeing you are, as you must confess, in search of happiness, why do you need so many arguments to persuade you to receive [it] when you are told where, and where alone, it may be found; when you are told where the highest, most perfect, everlasting, as well as only, happiness is to be found? If you search all the world over; if you could wander from the earth and go into all the various parts of this vast universe, and could spend a thousand ages in trying

every created thing, you would never find any happiness, any satisfaction, any satisfactory pleasure, till you come to the first and best
of beings.

Everything here upon earth has been tried already. Solomon tells
us that he set himself on purpose to try them, but he found nothing
but vexation of spirit. All these enjoyments have been tried already,
many millions of times, and have always proved ineffectual; there
never was a man yet seen, heard, or read of since the foundation of
the world, that was made a happy man by an affluence of these things.

Wherefore, seeing so many men in all past generations have tried
and found the world good for nothing for happiness, and you yourself, also, have been so foolish as to try the same, and have not yet
found satisfaction, why will you try any further? Why will you not be
persuaded to try this, also, and see if you can't find happiness in
religion, seeing that there was never one yet that have tried, that have
declared themselves not satisfied? If you make a trial, you will find
more and better satisfaction, a truer pleasure and delight, even in
this world, than ever you or any ever experienced in anything else:
a truly godly life is the most pleasant, joyful, and delightful life. The
wicked make the greatest laughter and noise outwardly, but laughter
and great noise is not always a sign of joy: but there are many that
hoot and shout as loud as anybody, that have hell begun within them
for all that; and if we examine, we shall find that the godly man lives
truly, internally, the merriest and most cheerful life. But this is nothing to what comes after. 'Tis true, 'tis the same sort of happiness that
is enjoyed in heaven, but it is but a drop of that ocean, but only some
few drops of those whole rivers of pleasure, that falls from heaven
upon the sanctified soul.

Thus for the first sort of motives.

Second. Consider what you will lose if you don't find God.

1. You will lose all your privileges and talents. You are privileged
by God above almost all the world: you live under the gospel, you
know the way to heaven, and may walk therein if you please. Now,
most of the world know nothing about heaven, and about Christ, as
you do, and so they perish for lack of vision.

What a thousand pities is it, now, that you should clear lose all this
advantage which you have above them, and for all the Bible, for all
the sabbath, for all the ordinances, which you have and they have
not, should at last be damned, with a worse damnation than they:
what a thousand pities is it to throw away all these so precious privileges, and make no use of them!

2. You will lose heaven. All losses are proportionably great and deplorable to the worth of the thing lost; now the happiness of heaven, because it is so great, and because it is eternal, is infinitely precious.

How do the children of men afflict themselves for infinitely smaller losses! They will say, "I might have had such an estate as easy as not, but I was a fool and have lost it. If I had but have taken care of myself, I might have been as rich, and lived as high, as any man in a thousand, but I was a fool and now the opportunity is gone and over." But how will sinners be afflicted in the other world when they see Abraham, afar off, and those holy men they have known, in his bosom; how will they roar out at their folly when they think, "All this same happiness was offered to me, many and many a time, but I was such a fool as to take no care about it, and now I am eternally deprived of all opportunities of obtaining it!"

3. You will lose all your worldly good things. You have no great sense of the happiness of heaven, and therefore to tell you that you will lose that don't much move you, perhaps; but it seems you make much of worldly good things by your so violently pursuing after them, and neglecting heaven for the sake of them; wherefore, 'tis to be hoped that you may be a little stirred up when you hear that you are like to lose them, too. If you continue sinfully, when you die you will clear lose them all, and the thoughts of them will torment you forever.

Now the godly man don't lose even his worldly good things, when he dies, but so improves them that he gets that good of them, that will stand by him forever: will go into the other world with him, and will afford immensely more comfort and pleasure there than here. And besides, when he leaves them, he is so far from losing them that he only exchanges for those, enjoyments that are infinitely better; yea, he exchanges the very affliction and troubles that attends, for a far more exceeding and eternal weight of glory.

But if you die a sinner, you clear lose all these, your dear enjoyments, and exchange them for torment and eternal misery.

4. If you don't find God, you will lose yourself. You will not only lose all that you enjoy, and all that you may enjoy, but you will lose yourself into the bargain; your being will entirely be lost to you, and you will wish that you had never been born, or that you might but be turned to nothing.

Thus for the two sorts of motives.

Third. Consider what you will get by seeking of other things and neglecting God. We have heard what you will lose; let us now see what you are like to get, and see whether it will balance. Certainly, if you be not persuaded, you expect to get something extraordinary by seeking something else. Wherefore, let us see what it is that you will really get by it.

1. You will get eternal shame and disgrace. If shame and disgrace is a desirable thing, 'tis true you will get that: you will [be] despised by God; you will be despised by angels; you will be despised by the saints; you will be forever despised and derided by devils; you will be mortally hated and despised by your fellow damned sinners. You will have none to go to; no, not those wretches that will be tormented with you: as in heaven there is nothing but pure love, one to another, so it will be directly contrary in hell; there will be nothing but perpetual, inveterate hatred.

2. You will get eternal pain and torment by it. Misery without mercy, pain without ease, fire without a drop of water, despair without hope; everything that is dreadful, dark, and horrible, without one beam of light, will be your reward, if you go on to neglect to seek God and seek other things.

Thus I have done with the three sorts of motive, to persuade you to set your heart and soul to seek the Lord, drawn from the consideration of what you will find if you find God, what you will lose if [you] don't find him, and what you will get if you pursue after other things and neglect to seek him.

Appendix to Fragment

I. *Use of Exh.* Here, let us of this congregation be, at this time, especially exhorted to set our hearts and souls to seek God. When we are more especially concerning ourselves with the affairs of God's temple, such things should be set about with a most solemn, devout spirit, with serious consideration, much prayer and meditation.[1]

How many offerings and sacrifices were made unto God by the children of Israel when the tabernacle was reared up amongst them, as you may see in the seventh chapter of Numbers; and so when the temple was dedicated, I Kgs. 8:63, "And Solomon offered a sacrifice of peace-offerings, which he offered unto the Lord, two and twenty thousand oxen, an hundred and twenty thousand sheep. So the king

---

1. Originally, JE began the next paragraph thus: "What a solemn charge does David give to the people to prepare their hearts to seek God, when the temple was about to be built amongst them." However, he deleted this opening in favor of the material involving Solomon.

and all the children of Israel dedicated the house of the Lord." We are not required to offer sacrifices of beasts, but we are to offer sacrifices of our hearts and the sacrifices of prayer, and the sacrifices of love, thankfulness, and obedience. Is. 1:11, 16–17, "I delight not in the blood of bullocks, or of lambs, or of he goats. . . . Wash ye, make you clean. Put away the evil of your doings from before mine eyes. Cease to do evil. Learn to do well."

It's a thing that incensed the anger of God, to behave lightly, inconsiderately, and without solemnity, when we concern ourselves in sacred matters and the affairs of God's house. God will not hold such guiltless: for this cause, God slew fifty thousand men of Bethshemesh (I Sam. 6:19).

Let us now, therefore, earnestly set ourselves to seek the favor, presence, and blessing [of God] in that affair which is before us. The success of his means and ordinances, and the ministry of the Word, depends on his blessing. If we don't now set ourselves to seek God, how can we expect any other, than that however God may bless the dispensation of his Word to others, yet not unto us, but make it a means of our hardening?

Let us all therefore earnestly seek to God, that he would now lift up the light of his countenance and shine forth, that he would appear and manifest his approbation and favor, that he would come down and dwell in the midst of us: dwell here in his house, as he hath done in times past, and give us to see his goings in his sanctuary; and would hereafter, from time to time, make the ministration of the gospel successful for the converting of many souls, and the edifying of saints. And let us not keep away, or drive away, God's Spirit by our carelessness and negligence, or by our sins, but seek him till he come and command his blessing upon us, even life forever more.

O NE of the most powerful of the early sermons, "Glorious Grace" is dominated by the spirit of celebration, even in its exhortations, and seems to belong to some celebratory occasion. So subtle are Edwards' occasional references that one is tempted to link the sermon with the Christmas season merely on the basis of two references to the angels' singing at the birth of Christ, not to mention the overall emphasis upon praising God for the gift of salvation through Christ. This supposition stretches the probable date of the sermon's composition, however, unless it was composed well in advance of its delivery. Furthermore, Edwards does not acknowledge Christmas in later sermons and these hints simply may have been part of the overall spirit of celebration.

Second only to this invocation of celebration is the sustained emphasis upon the essential dependence of the redeemed upon mere mercy in the context of the overall "work of redemption" through the gospel dispensation. Indeed, the Application of this sermon provides one of the first significant expositions of the anti-Arminian argument which was to receive a more systematic articulation in *God Glorified in Man's Dependence* (Boston, 1731) some nine years later. A defensive theological position carefully stated before an audience of professional peers, *God Glorified* would develop more theological subtleties, but the essential doctrine was well put in New York in the fall of 1722.

Rhetorically, this sermon is one of Edwards' most exuberant. Not only is the theme presented with elaborate repetition in the statement of the doctrine, but many passages, both of affirmation and denunciation, are developed through insistent *a fortiori* patterns of incremental repetition. The intensity of rhetoric is confirmed by an argumentative strategy which mediates a succession of surprises and paradoxes in the process of revealing the method of God in the work of redemption. This celebration of the workings of grace is thus reminiscent of the English Metaphysicals in its essential rhetorical and theological mentality; however, Edwards largely eschews their quaintness, or their attempts to realize the experience of surprise in verbal figures. He rather directs the reader to a referent beyond his text, an objective reality which embodies and manifests the strange grace of God's gospel dispensation.

* * *

The manuscript of Zech. 4:7 is relatively clean and free of major revisions. Those that are present, such as Edwards' shifting two paragraphs from the Doctrine to the Application, were made at the time of composition. Indeed, there is only one ink in the sermon, though a sign on the first page in a different ink indicates that it was repreached at Bolton, Connecticut. The octavo quire consists of the standard eight leaves with one additional leaf stitched into the center fold, again at the time of composition. All in all, then, the booklet provides evidence of a sermon that was left in its original state even when repreached a year or more later, apparently because it was unusually pleasing to Edwards. On the other hand, the sermon was apparently not preached in Northampton as were so many of these New York sermons.

GLORIOUS GRACE

ZECHARIAH 4:7.

*And he shall bring forth the headstone thereof with shouting, crying,
Grace, grace!*

THE mercy of God is that attribute which we, the fallen, sinful race
of Adam, stand in greatest need of, and God has been pleased, according to our needs, more gloriously to manifest this attribute than
any other. The wonders of divine grace are the greatest of all wonders. The wonders of divine power and wisdom in the making [of]
this great world are marvelous; other wonders of his justice in punishing sin are wonderful; many wonderful things have happened
since the creation of the world, but none like the wonders of grace.
"Grace, grace!" is the sound that the gospel rings with, "Grace,
grace!" will be that shout which will ring in heaven forever; and
perhaps what the angels sung at the birth of Christ, of God's good
will towards men, is the highest theme that ever they entered upon.

In order to understand the words of our text, we are to take notice
that the scope and design of the chapter is to comfort and encourage
the children of Israel, returned out of their Babylonish captivity, in
the building of Jerusalem and the temple: who it seems were very
much disheartened by reason of the opposition they met with in the
work, and the want of [the] external glory of the former temple before
the captivity, so that the priests and the Levites, and the chief of the
fathers, wept aloud as the rest shouted at the sight, as you may see
in Ezra 3:12, "But many of the priests and Levites, and chief of the
fathers, who were ancient men, that had seen the first house, when
the foundation of this house was laid before their eyes, wept with a
loud voice, and many shouted aloud for joy." You may see a full
account of their great oppositions and discouragements in the fourth
and fifth chapters.

The prophets, Haggai and Zechariah, were sent on this occasion
to comfort them under those discouragements, by foretelling the glo-

ries of the gospel should be displayed in this latter house, which should render the glories of it far beyond the glories of the former, notwithstanding it was so far exceeded in what is external. In Hag. 2:3–9,

> Who is left among you that saw this house in her first glory? and how do ye see it now? is it not in your eyes in comparison of it as nothing? Yet now be strong, O Zerubbabel, saith the Lord; and be strong, O Joshua, son of Josedech, the high priest; and be strong, all ye people of the land, saith the Lord, and work: for I am with you, saith the Lord of hosts: according to the word that I covenanted with you when ye came out of Egypt, so my spirit remaineth among you: fear ye not. For thus saith the Lord of hosts; Yet once, it is a little while, and I will shake the heavens, and the earth, and the sea, and the dry land; And I will shake all nations, and the desire of all nations shall come: and I will fill this house with glory, saith the Lord of hosts. The silver is mine, and the gold is mine, saith the Lord of hosts. The glory of this latter house shall be greater than of the former, saith the Lord of hosts: and in this place will I give peace, saith the Lord of hosts.

See also, in the third chapter of this book, at the eighth verse, "Hear now, O Joshua the high priest, thou and thy fellows that sit before thee: for they are men wondered at; for behold, I will bring forth my servant, the Branch." And the same subject is continued in this chapter, even the glorious grace of the gospel, which was to be manifested by Christ in this temple, particularly in our text, "and they shall bring forth the headstone with shouting, crying, Grace, grace unto it." The headstone is that which entirely crowns and finishes the whole work, signifying that the entire gospel dispensation was to be finished in mere grace.

This stone was to [be] brought with repeated shouting or rejoicings at the grace of God, signifying the admirableness and gloriousness of this grace.

DOCTRINE.

The gospel dispensation is finished wholly and entirely in free and glorious grace: there is glorious grace, shines in every part of the great work of redemption; the foundation is laid in grace, the superstructure is reared in grace, and the whole is finished in glorious grace.

If Adam had stood and persevered in obedience, he would have been made happy by mere bounty [and] goodness; for God was not obliged to reward Adam for his perfect obedience any otherwise than by covenant, for Adam by standing would not have merited happiness. But yet this grace would not have been such as the grace of the gospel, for he would have been saved upon the account of what he himself did, but the salvation of the gospel is given altogether freely. Rom. 11:6, "And if by grace, then it is no more works: otherwise grace is no more grace. But if it be of works, then it is no more grace; otherwise work is no more work."

That we may give you as full explication of this doctrine as we can in a little space, we shall first, show free grace shines forth in the distinct parts of this wondrous work of redemption; second, speak a little of the gloriousness of this grace.

[I.] But as to the first, every part of this work was performed of mere grace.

First. It was of free grace that God had any thoughts or designs of rescuing mankind after the fall. If there had not been an immense fountain of goodness in God, he would never have entertained any thoughts at all of ever redeeming us after our defection. Man was happy enough at first, and might have continued so to all eternity, if he would; he was not compelled to fall. If he had not willfully and sinfully rebelled against God, he would never have been driven forth, like an unworthy wretch, as he was. But although God had been so overflowing in his bounty to him as to make him head over the lower creation and ruler of all other creatures, and had planted a garden on purpose for his delight, and would have fixed him in an eternal happiness only on the reasonable condition of his obeying the easy commands of his maker; but yet notwithstanding all, he rebelled and turned over, from God to the devil, out of a wicked ambition of being a god himself—not content in that happy state that he was in as man—and so rebelled against God's authority.

Now who but God of boundless grace, would not have been provoked, after this, to leave him as he was, in the miserable state into which he had brought himself by his disobedience; resolving to help him no more, leaving him to himself and to the punishment he had deserved, leaving him in the devil's hands where he had thrown himself, not being contented in the arms of his Creator; who, but one of boundless grace, would ever have entertained any thoughts of finding out a way for his recovery?

God had no manner of need of us, or of our praises. He has enough in himself for himself, and neither needs nor desires any additions of happiness, and if he did need the worship of his creatures, he had thousands and ten-thousands of angels, and if he had not enough, he could create more; or, he could have glorified his justice in man's eternal destruction and ruin, and have with infinite ease created other beings, more perfect and glorious than man, eternally to sing his praises.

Second. But especially was it of rich and boundless grace that he gave his only Son for our restoration. By our fall, we are cast down so low into sin and misery, so deeply plunged into a most miserable and sinful condition, that it may truly be said, although all things are infinitely easy to God with respect to his omnipotency, yet with respect to God's holiness and justice, God himself could not redeem us without a great deal of cost, no, not without infinite costs; that is, not without the presence of that, that is of infinite worth and value, even the blood of his Son, and in proper speaking, the blood of God, of a divine person.

This was absolutely necessary in order to our redemption, because there was no other way of satisfying God's justice. When we were fallen, it was come to this: either we must die eternally, or the Son of God must spill his blood; either we, or God's own Son must suffer God's wrath, one of the two; either miserable worms of the dust that had deserved it, or the glorious, amiable, beautiful, and innocent Son of God. The fall of man brought it to this; it must be determined one way or t'other, and it was determined, by the strangely free and boundless grace of God, that this his own Son, should die that the offending worms might be freed, and set at liberty from their punishment, and that justice might make them happy. Here is grace indeed; well may we shout, "Grace, grace!" at this.

The heathens used to reckon that an only son slain in sacrifice was the greatest gift that could be offered to the gods. It was that, that they used sometimes to offer in times of great distress, and in some parts of the world it is constantly at this day performed. But we have a stranger thing than that declared to us in the gospel; not that men sacrificed their only sons to God, but that God gave his only Son to be slain, a sacrifice for man. God once commanded Abraham to offer up his only son to him, and perhaps the faith and love of Abraham may be looked upon as wonderful, that he was willing to perform it— there are few that would do it in these days—but if you wonder at that, how wonderful is it that, instead of Abraham's offering his only son to God, God should give his only Son to be offered for Abraham, and for every child of Abraham. Certainly, you will acknowledge this to be a wonder not to be paralleled.

And beside, God did not do this for friends, but for enemies and haters of him. He did not do it for loyal subjects, but for rebels; he did not do it for those that were his children, but for the children of the devil; he did not do it for those that were excellent, but for those that were more hateful than toads or vipers; he did not do it for those that could be any way profitable or advantageous to him, but for those that were so weak, that instead of profiting God, they were not able in the least to help themselves.

God has given even fallen man such a gift, that He has left nothing for man to do that he may be happy, but only to receive what is given him. Though he has sinned, yet God requires no amends to be made by him; He requires of him no restoration; if they will receive His Son of Him, He requires neither money nor price; he is to do no penance in order to be forgiven. What God offers, He offers freely. God offers man eternal happiness upon far more gracious terms since he is fallen than before; before, he was to do something himself for his happiness; he was to obey the law: but since he is fallen, God offers to save him for nothing, only if he will receive salvation as it is offered; that is, freely through Christ, by faith in Him.

Third. It was of mere grace that the Son was so freely willing to undertake our salvation. How cheerfully, yea how joyfully, did he undertake it, although he himself was the very person that was to suffer for man. Though He himself was to bear his sin and be made sin for him, yet how cheerfully doth He speak: Ps. 40:7–8, "Lo, I come: in the volume of the book it is written of me, I delight to do thy will, O God." He says, in Prov. 8:31, that his "delights were with the sons of men," for so did he love them that it seems he himself was willing to die in their room, rather than that they should be miserable. He freely undertook this out of mere love and pity, for he never was and never will be, repaid by them for his blood. 'Twas only that we might be happy.[1]

Fourth. The application of the redemption of the gospel, by the Holy Spirit, is of mere grace. Although God the Father has provided a savior for us, and Christ has come and died, and there is nothing wanting but our willing and hearty reception of Christ; yet we shall

---

1. Two paragraphs originally followed here, but JE moved them through key signs to a position at the end of the second use of the Application, p. 398.

eternally perish yet, if God is not gracious to us, and don't make application of Christ's benefits to our souls. We are dependent on free grace, even for ability to lay hold in Christ already offered, so entirely is the gospel dispensation of mere grace. Eph. 2:8–10, "For by grace are you saved through faith, and that not of yourselves: it is the gift of God." That is, we shall [be saved] freely and for nothing if we will but accept of Christ, but we are not able to do that of ourselves, but it is the free gift of God: "not of works, lest any man should boast, for we are his workmanship, created in Christ Jesus unto good works, which God hath before ordained that we should walk in them."[2]

II. We shall briefly speak to the gloriousness of this grace. As the grace of the gospel is altogether free, so it is glorious; the angels stoop down, with eyes full of wonder and joy, to look into, and shout for gladness and admiration, at the sight of it. How did the multitudes of heavenly hosts shout at the birth of Christ, crying, "Glory to God in the highest; on earth peace and good will towards men!" Well may the topstone of this house be brought forth with shouting, crying, "Grace, grace!" to it.

All the attributes of God, do illustriously shine forth in the face of Jesus Christ: his wisdom in so contriving his power in conquering death and the devil, and the hard and rocky hearts of depraved men; his justice in punishing sins of men rather upon his own dear Son, than let it go unpunished; but more especially, [in] his grace, that sweet attribute, he has magnified his mercy above all his names.

The grace of God, exhibited in the gospel, is glorious,

First. Because of the greatness of it. Every circumstance of the gospel, grace surprisingly heightens it; let us look on what part we will, we shall see enough to fill us and all the angels in heaven with admiration forever. If we consider it as the grace of God the Father, and consider his greatness, his holiness, his power and justice, immensity and eternity; if we diligently consider how great a being he is, who took such pity and compassion on mankind, it is enough to astonish us. Or, if we consider ourselves, on whom this great God has bestowed this grace, we are nothing but worms, yea less than worms, before God; and not only so, but sinful worms, worms swollen with enmity against God. If we consider him by whom we receive [grace], the Son of God who made heaven and, by his almighty power, [is]

2. This fourth subhead was inserted after the completion of the sermon, probably in conjunction with the transfer of the two paragraphs from the end of the third head.

equal with the Father; if we consider the greatness of what he did—
he died most ignominiously and painfully in our nature—it all infinitely heightens the grace of the gospel.

Second. Because of the glorious fruit of this. No less than salvation
and eternal glory are the fruits of this grace of the gospel; adoption,
union with Christ, communion with God, the indwelling of the Holy
Ghost, the heavenly happiness, the pleasure of the eternal paradise,
the new Jerusalem, the glorious and triumphant resurrection of the
body, and an everlasting reign with Christ in the height of glory, and
pleasure and happiness: no less than these things are the effects of
this marvelous grace.

What a vast difference is there between a poor, miserable sinner,
full of sin, condemned to hellfire, and, a saint shining forth in robes
of glory, and crowned with a crown of victory and triumph; but 'tis
no less difference than this, is made in the same man by the grace of
God in Christ.

APPLICATION.

I. Hence we learn, how they dishonor God and the gospel, who
depend on anything else but mere grace. The gospel is far the most
glorious manifestation of God's glory that ever was made to man, and
the glory of the gospel is free grace and mere mercy. Now those that
will not depend on this free grace, they do what they can to deprive
the gospel of this glory, and sully the glory of God therein shining
forth; they take away the praise, glory, and honor, that is due to God
by his free grace and mercy to men, and set up themselves as the
objects of it, as if their salvation at least partly, was owing to what
they have done.

This must needs be very provoking and highly affronting to God.
For miserable sinners, after they are fallen into such a miserable
estate that it is impossible they should be saved by any other means
than pure grace, and God is so gloriously rich in his goodness, as to
offer this free grace unto them out of pity to them: how provoking
must it be to God for these miserable, helpless wretches to attribute
any of their salvation to themselves!

It is not an opportunity to buy and procure our own salvation that
God offers, but an opportunity to lay hold on that salvation which is
already bought and procured for us; neither are we able to [do] this
of ourselves, it is the gift of God.

There are some, that hope to be saved quite in another way than ever the gospel proposed; that is, by their own righteousness, by being so good and doing so well, as that God shall take their goodness as sufficient to counterbalance their sin, that they have committed, and thereby they make their own goodness to equal value with Christ's blood. This conceit is very apt to creep into the proud heart of man.

Some openly profess to be able to merit salvation, as papists. Others hold that they are able to prepare and fit themselves for salvation already merited, or at least are able to do something towards it of themselves, and it is to be feared that many that don't openly profess either their own righteousness or their own strength, do very much depend upon both. By this doctrine, how much they dishonor the free grace of the gospel!

II. Let all be exhorted to accept the grace of the gospel. One would think, that there should be no need of such exhortations as this, but alas, such is the dreadful wickedness and the horrible ingratitude of man's heart, that he needs abundance of persuading and entreating to accept of God's kindness, when offered them. We should count it horrible ingratitude in a poor, necessitous creature, to refuse our help and kindness when we, out of mere pity to him, offer to relieve and help him. If you should see a man in extremity of distress, and in a perishing necessity of help and relief, and you should lay out yourself, with much labor and cost, out of compassion to him, that he might be relieved, how would you take it of him, if he should proudly and spitefully refuse it and snuff at it, instead of thanking you for it? Would you not look upon it as a very ungrateful, unreasonable, base thing? And why has not God a thousand times the cause, to look upon you as base and ungrateful, if you refuse his glorious grace in the gospel, that he offers you? When God saw mankind in a most necessitous condition, in the greatest and extremest distress, being exposed to hellfire and eternal death, from which it was impossible he should ever deliver himself, or that ever he should be delivered by any other means, He took pity on them, and brought them from the jaws of destruction by His own blood. Now what great ingratitude is it for them to refuse such grace as this?

But so it is: multitudes will not accept a free gift at the hands of the King of the World. They have the daring, horrible presumption as [to] refuse a kindness offered by God himself, and not to accept a gift at the hands of Jehovah, nor not his own Son, his own Son equal with himself. Yea, they'll not accept of him, though he dies for them; yea, though he dies a most tormenting death, though he dies that they may be delivered from hell, and that they may have heaven, they'll not accept of this gift, though they are in such necessity of it, that they must be miserable forever without it. Yea, although God the Father invites and importunes them, they'll not accept of it, though the Son of God himself knocks and calls at their door till his head is wet with the dew, and his locks with the drops of the night, arguing and pleading with them to accept of him for their own sakes, though he makes so many glorious promises, though he holds forth so many precious benefits to tempt them to happiness, perhaps for many years together, yet they obstinately refuse all. Was ever such ingratitude heard of, or can greater be conceived of?

What would you have God do for you, that you may accept of it? Is the gift that he offers too small, that you think it too little, for you to accept of? Don't God offer you his Son, and what could God offer more? Yea, we may say God himself has not a greater gift to offer. Did not the Son of God do enough for you, that you won't accept of him; did he [not] die, and what could he do more? Yea, we may say that the Son of God could not do a greater thing for man. Do you refuse because you want to be invited and wooed? You may hear him, from day to day, inviting of you, if you will but hearken. Or is it because you don't stand in need of God's grace? Don't you need it so much as that you must either receive it or be damned to all eternity, and what greater need can there possibly be?

Alas, miserable creatures that we are, instead of the gift of God offered in the gospel's not being great enough for us, we are not worthy of anything at all: we are less than the least of all God's mercies. Instead of deserving the dying Son of God, we are not worthy of the least crumb of bread, the least drop of water, or the least ray of light; instead of Christ's not having done enough for us by dying, in such pain and ignominy, we are not worthy that he should so much as look on us, instead of shedding his blood. We are not worthy that Christ should once make an offer of the least benefit, instead of his so long urging of us to be eternally happy.

Whoever continues to refuse Christ, will find hereafter, that instead of his having no need of him, that the least drop of his blood would have been more worth to them, than all the world; wherefore, let none be so ungrateful to God and so unwise for themselves, as to refuse the glorious grace of the gospel.[3]

3. This and the preceding paragraph were transferred to this place through key signs from the third subhead under the Doctrine, p. 394.

III. Let those who have been made partakers of this free and glorious grace of God, spend their lives much in praises and hallelujahs to God, for the wonders of his mercy in their redemption. To you, O redeemed of the Lord, doth this doctrine most directly apply itself; you are those who have been made partakers of all this glorious grace of which you have now heard. 'Tis you that God entertained thoughts of restoring after your miserable fall into dreadful depravity and corruption, and into danger of the dreadful misery that unavoidably follows upon it; 'tis for you in particular that God gave his Son, yea, his only Son, and sent him into the world; 'tis for you that the Son of God so freely gave himself; 'tis for you that he was born, died, rose again and ascended, and intercedes; 'tis to you that there the free application of the fruit of these things is made: all this is done perfectly and altogether freely, without any of your desert, without any of your righteousness or strength; wherefore, let your life be spent in praises to God. When you praise him in prayer, let it not be with coldness and indifferency; when you praise him in your closet, let your whole soul be active therein; when you praise him in singing, don't barely make a noise, without any stirring of affection in the heart, without any internal melody. Surely, you have reason to shout, cry, "Grace, grace, be the topstone of the temple!" Certainly, you don't want mercy and bounty to praise God; you only want a heart and lively affections to praise him with.

Surely, if the angels are so astonished at God's mercy to you, and do even shout with joy and admiration at the sight of God's grace to you, you yourself, on whom this grace is bestowed, have much more reason to shout.

Consider that great part of your happiness in heaven, to all eternity, will consist in this: in praising of God, for his free and glorious grace in redeeming you; and if you would spend more time about it on earth, you would find this world would be much more of a heaven to you than it is. Wherefore, do nothing while you are alive, but speak and think and live God's praises.

THE NAKEDNESS OF JOB

In "The Nakedness of Job" the nineteen-year-old preacher calls for a meditation upon death as the proper preparation for life. From the beginning, clearly, Edwards followed the traditional Christian method for putting human values in perspective, but an even more urgent matter for him here and in his later sermons is the subtler issue of human reality. For as he clearly states shortly after the statement of doctrine, the problem for men is not one of coming to terms with truth, but rather with reality: "All the world knows the truth of this doctrine perfectly well, but though they know, yet it don't seem at all real to them . . ." (p. 406). Calling attention to the reality within accepted truths, or discovering a rhetoric that would make truth real to his audience, was to become the central mission for Edwards as a preacher, and in this sermon that mission is fairly launched.

Although the image of the slipping foot occurs in the sermon, along with other materials that would one day be put to brilliant use in shaping the powerful *Sinners in the Hands of an Angry God,* the strategy of persuasion in the early sermon is markedly different from that employed in 1741. It is not that there is any euphemism in the New York sermon respecting death, but there is an assumption that merely *reminding* men of reality—when the truth of it is so obvious—should be sufficient mental preparation. And indeed, the sermon as a whole has a coolly rational decorum despite the force of the subject matter and Edwards' fine evocations of it.

Given the literary power of the book of Job, perhaps Edwards' most effective device in this sermon was the selection of his text, complemented by the specific preparation given it in the exegetical passages which introduce the statement of doctrine. Here, the interpretation of the ancient story as a "shadow of death" is a fine stroke for the preacher who would bring the full weight of the narrative to bear upon his doctrine. Moreover, through the vivid evocation of bodily dissolution in the Application, Edwards complements and fulfills the parable with concrete physicality, completing the exegetical cycle. The preacher's touch seems light, but his material becomes indelibly weighty;

indeed, the sermon is characterized by memorably fine passages, as if Edwards responded to the artistic power of the book of Job.

Formally striking, although not in a wholly agreeable sense, is the use of three statements of doctrine, only one of which actually functions as the doctrine for this sermon. That more than one doctrine might be deduced from the words was not unthinkable to Edwards, but his personal style tended away from the seventeenth-century practice of multiple doctrines; moreover, even in the seventeenth century doctrines were not normally introduced unless they were to be developed. Here, however, Edwards simply states that the doctrines are "useful" and that the one to be developed is his arbitrary choice of the moment ("upon which we shall at this time insist"). Since the first two doctrines are at least commented upon sufficiently to indicate their thematic import, it is not impossible that at the time of composing the sermon Edwards considered writing a sermon series upon this text, or at least a long and complex sermon of the old type. In any event, he developed only the last doctrine and there is no evidence that the other two doctrines were ever utilized for related sermons.

* * *

The octavo quire booklet of Job 1:21 is relatively neat and uncluttered: nearly a typical booklet for the single preaching unit sermon. The eight leaves reveal only light revision and, excepting the presence of the three doctrines and the absence of a large-letter "DOC" identifying the doctrine to be developed, the most striking feature of the booklet is the indication of at least five subheads under the doctrine, only two of which were developed. In the case of subheads *Three* and *Four* (as they would be designated in our scheme), large blank spaces were left in the booklet. These spaces confirm that at this time Edwards was in the habit of making a numbered outline in the booklet for much of the sermon and filling in the development in an order not necessarily corresponding to the numbered sequence. When he finally decided to distribute his thought in just two numbered subheads, he simply elided the first two, crossed out the third and fourth subhead headings, and gave the fifth the number 2. The resulting blank spaces under two of the undeveloped subheads illustrate the difficulties of the infolded quire when Edwards actually composed in the booklet: he had to estimate the space allotted to each point as well as the number of points or face being cramped in one place while wasting space in another. The combination of the two un-developed doctrines and the compressed development under the doctrine actually developed certainly suggests that this sermon is an instance of a large conception that was finally reduced in scope and complexity for reasons that are now obscure.

THE NAKEDNESS OF JOB

JOB 1:21.

*Naked came I out of my mother's womb, and naked shall I return
thither.*

W E have an instance in this chapter of one of the greatest men
in the world, in the most prosperous worldly estate and condition,
brought to be externally one of the meanest of men; brought from
seven thousand sheep, and three thousand camels, and five hundred
yoke of oxen, and five hundred she-asses, and a very great household,
all at once to nothing at all, as poor as the meanest beggar: a most
remarkable instance of the vanity of worldly honor, riches, and prosperity. How soon is it gone and lost; how many hundred, yea thousands of accidents, may deprive the most prosperous of all in a little
time, and make him most miserable and forlorn!

Here is a man that sat like a king and dwelt as a prince, but, as
yesterday and today, is become a miserable and forlorn beggar. Before
the messenger had finished his bad news, another came with more
of the like upon the back of it. First, he has the news of his servants'
being killed and his oxen and asses being taken, as you may see in
the fourteenth and fifteenth verses; but before he had done telling
this sad news to Job, there comes in another and brings him tidings
that fire from heaven had burnt up all his sheep, and servants that
kept them; and before he had done speaking there comes in another,
and tells him that the Chaldeans had carried away all his camels and
killed his servants; and before he had done, there came another with
the yet more dreadful news that his children were all suddenly killed,
as they were feasting together in their eldest brother's house.

And to what circumstances is this man, that just now was one of
the richest men in the world, brought to? Now most that read or hear
this remarkable history will doubtless acknowledge that, if such a
catastrophe was to happen to every man's estate, it would be enough
quite to wean him from the world. Almost every man will doubtless

say that, if they knew they should lose all their great estate and be deprived entirely of all their outward prosperity, as Job was, they would entertain no thought of striving and laying themselves out for a great estate in the world, seeing they must certainly in this manner be deprived of it, and they know not how soon. If it were so, men would not be so eager and earnest after riches, but would strive only for that that they could not be deprived of; all will grant [that] it would not be worth the while to do more.

But we may speak of it not only as a thing supposed, but as a thing that shall certainly be, for thus every man, however rich, shall certainly be deprived of all his goods, whether sheep, or oxen, or camels, or asses, or servants, or children; they shall be deprived of them as much as Job was, and he knows not how soon. Perhaps, when you read the history of Job, you read it as a strange thing that happened but once in the world; but, for the time to come, read it as a thing that happens daily, and frequently, for every man at death is as much deprived of all his worldly goods as Job was. The great men in the world, as kings, princes, and lords, when they die are as much deprived of all their outward prosperity as Job was: 'tis lost at once, and gone forever, never to be possessed more. Job's losses came indeed sudden, and in a little time one messenger came after another in a very strange manner, but the dying man is deprived of all his external prosperity and worldly good at once, at one breath, even his last breath. This history of Job is only a shadow of death; it is no more than happens to every man in the world.

This poverty that Job was reduced to puts him in mind of death, of which this was a shadow, whereby he and all men must be stripped of all these things and return, possessing nothing, into the earth from whence they come. It also remembrances him of the state he was born in: how he was born, naked and helpless, having nothing and depending entirely on others.

Job, at the news of his losses, shaved his head and rent his mantle, as is said in the verse before the text, so that now he was become literally and properly naked, as this also helped to put him in mind of the estate he was born in, and of the estate he must die in.

These three useful doctrines may be deduced from the words:

[DOCTRINE.]

I. That we bring nothing of our own into the world with us. By "coming naked from our mother's womb," can't be meant only that we come unclothed, but we come poor, miserable, helpless creatures, without either power or possession, spiritual or temporal; so that hereby we are taught[1] that all we receive, we receive from God, because we bring nothing with us. This appears to be Job's meaning, by this improvement Job makes of [it] in the ensuing part of the verse: "The Lord gave, and the Lord hath taken away; blessed be the name of the Lord."

II. [The second] doctrine is that the earth is the common mother of mankind. Job says, he came naked out of his mother's womb, and he shall return naked into his mother's womb again. What mother's womb shall Job return into again, but the bowels of his mother earth, out of which every man is made? Our bodies are made of the substance of the earth, as appears, because, when the body is rotten, it returns into the substance of the earth. God says to Adam, "Dust thou art, and unto dust thou shalt return." God was Adam's father and the earth was his mother; and by this same mother, out of whose bowels we come, are we nourished at her breast, for man lives by what he digs out of the earth by tillage. Now this doctrine, and the consideration of our mean original out of the earth, ought to teach us humility and so submission to God's will in all dispensations. The wise man would have us see that we are but beasts: what, shall man, whose body is made out of the ground, be proud of that body, whether of its beauty or its riches or honor, or shall man, that is made out of earth, proudly insult one another, for who makes us to differ from others? We are all born of the same mother earth, and thither we shall all return [Eccles. 3:18–20].

To this use it is that Job improves it; to teach him submission under God's hand, that he who was made out of earth as well as the meanest beggar, ought not to murmur when his estate is made as mean and low as theirs.

[III]. The last doctrine, upon which we shall at this time insist, is this:

> *When man dies, he is forever stripped*
> *of all earthly enjoyments.*

This must be what Job means when he says, "and naked shall I return thither again"; that he should return to the earth, stripped clean of all manner of worldly goods and possessions.

This doctrine is full of useful improvements, and is plain and cer-

---

1. Conjectural reading.

tain, and needs little proof or explication. All the world knows the truth of this doctrine perfectly well, but though they know, yet it don't seem at all real to them; for certainly, if it seemed a real thing to them that, in a little time, they must certainly have no more to do with the world, they would act wholly otherwise than they do. We very much need to be put in mind of these things; wherefore, my business [at] this time is only to jog our memories, for we cannot think too often of our latter end. There are these two things implied in the doctrine: First, that man, when he dies, can carry none of these earthly things out of the world with him; second, [that he] shall never enjoy any more of the like nature.

First. Man, when he dies, can carry none of these earthly things out of the world with him. If he possesses all the riches of the Indies, and governed the largest empire in the world, and the lives and fortune of all men upon earth in his hands, yet when death comes, he will strip him as naked as he was born, and will carry him out of the world with no more in his possession than the meanest beggar.

Death serves all alike; as he deals with the poor, so he deals with the rich: is not awed at the appearance of a proud palace, a numerous attendance, or a majestic countenance; pulls a king out of his throne, and summons him before the judgment seat of God, with as few compliments and as little ceremony as he takes the poor man out of his cottage. Death is as rude with emperors as with beggars, and handles one with as much gentleness as the other.

They are all alike in death's territories; one is no richer, no more honorable, than another in the grave, Job 3:14–19,

> With kings and counselors of the earth, which built desolate places for themselves; or with princes that had gold and silver, who filled their houses with silver; or as an hidden untimely birth, I had not been, as infants which never saw light. There the wicked cease from troubling, and there the weary be at rest; there the prisoners rest together; they hear not the voice of the oppressor. The small and the great are there, and the servant is free from his master.

Death, when he comes into kings' courts to perform his office, to fetch away kings and princes that used, as it were, to roll themselves in millions of money and drown themselves in pleasures: to carry them into the other world, he rends him away by force from all his money, and from all his pleasure. He will not allow him to carry away so much as one farthing out of all his shining treasures; forever shuts him out from any more earthly pleasures. His time for those things is ended. A poor creature; one drop of blood would be better than all; the least spark of true grace would be preferable to his kingdom.

Second. Man, after death, shall never more enjoy anything of the nature of these earthly things. He not only leaves all these goods and possessions in this world, but he shall never find any more such like possessions: never leaves house and land in one world, to inherit the like in another; never, when he leaves his bags of silver and gold here, to receive the like treasure elsewhere. No, but when once his soul is departed this life, he leaves all such like things to all eternity; he shall never fix his eyes on things anything like these any more at all. He is gone; he has taken a final farewell of all things of an earthly hue and appearance: he shall never any more be pleased with eating and drinking, never more have the pleasure of conversation of terrestrial friends. If ever they enjoy any pleasures after death, and be not fixed in eternal misery, they will be quite of another nature, exceeding different from them: the pleasures of another world are spiritual pleasures; the possessions are spiritual possessions, and the food is spiritual food, without any gross mixtures of flesh or earth.

As for the body, that will be in a condition uncapable of all enjoyment, as much as any common lump of clay; [it] shall be shut up in the silent grave and quickly moulder away to dust: and then of what advantage will pleasures, profits, and honors be to that? What is the dead body of a king the better for his having ruled a large and opulent kingdom, for his having been honored and respected in the world, for its once having been decked with jewels of gold and precious stones?

And as for the soul, the souls of the godly shall be brought to those enjoyments that are purely spiritual. Jesus Christ will be to them riches, honors, pleasures, and friends, and all things; and they shall forever feed on him, as the food of eternal life.

And as for the souls of the wicked, their dwelling place will be the lowest hell, where there is weeping and wailing and gnashing of teeth, and blackness of darkness forever. Instead of their former sensual pleasures, or anything like them, they shall feel incessant terrors: instead of their merry conversation, they shall have furies surrounding them, tearing and tormenting them; instead of eating and drinking, chambering and wantonness, rioting and drunkenness, they shall drink the dregs of the cup of God's fiery vengeance, and shall roar out forever, being enwrapped in eternal flames.

IMPROVEMENT.

I. *Use of Infor.*
[*First.*] From this doctrine, we may be instructed and informed that earthly riches and pleasure are not true riches and pleasure. Now all the worlds of good and bad are seeking after riches and pleasure; no man is to blame for seeking to be rich, or thirsting for pleasure, so that it be for true riches and true pleasure; but here is the case: some men are fools and pursue after shadows of riches, and shadows of pleasures, that the devil represents to them instead of the substance, and there are but a few that distinguish themselves from the common herd of human beasts, or rather beastly men, by seeking for true riches and true pleasures.

Now earthly riches and pleasures cannot be the true [riches and pleasures], because they presently leave us, disappointed and ashamed, and we can never obtain them more. These riches, which so suddenly leave us, cannot be called true riches any more than the shadow of a man that vanishes away as we attempt to lay hold of him, can be called a man; neither can those vanishing pleasures be called true pleasures, any more than the pleasure of a dream that leaves a man as sorrowful as ever when he awakens. The best locks and keys will not keep a man's silver and gold for him when he dies; he cannot hold it, it all slips between his fingers.

Now, that is the true riches that will stick by one, that there is no danger of losing, that one can hold by a sure tenor, in spite of death and all the world; and that is the true pleasure, whose delights never cease, and not that short, seventy-years' dream that returns no more, to all eternity.

Second. Hence we learn that we are not made for an earthly happiness. God certainly never made man for that sort of happiness which he cannot hold; he was never made for that happiness which, almost as soon as enjoyed, flies from us and leaves us disappointed. If this was the highest happiness we are made for—that happiness that would be unavoidably accompanied with those disappointments and frustrations that do more than counterbalance it—if we were made for this happiness, it would be our greatest wisdom to set our hearts upon it, for it is our wisdom to set our hearts upon that that we are made for; but as the case now stands, the more we set our hearts on those things, the more trouble and vexation, and the less satisfaction, do we find in them.

This, the wise heathen plainly saw, and for that reason taught[2] it as a great part of the wisdom of man, to abstract his thoughts and affections from all earthly things. Though they had no other knowledge of a future happiness than what naked reason taught them, even they discovered so much unsatisfactoriness and vexation of these enjoyments, that many of them, of their own choice, sequestered themselves from these things, and denied themselves even the common comforts of life.

[II. *Use of Exh.*] *First Exh.* Not to use these things as if we were to carry them out of the world with us. Worldly things are most commonly so used; the children of men are so full of madness and folly, as to love these things as much, and set as much by them, and rejoice at the attainment of them, and mourn for the loss of them, as much as if they were to endure here to all eternity, or as if the acquisition or loss of them affected their eternal state.

Now what madness and folly is it so to do! Such persons only make to themselves torment and vexation when there is no need of it; they fill themselves with the tormenting fears of death, whereby they must leave these things that they so dearly love, and when the time comes that they must be rent away from them, how doth it even tear their very heartstrings to be violently separated from that [to which] they cleaved, and even grew so fast to; whereas, those that don't set their affections upon them are easily separated from them.

What folly is it for a man, when he finds something that pleases him, that he can enjoy but a few minutes, to please himself with it as if he were to possess it always; and then, when it is taken from him, he is left disappointed and ashamed! They that would not be a torment to themselves here, and lay up torment for a deathbed, must follow the Apostle's direction, I Cor. 7:29–31,

> But this I say, brethren, the time is short. It remaineth that both they that have wives, be as though they had none; and they that weep, as though they wept not; and they that rejoice, [as though they rejoiced not;] and they that buy, as though they possessed

2. "Heathen" is JE's usual term for the classical authors of ancient Greece and Rome.

not; and they that use this world, as not abusing it: for the fashion of this world passeth away.

Such is the folly of the world. They pursue violently after the world, slave and tire themselves for a little of it, are exceeding anxious and careful about [it]. Their minds are gnawn with care and anxiety; they undergo abundance of difficulties for it, and will often violate their consciences, disobey their God, and go very near hellfire—so near as to scorch them—come so near to the pit that their feet are every moment ready to slip. Whey they lose the world, they mourn as if they had met with a loss that it is impossible should be repaired, either in this world or the next, and when they have got a little of the world, they please themselves with the thoughts of it as much as if they were sure they could never lose it, neither by death nor otherwise; and then, as soon as they have got a little of the world into their hands, death comes and lays hold of them, and hales them away from it all, naked and stripped of everything, into such a state as they seldom or never thought of. Before, they were careless and at ease, as if death were not wont to come into their parts of the world, but now they are in the greatest confusion imaginable; now they see, and tremble; now they are not a farthing the better for all their prosperity; now they mourn because they must leave their beloved estate, and must not carry any of it with them. How they wish they had not been so worldly, and had taken a little more pains for that which will stand by them! Thus the fools of this world act.

But as for the wise man, he will not be a self-tormentor. He neglects and despises the world; cares little for it, for he knows it can last him but a little while, and if he could keep it forever, 'twould do him little good. Wherefore, he seeks out for something better, that he don't fear losing, and then when death comes, he smiles in his face and says, "O death, where is thy sting? O grave, where is thy victory?"

Second Exh. Let all set themselves, with the greatest seriousness and diligence, to make sure of goods that death is not able to deprive them of. Every man knows he shall die; he cannot be ignorant of that. But yet they set themselves to the violent pursuit of earthly things as vigorously, and about heavenly things—if at all—as negligently and remissly, as if they were to remain here forevermore: just as if they had made a league with death and a covenant with the grave; just as if they secretly hoped that, although everybody else died, yet, they might be an exception from the general rule. Their strange folly is excellently represented in [Ps.] 49:11, "Their inward thought is, that their houses shall continue forever, and their dwelling places to all generations."

How many men are so foolish as inwardly to entertain this foolish thought? Not that any are so void of all sense and reason as to think they shall never die, when they really, seriously think of it, but *there* is the thing: they seldom think of it; it hardly ever starts into their thought, "It is but a little while and I must die, and never live here more." They very seldom think where, and how, and what their bodies will be a few years hence. They are now in life and health, stirring and moving about the world amongst the rest of the crowd of mankind; but they little think how, in a little time, they must lie buried in the ground, in the dark, still, and silent grave, rotting and putrifying, loathsome and filthy, by degrees turning to dust, and none taking notice of them, their flesh by degrees rotting off from their bones, leaving nothing but the ghastly skeleton.

They know all this, but when do they seriously think of it? They continue to act just as if they intended to live upon this earth always, and it is but seldom they seriously think otherwise; surely, if they did, they would be something concerned about something else than how to live prosperously here. The question, "What shall I do to be saved?" would be more frequently asked than it is.

They know that in all former generations, that used to make as great a stir in the world as they, are gone: they have no more to do here; they make no more noise in the world; they are no more seen walking about and taking pleasure in earthly things; Zech. 1:5, "Your fathers, where are they? and the prophets, do they live forever?"

Be persuaded for your own safety, to look a little forward and be concerned about your welfare an age hence, and not only what you shall eat, and what you shall drink, and wherewithal you shall be clothed for that little time you are to remain here. Frequently ask yourself the question, what you intend to do if death comes and summons you out of the world, and from all your earthly good things. If you are not prepared to die, you cannot resist the summons: none are able to grapple with the king of terrors. When death comes, he will hale you from all your dear enjoyments, whether you will or no, never to set your eye on those things more. And as there will be no encountering death, so neither will there be any entreating it; he'll not be wrought upon by cries and tears; he is altogether inexorable. He'll not wait for you one minute, that you may have a little opportunity to be better fitted and prepared to go with [him].

Consider whether you now are in such a state that you need not fear to meet death. If he should come immediately, should you meet him with terror and horror under dreadful apprehensions of going into another world, and leaving all these things forevermore? Or should you be able to look him cheerfully in the face, knowing that although you must be stripped of these enjoyments, yet death cannot take from you your heavenly happiness; knowing that although he takes you away from your earthly possessions, he cannot deprive you of your heavenly inheritance: though he takes you from your earthly friends, yet he is not able to separate you from your heavenly Father, nor from Jesus Christ, the spouse and bridegroom of your soul?

How would it be with you, if death should now lay hold of you? Would [he] find you asleep, or diligent at your work with your loins girt and your lamps burning? Do you live as circumspectly and watchfully, and keep the commands of God as strictly, as if you knew death would seize you tomorrow?

Let all examine themselves, and know whether they use this world just as if they would carry their earthly enjoyments into the other world with them, or whether they set their hearts chiefly on things which are not seen; and let all be exhorted to apply themselves immediately to the preparations for eternity. Set about [it] with the greatest seriousness and diligence, with the utmost vigor and most fixed resolution, for such things as concern eternal happiness or eternal misery are not to be trifled with, nor to be trusted to a mere peradventure; for what shall it profit you, if you gain the whole world, and lose your own soul?

A sermon predicating "the whole of Christianity" in its doctrine is certainly comprehensive, and one by Jonathan Edwards devoted to the "gloriousness and excellency" of God is certainly quintessential; one that encompasses both dimensions must thus represent a remarkable effort of synthesis. In fact, the very stretching necessary to unite such disparate dimensions and planes of Edwards' conceptual cosmos is an organizing principle of "God's Excellencies," a sermon in which the subject matter is frequently beyond "the outmost verge of our most outstretched thoughts."

Pastorally, Edwards explains the entire undertaking rather simply: we must have some idea of what we are worshipping in order to worship in a meaningful way. On a higher plane, we must be able to contemplate God in some sense, as this exercise is nothing less than the ultimate and chief end of man. Because God has graciously accommodated his divine attributes to the mind of man through the medium of the Word, there is hope for practical success in the enterprise. Like the inspired penmen of the Scriptures, Edwards conducts his survey of seven divine attributes through the medium of analogy so that men may comprehend within their limits.

The resulting sermon is simple and practical in plan and vocabulary, but Edwards' capacity for pursuit of the implications of biblical commonplaces on a plane of subtlety and wonder causes the reader to experience some "outstretched thoughts" as the seven attributes are explored in the Doctrine and weighed in the Application. The uncompromising testing of spiritual truths by human psychology, and the essential realism within the theological orthodoxy, are perhaps attributable to the optimism and confidence of youth in this case, though Edwards was to retain these traits far beyond his youth. Moreover, Edwards not only insists upon the "downward" validity of spiritual truth, but tests the "upward" capacity of human imagination by insisting upon the ultimate transformation of being into pure essence of experience upon union with God.

Although this sermon was certainly repreached only once and the manuscript shows little material evidence of having been widely employed, the range of its speculation and the variety of its literary resources have made it anticipatory of works as diverse in purpose and format as *Sinners in the Hands of an Angry God* and *God's End in the Creation,* to name just two. A poignant practical discourse and an untrammeled meditative excursion, this long sermon is finally evidence of Edwards' great ambition, personally and professionally, during this early phase of his career as he unabashedly tackled in its totality what was to become a favorite theme, the grandeur of God.

*   *   *

The sermon, written in two octavo quire booklets standard in form for the period and in good condition, was designed to be preached in two units correlating with the two booklets, the break coming just at the juncture of the Doctrine and Application. Perhaps the most remarkable feature of the manuscript is the presence of blank spaces, ranging from a few lines to a page, in both booklets. These spaces were apparently left when the development of the outline of heads either failed to fill the allotted pages, or when the outline itself was modified. Here, as in several sermons of this period, one can see the inefficiency of the infolded quire booklet when the preacher attempted composition in it (as opposed to copying in a text at least roughed out in scrap paper). In the second booklet, particularly, there is evidence of the juggling of heads and renumbering when an intermediate head in a numbered series was dropped.

The resulting sermon is rather well balanced in bulk and formal structure, each booklet containing nearly the same amount of exposition and each being formally dominated by a series of seven numbered heads. This formal symmetry was apparently on Edwards' mind, for he deleted a possible eighth head in each booklet in an apparent effort to keep the sermon within the time limitations of the pulpit, though the doctrinal heads correlate only generally with the applicatory heads and he could as easily have deleted two in one booklet and none in the other. Of course, in the latter case the divisions between preaching units and the Doctrine and Application would not have coincided, either.

GOD'S EXCELLENCIES

*For who in the heaven can be compared unto the Lord, and who
among the sons of the mighty can be likened unto the Lord?*

THIS book of Psalms has such an exalted devotion, and such a
spirit of evangelical grace every[where] breathed forth in it! Here are
such exalted expressions of the gloriousness of God, and even of the
excellency of Christ and his kingdom; there is so much of the gospel
doctrine, grace, and spirit, breaking out and shining in it, that it
seems to be carried clear above and beyond the strain and pitch of
the Old Testament, and almost brought up to the New. Almost the
whole book of Psalms has either a direct or indirect respect to Christ
and the gospel which he was to publish, particularly this Psalm
wherein is our text.

Of the ten penmen of these Psalms, Ethan the Ezrahite was the
penman of this. He was a man peculiarly noted for wisdom, as appears because the greatness of Solomon's wisdom is set forth by its
being greater than his; see I Kgs. 4:30–31, "And Solomon's wisdom
excelled the wisdom of all the children of the east country, and all
the wisdom of Egypt. For he was wiser than all men; than Ethan the
Ezrahite." This Ethan, in this Psalm, or rather the Spirit of God by
Ethan, gives us a most glorious prophecy of Christ. He begins it, as
it is very proper to begin a prophecy of this nature, by setting forth
the glorious excellencies, perfections, and works of God, for never
were God's perfections manifested so gloriously as they have been
manifested in the work of redemption; never did his infinite glories
so brightly shine forth as in the face of Jesus Christ.

Our text is part of this exordium, wherein the glory of Jehovah is
set forth by comparing of [it] with the highest of created beings. 'Tis
a usual thing in Scripture, to set forth the infinite perfections of God
by comparing of them with, and setting of them above, all finite

beings. Thus, the infinite greatness of God is set forth by his being greater than the whole universe, so that the heaven of heavens cannot contain him. His being from eternity is frequently set forth by his "being before the foundation of the world"; this expression is frequently used to express the eternity of the generation of the Son of God, and the eternity of the divine decrees. So the infinite excellency of Christ is described by his being the Rose of Sharon and Lily of the Valley, the most delightful, beautiful, and pleasing objects among created beings. So here in our text is another instance, wherein the infinite gloriousness and excellency of God is held forth to us, by its being so transcendent above the greatest and highest creature.

[1.] The comparison is first with the highest and most excellent creature in heaven, for who in heaven can be compared unto the Lord? There is none, of the angels or of those spotless, pure, wise, bright, and active spirits there, are worthy to be compared with him.

2. With the highest on earth: "Who among the sons of the mighty can be likened unto the Lord?" The great kings, princes, emperors, and monarchs of the world, that look like gods [to] the wondering and amazed eyes of men, are nothing to him, are not fit to be likened to him. See Job 34:19–20, "How much less to him who accepteth not the persons of princes, nor regardeth the rich more than the poor, for they all are the work of his hands. In a moment shall they die, and the people shall be troubled at midnight and pass away, and the mighty shall be taken away without hand."

DOCTRINE.

God is infinitely exalted in gloriousness and excellency above all created beings.

My design at this time [is] to endeavor, by God's help, to exhibit and set forth the greatness, gloriousness, and transcendent excellency of that God who made us, and whom we worship and adore.

It is of exceeding great importance that we should have right notions and conceptions of the nature, attributes, and perfections of God. It is the very foundation of all religion, both doctrinal and practical; it is to no purpose to worship God, except we know what we worship. It is to be feared, that there are many persons in these days that pretend to worship the true God, to whom it may be said, as Christ said to the woman of Samaria, "Ye worship ye know not what" [John 4:22]. For the Samaritans pretended to worship the same

God that the Jews did; they have some obscure, outside notions of God, that he is a great God, a God of great power, that he made the world and made them, and knows all things, etc., but [they] have not right apprehensions of the divine perfections.

Now it is impossible we should love, fear, and obey God as we ought, except we know what he is, and have right ideas of his perfections, that render him lovely and worthy to be feared and obeyed. Yea, it is impossible we should worship him, for it is not he that we worship, except we know what a being he is: it is something else; it is something we know not what; it is not Jehovah. Except we have some tolerable notion of him, we shall not worship any more than the Athenians did, who inscribed their altar to the Unknown God, and indeed the perfections of God are such a theme as the strongest, best instructed, and most knowing Christians know but infinitely little of; no, nor the bright intelligences of the higher world.

The most understanding there may spend all their lives' time, yea, an eternity, in learning and discovering more and more, and yet never arrive to a perfect knowledge; it is a bottomless ocean of wonders that we can never comprehend, but yet may with great pleasure and profit dive further into it. It would be greatly to the advantage of our souls, if we understood more of the excellency and gloriousness of God; wherefore, if what shall be said at this time shall be any help or assistance to any of us, the end of this sermon will be obtained.

This is the highest theme that ever man, that ever archangels, yea, that ever the man Christ Jesus, entered upon yet; yea, it is that theme which is, to speak after the manner of men, the highest contemplation, and the infinite happiness, of Jehovah himself.

What poor, miserable creatures, then, are we, to talk of the infinite and transcendent gloriousness of the great, eternal, and almighty Jehovah; what miserable work do worms of the dust make, when they get upon such a theme as this, which the very angels do stammer at?

But yet, although we are but worms and insects, less than insects, nothing at all, yea, less than nothing, yet so has God dignified us, that he has made [us] for this very end: to think and be astonished [at] his glorious perfections. And this is what we hope will be our business to all eternity; to think on, to delight [in], to speak of, and sing forth, the infinite excellencies of the Deity. He has made us capable of understanding so much of him here as is necessary in order to our acceptable worshipping and praising him, and he has instructed us, and taught us, as little ignorant babes and infants, and has helped our weak understanding by his instructions; he has told us what he is, has condescended to our poor capacities and described himself to us after the manner of men: as men, when they teach children, must teach them after their manner of thinking of things, and come down to their childish capacities, so has God taught us concerning himself.

Wherefore, I shall not presume to speak of the excellencies of God any further than he has taught and instructed us in his Word. I acknowledge, such a glorious, amazing, and astonishing and awful theme ought to be entered upon by mortals, by dust and ashes, with the greatest awe and reverence; with the deepest humility and fear, especially by such dust and ashes, and so likewise it also ought to be attended to at this time, by us all.

Wherefore, we shall proceed to show how vastly God is exalted above all the highest and most perfect of created beings: first, in duration; second, in greatness; third, in excellency and loveliness; fourth, in power; fifth, in wisdom; sixth, in holiness; seventh, in goodness and mercy. I choose rather to speak of these things comparatively, comparing of them with what is found in the creatures, because comparisons are a great help to our weakened, dull minds to conceive of things that are far out of the ken of our imaginations, and the outmost verge of our most outstretched thoughts; we are not so apt to conceive of the gloriousness of God, when considering objectively, as when compared with other things that we can easier conceive of, and because the Scripture generally takes the method of setting forth the divine perfections. But,

I. God is infinitely exalted above all creatures in duration, [even] the most ancient of all creatures. Neither the earth we stand upon, nor the heavens over our heads; the sun, moon, nor stars; nor the angels of God, can claim a duration of six thousand years, but what is this to the duration of the great [God] who is from everlasting? It is but a moment, no more than the twinkling of an eye.

God never had a beginning. If we run back in our thoughts forever; if we spend an eternity in going back, we shall never come to the beginning of God's duration, nor make any approach towards it, but at last all that we have thought of, is but as a moment to that which yet remains behind unthought of; if the whole universe, from one side of the creation to the other, was stuffed full [of] rolls of figures of [years], it would make no approach to the beginning of the Ancient of Days. How are we lost and confounded, amazed and astonished, when we think of God's being from eternity; yea, how are angels lost, here; how are they yet lost, although they have spent their short past duration in sweet, but amazed thoughts upon it: Ps. 90:2,4, "Before the mountains were brought forth, or ever thou hadst formed the earth and the world, from everlasting to everlasting, thou art God. For a thousand years in thy sight, are but as yesterday when it is past, and as a watch of the night."

While God never was made, it is necessary that that which hath a beginning must have some cause, some author that gave it a beginning, but God never had a beginning; there was none before him, and therefore none that gave him his being. He thanks no one for his being; doth not, nor ever did depend upon any for it, but receives his being from himself, and depends alone on himself. Neither doth he thank anyone for anything he enjoys: his power, his wisdom, his excellency, his glory, his honor, and [his] authority are his own, and received from none other; he possesses them and he will possess them: he is powerful and he will be powerful; he is glorious and he will be glorious; he is infinitely honorable, but he receives his honor from himself; he is infinitely happy and he will be infinitely happy; he reigns and rules over the whole universe, and he will rule and do what he pleases, in the armies of heaven and amongst the inhabitants of the earth. Poor nothing creature can do nothing towards controlling of [Him]; they, with all their power conjoined, which is but weakness, can't deprive Jehovah of any of these things. He was just the same, in all respects, from all eternity as he is now; as he was, infinite ages before the foundations of the world were laid, so he is now and so he will be, with exactly the same glory and happiness uninterrupted, immovable and unchangeable, the same yesterday, today, and forever.

II. God is infinitely exalted above all created beings in greatness. This earth appears to us as a very great thing. When we think of the large countries and continents, the vast oceans, and the great distance between one country and another, the whole, together, appears very great and vast; but especially doth the great universe surprise us with its greatness, to which, without doubt, this vast earth, as we call it, is less than any mote or dust, that ever we saw, is to the whole earth; but how shall we be surprised when we think that all this vast creation, making the most of it we can, is infinitely less, when compared with the greatness of God, than the least discernible atom is to the whole creation! This is the most certain truth.

O how great doth God seem, when we look upon the universal creation as no more than one of those motes that swims in the air! How great is God; how little is the universe in comparison of him, how inconsiderable and good for nothing. Alas, if God is so great and the universe so little, what are our little, swelling kings, princes, and emperors; what is become of our great and mighty men, that scare all the world with their greatness and pride; where will our bold and impudent blasphemers, and common swearers that take God's name in vain so merrily, appear? I can't but mention these things before I come to the application: how may the angels well spend their eviternity in meditating upon this infinitely great and glorious Being! What miserable creatures are we all, what nothings, what worms; how may we well turn ourselves into nothing, when we come into the presence of so great a God!

III. God is infinitely exalted above all created beings in excellency and loveliness. It all runs upon infinites in God: so great as is his duration, so great as is his being and essence, so great is his excellency and loveliness. His excellency excels all other excellencies that ever were seen or heard of, as much as his being exceeds created beings in greatness. It must needs be so: for all other excellencies proceed from him as the fountain, for he has made them all; he has made all things that are excellent, and therefore must have given them their excellency, and so must have all that excellency in himself, or else could not have given it. He must have all the glories, perfections, and beauties of the whole creation in himself in an infinite degree, for they all proceed from him, as beams do from the sun, and [he] is as much more excellent than they all, as the whole sun is than one single ray.

We admire at the beauty of creation, at the beautiful order of it, at the glory of the sun, moon, and stars. The sun appears very bright and glorious; so beautiful doth it appear that many nations take it to be the supreme God, and worship it accordingly, but we have much more reason from the beauty of the sun to admire at the invisible glory of that God whose fingers have formed it, and to say, as one that was imprisoned by virtue of the Spanish Inquisition and was kept in a dark dungeon three years from the sight of the sun, when he was brought forth into the light to his martyrdom, he, greatly admiring at the beauty of the sun which he had not seen so long, being astonished at it, cries out that he wondered any man could worship anything but the maker of that glorious creature, having respect to the idolatry of the papists.[1]

The beauty of trees, plants, and flowers, with which God has bespangled the face of the earth, is delightful; the beautiful frame of the body of man, especially in its perfection, is astonishing; the beauty of the moon and stars is wonderful; the beauty of [the] highest heavens is transcendent; the excellency of angels and the saints in light is very glorious: but it is all deformity and darkness in comparison of the brighter glories and beauties of the Creator of all, for "behold even to the moon, and it shineth not" (Job 25:5); that is, think of the excellency of God and the moon will not seem to shine to you, God's excellency so much outshines [it]. And the stars are not pure in his sight, and so we know that at the great day when God appears, the sun shall be turned into darkness, shall hide his face as if he were ashamed to see himself so much outshined; and the very angels, they hide their faces before him; the highest heavens are not clean in his sight, and he charges his angels with folly.

In fine, God's is an infinite excellency, infinite glory, and beauty itself; he is an infinite, eternal, and immutable excellency; he is not only an infinitely excellent being, but a being that is infinite excellency, beauty, and loveliness.

IV. God infinitely exceeds all created beings in power. If we look at might and strength, where can we find another being that can cause a great world to be or not to be, at a word, when he will; that can do everything that he pleases with infinite ease; that can manage a world, and keep all the various parts of it in such orderly and harmonious motion, who can manage such great bodies as the sun, moon, and stars, and can give what laws to them he pleases?

There are many of the princes of the earth that have great power, and that rule over great part of the earth, and have the lives and fortunes of their subjects in their hands; but what are these to him who is king of the whole earth, who is King of Kings and Lord of Lords; who rules over kings and emperors, and has them as much in his power as he has the ants and flies, pulls down one and sets up another at his pleasure; who oversees all the kingdoms and governments in the world, and manages the affairs of them just as he pleases.

1. This carefully elaborated exemplum, with its gratuitous swipe at the Roman Catholic church, is obviously from a collection of martyrs' lives such as John Foxe's *Acts and Monuments,* though I have been unable to find the account in Foxe or in any similar book to which JE is known to have had access.

When he pleases, one king must die, and who he pleases must reign in his room; armies conquer or are conquered according as he will have it: "The king's heart is in the hand of the Lord, and he turns them as the rivers of water" [Prov. 21:1]. Thus he holds an absolute and uncontrollable government in the world; and thus he has done from the beginning, and thus he will do to the end of all things. Neither is his dominion confined to the children of men, but he rules the whole creation. He gives commands to the seas, and has appointed them bounds which they cannot pass; "which removeth the mountains, and they know it not who overturneth them in his anger; which shaketh the earth out of its place, and the pillars thereof tremble; who commandeth the sun and it riseth not; who sealeth up the stars, which maketh Arcturus and Orion, and the chambers of the south; who doth great things past finding out; yea, wonders without number" [Job 9:5–7, 9–10].

What a vast and uncontrollable dominion hath the almighty God. The kings of the earth are not worthy of the name, for they are not able to execute their authority in their narrow bounds, except by the power and assistance of their subjects, but God rules most absolutely the whole universe by himself; kings rule, perhaps sometimes for forty years, but God's kingdom is an everlasting kingdom, and of his dominion there is no end. Well, therefore, may he be said to be the blessed and only potentate, King of Kings, and Lord of Lords.

V. God is infinitely exalted above all created beings in wisdom. The wisest of men, how little do they know, how frequently are they deceived and frustrated, and their wisdom turned to foolishness, their politic designs undermined; but when was the time that God's wisdom failed, that he did not obtain his end, although all the bleak army of hell are continually endeavoring to counterwork him? When was it that God altered his mind and purpose, or took a wrong step in the government of the world?

Solomon was sensible that there was need of uncommon and extraordinary wisdom to rule such a kingdom as he had; but what wisdom, what vast knowledge and infinite penetration must he have, who has every being in the world to rule and govern; who rules every thought, and every purpose, every motion and action, not only of angels and men, but of every creature, great and small, even to every little atom in the whole creation, and that forever and ever? What infinite wisdom and knowledge is necessary and requisite in order to this! But this God doth; this he hath done and will do. All the changes and alterations that happen in all the world, heaven and earth, whether great or never so small, he knows it altogether, even to the least insect that crawls upon the earth, or dust that flies in the air, and it is all from his disposal, and according to his eternal determination.

But God's wisdom and omnisciency shines clearest of all in his perfect knowledge of himself, who is the infinite object of his own knowledge. That eternity of his, whereby he was from everlasting to everlasting, which so confounds us miserable worms, is clearly understood by him with the greatest ease, at one simple view; he also comprehends his own infinite greatness and excellency, which can be done by none but an infinite understanding. Well might the Apostle cry out:

> O the depths of the riches both of the wisdom and knowledge of God! how unsearchable are his judgments, and his ways past finding out! For who hath known the mind of the Lord, or who hath been his counsellor; or who hath first given to him, and it shall be recompensed to him again? For of him and through him, and to him, are all things: to whom be glory forever. Amen [Rom. 11:33–36].

VI. God is infinitely exalted above all created beings in holiness. Holiness is the highest sort of excellency or perfection that ever the creature attains unto; 'tis the highest beauty that shines in the creation.

Now God is infinitely holy, and infinitely exalted therein, above the holy angels and all creatures; there is not the least tincture of defilement or pollution in the Deity, but he is infinitely far from it: he is all pure light, without mixture of darkness; he hates and abhors sin above all things, 'tis what is directly contrary to his nature. This, his great holiness, has he made known to us by his justice, truth, and faithfulness in all his dispensations towards us, and by the pure holiness of his laws and commands.

Holiness used to be for a distinguishing attribute between the God of Israel and other gods, Dan. 4:8, "But at last Daniel came in before me, whose name is Belteshazzar, according to the name of my God, and in whom is the spirit of the holy gods"; and so in the next verse, "because I know the holy gods is in thee." Likewise, in the eighteenth verse,[2] "the Holy One" is a name that God seems to delight [in]. 'Tis

2. That is, Ps. 89:18.

that attribute which continually ravishes the seraphims, and causes them continually to cry in their praises, without ceasing, "holy, holy, holy." This is the sound with which the highest heaven, the palace of God, perpetually rings, and [it] will ring on earth in the glorious times that are hastening.

VII. God is infinitely exalted above all created beings in goodness. Goodness and royal bounty, mercy, and clemency is the glory of earthly monarchs and princes, but in this is the Lord, our God, infinitely exalted above them. God delights in the welfare and prosperity of his creatures; he delights in making of them exceeding happy and blessed, if they will but accept of the happiness which he offers.

All creatures do continually live upon the bounty of God; he maintains the whole creation of his mere goodness: every good thing that is enjoyed is a part of his bounty. When kings are bountiful, and dispense good things to their subjects, they do but give that which the Almighty before gave to them. So merciful and so full of pity is God, that when miserable man, whom He had no need of, who did Him no good, nor could be of any advantage to Him, had made himself miserable by his rebellion against God, He took such pity on him that He sent His only Son to undergo his torment for him, that he might be delivered and set free. And now He offers freely, to bestow upon those rebels, complete and perfect happiness to all eternity upon this, His Son's account. There never was such an instance of goodness, mercy, pity, and compassion since the world began; all the mercy and goodness amongst creatures fall infinitely short of it: this is goodness that never was, never will, never can be paralleled by any other being.[3]

Thus we have briefly insisted upon the glorious—infinitely glorious—perfections of that God which we profess. All that we can say is but clouds and darkness to the reality: the attributes of God, these infinite perfections, cannot be set forth by the eloquence of an angel, much less by mortal tongue. How much too little is the space of one sermon, to speak of that which angels spend an eternity in! This is that being which we worship, to whom we pray and sing praises; whom we are met together this day to worship as he has instituted, and whose word we have heard at this time.

So glorious and so excellent is our God; such a being is he that

---

3. Leaf eight recto has been left blank, apparently for the development of an eighth head concerning "his wonderful works" which was finally rejected.

made us, that made these bodies and these souls, and continually upholds us, that keeps us alive, keeps our breath playing in our nostrils; that continually sees us, is present everywhere, is present here now, and sees all our thoughts and knows whether we have any fear of him or love to him, and how we are affected by the consideration of his glorious perfections and wondrous works, and whether or no we regard his holy commands, or are moved by his gracious promises, or terrified by his dreadful threatenings.[4]

APPLICATION.

We are now come to make some improvement of this glorious truth; indeed, the whole of Christianity follows as an improvement from this doctrine. The infinite excellency, greatness, and glory of God is the foundation of all religion, for except we believe the perfections of God, we shall never worship him and love him as he ought to be worshipped and loved; except we believe his power and justice and holiness, we shall not fear him and stand in awe of him, and be afraid to violate his commands; except we believe his omnisciency, we shall not act as under his all-seeing eye, and as those who are to be judged by him. Except we believe his mercy and goodness, we shall not praise him with a grateful sense thereof, but if once our eyes were but opened, and God makes a discovery to our souls of his own gloriousness and excellency, how should we reverence all his commands and be afraid to sin against him; how should we abhor ourselves and repent in dust and ashes; how should we love the Word of God, religion, and religious persons, and everything that hath [the] least shadow of the divine perfections! But we shall improve this doc-

---

4. Here ends the first preaching unit. The following recapitulation heads the second preaching unit:

Psalm 89:6, "For who in heaven can be compared unto the Lord, and who among the sons of the mighty can be likened unto the Lord?"

Doctrine. That God is infinitely exalted in gloriousness and excellency above all created beings.

We have already handled the explicatory part of this doctrine, and have briefly insisted upon this glorious, transcendent, infinite, perfection of the deity, and shown how all creatures, even the highest, greatest, and most excellent of them, are as nothing before him, and that there none in heaven are to be compared to him, nor any among the sons of the mighty are worthy to be likened to him in duration, in greatness, gloriousness, excellency, or loveliness; in great power, and wisdom, or transcendently bright holiness, and amazing goodness, bounty, and mercy.

trine at present only in a few uses, which do most immediately and directly offer themselves from this doctrine: first, in a use of instruction; second, of exhortation; third, of consolation.

I. *Use of Instr.*

[*First.*] If he be such an excellent being, how dreadful is sin against [him]. There are very few that conceived what a dreadful thing it is to sin against the infinitely excellent, great, and glorious Jehovah. The aggravations of sin are really infinite, infinite in greatness and almost infinite in number, for it is committed against an infinitely great and powerful God, one that has infinite authority: this alone is an infinite aggravation of sin, but then it is committed also against an infinitely lovely and excellent God, and that is another infinite aggravation, and also against an infinitely holy God, and one that hates sin with infinite hatred, and besides that, against an infinitely good and merciful God. Each of these are infinite aggravations of sin, and render it an infinite evil.

But consider: sin is committed against that God that made us and preserves us, feeds us and clothes us, and which is more than all, has sent his Son into the world to redeem us, his Son that he infinitely loved, and has been so gracious as to make him known to us, and to invite us to accept of him and be happy after our rebellion; but time would fail to enumerate all the aggravations of sin.

Second. How dreadful must his wrath be! If God [is] infinitely great and powerful, how terrible must his wrath and anger be; what a miserable creature—how inexpressibly miserable—must a poor, weak, sinner be in the hands of an angry and enraged God, who can shake the whole earth in pieces in a moment, and can annihilate the whole universe in the twinkling of an eye. It is dreadful to fall in[to] the paws of a bear robbed of her whelps, but what is it to fall into the hands of an almighty God that is angry and irreconcilable, as he will be to sinners after this life?

You may be sure that sin, persisted in, makes him exceeding angry. Without doubt, it makes God angry to see that he is slighted, and his laws trampled upon, by poor dust and ashes that he has made, and that depend upon him for life and breath and all things. Without doubt, God is made very angry when he sends his only Son into the world, out of pity to poor creatures, to die for them: to have him rejected and despised, and the salvation offered by him slighted, and the glorious gospel mocked. You can't suppose that God sees these things without being very angry; you can't think but that, when God calls for [a] matter of ten, twenty, or thirty years together upon a perishing sinner to come to Him for deliverance, and promises him, if he will come He will give him eternal happiness, and the sinner all the while contumeliously turns his back and stops his ears: you can't think but that it must needs incense the wrath of God enough to make him exceeding miserable, nor you can't doubt but that God, being of infinite power, can make him just as miserable as He pleases. O what is a worm, to bear the weight of the anger of so great a being?

Third. How hath he honored us, in that he hath made us to glorify and enjoy him to all eternity; how are we dignified by our Maker, who hath made us for so high and excellent an end! He has made other creatures for his own glory, but they are passive in it: the sun glorifies God by shining, and the trees by growing, and all things by performing the laws of nature which God has given them. But God has made us actually to glorify, to behold his excellencies and to admire them, and to be made forever happy in the enjoyment of them.[5]

Fourth. If he be so great and glorious, what an amazing thing it is that he should take upon him the human nature and die for men! He, who was born of the Virgin Mary, that was mocked amongst the Jews and soldiers, that was condemned by Pilate, and suffered between two thieves upon the cross without the gates of Jerusalem: he was this glorious God, that is infinitely exalted above all created beings, which we have been speaking of to you. This is enough to amaze us, and strike us with astonishment.

Certainly, it is no small thing for God to become man and die; this is worthy to be wondered at. 'Tis certainly a very strange thing to see him that is from everlasting to everlasting, the same yesterday, today, and forever; immutable, unchangeable, infinite in his essence, so that the whole universe is as nothing to him; omnipotent, omniscient, and omnipresent, and all-sufficient, who made heaven and earth by the word of his power, and reigns over the creation: I say, to [see] him dying like a malefactor, in the flesh![6]

---

5. Leaves two verso and three recto of the second booklet are each half blank, composing a blank page at this point, primarily the result of JE's abandoning the development of a subhead which would have discussed "how much hath [God] condescended to be concerned for our welfare."

6. Following this sentence in the MS, inserted in a blank space left when the sermon was composed, is a passage prepared for a later preaching. The passage is abbreviated if not entirely an outline:

When we think upon that being which is without beginning of days or end of years, whose goings forth are from everlasting, who had a being endless ages

Fifth. How highly are we privileged, in that he hath made known himself to us! How many poor, miserable, blinded and deluded creatures are deifying molten gold and silver, or carved wood and stone, because they know of no God that is more excellent! Alas, how miserably doth a dumb, lifeless stock serve, in the room of a being that the heaven of heavens cannot contain, and whose perfections [and] glories are as infinite as his being! Others give themselves to worship him who is the most hateful, vile, cursed, cruel, malicious creature in the creation: even the devil, instead of a glorious, transcendently lovely, thrice holy, and exceeding good and merciful God.

Such Egyptian darkness are they under, but to us hath God shined, and although there is darkness all around us, yet with us there is light, as it was with the children of Israel in Egypt. The Sun of Righteousness stands still in our hemisphere, and sheds down his lovely beams upon our heads, revealing unto us the blessed and glorious God.

Many nations, they worship base and abominable gods, but if it is asked of us what god we worship, we may answer that we worship infinite excellency, infinite perfection and loveliness; for this is our God, and certainly that God that is infinite perfection, itself, is the most perfect of all. What a vast difference is there betwixt a God that is infinite excellency in the abstract, and bulls and serpents, wild beasts and devils, which go for gods amongst some of the poor deluded world. How highly has God favored us; how has God distinguished us; what cause have we of thankfulness, that we are born where the true God is known![7]

Sixth. How great must be the happiness of the enjoyment of him. The happiness of society, and the enjoyment of entire friends, is one

---

before the foundation of the world, who had no beginning: is it not enough to make us wonder, to see this God hanging upon the cross in the flesh?

When we think of that being who fills heaven and earth, etc.

When we behold the heavens . . .

When we look upon the sun . . .

When we think on the earth, how he holds it up by his power . . .

When we think on the thunder, of his power, the voice of the Lord which is so full of majesty: "that voice of the Lord which breaketh the cedars, which maketh them to skip like a calf; Lebanon and Sirion like a young unicorn; that voice of the Lord which divideth the flames of fire; that voice of the Lord which shaketh the wilderness; that voice of the Lord which maketh the hinds to calve, and discovereth the forests" [Ps. 29:5–9].

7. This subhead was originally written *after* the sixth subhead in the sermon booklet and has been placed in this position in accordance with JE's numbering.

of the highest sorts of pleasures, next to the pleasures of religion; if that be so sweet, how inexpressibly sweet and delightful must it be to enjoy this excellent being, who is infinitely more excellent, more lovely, than the most perfect, than any of our fellow creatures. There is inexpressibly more pleasure and delight in the enjoyment of God, than in the enjoyment of the most excellent, dear, and entire friends upon earth, and that upon these several accounts:

1. God is every way transcendently more amiable, than the most perfect and lovely of all our fellow creatures. If men take great delight and pleasure in beholding and enjoying the perfections and beauties of their fellow mortals, with what ecstasies, with what sweet rapture, will the sweet glories and beauties of the blessed God be beheld and enjoyed!

2. God loves those that he admits to the enjoyment of him with far greater love than the highest love of fellow creatures.

3. Those that enjoy God shall love him with transcendently greater love than it is possible to love the most lovely creature, so that the love will be mutual; the glorified saint shall be all transformed to love to God, and shall be all transformed to joy at the thought of God's so dearly loving him.

4. The glorified saint shall be more nearly united to God than ever the best friends are united here in this world. They shall be received into the closest union with God: we represent it by "being embraced in God's arms," but that is too faint a shadow to represent the close union that there will be; the very soul of the saint shall be united to God, and God shall be in them, in their very souls, by his glorious presence.

5. They shall more fully enjoy God than the nearest friends. The enjoyment of friends is not full and satisfying; it is frequently interrupted; but it is not so with respect to God and the glorified saint, but the enjoyment will be entire, to the constant full satisfaction of the enlarged desires of the soul, and it shall be constant and without interruption, shall continue to the same height, and shall rise and increase to all eternity.

6. The sweet relish of these enjoyments shall never decrease or be diminished. In all temporal enjoyments, one has enough of it presently; we are quickly weary of them and want some new sort of delights, but in heaven the joys will be so full, and so great, and so sweet, that the relish of them shall hold; and there will be as high, as sweet, and [as] ravishing delight in the enjoyment of God at the end

of millions of ages, as there was the first hour. All these things meeting together, there must needs result an unutterable delight and unimaginable pleasure; the saint will be transformed to be all pure holiness, all light, all understanding, all vision, all love, all joy and delight; they shall not only, as it were, be full of love and full of joy, but their very souls will be transformed to love and to joy, and exceeding excellent pleasure.

Seventh. How excellent are they who are sanctified, and have their souls conformed unto him. 'Tis a wonder that a creature should ever be so highly honored, as to be made conformed to the image of God, as much a wonder as that they should be allowed the enjoyment of him. Sanctification is as great, yea, a greater favor done to the creature, than glorification: the creature is more honored by being made like unto God in holiness, than in happiness; the image and likeness of God upon the creature exalts it and honors it more, than the fruition of him.

As God is infinitely exalted above all creatures in excellency and perfection, as you have heard, so those creatures that are sanctified and made like him, and have the image of God drawn upon them by the Holy Spirit, are very much exalted above all other creatures that are not; they are made more excellent, more lovely, and more honorable, than kings and princes, and emperors and potentates.

That man that is sanctified and made holy, has more excellency than all the wicked men in the world, and is more honorable, and will be honored more, than all the rich and powerful men upon earth, put together, that are destitute of holiness. And why? Because those that are holy are made like unto God, have the image of that God before whom all the kings of the earth are as nothing.

Holiness is the very beauty and loveliness of Jehovah himself. 'Tis the excellency of his excellencies, the beauty of his beauties, the perfection of his infinite perfections, and the glory of his attributes. What an honor, then, must it be to a creature who is infinitely below God, and less than he, to be beautified and adorned with this beauty, with that beauty which is the highest beauty of God himself, even holiness. The highest honor of angels is their holiness. 'Tis astonishing that God should make even the angels, or any creature, in his own likeness, but how much more admirable is it that God should sanctify sinners—loathsome and abominable creatures—and make them like to himself.

II. *Use of Exh.* To all, immediately to seek after his love and favor.

It is a dreadful thing, as you have heard, to have such as God is, an enemy, to have him our enemy, that can do what he pleases with us, can execute his vengeance upon us how and when he pleases. Certainly, it is well worth our while to strive, if it be possible, to make such an one our friend, to get him to be on our side; for if he is for us, who can be against us?

Men generally seek very much for the friendship of those that have power in their hands, and can manage things for or against us as they list; they are generally careful how they fall out with them, that have either their goods or their lives in their hands, and love to make friends with those whose friendship they hope to be profited by. And yet, they are such fools as to neglect to make friends with him who holds the universe in his hands; who has them and all other men every moment in his power, can kill, ruin, destroy, and make miserable in a moment, only by bare willing of it; who can not only take away their estates and their lives, but make them so miserable to all eternity, body and soul, as you have heard. They are very much afraid how they offend a king, for then they know they endanger their outward prosperity, and it may be their heads, but don't care how much they offend, affront, contemn, and openly despise almighty God, who has kings as much as them in his hands, and in whose hands all the kings in the world are mere nothing and vanity, that he regards not nor cares for. [He] can kill them and make them miserable, as easy as the least infant; he regards not the persons of princes: princes or not princes, 'tis all one to God. But yet they are not at all concerned about offending God, as if his anger were not to be regarded any more than the anger of a child, as if he, were [he] never so angry, could do them no hurt. Or else, as if he were so unwise that he had not wisdom enough to take care of his own honor, but would let men dishonor him without making them to know how dreadful a thing it is to offend him; as if he gave out laws and commands, but never intended to take any care to see that they were performed; as if all his dreadful threatenings of hellfire, outer darkness, and the final doom at the Day of Judgment, were nothing but a mere bugbear to fright men with. They see that God don't punish them yet; they see he lets them alone, lets them live and breathe, and sin on as much as they please; and so they take encouragement to [be] fearless and regardless, are as if it would be so always, not considering that God's ways are not as our ways, nor his thoughts as our thoughts. Man, when he is affronted, must be revenged forthwith; thus Nebuchadnezzar, when disobeyed by Shadrach, Mesheck, and Abednego, that his countenance changed and [he] was in haste to have them cast into the burning, fiery furnace. Many [are the] men that refuse as absolutely to obey God as they did to obey Nebuchadnezzar, but yet He bears with them and lets them go on.

But God is not subject to passion. He has sinners always in his power; he can punish them when he thinks best; there is none of their sin is missed; they are all taken notice of; they are all marked down, and shall every one have a full and complete reward when the time comes. However they may think that they can sin unobserved, the longer it is in coming, the more dreadful will it be when it comes. Men neglect to seek the favor of God, as if his favor was not to be regarded, as if one would never be much the better for having his love; as if he were not able to make us happy, or bestow that upon us that it would be worth the while to please him for. But how different will they find it in a few years' time, and perhaps in much less; they will then see that, although sentence against their evil works was not speedily executed, yet their damnation was not asleep, that God did not forget to set down their sins in the book of his remembrance. They will see that he takes more care of his own honor, and the honor of his laws, than they thought; they will see that it is a more dreadful thing to slight and despise God's threatenings than they imagined, and that a friendship and reconciliation with God is truly to be valued and highly prized, vastly above everything else, and his anger more to be feared than they were sensible of.

The reason why some men neglect to seek the favor of God is because they foolishly presume on his mercy and goodness. They hear that God is infinitely merciful and that he delights not in the death of a sinner, but had rather he should turn and live; and thence they take encouragement still to go on in disobedience to this same God, whose mercy they presume upon. To such, I say: Although God is infinitely merciful and gracious, yet he never bestowed his grace yet upon any of those that took encouragement from his mercy, finally to persist in wickedness; he has declared positively that, without holiness, no man shall see the Lord. Although mercy is freely offered to all, yet God never yet compelled any to be holy that they might be happy. 'Tis absolutely impossible that those who persist in wickedness until death should be made happy after death, for as the tree falleth, so it lieth; God never sanctifies a wicked soul after it is separated from the body, for that, in Rev. 22:11, is pronounced upon all separated souls: "He that is unjust, let him be unjust still; and he which is filthy, let him be filthy still; and he that is righteous, let him be righteous still; and he that is holy, let him be holy still."

So that if they are wicked when they die, they must be wicked to eternity, and if they are wicked, it is impossible they should be happy; it is impossible that they should be admitted into heaven, where it is impossible that any unclean thing should enter. Nothing unsanctified can come there to defile the heavenly palace: no wicked monster will be found amongst those pure and spotless, bright and glorious, inhabitants of the New Jerusalem. See Rev. 21:27, "And there shall in no wise enter into it anything that defileth, neither whatsoever worketh abomination, or maketh a lie: but they that are written in the Lamb's book of life." You see that God saith, it shall *in no wise*; so that it is the greatest madness and folly, to presume upon the mercy of God and yet continue in wickedness, for you may know certainly that however merciful God is, if death finds you so doing, you will certainly be miserable.[8]

There is nothing in God's mercy that is any matter of encouragement to any but returning sinners. He has said indeed that he delights not in the death of a sinner; but what follows, He had rather he should turn and live, for God is not willing he should live without turning, but had rather he should turn and live. There is no more encouragement given to any sinners, but returning sinners, than there is to the fallen angels. God has given no more encouragement that he will save those sinners that go on in their sins without turning, than he has that he will save devils that are already damned; and there is as much reason for the devils to hope to be delivered out of hell because God is merciful, as there is for sinners to take encouragement from God's mercy to go on in their sins.

God is infinitely merciful and gracious, it is true; so also he is infinitely just, and as he honors his mercy upon repenting and returning sinners—those that forsake all their sins—so he will honor his justice upon all those that go on in wickedness. God will vindicate his own honor, and when men dishonor him by living all their lives' time in sin, so he will be honored upon them in their everlasting misery. 'Tis a wonder that any can imagine that they may be saved, though they don't intend to forsake their sins, when Christ has expressly told us that few obtain heaven, in comparison of those who

8. Ed. italics.

are thrown into destruction and perdition. If many of those that seek shall not be able, how shall they enter who don't seek; if of those that run, few obtain the prize, how shall they obtain who stand still? I Pet. 4:18, "And if the righteous scarcely be saved, where [shall] the ungodly and [the] sinner appear?"

As there is no encouragement in the Scripture of God's saving such, so neither are there any instances of mercy upon those that did not turn from their sin. A whole world at once was destroyed because they would not turn at the preaching of Noah, and most of their souls, if not all, were sent to hell, as appears by I Pet. 3:19–20. God had no mercy on the cities of Sodom and Gomorrah; God had no mercy on Judas; he had no mercy on the five foolish virgins that slumbered and slept and suffered their lamps to go out, and when they called and knocked at the door, there was no entrance nor admittance to be had, although they sought with great importunity.

III. *Use of Consola.* To all true Christians: you have heard what a superlatively excellent being your God is. His excellencies are all matter of joy and comfort to you; you may sit and meditate upon them with pleasure and delight. The thoughts of the greatness, power, holiness, and justice of God is matter of terror to the wicked, and will be matter of horrible amazement to them forever; but it is all comfortable and rejoicing to you. The most terrible and dreadful of all God's attributes need not to be terrible, but comfortable to you. You may think of his great power, of his terrible majesty, of his vindictive justice, with joy, as well as of his mercy and goodness; you may think of his being a consuming fire joyfully, as well as of his being the Rose of Sharon and Lily of the Valley, for all his attributes are on your side: his justice and holiness, as well as his pity, love, and compassion. You may think of his descending from heaven to judgment in his dreadful majesty, and all the world rent to pieces before him with earthquakes and thunder and lightning, and devils and wicked men trembling in inexpressible horror and amazement at the sight of him, with as much comfort as you may think of him hanging upon the cross. You are delivered from the wrath of this dreadful Being, are got into Christ, a safe refuge from all danger, and where you never need to fear the feeling of His vengeance. His wrath is to be poured out on his enemies, but you are safe and need not fear: you are out of the way of that stream of brimstone which kindles hellfire, and are come to Mount Sion, the city of the living God, to the heavenly Jerusalem, to an innumerable company of angels, to the

General Assembly and church of the first-born which are written in heaven, and to God the Judge of all, and to the spirits of just men made perfect, and to Jesus the mediator of the new covenant, and to the blood of sprinkling that speaks better things than the blood of Abel.

This God, to whom there is none in heaven to be compared, nor any among the sons of the mighty to be likened; this God who is from everlasting to everlasting, an infinitely powerful, wise, holy, and lovely being, who is the alpha and omega, the beginning and the end, is your God: he is reconciled to you and is become your friend; there is a friendship between you and the Almighty; you are become acquainted with him, and he has made known himself to you, and communicates himself to you, converses with you as a friend, dwells with you, and in you, by his Holy Spirit. Yea, he has taken you into a nearer relation to him: he is become your father, and owns you for his child, and doth by you, and will do by you, as a child; he cares for you, will see that you are provided [for], will see that you never shall want anything that will be useful to you. He has made you one of his heirs, and a co-heir with his Son, and will bestow an inheritance upon you, as it is bestowed upon a child of the King of Kings.

You are now in some measure sanctified, and have the image of God upon your souls, but hereafter, when God shall receive you, his dear child, into his arms, and shall admit you to the perfect enjoyment of him as your portion, you will be entirely transformed into his likeness, for you shall see him as he is. The consideration of having such a glorious God for your God, your friend, your father, and your portion, and that you shall eternally enjoy him as such, is enough to make you despise all worldly afflictions and adversities, and even death itself, and to trample them under your feet.

THE DUTY OF HEARKENING TO GOD'S VOICE

THIS is very much a sermon of voices, some merely named, others dramatized in monologue and dialogue. There is the voice of the Psalmist, the fourfold voice of God, the voice of Satan, the voices of self-deceiving sinners, and of course the voice of the preacher. Through seemingly casual and yet intricate patterns these voices adumbrate the individual's quest of redemption. An important sidelight of this process is a differentiation and cataloguing of voices, as in the third subhead under the first proposition of the Doctrine where the voices of the Word, and not incidentally the homiletical voices of the preacher, are distinguished.

On the merely formal level, God and Satan are given a kind of parity: the Doctrine is dominated by the exposition of the "four voices of God" while the Application is dominated by the four temptations of Satan. The rationale for such parity is not only dramatic but psychological, for in the mind of the "natural man" Satan may have the only voice, and in any human mind that has not been wholly transfigured by sanctification, the voice of Satan is likely to seem as imposing as God's. The entire struggle is thus depicted as a mental one and the time-frame is, as in all awakening sermons, the present moment. God and Satan vie for the *now* of the human heart: the future is secret, even illusory, and hardly more than a trap in itself. But it is in the moment, and from moment to moment, that God, Satan, and the preacher work.

As much an awakening sermon as *Sinners in the Hands of an Angry God* (and anticipating some of its metaphors), "The Duty of Hearkening to God's Voice" is nevertheless characterized by a consistent tone of reasonableness, occasionally leavened by a consciously humorous turn of phrase. Still, the overarching urgency and concern become apparent when the voice of the preacher moves to the forefront, and even stepping into hell and falling into the hands of God are introduced as emphatic images. As in the case of other New York sermons, this sermon seems gentler and its author more optimistic concerning the power of rational argument to effect the awakening

436

of men than do many later sermons of the same type. Perhaps anticipatory of the more ruthless exploitation of sensation in later hortatory sermons is the use of a Yale College tragedy in repreaching
during Edwards' tutorship.

* * *

The sermon booklet is a complete octavo quire into which an additional ninth leaf was pinned between the first and second leaves.
The material on this leaf, supplemented elsewhere by a few minor
interlineations and a couple of paragraph-size deletions in the same
ink, apparently pertains to the subsequent preaching of the sermon
during Edwards' tutorship. (A third ink in a Bolton symbol and in
one correction on the first page indicates an earlier repreaching during 1723–24). The passages on the added leaf are printed below in
an Appendix. It is perhaps noteworthy that in two places, one at the
time of the sermon's composition, Edwards reversed the order of
entire heads after writing them, as is indicated in the notes below.

THE DUTY OF HEARKENING TO GOD'S VOICE

PSALM 95:7–8.

Today if ye will hear his voice, harden not your heart.

'T IS a prudential maxim amongst all mankind: the things of the greatest concern should be done first. It is so plain and evident that no man can deny or question it. It is evidently a great piece of folly for a man, when his house is on fire, to spend his time in endeavoring to save some useless trifles, and in the meanwhile suffer the most precious and valuable things to be lost. It is just such a piece of folly for a man to spend all his lifetime about money, meat, drink, and clothing, and in the meanwhile take no care of himself or his everlasting welfare, but suffers his soul to run to ruin while he is busy about worldly baubles. But yet the world is full of such that do thus. They postpone the affairs of their souls to all other affairs, and take less care about losing body and soul in hellfire than in saving that which cannot profit them; and although God himself calls upon them, and entreats them to save themselves, yet they will not hearken to him, but turn him off, telling him practically that when they have a more convenient season, they will afford time to hear what he has to say to them.

Against this foolish and wicked way of acting, we are warned in our text. The Psalmist, as you may observe, is here calling upon the children of Israel, God's professing people, to praise and worship him: "O come, let us sing unto the Lord: let us make a joyful noise unto the rock of our salvation" [Ps. 95:1]. This rock of their salvation, that is, their God, that has been such a bulwark and defense from the very beginning until now, and has taken a more peculiar care of us, more than any nation upon earth, has been a defense to us like an impregnable rock, who wonderfully brought us out of Egypt, and saved us from our cruel enemies with an outstretched arm, and miraculously led and preserved us in the wilderness: "Come, let us wor-

438

ship and bow down, and kneel before our maker" [v.6]—the maker of our bodies and souls, and our Maker as his peculiar people—"for he is our God; and we are the people of his pasture, and the sheep of his hand" [v.7]. God has acted the part of a shepherd to us all along: he defended us from the Egyptians, who were like ravening wolves; he fed us in the wilderness as his flocks; wherefore, let it not be now as it was then. You then ungratefully rejected and despised this, your God, and lightly esteemed this rock of your salvation, but let it not be so now.[1] "Today if ye will hear his voice, harden not your heart, as in the provocation, as in the day of temptation in the wilderness" [vv.7–8], in the words of the text.

Obs. 1. A duty exhorted to: hearing the voice of God; hearkening to his commands, his offers, his invitations, his promises, and his threatenings. Hear them not only with the ear, but with the heart; attend unto this voice, and act according to it.

[*Obs.*] 2. A sin dehorted from, or warned against: hardening of the heart, persisting still, obstinately, against God's commands and calls.

[*Obs.*] 3. The times wherein they are exhorted thus to do: today, immediately, and without delay. If you ever intend to hear the voice of God at all, hear him today and harden your hearts no longer. But why must we hearken to the voice?

(1) Because delaying longer will be a just provocation to God. "Harden not your hearts, as in the provocation, as your fathers did then, with whom I was so provoked that I sware in my wrath, that they should never enter into my rest" [Heb. 3:8–11].

(2) Because it is your highest interest. If you ever intend to hear his voice, hear it now: now is the time. The manner of expression seems to hold forth that it is now or never, of the same import as II Cor. 6:2, "Now is the accepted time; now is the day of salvation." From the words thus explained, we shall offer to your attention this doctrine:

DOCTRINE.

It is our great duty forthwith, without any delay, to hearken to God's voice.

There is no excuse for us to put it off one day. No circumstances, whatever, will be found sufficient to excuse this, for now is the time

---

1. The dramatically literal identification of modern Christians with ancient Hebrews is an unusual device for JE, another indication of the experimental homiletics which are variously evident in these early sermons.

that God requires; now is the only time we are sure of, and now is the only accepted time. Here,

I. We shall show what is God's voice that we are to hearken to.

II. We shall show how very sinful it is to delay to hearken to it.

I. But the voice of God that we are forthwith to hearken to is fourfold.[2]

First. There is his creating voice; that is, the voice of God by the creatures. The whole creation of God preaches to us; its creatures declare to us his majesty, his wisdom and power, and mercy: Ps. 19:1–2,[4], "The heavens declare the glory of God; and the firmament showeth his handiwork. Day unto day uttereth speech, and night unto night showeth knowledge. Their line is gone out through all the earth, and their words to the end of the world." Job 12:7–8, "But ask now the beasts, and they shall teach thee; and the fowls of the air, and they shall tell thee: or speak to the earth, and it shall teach thee: and the fishes of the sea shall declare unto thee." [See also] Rom. 1:19–20. If we look to the heavens or the earth; or birds, beasts, or fishes; or plants and trees: if we do but take notice of it, they all declare to us that we ought to worship, to fear, to love and obey, the God that made all these things. The workmanship of God in our own bodies and souls proclaims aloud the same: all the creatures do declare the same thing.

Second. There is God's providential voice. The providence of God preaches aloud to us our duty, and warns us of sin and danger; God so orders all his dispensations towards us, that his voice may be heard in them, to which it behooves us to listen and hearken. There is a voice of God in mercies which aloud calls us to love and thankfulness to God; there is also the voice of God to be heard in judgment, evidently reproving and rebuking of us for our sins and misdeeds, and warning of us to flee from the wrath to come, and calling to us to return unto the Lord that he may have mercy on us, and to our God that he may abundantly pardon us.

We may also hear the voice of God in his providential dealing with others; by his providence in the world, in the overturnings and changes, and revolutions of nations. God may be seen, and his voice heard, by his judgments upon those that are round about us. We are called upon to learn righteousness, lest it should be our turn next;

2. The first and second subheads following were written in reverse order in the MS but were numbered to indicate the present order. Number two (in the present order) was renumbered at the time that number one was written.

by the death of others, whether by diseases or accidents, we are called upon to prepare for our last change, and many other instances of God's voice in his providence might be given.

Third. There is the voice of God in his Word: his voice to us in the Scriptures, and his voice by his ministers and ambassadors. There is God's thundering, terrible, awful voice of commands and dreadful threatenings in his holy law; and there is a sweet, gracious, and compassionate voice, calling and inviting of us to blessedness and most glorious benefits, making offers of his Son to be our Savior and Redeemer, making offers of his blood to cleanse us, of his righteousness to justify us, of his Spirit to sanctify us, and of his glory to glorify us. There is God's inviting voice, wherein he condescends to call and invite us to come to him that we may have life. There is his entreating voice, for God humbles himself even to entreat and urge and persuade, and use arguments with worms, to knock at their door till his head is wet with the dew, and his locks with the drops of the night; such a voice as that, Rev. 3:20, "Behold, I stand at the door, and knock: if any man hear my voice, and open the door, I will come in to him, and sup with him, and he with me." Such an expostulating voice as that, Hos. 11:8, "How shall I give thee up, Ephraim? How shall I deliver thee, Israel? How shall I make thee as Admah? How shall I set thee as Zeboim? Mine heart is turned within me, my repentings are kindled together." There is God's warning voice, whereby he graciously forewarns of evil, that we may shun and avoid it. And there is his directing voice, whereby he points out to us, as father to a child, the best way, the safe and sure road, and tells us how we may avoid dangers and enemies, and how we may find happiness. This voice is the voice of God, that we are forthwith to hearken to without any procrastination.

Fourth. There is God's voice by his Holy Spirit. God not only calls upon us by the external call of his Word, but likewise by the internal call of his Spirit. As the devil is continually plying of us by his temptations, the Holy Spirit is also frequently moving upon the heart, and making his gracious calls to us; which motions of his are frequently rejected by sinners, who grieve the Holy Ghost by hearkening rather unto the devil than to him.

II. We are come, in the second place, to consider how sinful it is, not immediately to hearken to this voice of God to us, but to put off and delay to hear him.

First. It is a most provoking kind of disobedience. What a provoking thing it is, when God himself commands, for man to delay to obey: when God says, "Now," for the sinner to say, "No, not now, but when I have a more convenient opportunity; when I have more leisure from other things, and when I find myself more disposed to it than I do now." How provoking is this; is not this enough to fetch fire from heaven? How provoking it is for the sinner, when God says, "Do this today, while it is called today," to delay for whole weeks and months; yea, year after year to do it, upon no other excuse but only the man, he is not disposed to obey God at this time, because he finds no inclination to set about the work that God commands so soon as he orders, and therefore God must wait till he finds a greater inclination to it.

Is not this enough to incense God's anger to a most vehement flame, and to cause it to burn to the lowest hell? Is not this enough to rouse God's justice, and draw down thunder and lightning upon the heads of such rebels? Especially considering that God has commanded so often and so positively, and has enforced his laws with so many promises and threats, and besides has been so gracious as to persuade, invite, and entreat in such a condescending manner, how provoking is this: where is a prince that will bear this in a subject? Where is a master that will bear this in a servant, when the master commands this to be done forthwith, for the servant to reply, "No, stay till I please"? How much more provoking is it to delay, from year to year, to do that which God commands to be done today, while it is called today.

What a provoking abuse is it of God's mercy, for sinners to take occasion from it to dare to go on in sin, which should allure ['em][3] to obedience; what base dealing is this with God, to disobey him the more and deal the worse by him, because he is merciful. For us to dishonor God the more, because he is good and gracious: that is doing what in us lies to render evil to God for his goodness to us. What greater ingratitude can there be? How provoking must such a presumption upon God's mercy needs be to him, to take encouragement from it still to continue in sin![4]

Second. There is great contempt cast upon God by thus putting off and delaying our duty. Hereby, God is put last and set in the lowest

3. MS: "is."

4. In a later version for repreaching, this paragraph was given a separate heading: "3. A great abuse of his patience and forbearance." Apparently the paragraph was to be read after the second subhead which follows here.

place, as if he was least to be regarded of anything: God's business must be done the last, as if it were no great matter whether it was ever done at all or no, as if other things were a great deal more to be regarded than him. This is the language of their practice: "God has his demands, it is true; he requires of us to do such and such things. The devil, and lusts, and the world have their demands, too, and God must stand by and wait till they are served first." As if God's turn did not come till the last, till all other things were served! Even sin and the devil must have their share before God has his. He himself must be served first, and then God: so the sinner that delays to do his duty places God in the lowest place; he puts the devil at God's right hand, and every filthy lust and nasty pleasure must be served before Him, and all the creatures must be served before their Creator. What contempt is this upon the Majesty of heaven and earth, the great and everlasting Jehovah, King of Kings and Lord of Lords, the blessed and only Potentate, who only hath immortality!

But such contempt as this, those that delay to hear God's voice do most certainly cast on God, for they delay to hearken to him upon no other account, but for the sake of their ease and pleasure, and sinful desires; and thereby they place Jehovah in the last and lowest place, lowest in their affections and last as to time, for they will give the world and their pleasure their youth and full strength, the bloom of their life, but God must be turned off with old age, with decrepit years, with a decayed mind and body. God must even take up with old age, or else he must have none at all; or else he must have only a little time upon their deathbeds, when they are just taking their leave of the world, when their body begins to totter and is just upon falling: then they will begin, it may be, to think of God and have thoughts of obeying him, but not before.

Thus we have briefly shown what is intended by the voice of God: his fourfold voice; his creating, his providential, his verbal, and spiritual voice; and also, what a dreadful sin is the delaying to hear this voice of God. We now proceed to the Improvement.

APPLICATION.

The use we shall make of this is to endeavor to set home this duty of speedy and undelayed hearkening to the voice of God, and persuade everyone to it. We have already heard most powerful motives to it, drawn from the great and heinous sinfulness of the neglect.

What a provoking sin it is, and what is thereby cast upon God! We shall now, in the Application, endeavor if possible to exhort all to hear the voice of God today, while it is called today, that what we shall say may be more effectual to all of us.

We shall first show what are the common temptations by which the devil persuades men to put off and procrastinate [in] the work of their souls; and second, shall endeavor to offer some motive to a speedy and immediate hearkening to the voice of God. We shall first endeavor, God helping and assisting, to discover Satan's foundation, whereby he supports this sin of delaying and putting to another time, and then shall endeavor to move and persuade to the contrary.

I. But,

[*First.*] The first temptation, whereby Satan tempts men to this sin of putting off religion, is the proposal of ease: he tells them it will be most for their ease. He tells them, "If you set immediately about religion, you must betake yourself to a very difficult and laborious work; you must give up your ease and sloth, and must labor and run, and fight and wrestle, and must be continually laborious and active in the service of God. And is it not better for you to enjoy your ease a while longer than immediately to give it up, never to expect any more in this world? And is it not better to live at ease and be unconcerned, and to enjoy your liberty a while longer, than to go immediately to wrestle against flesh and blood, and resist your own natural inclinations? You may well enough have your ease, and sleep quietly in a whole skin yet for several years, and enjoy your liberty, and then there will be time enough, and enough to appease God's anger, and make your peace with him."

Second. The second temptation is pleasure. The wicked man hears such suggestions as these within himself: "If I resolve to go immediately about religion, I must depend [on] being at once deprived of all such and such pleasures and delights. I must never more gratify such and such a dear inclination; I must never more expect to enjoy that darling pleasure, or such a vice. Yea, I must take my leave of all such like satisfactions; I must always be forced to keep my mouth with bit and bridle, and I must make a covenant with my eyes, and must shut up my senses, and shut out pleasures, and jollity, and merriment. And why should I do this now, immediately, today? Why in such great haste? Is it not better to enjoy these pleasures a little longer; what need of being in a hurry about it? Why today? Will not tomorrow do as well? Will it [not] be in all respects as well if I begin the next year, or a five or six years hence? And by this means of putting of it off till two or three years hence, I shall gain a great deal: I shall get several years' pleasure by it, and is it not better to enjoy two or three years of pleasure, than to give up my pleasures now, today? If I begin the next year, or some years hence, I shall have time enough to prepare to die, and when I am prepared, I am prepared, and it is as well as if I had prepared never so soon."

Third. They are tempted to delay the work of religion, and hearkening to the voice of God, by a foolish expectation of long life. Although one in twenty don't live to old age, yet they foolishly expect it without any manner of reason in the world; but yet Satan will keep putting of it into their heads that they shall live long, and see many days. They see some live long, and say they to themselves, "Why may not I, as well as others?" They also see more that die in youth, but yet they say not to themselves, "Why may not I, as well as they?" But so Satan will have them believe, and so they would have it, and so they are tempted to leave their work, being unconcerned about it a long time. Satan promises time enough, and they are so foolish as to believe him.

Fourth. The fourth temptation, which moves them to put off soul concerns, is a presumption upon the mercy of God. They say to themselves, "God is very merciful and full of pity, and although I do delay religion, yet he will not refuse to show me mercy when I call upon him, and cry unto him in distress for fear of hell. I will make a confession, then, of all my sins, and God is easily moved to forgive and pardon. When I am old, there will be time enough to confess my sin and to turn to God; there will be time enough to move the pity of such a merciful God. His anger is easily appeased, and crying a few times, 'The Lord have mercy upon me!' is sufficient. He'll not cast into hell them that call upon him."

Thus they presume upon God's mercy, not considering that God is a consuming fire, as well as the Lord God, gracious and merciful; nor considering that he will not always strive with men, and has so declared; nor considering that God has declared that he will not be mocked, and that those that will not hear when he cries, so neither will he hear when they cry unto him: he will mock and deride them, poor deluded souls, thus to presume to God's mercy, which they so abuse. God will make such know; that it is a terrible thing to fall into the hands of the living God!

Thus we have briefly shown how miserable men are tempted to

delay, and procrastinate their duty of hearkening to the voice of God. By these voices it is, the poor sinners are baited to hell: thus they are allured on, from step to step, till they are surprised with the flames of hell. Some are tempted to delay only a little while, perhaps a few months; others intend to wait some years first, perhaps till such a thing is done, till they are settled in the world. They hope sometime or other for a more convenient opportunity, when they have less business upon their hands; now they have other business to mind; they have other things to take care of; they can't spare time for religion. Some intend to put off till they are old, others till they lie upon a bed of sickness, and expect to die and leave the world.

Young persons are tempted to put off till they are middle-aged because they think they have time enough before them, and there is no need of being in a hurry. This is their time of pleasure, and they are resolved never to throw away the best of their time upon religion. Middle-aged persons are tempted to put off till they are old, for they think it will not be long past[5] now, and when old age comes they shall have nothing else to do but to be religious, and the old age is good for nothing else but to be religious in. When old age comes, then they [find] some are so hardened, so dreadfully and desperately hardened, that there is no thought of another world moves them at all. Others put off this work till their deathbed; others are tempted to despair. And so the old serpent, by one contrivance or other, gets almost all mankind into his possession.

II. We are come to offer some motives, to persuade to immediate setting about religion and the duties of it, and to dissuade from procrastination; which, if duly considered, will be sufficient entirely to overthrow all the temptations of Satan against it.

First. Consider, the longer you delay, the more you will be hardened in sin. Sin gains strength every minute that it remains unforsaken and unrepented of; it cleaves faster and faster into the soul; the lusts are continually renewing and redoubling their strength. When man first comes into the world, his corruptions are weak and tender, like young whelps, but the longer they are suffered to continue, the more they become like old lions, till there is no encountering of them.

Man, when he first comes into the world, is like a young twig, easily bent; but the longer you suffer yourself to grow at random, the more you will be like an inflexible tree: your heart hardens so fast, that

5. Conjectural reading.

you will find the work of religion much more difficult the longer delayed. It will never be so easy as it is now with you. If your heart is so hard now, as that you dare to put off religion so long, when that time comes it will be so much harder that you will dare to put it off yet longer. And so your heart will grow harder and harder; for all the while you delay, the devil is very busy in strengthening his interest, and contriving how to fortify against the time comes. So that 'tis the greatest folly imaginable so to procrastinate, because the work grows continually more and more difficult.

Second. The longer you delay and put off religion, the more bitter will be your repentance when the time comes. You keep continually making work for repentance; thus, old converts—those few that they are—find most bitter work on't, to what young persons do, and sometimes they don't get over it till death, but hang down their heads like a bulrush all their days. Dreadful is the load of their sin when they come to feel the weight of it, when all their sins are set in order before them.

Third. The longer religion is delayed, the less progress will you have opportunity to make. If you set out early, you may make a glorious progress in your Christian course; you may flourish like a palm tree in the courtyards of God, but those that begin late are like to make but little progress, and to do but little good. If you ever intend to be religious, it is certainly your wisest and best way to be as religious as you can; if you take heaven for your happiness, it is the best way to obtain as much of this happiness as is possibly attainable.

Fourth. The longer you delay, the less assurance and spiritual comfort it is like you will have. The most assured Christians are commonly those that turned to God in their youth; they find, as it were, a heaven upon earth. They have the pleasure of thinking that they, for their parts, have given God the best of their days, their youth, their strength, the bloom of their life, and have for God's sake resisted the temptations of youth, and those violent lusts and temptations which are most powerful then, of any time. This is an acceptable sacrifice to God, and he graciously rewards it with abundance of joy and comfort, and much assurance—which late converts seldom attain to, but rather travail all their lives' time with bitter reflections on their having given the best of their days to the devil.

Fifth. This delaying to hear God's voice is so provoking a sin, that there is great danger of God's being provoked by it to give them up, and to strive no more with them. God's Spirit shall not always strive with men: God will not be mocked. It is very provoking when God commands a man to do such a thing now, for him to defer and delay it for the sake of his ease and pleasure; God may well be provoked to swear in his wrath that those that do thus shall never enter into his rest, and sometimes is provoked to give them up to the devil, whom they so industriously serve, whose service they chose before his. He bids them go to the gods whom they have served: let them deliver them. He resolves that he will not, and he gives them over to judicial hardness of heart, and never more knocks at the door of their heart by his Holy Spirit, but lets the devil have uninterrupted possession.

Sixth. If you put off religion, intending to set about it at a more convenient opportunity, there is great danger of your mind's changing before that time comes. How very frequently is it thus! How many at first think they will only defer religion a little while, [but] afterwards put it off farther still, and when the time comes they had picked upon, they put it off a little longer still, till the devil has got them. There is greater danger of your so doing; thousands—yea, doubtless millions—of souls have thus been lost.

Seventh. Consider the great uncertainty of life: what assurance have you that you shall live till that time comes in which you propose to begin to be religious? Have you made an agreement with death, or a covenant with the grave, or have God and you made a bargain that he shall not cut you down before such a time? Don't you believe that multitudes in the world die every day, that intended as you do, before the time they proposed comes: don't you believe that hundreds of thousands are now in hell that were as full of good intentions as you are? What assurance have you, that you shall live five or six years longer? Supposing death should come by some disease and tumble you into your grave, or some accident should suddenly throw you out of the world: what a miserable condition you would be in! Where, then, would be your spider's web of projections and fair intentions; what, then, would become of your hopes of long life?

Eighth. Consider the sad instances you have seen in others. You may safely conclude that there is hardly anyone, whatever, but what intends sometime or other [to] become religious; but what becomes of all their intentions? How many have you reason to fear for: all that die in sin and are damned forever. How [many] middle-aged and old sinners are there, which are yet as unconcerned as when they were young? Wherefore, be forewarned immediately to flee from the wrath to come, for now is the accepted time: now is the day of salvation.

Appendix to Ps. 95:7–8

This is in contradistinction, both to that time that is past—and so the sense is, though in times past [you] have not hearkened to God's voice, as when you provoked God in the wilderness and hardened your hearts there, and have for a long time refused to yield. Yet even to this day, after so long a time, God is willing to accept you and to admit you into his rest, which your fathers fell short of. It seems to be interpreted by the Apostle: Heb. 4:7, "Again, he limiteth a certain day, saying in David, Today, after so long a time, if ye will hear his voice, harden not your hearts"—Or with respect to that which is to come, and then the sense is that we ought to hear his voice without delay.[1]

* * *

Eighth.[2] Let us consider the awful instances of our frailty, the uncertainty of life that we have seen, and especially, those that God has lately given us by the removal of two of the members of the college, in the bloom of their [life], soon one after another; and by bringing another to the very gates of death, if yet alive, who had as many reasons for depending on a long life as, perhaps, any in this congregation. And, perhaps, whatever we can say as flattering ourselves that we shall have a longer time and space to repent in, they could say a few days ago; but yet, they are gone, and the strength and skill of man could not prevent it.[3]

Herein is the misery of man: that, however awful instances are given of this nature, and warnings by the death of others, they will flatter themselves that none can say that they shall die before they are old, and therefore flatter themselves till they are sure of it, and

---

1. This passage, on the recto of the inserted leaf, is probably to be added to a paragraph in the textual exegesis, possibly the third observation, although there is no key sign.

2. This head, on the verso of the inserted leaf, is a second version of the eighth consideration under the Application.

3. Neither the New Haven town records nor those of Yale College mention a single fatal accident or epidemic involving two or more Yale undergraduates in the spring of 1726, the most probable date of this addition.

they see death approaching them and feel that he [is] begging to lay hold on them, when it is generally too late.

Let us, therefore, hear God's voice this day and not harden our hearts before we hear his terrible voice summoning us out of the world, or that midnight cry. His voice now to us indeed is terrible, but if we hear it, 'twill prove merciful; then, if we harden our hearts till that time, 'twill be terrible, and to us only miserable and dreadful. Now 'tis corrective; then, 'twill be only penal. Today, while it is called today, let us heed God's voice, for the time is coming—how soon, we know not when: it may be today, even today—without farther delay, you must depart out of this world.

CHRISTIAN SAFETY

THIS systematic exposition of that which, Edwards admits, can be "fully understood only by those who have it," is distinctly reminiscent of "Christian Happiness." Both sermons attempt fairly precise definitions of uncommon states of mind or rare dimensions of experience. The neat, carefully elaborated structure of definition in "Christian Safety" is indicative of an essentially rationalistic bias at this time in Edwards' homiletical approach: never mechanical, but pedagogically intrepid in persistently defining a most elusive exultation in the plainest idiom and within a highly analytic structure. The seven subheads under the affirmative proof of the first proposition under the Doctrine, culminating in a summary of the argument in the seventh subhead, present the most impressive illustration of this argumentative strategy. While the style is remarkably free of rhetorical weapons such as imagery and metaphor (excepting of course those in biblical quotations), there is yet a remarkable quality, a referential specificity respecting an entire tradition of homiletics, to be observed throughout the sermon. It is as if Edwards knew his auditory to be familiar with the entire argument and its conventional embellishments, and wished not so much to provide a new argument—least of all a new series of potentially distracting homiletical embellishments—as to indicate the underlying rationale, the bone structure of the orthodoxy.

Such an essential discussion seems to have been well received; at least Edwards found it useful, for he repreached the sermon subsequently on at least three occasions, at Bolton, Glastonbury, and Northampton. Although the sermon was revised with some care on one occasion (see footnotes to the text), the most interesting revision may have occurred during the sermon's composition. Edwards seems to have begun the first draft of the Application with a meditation upon God's mercy and goodness but soon decided that a direct address to the people was more appropriate at this point. He consequently struck out what he had written and eventually completed the sermon with only two exhortations, a rather underdeveloped Application for a regular sermon. However, if it is assumed that the sermon was finally devised to function as a lecture, with its characteristic brief Application, the assumption is substantiated by the doctrinal exposition of the sermon which from the start is relatively analytical and formally didactic. Certainly the sermon has many of the traits of the lecture and may have functioned as one, albeit one with a strong hortatory element.

Within the sermon, and in some respects buried, is the crux of trust in God as defined by Edwards: "we fly from [God] as we would from a mortal enemy . . . till he discovers his excellency and loveliness to us, and powerfully changes us and causes us to love him" (p. 456). This experiential, aesthetic paradigm suggests the essential Edwards of the New York pastorate; it was peculiarly a time of spiritual adventure for him, a time of the romance of the spirit.

* * *

The octavo quire of this sermon's manuscript booklet is neat and ostensibly conventional: no appended leaves or dismembered parts. However, the changes in ink and some strategic keying signs, not to mention one rather large blank space near the beginning, indicate more problems with composing in a pre-stitched booklet of eight infolded leaves. Again Edwards clearly attempted to block out at least parts of the sermon, leaving what he took to be appropriate spaces for development. In some places he left too much, as is indicated by a blank or by his inability to fill up the space until further development was made in conjunction with repreaching years later, and in some places the writing is squeezed, indicating that he had left too little. But at the beginning of the Application a combination of factors stemming from his effort to block out the text caused considerable difficulty when he altered the plan and proportions of the Application after having begun composition under more than one heading. The complex details of his predicament are explained below in the textual notes. Edwards clearly wished to save time by not making more than one complete draft of his sermon, but his early attempts to block out the text and then compose heads out of their formal sequence proved troublesome when conjoined with an inflexible booklet.

CHRISTIAN SAFETY

PROVERBS 29:25.

But whoso putteth his trust in the Lord shall be safe.

G OD is the chief, yea, the all and only good to the godly; he is all in all to them; he is all their good, and their only defense from evil. He is called in Scripture by the names of all those things from which we either receive good, or are defended from evil: he is frequently called the father, the guide, the friend, the savior, the redeemer, the light, the life, the portion and inheritance, the shield and buckler, the strong tower and hiding place, of those that are his.

And who are those that are his, but those that trust in him? There wants nothing to make a man one of His, but his being willing. It is said in our text that those that trust in God are safe, and it is said in the next chapter, at the fifth verse, to the same purpose: he is a shield to them that put their trust in him; and, in many other places to the same purpose, he is called their refuge in time of trouble, a strong rock, and a wall of fire round about them that fear him.

In the words, observe: first, the subject spoken of, and that is he that puts his trust in the Lord. Second, what is asserted of him, that he shall be safe; [and] third, the universality of it: "whoso putteth his trust in the Lord," however mean and low their state in this world. The poorest beggar that trusts in God, He will be his safeguard and will take him into his gracious protection.[1]

---

1. At the end of this sentence, JE added an amplification in a later ink, probably for the Glastonbury repreaching: "or even those that have been the greatest sinners, God's mercy and grace being unbounded through Christ." And after a blank space of about five lines: "Though they ben't safe from those things that are in themselves evil, yet they are safe from the evil of those things." (The two are apparently separate statements.)

DOCTRINE.

They are safe that trust in God.

I. What the trusting in God here spoken of is.
II. That they are safe that so trust in him.
III. Give the reasons of the doctrine.

I. What is trust in God? It is indeed difficult for those to be made to understand what it is, that have never experienced it. There is that sweet repose and rest in it that cannot be expressed, and is fully understood only by those who have it;[2] but yet, everyone may be made to understand so much of it as to know whether or no he has it, and so may know whether he is safe or no. For our doctrine is reciprocal: as all that trust in God are safe, so none are safe, but they that trust in God, but are in a dreadful, dangerous condition, continually exposed to ruin on all sides, without anything to safeguard them.

Wherefore, that we may not be mistaken in the nature of trust in God, and so be mistaken about our own safety, I shall show, first, what this trust is not; second, what it is.

First. Negatively:

[1.] It is not barely a desiring that God would deliver us from evil, and bestow good things upon us. A man may wish that God would defend him from misery and make him happy, that yet dare not trust himself with Him, but must have something else to depend upon. They don't care to trust in such a defense as God; they don't care to leave themselves entirely in his hands, but must have some other fortress of their own building. Beside the fountain of living waters, they will have a cistern of their own building. The children of Judah, when the Chaldeans came against Jerusalem; they doubtless wished that God would deliver them, but yet they would not trust him, but would have the king of Egypt, too, if God should fail.

2. Nor is barely a hoping that God will [bestow] blessing and salvation upon them [sufficient]. There is a hoping in God that is false, and the hope of a hypocrite that will come to nothing when God takes away his soul; and there is a sort of hope in God that all men have: that is, they hope when they die that God will receive them to happiness; neither can this be said to be a trusting in him, for at this rate

2. Originally, "have it" was "experience it," but JE revised the phrase during composition of the sermon. Later, the statement was again revised for a subsequent preaching thus: ". . . is fully understood any other way but by the teachings of God's spirit."

the wickedest man upon earth would trust in God, and be safe and yet continue wicked.

Second. But affirmatively, there must be these following things in order to a right trust in God:

1. There must [be] a lively sense of our need of him, and the insufficiency of all other confidences. If we see not our great and perishing need of help and relief, we shall never come to God for relief, because we shall think we can do without him; and except we see that nothing else is sufficient to afford us help but God alone, we neglect to come to God, and seek something else [in which] to put our confidence. Such is man's natural enmity against God, that he had rather trust in anything in the world, than God.

2. There must be a firm belief of his all-sufficiency. After we have seen our need and necessity, that we are poor, wretched, blind, and naked, and stand in great need of help, the next thing is to see where the help is to be had: we must see who is able to help us, before we shall come to him for help. After we have seen our own insufficiency, and the insufficiency of everything else but God; after we have seen that there is nothing else to take hold of, but we must take hold on God or perish, then we must see God's all-sufficiency, and that there is enough in him for us. We must believe his almighty power, that he is able to do everything for us that we need to have done.

3. There must be a firm belief of God's merciful nature, and that he is willing to help us and do for us: a trusting in God is a trusting in his mercy and goodness. Many are kept from trusting in God, because they think they have committed so much sin that there is not mercy in God enough for them. He therefore must be sensible, that there is mercy enough, as well as power enough, [to] save the most vile returning sinner.

4. A firm belief of God's truth and faithfulness to his promises: there is no trusting in God without a firm belief of the Word of God, and the revelation he has made concerning himself, especially his gracious promises. As men will not trust men, except they think them faithful to their trusts, so they will never trust God till he sees His faithfulness. It is a contradiction to suppose that a man can quietly and sweetly commit himself, soul and body, forever into His hands, when he at the same time questions whether He will be true to his trust.

5. A love to God: there is no such thing as trusting in God, as long as we are enemies to him and hate him; it is not possible we should

come to God, and sweetly repose our souls upon him, as long as we have an aversion and antipathy to him, as we all naturally [do]. As soon as we come into this world, and look behind us upon him that has just made us, we fly from him as we would from a mortal enemy, and instead of trusting in him continue to run with all our might from him, till he discovers his excellency and loveliness to us, and powerfully changes us and causes us to love him: then we shall venture quietly to rely upon him, and rest in him.

6. A hope in him, that he will bestow his mercy on us: neither can we be said to trust in God, except we hope that he will bestow upon us what we trust in him for. How can we trust in God for that we don't believe, nor hope that he will ever bestow upon us what we trust in him for? Therefore, when once we are come to this hope, arising from this belief of, and love to God, there remains nothing but to [trust in him].[3]

7. A rest and satisfaction in the soul, arising from such a belief of, love to, and hope in God. The sight of his great necessity and danger makes him restless and uneasy: when he sees danger all around him, and destruction every minute ready to take hold of him, and sees nothing that he can trust to, he must needs be very restless and in a very uneasy state. But, when he sees a God that can save him, and stands ready, and is very willing to do it, and besides that has given his word and oath that he will do it, if he will depend upon Him; when he sees that God is excellent and lovely, and worthy to be trusted and depended on: he then hopes in God, and places his dependence there, and so no more fears those evils that he was in danger of before. There follows a rest, satisfaction, and repose in the soul, relying upon God; this rest in God, and satisfaction from believing in him, loving of him, and hoping in him, is that trust that we speak of.

II. All those that thus trust in God are safe. We shall show, first, what they are safe from; second, how they are safe.

[*First.* What they are safe from.]

1. They are safe with respect to temporal evils. Their faith and trust lifts them so high that they are above clouds, storms, and tempests; worldly afflictions do often happen to them, but the evil of them don't befall them. They may be exposed to difficulties, losses, and troubles, but he is not properly in danger of them, except as [he]

---

3. This sentence was left incomplete and is followed by a blank space sufficient to hold at least two lines of writing.

may be said to be in danger of that which can't do him any hurt: a true Christian may perhaps be exposed to be burnt at the stake, but not to be in danger of it, except it is proper to say that he is "in danger" of being crowned with a crown of glory. Let sickness or health, poverty or riches, honor [or] dishonor, wars, famine, or pestilence, or whatever will, come; he that trusts in God is safe.

2. They are safe from death. Those that are in Christ, are as truly safe from death as those that are with him in glory, because they are safe from any hurt that death can do them. Death is turned into a blessing, and there is a great deal of mercy showed in the death of a saint: He doth thereby graciously and kindly receive them to happiness. God stands by his dying children, and while their bodies are languishing, he is the physician of their souls; his angels guard them, and are ready to receive their departing spirits.

3. They are safe from the devil. While they trust in God, they need not fear the devil; he is full of spite and malice against them, but he cannot hurt them. The devil knows this: that if once they come to place their confidence in God, they are out of his reach, and this makes him so violent to hinder men from it. He knows that when God has taken them into His protection, they are not for him; he has no hopes of getting them: the devil, with all his army, with all the powers of hell conjoined, can't come at them[4] with all their rage and fury, and it will not be long before God will give them a glorious triumph over them.

4. They are safe from hell. As the danger of hell is a danger that is above all others to be dreaded, because nothing else that we can be in danger of is comparable [to] it, no other misery but what is as nothing to it; so safety from it is desirable above all safeties. Now, there is nothing else whereby a man can be safe from hell, but trusting in God.[5]

Second. How are they safe? I answer, because nothing can hurt

---

4. MS: "him."

5. This head was amplified for a later preaching through the following addition in a space originally left blank:

> Other persons, in all their occasions through the whole course of their lives, whether they labor or rest, whether they rejoice or are in heaviness, are in continual danger of being swallowed up in this dreadful pit from whence there is no return; but the souls of those that put their trust in God are in his hands, and none can pluck them thence. If believers in him are damned, it must be because there is someone stronger than the Almighty, so as to rend them from the arms of his mercy.

them. I Pet. 3:13, "Who is he that will harm you, if ye be followers of that which is good?" There is nothing that can do them any harm; wicked men, do what they will, cannot do them any hurt. Wicked men often are spiteful, malicious; envying and hating the godly, [they] exercise all their wit and power against them, but it is to no purpose. They trust in God; God is on their side. What can a wicked man do [to] him whom God defends and fights for? This discouraged the proud Egyptians when pursuing after Israel through the Red Sea, Ex. 14:25, "The Egyptians said, Let us flee from the face of Israel; for the Lord fighteth for them against the Egyptians."

Nero and Diocletian, and other persecutors, did the Christians no real hurt when they ordered them to be burnt; neither could they hurt them with all their power, though they were very powerful emperors, but the Christians would sometimes thank them for their sentence against them.[6]

The sting of death is taken away, and the poison of afflictions: all these things are made harmless, yea, profitable and gainful, to him that trusts in God. These are poisonous serpents in themselves, but God takes away their poison. That prophecy in Is. 11:6–9 is fulfilled upon all true Christians:

> The wolf also shall dwell with the lamb, and the leopard shall lie down with the kid; the calf and the young lion and the fatling together; and a little child shall lead them. And the cow and the bear shall feed; their young ones shall lie down together; and the lion shall eat straw like the ox. And the sucking child shall play on the hole of the asp, and the weaned child shall put his hand on the cockatrice' den. They shall not hurt nor destroy in all my holy mountain: for the earth shall be full of the knowledge of the Lord, as the waters cover the sea.

The mystical sense of which prophecy is, that all these things that are hurtful in themselves shall become harmless to the godly. As also is that promise, partly accomplished upon every true believer: Mark 16:18, "And they shall take up serpents; and if they drink any deadly thing, it shall not hurt them." Satan cannot hurt them; all the powers

---

6. Nero and Diocletian were the first and last instigators of the ten major Roman persecutions of the Christians over a span of about two hundred forty years. This passage probably refers more specifically to the martyrdom of Romanus under the Diocletian persecution. See Foxe's *Acts and Monuments*.

of darkness, with all their spite and malice, can do them no harm, and the flames of hell cannot reach them.

III. Now follow the reasons of the doctrine.

First. Because none are strong enough to encounter that God that protects them. All those that fly to God for refuge, he will protect; and if God protects them, it is to no purpose for all the world to endeavor to hurt them. That God is their shield, buckler, and high tower, before whom all the world is as nothing.

If he wills that a man shall be happy, all the world can't make him unhappy; Job 34:29, "When he giveth quietness, who can make trouble?"

Those that trust in God are his favorites, his dear ones. Devils, the prince of devils, and wicked men, although kings and emperors, would fight against Jehovah, the Almighty God, to as much purpose as they endeavor to hurt those that trust in him.

Second. Jesus Christ has overcome all their enemies. He has overcome this world, as he tells us, John 16:33, "In the world ye shall have tribulation; but be of good cheer, I have overcome the world." Christ has overcome the afflictions of this world; he met with abundance of them, but he went through them all and overcame them. He has overcome the pomps and glories of this world: when the devil carried him to an exceeding high mountain, and made a pompous [show] of all the kingdoms of the world, he rejected and despised them.

He has overcome the devil; he has bruised his head and given him his mortal wound, Col. 2:15, "And having spoiled principalities and powers, he made a show of them openly, triumphing over them in it."

Third. Their happiness is of such a nature, as nothing can deprive them of. It is not a carnal, earthly, and worldly happiness, that is thrown down with every breath of wind, but is a spiritual happiness which is stable as a rock, and can be no more moved by storms and tempests than a mountain.

"Fear not," says Christ, "those that kill the body, and after that have no more that they can do."[7] They may cut and mangle the body as much as they please; they cannot deprive of peace of conscience, and joy in the Holy Ghost. Some of the martyrs used to be cheerful while

---

7. Matt. 10:28 is JE's source, though his language is inexact and this passage functions not so much as a substantive quotation as it does a dramatic representation.

their flesh and blood was frying in the fire, and in despite of the malice of the persecutors: yea, a man would be happy in hell-flames, if he enjoyed communion with God there. For these reasons, he is always safe that puts his trust in God.

IMPROVEMENT.

[I.] *Exh.* To all, to put their trust in God.[8] Certainly, it is very desirable to be safe and out of danger. Now, those that trust in God, as you have heard, are safe with respect to temporal evils, safe with respect to death, the malice of the devil, and hell-torments. Wicked men know they are not safe with respect to these things, and this makes [them] always afraid. They are so fearful and pusillanimous, that they flee when no man pursues (Prov. 28:1). They are, all their lives-time, subject to bondage by fears of death, except they are so accustomed unto presumptuous sinning that they are come to a beastly thoughtlessness, or rather the stupidity of stones: for the ox knows his owner, and the ass his master's crib; the swallow knows the time of her coming, and of her going to avoid the winter; and the ant provides in summer, and lays up in harvest.[9]

But most wicked men, that have heard of hell, have those internal uneasinesses, arising from the thought of their unsafeness, that a wise man would not endure upon any worldly consideration, although they [don't] dare manifest it outwardly. For Solomon tells us, in Prov. 14:9, "the fools mock at sin"; that is, as if they did not regard, and never

8. In the MS, this head actually begins on the third page of the Improvement. JE originally numbered for two heads at the start of the Improvement but rejected his first effort at an opening head (eleven lines) on the first page; he then left the second page blank and began writing again after drawing a heavy line at the top of the third page. He wrote a little more than two pages until he apparently ran up against a head written previously (the second exhortation), at which time he turned back and continued on the blank second page. Thus, the two exhortations which now compose the Improvement were originally intended to follow two earlier heads—inferences or uses of information—the first of which was rejected and the second of which was never written.

When the sermon was revised for repreaching, four brief passages were interpolated at separate points near the beginning of the Improvement, the first of which gives the sense of what JE had originally attempted to establish at the outset of the Improvement: "Hence we learn that 'tis our fault alone that we are in danger of misery. There is no need of it: there is a refuge, the gates of which stand open to us, and we may fly to it, if we please, and be safe. If we are lost, therefore, it will be because we are, by just interpretation, lovers of death."

9. All of these gnomic expressions are drawn from the Scripture, from Is. 1:3, Jer. 8:7, and Prov. 6:6–8, respectively.

felt any twinges of conscience for, the committing of it; yet in the next verse, he says that the heart knows his own bitterness. The other men cannot perceive it, yet he himself feels it; and, in the thirteenth verse, that "in laughter the heart is sorrowful, and the end of that mirth is heaviness."

They that don't trust in God, when afflictions come, they have nowhere to go, must stand and bear them. Neither have wicked men such abundance of patience that they can stand quietly and bear the brunt of troubles, disappointments, and losses, without any remedy: they have neither any refuge or defense to fly to from afflictions, nor patience to bear them. They are in a miserable condition, for they have nothing to ease them, or defend them; they can't comfort themselves and say, "those afflictions are from a father," for they are inflicted by him whom they have made their dreadful enemy, and is angry with them every day; Ps. 7:11, "God is angry with the wicked every day." They can't say, to comfort themselves, that "those things shall surely work together for my good," for there is no such promise to any but those that love God.

It is said, Ps. 112:7, that "the godly man shall not be afraid of evil tidings." His heart is fixed, trusting in God; if he hears news of wars, or pestilence, or anything else whereby his life is in danger, he shall not be afraid: "Let it come, if it will. 'Tis of my Father's ordering, and I know he loves me [as] his child, and will never do anything to me but out of love."

Now, such evil tidings put the wicked into a terrible consternation. They are dreadfully frightened at the sight of death upon his pale horse, because they know hell comes behind him (Rev. 6:8).

The most bold and daring of sinners are the worst cowards upon a deathbed. How do they fear and tremble; how do they shrink back; how do their proud hearts tremble at the sight of his frightful face: when those that they used to laugh at and ridicule as strict and precise, that dared [not] swear, or say any[thing], and dare [not behave] so courageously as they used [to], yet can meet death as bold as lions, because they know they are safe, and nothing can hurt them because they trust in God, who, they know, is able to keep that which they have committed to him (II Tim. 1:12).

As they that trust in God are safe from everything, so those that don't trust in him are safe from nothing. If God be for us, who shall be against us; but if God be against us, who shall be for us? For be sure, everything else will be against us: angels will be against us; the godly will be against us. Although they endeavor to recall us, yet it will prove to our hardening, and so turn to our misery. Wicked men will be against us, for though they will seem to like us the better for being on their side, yet they are but the devil's instruments to entice us to come to hell with them.

The devil, we know, is against us, for he wants nothing but to have us with him in hell, that he may torment us. Worldly prosperities will be against [us], and afflictions will be against us; life will be against us, and death will be against us, and whom shall we go to [to] find that, that will be for us? Certainly, we shall be very unsafe in the midst of so many that are against us. There is hardly anything but may be a door to let the wicked man down into the pit.

How happy, then, is it for us, when God is on our side. Then all these things shall be for us: how happy it is to be so safe. Who would not get into that tower that will defend us from every evil thing? How well is it worth our while to trust in God, if that is all we need to do to be safe.

Wherefore, let us all be exhorted, immediately to put our confidence in him, to cast our burden upon [him], to commit our way unto him, to dedicate ourselves to him, and deliver up our bodies and souls into his hands; and so go fearless on through this world, neither fearing men, death, nor the devil. Ps. 11:1, "In the Lord put I my trust: how say ye to my soul, flee as a bird to her mountain?"

[II.] *Exh.* Particularly to the godly, to trust and rely on God. Surely God's own children may venture to trust in God! Labor to get an assurance of your being one of his adopted ones, one that he loves, and one that has a right to the privileges of the sons of God, and you need not be afraid to put your trust in him.

Whatever difficulties you may be under, whatever trials and afflictions, you may say, as Job did, "Though he slay me, yet will I trust in him." Let him do with me what he please; whatever afflictions he orders to me, I know I am his child, one of his family, and have an interest in his Son, and I will place my confidence in him, and let him do what he will with me.

Surely a child of God, one that Christ died for, one that God dearly loves, one to whom God has promised that all things shall surely work together for his good, may very safely do thus without any danger. God never yet failed any of his children that thus trusted in him. They that thus trusted in God have never yet found occasion to be ashamed because of their disappointments: Ps 37:5–7, "Commit thy way unto the Lord; trust also in him, and he shall bring it to pass. And he shall bring forth thy righteousness as the light, and thy judgment as the noonday. Rest in the Lord, and wait patiently; fret not thyself because of him who prospereth in his way, because of the man who bringeth wicked devices to pass;" Ps. 55:22, "Cast thy burden upon the Lord, and he shall sustain thee; he shall never suffer thy righteousness to be moved."

Surely you can believe God, when he so positively promises; for "God is not a man that he should lie, nor the son of man that he should repent: hath he said, and shall he not do it; or hath he spoken, and shall he not make it good?" [Num. 23:19].

Certainly, if you were fully resolved to trust in God, and to give yourself up entirely into his hands and let him do as he will, trusting in his mercy through his Son, Jesus Christ, who died for you; you need not to afflict yourself, but might lie down and sleep and awake, the Lord sustaining of you. You will not find yourself disappointed, but though sorrow continue for a night, yet joy would come in the morning.

A child of God may come with boldness up to the throne of grace, and say, "Lord, surely I am thy servant; I am thy servant. I am thy child; thou hast made a covenant with me and with my dear Savior for me. I am a member of thy Son and will trust in thee, whatsoever thou doest to me, whatever afflictions thou layest upon me."

Jonah, although he was in the fish's belly, and there was no manner of appearance of ever being delivered—for what hope can a man have of deliverance that is swallowed by a whale?—but yet he trusted in God: he prayed unto him, and looked towards his holy temple. The floods compassed him about, the billows and the waves passed over him; the waters compassed him about, even to the soul; the depths closed him about, the weeds were wrapped about his head; he went down to the bottoms of the mountains, the earth with her bars was about him: now, what hope could there be for such a man, in this condition? But yet, he says, "I will look again towards thy holy temple" (Jonah 2:4). And what was the effect of it? See the last verse, "And the Lord spake unto the fish, and it vomited up Jonah upon the dry land" [Jonah 2:10].

They that thus trust in God are certainly safe in whatever condition they are in: they are safe in affliction, and safe in prosperity. Jonah was as safe in the fish's belly, down under the bottoms of the mountains, as if he had been in a strong tower, for he trusted in God and he was in God's hand. God's mercy and love is a bulwark and defense, so strong that the forces of all the creation are not able to hurt us therein.

Whatever God doth to those who are his children, he doth as a father. It is all from love and tender affection; wherefore, if they meet with affliction, they ought patiently to receive it, considering that their Heavenly Father orders it out of love to them. And though they cannot see God's gracious design in it now, yet they will see hereafter, and will break forth into singing praises to God for his merciful inflicting of them.

If God gives them prosperity, they ought to receive it joyfully and gladly, as a gift of their kind Father, knowing that God sends it to them as children. Now, the wicked can't have this comfort in their outward good things, because they don't trust in God. The godly are nourished and provided for of God, as children are provided for by a father; but the wicked know not but that they are fed as beasts are fed, and fatted for the slaughter.

Wherefore, whatsoever your state and condition be, throw by all other confidences, and resolve to trust in God, and cast your whole burden upon him; for it is [good] for a man to hope, and quietly to wait, for the salvation of the Lord.

THE WAY OF HOLINESS

ANOTHER early effort in seminal definition, "The Way of Holiness" is much more a definition of holiness than an attempt to provide a "way" or practical guide to it. The prior existence of such a guide is established by mentioning the most relevant portions of the Scriptures, but Edwards eschews sustained analysis of them, even in the Application. Such an undertaking in practical theology would be beyond the scope of any one sermon, in any case, and would not be realized until many years later when, in 1738, Edwards composed the sermon series eventually published as *Charity and its Fruits* (1852). But in this sermon one encounters an exalted meditation upon the concept of existential holiness, culminating in a final evocation of the sanctified soul that seems remarkably sentimental, even self-indulgent, for Edwards.

That the sermon had intellectual importance for Edwards is indicated by the presence of its concluding paragraphs in the first, inaugural entry of what was to become his vast "Miscellanies." But probably before the sermon and certainly before the notebook entry was composed, Edwards entered in his "Diary" the following notation:

> [*Dec.* 22 [1722], *Saturday.* This day, revived by God's Holy Spirit; affected with the sense of the excellency of holiness; felt more exercise of love to Christ, than usual. Have, also, felt sensible repentance for sin, because it was committed against so merciful and good a God. (Dwight, *Life,* p. 76.)

The personal, spiritual importance of Edwards' preoccupation with holiness is embodied in this entry which was made near the probable time of the sermon's composition. That this moment, theologically rationalized in the sermon and distilled in the notebook entry, made a lasting impression upon Edwards is substantiated by a passage written years later in the "Personal Narrative":

> Holiness, as I then wrote down some of my contemplations on it, appeared to me to be of a sweet, pleasant, charming, serene,

calm nature. It seemed to me, it brought an inexpressible purity, brightness, peacefulness and ravishment to the soul: and that it made the soul like a field or garden of God, with all manner of pleasant flowers; that is all pleasant, delightful and undisturbed; enjoying a sweet calm, and the gently vivifying beams of the sun. The soul of a true Christian, as I then wrote [in] my meditations, appeared like such a little white flower as we see in the spring of the year; low and humble on the ground, opening its bosom to receive the pleasant beams of the sun's glory; rejoicing as it were, in a calm rapture; diffusing around a sweet fragrancy; standing peacefully and lovingly, in the midst of other flowers round about; all in like manner opening their bosoms to drink in the light of the sun.

There was no part of creature-holiness that I then, and at other times, had so great a sense of the loveliness of, as humility, brokenness of heart and poverty of spirit: and there was nothing that I had such a spirit to long for. My heart as it were panted after this, to lie low before God, and in the dust; that I might be nothing, and that God might be all; that I might become as a little child. (Hopkins, *Life*, pp. 29–30.)

"Diary," sermon, "Miscellanies" entry, and finally a generation later, "Personal Narrative" focus upon this brilliant moment of the New York period and its enduring impact. As the first and only public statement correlating directly with it, the sermon clearly presents matter of deep and lasting significance for an understanding of Edwards himself, not least of all in its imagery and tonality. In reading the sermon, one is privy to an experiential paradigm in its earliest full expression which was to remain a touchstone throughout Edwards' life.

For all the apparent personal significance of the sermon, however, it does not seem to have been repreached. This is unusual, particularly in the early years when Edwards did not have a large number of sermons to draw upon. Does this indicate that the sermon was not as well received by the first auditory as Edwards would have liked, or does it suggest that such passages as those which inspired him, or revealed the sources of his inspiration, were too intimate for him to air publicly in later years? The vision of cosmic order, the unification of power and reason, joy and goodness, of God, Christ, and the redeemed soul: all these affirmations of the ultimate oneness may have struck Edwards as something requiring more circumspect presentation in the years after his New York pastorate. In Northampton, of course, he was no longer preaching to an intense splinter group. Whatever the case, the sermon remains a vivid memorial of the New York period.

* * *

The eight-leaved octavo booklet of this sermon is fairly neat, with only a few rub-outs and deletions. The booklet does not show signs of later revision, or for that matter of much wear. The text, like many of those from this period, is meticulously elaborated through formal divisions, the utmost care being given to points of transition.

THE WAY OF HOLINESS

ISAIAH 35:8.

And an highway shall be there, and a way, and it shall be called the
way of holiness; the unclean shall not pass over it.

THIS book of Isaiah speaks so much of Christ, gives such a particular account of the birth, life, miracles and passion, and of the gospel state, that it has been called a fifth Gospel. In this chapter is contained a glorious prophecy of the evangelical state:

1. We have a description of the flourishing state of Christ's kingdom in the two first verses, in the conversion and enlightening of the heathen, here compared to a wilderness, and a desert, solitary place:

> The wilderness and the solitary place shall be glad for them; and the desert shall rejoice, and blossom as the rose. It shall blossom abundantly and rejoice, even with joy and singing; the glory of Lebanon shall be given unto it, the excellency of Carmel and Sharon, they shall see the glory of the Lord, and the excellency of our God.

2. The great privileges and precious advantages of the gospel, in the five following verses wherein the strength, the courage, the reward, the salvation, the light and understanding, comforts and joys, that are conferred thereby, are very aptly described and set forth:

> Strengthen ye the weak hands and confirm the feeble knees. Say to them that are of a fearful heart, Be strong, fear not; behold, your God will come with vengeance, even God with a recompence; he will come and save you. Then the eyes of the blind shall be opened, and the ears of the deaf shall be unstopped. Then shall the lame man leap as an hart, and the tongue of the dumb sing: for in the wilderness shall waters break out, and streams in the desert. And the parched ground shall become a pool, and the

thirsty land springs of water: in the habitation of dragons, where each lay, shall be grass with reeds and rushes.

3. The nature of the gospel, and way of salvation therein brought to light. First, the holy nature of it, in the eighth and ninth verses:

And an highway shall be there, and it shall be called the way of holiness; the unclean shall not pass over it, but it shall be for those: the wayfaring men, though fools, shall not err therein. No lion shall be there, nor any ravenous beast shall go up thereon, it shall not be found there; but the redeemed shall walk there.

Second, the joyful nature of it, "And the ransomed of the Lord shall return, and come to Zion with songs and everlasting joy upon their heads: they shall obtain joy and gladness, and sorrow and sighing shall flee away" [v.10].

Obs. 1. Observe in our text the subject spoken, that is, the way to salvation: "An highway shall be there, and a way." This highway is the common and only way to heaven, for the way to heaven is but one. There is none ever get to heaven except they walk in this way: some men don't get to heaven one way and others another, but it is one highway that is always traveled by those that obtain heaven.

It is the same narrow way that Christ tells us of. Some don't go to heaven in a broad way, and others in a narrow; some in an easy and others in a difficult way; some in a way of self-denial and mortification, and others in a way of enjoyment of their lusts and sinful pleasures; some up hill and others down: but the way to heaven is the same, and it is the highway here spoken of. There is only one highway, or common road, and no bypaths that some few go to heaven in, as exceptions from the rest.

If we seek never so diligently, we shall never find out an easier way to heaven than that which Christ has revealed to us. We cannot find a broader way, but if we go to heaven, the way is so narrow that we must rub hard to get along and press forward. The kingdom of heaven must suffer violence; it must be taken by force, or else it never will be taken at all. If we don't go by the footsteps of the flock, we shall never find the place where Christ feeds, and where he makes his flock to rest at noon.

It appears that the way here spoken of is the way of salvation, by the last verse of the chapter. When speaking of this way, it is said, "the ransomed of the Lord shall return and come to Zion," etc. "Zion" is the common appellation by which, in the Old Testament, the church both militant and triumphant is signified.

Obs. 2. In the words observe the holy nature of this way described: first, by the name by which it is called, "the way of holiness"; "and it shall be called the way of holiness." Secondly, the holiness of those that travel in it, and its purity from those that are unclean, or unholy; "the unclean shall not pass over it." No wicked person shall ever travel in this way of holiness. To the same purpose is the next verse, "No lion shall be there, nor any ravenous beast shall go up thereon, it shall not be found there." That is, none of the wicked men of this world, which are like lions or ravenous beasts more than like men: in their eager raging and lustful appetites and evil affections, or by their insatiable covetousness, are like hungry wolves, are violently set upon the world and will have it, whether by right or by wrong. Or make themselves like ravenous beasts by their proud, invidious, malicious dispositions, which is directly contrary to a Christian spirit and temper. They are more like wild beasts than Christians, that are wrongful and injurious, are all for themselves and the satisfying their own appetites, and care nothing for the welfare of others, their fellow-men that are of the same blood, make a god of their bellies, and therein resemble tigers and wolves.

"Now," says the Prophet, "none such shall go upon this highway to Zion; such unclean and ravenous beasts shall not be found there. No, but the redeemed shall walk there, and the ransomed of the Lord shall return and come to Zion." This way is a way of holiness and not to be defiled by wicked persons. That in Rev. 21:27 will serve well for an explication of these words: "And there shall in no wise enter into it anything that defileth, neither whatsoever worketh abomination or maketh a lie, but they which are written in the Lamb's book of life."

DOCTRINE.

Those only that are holy are in the way to heaven.

Many are not sensible enough of the necessity of holiness in order to salvation. Everyone hopes for heaven, but if everyone that hoped for heaven ever got there, heaven by this time would have been full of murderers, adulterers, common swearers, drunkards, thieves, robbers, and licentious debauchers. It would have been full of all manner of wickedness and wicked men, such as the earth abounds with at this day. There would have been those there that are no better than wild beasts, howling wolves, and poisonous serpents; yea, devils incarnate, as Judas was.

What a wretched place would the highest heavens have been by this time if it were so: that pure, undefiled, light and glorious place, the heavenly temple, would be as the temple of Jerusalem was in Christ's time, a den of thieves; and the royal palace of the Most High, the holy metropolis of the creation, would be turned into a mere hell. There would be no happiness there for those that are holy. What a horrible, dreadful confusion would there be if the glorious presence of God the Father; the glorified Lamb of God; and the Heavenly Dove, spirit of all grace and original of all holiness; the spotless, glorified saints; the holy angels; and wicked men, beasts and devils [were] all mixed up together!

Therefore, it behooves us all to be sensible of the necessity of holiness in order to salvation; of the necessity of real, hearty and sincere, inward and spiritual holiness, such as will stand by us forever and will not leave us at death, that sinners may not be so foolish as to entertain hopes of heaven, except they intend forthwith to set about repentance and reformation of heart and life. Wherefore, this is what we are now upon: to show the necessity of holiness, and this we shall do in these three things.

I. Show what holiness is.
II. That those that have it not are not in the way to heaven.
III. The reasons why it must needs be so.

I. What is holiness? I shall answer to this question in three things which fully comprehend the nature of holiness, which are not in themselves distinct as so many parts of holiness, but the same thing in three different lights, to give us the fuller understanding of it.

First. Holiness is a conformity of the heart and the life unto God. Whatever outward appearance men may make by their external actions, as if they were holy, yet if it proceeds not from a most inward, hearty and sincere holiness within, it is nothing. Amaziah did that which was right in the sight of the Lord, but not with a perfect heart; all that he did was not acceptable to God, who searcheth the hearts and trieth the reins of the children of men, and must be worshipped in spirit and in truth.[1]

And whatever holiness they may pretend to have in their hearts, whatever hypocritical pangs of affection they may have had, it is all to no purpose except it manifest itself in the holiness of their lives and conversations: Jas. 1:26–27, "If any man among you seem to be religious, and bridleth not his tongue but deceiveth his own heart, this man's religion is vain. Pure religion and undefiled before God and the Father is this, to visit the fatherless and widows in their affliction, and to keep himself unspotted from the world." And in the second chapter, eighteenth verse: "Yea, a man may say, Thou hast faith, and I have works: show me thy faith without thy works, and I will show thee my faith by my works." And in the nineteenth [and] twentieth verses, "Thou believest that there is one God; thou doest well: the devils also believe and tremble. But wilt thou know, O vain man, that faith without works is dead?" So that there must be a conformity of both heart and life to God, in order to true holiness.

Holiness is the image of God, his likeness, in him that is holy. By being conformed unto God is not meant a conformity to him in his eternity, or infinity, or infinite power. These are God's inimitable and incommunicable attributes; but a conformity to his will, whereby he wills things that are just, right, and truly excellent and lovely; whereby he wills real perfection, and goodness; and perfectly abhors everything that is really evil, unjust, and unreasonable. And it is not only a willing as God wills, but also a doing as he doth: in acting holily and justly and wisely and mercifully, like him. It must become natural thus to be, and thus to act; it must be the constant inclination and new nature of the soul, and then the man is holy, and not before.

Second. It is a conformity to Jesus Christ. Christ Jesus is perfectly conformed unto God, for he is God. He is his express image. Now Christ is nearer to us in some respects than God the Father, for he is our Mediator and is more immediately conversant with us; John 1:18, "No man hath seen God at any time; the only begotten Son, who is in the bosom of the Father, he hath declared him." Jesus Christ, he has been with us in the flesh and as one of us he appeared in the form of a servant, and we have seen his holiness brightly shining forth in all his actions. We have seen his holy life; we have a copy drawn, and an example set for us.

1. King Amaziah's career is discussed in II Kgs. 14, and the particular issue taken up by JE is alluded to in II Kgs. 14:3–4. This is not the priest Amaziah of Amos 7:10.

Now holiness is a conformity unto this copy: he that copies after Jesus Christ, after that copy which he has set us and which is delivered to us by the evangelists, is holy. He that diligently observes the life of Christ in the New Testament need not be at a loss to know what holiness is. Christ commands us to follow his example: Matt. 11:29, "Take my yoke upon you and learn of me, for I am meek and lowly in heart, and ye shall find rest unto your souls."

Have you ever read the four Gospels, and did you not observe in the life of Christ wonderful instances of humility, love to God, love to religion; wonderful instances of zeal for God's glory, steadfastness in resisting temptations, entire trust and reliance on God, strict adherence to all his commands; astonishing instances of condescension, humility, meekness, lowliness, love to men, love to his enemies, charity and patience? Why, this is holiness. When we imitate Christ in these things, then are we holy, and not till then.

Third. Holiness is a conformity to God's laws and commands. When all God's laws without exception are written in our hearts, then are we holy. If you can go along with David in Psalm 119, where he speaks of his love and delight in God's law, in your own experience; when a man feels in some good measure what David declares concerning himself towards the law of God, then may God's law be said to be written in his heart. By God's law I mean all his precepts and commands, especially as they are delivered to us in the gospel, which is the fulfillment of the law of God. If you feel Christ's Sermon upon the Mount engraven on the fleshly tables of your hearts, you are truly sanctified.

The new covenant is written in the hearts of those that are sanctified, of which the prophet Jeremiah speaks, 31:31,33, "Behold, the days come, saith the Lord, that I will make a new covenant with the house of Israel, and with the house of Judah. This shall be my covenant, that I will make with the house of Israel; after those days, saith the Lord, I will put my law in their inward parts, and write it in their hearts; and will be their God, and they shall be my people."

The commands and precepts which God has given us are all pure, perfect, and holy. They are the holiness of God in writing, and, when the soul is conformed to them, they have holiness of God upon their hearts; II Cor. 3:3, "Forasmuch as ye are manifestly declared to be the epistle of Christ ministered by us, written not with ink, but with the spirit of the living God; not in tables of stone, but in the fleshly tables of the heart." When the soul is molded and fashioned according to the image of God, the example of Christ, and the rules of the gospel, then it is holy, and not else.

II. Those that have not this holiness are not in the way to heaven. Those that are not thus conformed to God, to Christ, and God's commands, are not in the way to heaven and happiness; they are not traveling that road; the road they are in will never bring them there. Whatever hopes and expectations they may have, they will never reach heaven to eternity except they alter their course, turn about, and steer [towards] another point; for the way is a way of holiness, and the unclean shall not pass over it. Christ said that it was easier for a camel to go through the eye of a needle, than for a rich man to enter into heaven, but yet he left it absolutely possible with God that it might be; but he said positively and without exception that except a man be born again, he cannot see the kingdom of God. None but those that are holy are in the way to heaven, whatever profession they may make, whatever church they may be in: for in Christ Jesus neither circumcision availeth anything nor uncircumcision, but a new creature.

Whatever external acts of religion they may perform, however they may be constant attendants on the public [or] family worship, and live outwardly moral lives; yea, what is more, if they speak with the tongues of men and angels, though they could prophesy and understand all mysteries and all knowledge, and though they have faith that they can remove mountains; though they bestow all their goods to feed the poor, and though they give their very bodies to be burnt: yet if they have not charity or holiness—which is the same thing, for by charity is intended love to God as well as man—though they have and do all those things, yet they are nothing; they are as a sounding brass or a tinkling cymbal (see I Cor. 13). It is good that we should be thoroughly convinced of the most absolute and indispensable necessity of a real, spiritual, active and vital—yea, immortal—holiness.

III. We shall now, in the third place, give the reasons why none that are not holy can[2] be in the way to heaven, and why those who never are so can never obtain the happiness thereof.

First. 'Tis contrary to God's justice, to make a wicked man eternally happy. God is a God of infinite justice, and his justice (to speak after the manner of men) "obliges" him to punish sin eternally; sin must be punished, the sins of all men must be punished. If the sinner

2. MS: "cannot."

retains his sin, and it is not washed off by the blood of Christ, and he purified and sanctified and made holy, it must be punished upon him. If he is sanctified, his sin has been already punished in the passion of Christ, but if not, it still remains to be punished in his eternal ruin and misery; for God has said that he is a holy and jealous God, and will by no means clear the guilty. It is reckoned amongst the rest of God's attributes which he proclaims in Ex. 34:7 and Num. 14:18.

Second. 'Tis impossible by reason of God's holiness, that anything should be united to God and brought to the enjoyment of him which is not holy. Now is it possible that a God of infinite holiness, that is perfect and hates sin with perfect hatred, that is infinitely lovely and excellent, should embrace in his arms a filthy, abominable creature, a hideous, detestable monster, more hateful than a toad and more poisonous than a viper? But so hateful, base, and abominable is every unsanctified man, even the best hypocrite and most painted sepulchres of them all.

How impossible is it that this should be, that such loathsome beings, the picture of the devil, should be united to God: should be a member of Christ, a child of God, be made happy in the enjoyment of his love and the smiles of his countenance, should be in God and God in them? It is therefore as impossible for an unholy thing to be admitted unto the happiness of heaven as it is for God not to be, or be turned to nothing. For it is as impossible that God should love sin as it is for him to cease to be, and it is as impossible for him to love a wicked man that has not his sin purified, and it is as impossible for him to enjoy the happiness of heaven except God love him, for the happiness of heaven consists in the enjoyment of God's love.

Third. It would defile heaven and interrupt the happiness of the saints and angels. It would defile that holy place, the Holy of Holies, and would fright and terrify the sanctified spirits, and obstruct them in their delightful ecstasies of devotion, and [his] praise would quite confound the heavenly society. How would one unsanctified person interrupt their happiness, and fill those regions all over with the loathsome stench of his sin and filthiness!

Fourth. The nature of sin necessarily implies[3] misery. That soul that remains sinful must of a necessity of nature remain miserable, for it is impossible there should be any happiness where such a hateful

3. MS: "infers."

thing as sin reigns and bears rule. Sin is the most cruel tyrant that ever ruled, seeks nothing but the misery of his subjects; as in the very keeping [of] God's commands there is great reward, so in the very breaking of them there is great punishment.

Sin is a woeful confusion and dreadful disorder in the soul, whereby everything is put out of place, reason trampled under foot and passion advanced in the room of it, conscience dethroned and abominable lusts reigning. As long as it is so, there will unavoidably be a dreadful confusion and perturbation in the mind; the soul will be full of worry, perplexities, uneasinesses, storms and frights, and thus it must necessarily be to all eternity, except the Spirit of God puts all to rights. So that if it were possible that God should desire to make a wicked [man] happy while he is wicked, the nature of the thing would not allow of it, but it would be simply and absolutely impossible.

Thus I have given some reasons of the doctrine, why it must needs be that those that are not holy cannot be in the way to heaven. Many more reasons might be offered, which the time will not allow to take notice of at this time; but these alone would have been enough to certify us that none but those who are holy ever attain to a crown of glory, if God had not expressly said that without holiness no man should see the Lord.

Wherefore, the

APPLICATION.[4]

We shall apply this doctrine in three uses: first, of inference; second, of trial or self-examination; third, of exhortation.

I. [*Use*] *of Inf.* If it be so that none but those that are holy are in the way to heaven, how many poor creatures are there that think they are in the way to heaven who are not? There are many that think that they are undoubtedly in the way to heaven, and without question shall enter there at last, that have not the least grain of true holiness, that manifest none in their lives and conversations, of whom we may be certain that either they have no holiness at all, or that which they have is a dormant, inactive sort—which is in effect to be certain that there is none. There are a great many others that are not so distinctly and plainly perceived, that have nothing but what is external, the shell without the kernel. Vast multitudes are of these two kinds.

4. MS: "Application follows."

What a pitiable, miserable condition are they in: to step out of this world into an uncertain eternity, with an expectation of finding themselves exceeding happy and blessed in the highest heaven, and all at once find themselves deceived, and are undeceived, finding themselves sinking in the bottomless pit!

II. [*Use*] *of Trial.* If none are in the way to heaven but those that are holy, let us try and examine ourselves by this doctrine to see whereabouts we are, and see whether or no we are in the way to heaven. To know which way we are going, whether towards Canaan or Egypt, whether towards heaven or hell; for if we think ourselves in the road to heaven, and are going to the place of torment all the while, and continue deceived, without doubt fire and brimstone will undeceive us. If we find ourselves in the broad way to destruction, how dare we stir a step further? If we would know whether we are holy or no, let us try ourselves by these five following things:

First. Meditate on the holiness of God, and see if you cannot see a conformity, a *likeness* in your mind. There is no likeness or comparison in degree—we speak not of that—but yet there is a likeness in *nature* between God and the soul of the believer. The holy soul, when it thinks and meditates upon God's nature, finds a pleasure and delight, because there is an agreeableness in his new nature to the divine perfections. If those that think themselves in the way to heaven, that are unholy in the meantime in their hearts, would compare themselves and their nature to the holy nature of God, such a glorious light as the holiness of God would quickly discover their rottenness and unsoundness.

Second. See if you can see any resemblance in your life to the life of Christ. It is not supposed that ever any copy comes near to this original, nor ever will; but yet they may perceive whether the same spirit, the same temper and disposition, in a lesser degree be in them, that was manifested by the life and conversation of Jesus Christ.

Third. Is there an agreeableness between your souls and the Word of God? The Bible is the epistle of Christ that he has written to us; now, if the same epistle is also written in our hearts that is written in the Scriptures, it may be found out by comparing. Have you love to all God's commands and a respect to them in your actions? Is it your delight to obey and hearken to the will of God? Do you obey them of choice? Is it what you would choose to do if God had not threatened to punish the breach of them?

Fourth. Do you find by a comparison a likeness and agreeableness between your hearts and lives, and the hearts and lives of those holy men that we [are] assured were such by the Word of God? Do you walk with God as Enoch did, [or] distinguish yourselves by your piety in the midst of wicked examples as Noah did? And when you read the lives of Abraham, Isaac, Jacob, Moses, and the prophets, wherein holiness is drawn to the life, you may viewing so exact a picture discover whether you have not the root of the matter in you, though it be much obscurer in you than in them. When we read the Psalms of David, we may clearly see what David's holiness was by that spirit that is breathed there; when we read the Epistles of the apostles, we may know what is a truly evangelical spirit, and whether such a spirit reigns in our souls.

Fifth. Do you in a measure imitate the saints and angels in heaven? They spend their duration to the glory of God; they love him above all things, are delighted with the beauties of Jesus Christ, entirely love one another, and hate sin. And those that are holy on earth have also a resemblance and imitation of them: they are of an heavenly temper, of heavenly lives and conversations.

III. [*Use of*] *Exh.* Exhort all to holiness. You have heard what holiness is and of the necessity of it, the absolute necessity in order to escaping hell; what we must have or die forever, must be forever forsaken.[5] Now, nothing is so necessary to us as holiness; other things may be necessary to discover this life, and things that are necessary men will strive for with all their might, if there is a probability of obtaining of them. How much more is that to be sought after, without which we shall [fare] infinitely worse than die ten thousand deaths!

This is motive enough without any other; for what can be a greater motive than necessity? But besides that, if it were not necessary, the amiable and excellent nature of it is enough to make it worthy the most earnest seeking after.

Holiness is a most beautiful, lovely thing. Men are apt to drink in strange notions of holiness from their childhood, as if it were a melancholy, morose, sour, and unpleasant thing; but there is nothing in it but what is sweet and ravishingly lovely. 'Tis the highest beauty and amiableness, vastly above all other beauties; 'tis a divine beauty, makes the soul heavenly and far purer than anything here on earth—this world is like mire and filth and defilement [compared] to that soul which is sanctified—'tis of a sweet, lovely, delightful, serene, calm,

5. MS: "for."

and still nature. 'Tis almost too high a beauty for any creature to be adorned with; it makes the soul a little, amiable, and delightful image of the blessed Jehovah. How may angels stand with pleased, delighted, and charmed eyes, and look and look with smiles of pleasure upon that soul that is holy!

Christian holiness is above all the heathen virtue, of a more bright and pure nature, more serene, calm, peaceful, and delightsome. What a sweet calmness, what a calm ecstacy, doth it bring to the soul! Of what a meek and humble nature is true holiness; how peaceful and quiet. How doth it change the soul, and make it more pure, more bright, and more excellent than other beings.[6]

6. The language in the last two paragraphs of this sermon is nearly identical with that in the first entry of JE's "Miscellanies," "Of Holiness":

a Of Holiness.

Holiness is a most beautiful and lovely thing. We drink in strange notions of holiness from our childhood, as if it were a melancholy, [morose, sour,] and unpleasant thing; but there is nothing in it but what is sweet and ravishingly lovely. 'Tis the highest beauty and amiableness, vastly above all other beauties; 'tis a divine beauty, makes the soul heavenly and far purer than anything here on earth (this world is like mire and filth and defilement, to that soul which is sanctified); 'tis of a sweet, pleasant, charming, lovely, amiable, delightful, serene, calm, and still nature; 'tis almost too high a beauty for any creature to be adorned with. It makes the soul a little, sweet, and delightful image of the blessed Jehovah. O how may angels stand, with pleased, delighted, and charmed eye, and look and look with smiles of pleasure upon their lips, upon that soul that is holy; how may they hover over such a soul, to delight to behold such loveliness! How is it above all the heathen virtues, of a more light, bright, and pure nature, more serene and calm, more peaceful and delightsome! What a sweet calmness, what a calm ecstasy, doth it bring to the soul! How doth it make the soul [to] love itself; how doth it make the pure sensible world [to] love it; yea, how doth God love it and delight in it; how do even the whole creation—the sun, the fields, and trees—love a humble holiness; how doth all the world congratulate, embrace, and sing to a sanctified soul! O, of what a sweet, humble nature is holiness; how peaceful and loving [of] all things but sin; of how refined and exalted a nature is it! How doth it clear change the soul and make it more excellent than other beings. How is it possible that such a divine thing should be on earth? . . .

The passage continues for another two hundred words, including the white flower image which figures prominently in the "Personal Narrative" version quoted in the headnote.

THE DUTY OF SELF-EXAMINATION

In a sermon with strong overtones of the Puritan meditative tradition, Edwards insists upon the conscious control of thought as prerequisite to salvation: the whole of religion is founded upon "most deliberate consideration"; words follow thought, and action follows words. Thus the serious, realistic person will study the Bible, and perhaps its secondary literature such as sermons, seeking the standards by which to evaluate himself in an unceasing, virtually habitual effort of self-appraisal. The reprobate mind, on the other hand, perversely refuses to act other than do animals, trusting in impulse and appetite when man has been specifically directed by his Creator to think.

The Exordium or opening of the sermon is interesting for its meditation upon animals and the natural world, eschewing for a space the usual textual exegesis. Immediately we are introduced to the wonderful phenomenon of instinctual life in nature, if only to be reminded that we are not of that world but are creatures of "reason and understanding." Throughout the remainder of the sermon Edwards sustains the contrast between the natural world which exists only once and for a time, and man who in his lifetime must prepare for an anti-world that will be his for eternity. If he follows God's directions, that anti-world will be heaven; if not, hell. The important point is Edwards' insistence upon the conscious, rational control of thoughts *and* affections to shape this destiny. One's breath is in God's hands from moment to moment, but one's eternal state is a matter of personal mentality.

To a modern reader, "The Duty of Self-Examination" may seem peculiar in its focus. It appears to be essentially moral in its exhortations to "consider your ways," and one might well think of social behavior upon first hearing the injunction. However, the entire argument of the sermon is focused upon *self*; that is, the isolated self, before God and in juxtaposition to "the world." There is a brief passage referring to the social dimension of gracious conduct, but it is all but lost amid the unabashed and unremitting appeals to a higher selfishness. One must save himself at all costs, and in order to do so he must in practice separate himself from "the world" and thus from most of mankind. Inevitably, the argument is largely negative in specifics, and only the conclusion stresses the essential optimism of one who would truly improve himself through self-analysis and meditative discipline. This is the Edwards of the "Diary" and "Resolutions," striving mightily for perfection in the prescribed way of holiness and not giving a hoot for modern man's "well-adjusted personality" or, for that matter, Benjamin Franklin's success and reputation among his fellows. In such sermons the implacable radicalism of Edwards and the Puritan tradition becomes inescapable: only two ways are available, only two forces are at play in the world, and only one issue is ultimately meaningful. One opts either for God's ways and salvation or the devil's and damnation.

The style of the sermon reflects the delicate Calvinistic balance between skepticism and hope, and the rhetoric manifests a combination of tenderness and urgency. Through such devices as the repetition of the word "consider(ation)" and the insistent references to the brevity and fragility of life, Edwards creates a remarkable intensity of statement. It is all the more remarkable when one considers his avoidance of particularistic descriptions and his preoccupation with abstract methods of spiritual discipline.

* * *

The octavo quire booklet has been extended by the addition of a single ninth leaf (now quite tattered) containing a half-page of writing. This material was added in Northampton in no less than the fourth ink to be found in the manuscript. It seems evident that the sermon was thus preached at least three times after the original delivery, although shorthand indicates repreachings only in Bolton and Northampton. Like many of the New York sermons, this has a relatively long Doctrine and brief Application. Although the proportions alone probably do not warrant identifying it as a lecture, the pedagogical cast of the message lends greater weight to the hypothesis that the sermon may have functioned as a lecture.

THE DUTY OF SELF-EXAMINATION

HAGGAI 1:5.

Now therefore thus saith the Lord of hosts: Consider your ways.

IT is the property of a beast to do things without any reflection or consideration, but to go just as their animal appetites lead them. They neither premeditate what to do in time to come, nor reflect on what they have done in time past. God has made their sense and their natural instinct their guide, and therefore hath made these far more perfect in them than in man. But the Almighty has given us something to be guided by, besides outward impulses upon our senses. He has given us a higher faculty, even reason and understanding, that we might be guided by consideration in things that we set about. The bees and the ants, they have natural instinct to prompt them to provide in summer against winter, and diligently to improve their best opportunities for gathering and laying up their food. Natural instinct teaches the swallow to know the time of her coming and going.

But God has left us without these instincts because he expects we should use those powers he has given for our own safety and advantage; he expects that we should improve our power of thinking and considering, that he has given us, by looking forward to see what is like to befall a little while hence, and make preparation for it against it comes. He expects, seeing he has made us capable of understanding and knowing future things that he has revealed, that we should consider them and provide for them: that we should make provision not only for this life, like the beasts that perish and have no other state to provide for, but also for the life that is to come, and consider what will become of us after death as well as before it.

'Tis this duty of consideration that God presses on the people of Israel by his prophet, Haggai. The people being returned out of captivity, and being about to build the temple again, were discouraged in the attempt; for it seems they were not zealous enough about [it] and a little matter would discourage them, and therefore they began to make excuses. They pleaded that the time was not yet come to build the house of the Lord, as you may see in the second verse: "Thus speaketh the Lord of hosts, saying, This people say, The time is not come, the time the Lord's house should be built." That is, that the time that God had appointed and ordained that this house should be built was not yet come, an excuse. Much of the like nature, taken from God's decrees, many make use of in these days to excuse them from setting about their duty and the work of their souls; for say they, "The decrees of God must be fulfilled, let me do what I will," but God reproves such kind of excuses in our text. They did not make use of this to excuse them from building their own houses, though they try to excuse themselves by it from building the house of God. See what God says to this in the fourth verse: "Is it time for you, O ye, to dwell in your cieled houses, and this house lie waste?" As much as to say, "Ye say the time is not come to build the house of the Lord, but never ask the question whether the time is come to build your own houses. Surely it is not a time for you to dwell in your own houses, and [be] kept at home and be at ease, as long as my house lies waste." See again in the ninth verse: "Ye looked for much, and lo, it came to little; and when ye brought it home, I did blow upon it. Why? saith the Lord of hosts. Because of mine house that is waste, and ye run every man to his own house." Thus they, like many others in these days, neglected the glory of God for your own particular advantage. They were very apt to make excuses, to excuse them from serving of God, but they plead nothing to excuse them from serving themselves.

Wherefore, says God in our text, "Consider your ways." And again in the seventh verse, "Consider your ways." Consider what you do. Ye wonder why you have not a greater blessing on your labor. In the sixth verse: "Ye have sown much, and bring in little; ye eat, and have not enough; ye drink, but ye are not filled with drink; ye clothe you, but there is none warm; and he that earneth wages earneth wages to put into a bag with holes." In the ninth verse, "Ye looked for much, and lo, it came to little." The reason is, ye neglect the house of the Lord and run every man to his own house. That is the reason it is thus. In the tenth and eleventh verses:

> Therefore the heaven over you is stayed from dew, and the earth is stayed from her fruit; I called for a drought upon the land,

and upon the mountains, and upon the corn, and upon the new wine, and upon the oil, and upon that which the ground bringeth forth, and upon men, and upon cattle, and upon all the labor of the hands.

The reason is plain; you might easily know the reason if ye would but consider your ways. In the text, observe:

1. The duty commanded; that is, consideration of our ways: to consider and see what we do, and what is the tendency of it.

2. The solemn manner of introducing it: "Now therefore thus saith the Lord of hosts." This is no small matter, but a duty of grand importance, for the Lord of hosts commands it. Take particular notice of it. 'Tis the special particular command of Jehovah Sabaoth. The same is also signified by the repetition of it, again in the like solemn manner, in the seventh verse.

DOCTRINE.

'Tis our most important duty to consider our ways.

This duty of consideration of our ways, I think is fully implied in these three things:

I. What our ways ought to be.
II. What they have been in times past.
III. What they now are.

I. We ought to consider what our ways ought [to be]. It ought to be our greatest inquiry: What ought I do? That question in Acts 9:6 ought to be the grand question: "Lord, what wouldst thou have me to do?" This is a thing woefully neglected by most of this wicked generation. They never consider what they ought to do, care not what is their duty, nor what is contrary to their duty. Their care is what will get them the most money and the most bodily pleasure.

Nothing so much concerns us as to know our duty, that we may do it; for we must be miserable if we don't do it. And God has been so gracious to us as to reveal our duty to us, so that we may know it if we will, only at [the] cheap rate of reading and considering. Our privileges in this respect [are] above most of the world's, and yet for all this many never consider what is their duty. We ought to be diligent to know what those things are which God has commanded, seeing he has commanded them. We ought frequently to consider what are our obligations to our duty, and to meditate on the reasonableness of it: to think what an absolute right God has to our service; how great and excellent a being he is, and what he deserves of us upon that account; to consider that he has made us, and how just it is we should obey him upon that account; to consider what we receive from him, and what is due from us to him on that account. We ought not to eat and drink like beasts, never considering whence these good things come. Nay, we ought not to breathe like beasts, without considering who it is that gives us our breath, without considering the God in whose hand our breath is; for every breath we draw is a mercy of God that we do not deserve.

Especially we ought to consider what God has done for our soul's welfare, and what is due to him on that account; surely, a man of reason will consider these things. Certainly we ought not to act worse than beasts, to live by the kindness of a merciful being and never once consider what we shall render to him for all his benefits towards us.

II. We ought to consider what our ways have been in time past. Have we not cause to repent and mourn when we reflect on past actions? Don't conscience tell us, "there you ought not to have done, seeing you have done foolishly; herein you did basely and unworthily"? How have we lived and how have we acted; what has been our course? Certainly we ought not to live without reflection. Why have we our memory given us? Is not one of the principal uses of [it] to reflect on our past actions? We ought to look back and see where we have missed it, see where we have moved out of the right way; see where we have stumbled and fallen, and see where are the rocks that we have suffered shipwreck upon [in] time past, that we may avoid them.

We ought frequently to consider whether our ways have been in all respects as they ought to be, whether they could not have been better, and to be nice and critical in searching for faults in our behavior. Some men stifle and muzzle their consciences when [they are] about to tell them of their past actions, which is a certain sign that they are very bad; but conscience ought not to be [by] any means to be restrained, but to have full liberty to tell us of all our faults, and set the heinousness of them before us. Yea, we ought instead of stifling it to assist it; for conscience is our best friend in this world when its rebukes are severest.

III. We ought to consider what our ways now are. This is what is chiefly respected in our text: first, the nature of our ways; second, what is their tendency; third, what will be the end of our ways.

First. We ought to consider the nature of our ways, whether they are good or bad, right or wrong. Are ours ways of wickedness or ways of godliness; is the race that we run the Christian race, or the race of the devil? Are we careful to observe all the laws of God and do as he directs and commands, and endeavor to please him in all that we do and thereby recommend ourselves to his favor; or do we do just as the devil would have us? Do we rather choose to hearken to him than to the God that made us, follow after him that will lead us to hell than him that will conduct us to heaven?

We ought to consider which has the greatest influence upon us: our carnal appetites, or the promises and threatenings of God's Word. When there is set before us a self-denying, mortifying duty and a pleasant sin, for us to take our choice, the sinful pleasure and delight allures and entices on one side, and the favor of God and heaven invites on the other. Which do we choose, which has the greatest influence upon us: the vain show that the devil makes to us of pleasure, or else the offers and promises of God?

Do we live to the world, or do we live to God? Has the world the victory in our hearts over all principles of goodness? Which do we choose: to be rich or to be holy; to feed sumptuously to please our appetite with meat and drink, or to feed on Jesus Christ, the bread that came down from heaven, the heavenly food; to have our bodies finely arrayed, or our souls clothed with meekness and humility, and the righteousness of Christ; to dwell in stately houses, or to have our souls made the temples of the Holy Ghost?

1. We ought to consider the nature of our thoughts. How are the faculties of our souls chiefly employed; are our thoughts and our affections chiefly exercised upon earthly things, about what we shall eat, what we shall drink, and wherewithal we shall be clothed? Are our minds set chiefly on vanities and trifles that are of little profit or advantage? Do we suffer our thoughts to rove to the ends of the earth? Do we give our thoughts the reins to go where they incline, sometimes upon the pleasing objects of concupiscence and the lusts of the flesh; sometimes after the objects of covetousness and the lusts of the eyes; sometimes after the objects of ambitious desires and haughty expectations led and governed by the pride of life, [and] at other times about things of no advantage or importance? Are our thoughts thus employed?

Or do we restrain them, and keep them chiefly exercised upon heavenly objects? Do we think mostly about our Creator and Redeemer, the glory of God, our salvation and the welfare of our souls, the state we are in and the eternal estate we are to be in after this life? Do we think most of that which most concerns us and is of greatest importance to us? Do we think most of those things which are the most excellent and are most worthy of our thoughts: how is it with us in this respect?

2. We ought to consider our words. Words commonly follow thoughts: if the thoughts are much upon religion, certainly our tongues will be apt sometimes to be upon the same subject; but if the thoughts are mostly vain, the words will be likewise vain and to little purpose. Matt. 12:34, "O generation of vipers, how can ye, being evil, speak of good things, for out of the abundance of the heart the mouth speaketh." For if the tongue is bad, we may judge the man bad also. Commonly, as is the tongue so is the man. The apostle James compares it to a bridle by which the horses are turned about, and to the helm of a ship by which the whole ship is guided (Jas. 3:3–4), thereby intimating that the whole man is commonly as the tongue is.

Wherefore, in this respect we ought to consider our ways by considering whether our words are good or bad, profitable or unprofitable. We are directed how the words of Christians ought to be: "Let the word of Christ dwell in you richly in all wisdom; teaching and admonishing one another [. . .] and whatsoever ye do in word or deed, do all in the name of the Lord Jesus, giving thanks to God and the Father by him" (Col. 3:16–17). "Let your speech be alway with grace, seasoned with salt, that ye may know how ye ought to answer every man" (Col. 4:6). How far is the practice of most nominal Christians from [this], just as if these commands were not in force now in these days as they were in the apostles', just as [if] this age were exempted. Wherefore, we ought to consider how it is with us, whether we follow these directions. If we do not, here is a command stands against us.

3. We ought also to consider the nature of our actions. Thoughts, words, and actions go all together.

(1) We ought to consider the nature of our actions which respect God: whether they are done in his service and to his glory; whether all that we do is part of the work that God has appointed for us and commanded, for everything that we do that is not part of God's service is part of the devil's service. "Whatever is not of faith is sin" (Rom. 14:23).

(2) We ought to consider the nature of those actions which nextly respect ourselves: whether we live soberly and humbly, chastely and temperately; whether we are patient in afflictions and deny and mortify our evil desires and curb unruly passions or no, and keep under our bodies and bring them into subjection or no.

(3) We ought to consider the nature of our actions which directly respect our neighbor, with respect to justice, charity, beneficence, and the like.

Thus, all our actions ought to be strictly examined and tried, and not only barely to consider the outward action as it is in itself: but also from what principle our actions do arise from; what internal principle we act and live [by], for actions are either good or bad according to the principle whence they arise. We must consider whether what we do, we do from a love to God and his commands, or whether from a love to ourselves—that is, to our flesh—love to this world, and love to sin. We ought diligently to consider why it is that we pray and read and hear and sing Psalms, whether out of love of reputation and fear of disgrace; or whether only from custom, education, and fashion; or whether we do it from love to God and godliness. For otherwise, all these things are good for nothing: we are but emptiness and vanity, a sounding brass and a tinkling cymbal. Thus the nature of all our actions ought to be strictly examined and considered by us.

Second. We ought to consider the tendency of our actions. We ought not to go blindly along through this world and never inquire which way we are going, and where the path we are in will lead us at last; for there is but one path that leads to happiness, but innumerable paths lead to destruction. We ought always to consider whether the way we are in leads to our misery or to our felicity, whether they tend to ruin us or to make us blessed. How doth the blind, inconsiderate man know but that the next step will bring him to the pit, and will put him past recovery?

Third.[1] We ought to consider what will be the end of our ways. Where are our ways like to end, or what will the course we now follow at last bring us to? Every man is in the way to heaven or the way to hell, and the way that we are now in, if pursued, will certainly bring us to one or the other of these.

If wicked men did but consider what will be the dreadful end of

---

1. MS: "2."

the ways they are in, how would they be startled and affrighted, for their path is the way to hell, leading down to the chambers of death! They go like oxen to the slaughter; their ways lead down into the hideous den of the old serpent, where those that come never return again.

Certainly, therefore, it behooves us to examine, according to the best of our light, what is like to [be] the upshot and event of our present course of living; frequently to ask ourselves: "Where will this path that I am now in lead to in the end? What will be the fruit of these actions? When I die and go into another world, will it be unspeakable torments, or immortal glory?"

APPLICATION.

Thus you have heard this duty of consideration explained: a duty which we all know is miserably neglected in the world, although it be what above all others most directly respects our own safety. When God, the Lord of hosts, most solemnly and repeatedly says, as he doth in our text and context, "Consider your ways," he doth as it were only say to us, take care of your own safety. But yet how inconsiderately do most men go on, so that one that did not know human nature better would judge that the Almighty in the creation had denied most men the power of consideration; for, though this life is but a short race, it never comes about but once and this never-returning life is that that we are to act for eternity in, yet we all know how most men live. But it is not because God has not given them the power of consideration, nor is it because they have not light and knowledge, but it is because they have reprobate minds, and have brought themselves down very near to the level of thoughtless, poor inconsiderate beasts, by their sins.

But that it not be so with us, let us hearken to that solemn command of the Lord of hosts to us in our text to consider our ways; and that we may be assisted so to do, let us lend our attention to the following motives and directions.

[I. *Motives*]

First. For motive, consider the great danger we are in in this world, in what danger of losing our souls and dropping into remediless misery. We are surrounded and encompassed with dangers on every side, within and without. Without us we have enemies everywhere lying in ambush for us, and within our own breasts we have enemies armed with poisoned arrows and deadly weapons. They are all conspiring our hurt, yea, our greatest hurt, our irrecoverable overthrow. The enemies within are assistants to our enemies without, and our enemies without spur on our internal enemies. The world allures and entices us; the devil, he makes the fairest show and representation of the world[2] that possibly he can, as he did to our souls.[3] The world shoots fiery darts at our souls, and the devil adds a new force to them as they come along. The devil, he is laying snares for us, and the world helps the devil; and both join in with our lusts, and betwixt them all three thus combined, thousands of inconsiderate souls are carried down into destruction as a foolish ox to the slaughter. If we will not consider in such danger as this, when will we consider? If a man will not consider in the midst of an army of enemies, we may justly look upon him as foolish to the last degree.

Wherefore, let all consider for their own safety: consider what danger they are in, and by what means they may escape this danger. Let none think themselves so free from danger as to be escaped from this duty of consideration. Every inconsiderate man is in danger of eternal ruin, for it is a thing essential to a man in Christ, and so out of danger of hell, that he be considerate. All have need of consideration. Every truly godly man accounts the danger of offending his God greater than the wicked esteem the danger of burning in hell. Wherefore, consider your ways, for you are every moment in danger of being drawn into an offence of your Maker, and so thereby of losing the light of his countenance and the manifestation of his favor, and of being deprived of your own comfort and exposing yourself to remorse of conscience.

Second. Consider that there can be no effectual amendment of heart and life without consideration; that is, no such change as will be lasting and permanent, and will stand us in [good] stead at death and judgment. For this is always the very first step towards amendment; there can be nothing done before it: Ps. 119:59–60, "I thought on my ways, and turned my feet unto thy testimonies. I made haste, and delayed not to keep thy commandments." When David considered his ways, the duty commanded in our text, then he betook himself to a better course of life, and turned his feet into God's testimonies.

---

2. "Of the world" is an insertion, but it appears to be in an ink very similar to that of the original text.

3. "Souls" is a conjectural reading.

When he saw the danger he was in and considered the tendency of his former ways, he made haste and delayed not to keep God's commandments; he fled from his former course as from the most imminent danger.

Wherefore, if ever we intend to come to any amendment in our lives, we must begin with consideration; for there is no true religion but what is founded on most deliberate consideration.

Third. Let the thought of the good effects of consideration move you to it. It causes men to act wisely, and like rational creatures to consult their own safety and fly danger. A man that considers will never be easy till he is well-assured that he is safe, till he is gotten into a safe bulwark and defense. The effect of due consideration is commonly to bring men to Christ, the only safe refuge.

Inconsiderate, wicked men are yet so sensible without consideration of the state they are in, that they dare not consider for fear of being frightened and terrified, and having their carnal ease disturbed. But the man that is in Christ, he can behold his own state with joy, for some of the greatest joys of good men in this life arise from the thoughts of their safety in the arms of their Redeemer.

II. [*Direct.*] That you may consider to more profit and advantage, follow these directions:

First. Consider speedily, for the time is coming wherein it will be too late. The damned do consider, but now consideration doth them no good, but only torments them. They consider their ways now; they spend all their time in considering, in tormenting consideration. They now consider all their wicked practices while on earth: they consider the advantages they were under, and the precious opportunities they enjoyed; they consider now the obligations they were under to duty, and the aggravations of their disobedience, the prodigious folly of their ways, but these considerations are like scalding brimstone to them. But if we consider now, speedily, it will be to our eternal advantage, but if we delay and remain inconsiderately wicked, we know not how soon this life will be over.

Second. Consider seriously, with the greatest application of mind. 'Tis diligent and serious consideration alone that is like to have its effect upon us.

Third. Consider often, not once or twice but daily and continually, not only a little while after hearing a sermon or something remarkable in God's providence towards [you], as upon a sick bed, under affliction, or some particular circumstance; but let it be constant, lying down and rising up, on visit or home and as we walk by the way, when we labor and when we rest, and in all circumstances. By this means our minds will by degrees grow better and better, and we shall get a habit of consideration, and prudent acting and living.[4]

4. The following passage, written upon a loose leaf and having no key signs linking it to a particular passage in the sermon, is a Northampton addition which seems to belong to the Application, possibly constituting a final head. The leaf has a badly worn edge, and lacunae in the text resulting from it are represented by ellipses.

That persons may not make a wrong improvement of the doctrine; least they should be discouraged from seeking and striving, fearing and almost concluding that God has given them over:

Consider all those that are faithful in using means for their salvation, are so far convinced and are . . . they dare not allowedly commit sin. They are under a sense and impression of God's all-seeing eye . . . so much of a fear of his wrath that it makes them diligent in using means in seeking conversion. I say, one such may conclude that God has not given them up to sin, for God is striving with them, and them that he strives with he has not forsaken; 'tis a day of grace with them. But all such as have continued long in sin and find they are still stupid and senseless, truly they have great reason to fear and be awakened.

POVERTY OF SPIRIT

I N this lecturely sermon Edwards propounds in considerable detail the doctrine of poverty of spirit, as derived from Christ's Sermon on the Mount. The textual exegesis is one of Edwards' more imaginative, consisting of the simple and efficient juxtaposition of the two liberators, Moses and Christ, their mountains, and their dispensations. The remainder of the sermon is probably less remarkable in the exposition of poverty of spirit, its justifications and rewards. The brief Application is intensified, however, through allusion to the heroic efforts of the blinded Samson to achieve an earthly redemption in destroying the temple of Dagon. Here, the blinded slave of the Philistines is equated with the natural man who is a slave of the world, sin, and Satan. The preacher exhorts his listeners at the beginning of the Application to overthrow the pillars of pride and worldly-mindedness which prop up the temple of unbelief, whatever the implied worldly risk. The Samsonian motif of blindness is then deftly invoked from time to time until the very last sentence of the sermon which concludes with a reference to the opening of spiritual eyes. Such typological devices, in opening and concluding the sermon, complement one another and enforce the idea that Christ's burden is lighter and his reward infinitely greater than those types of redemption presented in the Old Testament.

While the lengthy Doctrine is not enlivened by similar literary resources, the exposition is carefully structured, points are meticulously summarized, and the whole is charged with the energy of applied critical thought. Sometimes, as in the brief exploration of false humility (pp. 498–99), Edwards' analytical zest is nearly effervescent. Never really personal or local, his discussion nevertheless achieves significant psychological specificity. The paradoxical elevation within humiliation so essential to the Christian vision of redemption is the central concern of the Doctrine, and all aspects of the notion are explored until the whole scheme of the heavenly, earthly, and infernal, including the place of the redeemed and the unredeemed in it, is revealed. Though only implicitly and generally, there is a final coalescence of the approachable Mount of Christ's message, the preacher's appeal for simultaneous self-abasement and exultation, and the image of the humiliated hero who triumphs in his self-destruction as, blinded, he finally perceives a way to serve both God and himself. The sermon may not appear remarkably neat as a literary construct, but it efficiently manifests the essentially revolutionary spirit of the gospel.

* * *

The octavo booklet of this sermon manuscript is in good condition and the revisions within it for at least three repreachings at Bolton, Glastonbury, and Northampton are not heavy. Indeed, the sermon seems to have been revised on only two occasions, the major modification being the addition of a half-page of writing at the end for the Northampton preaching. Probably as a result of Edwards' attempt to block out the sermon booklet in advance of composing the substance, there are some difficulties apparent in the arrangement of the text; for instance, one numbered subhead had to be inserted behind what should have been the succeeding major head, and the summary paragraph of the Doctrine was inserted after "Application" had been written across the page. Shorthand records of repreaching in this booklet are among the more detailed of the New York sermons, including at least one symbol for which the meaning has not been ascertained.

POVERTY OF SPIRIT

MATTHEW 5:3.

Blessed are the poor in spirit: for theirs is the kingdom of heaven.

THE old law was once delivered from a mountain, shaking and trembling exceedingly with thunder and lightning, and a dreadful voice; so that Moses said, "I exceedingly fear and quake," and the people desired that they might not hear that voice, for it was so terrible they could not bear it. Thus the fiery law was delivered from a mount that might not be touched, and if so much as a beast touched it, he was to be stoned or shot through. In this dreadful manner was the law of Moses delivered from a mountain.

Here, also, we have the precepts of, and blessings of the gospel delivered from a mountain: from the God himself as well as the other; yea, more immediately, but as the gospel is very different from the law that cries, "Cursed be everyone that continueth not in all things written in the law to do them," the voice that is now heard, the sweet voice of Jesus Christ, [dwells] on blessings and not curses.[1] The old law was delivered with a dreadful voice, so that the children of Israel could not bear [it]. Here the gospel is delivered with a sweet voice of Christ, into whose lips grace is poured; here is a voice from the lips of God become man, so that all may hear it without trembling. 'Tis a sweet voice and not a dreadful sound; 'tis blessings and not curses. The mount from whence Christ delivered this sermon was not a mount that must have limits and bounds far about it, which if any transgressed he was to be shot through, but all might freely go up to the top of the mountain and hear their Creator speak to them and deliver his glorious gospel. In the wilderness of Sinai, only Moses was admitted to the great privilege of being spoken to by God face to

1. The contrast of the two mountain-given codes through the disparate settings and moods involves the account of God's speaking to Moses, particularly Ex. 19:11–16, and the Sermon on the Mount, Matt. 5:1ff. The contrast is made explicit in Heb. 12:18–24.

face; but here all are freely admitted to hear their Creator speak to them in a meek and lowly manner, as familiarly as they speak one with another, more familiarly than God spoke to Moses alone. Here they were freely admitted to see his face, not only see a representation or similitude by which God manifested himself, as Moses did, but actually to see that body, enlivened by that soul, which God had assumed into a personal union with himself, to be the same in person with him forever more. Here they might hear his familiar voice without being overcome with dread. They might freely converse with [him]: he was willing to receive all that came to him, and to condescend to them so far as even to wash their feet.

The words of our text are the beginning of this sermon: "And seeing the multitudes, he went up into a mountain; and when he was set, his disciples came unto him. And he opened his mouth, and taught them, saying, Blessed are the poor in spirit, for theirs is the kingdom of heaven." He sets out with these words, by pronouncing, "Blessed [are] the poor in spirit." He begins with that which is the very foundation of Christianity: humility, weanedness from the world, and poverty of spirit. How sweet, how lovely is a Christian temper of soul founded on poverty of spirit, meekness and lowliness of mind. How excellent are its precepts.

In the words are three things to be taken notice of: first, the persons here spoken of, the poor in spirit, which we shall explain in the following discourse. Second, what is here declared of them: they are pronounced blessed; they are happy and blessed persons, however they may be esteemed to be a melancholy, dull sort of people by the merry and yet miserable men of this world. Yet Christ pronounces them blessed and happy. The poorer they are in spirit, the richer they are; they are happier than monarchs and princes. Third, the reason of their blessedness given: because theirs is the kingdom of heaven.

There is no need of much varying the words in this doctrine:

DOCTRINE.

Those persons that are poor in spirit are happy and blessed, because the kingdom of heaven is theirs.[2]

The kingdom of heaven is mentioned twice in these beatitudes: in our text, as the blessing of the poor in spirit; and again in the tenth

2. In the Northampton revision of the statement of doctrine, JE deleted "because the kingdom of heaven is theirs" and substituted "in a right and title to the kingdom of heaven."

verse, as the blessing of those that are persecuted for righteousness. You may observe the blessing in everyone to be suitable to the condition or disposition. In our text, a kingdom—yea, the heavenly kingdom—is promised to the poor in spirit, such riches being a suitable motive to poverty of spirit; and so to the persecuted for righteousness' sake, as a suitable encouragement to those that by persecution lose all in this world: they shall receive a hundred-fold in the next, and so comforting as a suitable encouragement to mourners; inheriting the earth, the meek, who are not proud and lifted up with their possessions, and so satisfaction to those that hunger and thirst for righteousness. Mercy is promised as a blessing suitable for the merciful; seeing of God, a suitable blessing to the pure in heart, because they are pure and fit to come into his presence; a becoming God's children, a blessing suitable to peacemakers, for how disagreeable it [is] for those that are children of the same heavenly Father to fight and contend, one with another, who are of the same family of God.

That we may give you the full meaning and force of the text and doctrine, as far as we can, we shall:

I. Describe a person that is poor in spirit.
II. Show that the kingdom of heaven is theirs.
III. Why God bestows the kingdom of heaven on such.
IV. That they are blessed on that account.

I. But we shall describe a person poor in spirit as well, that you may see of what an excellent, lovely temper and disposition true Christians are of, of what an amiable disposition these are of that are conformed to the gospel, and have Jesus Christ dwelling in their hearts and souls by his Holy Spirit, as that you may [see] how such are happy and blessed. This, therefore, we shall do in these following things:

First. One that is poor in spirit is one that is sensible of his own littleness, weakness, and poverty. He sees the greatness, the glory and majesty of the great Jehovah, and how doth he sink into nothing in his own eyes at the sight! After he has been employing his wondering and amazed eyes in viewing the majesty and glory and excellent beauty of God, and is filled with sweet astonishment; when he comes to turn his eyes inward upon himself, and sees what a little, miserable, helpless creature he is: how is he humbled, what low thoughts has he of himself, how doth he annihilate himself in the presence of this great God! He then sees that he is not so much as worthy that so glorious a being as God should take any notice of him. He wonders with himself how such a little, despicable, miserable creature as he, comes to be regarded of God, that he is not entirely neglected by Him and left out of His notice, as a despicable creature not worthy regarding.

He sees himself weak and altogether helpless, a miserable wretch that must die and perish except God helps him, and so he renounces his own strength, for he sees it is nothing.

He is one that is sensible of his own poverty, sees he has nothing of his own; he strips himself of all that he used to account his riches, and esteems them as dung. When he comes into the presence of God, he comes as a beggar without money and without price.

Second. He that is poor in spirit is one that is sensible of his own filthiness by sin. He looks on his own heart with loathing and abhorrence; it makes him sick at the heart [to see] it: so much filth, so much sin within himself. He is one that truly loathes sin and detests it above all things, and it is his greatest burden that he still carries remainders of this hateful corruption; it is like a stench in his nostrils all his life.

He is sensible of his original sin and corruption, that his heart by nature is only evil and that continually. How doth he abhor himself when he sees himself by nature to be a young viper, full of poison against his Creator. How doth he abhor himself when he calls to mind how he has affronted a merciful God. He sees how hateful his sins are.

Third. A person that is poor in spirit is one who has a contrite, truly humbled spirit. Contrition and humiliation are some of the principal things appertaining to poverty of spirit. The true humiliation of one poor in spirit is vastly different from the pretended, false humility of others. The pride of natural men will work one way or other. This great part of corruption that we derive from Adam will never be unoperative in any but those that are truly born again. Some are proud of their wealth and outward estate; others are proud, in the greatest poverty, of supposed perfections of body or mind; or else, as many foolish persons in these days, are proud of their imperfections, yea, of their sins. They glory in their shame. They are proud of those things whereby they are like beasts and devils. Some are proud of swearing, others take a pride in wantonness; they most esteem themselves when they are most bold and daring in their own destruction: he is the best man among them that runs with most hellish boldness on God, even on his neck and the thick bosses of his buckler. There are multitudes of such, as I believe almost everyone knows, so some are proud of their religion, others of their irreligion, and some are proud of humility. So pride will work one way or other in all natural men.

But the poor in spirit is vastly different from all these: though they have some remains of pride in them, yet it is but a remainder. Pride is mortified; he is truly humbled before God; his heart is broken and softened and deeply humbled for sin. He don't say "I have sinned," as Saul did, for spearing Agag, King of the Amalekites, and the best of the cattle, alive, when Samuel was sent with a terrible message to him (I Sam. 15:24), but as David did when Nathan tells him, "Thou art the man." And the fifty-first Psalm, David's penitential psalm on this occasion, is the language of his heart: he cries out as Job did when God had reproved him by a voice out of the whirlwind, "I abhor myself, and repent in dust and ashes."

Fourth. Another part of poverty of spirit is the fear of God: a fear of him as a child fears his father, is afraid to offend him, bears a great awe and dread of his majesty, authority, and power above all things; fears his anger, trembles at his Holy Word. This is reckoned by God as one part of poverty of spirit; Is. 66:2, "but to this man will I look, even to him that is poor"—that is, poor in spirit—"and of a contrite spirit, and trembleth at my Word."

Fifth. He that is poor in spirit is one that despises the world. However wealthy he may be, yet he despises his wealth and keeps his heart from [it], and so is poor in spirit. He neglects and rejects the world, lives above it, suffers not his soul to be ensnared by the deceitfulness of riches, hath not his heart lifted up by these things: he is crucified to the world, and the world is crucified to him. He don't esteem himself because of prosperity or honor of the world; he empties his soul of the world, leaves it all to others. He is a pilgrim and stranger in the earth; his riches are not here, but beyond this life.

Sixth.[3] He that is poor in spirit is one that is full of meekness, lowliness, in his carriage towards other men. He don't act with superciliousness and haughtiness as those that esteem themselves above other of their fellow creatures, but is rather at all times to esteem others better than himself, to place himself last in his own esteem.

---

3. This head was originally written after the second proposition (below), apparently as an afterthought.

He delights in condescension to his inferiors, and submission to superiors.[4]

In short, poverty of spirit is a comprehensive thing that implies great humiliation and abasement in the sight of God, deep contrition for sin, a deep sense of our own poverty and weakness of ourselves, a sense of the meanness and insufficiency of our own righteousness, a slighting and despising the world, a heavenly sweet humility in our deportment towards others as the children of God.

II. The second thing proposed was that the kingdom of heaven doth belong to those that are thus poor in spirit. They are little and low in their own eyes, but God will advance them to be greater than the kings of the earth. They have seen themselves to be vile and filthy, but God will take away their filthy garments, and clothe them with royal apparel, shining with glory. They shall be made beautiful, with a beauty that transcends all that any creature here below can boast of.

The kingdom of heaven is sometimes to be understood of Christ's heavenly kingdom here on earth, for Christ's kingdom is not of an earthly but a heavenly nature; at other times, of the glorious state of the saints in heaven, to which estate only those that are poor shall be advanced.

III. As for the reasons why God will bestow the kingdom of heaven only on the poor in spirit:

First. They are the only fit persons to receive it. These sinful, wicked men that, since[5] they are sinful, wicked, and abominable, are not fit to be advanced to glory: they are not in a fit disposition of soul to be thus honored and advanced. God will not advance the proud, will not give the kingdom of heaven to those that are not truly humble. To give heaven to those men who have never been truly humbled, and had their hearts broken for their sin, and sensible of their own vileness, would have been like continuing the fallen angels in heaven after the fall.

If those that are not poor in spirit act proud of their miserable worldly possessions and honors, what then would they be if they were advanced to the glory of heaven? If they were so advanced, they would not be contented to be joint heirs with Christ, but would be

4. For JE, the word "condescend" has no pejorative connotations; on the contrary, it implies here a very admirable, Christian humility.

5. MS: "although." Apparently JE originally had a different syntactical structure in mind, requiring an adversative clause rather than simple consequence, and failed to alter the conjunction when he altered the rest.

for pulling God out of his throne and getting into it themselves, as the angels which fell were.

Wherefore, God will not advance those that are not poor in spirit, but will depress them into the lowest disgrace and misery, and will bestow heaven alone on humble, contrite souls.

Second. Those that are not poor in spirit will not receive the kingdom of heaven as it is offered to them; wherefore, God will not bestow it upon them. They esteem themselves to be rich already, and therefore will not receive the kingdom of heaven as given out of mercy, pity, and free grace. They don't see that they are worthy to be objects of pity; they don't see themselves to be miserable, but till that is, God will never make them happy. God offers eternal life to them as a free gift, but they are for receiving it as a debt, and for challenging of it, instead of humbly praying for it; at least they are ready to expect [it] on the account of their own righteousness, so that they come with money in their hand and not as beggars, but God don't offer salvation on these terms.

Third. The third reason why God will not bestow the kingdom of heaven on any others but the poor in spirit, is because they take up with a portion here in this world. They are not concerned about the kingdom of heaven. If they could obtain an earthly kingdom, they would be glad, would rejoice with all their hearts, and they also choose not to be miserable in hell when they die; but as for the kingdom of heaven, they raise not their thoughts to that, but keep them down upon the ground. They take their heaven here: they are worldly men that have their portion in this life, and they are to have none in the next life but a portion of misery.

IV. [The] fourth thing was that the poor in spirit are happy and blessed on this account: these men that the world esteems to be miserable because they deny themselves sinful pleasures, they are the only happy men. These whom the world esteems to be poor because they are poor in spirit, they are the only rich. The world deems them to be dishonorable, but they are the only honorable. They indeed endeavor to dishonor them, but they are nevertheless happy for them, as long as God honors them and Christ loves them. Worldly men are proud of their riches and despise the poor in spirit, but the poor in spirit despise all their wealth and pity them. They are got above such childish things.

How blessed are the poor in spirit; they are blessed in all conditions. If they are in a cottage, they are blessed. If they are in prison, they are blessed. If they are in the flames, they are happy and blessed for this reason, because they are heirs of the kingdom which nothing can take from them. God will abase the proud and bring them down, but those that humble themselves, God will advance: "He resists the proud, but he gives grace to the humble" [Jas. 4:6]; "A man's pride shall bring him low, but honor shall uphold the humble spirit" (Prov. 29:23); "Better it is to be of a humble spirit with the lowly, than to divide the spoil with the strong" (Prov. 16:19).⁶ God says he will dwell with him that is of a humble and contrite spirit. They may well rejoice in all manner of troubles and sorrows: "As sorrowful, yet always rejoicing; as poor, yet making many rich; as having nothing, yet possessing all things" (II Cor. 6:10). The poor in spirit leaves all this world, in his heart and affections, for Christ, but he shall receive an hundredfold for it:

> Then Peter began to say unto him, Lo, we have left all, and have followed thee. And Jesus answered and said, There is no man that hath left house, or brethren, or sisters, or father, or mother, or wife, or children, or lands, for my sake, and the gospel's, but he shall receive an hundredfold now in this time, houses, and brethren, and sisters, and mothers, and children, and lands [. . .] and in the world to come eternal life (Mark 10:28–30).

God hath chosen the poor of this world, rich in faith and heirs of the kingdom. God hath chosen none but the poor of this world; that is, the poor in spirit who are joint-heirs with Jesus Christ.

Thus we have gone through the explication of this doctrine. We have shown what excellent and lovely temper and disposition that is that is meant by poverty of spirit, consisting in an abstraction of the heart from the world, in abasement, contrition, humility and lowliness of mind, and that the kingdom of heaven appertains to such; and have given the reasons why God will bestow the kingdom of heaven on such only as are thus poor in spirit, and how happy, blessed they are upon that account.⁷ We shall now make some short improvement of this doctrine.

---

6. The Bible (AV) gives "proud" rather than "strong."

7. Originally JE wrote, "God will not bestow the kingdom of heaven on such as are not thus poor in spirit," but revised it to the present "such only as are thus poor" during the period of composition. In making the revision, he neglected to delete the first "not," a correction which has been made here.

APPLICATION.

I. Hence we learn what we must expect to mortify if ever we propose to obtain the kingdom of heaven: even pride and worldly-mindedness. For the poor in spirit only shall obtain heaven; therefore, they only are blessed. Pride and worldly-mindedness are the two great obstacles that hinder from the reception of the benefits that are offered in the gospel, the two great props of unbelief, the main pillars of the body of sin. We must therefore bow ourselves with all our might on those two pillars, calling upon God to help as Samson did, that the whole house, the building that Satan has reared in our hearts—his kingdom—may fall.

We must become poor in spirit, as you have heard, before we shall have any right to heaven. We must be sensible of our own filthiness by reason of sin. We must be sensible of our own littleness, of our own poverty. We must become beggars before we are kings: there are none now reigning with Christ in heaven and are crowned with glory and sit in the throne of Christ, but what while on earth[8] came humble at the throne of grace as poor perishing beggars. Those that are now in misery in torments with Dives are those that were never truly humbled for sin, never saw themselves to be poor, wretched, blind, and naked. We must mortify that disposition that so makes us hate to come up to the humble terms of the gospel, that makes us so to fly from Jesus Christ, so averse to a reception of him and the blessings he holds in his hands, that is freely, without money and without price.

We must mortify that disposition that makes our hearts so cleave to earthly things, so that it would be even as death to us to be deprived of them. For those that are rich in this sense are directly contrary to the poor in spirit: it is easier for a camel to go through the eye of a needle, than for such rich men to enter into the kingdom of heaven.

II. Hence we learn what great cause we have to lament the pride, luxury, and covetousness of the present. How lamentable is it to consider how few there are that have a right to the kingdom; for we are assured by our text and doctrine that the kingdom of heaven is appropriated to the poor in spirit, and so that none that are not thus poor in spirit have a right to it. But how few are there thus poor in spirit: how few there are that are blessed! Those few that are poor in spirit are blessed, that are found to be really humble, contrite ones

8. Word inserted by JE in a later ink to correct an omission.

that live above the world, that have purged their souls from the dregs of earthly-mindedness, and have taken up with God as their portion. These are happy, but all the rest are miserable; these are blessed, but all the rest are cursed; these are under the blessing of the gospel, but all the rest are under the curse of the law.

How full is the world of pride and covetousness; how little appearance is there of Christian lowliness, humility, and heavenly-mindedness. Let everyone answer for himself how doth this call for our wailing and lamentation, how lamentable is it that so few of mankind obtain the kingdom of heaven.

III. Let those that are poor in spirit be comforted by this doctrine. Christ Jesus tells you that you are blessed. Is not our text a sweet and pleasant voice to you? Don't you hear it with pleasure and joy? 'Tis enough to fill you with ecstasy of joy. I speak to those that are poor in spirit, that have their hearts broken for sin and weaned from the world, and have truly humble minds: blessed are you, poor in spirit, for yours is the kingdom of heaven. You are not become poor in spirit for nothing. You have stripped your souls of the world, cast in your affections, and are become poor in spirit with respect to the world but rich with respect to heaven, [so] that the kings of the earth are poor in comparison of you; their crowns and robes are but beggars' rags in comparison with those robes you are to be covered with. Whatever your estate be with respect to worldly prosperity, God is yours and Christ is yours, and the kingdom of heaven is yours.

IV. Let all be exhorted by this doctrine to poverty of spirit. We cannot offer you a more powerful motive to poverty of spirit; yea, God cannot offer you more. This is the highest, most excellent inheritance, that most excellent kingdom in the universe. Be assured this kingdom of heaven is something very excellent and worthy of your acceptance, worthy of your most diligent pursuit; the expression "the kingdom of heaven" exhibits to us the highest and most glorious estate in the world:

First. A kingdom, the station of a king, is the highest station among men; these are the top of this lower creation. They are at the highest pitch of honor, power, and dignity.

Second. This kingdom being the kingdom of heaven, which is the palace of the universe, the most honorable and excellent part of it, holds forth that this state is the most glorious that creatures are advanced to.

Certainly, then, here is motive enough to poverty of spirit; here is motive enough to reject the world and all in its glories. If there were nothing else but even the grace of poverty of spirit itself, [it] is of such an excellent, lovely nature that one would think [it] should be enough to charm us to it. All men hate pride and covetousness in others and will praise the contrary virtues, however destitute they are of it; but how much more would they if they had their eyes opened and their blindness, that hinders them from beholding spiritual beauties, [conquered]? Without doubt, that which is amiable enough to attract and ravish the eyes of the Creator would appear charming to us if our eyes were open.[9]

9. When revising his sermon for a Northampton repreaching, JE added the following paragraph to the original text at this place:

'Tis not only that pride that runs out into an affectation of grandeur and pomp in living amongst men, an affectation of stateliness in garb, in building, and being superior to others in outward appearance; I say, 'tis not only thus that is opposite to being poor in spirit, or that I now warn you against them. Pride in a cottage and pride in rags that prevents men's humbly coming to God through Christ, that makes men fond of their own goodness and righteousness, and ben't to ascribe that glory that is due to God alone to themselves; this pride is equally devouring to the soul. It is the same principle of pride; however, it runs out to different things and exercises itself in a different way. Many that account themselves humble have much of this sort of pride, and 'tis that which all unregenerate men are guilty of to a damning degree. Let your heart be prepared, by a lowly and humble disposition and a weanedness from the world's vanities and glories, to receive God with all his glory and majesty, to embrace Christ Jesus with his honor and beauty, and from him to receive as a free gift and the effect of wonderful grace the riches and the honors and the glories of the kingdom of heaven.

"TRUE Repentance Required" should probably be classed as a preparatory sermon, though it might even be specified as an awakening sermon if one does not require the hellfire vehemence found in many awakening sermons as a sine qua non of the type. Certainly the element of urgency is present, as is the radical assessment of the human condition and the equally radical call to action: however, the burden of the sermon is instruction and the lengthy Doctrine's very complexity contributes a discursive quality. Immediate and profound repentance is the preacher's theme, but rather than merely reiterate and amplify it, Edwards chooses to explore its history and its justification in a rather pedagogical spirit.

Immediately following the statement of doctrine, Edwards declares his intent to address aspects of faith, metaphysics, and psychology which bear upon the process of conversion, and indeed there is little that in any way qualifies the overall issue which he does not touch upon. From original sin to redemption through love, from the law to the covenant of grace, from the fear of damnation to shame at dishonoring a beloved God, from natural selfishness to a wholly new (Christian) mentality: the theoretical issues and general processes involved in awakening and conversion are all here and some are discussed memorably, considering the limitations of the sermon form. Perhaps more than anything else it is the very scope of this sermon that causes hesitation before one classifies it with the practical awakening sermons of a more conventional form.

As in many of the New York sermons, there is a preoccupation with definitions and fundamentals that are assumed in comparable sermons of a later period. Rather than focusing sharply upon the immediate predicament of the natural man, Edwards presents the range of contextual factors which justify the very emphasis upon conversion in the first place. But having established the context, Edwards pursues the troubling implications with economy and vigor.

Well before the sermon's conclusion, the direct idiom of the awakening sermon has been brought into play: the sinner has been identified, alerted to his need, and exhorted to action. The overall tone of the sermon may be that of rational persuasion, but the message is as radical in its demands and assurances as any awakening sermon of later years.

A significant note in this youthul effort at definition is the recurrent emphasis upon the inevitable variables within an authentic conversion experience. Thus Edwards stresses that it is the "nature" of the thought and the "principle" from which the action proceeds, rather than the outward manifestation of either, that differentiate the authentic from the inauthentic. While not original and in some respects reflecting his father's views, such qualification in the midst of an effort in exhaustive specification testifies to Edwards' respect for the complexity of human experience and his habitual judiciousness even during the heat of argument. Those actuating gracious principles remain, in any case, a practical mystery within Edwards' extended exploration of the nature of repentance. That such a position may have been founded in Edwards' own experience of conversion is suggested in his "Diary" meditations, particularly that for August 12, 1723, in which he discovers discrepancies between his own experience and the traditional Puritan morphology of conversion.

* * *

A single preaching unit, or one octavo quire in length, the sermon manuscript is generally neat with only two or three major crossouts or insertions. The presence of three inks, including one represented only in the sign for Bolton, suggests that the sermon was repreached at least twice, perhaps including a guest appearance in the East Windsor pulpit of Timothy Edwards, although it was apparently not selected for repreaching in Northampton. One of the more interesting aspects of the manuscript is a substantial passage written on the originally blank last page in a later ink. The passage is a meditation upon the elect as strangers and pilgrims in this world, but it is not keyed to any part of the manuscript and was probably not intended as an addition to the sermon. Indeed, the number of deletions and rephrasings it contains suggests that

Edwards may simply have worked out a passage for another sermon on the blank back of this one. (There are even some mathematical calculations intervening between the passage and the end
of the original sermon in yet another ink.)

TRUE REPENTANCE REQUIRED

I tell you, Nay: but, except ye repent, ye shall all likewise perish.

Under the Law, worldly comforts and blessings were dispensed in some measure proportionably to their uprightness or impiety, though there were even then some exceptions from this general rule to lead the observers to the consideration, and expectation, of another state wherein God would reward all according to their works, as God frequently assured his people under the Mosaic Dispensation he would certainly do. Wherefore, they seeing that it was not done always in this [world], must unavoidably expect another state to succeed, as it is manifest they did expect by several passages in the book [of] Job, and Psalms, and elsewhere.

But worldly rewards and punishments were sanctions that were chiefly insisted upon before the publishing of the gospel, as may be seen by reading the book of Deuteronomy, which very much consists[1] of promises and threatenings of this nature to enforce the observation and obedience of the Law.

And we have many instances of the bestowment of such temporal rewards upon the godly, and inflicting worldly adversities on the wicked; many upon the children of Israel the while they were in the wilderness, frequent instances under the judges, and afterwards under the kings. Thus, Saul and his family were blotted out for their transgression; and David, being a man after God's own heart, greatly flourished and prospered, and after him his son, Solomon, while he remained steadfast to his duty, and as he fell from it his glory fell with him. And so it constantly went well or ill with their kings, even to the captivity into Babylon, according as they feared the Lord or

---

1. MS: "which is very much consists." JE revised wording at this point and neglected to delete "is" along with "principally composed."

forsook him. This was needful for the infant state and childhood of the church to keep them from sin and awe them to obedience, when they enjoyed so much less light than we do.

But when Christ came into the world, the sanctions of God's commands are no more outward, and worldly prosperity and adversity; but, heaven and hell, eternal misery and eternal blessedness, fire and brimstone or light and glory, a bottomless gulf of misery or else rivers of pleasure forevermore.

So that now we need not to [be] stumbled at all by the great worldly prosperity of some of the wicked, and the great adversity of some of the godly. When we see a wicked [person] flourishing and spreading himself like a green bay tree, we suddenly may curse his habitation. When we see sinful and debauched men rolling in heaps of silver and gold, dwelling in proud palaces and decked in gorgeous apparel, and glutted with the fat and drunken with the sweet, we may well weep over him out of pity to him, considering what a poor, miserable wretch he is. We may pronounce the lifeless stocks and stones blessed in comparison of him.

And if we see a godly man oppressed, afflicted, vexed, and parched with worldly afflictions and adversities, yea, frying at the stake, we may well admire at their happiness and pronounce them thrice happy and blessed.

We have no cause to be stumbled at all because Nero, the wicked tyrant, reigned over all the earth and was drowned in worldly pleasures, and the poor Christians—or rather the blessed and thrice happy Christians—martyred and roasted, and fried, and cast to wild beasts, and crucified and put to all manner of the worst of deaths. What should we think if our eyes were opened and should see the difference of their states as they are now? Wherefore, Christ commands and instructs us in the beginning of this chapter, not to judge of the internal state of the souls of men by their outward condition, seeing that this state was not an estate of rewards and punishment, but of probation.

For says Christ, "Suppose ye that these Galilaeans were sinners above all the Galilaeans because they suffered such things as those eighteen, on whom the Tower of Siloam fell, and slew them? Think ye that they were sinners above all that dwelt in Jerusalem? I tell you, Nay: but, except ye repent, ye shall all likewise perish" [Luke 13:2–5].

In the words observe two things: first, a solemn preface, "I tell you, Nay"; "I assure you, it is as I declare unto you." Second, the assertion itself, "except ye repent, ye shall all likewise perish"; in which observe, first, the thing presupposed, and that is the danger of perishing; second, the means without which it cannot be escaped, to wit, repentance: "except ye repent."

DOCTRINE.

Without true repentance for sin, there is no escaping eternal ruin.

This is a truth that is either not believed, or not understood, or not sensibly felt by the greatest part of mankind: for if they believed that, except they truly repented, they must be miserable forevermore, how could they live as they do, except they did not understand it and did not know what repentance is; or if they did understand it, scarcely ever thought of it, and when they did think of it, but slightily and not seriously? Wherefore, I have chosen to insist upon this subject at this time, and I shall handle it in the following method:
We shall show,

I. That all men before repentance are sinners.
II. What true repentance of sin is.
III. That without such a repentance, there is no escaping eternal ruin.

I. All men, without exception, are concluded under sin. They are all in the first place sinners; there never was any man that was so free from sin, but that he stood in such necessity of repentance that, without it, it would be impossible for him to escape eternal ruin and perdition. Gal. 3:22, "But the Scripture hath concluded all under sin."

Christ's coming into the world to save sinners supposes that all men are sinners, for Christ comes to save none but sinners; for those that are not sinners have no need of Christ's salvation, for he came to save his people from their sins. His name, Jesus, was given to him because he should save his people from their sins, Matt. 1:21. The Messiah came into the world "to finish the transgression, and to make an end of sins, and to make reconciliation for iniquity" (Dan. 9:24). "He was wounded for our transgressions, he was bruised for our iniquities: the chastisement of our peace was upon him, and with his stripes we are healed" (Is. 53:5).

Now all this would be false and absurd, except all men are sinners;

for Christ's incarnation, his life, his righteousness, his death, his resurrection, ascension, and intercession are to no purpose to those that
are not sinners. Christ did not come to seek and save that which was
never lost, nor did he come to call righteous men to repentance; so
that, except some men get to heaven by some other way besides
Christ, all men are certainly sinners and must see themselves to be
such, or else they will never be saved by him.

First. All men are guilty of Adam's first sin. Adam was our common
father and representative who stood in our room: we were all in his
loins. The covenant which he broke was made with us all, and for us
all in him; it cannot be supposed that the covenant that God made
with Adam, He made only for his single person. That is ridiculous,
for at that rate there must be a particular covenant made with every
particular person, in all nations and ages. We might know that we
are guilty of Adam's sin because we see that the effects of it are
transmitted down to all his posterity; which if it were not so, there
would be no more reason for than that all the world should feel the
effect of every particular man's sin in these days.

But we have something that is more sure, whereunto we do well if
we give heed: Rom. 5:12, "Wherefore, as by one man sin entered
into the world, [and] death by sin; so death passed upon all men, for
that all have sinned"; which is as much as if the Apostle had expressly
said, "All men have sinned in one man." Verse 15, "For if through
the offence of one many be dead"; in v. 16, "for the judgment was
by one to condemnation"; v. 17, "for if by one man's offence death
reigned by one"; v. 18, "therefore as by the offence of one judgment
came upon all men to condemnation"; and v. 19, "for as by one man's
disobedience many were made sinners." Also, I Cor. 15:21–22, "For
since by Adam came death, by man also came the resurrection of the
dead, for as in Adam all die, so in Christ shall all be made alive."

Second. All men are born with a dreadful depravity of nature. We
come into the world as full of poison as young vipers or any deadly
serpent. There are in us the seeds of all sins, even murder, idolatry,
blasphemy, and the worst sins that are ever committed; and this appears because that the natural corruption of nature has been stirred
up to that degree as to produce these sins. The Scripture tells us we
are all by nature children of wrath, that none can bring a clean thing
out of an unclean, that we are shapen in iniquity and conceived in
sin, that the old man is corrupt, that we need to be born again and

to be created anew that we may bear the image of the last Adam, as we have of the first.

Every man experiences this law of sin, this body of death and root of bitterness, and must also see his own hatefulness by reason of it, or is lost forever.

Third. All are guilty of actual transgressions. Job 9:2–3, "I know it is so of a truth, but how should man be just with God? If he contend with him, he cannot answer him one of a thousand." And in the thirtieth and thirty-first verses, "If I wash myself with snow water, and make my hands never so clean; yet shall thou plunge me in the ditch, and mine own clothes shall abhor me." The best and most just man upon earth is not free from actual sins, but what a vast difference is there between a man before and after repentance and regeneration. The life of man before repentance is one continued act of sin.

II. We are come to show what that true repentance of sin is that is so absolutely necessary in order to salvation from everlasting perdition, that we all know what that thing is which we must do or perish. I shall answer to this, and endeavor to give you to understand what it is in these two things which are the parts of it: first, it is a godly contrition for sin; second, a turning from it.

First. A godly contrition for sin. Sin cleaves by nature fast to our souls: 'tis grown into us, firmly fixed in our very nature. This hideous, dreadful, most poisonous, loathsome monster clasps us round so close by nature that it has fixed his claws even to the very center of our souls; and it cleaves faster to us as we grow older, and therefore it cannot be rent from us without rending our hearts. The heart is so hard that it cannot be softened without breaking of it in pieces.

Therefore, there must be a contrition and godly sorrow for sin. The sinner must look back on his past life and actions with a hearty grief, and it must break his heart in pieces to think of it. It must break his heart to think how base and vile he has been, and how filthily and sinfully he has done. True repentance melts the soul down. To think how he has disobeyed God, offended his Maker and dishonored His Holy Name, makes his very heart like melted wax in the midst of his bowels.

True contrition may be known by the principle it arises from, and the effect it produces in the heart:

1. By the principle it arises from, and that is love to God and the

Lord Jesus Christ. The sinner, thinking of the merciful nature of God, thinking of his great compassion and pity manifested to men, he sees that God is really exceeding merciful and compassionate. He wonders that God should so condescend to the children of men. He sees that really and truly God has shown an unparalleled goodness and a most sweet, condescending compassion in that act of sending his Son into the world. He admires the goodness of God herein; he wonders that so great and glorious a God should be so full of pity and compassion. What, the King of the Universe, the Infinite God, the Eternal Jehovah pity man at this rate?

Such thoughts as these make him to love God, and think him most excellent and lovely, that ever he should be so full of mercy and pity, that ever he should be so exceeding gracious; that ever so great a God, that has been so much affronted by proud worms, should be so full of goodness and astonishing clemency as to take pity on them, instead of punishing them, especially when he considers that he is one of those wretched rebels whom He so pitied. This makes him to love this so good God above all things in the world; his very soul is all drawn out: how doth it melt with such thoughts, how doth it flow in streams of love!

And then when he reflects on his sin, as [on] his vileness, on his disobedience to this so lovely God, his proud and contemptuous behavior towards him, how he dishonored him by his unreasonable, most ungrateful disobedience—that ever he should be so ungrateful and so vile: then what sorrow, what grief, what deep contrition follows! How doth he loathe himself; how is [he] angry with himself! See the motions that the penitent feels at this time excellently represented by the Apostle: II Cor. 7:11, "For behold this same thing, that ye sorrowed after a godly sort, what carefulness it wrought in you; yea, what clearing of yourselves; yea, what indignation; yea, what fear; yea, what vehement desire; yea, what zeal; yea, what revenge!"

I do not say that a true penitent's thoughts always run exactly in this order, but I say that they are of this nature, and do arise from this principle.

2. The effect of this contrition is a deep humiliation. When the sinner thus reflects on his vile and abominable sins, how humble doth it make him; how doth he bring himself even to the dust before God. "What a hateful and vile creature am I, that have thus done; how unworthy am I of any look or the least smile from God. That ever I should be so monstrously ungrateful, that ever I should be such a

base wretch . . .": such thoughts as these make the proud heart that before used to lift itself up against God come down low before the throne of grace. He don't hesitate any longer whether he had best to depend on his own righteousness; he abhors the very thought of offering that to God which so vile a creature as he has done, with hopes of God's accepting of it as an amends for his sin. He does not desire in the least to have any of the praise of his own salvation; he sees he is unworthy of it: he had rather that Christ should have it all. He had rather depend entirely on Christ and be saved entirely on his account. He abhors the thoughts of having part of that praise which belongs to Christ; he sees plainly that it all belongs to Him. This humiliation, which is the effect of godly contrition, is not always to the same degree; but it is always of the same nature, and this is the nature of it.

Second. The second part of repentance is a turning from sin. When once the heart has been thus broken for sin, it shall be forsaken; when once the sinner hath thus seen the vileness of it, he takes his leave of [it]—bids it an eternal adieu, desires to have no more to do with it. It was his darling in time past, that he used to take delight in and loved above all things, that he used to hug and embrace; but now he bids it be gone at an infinite distance and never have anything more to do with him. He desires no more on't: he sees it to be the hatefulest monster in the world, and therefore desires never to converse with it any longer.

1. There is a turning of the heart. Before he loved it most dearly, but now mortally hates it: it stinks in his nostrils and is exceeding offensive to him. He now loves that which is excellent and truly lovely, and that which is more contrary to sin than light is to darkness, even God and holiness. He delights in God and chooses to converse with him. He will have no more to do with that that was the occasion of so much torment and misery to his dear Redeemer.

2. A change of life. He now acts from other principles, for other ends and designs than he did before. There is a great deal of difference in the way that leads down to the chambers of death which he used to walk in, and the pathway of life which he walks in now. Before, the devil led, and hast governed; but now the Holy Ghost leads and guides, and he is governed by a vital principle of true holiness. This is the true repentance which our text and doctrine speak of.

III. Without such a repentance as this, there is no escaping eternal ruin. Except our hearts are thus broken and melted down, as you have heard; except there be such a hearty grief for sin because it is committed against so good [a] Creator, Preserver, and Redeemer; except there be such a humiliation, such a contrition and sorrow that shall make the heart thus humble; except there be such a change of heart, from dear love to sin to mortal hatred, and from hatred to God to the dearest love to him: there is no way to be found out whereby a man may escape eternal ruin. All the world can't deliver him out of the jaws of hell.[2]

Who can be so unreasonable as to think that God, that has been so affronted, will save a sinner that don't, and won't repent; [that][3] neither is sorry for it, or if he does repent, repents it only because he is like to be damned for it? This is not being sorry for sin, but a being sorry that he is in danger of damnation.

But God has declared that it shall not be so, and Christ has declared that except we repent, we shall all likewise perish:

> Because I had called, and ye refused; I have stretched out mine hand, and no man regarded; but ye have set at naught all my counsel, and would none of my reproof: I also will laugh at your calamity; and mock when your fear cometh; when your fear cometh as desolation, and destruction as a whirlwind; when distress and anguish cometh upon you. Then shall they call upon me, and I will not answer; they shall seek me early, but shall not find me. For that they hated knowledge, and did not choose the fear of the Lord: they would none of my counsel; they despised all my reproof. Therefore shall they eat of the fruit of their own way, and be filled with their own devices (Prov. 1:24–31).

IMPROVEMENT.

I. Hence we see that all those that think they are in a state of salvation that never experienced a repentance of this nature are certainly deceived. 'Tis to be feared there are many such, many who never yet found any such contrition and melting of the soul at the reflection on their past sins; never found such a hearty grief because they sinned against that God which they now love, which they now

---

2. A three-line block insert in a later ink occurs at this point. It reads: "Not because repentance makes any satisfaction. [It is] unsuitable and impossible to glorify [God] by one not separated from sin."

3. MS: "It."

see to be most lovely; never found half so much sorrow for this offending and dishonoring and contemning God as they would feel if they had so wronged, dishonored, and injured an earthly friend that they very dearly love. They would be heartily sorry and grieved that ever they had dishonored and wronged so good a friend, one that they so entirely love, and their very heart would even break at the thought of it, and perhaps they would hardly ever be reconciled to themselves again for it.

But they repent of their affronting and dishonoring God, not because they think he is lovely, because he is a dear friend and a tender father: the thoughts of that don't grieve them at all, but they are grieved to think that they are like to burn in fire and brimstone. This perhaps has grieved them; or they may be grieved that they have lost their credit by it, or something of that nature.

II. How happy are they who have already truly repented. They are happy they are free from the reigning power of sin, from the power of hell. They have reason to rejoice that they are got rid of the guilt of their sin, rid of the slavish fears of death, and may think of eternal fire and brimstone without being terrified. They may lie down with quiet in this world, and they may lie down with peace and quiet in the grave, and never need to fear lying down in eternal misery.

III. Let [us] from this doctrine be persuaded, first, to a speedy; and second, to a constant, repentance.

First. To a speedy. By "speedy" I mean to go about it immediately, without any interval of time at all. Whoever says, "I will not repent yet," in effect tells the Almighty that he does not regard his threatenings so much but that he intends to disobey him a while longer; and when God says, "now," he says, "No, not now, but when I please, when I have the most convenient opportunity." It is evident that this is the language of such a practice, and would be evident to them if they were not resolved not to think of it. How just now would it be with God to say to such an one, "Thou fool, thy soul shall be taken from thee long before that time comes," as he doth say so to a great many of such procrastinators.

1. Consider first that the later repentance is, the more bitter, the more we shall have to repent of: young penitents have easy work of it to what old sinners have. If the twig be bent while it is young, [it can be done] easily, but when it is grown to a tree 'tis almost impossible to bend it, and [it] can't be done without breaking.

2. If we defer our repentance till some other time, when we come to repent we must repent of this among the rest of our sins: that we put off the work of repentance. Now how ridiculous is it to put off repentance with such an expectation of repenting of that, when we know at the same time that we shall bitterly repent it, and intend to repent it. And if we intended it not, dared not to do it, one would think that an expectation of repenting of it hereafter should terrify us from it and not encourage us to it.

3. If you think it is too soon now, hereafter the devil will tell us 'tis too late. Now he says 'tis too soon, and 'tis his way so to do till they become either damned or old. If by telling them 'tis too soon he can but persuade them to put off till old age, then he changes his voice and tells them 'tis too late; and thus poor creatures are deluded and drawn on by the devil's wiles and temptations till they are past hope, and he has made sure of them. While young, they are encouraged to delay by the expectation of time enough hereafter, and when they are old, they are quite discouraged and disheartened with the thought of its being too late. He first tells them perhaps of delaying only a few years; when that time comes, he has another bait to draw them on a little further, and thus this devouring lion draws them on by little and little, further and further, till they have passed the line and are past recovery. And thus that old serpent fills his den with sinners that he has taken in his snares and traps.

Second. Be persuaded to a constant repentance. None must think they have done with repentance when the first act of repentance is over. No, but we should frequently be reflecting on our old sins and lamenting of them before God. This frequent lamenting of sin will not decrease, but increase our comfort: for daily lamentation, contrition, and humiliation, we shall be largely repaid by the Holy Ghost, even [in] this world, by spiritual joys and delights. For by our thus frequently lamenting of our past sins, our hatred and aversion to sin increases and grows, and also our love to God, and consequently our joy and delight.

Besides repenting of old sins that are committed before conversion, there are sins that are daily committed by the godly and therefore are daily to be repented of. It is our duty and our interest so to do, and what if we do we shall never have cause to repent of.[4]

4. More than a half-page of later writing appears on the verso of the sermon booklet's last leaf. The passage defines Christians as strangers and pilgrims in this world. It seems not to be related to this sermon and there are no key signs, so it is not reproduced here.

LIFE THROUGH CHRIST ALONE

THEMATICALLY a christological meditation, and an awakening sermon in argument and rhetoric, "Life through Christ Alone" is an unusual if not unique sermon. In most cases, such urgency as suffuses this sermon would be associated with images of damnation and expressions of divine disapprobation. However, this sermon not only avoids most of the overt threatening of the awakening sermon but becomes increasingly positive in its argument as it becomes more urgent in tone.

The overall argumentative strategy is characteristic of Edwards in that it moves through a rigorously systematic exposition from a denial of alternatives to a careful elaboration of particulars which identify the subject. Such a "rhetoric of logic"—for that is precisely what it is—prepares the auditory for a final series of urgent interrogations which again tend to establish the thesis by eliminating alternatives. The overall process, entailing as it does the drama of investigation, generates considerable tension by mediating between the extremes of urgent hope and fearful anxiety. In this case the result is an unusually fine balance of hope and anxiety.

A seemingly exhaustive sermon, "Life through Christ Alone" moves from point to point rapidly and there is little literary embellishment of any one point: expression is vivid but imagery is minimal, most of the vividness resulting from an absence of peripheral images in any one passage rather than from the fullness with which images are elaborated. The rapid pace is enhanced by the staccato querying of the auditors, particularly within the Application. Perhaps because he was aware of this quality and was not wholly happy with it, Edwards inserted a number of passages for a Northampton repreaching of the sermon which seem calculated primarily to expand points that are already clearly established.

Of all the New York period sermons, this is probably the most thoroughly christological, comparable in its focus to "The Excellency of Jesus Christ" (1738), although the focus of the New York sermon is sharply delimited to the Redeemer role, unlike the more complex conception of the later sermon. There is no specific occasional context, but given the character of this sermon it is tempting to associate it with the sacrament. While the urgency is perhaps atypical of a sacrament sermon, the theme would certainly be appropriate, and there are few rivals among other sermons from the period.

* * *

The octavo quire booklet has been enlarged by the insertion of a two-leaf unit just before the last leaf, making ten leaves in all. The insert contains two separate passages, unkeyed but obviously to be inserted in the text at the appropriate points (see footnotes to the sermon). These passages are just two of a series of amplifications Edwards made when preparing the sermon for repreaching in Northampton during his first years there. The other insertions were made mostly in blank spaces at the ends of heads and not all of the blanks have yet been filled in. These blanks result from the blocking out of the sermon in an outline of numbered heads and a subsequent filling in of them without regard to formal order in the booklet. This sermon is thus one more example of Edwards' growing tendency to compose in the sermon booklet, even when the makeup of the booklet did not lend itself to the process, since Edwards seems to have been unable to predict accurately how much space a point would require and the octavo quire is an inflexible unit. In this case, he seems to have left the argument less fully developed than he at first planned, as many of the Northampton insertions could be made without any cramping. There is still a vacant space in the middle of the booklet of about a third of a page. Still, the sermon was apparently one Edwards liked or found useful, since shorthand signs and varying inks indicate that he repreached it twice or more, probably in Bolton, Connecticut, and in Northampton.

LIFE THROUGH CHRIST ALONE

JOHN 6:68.

*Then Simon Peter answered him, Lord, to whom should we go? thou
hast the words of eternal life.*

THE least happiness or the least misery that is eternal is more to
be regarded [than] the greatest happiness or the greatest misery that
is but temporal and will have an end; so that the smallest additions
to our eternal happiness and treasure in heaven is of more value than
the greatest additions to our outward prosperity, because there is no
proportion at all between the greatest finite and least infinite, the
greatest temporal and the least eternal, the one so much exceeds the
other.[1]

Much more is a great and unspeakable happiness that is eternal:
of infinitely more value than the little pleasures that last but a few
days, and therefore, the grand question should be, "What shall I do
to obtain eternal life?" and this life in comparison of it be neglected
and overlooked and counted as not worth the taking notice of with
it.

It seems as if this was a great question amongst the Jewish rabbis
about the time of Christ's coming into the world, what was the condition of eternal life, for all believed [in] a future state of happiness
but only the Sadducees. But the question was how it was to be obtained; this they expected the Messiah would plainly tell them when
he came into the world.

And accordingly, our blessed Savior fully and clearly resolved this
question while he was on earth, for he tells us that he himself is the
way, the truth, and the life. It was his prophetical office to teach us

1. For a later preaching of the sermon, JE formulated a new introductory sentence to
be inserted at the head of the textual exegesis: "Our eternal condition is that which infinitely more deserves our care and concern than anything else."

the way to eternal life. 'Tis his priestly office to purchase it for us, and it is his kingly office, by his almighty power, to bring us to it.

Christ Jesus had been fully instructing his disciples and others in these things in this chapter in an excellent discourse to them and to some of the multitude that he had miraculously fed with five loaves and two fishes, occasioned by their asking him this same grand question about the condition of eternal life, in the twenty-eighth verse, "What shall we do, that we may work the works of God?" That is, "What shall we do that we may do that work which God has appointed in order to everlasting life?"

Christ fully answers them this question in the ensuing excellent discourse. He tells them in it that the work of God was to believe on him; that he that believes on him should [have] everlasting life; that he is the bread of life, and that he that eats this bread should hunger nor thirst no more, and should never die.

But the effect these heavenly instructions had upon them, instead of moving them to come to Jesus and believe on him that they might have this everlasting life, was quite the contrary: their final departure from him, in the sixty-sixth verse, "From that time many of his disciples went back, and walked no more with him. Then Jesus said to the twelve, Will ye also go away?" This is the occasion of these words of Peter in our text, "Lord, to whom should we go? thou hast the words of eternal life." We do believe that thou alone canst teach us the way to everlasting life. We believe that it is as thou sayest, that believing in thee is the work which God requires of us, to do [so] that we may receive everlasting [life]. We believe that thou are the bread of life, and if we leave thee, we can find none else by whom we may obtain everlasting life; for we believe that thou art the Christ, the Son of the living God, that was to come and teach us and lead us to eternal happiness.

In the words observe a twofold assertion: first, that Christ has the words of eternal life; that is, that he has the dispensing and communication of eternal life, his word being the means of communication. Second, that none else has the words of eternal life, strongly implied in this interrogation, "To whom shall we go?" There is none else we can go to, but to thee alone.

DOCTRINE.

It is by Christ alone that eternal life is ever communicated to men.

It was by Christ that eternal life has been communicated from the foundation of the world. It was by Christ that holy men in the old world, before the flood, received life; 'twas by faith in him that Enoch was translated; 'twas by the reception of Christ that Abraham received eternal life; 'twas [by] faith in him Moses received eternal happiness, that faith whereby he esteemed the reproach of Christ greater riches than the treasures of Egypt. It was by Christ and him alone that Job, Samuel, David, and the prophets were saved; he is the lamb slain from the foundation of the world, in whose blood the godly have been washed and with whose righteousness they have been clothed—never ever have been or ever will be saved any other way to the end of this world. There is none else can communicate eternal life to us, or deliver us from eternal death.

I. We cannot obtain it by ourselves. Our own strength, our own righteousness, our own suffering, are all good for nothing to procure this life we speak of. If we make our ways never so clean, if we worship God never so well, if we sacrifice thousands of rams and ten thousands of rivers of oil, yea, if man should sacrifice the fruit of his body for the sin of his soul, it is nothing.

Abraham's being so freely willing to offer his only son, Isaac, was not sufficient to satisfy God for the least of Abraham's sins, not for the least wrong thought and sinful action; but it was Christ that satisfied for Abraham's sin, and it was through that faith in Him by which he offered him up that he received pardon of sin and eternal life, and it was for His sake that this action of his was accepted and rewarded.

II. All the world can't procure eternal life for us. If all the men in the world should offer to be crucified for the sake of one man, it would be absolutely to no purpose; instead of satisfying for all our sins, they could not satisfy for one of them; instead of procuring eternal life, they could not procure one drop of water for us in hell: the flames of hell would not be at all the cooler for it. They are not able to pay one farthing of all that ten thousand talents which we owe, but we must have been in hell till we had paid the uttermost farthing, notwithstanding all that they could do or suffer; and so,

III. Neither could angels help us. If the archangel, the chief angel in heaven, with all the rest of those bright, excellent, and glorious spirits, should assume human bodies and all undergo as much disgrace as Christ did, and should hang upon crosses in pain and intolerable torment thousands of years, 'twould be to as little purpose.

[IV.][2] 'Tis the Lamb of God alone that can take away the sins of

2. The MS originally had neither head number nor indentation at this point; however,

the world, and it is the Lion of the tribe of Judah alone that is strong enough to work our way through to everlasting happiness. The reasons why it is so are:

First. None else is able to endure the wrath of God against sin. God's hatred of sin and his wrath against it are infinite, and no finite person can bear such an infinite weight. No angel or man could have held out to bear what Christ bore, but before the [agony] grew to that height as to cause them to sweat blood as Christ did, their strength would fail, and they would relent. Now, Christ was able to lay down his life, and was able to take it again of himself.

Second. The suffering and righteousness of none but Christ could have been sufficient and satisfactory. The least sin deserves eternal punishment, and the suffering of none but of an infinite person can be equivalent to eternal sufferings. Christ is an infinite person, and he is one that the Father loves with an infinite love; and therefore whatever he doth is accepted upon his own account, upon the account of that love which the Father hath to him.

Third. None other is of power and wisdom and grace enough to fit us for, to bring us to, and make us eternally happy in heaven, but Christ alone. Our old natures must be destroyed, or else heaven, although it be bought for us, cannot be bestowed upon us. We must be sanctified and made holy, and all the men and angels in the universe can't do that; they have not power enough to raze³ out the old image of Satan, nor skills enough to draw the image of God upon our souls. This [is] a work of the almighty power and wisdom of God, which is Christ: I Cor. 1:24, "Christ the power of God, and wisdom of God"; Eph 1:19, "And what is the exceeding greatness of his power to us-ward who believe, according to the working of his mighty power."

There is none else that can fill our hearts with grace: we must receive of his fullness and grace for grace. 'Tis he alone that has received the Spirit without measure: "For he whom God hath sent speaketh the words of God, for God giveth not the spirit by measure unto him" (John 3:34). He is an infinite vessel; he has enough for himself and for us too, but it is not so with angels.

JE perceived that it was a division of significance and drew a heavy line before it in the text. Here the inserted number indicates the head's actual place in the structure of the sermon, including the subheads under it.

3. MS: "race." The word "raze" (or arch. "race") suggests scraping as with the blade of a knife, a method of erasure sometimes employed by JE in his manuscripts.

None else can give us spiritual wisdom, for none know the things of the Spirit; and Christ alone can send into our hearts the Holy Spirit to dwell in us, to teach us heavenly things.

There is no other vine that we can [be] ingrafted into, that can communicate vital and spiritual nourishment, and, at last eternal life unto us but Christ alone, by whom and for whom are all things, who is before all things, by whom all things consist. There needs an almighty power to give us our natural life, and less will not suffice to give us our spiritual.

There is no one else can conquer our enemies but Christ alone: that can conquer the world; that can triumph over the devil and make a show of him openly, as Christ did upon the cross; that overcame death and break his bands, that can take away his sting, and that can raise us up at the last day.

Or that [can] make us happy when we get into the other world. Christ Jesus is the only source and fountain of true happiness; 'tis he alone that can fill the soul and satisfy it forever.

Christ Jesus is the only complete Redeemer that has worthiness enough, that has power, wisdom, and an inexhaustible fountain of grace, sufficient for our spiritual life here and our eternal life hereafter.

In these several respects eternal life is communicated by Christ:

1. He has bought it for us. If we had not sinned, God would have given us eternal life upon the account of our obedience. But by our sin we have lost it and Christ alone can redeem it, seeing divine justice must be satisfied and it would not have been just with God to let sin go unpunished. Christ so loved the offender that, rather than he should die, He would pay all that justice demanded, and [that] He has done, so that justice is paid and everlasting life is purchased and is to be received, without any money or price, by those that will come to Christ for it.[4]

2. By preparing a place for them in heaven. Christ having been here on earth and done all that was necessary towards satisfying and

---

4. In this and the two succeeding heads JE later added amplifications of the material in blank spaces left at the time of composition. The following passage was added at this point:

> Eternal life was not bought by silver and gold, and such corruptible things, but by the precious blood of the Son of God (I Pet. 1:18). Christ's life went for ours. So great a thing as eternal life, so infinite [a] blessing, was not purchased by anything but that which in God's sight was of infinite value: even the blood and obedience of his own and only Son.

purchasing heaven, he is gone to heaven to prepare for those that come to him: to intercede with the Father and plead his obedience, his passion, for them. John 14:2–3, "In my Father's house are many mansions: if it were not so, I would have told you. I go to prepare a place for you, and if I go to prepare a place for you, I will come again and receive you to myself, that where I am, there ye may be also."[5]

3. By leading and conducting of them to eternal life, by his Word and Spirit and mighty power. The Scriptures, which are our rule to go to heaven by, are the word of Christ;[6] the ministers of the gospel speak nothing otherwise than representing their great master, Jesus Christ. That Holy Spirit by which Christians are led, and guided to heaven, is the Spirit of Christ: he dwells with them and in them by his Spirit. That power by which they, when they have believed, are brought on in the way to eternal life, through all obstacles and oppositions, in spite of all the powers of darkness, is the power of Christ. John 10:28, "And I give unto them eternal life; and they shall never perish, neither shall any pluck them out of my hand."[7]

4. By communicating and infusing grace and holiness, which is the principle of eternal life. The spiritual life [through] which the souls of the saints are alive unto God, and do live to him, is the beginning of life eternal. 'Tis the same life, but only in a far less degree. Holiness, love to God, and the love of the saints is the very life of a Christian in this world, and the same is his life forever, but only in its perfection.

Grace and holiness is the same in this world as in the next: but only in this life it is like a spark, but there shall be like a flame; here mixed with much sin, which is the death of the soul, which quenches the

---

5. At this point the following passage was later inserted:

Though Christ is in heaven and we on earth yet, and so he is at a great distance as to place, yet he is not unmindful of us but is continually doing for us. He is as it were making ready for those friends of his he expects home to his Father's house. He is preparing things for the reception of his spouse.

6. MS: "and they are the word of Christ."

7. At this point the third of the amplifications was added:

God the Father has committed the care of all the church, of all the redeemed, unto our ascended Redeemer; and it is his care that preserves his people in all changes. He watches over them night and day; he restrains the power of Satan in all his attempts against them; he directs them in difficulties and finds out their way for them; he fights against all their enemies and carries them through all the opposition they make in their way to eternal life.

After this insert, about one third of a page remains blank.

exercises of grace as water quenches the fire, but there they shall be pure and undefiled, perfectly free from the least stain of sin. They shall be all life and vigor in the exercises of divine love; there shall be no darkness or dullness, which the best complain of in this world. They shall be active as angels; their souls shall be full and overflowing with an active, sprightly holiness, love and joy.

5. By raising from the dead. The resurrection is four times mentioned in the chapter of our text as a means whereby he will bestow eternal life on those that believe: in the thirty-ninth verse, "And this is my Father's will which hath sent me, that of all which he hath given me I should lose nothing, but should raise it up again at the last day." In the fortieth verse, "And this is the will of him that sent me, that every one which seeth the Son, and believeth on him, may have everlasting life: and I will raise him up at the last day." In the forty-fourth, "No man can come unto me, except the Father which hath sent me draw him, and I will raise him up at the last day." In the fifty-fourth verse, "Whoso eateth my flesh, and drinketh my blood, hath eternal life; and I will raise him up at the last day."

The wicked shall be raised, too, but not to life; but theirs shall be the resurrection of damnation. But the true Christian shall rise to life and eternal joy: their bodies also shall partake of eternal life, for it is sown a natural but shall be raised a spiritual; sown in corruption but raised in incorruption; sown in weakness but raised in power; sown in dishonor but raised in glory [I Cor. 15:42–44].

6. Christ is the eternal life of the believer. He is the life of the soul in this world, and will be the life of it to all eternity. Christ is all the life that a believer desires or hopes for. When Christ is present the soul is alive, but when absent, it is dead; and when the soul is present with Christ, then the soul enjoys eternal life: Col. 3:4, "When Christ, who is our life, shall appear"; I John 5:20, "And we know that the Son of God is come, and hath given us understanding, that we may know him that is true, and we are in him that is true, even in his Son Jesus Christ. This is the true God and eternal life."

APPLICATION.

From this doctrine we shall take occasion,

I. To invite those that are lost and undone to come to him who has the words of eternal life.[8] It is enough to make one full of pity, to weep bitterly with tears of grief and compassion, to see how miserable men, that have lost their God by their sin and have foolishly forsaken him, do wander about like desolate persons, bewildered and lost, miserably deceived, having no hope without God in the world:

Wandering in this world, which is a wilderness hideous and dreadful, full of ravening wolves, roaring lions and fiery serpents that are ready to devour us, without any manner of defense or safeguard; wandering in this dark and horrible place, full of snares, pits and gins that the devil has laid for them, without any manner of guide, director or preserver.

Led about like poor wretched captives, condemned to the flames by the devil at his will, having hell before them, waiting for them and ready to swallow them, without any Redeemer or Savior to deliver them.

To see them thus hurried about by Satan in such a miserable plight, naked and miserable, blindfolded and bound with shackles and chains, poor, famished, languishing, sick and dying, under no one's care but the devil's.

And at the same time to see them so infatuated and cheated by the devil that they are ignorant of all this, are going to be miserable but are so drunken and intoxicated by the devil's potion that he has given them, that they are not sensible of, poor creatures are led away by the devil to the slaughter, are enticed along by his shows, vanities and lies, and know nothing of the matter till the fatal stroke is given.

This their condition is enough to make the hearts of the godly, who have their eyes opened, even to melt with pity at the sight and view of it.

'Tis enough to amaze to see their folly, when Christ so freely offers them life, light and salvation, that yet they will choose to follow these lies of the devil. To see how many have come to Christ, have been called out of darkness into marvelous light, and have been made safe and happy at once, and they also have the same offer and yet foolishly refuse to hearken to it.

Let me ask such Peter's question, "Whither will you go?" You will not receive Christ: whither do you propose to go; where do you think to find anyone else that hath the words of eternal life? To whom will

---

8. This head was later designated: "I. Use of awakening to those who reject Jesus Christ."

you flee for help; where do poor, cheated souls think to find another Savior? Is there ever another God that delivers you from the wrath of this God, who is Jehovah; is there ever another mighty Savior that you think will do as well as Christ; is there ever another captain that you intend to list[9] under that can by his almighty power deliver you from all evil, that can conquer all your enemies and bestow an eternal crown and kingdom upon you? Do you expect to find another Savior, of another kind, that will indulge you and let you go on in sin as much as you please?

Where is this other Savior that you are going to and trust in? Who is he? In what part of the world does he dwell? Let us know. This other Savior will be found to be only that old serpent, the devil: it will come to this at last. Well, and what do you expect of the devil? Is he able to save you; is he able to fight against God and overcome him? Will he ever bestow eternal life upon you; has he the words of eternal life? Has he got a heaven, too, that you expect to enjoy a better heaven than the heaven into which Christ is ascended?

What is it that you think to receive of him? Don't you think that he intends to ruin and destroy, and forever to torment you when he has once got you in his power?

Why, then, do you follow after him so diligently, as if [it] could give you eternal life; a handsome, extraordinary thing to bestow upon you?

Or is there anyone else that has the words of eternal life? Is it riches and pleasure and worldly prosperity? Can you suck eternal life out of them, or to whom will you go? Certainly you expect eternal life, or something as good as eternal life, from some being or other; and who is it? Consider and see who it is.

If you don't come to Christ, consider what you intend to do. Something must be done or you are miserable forever. Now what is that thing that you have thought? Will you let yourself alone and be unconcerned about eternal life, and let yourself go down into [hell] as fast as the devil and your lusts can carry you?

If you don't intend so to neglect yourself, but intend to do something, what is it except you come to Jesus Christ? Will you put trust in your own performances: will you give your goods to the poor or do some very good deed and so depend upon that, and think that

---

9. "List" is an earlier form of "enlist."

God is obliged to you for it, or that you make amends for your sins by it?

Will you be much in prayer and reading the Scriptures, and the duties of divine worship, and think by them to procure everlasting life? This will not do: you can't do more in duties than what is duty, and whatsoever is done therein that is not your indispensable duty is sin. What other project yet have you in your minds?

All projects and contrivances are vain and senseless but only that way which infinite wisdom has contrived, and none but infinite wisdom could project, even the dying Son of God. If there is any cheaper way of getting to heaven than the blood of the Son of God, that you can think of, doubtless God would have thought of it before you, and so Christ's blood might have been spared.[1] Wherefore, stand no longer, for if ever you get to heaven any other way than by faith in Christ, it will be because you are wiser than God. Come, therefore, to this rock at last; for hitherto you have been wandering about like Noah's dove and have found no rest for the sole of your foot, nor never will till you return to this ark.

Come, therefore, and trust in him, and yield yourself to him, sweetly reposing yourself on him: for he hath the words of eternal life.

II. Let us be exhorted from this consideration, that there is none else to go to, never to depart from Christ; for if we depart from [him], to whom will we go? Let us, therefore, keep close to him; let us follow him wheresoever he goes.

We then depart from Christ when we fall into sin, especially when we sin against our own consciences. It is a turning our backs upon the blessed Jesus, and a hearkening to his enemy.

Will you sinfully, basely and ungratefully, leave Christ for the sake of other things? Will you leave him who has the words of eternal life for the sake of the world, for the sake of vanities and trifles? Will you leave him who died for you for the sake of wicked examples, and for fear of losing your credit and reputation? Will you leave him who

---

1. Following this sentence is a later interlineation which converts the remaining lines in this head into a separate subhead: "2. Be invited to come to this Savior." This statement evidently should be followed by the first of two passages on a pinned-in leaf, though there are no key signs. The passage is the first in the appendix to this sermon. After reading the inserted passage, the reader should pick up the original text at the next sentence, i.e., "Wherefore, stand no longer . . ." This is essentially the method JE followed in reading the sermon in Northampton.

wrought so hard for you that he even sweat drops of blood? Will you not deny yourself for him, and take upon you his easy yoke and his light burden, who bore the heavy burden of God's wrath upon him for you? Can't you kill your lusts for his sake, who himself was killed for you?

Consider how constant and steady Christ was for you, in the midst of all those great temptations with which he was assaulted. If he had not continued constant in resisting them, you must have perished without hope or remedy.

What would have become of you to all eternity, if Christ, when he came to look death in the face and saw that he was condemned and must be crucified, had repented that he had undertaken your salvation? He might easily have avoided his crucifixion, but he loved you constantly, steadily, and to the end; and patiently bore his agonies, the derision of men, the crown of thorns, the scourging; patiently bore his heavy cross, and patiently was nailed to it and died upon it.

But if you will not continue steadfast to your Redeemer for his sake, do it for your own; for he has not the benefit of it, but yourself. For if you leave Christ, whither will you go? By departing from him, you foolishly cast yourself off from a sure and safe rock into the midst of the tempestuous and boisterous sea.

Wherefore, be persuaded to continue steadfast to him and not depart from him, never to commit any known sin, whatever temptations you may be assaulted with.[2]

Appendix to John 6:68

For there is no other way, there is nowhere else that you can go. You must come hither or perish. You had better, therefore, leave off all attempts of getting salvation in any other way, leave off building upon your own righteousness and yield yourself to Christ Jesus. He is the only Savior, and he is a very glorious one; he is all-sufficient, able to save to the uttermost, able to do everything for you that you need should be done. He is willing to receive you: he calls you, he nears you, he opens his arms to receive you.

2. At this point it is likely the second addition, printed in the appendix to the sermon, should be appended. Although there are no key signs, the content of the head suggests locating it here. The number "4" at the top of the head does not correlate with the numbering of the original text which is reprinted here; however, renumbering for the Northampton repreaching involved renumbering the above head "3," thus eliminating the problem in numerical sequence.

* * *

4. Let those that do believe highly prize Jesus Christ; that Savior that is your Savior, and in whose name [you] have believed, whom you have chosen, is the only Savior. There is no other name given under heaven whereby you could have been saved; you could have gone nowhere else but only where you did go. That act of choosing Jesus Christ and yielding yourself to him was the wisest act that ever you did in your life.

If you had not chosen him, you would have been in the like miserable condition that many others of your neighbors are in: subject to the wrath and curse of God, exposed to hellfire, quite uncertain whether ever you should be saved or no. 'Tis owing only to him that your sins are now all pardoned and you brought into a state of favor with God, and are reconciled to him and have a right to heaven and eternal blessedness in God's kingdom and glory.

Wherefore, prize this favor. Behold your safety in him; view the strength of this high tower; view the horrid dangers that are without, that in this tower you are secure from. See what miseries others that are out of Jesus Christ are subject [to]; and rejoice in the Lord Jesus that you are so secure in him and in a way certainly to be made the possessors of glory by him, that you are already the heirs of it and have indefeasable right to it. Bless yourselves in Christ Jesus, and let your soul the more sweetly rest in the arms of his redeeming love.

CHRIST, THE LIGHT OF THE WORLD

A remarkably unified piece, "Christ, the Light of the World" is Edwards' earliest extant sermon to have a metaphor wholly adequate to the rhetorical foundation of its argument. Although Christ is the stated subject of this christological meditation, it is the metaphor of light that distinguishes the sermon, imparting to it an organic unity generally associated with literary forms of a later period. The traditional sermon form is emphatically present, of course, and it does preserve a sense of order and sustain momentum within an argument that threatens to become an exercise in liberal (if not free) association.

For Edwards, the "most excellent and glorious similitude" of light is not only scriptural, but it links Scripture and nature in such a way that simple phenomena relating to the sun metaphorically interpret Scripture to the informed heart. In the third subhead under the second Proposition of the Doctrine, Edwards illustrates the process in five parallels or analogies which constitute a remarkable extended simile. Not only is Christ here identified with the sun and its rays, but Edwards ultimately establishes a hierarchy of rays, commencing with God the Father and extending through Christ, the Bible, and the interpreted Word (especially in preaching). Finally, the Holy Spirit, operating within the heart of the redeemed, completes the cycle of accommodation through which the fountain of God's love becomes the "indwelling light" which transfigures the heart and vision of the redeemed person.

The "enlightened" person no longer operates on the level of theoretical truth in spiritual affairs, but rather is able to apprehend *reality*: he is "really *sensible* of the truth . . ." (p. 539). In practice, the individual is most likely to have received such an orientation through the medium of preaching, for Edwards insists that "faith comes by hearing, and hearing by the word preached" (p. 542). Having arrived at such a simple and concrete accommodation in his heart, he is no longer in the position of merely weighing arguments but can rely upon the intuitive differentiation of the real from the unreal. The real is verifiable because to the mind enlightened by the rays of

Christ's presence, the subject of his consideration has been imparted and is *possessed* by him: he is no longer considering someone else's point—even God's—but rather a dimension of personal experience.

This conception of a world permeated by the rays of God's illuminating spirit (particularly through Christ) was to endure, intensify, and in some respects be refined during the succeeding years. Edwards would return in the not distant future to the theme in a sermon on Jas. 1:17 (1728), and most memorably in 1735 with the sermon printed as *A Divine and Supernatural Light.* In all these sermons, it is the notion of a supernatural radiation that Edwards finds most compelling as a representation of the process of accommodation between the divine and the human.

* * *

A single octavo quire booklet neatly contains the sermon without either blank spaces or much cramped writing, probably indicating the use of a preliminary draft. The proportions of the sermon are more like those of later years than many from this period in that less space is devoted to the Doctrine, although the textual exegesis is a trifle longer than usual. But the most remarkable feature of the manuscript may be the presence of three Northampton symbols, at least two of which are in different inks. This seems to indicate that the sermon was repreached at least twice in Northampton, perhaps thrice. There is also a sign indicating an earlier Bolton repreaching.

CHRIST, THE LIGHT OF THE WORLD

JOHN 8:12.

I am the light of the world.

THERE is scarcely anything that is excellent, beautiful, pleasant, or profitable but what is used in the Scripture as an emblem of Christ. He is called a lion for his great power, victory, and glorious conquests; he is called a lamb for his great love, pity, and compassion: for that merciful, compassionate, condescending, lamblike disposition of his; for his humility, meekness, and great patience, and because he was slain like a lamb. He was brought as a lamb to the slaughter, so he opened not his mouth.[1] He is called the bread of life and water of life, for the spiritual refreshment and nourishment he gives to the soul; he is called the true vine, because he communicates life to his members, and yields that comfort to the soul that refreshes it as the fruit of the vine doth the body; he is called life, for he is the life of the soul. He is called a rose and lily, and other such similitudes, because of his transcendent beauty and fragrancy. He is called the bright and morning star, and the sun of righteousness; and in our text, the light of the world, of which it is our business at present to speak. In the words, observe:

1. The thing to which Christ compares himself: light, a most excellent and glorious similitude. God the Father is an infinite fountain of light, but Jesus Christ is the communication of this light. Some compare God the Father to the sun and Jesus Christ to the light that streams forth from him by which the world is enlightened. God the Father, in himself, was never seen: 'tis God the Son that has been the light that hath revealed him. God is an infinitely bright and glorious being, but Jesus Christ is that brightness of his glory by which he is

---

1. Following this sentence is another, deleted in the ink of composition, which introduces the emblem of the bridegroom: "He is called a bridegroom for the great joy and delight he brings to believers, and rejoices over them as a bridegroom rejoiceth over his bride."

revealed to us: "No man hath seen God at any time, but the only begotten Son, which is in the bosom of the Father, he hath declared him" (John 1:18). It was the Son of God, the second person in the Trinity, that all along appeared to the patriarchs, that manifested himself to Adam and Abraham, Isaac and Jacob, that appeared to Moses in the burning bush, and went before the children of Israel in a pillar of cloud by day and a pillar of fire by night, that descended on mount Sinai, that was seen by Moses and spake to him face to face as a man speaks to his friend, that dwelt between the cherubims: 'twas the same Jesus Christ that afterwards appeared in the form of sinful flesh and took on him our natures, and said, "before Abraham was, I am," that here compares himself to light.

2. Observe the universality and extensiveness of this light. I am the light of the world, the light of the whole world, as the sun is. As they have not one sun in one part of the world and another in another, but all that are not blind are enlightened by the same sun, so neither is there one Messiah in one part of the world and another Messiah in another part of the world, but all that are not blind are enlightened by the same Messiah. There are these three things implied in Christ's being the light of the world:

(1) That he is the only light by which any in the world can be enlightened. Those that be not enlightened by this light must remain in darkness, for there is no other light by which they can be enlightened.

(2) All the world may be enlightened by it; it is a light that is offered to all the world; an universal offer is made of this light; the partition wall by which the Jews were shut up from all other nations is now broken down. Christ came not only to enlighten the Jews, but all nations: "That was the true Light, that lighteth every man that cometh into the world" (John 1:9).

(3) The world in general will in process of time be enlightened by him: when these glorious times shall come wherein all nations shall flow to the mountain of the Lord's house (Is. 2:2) and the name of Christ shall be among the Gentiles, "from the rising of the sun even to the going down of the same, and incense shall be offered in every place to his name, and a pure offering" (Mal. 1:11); "when they shall teach no more every man his neighbor, and every man his brother, saying, Know the Lord, for they shall all know him, from the least to the greatest" (Jer. 31:34).

This matter cannot be more fully and comprehensively expressed than it is in our text. Wherefore, take the text for a doctrine, thus:

DOCTRINE.

Jesus Christ is the light of the world.

We propose thus to handle this doctrine:
I. To show how the world is in darkness without Christ.
II. How it is enlightened by him.
III. To show by what means Christ communicates his light.

I. The world is in darkness without Christ. Without this sun to enlighten it, the world would always continue in a dreadful, gloomy night of darkness; perpetual midnight, without him, would forever have reigned upon this earth. This is the sun by whose beams alone the shades of spiritual darkness can be made to flee. The darkness that the world is in without Christ may be taken these two ways:

First. For that barbarous idolatry and superstition which the devil has introduced into the world. The world in general has been all overwhelmed with this kind of darkness, insomuch that Satan is called the god of this world, he being worshipped as God from one end of the earth to the other, and the prince of the power of the air. The world in general had for many ages been darkened, before Christ came into it, with a midnight of barbarous polytheism and idolatry, and Satan domineered in an uncontrolled dominion over the miserable, blinded world—in which delusions the greater part of the world still remains—II Cor. 4:4, "In whom the god of this world hath blinded the minds of them which believe not, lest the light of the glorious gospel of Christ, who is the image of God, should shine unto them."

It would be endless to give an account of the barbarous ignorance and sottish, foolish idolatries of the poor, deluded heathen world; how some worship one thing and some another: birds, beasts, insects, fishes, serpents, idols, devils, diseases, fire, water, earth, and air. There is hardly anything but what has been deified and worshipped by one nation [or] another, and their barbarous manner of worshipping them is no less ridiculous: some by burning their children, some by most lascivious actions, others by cutting and tormenting themselves, and innumerable other ridiculous ways.

This is one part of the darkness that Christ came into the world to dissipate. There was a kind of universal night of this darkness over the world before Christ came; all nations were benighted by it. But when Christ came and began to appear like the rising sun, this darkness presently fled from [a] great part of the world, and the nations began to have their eyes enlightened in the knowledge of the true God and Jesus Christ, the Mediator (Luke 2:32, Acts 13:47).

Second. The darkness that Christ came to dissipate is the spiritual darkness that all men by nature are in. Dreadful is our blindness and ignorance by nature; our souls are naturally like a dark, hideous dungeon where the sun, moon, nor stars never found an entrance for their beams. How dull[2] are men while in their natural state of ignorance and unbelief! Their eyes are closed that they cannot see, and their ears heavy like the deaf adder that cannot hear the voice of charmers charming never so wisely. How blind are they to spiritual things; how impossible is it for any but God to persuade them of their danger, and of the importance of things of eternity, although it be as plain as the sun that those things which will last forever are a thousand times more to be regarded than those that will presently have an end; yet how impossible is it to persuade men of it, so full are their minds of darkness. How blind are they when they look on God! They can see nothing excellent or lovely in him, although he is infinitely glorious and infinitely amiable, and his glories appear everywhere throughout the whole creation; there is nothing that we converse with, but what God may easily be seen in it by those whose minds are not full of darkness.

So blind are men by nature that they cannot see the hateful nature of sin, that odious thing, nor the excellency of holiness. They are so full of blindness and darkness that they madly run upon their own ruin, like a blind man that runs into a pit and knows it not.

Thus we have shown how the world is in darkness without Christ; we are now come in the

II. [Second] place to show how Christ is the light of the world. Here we shall show how Christ is the same to our souls as light is to our bodies.

First. 'Tis the property of light to make manifest; that is, to cause things to appear and be seen: without light, nothing can be seen; all things lie hid; nothing can be discerned by the most piercing sight without some light. But when light comes, then things are made to appear; then things may be seen distinctly as they are in their various

---

2. MS: "full," probably because it is written in above a deleted "feeble" and the "f " was transferred inadvertently.

forms, figures, and colors. So Jesus Christ enlightens the soul that comes unto him, makes glorious things manifest to him that he never saw before. When a man is enlightened savingly by Christ, he is as it were brought into a new world; he may say, "Once I was blind, but now I see." He sees then that he was in darkness before; though he was not sensible of it till now, he is like one that was born and brought up in a cave, where is nothing but darkness, but now is brought out into the lightsome world, enlightened by the beams of the sun, and greatly admires and wonders at those things which he never saw before, looks and gazes with sweet astonishment on the pleasing variety of things that are discovered by the light unto him. He now sees things in their true shapes and colors that he never saw before: how he sees his own vileness and filthiness, which he had often heard of before but never believed. He now sees plain enough the glory of Christ: he, while in his dark cave, had been often told what a glorious thing [the] sun was, but he had no notion of it till now. But now he sees with his own eyes, how doth he delight to behold the beauties of this light of the world!

He had often before heard many discourses about religion, about God and Jesus Christ, heaven and hell, free grace and mercy, the excellency of religion and the glorious mysteries of the gospel, but it all seemed as a strange thing to him before; but now he is enlightened by Christ, he sees with his own eyes and admires and is astonished, as being really sensible of the truth of these things.

Second. Another property of light is to be beautiful and pleasant to behold. How dreadful is it to be in horrid darkness, how horrible is it to nature; and how pleasing is the light, how agreeable is it to the eyes. Men manifest it as soon as they are born: how glorious and beautiful is the sun to behold; what a dismal, gloomy, dreadful place would this world be if it were not for the light. What is more beautiful and glorious that can be beheld with bodily eyes than the light?

So, likewise, Jesus Christ is infinitely the most beautiful and glorious object in the world. When the soul is enlightened by Christ to behold him, the soul is greatly delighted with the sight of him, as a little infant is delighted when gazing at the light. 'Tis a far more pleasant thing to behold Jesus Christ than to look on the sun in his meridian glory, for Jesus Christ is an infinite excellency and beauty.

Third. And lastly, light is of a quickening, reviving, and refreshing nature. It revives one that hath been long in darkness again to behold the light; so Christ Jesus revives the souls that come unto him by faith. Here you may run a parallel between the sun and Jesus Christ, the Sun of Righteousness.

1. As the sun, when it rises, all things are thereby revived and awakened out of sleep and silence, so when Jesus Christ shines into the souls of men, they are revived out of their deep and dead sleep of sin. When the sun arises, the world that before was all still and silent, and seemed to be dead, now is[3] revived and raised up by the light thereof, and all things begin to stir and move: things seem to have new life put into them; man rises out of his sleep and sets about his business; the husbandman goeth forth to his labor, the beasts come out of their dens, the birds begin to sing and chant forth their notes, and the world is again put into motion. So it is in spiritual matters with respect to Christ. Before he shines into men's souls, they are dead and dull in a deep sleep, are not diligent at their work, but lie still and sleep and do nothing respecting their souls. All their affections are dead, dull and lifeless; their understandings are darkened with the dark shades of spiritual night, and there is nothing but spiritual sleep and death in their souls.

But when Christ arises upon them, then all things begin to revive, the will and affections begin to move, and they set about the work they have to do. They are now awakened out of their sleep: whereas they were still before, now they begin to be diligent and industrious; whereas they were silent before, now they begin to sing forth God's praises. Their graces now begin to be put into exercise, as flowers send forth a fragrancy when the sun shines upon them.

2. As the sun by his returning influences causes clouds and storms and cold to fly before it, so doth Jesus Christ, the cold, tempests, and clouds of the soul. In the winter season, the heavens are frequently overcast with clouds that hide the pleasing light of the sun; the air is disturbed with winds, storms and tempests, and all things are chilled with frost and cold. The rivers and streams are shut up with ice, the earth is covered with snow, and all things look dreadful; but when the sun returns with its warming influences, the heavens are cleared of dark clouds and the air stilled from tempests, the ice and snow and cold are fled. So the souls of men in their natural state are like winter, perpetually disturbed with the storms of lust and vice, and a raging conscience; their souls are all beclouded with sin and spiritual

3. MS: "are."

darkness. But when Christ comes with his warming influences, things are far otherwise: their minds are calm and serene, warmed with holiness and religion, and the clear sunshine of spiritual comfort.

3. As when the sun returns in the spring, the frozen earth is opened, mollified and softened, so by the beams of the Sun of Righteousness the stony, rocky, adamantine hearts of men are thawed, mellowed and softened, and made fit to receive the seeds of grace. In the winter, the face of the earth is closed and shut up as a stone, unfit for anything to be sown in it, but is loosened in the spring by the warm beams of the sun; so [is] the heart in its natural state frozen and like the stony ground, so that the seeds of God's Word take no rooting in it, but is as if we should cast seed upon the bare rock. But when Christ melts the heart by shining upon it, the seed then sinks into it and takes root and begins to germinate and spring forth.

4. As the sun revives the plants and trees and fruits of the earth, so Christ Jesus by his spiritual light revives the soul and causes it to bring forth fruit. In the winter, the trees are stripped of their leaves and fruit, and stand naked, cease growing, and seem to be dead; the grass and herbs are killed, and all things have the appearance of death upon them. But when the sun returns, then all things have the appearance of a resurrection: things revive again, the trees and fields put on their green livery and begin to bud forth, anew, and flourish and grow. The grass and herbs begin to peep forth out of the ground, and all things look green and flourishing: the fields, meadows, and woods seem to rejoice, and the birds sing a welcome to the returning spring. The fields and trees are adorned with beautiful and fragrant flowers.

Just such an alteration is made in the soul at conversion by Jesus Christ, only far more glorious:

> My beloved spake, and said unto me, Rise up, my love, my fair one, and come away. For, lo, the winter is past, the rain is over and gone; the flowers appear on the earth; the time of the singing of birds is come, and the voice of the turtle is heard in our land; the fig tree putteth forth her green figs, and the vines with the tender grape give a good smell. Arise, my love, my fair one, and come away (Cant. 2:10–13).

In conversion, graces do spring forth in the soul which are like the sweet flowers that adorn the face of the earth in the spring, and like the sweet melody of singing birds. The soul of one upon whom Christ has shined differs as much from the souls of the wicked as the earth, beautified with the vernal sunbeams, and, when covered with ice and snow, and vexed with storms in the dead of winter.

5. And lastly, as the sun by his influences causes the fruits of the earth to grow and increase, fit for the harvest, so Christ by his spiritual influences increases graces and fits for glory. All the fruits of the earth are brought to perfection by the sun; so all the graces of the soul do continue to be increased and ripened by the light that Christ gives, till at length all is perfected in glory. Thus, as the sun is the light of the corporeal world, the great light by which the whole earth is enlightened and enlivened, so Jesus Christ is a far more glorious light of the spiritual world, by which all that are saved are enlightened and quickened. This is a sun by whom the sun in the firmament is created and upheld, to whom our bodily sun is but a shadow, is but as darkness to this infinite fountain of glorious light, and the great light of the world.

III. The third thing proposed was to show how this light of the world communicates his light to the souls of men. I answer:

First. By his Holy Word. Jesus Christ himself is the essential Word of God, of whom the word written and preached is but an emanation: Christ is the sun, and the word written and preached are the rays. The Word of God is frequently compared to light; it pierces as light into the dark recesses of the heart, and reveals the secret and hidden thoughts of [men]. Many of the properties of light are applied to the Word of God:

> The law of the Lord is perfect, converting the soul; the testimony of the Lord is sure, making wise the simple. The statutes of the Lord are right, rejoicing the heart; the commandment of the Lord is pure, enlightening the eyes. The fear of the Lord is clean, enduring forever; the judgments of the Lord are true and righteous altogether (Ps. 19:7–9). For the word of God is quick and powerful, sharper than any two-edged sword, piercing even to the dividing asunder of soul and spirit, and of the joints and marrow, and is a discerner of the thoughts and intents of the heart (Heb. 4:12).

But God has more especially made the word preached efficacious to the enlightening [of] the soul. Faith comes by hearing, and hearing by the word preached: Rom. 10:14, "How then shall they call on him in whom they have not believed, and how shall they believe in him of whom they have not heard, and how shall they hear without a preacher?"

Second. But Christ enlightens the soul by his Holy Spirit. Although the word be quick and powerful, yet it is nothing; it is but a dead letter without the application of the Holy Spirit. Though it be sharper than a two-edged sword, it cannot divide a rocky heart except [it be] managed by an Almighty hand; the hammer will not break this rock in pieces, except God smites with it: but Jesus Christ, when he enlightens the mind, sends forth the Holy Spirit to dwell in the soul, to be as a continual internal light to manifest and make known spiritual things to the believer.[4]

Thus we have shown how Jesus Christ is the light of the world. We shall now briefly apply this doctrine.

APPLICATION.

[I. *Use of Instr.*]

First. Is it so that Jesus Christ is the light of the world? From hence we may learn one great reason why wicked men are so shy of Jesus Christ and so adverse to come unto him: for fear their deeds should be made manifest. Those that use themselves to wicked courses love to keep in darkness as much as they can. They hate the light; it is as the shadow of death to them:

> In the dark they dig through houses which they had marked for themselves in the daytime; they know not the light, for the morning is to them even as the shadow of death: if one know them, they are in the terrors of the shadow of death (Job 24:16–17). And this is the condemnation, that light is come into the world and men loved darkness rather than light, because their deeds are evil. For everyone that doeth evil hateth the light, neither cometh to the light, lest his deeds should be reproved (John 3:19–20).

Wicked men are terribly afraid of conviction, dreadfully afraid of their own conscience, and do what they can to put out the light of it. The light of conscience is a perpetual torment to them, will not let them alone to sit peaceably and quietly, and they know if they come

4. In this passage JE particularly anticipates the central concept of *A Divine and Supernatural Light* (1735), the "indwelling light" that seems so close to the Quaker "inner light," but apparently without admitting of such Antinomian revelatory autonomy.

to Christ that they must give their conscience full liberty: let it blaze out without restraint; must let it speak to them with open mouth.

They know how contrary their practices are to Jesus Christ, the Light of the World, and his glorious gospel; as contrary as darkness is to the light. They know, if they come to Christ, they must repent and mourn for their sins, must have their hearts broken for it, must forsake and repent of all their former courses, must undo all that they have done by repentance, must utterly forsake that which they used to count their greatest happiness, and for the time to come look upon it as their greatest misery and shun and avoid it as such. And they can't bear to think of that; they can't bear the thoughts of this contrition and confession, repentance and humiliation. They can't bear the thoughts of forsaking all their sins and mortifying all their lusts without retaining one, for Jesus is pure light, and without the least spot of darkness. No darkness can endure this light; I John 1:5–6, "This then is the message which we have heard of him and declare unto you, that God is light and in him is no darkness at all. If we say that we have fellowship with him, and walk in darkness, we lie and do not the truth."

This forsaking all their sins and every lust is the thing they stick at, if it were but some sins. They would not so much hesitate if they might but retain such a darling sin, such a dear lust, but only that one. They should not be so shy of Christ if they might but retain one or two little sins; they would come but [for] that they may not do. He that cometh unto Jesus Christ must bring none of Christ's enemies in his arms.

Second. Is Christ Jesus the light of the world? What glorious times will those be when all nations shall submit themselves to him, when this glorious light shall shine into every dark corner of the earth, and shall shine much more brightly and gloriously than ever before. It will be like the rising of the sun after a long night of darkness, after the thick darkness had been ruling and reigning over all nations and poor mankind had been groping about in gross darkness for many ages. When this glorious morning comes, then those that never saw light before shall see it and be astonished at its glory. Then the world, which has been in a kind of dead sleep for this many ages, shall rouse up and begin [to] open their eyes and look forth to behold this glorious light of the world; then will the sweet music of God's praises begin to be heard.

Then will Christ say unto his spouse, as in Is. 60, at the beginning:

"Arise, shine; for thy light is come, for the glory of the Lord is risen upon thee. For the Gentiles shall then come unto her light, and kings to the brightness of her rising." Now, indeed, darkness covers the earth and gross darkness the people, but the Lord shall arise upon his church and his glory shall be seen upon her.[5] Then shall "the light of the moon be as the light of the sun, and the light of the sun shall be sevenfold" (Is. 30:26). The world has had a long winter of sin and ignorance; for many ages has the Sun of Righteousness been in the Tropic of Capricorn; but when this time comes the world will enjoy a glorious spring: then holiness and God's kingdom shall revive as the fields and trees revive in spring. Then shall the time come when all creatures shall praise the Lord, and the mountains shall break forth into singing and all the trees of the field shall clap their hands:

> For ye shall go out with joy, and be led forth with peace; the mountains and the hills shall break forth before you into singing, and all the trees of the field shall clap their hands. Instead of the thorn shall come up the fir tree, and instead of the briar shall come up the myrtle tree; and it shall be to the Lord for a name, for an everlasting sign that shall not be cut off (Is. 55:12–13).

II. *Use of Exh.*

First. If Christ Jesus is the light of the world, let all be exhorted to come unto him. Hear what Christ says in the latter part of the verse of our text: "He that followeth me shall not walk in darkness, but shall have the light of life." Consider how much light is preferable to darkness.

1. How uncomfortable is darkness. If you love darkness rather than light, it is a certain sign that your nature is horribly depraved, for to love darkness is against nature.

2. How dangerous is it to walk in darkness, not knowing which way we go, groping about in this world so full of dangers—so full of enemies, so full of snares and pits—without knowing how near we are every moment to the pit of misery. Truly we had need to have our eyes open in such a dangerous state as we are in [in] this world; we had need to have the best light instead of groping in darkness.

3. Consider that those that walk in darkness in this world will be cast into outer darkness where there is weeping and wailing and

---

5. The quotation involves fairly free use of Is. 60:1,3 while the following sentence is a paraphrase of 60:2.

gnashing of teeth, and blackness of darkness forever. Now we have the Light of the World offered to us; we may come unto him if we will, and he will enlighten us.

If you desire to have your soul raised out from a hideous, yea, a hellish night of darkness, and to have a heavenly light shine into it, come to this Light of the World. Receive him and trust in him, and you will find that hitherto you have been in darkness; that your soul has been in a wintry state and condition till then, when your soul shall be warmed, enlivened, quickened, comforted, and refreshed by the beams of this glorious sun.

Second. The second exhortation is to all that live under the gospel. The exhortation is that in John 12:35–36, "Yet a little while the light is with you. Walk while you have the light, lest darkness come upon you: for he that walketh in darkness knoweth not whither he goeth. While ye have the light, believe in the light, that ye may be the children of light." Now the light of the gospel shines upon you; now is your only opportunity: how soon your sun will set you know not; the Sun of Righteousness more commonly sets before than after noon, and very seldom reaches the western horizon.

Third. [The third] exhortation is to those who are the children of light. 'Tis that in Eph. 5:8, "For ye were sometimes darkness, but now are ye light in the Lord: walk as children of light." Your souls were once filled with the same darkness of spiritual ignorance and blindness, but Christ has enlightened your minds. Wherefore, no more act and walk as the children of darkness. O, what reason have you to live to the praise and glory of God, who has called you out of darkness into marvellous light, and walk worthy of the vocation by which ye are called. Wherefore, as God which has called you is holy, so be ye holy in all manner of conversation.

THE Puritan "plain style" is exemplified in this sermon to a degree that is unusual for Edwards at any period. Carefully composed, symmetrical in form, and remarkably clear in its expression, "Dedication to God" is devoid of vivid images, figures, and tropes, or anything else that might mitigate the spareness of its rhetoric. Moreover, although the issue of reason is an explicit part of the argument, there is little in the way of subtle or brilliant argumentation: even such cool aesthetics as those of logical exposition are restrained, and much of the sermon is asserted rather than argued. (For that matter, even "Scripture proofs" are remarkably rare.) But that this effect was calculated rather than the result of the sermon's being composed on an off-day is borne out by the fact that several significant additions made years later in Northampton for a repreaching are all in the same style: no ornaments were added; points were merely amplified (see textual footnotes).

The terms of the sermon are those traditional opposed poles of Christian discourse, "God" and "the world, the flesh, and the devil," concepts neither remarkably precise nor vivid, yet as familiar and essential as small change in the pocket. The operative element in the argument—"the great duty of self-dedication"—is likewise neither novel nor unusual in its application. It would thus seem that Edwards has the basic ingredients for dullness or even triteness prominently disposed within his sermon, and it is true that "Dedication to God" is not colorful or brilliant in the accepted sense, either from the standpoint of theology or literature. Yet a careful reading of it reveals a mysterious rhetorical vitality and argumentative intensity. In fact, the effect brings to mind that portion of the "Personal Narrative" in which Edwards recounts his discovery of the majesty of God in a passage of Scripture. The episode is related in Samuel Hopkins' *Life* (Boston, 1765):

> The first that I remember that ever I found anything of that sort of inward, sweet delight in God and divine things, that I have

lived much in since, was on reading those words, I Tim. 1:17, "Now unto the King eternal, immortal, invisible, the only wise God, be honor and glory forever and ever, Amen." As I read the words, there came into my soul, and was as it were diffused through it, a sense of the glory of the Divine Being; a new sense, quite different from anything I ever experienced before. Never any words of Scripture seemed to me as these words did. . . . I kept saying, and as it were singing over these words of Scripture to myself; and went to prayer, to pray to God that I might enjoy him; and prayed in a manner quite different from what I used to do, with a new sort of affection. (P. 25)

Years later, recollecting in tranquility, Edwards tells how words, neither colorful nor profound in themselves, may serve to evoke a profound, unforgettable experience if they should be the *right* words. Wit and even wisdom, on the other hand, may virtually distract, or dilute the sense of the actual, through their own intense manifestation.

Such a sense of the actual may in fact be the transfiguring ingredient within the otherwise unremarkable sermon presented here. Given his own experience as recounted above, Edwards would certainly be inclined to trust in the power of spare statement of the actual, even when mediated by the formal constraints of the sermon as he practiced it, when the job at hand was the communication of an intensely experienced religious conviction. That such a moment of private conviction underlay this sermon is suggested by another passage published in the Hopkins volume: this time, however, not one representing Edwards' recollections in later life, but one written in the "Diary," apparently within days of "Dedication to God" and recounting an ongoing experience.

Saturday, Jan. 12, 1723, in the morning. I have this day solemnly renewed my baptismal covenant and self-dedication, which I renewed when I was received into the communion of the church. I have been before God; and have given myself, all that I am and have to God, so that I am not in any respect my own: I can challenge no right in myself; I can challenge no right in this understanding, this will, these affections that are in me; neither have I any right to this body, or any of its members: no right to this tongue, these hands, nor feet: no right to these senses, these eyes, these ears, this smell or taste. I have given myself clear away, and have not retained anything as my own. . . . I have this morning told Him that I did take Him for my whole portion and felicity, looking on nothing else as any part of my happiness, nor acting as if it were; and his law for the constant rule of my obedience: and would fight with all my might against the world, the flesh, and the devil to the end of my life. (Pp. 11–12)

Here and throughout the remainder of this long entry, as well as in the two related resolutions and the subsequent entry for January 14, Edwards clearly presents the personal context of his sermon. Indeed, it is most likely that the sermon was written very near the above date, since there was another falling off of inspiration a few days later, according to the "Diary." In any event, it should be noted that Edwards follows the precedent of the Apostle, as he is careful to point out in the sermon's textual exegesis, in moving from the idiom of inspired reflection to the appeal of reason as he undertakes the public inculcation of those duties which are predicated upon such deep religious conviction.

* * *

The octavo quire of the sermon booklet is standard and fairly neat, although there are some crossouts, in addition to the usual corrections, that apparently result from Edwards' having laid out the sermon's major heads beforehand and his having to overrun some of them when the argument took more space to develop than anticipated. On the other hand, several heads were not filled until a later preaching in Northampton for which Edwards made seven substantial additions, six of which he was able to insert in blank spaces at the ends of heads. The first insertion, however, was too large for any blank space, being a page in length, and had in any case to be written where there was no convenient blank. Thus Edwards wrote the insertion on the first page of a two-leaf octavo fold which he must have wrapped about the existing sermon as there are no stitching holes in the fold matching those of the original booklet. Having finished with the repreaching of the sermon on Rom. 12:1, Edwards utilized the verso and the remaining leaf of the fold in a sermon on Matt. 11:28

where they now constitute the first and last leaves of the sermon booklet. Unlike most sermons, Matt. 11:28 begins on an inside page.

Shorthand signs and varying inks suggest that this sermon may have been repreached twice in Northampton and possibly in Bolton, Connecticut.

DEDICATION TO GOD

ROMANS 12:1.

I beseech you therefore, brethren, by the mercies of God, that ye present your bodies a living sacrifice, holy, acceptable to God, which is your reasonable service.

THE Apostle, in the foregoing part of this epistle having insisted upon the great doctrines of Christianity, against Jews and heathens, and clearly proved and brightly illustrated those gospel truths which are so bright and glorious, the Apostle breaks out in a sort of a rapture at the conclusion of the doctrinal part of the epistle in the last words of the foregoing chapter:

> O the depth of the riches both of the wisdom and knowledge of God! How unsearchable are his judgments, and his ways past finding out! For who hath known the mind of the Lord, or who hath been his counsellor? Or who hath first given to him, and it shall be recompensed to him again? For of him, and through him, and to him are all things: to whom be glory forever. Amen [Rom. 11:33–36].

And now he begins in this twelfth chapter the practical part of the epistle, as an improvement of the foregoing glorious truths, and this he begins with the words of our text, with urging this greatest of all the duties of a Christian: of offering up ourselves to God. The Apostle begins with this because it comprehends all other duties. At this present time, we shall only consider these two things in the words:

1. The duty enjoined and urged, and that is the presenting our bodies, which is to be understood metonymically of our whole per-

sons—body and soul—a living sacrifice to God.[1] The sacrifices that were enjoined under the law were of bulls, goats, and calves, etc., which were but types of the great sacrifice of the gospel: Jesus Christ, who was once offered up. And therefore, all the standing sacrifices that remain are of our own bodies which we are to offer up alive to God.

2. The argument by which it is urged, and that is that it is our most reasonable service; most reasonable by reason of those things of which the Apostle had been speaking in the foregoing part of the epistle.[2]

DOCTRINE.

'Tis our most reasonable duty to offer and give ourselves up to God.

We are now to speak something of the great duty of self-dedication. It is the greatest, most comprehensive and necessary, of all duties.

---

1. A key sign at this place indicates the point of insertion for a passage now bound with a sermon on Matt. 11:28 (1726). The insertion was made in Northampton in order to amplify the exegetical material for a repreaching. The inserted passage is as follows:

We find it [a] notion as general amongst men as the being of God, that as [we] receive and expect many things from him, so that something that is ours should be devoted and given to him. And however unreasonable it is to imagine that God can be profited by any of our gifts, yet the light of nature taught all mankind that our gratitude to heaven ought to be manifested at our expense.

Agreeable to this was the practice of all nations, and that time out of mind, who used to make offerings of their goods and possessions, of their cattle slain and consumed in sacrifice and sometimes even of the fruit of their bodies, from a true opinion that nothing that we have is too dear and precious to be offered to the deity, however it was ill-directed and misguided.

There was also the same usage in that nation that was God's peculiar people and the only nation of all upon the face of the earth that professed the true religion and [established practice] upon a better foundation, even their custom by divine appointment to offer up the first fruits of their land: their corn, their silver and gold, their wine and their oil, and their cattle. But the sacrifice here enjoined is the sacrifice of ourselves.

2. At this point occurs the first of six amplifications made at the same time as that from the Matt. 11:28 sermon noted above, but in blank spaces within the sermon manuscript. The passage added is as follows:

This may be taken as including these two things: First, a service in itself proper and reasonable to be offered to God, in distinction to the sacrifices under the law of slain beasts which were not reasonable sacrifices in themselves, only as they typified something else; for otherwise, what propriety could there be in offering flesh and blood to God who can't hunger nor thirst? Second, reasonable upon the account of the many obligations that lie upon us to do it, that make it a very reasonable thing that it should be done.

All other duties, internal and external—faith, repentance, hope, charity, obedience, and good works—are included. 'Tis a duty more necessary than by many is imagined. Many think that God's love and favor belongs to them, but yet never act as if they belonged to God, but as if they were their own and had a right to themselves: as if God had nothing to do with them any further than to make them happy. They imagine that God loves them so much as to bestow everlasting life upon them, and yet at the same time they don't love him so well as to obey his commands.

Now it behooves us all to know that God never looks upon us as his, to make us happy, till we have given ourselves entirely to him and look upon ourselves as his, to obey his laws and in all things submit to his will. 'Tis this giving ourselves to God is the very thing that alone gives us a right to the privileges of the sons of God, and makes us partakers of the benefits purchased by his dear and only Son; for until we have given ourselves to God, and have offered ourselves as a sacrifice to him, we belong to the devil and he claims a right to us. For we have all in effect given ourselves to him by sin, and except we can show another deed whereby we have given ourselves to God, whereby that is disannulled, when we come to die he will certainly stand ready at our deathbeds, and will lay hold of us as his own, as those that are his servants, that have sold and given themselves to him, and will violently hurry us away to hell, his own habitation. Wherefore, seeing this offering ourselves to God is such an important duty that so much concerns us and is so necessary, we shall:

I. Show what it is, and
II. Show how reasonable a duty it is.

I. What is offering or giving ourselves up to God? You may take the whole of this duty as included in these four things: first, an absolute renunciation of the world, the flesh, and the devil; second, a joyful receiving of God as our whole portion and happiness; third, a willing embracing all his commands; and fourth, a resignation to his will.

First. There must be an absolute renunciation of the flesh, the world, and the devil. If we pretend to give ourselves to God, we must give ourselves to him entirely, and wholly, and heartily. God will not accept of any if we keep back a part. The flesh, the world, and the devil are God's most irreconcilable enemies. There is no such thing as belonging to God and yet to his enemies, or belonging partly to

God and partly to his enemies; we cannot serve God and mammon, but we must give ourselves altogether to God, or else belong altogether to his adversaries.

If we would offer ourselves to God, we must renounce the flesh: that slothfulness, that love to ease and pleasure which makes us hate to set about religion in good earnest, which makes us hate to leave sin and hate to deny ourselves, must be renounced and parted with. We must give ourselves away from ourselves, and never more challenge any right to ourselves to please ourselves, any otherwise than as we please God. We must no more challenge any right to these understandings, these wills, these affections, these bodies, or these senses. We must look upon them as entirely belonging to God, and altogether his own; and from that day forth that we give ourselves to God, we must no more till we die expect to gratify any of our lusts: no more expect any slothful ease or rest, no more expect to gratify the flesh and any of its appetites, but must take our eternal leave of them.

The world must also be renounced. We must that day take our hearts off from worldly pomp, show, or prosperity, and no more set our hearts upon them, or to pride ourselves in the possession and enjoyment of them, or to be over-anxious about [them]: never so much to regard them as to make the least of God's commands turn aside for them, and to regard them no otherwise than as a staff to help us in our journey to heaven. Worldly glory, worldly pleasure, and worldly riches must all be renounced at once.

We must renounce the devil and resolve no longer to serve him, as we have done in time past; no more to hearken to him, however he tempts us, whatever allurements he sets before us, or whatever difficulties he represents to affright us from our duty. This is the most difficult part of this great and necessary duty of giving ourselves to God, but yet no more difficult than must be complied with. 'Tis the best and the worst; 'tis the hardest, and yet never anyone that ever got to heaven found it easier.

Second. A joyful receiving of God as our whole portion and happiness. This world and the pleasing of the flesh being renounced, we must no more look upon them as our happiness; we must no more suffer our hearts to rest upon them as our portion, but God must be taken and rested in as all the felicity of our souls. If we have not so given ourselves to God as to be contented in him as a sufficient and satisfying happiness, without hankering, looking back and longing after our old masters, the flesh, the world, and the devil, and their pleasure, we have not given ourselves to God in a right manner.[3]

Third. A willing embracing all God's commands, and a devoting ourselves to his service and glory. It is a giving ourselves up to God as servants, and receiving him as sovereign, God and King over our souls and bodies, over all our powers and all our actions. 'Tis a giving our understandings to him to be enlightened, and to be exercised in thinking upon him. 'Tis a giving our wills to him, to be guided and exercised in choosing of him above all things. 'Tis a giving our affections to him to be governed and exercised in loving him, and what he loves, and hating what he hates. 'Tis a giving all our executive powers to him to be employed wholly in his service.

Fourth. A resignation to his will. If God receives us as his own, he will dispose of us as he pleases; for he will do what he will with his own. Therefore, if we profess to give ourselves to God, we must cast ourselves and all our affairs upon his will, to be at his disposal, trusting in his mercy, goodness, and promises. As one man cannot be said entirely to give a thing to another, except he gives him the liberty of disposing of it as he pleases; so neither can man be said to offer himself a living sacrifice to God, except he entirely gives himself up to God's will, trusting in his mercy.

II. It is our most reasonable duty thus to give ourselves to God. However difficult and self-denying it may seem, yet it is exceeding reasonable that we should do it, and that for these four reasons:

First. We of right belong to God by creation, and therefore it is most reasonable that we should offer ourselves to him. When we give ourselves to God, we do but give his own, that that he has made for himself, that which he has formed for his own use and service.[4]

---

3. This head was also amplified by inserting the following passage:

We can't divide ourselves and give God a part, and mammon a part, and our sensual pleasures a part: but God must have all. Our love to him must govern all our love; our desires after him must govern all our desires; our joy in him must be above all our joy. The love of him and desires after him must take full possession of our hearts.

4. A fourth amplification was made by the insertion of the following material at this point:

Certainly, that which God gives being to, its being is his; for what God gives, and comes wholly from God, is God's except he quits his right to it. That which God gives being to is as much God's as his own being is. That that is the effect of his power is as much God's as the power that effected [it]. The thing is exceeding plain and even self-evident. Therefore, if God made our souls, our souls are his; if God made our bodies, our bodies are his; if he made our understand-

Second. We of right belong to God by preservation. As we are God's because we could never have been if it had not been for God's creation, so we are his because we cannot be one moment longer without his preservation. He is the God in whose hand our breath is, and whose are all our ways: in whom we live, move, and have our being.

He preserves us from annihilation; we should immediately drop into nothing if he did not uphold us. He preserves us from death; we are fed and nourished and clothed, and thereby kept alive by him. He preserves us from the devil; the devil stands ready to lay hold of us as soon as ever he has the liberty, and we should long ere this time have been in his tormenting, cruel hands if God by his almighty power had not kept him off, and of his goodness preserved us from him. 'Tis by God that our well-being is preserved. All our good things, all the comforts, temporal and spiritual, that we enjoy are by him given to us and by him preserved. We are not able to retain them if God pleases to take them from us. We are not able, without God, to preserve ourselves from death, to preserve ourselves from the hands of Satan, one moment. How reasonable, therefore, is it that we should give ourselves to God who so constantly preserves us; and how just would it be with God to leave us to fall into the hands of Satan, except we will give ourselves to him, for God is not bound to preserve us one moment longer. He does only from his free mercy and goodness.

Third. We are God's by redemption: "What? know ye not that your body is the temple of the Holy Ghost which is in you, which ye have of God, and ye are not your own? For ye are bought with a price; therefore glorify God in your body and in your spirit, which are God's" (I Cor. 6:19–20).

Fourth. 'Tis our most reasonable duty because God gives us such glorious encouragement. His mercy has been so redundant and overflowing that, although he has an absolute right to us, a threefold right, whereby we are bound to give ourselves to God; and although it is for our advantage and not his for us to give ourselves to him, for we must be either God's or the devil's, yet he has promised eternal happiness as a free reward of such a sacrifice.

APPLICATION.

The use of this doctrine is to persuade all to present themselves a living sacrifice, holy and acceptable to God, which is your reasonable

---

ings, our understandings are his; if God gave us our bodily strength, that strength is his; and if he gave us our outward possessions, they must likewise be his.

service. However hard it may seem to you thus quite to renounce the flesh, the world, and the devil; to give yourselves entirely and altogether to God, and to look upon yourself no longer as your own, to take up satisfied with God as your whole happiness, leaving all those other happinesses and pleasures to embrace all the laws and commands of God, the most difficult as well as the most easy; however difficult it may seem to be entirely resigned to God's will and be at his disposal, yet you see how reasonable a thing it is, for we belong to God. He challenges a right in us, and what if it seem hard to us to give God that which is his own, yet certainly it [is] most reasonable it should be done and nothing will excuse our neglect of it.

And beside, if you consider these following motives to the duty, you will find that they far outweigh the difficulties you imagine:

[I. *Motives.*]

First. A refusing to do it is a denying your baptism. You have done this in your baptism: you have already given yourself to God the Father, the Son, and the Holy Ghost; have devoted yourself to him, renounced the world, the devil, and yourselves, and have given yourselves to God and disclaimed all right in yourselves—that is, if you will stand to your baptism and pretend to be a Christian. I acknowledge, if you renounce your baptism and turn atheists or heathen, this motive loses its force with you; but if you acknowledge your baptism, you must give yourself to God, and that entirely, however difficult it may seem to you, for therein you promised you would so do to the end of your lives. You must do [it], that is, you cannot help or avoid doing one of these three things. It is left with you which you will choose: either renounce and become an atheist, or else own your baptism and the solemn vows and promises you made therein and, at the same time, wilfully and obstinately live in the continual breach of them, or else give yourself to God as a living sacrifice to him.

Second. God will receive those that heartily give themselves to him as his own peculiar treasure. The privileges and great advantages of thus offering yourself to God infinitely outweigh the self-denial and mortification of it: the difficulties vanish into nothing when compared with them. For you will [be] received by the Almighty as his peculiar treasure. If you set yourself apart for him, he will receive you and set you apart for himself, as a man sets apart some precious gem: "The Lord hath set apart him that is godly for himself" (Ps. 4:3).

Third. They that heartily give themselves to God are sure of his love and favor and protection. Although you are vile and hateful and unworthy to be accepted of God, yet he will willingly receive you as his own; will receive you as his charge and trust, will have you as a child, will keep you as a treasure. Then you may [be] certain of his love and favor, certain of his guidance in all your ways, certain that no evil shall befall you, certain that whatever befalls you it is for your good; for you know and are certain that you are God's, for you have given yourself to him, and therefore you are certain that he will do by you in all respects as to one that is his. You may lie and rest quietly and securely in the midst of storms and tempests, fearing nothing, knowing that you are in God's hands where nothing can hurt you.[5]

Fourth. They are sure of the happiness of heaven hereafter. After God has received you as his own, God will make it his business to make you happy: to make you beautiful and amiable with grace and holiness and his lovely image, and to destroy sin which he so hates. He will make it his business to prepare you for happiness and afterwards to bestow it upon you, for God loves to see his own image and likeness upon all that he receives as his, both in holiness and happiness. He don't love to see that which is his own to be either sinful or miserable, nor will he allow it. When you give yourself to God, if you do it aright, you do it out of love to him, and if he receives you as he certainly will, he will receive you into his love. And he will surely make that happy which he so loves as to take to be his own, for when he receives them from love, he takes them for that very end and for no other purpose than to make them happy and blessed forever.

Those that give themselves to God and resign themselves to his will, will find that his will is nothing but their eternal welfare and happiness. They never need to fear to trust God, not knowing what his will [will] be; for as soon as you have heartily and entirely given yourself to him and retain nothing, God will set himself to make you happy. You are sure that he will do nothing to you while here but what will end in your glorious happiness hereafter. And when you die, you shall be received unto God as his own, very near to himself, into the closest union, and he will completely fill you with happiness.

---

5. This head was amplified by the insertion of the following:

'Tis indeed wonderful that the infinite God will so graciously accept of such a gift as the dedication of ourselves, for we are poor, forlorn, loathsome creatures; but yet such is the mercy of God that if we will come to him and render up ourselves to him, he'll receive [us] into his favor and will bestow upon us his everlasting love. He will set his heart upon us as his jewels, and will be tender of us as of the apple of his eye.

If you give yourself to God to obey him, he will receive you as his to make you blessed. If you give yourself to God, he will also give himself to you. You give yourself to him to be his servant; he will give himself to you to be your portion and everlasting happiness, and thereby you are sure of eternal glory, because the infinite source and fountain of eternal glory is yours already. He has given himself to you and you need not fear enjoying what God has made yours. Thereby you become possessed of all things, because the maker, governor, and possessor of all things is yours. He has given himself to you.

If you have given yourself to God sincerely, you are become a member of his Son, and as it is impossible that either sin or misery should be in the glorified Son of God, so it is impossible that sin or misery should long remain in any of his members.

[II.] Directions.

First. Frequently renew this dedication or giving yourself to God. Let not barely a consent to your baptism suffice. There are many that pretend to assent to their baptism that don't truly do it, but if they don't speak, yet they live forth a renunciation of it. You cannot truly consent to your baptism, except you again act over solemnly and heartily and sincerely what you then did, and so make it your own act. Frequently come before God in your closet, and there heartily give yourself to him. Beg of him to accept of you. Renounce all right in yourself, and humbly tell him that you receive [him] as your whole portion and happiness, and that you will be devoted to his glory. Tell him that you do and will receive his commands—every one of them—with all the difficulties that do or can possibly attend them. Let this be very frequently done, for unspeakable are the advantages of it.

Second. Never act anymore as if you were your own. You must consider that in giving yourself to God, you have cast off all pretenses to a right in yourself, and if you go afterwards to act as if you were your own, you thereby deny what you [have] done. You give and take away again: you have given all your powers and faculties to God, and yet you take them and make use of them as if they were your own. If you don't give yourself to God entirely, it is not worth your while to pretend to give yourself to him at all; for he will accept of no other self-dedication but what is entire. For what do you mean by giving yourself to God except devoting all your powers to him, to be used entirely for him and not for yourself, to act for the time to come as

his and not as your own? Now, you will act as if you were your own
and not as God's if you do these following things:

1. You will act as if you were your own if you do anything but what
is to the glory of God, and don't make the glorifying of him your
chief business. If you do anything for the devil, anything for any one
of your lusts, or anything merely for the world, or indeed merely and
only for yourself, you thereby go from God again to your old masters,
and serve them. You thereby take yourself away from God and challenge a right in yourselves again.[6]

2. You act as if you were your own, if you omit any duty or commit
any sin for the sake of your own ease or pleasure. You are no longer
to look at your own ease or your own pleasure or profit any farther
than they respect and help religion and God's glory, for you are to
remember that you are not your own, to please yourself, but God's
to please him.

Wherefore, the neglect of difficult duties, or the commission of
pleasant or profitable sins, is a reaffirming a right to yourself, and a
direct breach of your former act. Wherefore remember, whenever
you are assaulted by the temptations of ease, profit, or pleasure, that
you are not your own, and that you have renounced these things and
given yourself wholly to God.

3. You act as if you were your own when you trust to yourself.
This is directly contrary to a resignation to the will of God, and is in
no wise consistent with it. Did you give yourself into the hands of
God, trusting in him to be guided, directed, assisted and helped by
him, and do you notwithstanding again place some trust in your own

6. This head was amplified by the following insertion:
   Seeing that we ourselves and all our powers are God's, every exercise of these
powers should be God's too. And therefore, every action that does not tend to
God and has not a respect to him is a theft from God. When we do anything not
for God's glory, we use that that is God's in a manner that we have no leave to
use it; we use God's talents about that which he did not lend it to us for. God has
lent us many talents: our power of understanding is one, our senses are others,
our powers of bodily action are others, and our substance is another. And God,
when he put these talents into our hands, he did not do it for us to improve for
ourselves, but for him. We are to be stewards and servants to do his service with
them. Those talents are God's own, and therefore the interest of them should also
be his own. Matt. 25:27, "Thou oughtest to have put my money to the exchangers,
and then at my coming I should have received my own with usury." If we therefore
take any of this money and turn it wholly to our own interest, having no respect
to God, we steal it from him.

strength or righteousness, both which you renounced when you gave yourself to God?[7]

4. You act as if you were your own when you murmur at afflictions. Did you commit yourself to God, and tell him that you resigned yourself to his will and pleasure, to do what he would with you? Did you give yourself to him, and yet murmur when God orders afflictions for you? What did you mean when you pretended to present yourself to God: to be done with as he pleased, or as you please? Did you retain a right to choose for yourself, to choose what you thought best should befall you, or did you leave it with God, and trust it with him to do what he would with his own? If you did, why do you murmur and fret and be uneasy when you are afflicted? Is not that God's that he thinks best to afflict?

Consider you have given yourself to God and you are not your own: it is not for you to murmur, for you have no right in yourself but belong to God, if you have trusted yourself with him.

5. You act as if you were your own if you are proud, malicious, invidious, and revengeful. How ridiculous is it for a man to be proud of that which is not his own; so how ridiculous will it be for you to be proud of yourself, or your own powers or qualifications, which you have given away entirely to God. Remember, therefore, whenever you feel any motion of pride, that you have given yourself with all your powers to God and have disclaimed all right in them. Remember, when you have done any good action, that you are not your own and that God only made you the instrument of it. Remember, when you are wronged and injured and affronted by others, that that which they wrong is God's and not your own, and suffer no motions of malice or revenge. God will take care and avenge his own.

6. If you are uncharitable; if you neglect the welfare of your fellow-creatures; if you are not ready, freely and without grudging, to distribute to the needs and necessities of others; if you withhold your hand from doing good to your fellow-Christians upon all occasions

7. This head was amplified by the following addition:

By trusting in ourselves, we act as if we were our own disposers, as [if] it were with us to make ourselves thus or thus, or to obtain by our own efficiency our own welfare. But if we are God's, God will dispose of us as he pleases, for God disposes as he will of his own: he don't leave it with men to save, to help, and make happy that which is not theirs but his. And therefore, if men give themselves with God and trust in him, and not in themselves [. . .]

JE did not complete the last sentence in this passage.

for a needless fear of hurting yourself: you act as if you were your own. You are to remember that you have given yourself to God with all that you have; for if you are God's, what you possess is his too, and not your own, neither have you the liberty of disposing of it according to your own inclinations, for your outward ease and prosperity, without respect to God's glory and the good of others.

If you have offered yourself and all that you have to God, you need not think it hard to distribute freely, liberally, and charitably of God's own to his creatures, that bear his image and likeness as well as you; but especially to those who are his own children, and are the members of Christ. Wherefore, if you pretend to make an offering of yourself to God, don't withhold what you possess: Prov. 19:17, "He that hath pity on the poor lendeth to the Lord." Matt. 25:35–36, "I was an hungered, and ye gave me meat; I was thirsty, and ye gave me drink; I was a stranger, and ye took me in; naked, and ye clothed me; I was sick, and ye visited me; I was in prison, and ye came unto me." And the fortieth verse, "Verily I say unto you, Inasmuch as ye have done it to one of the least of my brethren, ye have done it unto me."

LIVING TO CHRIST and DYING TO GAIN

"Living to Christ" and "Dying to Gain" constitute a true pair of sermons. That is, while each sermon is an independent and fully developed literary unit which can be preached separately from the other, the sermons not only divide a single brief verse of Scripture, but a reference to "the forenoon" near the end of the second sermon's textual exegesis confirms the original function of the pair as morning and afternoon segments of a single sabbath's preaching. Analysis of the inks involved in the complex revisions of the sermons reveals that they were probably preached as separate sermons also, the second of the two apparently having been repreached more often than the first.

The essential unity of the pair transcends the merely formal aspects of text and doctrine, however, and derives primarily from the paradoxical use of the terms "life" and "death" as understood in the light of Christian doctrine. The Christian life is thus predicated upon a death—even a kind of crucifixion—of the "normal" earthly life; consequently, true Christians are already in a sense dead and resurrected in this life in order that they may become part of the living Christ. On the other hand, the second sermon stresses the absolute value of physical death to the Christian as it liberates him from pain and sorrow, and secures the highest joys and pleasures for him. The language of the sermons is generally plain, practical, and relatively free of theological niceties, yet the great common denominator or linchpin of the pair is the virtually metaphysical play upon the concepts of life and death. The idiom is predominantly literal and in a sense modern, especially when compared to that of John Donne or George Herbert, yet the emphatic juxtaposition of levels of being parallels the radical verbal conjunctions of the metaphysical poets. The style may be different, but the mentality is much the same, deriving as it does from the underlying doctrines themselves.

The level of paradox and irony so apparent in both sermons extends even to the arrangement of the sermons. Thus, though the first is nominally about living and the second about dying, the reverse is true when the essential message is considered, and the Edwardsean tendency to argue from negative to positive is preserved in the larger as well as in the smaller literary units.

Imagery plays a significant role in both sermons. It is generalized yet vivid, simple in visualization yet subtle in implication. The imagery of light is especially important to the discussion of divine influences, and this pattern of images culminates in a striking passage depicting the saint's glorification in the second sermon's fourth subhead under the second proposition of the Doctrine. But beyond the immediate metaphor of light is the more abstract proposition that action follows vision, including an emphasis upon the correlation between perception and conduct. Many other visual images are employed throughout both sermons, but they are always integral to the thematic development and hardly appear as embellishment.

The end of the thematic development is nothing less than the abolition of the life vs. death dichotomy which imprisons and threatens all natural men. That primal fear is putatively allayed by an awareness that death brings life and life death in direct proportion to one's transcendent identification with Christ. Like the Apostle, Edwards insists, converts can literally contemplate life and death indifferently when their existence is united with one who is beyond both life and death. This pair of sermons thus enlarges upon a thematic preoccupation with the triumph over fear of pain and death which is so noticeable in the sermons of the New York period. From "Christian Happiness" on, Edwards insists upon the most radical implications of the fruits of Christian faith for the individual.

* * *

The two octavo booklets which correlate with the two sermons comprise ten and eleven leaves, respectively. Both sermons are thus somewhat longer than the usual octavo preaching unit. The most remarkable aspect of the manuscripts, however, is that neither has its original first leaf, putting the original opening of the texts somewhat in doubt. Since both sermons contain the concluding portions of the original textual exegeses, the newer portions constituting only about half of the existing exegeses, it is apparent that the sermons were originally preached from the Phil. 1:21 text. In any case, the situation is sufficiently awkward to warrant a departure from the standard practice of printing such subsequent additions and revisions in an appendix. For the reader's convenience, the sermons begin with the existing (later) openings of the text. The junctures of the later with the original portions are noted in footnotes.

As for the peculiarities of the individual manuscripts, beyond the similarity of the replaced openings there are similar general traits, but even more obvious differences. The first sermon is by far the simpler bibliographically, having only one level of revision beyond the original text and involving fewer insertions. In addition to the replaced first leaf, a double leaf of added "particulars" has been stitched to the end of the original sermon. This entire operation is fairly neat, the only peculiarity being that the sermon now begins on the verso of the first leaf.

The second sermon, by contrast, contains a number of alterations beyond the scope of those in the first. Although the device of cutting off the first leaf is the same, thereafter differences abound. The replaced first leaf is here actually a wrap-around leaf comprising new first and last leaves. The last leaf contains a set of directions to be inserted in the text on the recto of the penultimate leaf (printed below in the appendix to the sermon). The place of insertion is designated by a key sign. In the centerfold of the booklet is stitched a two-leaf fold containing several separate passages which are to be distributed likewise according to key signs. These additions, involving three inks beyond that of the original sermon, are printed in footnotes, most of them being brief amplifications. The second booklet thus presents a rather choppy surface as a manuscript, causing one to wonder how Edwards could have read from it in the pulpit as this would have necessitated much flipping through pages. It also illustrates the difficulty of adding to or otherwise modifying an octavo quire of infolded leaves, a problem that apparently became increasingly annoying to Edwards as his duties were expanded and he attempted to re-use earlier sermons in the Northampton pastorate.

LIVING TO CHRIST

PHILIPPIANS 1:21.

For to me to live is Christ.

THE Apostle when he wrote this epistle was at Rome, as appears by the twenty-second verse of the last chapter, where he tells the Philippians that the saints of Caesar's household saluted them. He was also a prisoner at Rome, as appears by the thirteenth verse,[1] "so that my bonds in Christ are manifest in all the palace"; that is, in Caesar's court.

He was a prisoner for the gospel because he preached the gospel of Jesus Christ, as plainly appears by the context. You may remember the account we have in the Acts, how he was apprehended by the Jews and brought before Felix and Festus and King Agrippa, and appealed to Caesar and was sent to Rome to be tried by Caesar.

He was in prison at Rome waiting for his trial and was uncertain what the issue would be, whether he should be condemned and put to death or cleared. When he wrote this epistle, and that is the occasion of these words of our text, the Apostle being soon to be tried for his life and being doubtful how the case would go, had death brought into a very near view to him: life and death were set before his eyes. And they both appear lovely to him, so that he is at a loss which is the most eligible: "For to live is Christ, and to die is gain."

When he says, for him, "to live is Christ," the meaning of it is his living longer would be for the promoting of the kingdom and interest and honor of Christ in the world; it would be for the benefit of the church of Christ, which is the body of Christ,[2] [the] mystical body of Christ, and to convert sinners and advance Christ's kingdom. Where-

1. Here, without warning, JE has returned to the first chapter.
2. The entire first page of the sermon MS, which concludes at this point, was supplied by JE at a later date. It is printed here rather than in the Appendix to provide a formal beginning for the sermon.

fore, he says, for him "to live is Christ," the spiritual meaning of which words so comprehensively exhibits to us the life of a Christian, or rather a Christian life, that can hardly be expressed in other words.

Christ lives and dwells in the heart of every believer; yea, Christ is the very life of the Christian. He dwells in him as his life; as the vital heart and spirit seated in the heart is the life of the body, so Christ is spiritually the life of the soul, as vital heart and enlivening spirit seated therein.

And as from the internal life of the body flow all the external vital actions, so from the indwelling of Christ, as of a spiritual life, it follows that the true Christian will live to Christ and will manifest the life of Christ in all his actions. Wherefore, this is the proposition we are now to insist upon:

DOCTRINE.

Everyone that is a true Christian lives to Christ.

Our business in explaining this doctrine is to show how believers live to Christ, and what is meant by living to him; and therein briefly to describe a Christian life, and the principles, actions, and aims of the life of a believer, as distinguished from the life of all others. That we may do this, we shall

I. Show what is prerequisite, or what necessarily precedes a living to Christ.

II. From what true life to Christ arises, or from what principles this life springs.

III. Describe what is meant by living to Christ.

I. But as to those things that precede a living to Christ. They are these: a dying to sin, to self, and the world. The life of a true Christian whereby he lives to Christ is a new life; it is called a resurrection from the dead, as well as regeneration. 'Tis this sort of resurrection is spoken of [in] John 5:25, "Verily, verily, I say unto you, the hour is coming, and now is, that the dead shall hear the voice of the Son of God, and they that hear shall live." 'Tis this sort of resurrection that Ezekiel speaks of in his vision of the valley of dry bones, and the Apostle in the sixth [chapter] of Romans: "Therefore we are buried with him in baptism into death, that like as Christ was raised up from the dead by the glory of the Father, so we also should walk in newness of life"; and in Eph. 2:5–6, "Even when we were dead in sins, hath he quickened [us] together with Christ (by grace ye are saved), and hath raised us up together, to sit together in heavenly places in Christ Jesus," and frequently elsewhere.

Now there is a death that must precede this resurrection. 'Tis true we are all naturally dead in sin, but this death consists in living to the devil; but this sort of life must go out and be extinct as a candle before we can live the life of Christ and to his glory. The life that we naturally live to Satan must be destroyed before we are raised again to the spiritual life of Christ. This is most reasonable, for how is it possible that the Christian life should begin till the devilish life ends? What the Apostle says of the resurrection of the body, I Cor. 15:36, "that [which] thou sowest is not quickened, except it die," is also very true of the spiritual resurrection to the life of Christ.

First. Therefore, the true Christian, before he lives to Christ, dies unto sin. Of this sort of death the Apostle speaks in Rom. 6:2, "How shall we that are dead to sin live any longer therein?" and I Pet. 2:24, "Who his own self bore our sins in his own body on the tree, that we, being dead unto sin, should live unto righteousness; by whose stripes ye were healed."

This dying unto sin is a true and godly repentance, and hatred of it. By repentance sin receives his deadly wound, such a wound as is never cured, but increases until it has quite deprived the body of sin of all its life. True repentance may very properly be called a dying unto sin, because in that sorrow and contrition, and turning of the heart, the power and activity of sin dies: the sinner's inclination to sin, his love of it, his relish and taste, and the false pleasure he used to experience in it, vanishes and dies; and he relishes sin no more than a dead man relishes food, and so may be said to be dead to sin. Life consists in activity, and the life of sin consists in the activity of it, but by repentance and godly sorrow sin—that is, sinful inclinations are no more active as before—but lies as that that is dead, as there are some remaining motions of sin, but 'tis only like the struggles of one that is dying, and not as the activeness of him that has his life whole in him.

Second. The true Christian dies to the world of this sort of death which is necessary in order to living to Christ. The Apostle speaks, in Gal. 6:14, where he says, "The world was crucified unto him, and he to the world." This dying to the world is the loosening of the mind from the follies, vanities, pleasures, and glories of the world. 'Tis the dying of covetousness and worldly-mindedness. The sinner that is alive to the world suffers worldly thoughts, earthly inclinations, terrestrial pleasures and appetites to live in him, and he lives to them [in] that he spends his life in and after these things, and looks on them as his life.

But he that is dead to the world, these inclinations, these eager thoughts and earnest desires, die and vanish away; these were as natural to him before as life itself, and [he] loved them as well because he placed the happiness of his very life in them, but now this worldly nature is mortified, and his worldly life is extinct.

This also is very aptly and properly called death; for the vanishing of worldly inclinations can't be better represented than by a dying to the world, for the true Christian is as it were dead to these things, as one that is out of his element. Worldly pomps and fine shows, the shining of silver and gold, move him not because he is dead and is alive only to Christ.

Third. He dies to himself. By dying to ourselves is not to be understood a choosing that which is to our own hurt, as it were not to love ourselves. The true Christian is furthest of all from that, for none consults his own happiness so much as he that lives to Christ. 'Tis the wicked man that loves his own death and chooses it before life, and runs himself like a fool into his own destruction and ruin, into his own eternal misery.

But by dying to ourselves, we mean the mortifying of that false, inordinate, irregular, mistaken self-love, whereby we seek to please only ourselves and none else, seek our own present pleasure without consideration of our future state. Now this strong inclination to please and pamper ourselves must die within us, and we must die to that: we must die to our lusts and to our natural corruptions, by mortification and the deepest humility, and a mean and lowly thought of ourselves. This dying to ourselves is very frequently spoken of in the Word of God:

> He that findeth his life shall lose it, and he that loseth his life for my sake shall find it (Matt. 10:39). If any man come unto me and hate not his father and mother, and wife and children, and brethren and sisters, yea, and his own life also, he cannot be my disciple (Luke 14:26). And if Christ be in you, the body is dead because of sin; but the spirit is life because of righteousness (Rom. 8:10).

The same is spoken of [in] Gal. 2:20 and 5:24, but it would be endless to mention all the places that speak of mortification.

This killing of our lusts and corruptions, such as pride, concupiscence, carnal appetites, revenge, etc., is very well called the hating of our own lives; for it [is] a hating of that which once was accounted as the whole happiness and satisfaction of our life. The true Christian doth truly hate his own life; that is, he hates that life of his which is his own and distinct from the life of Christ. As he is a branch ingrafted into the true vine, he hates all other life than that he derives from the vine: he hates that life that is derived from his own root and not from the common stock. As he is a member of Christ, he hates that life that is not derived from the head. Before he was ingrafted into Christ, he had no other life but that he derived from his own root, and afterwards he hates that life. And so it is necessary to hate our own life. Thus we have shown what necessarily precedes a living to Christ. We go on

II. In the second place, to show from what principle it is that a true believer lives to Christ: what is the internal principle of life that causes him thus to live to Christ.

I answer in one word: Christ himself lives in the soul of a true Christian, and influences and actuates him by his Holy Spirit. When sin and the love of the world, and fleshly lusts and self-love, which before were the principle of their life, [are mortified], then Christ enters in their room and makes his abode in the same heart where sin, lust, and the devil formerly dwelt; and he enlivens and actuates the Christian by his Holy Spirit as by refreshing, warming beams of light diffused around in the soul, which scatter the darkness and is like a vital heat which destroys the coldness and deadness of the heart.

That branch that before lay withered, dry and dead upon the ground is now taken up and ingrafted into the true vine, from whence it receives life and becomes green and flourishing, and sprouts forth in pleasant branches.

The soul is united to Christ, and therefore partakes of his life: he lives in Christ and Christ lives in him, yea, not only lives in him but is his life. He is invigorated with him, with his Holy Spirit which is diffused as new life all over his soul.

And from this principle it is that the true Christian lives to Christ; 'tis because Christ lives in and is the life of the true Christian: "I live; yet not I, but Christ liveth in me" (Gal. 2:20). The life of a Christian proceeds from the same person it is directed to. He is the beginning and the ending of it; and as he is the alpha and omega of all things, so he is the alpha and omega of the Christian life.

Thus we have shown which way Christians come to live to Christ, by dying to sin, to the world, and to themselves; and then, from what it is that they thus live: from Christ's dwelling as a principle of life in the soul.

III. We are come in the third place to show how they live to Christ, or as the Apostle expresses, how for them to live *is* Christ. I know the Apostle has a most immediate respect to his propagating the gospel and glorifying of Christ by preaching his doctrine; but it has a larger sense, according to other such like expressions in his epistles, even such a living to Christ as in every true Christian follows his dying to sin.

First. By living to Christ is meant a life conformed to his life in his great condescension, meekness, lowliness and humility; in his love to God, in his zeal for his glory, in his contempt of the world, in his hatred unto sin, in his steadfast resisting the temptations of the devil, in his resignation to God's will; in his patience in suffering injuries, pains, and reproaches, in his great love to mankind, in his forgiving injuries and praying from his heart for his enemies, in his constant doing of good:

> John 13:15, For I have given you an example that ye should do as I have done to you. Acts 10:38, How God anointed Jesus of Nazareth with the Holy Ghost and with power, who went about doing good. I Pet. 2:21–24, For even hereunto are ye called, because Christ also suffered for us, leaving us an example, that ye should follow his steps: who did no sin, neither was guile found in his mouth; who, when he was reviled, reviled not again; when he suffered, he threatened not, but committed himself to him who judgeth righteously; who his own self bare our sins in his own body on the tree, that we being dead to sin, should live unto righteousness; by whose stripes ye were healed.

Whosoever has Christ himself dwelling in his soul as a principle of life, will live comformably unto that principle. Whosoever don't in a good measure follow the example of Christ, of him it cannot be said that for him to live is Christ.

Second. A living to Christ is a living according to his rule and precept in the gospel. The rules of the gospel are exceeding contrary to flesh and blood; to keep strictly to them is like cutting off a right hand and plucking out a right eye. They are what sinners hate to come to. But now even the hardest of them all will be easy and exceeding pleasant to those that are dead to themselves, to sin, and the world; and however grating it may be to the body of sin, no man [can] be said to live to Christ except he take up his cross and follow him.

Third. And principally, a living to Christ, or a living Christ is a living to his honor and glory.[3] This every true Christian doth. He makes Jesus Christ the highest end of his actions; his principal aim and design, which will be followed more eagerly than any whatsoever, and more earnestly than any other whatsoever, is the honor of Christ. He aims his whole life at this as his great design, as his chief business. He has Christ in his eye in the whole train of the successive actions of his life. He is heartily grieved and troubled when Christ is not glorified but dishonored, especially when he himself dishonors him. He greatly rejoices when he sees or hears of anything done that is signally to his honor and the advancement of his kingdom.

His principal endeavor is to do something towards the destruction of the kingdom of Satan, and the setting up [of] the kingdom of Christ in his own soul and in the world, and gladly lays hold on all opportunities so to do.

He acts from a heavenly principle, and aims at more heavenly things than are under the sun. His faith enlarges his understanding and clarifies the eye of his soul, so that he can view the highest heavens at a distance and have a delightful prospect of Christ in glory; and therefore endeavors to act and live continually worthy of the profession he makes of his name. There is some image of the beauty of Christ derived upon his soul; it appears in his words and actions, and may be seen in his life and walk.

APPLICATION.

[I.] From hence we may infer what a vast difference there is between the life [of] a true Christian and the life of Christless persons.

---

3. This third head was later renumbered "4" and the following heading inserted above it: "3. Living a life of faith in Christ, or a living upon Christ." There is no further development or signs of paper having been attached at this point. The head could have been preached *extempore*, though that is unlikely. On the same page, a line is inserted in the bottom margin and deleted in the ink of composition: "living a life of dependence upon him." This appears to have been an attempt at clarifying the inserted heading, and both insertions are in the same ink.

How vastly different is a living to Christ from that life which is commonly lived by the men of this world. How few are those of whom it may be said, for them to live is Christ. Yea, may it not rather be said, for them to live is the devil? I may appeal to the observation of everyone who has had his eyes open but a little while in this wicked world, how exceeding far the generality of men are from living to Christ; how lamentable is it to see how little, how very little, there is of Christian life appearing in the world, how little of Christ is to be seen in the walk and actions of the generality of miserable mankind.

How few are there that ever died to sin, that have found their sinful inclinations dying and gasping within them. How far are the most of the sons and daughters of men from dying to the world, and being crucified thereto. Is not all the world merely alive, from the great stir that is made after the world? How do men spend themselves, with all the life they have, after worldly things. How far are [they] from dying to themselves, and to their self-love. How doth almost everyone seek only his own particular advantage, profit, and pleasure, neglecting both the glory of Christ and the good of his fellow men.

How vast is the difference between the man of this world and the true Christian. Christ himself, the power and wisdom of God, dwells in the heart of the one and fills his soul with a divine light, a spiritual fragrancy, and heavenly grace. The devil takes up his abode in the heart of the other and fills it with darkness, with loathsome filth and defilement, with the smoke of the bottomless pit, and with the stink of the brimstone of hell.

Christ himself is the life of the one, by which his soul is acted and enlivened; but Satan is the life—or rather the death—of the other, fills him with deadness and dullness, and a strange stupor and lethargy, and makes him inactive in everything but when he is employed in his own ruin.

The heavenly image of the Son of God, the brightness of God's glory, is derived upon the soul of the one; but the picture of Satan on the other. The one follows the example of Christ and imitates those sweet graces that appeared in the Lamb of God: of heavenly meekness, patience, condescension, charity, etc. The other follows Satan as his grand pattern in pride, ambition, malice, hatred, revenge, and deceit.

The one follows the excellent rules, the self-denying gospel precepts, takes Christ's yoke upon him and bears his burden; the other rather chooses to hearken to the whispers of the devil, though he whispers him on and draws him to hell.

The one makes Christ the very chief end of his living, and lives and acts and strives for his glory more than anything in the whole world. The other little regards him, seldom thinks of him, cares very little if at all whether he is glorified or no.

The one is sensibly touched when he hears of anything done for Christ; the other feels it not, not caring which way it goes, whether for Christ or Satan: Christ's kingdom and glory is advanced by the one, the devil's by the other.

In short, the one in the whole of his life has his soul chiefly set upon heaven and on the glories of Christ there, having his mind lifted above the ground by faith; the other spends his days in grovelling in the dirt, makes his mind much like a mole or muckworm, feeding on dirt and dung, and seldom lifts his mind any higher than the surface of the earth he treads on. Such a vast difference there is between a true Christian and a Christless person.

II. Will every true Christian live to Christ? Then this doctrine gives everyone occasion to examine and try themselves, whether they be true Christians or no. We may be assured by our text that none have an interest in Christ but those that live to him, that live to his glory. You have heard what a vast difference there is between a believer and [an] unbeliever; all this affords matter for the trial of yourself: wherefore, ask yourself whether you ever experienced a mortification of sin and lust and worldly inclinations, whereby your heart and life has been changed and altered from the flesh, sin, and the world, unto Jesus Christ.

Do you in a good degree follow Christ's example? Do you despise the world and its vanities? Are you humble and meek and patient, as your blessed pattern? Do you come up to the gospel rules, particularly to those in Christ's Sermon on the Mount, which is a summary of all the rules of the gospel?

Do you truly and really make the glory of Christ what you desire and aim at above anything else whatever, whether it be worldly goods, possessions, honor, reputation, or pleasure? Has your life been, as it is now, a life by which Christ is honored? Has Christ had any more honor in the world for your living in it? Examine and prove yourself, for most certainly, whoever don't live to Christ and his glory in this world, shall never live with him and in his glory in the world to come.

How many professors of Christianity have you seen in the world (I may ask everyone that is come to years of understanding) for whose lives Christ has not anything the more honor in the world, except it be eventually; and let everyone ask himself whether he is not one of those? If so, our doctrine assures you, you are none of Christ's.

III. A third use of this doctrine is to exhort all to live more to Christ, seeing that every true Christian, while he doth live, lives to him. Let those who are not true Christians change their lives and live no longer to the devil, but to Christ, that they may have an interest in him. And let those that are true Christians yet change their lives, for the lives of the best need an alteration, and true converts themselves need to be converted. Wherefore, I say, can such change their lives and live more to Christ than they have done, that that which true believers desire above anything else, even the honor of Christ, may be advanced, and that you yourselves may have a clearer evidence that you are true Christians; that you may enjoy more comfort, joy and pleasure here, and more happiness hereafter?

The best, if they examine themselves, will find deficiencies enough to make them blush, and it would be greatly to their advantage if they would often compare their lives with the life of Christ and see how far their humility, meekness, and charity falls short of his; if they would compare their lives to the gospel rule and see wherein they fall short; if they would let their consciences frequently whisper to them this question: how much the better is the honor of Christ in the world for my living in it? Wherefore, let all be exhorted and persuaded so to do.[4]

Appendix to Philippians 1:21

Particularly.

First. Let those that [have] hopes of themselves that they are true Christians labor more and more to promote the life of Christ in their own hearts. Labor for the increase of grace and to abound in the exercises of it. Don't content yourself with that, that you are converted and are in a state of favor with God; but pray and strive for greater degrees of holiness, for greater and brighter discoveries of God's glory and of the excellency and loveliness of Jesus Christ, and that your heart may be more filled with love to Jesus and with desires after him. Strive to abound more in a Christian temper, in a humble, submissive, meek, patient, and charitable disposition: I Thess. 4:1,

---

4. At this point two full leaves of material were added for the later preaching. They follow in the Appendix to this sermon.

"Furthermore then we beseech you, brethren, and exhort you by the Lord Jesus, that as ye have received of us how ye ought to walk and to please God, so ye would abound more and more"; and in the tenth verse, "We beseech you, brethren, that ye increase more and more." Faith, knowledge, and temperance, and patience, and godliness, and brotherly kindness, and charity, should not only be in Christians, but they should abound in them (II Pet. 1:6–8).

The apostle Paul, as holy a man as he was, he pressed forward still and did not rest in past attainments. If you are a true Christian, you do hunger and thirst after righteousness. It is as natural to a sanctified nature to desire grace and hunger for that, as it is for our bodies to crave food: wherefore, let this appetite be increased and pursued. Strive to be more like Jesus Christ, more as you hope to be in heaven. As God, who has called you is holy, so strive to be holy in all manner of conversation.

For this end, be more prayerful, more frequent and more earnest in your approaches to the throne of grace; and besides your set times of prayer, let your [heart] be frequently lifted up to God when you are about your ordinary affairs.

And be more frequent and careful in reading the Holy Scriptures. Endeavor to read them with understanding and a particular applying of them to your own case. Be more frequent in your meditations upon God and Jesus, the wonderful love and grace of God and another world, and the blessedness of heaven.

And be more frequent in examining yourself, in searching and trying your hearts and your ways, to see when you have turned aside from the path of duty, and wherein your life needs amendment. Be more frequent in religious conversation, in speaking of the things of a spiritual and eternal nature: let your tongue be oftener employed about the great things which God has revealed in the gospel.

And be more exact in your walk, more in acts of obedience. There is nothing that tends so much to increase grace as the exercise of it in good works.

Second. Use all possible endeavors and improve all opportunities that God puts into your hands for promoting the kingdom and interest of Jesus Christ amongst men. Use all endeavors to be some way or other instrumental of bringing souls to Jesus Christ. This is the work which Christ is carrying on in the world; let Christians be fellow-workers with him, let them all in their places carry on the same design.

There is no man but what God gives opportunity of doing considerable this way if he would seek opportunities and improve them. If every converted man and woman did what they could this way, there would many fewer souls go to hell than now do.

1. A great deal might be done by example if Christians were up to the rules of the gospel. If they did so, their light would so shine before men that they, seeing their good works, would glorify their Heavenly Father. There is a brightness and glory in a Christian life that, if it did appear in its own proper colors in all Christians, would exceedingly tend to the credit and honor of religion, and to the turning men from sin to God. As the ill examples of those that go for godly tend exceedingly to hurt religion and to encourage wickedness, so when they set an example of a sincere, universal, unaffected piety, humility, and charity, it has a wonderful influence to the contrary.

2. By discountenancing of sin and wickedness, and doing your part that open wickedness may be punished and purged away. Men by their neglects this way may become partakers of other men's sins and may have other men's sins to answer for another day; and not only the sins of particular persons, but also the impurity and uncleanness of the church: and the defilement of God's ordinances is like to be laid to their charge, and a heavy charge it will be. Therefore, we may expect at least of godly men that they will not allow no such neglect in themselves as they desire any spiritual benefit by ordinances, or hope to meet with Christ at his table.

3. By parents bringing up their children for Christ. If persons have no other opportunity, yet they have opportunities in their own families that they have the government and the instruction of, of doing a great deal for Jesus Christ. And indeed, heads of families have the greatest opportunity and are under the greatest advantages with respect to them that are under their roof of anybody whatsoever. A Christian family is as it were a little church and commonwealth by itself, and the head of the family has more advantage in his little community to promote religion than ministers have in congregation, and magistrates in the commonwealth, they being always with them and having them at continual command, and having always opportunities of instructing them. If parents did what they might do this way, multitudes of souls might be saved by their means, and a great increase and addition might be made to the kingdom of Jesus Christ: "Train up a child in the way he should go, and when he is old he will not depart from it" (Prov. 22:6).

I entreat all Christians that desire to live to Christ, and to promote his interest in the world, to remember and to follow these directions.

DYING TO GAIN

PHILIPPIANS 1:21.

And to die is gain.

T HE Apostle, when he wrote this epistle, was a prisoner for the gospel and was to be tried for his life, as appears by the context. And as it is natural in adversity to desire that those that are dear to us should be acquainted with our circumstances, and to communicate our minds to those who are our nearest friends when life hangs in doubt before us, and either receive support and consolation from them or give our friendly advice and comforting counsel to them; so the Apostle here acquaints the Philippians of his present circumstances and improves them for their strengthening and comfort, they being some of his spiritual children and those that he had a very tender affection to in Christ. As in the third and fourth verses, "I thank my God upon every remembrance of you, always in every prayer of mine for you all making request with joy," and in the eighth verse, "For God is my record, how greatly I long after you all in the bowels of Jesus Christ," and he tells in the twelfth verse and following verses them, for their comfort (for he for his own part was not in the least disconsolate), that his bonds had not been a hindrance to the spreading of the gospel, but that it was so turned by providence that it rather made for its furtherance. For the imprisonment of one that had been so eminent for his labors in Christ in all parts of the world made people take notice of the occasion of it, and put them upon inquiring about the doctrine that he had taught and for which he was made a prisoner; but Christianity never loses anything by being inquired into. And then the seeing of his sufferings and a sense of the injustice and unreasonableness of them, and seeing his courage and constancy under them, made other Christians the more resolute and courageous to defend Paul's doctrine and to speak the Word without fear.

579

And others were excited to preach Christ because they envied him the honor of being so eminent, and strove to acquire that honor to themselves. All which gives occasion to the Apostle to rejoice in his bonds, being confident, as he says in the nineteenth and twentieth verses, that all those things will be for the best and turn to those ends which he sought for, and that he should be enabled through their prayer and the assistance of Christ's spirit to behave himself so without shame or fear, whether his life was spared or he was put to death, that the Christian cause should receive honor and advantage by him, and that Christ should be magnified in his body, whether by a life or death. For, says he, let it come out how it will, I have no reason to be fearful and cowardly, for if I live it will be Christ: I shall [have] further opportunity of promoting his cause in the world, and it will be for the edifying and growth of the church, which is the body of Christ; and if I die it will be my advantage and benefit: I shall lose nothing by it, but shall be a great gainer. So that if it were left to my choice, I should hardly know which to choose. As in the two verses following the text: "Yet what I shall choose I wot not. For I am in a strait between two, having a desire to depart and to be with Christ, which is far better; nevertheless, to abide in the flesh is more needful for you" (Phil. 1:22–24).

In the latter part of the verse which we have chosen to insist upon are to be observed the person, the change, and the event of that change. The person is the apostle Paul; what he asserts of himself is not as apostle but as a Christian, as he is one for whom to live is Christ. The change is death, a change that is above all others dreaded by men; and yet the event of it to the subject of it is gain, being that which is the object of every man's pursuit.[1] For he says, if he lives 'tis Christ, and if he dies 'tis his gain; and in the verse foregoing, "so now also Christ shall be magnified in my body, whether it be by life, or by death." Such is the happy and blessed estate of a true Christian that, whatever condition and circumstances God places him in, he is sure of obtaining the two great ends for which he lives, and in comparison of which he desires nothing else, even his spiritual gain and the honor of Christ. For Christ, who is made head over all things to the church, will have all things so disposed as shall be most to His own glory and the welfare of His members; so that whether he die

1. The first two pages of this sermon booklet, which conclude at this point, were supplied by JE at a later date. As in the first sermon, the later additions are printed here for considerations of form and the reader's convenience.

or live, or whatever becomes of him, he attains his end: "For whether we live, we live unto the Lord; and whether we die, we die unto the Lord: whether we live therefore, or die, we are the Lord's" (Rom. 14:8).

The Apostle, he knew not therefore which of the two to choose; he says, "yet what I shall choose I wot not," for his desire of Christ's glory caused him both to desire to die and to live, for he desired to die for no other reason but because he longed to be with Christ, being in haste to be glorifying of him there and singing his praises. For if it were not that we may live to the honor of Christ while here, a day gained upon earth would be a day lost in heaven; as the Apostle says, "I am in a strait betwixt two, having a desire to depart and to be with Christ, which is far better. Nevertheless, to abide in the flesh is more needful for you."

In the forenoon,[2] we have spoken to the former of these, to the first part of the verse, "for me to live is Christ," and showed how the life of every true Christian, as long as he lives, will be to the glory of Christ. We shall now speak to the latter part, that all believers may be entirely easy and resigned, unconcerned about living and dying, knowing that if God orders them life, it will be for the glory of Christ, and if death, it will be their gain, that they may cheerfully go forwards, let what will come. Wherefore, the doctrine from this part of the verse is this:

DOCTRINE.

Death is gain to the true Christian.

Yea, I may say "the gain," because death is not any small gain, a little matter gained that is not worth minding; but it is inestimable, inconceivable gain: yea, it is all his gain, for all the gain of a Christian is in heaven and not upon earth, and by his death he is brought to the possession of all this gain. If he were to live here upon earth always in these gross bodies of clay, he would be forever kept from his heavenly inheritance which is his all.

By his death he is brought to the actual possession of all his happiness, of all Christ's benefits. It is all on the other side [of] the grave;

2. The reference makes clear that this pair of sermons was originally designed to be preached in the morning and afternoon sessions of the same sabbath service. Often, as in the case of "The Value of Salvation" (above p. 322n.), a single literary sermon would be made long enough to be thus divided between the two sessions.

this valley must be passed before we can come to it. So that seeing if
the believer was to continue always in these earthly animal bodies, he
would entirely lose his heavenly treasure, which is all his gain. Therefore, dying and a separation from those tabernacles, when God thinks
it is the fittest and best time that we should, is his gain.

We have already in the forenoon told you who are true Christians.
We are told in the former part of the verse: there they are described
to us by a certain mark and character. Those only are true Christians
that live to Christ, of whom it may be said, for them to live is Christ;
of them only may it also be said, for them to die is gain. Whatever
goodness any may pretend to, it is all nothing except they live Christ,
except their lives are lives whereby Christ is honored and glorified.
If Christ has no honor by their lives, as if their lives in general be
not for him and to the advancement of the honor of Christ, they live
for the devil and not for him, and hereafter they shall live with the
devil and not with him. But to proceed.

That we may truly describe the gainfulness of the death of a believer, that we may see as justly as may be how much is gained by it,
I shall set before you what may be supposed to be evil or terrible in
the death of a believer; on one side, and what is desirable and gainful
in it on the other, that we may compare the one with the other.

I. But as to that which may seem at first something terrible in the
death of a saint.

First. That is, a leaving of all worldly comfort and good things,[3]
which are given to us for no other end than to prepare us for death:
are good for nothing at all else, but only to fit us to leave them. Of
what use is a staff when one has got to his journey's end? Or suppose
one had a whole back-burden of staves for travel with, and [to] help
us on our journey. Why should we be unwilling to part with them
when we are got home to our own country, to rest forever in our
father's house? What a folly would it be, still to desire to carry the
burden of them when they do us no good in the world, but only to
burden.

---

3. At approximately this point, the following words were to be inserted for a later
preaching:

> Whatever is pleasing or gratifying to the external senses: those things are indeed
> good things and fruits of God's bounty to us, and 'tis reasonable that pleasure
> and comfort should be taken in them. These things must all be parted with, and
> that forever, and they must not only have no more to do with those things, but
> with nothing of the like nature forever.

These worldly good things are given for no other use than to help us forward on our way to heaven, as a staff, and if we could carry all of them through death with us, and might have the liberty of the full enjoyment of them, they would be nothing but a mere burden, slavery, torment. Solomon has declared that they are nothing but vexation of spirit, even in this world. If so, what a burden and vexation would they be in that where there is no manner of use for them!

What great matter is it to a Christian to leave these vain things which are utterly incapable of yielding any true satisfaction, but yield so much true vexation to the mind? What is silver and gold, what is pomp and honor good for? There is nothing in them that is in itself any way valuable, but only and merely as they respect another world. It can't be much for him to leave those things, whose heart is loosed from them as the heart of every true Christian is: why should one that is dead to [the] world be afraid to leave them by death?

But then besides, although the Christian when he dies leaves all worldly good things, yet he don't lose the good of them; he carries all the good of them out of the world with him into the other. He gets their spiritual good out of them that will stick by him forever, and why should the bee regard the flower after he has sucked all the honey out of it?

Second. At death the believer must leave his friends and relations.[4] He leaves the persons, 'tis true, but he don't leave the relation, for he enjoys them all in God: John 15:14–15, "Ye are my friends, if ye do whatsoever I command you. Henceforth I call you not servants; for the servant knoweth not what the lord doth, but I have called you friends." Must you leave your parents, you go to your heavenly Father. Must you leave brethren or sisters, Christ is not ashamed to call you brethren: "Whosoever shall do the will of my Father which is in heaven, the same is my brother, and sister, and mother" (Matt. 12:50).

[Should][5] you be by death separated from your husband or wife, know ye not that ye are espoused to Jesus Christ? You shall not only find all your relations completed and made up in Jesus Christ, but

4. Here the following passage was inserted for a later preaching:
   This is a far more grievous and melancholy circumstance of death to the ingenuous mind than the parting with the profits and honors and sensitive pleasures of the world. What sorrow and mourning is often occasioned by the loss [of] a near relation or dear friend, but at death leave is taken of all at once. All their tears and sighs over us when departing will not save, and the last time that ever we shall behold them [they] will be expressing their fears in tears.
5. MS: "Shall."

shall become nearly related [to] the whole triumphant and glorified family of God. You shall leave a few friends and relations to go to the employment of thousands nearer, dearer, and far more excellent than any upon earth.

And besides all this, you don't leave your friends forever; that is, not any of those that are truly excellent and desirable, whom God hath sanctified and made holy, and so worthy to be the objects of your love in the other world: them you shall meet again in glory. You shall meet them in heaven and at the resurrection of the just, and shall never part more.

Third. The believer must endure the pain of dying,[6] a little short pain that endures for a few minutes before it ceases, perhaps not a quarter so much as is frequently endured in the life-time, perhaps not near so much as many endure in one fit of the gout or stone. But who would not be willing to endure a few minutes' short pain to get rid of a life full of pain? 'Tis only a sharp medicine that effectually cures of a long and most painful distemper—yea, forever cures of all pain.

Fourth. But finally, believers must at death undergo that separation of soul and body,[7] those two dear companions, which is so contrary to human nature. 'Tis true they go out of a rotten, filthy, loathsome, infected house of clay and tabernacle of dust, to go into a light mansion of glory and blessedness. Hear what the Apostle says to this:

> For we know that if the earthly house of this tabernacle were dissolved, we have a building of God, an house not made with hands, eternal in the heavens. For in this we groan, earnestly desiring to be clothed upon with our house which is from heaven, if so be that being clothed we shall not be found naked; for we

6. The following reflection was keyed to this place for a later preaching. Note that the addition assumes a plural "pains" in the first clause.

> which are sometimes doubtless very great, and the pains of death may be peculiar to themselves and the more feared because none beforehand knows what they are because those that die before us cannot tell us.

7. At approximately this point, replacing the remainder of the sentence, the following (incomplete) amplification was added for a later preaching:

> This is something afflictive and grievous in death that is different from the pain of dying. For God has made the human spirit with a design that it should be united to a body, created with a nature and inclination adapted to that, its designed state. So that the human soul has a natural inclination to be united to, and to exert itself by a body: so that this separation absolutely considered, and abstractedly from other circumstances, is terrible to nature. That dear friends must part at death is . . .

that are in this tabernacle do groan earnestly, being burdened, not for that we would be unclothed, but clothed upon that mortality might be swallowed up of life (II Cor. 5:1–4).

And besides, the Christian has the certain faith of the resurrection, of his return to the body again. Now faith is the substance of things not seen, so that his faith of it makes it even present to him and causes the separation to be as it were no separation, because it is but a short parting with a certain hope of meeting again.

Thus we have shown you the worst of the death of a saint. This is the worst that can be made of it. This is all that you can pretend to be evil or terrible in it, and we have shown that there is nothing really terrible, but only in appearance. Now on the other hand,

[II.] We shall endeavor to show you the advantages of the true Christian's death. We have set before you what appears dark in it, in the darkest hue and form it will bare; we shall now endeavor to make a representation of what is light and glorious in it, that you may see how much is the gain of it.

First. At death all the troubles and afflictions of a true Christian are come to an eternal end. This life is nothing but a continued chain of troubles and sorrows. We commonly come weeping and crying into the world, and sighing and sobbing we continue in the world, and gasping and groaning we go out of the world. There are none, no, not the most prosperous and successful, but what every day meet with griefs for past evils, uneasiness for present evil, and fear and anxieties for future evils. The heart knows its own bitterness. If there were no higher sort of happiness than what is earthly, men would really be the most miserable of any sort of creatures upon earth; for beasts are only afflicted with present pains, without grieving for past or fearing future, but man besides that he feels as much present pain as the generality of beasts, he feels past misfortunes for a great while, which doubles it, and is tormented with the expectation of future ones, which makes it threefold.

But death is a final and everlasting end put to all afflictions, for every man upon earth finds more uneasiness in a minute than sanctified souls departed will feel in all eternity. 'Tis true he takes his leave of all worldly good things, but he also at the same time shakes hands and bids adieu forever to troubles of every sort. This is the first part of the gain of the death [of a true Christian]. This is the first thing that is gained by it: a full and perfect deliverance from affliction, and that eternally.

Second. The second thing is a perfect and eternal freedom from sin as the body is put off and all remainders of sin are put off with it, and the soul ascends pure into the hands of its maker as it at first came pure out of them. Indwelling sin is the greatest burden of a true believer and tends to make him long to be rid of the body that he may be delivered from the body of sin, makes him ready to cry out, "A wretched man that I am, who shall deliver me from the body of this death?" A true Christian desires more earnestly to be delivered from sin than afflictions; the remainders of corruption are like thorns in his side and pricks in his eyes, like a continual offensive stench in his nostrils that he earnestly desires to be freed from. Now when the body is forsaken, 'tis all cast behind: he shall never more be afflicted with the loathsome and abominable thing, sin.

Third. Death is a perfect freedom from temptation. The devil endeavors with all his might to disturb the peace and calm of a believing soul, and interrupt its spiritual pleasures by the injections of hellish temptations and devilish suggestions, and so the Christian is very frequently afflicted with this grand adversary. But death puts him out of reach; he, like his great Lord Jesus Christ, triumphs over the devil by dying.

Fourth. At death the believer not only gains a perfect and eternal deliverance from sin and temptation, but is adorned with a perfect and glorious holiness. The work of sanctification is then completed, and the beautiful image of God has then its finishing strokes by the pencil of God, and begins to shine forth with a heavenly beauty like a seraphim. Then that grace which was so suppressed and kept under by the devil and the remainders of corruption begins to find itself at liberty, and breaks out and flames forth in pure flames, and the soul begins to shine like the brightness of the firmament.

Fifth. By death the true believer is brought to the possession of all those heavenly riches, honors, and glorious pleasures that were laid up by Christ for him. Being thus made gloriously beautiful, with perfect holiness, he is embraced in the arms of his glorified Redeemer and is conducted to the infinite treasure that was laid up for him, has his crown of glory placed on his head and is led to the rivers of pleasure that flow at God's right hand, is set down at the eternal banquet of heaven, and is eternally entertained in the heavenly music of God's praises that are sung by choirs of angels above, resting forever in the arms of a glorious Christ, forever delighted in his sweet embraces. 'Tis this, and no less than this, that death brings the true

Christian to: this is the gain of dying, this is instead of those worthless, miserable, wretched, dull, earthly vanities which he left behind. No less than this is the gain of a Christian's death.

Sixth. And lastly, the death of a Christian is in order to a more glorious resurrection. It may be said that the Christian gains the resurrection by it, for that that we sow is not quickened except it die; so the body must die before it can be quickened with eternal life. So that death is even gainful to the body itself, as well as the soul, for thereby it will gain that glorious and beautiful and immortal form which it will then put on.[8]

APPLICATION.

This doctrine, if rightly improved, will be of universal use and benefit because it is that which concerns everyone. This dying is not a thing that some must undergo and not others, but everyone must die. It is appointed to all men once to die.

I. Hence learn the reason why true Christians die as well as other men. Death temporal is one part of the threatening of the law, from

---

8. At this place JE later added a substantial amplification upon corporeal resurrection, not only to develop the head but to conclude the Doctrine properly:

There is such a pravity brought upon our nature, upon our corporeal part, that there is no amending of it without disturbing of it. The frame must be taken to pieces in order to so glorious a piece of workmanship as the bodies of the saints will be hereafter: they lay down their bodies for a time that they may lay down their infirmities and deformities forever, and that they may receive them in power and great glory. This crazy tabernacle is taken down that a glorious temple may be reared up.

It is agreeable to the nature of the human soul to be united to a body and by it to exert itself; it certainly will be very agreeable to it to be united to a body so refined, glorious and perfect.

If you would know what is gained by this dissolution of the body and know what the body gains by it, see the difference between the body dying and the body raised again: I Cor. 15:43–44, "It is sown in dishonor; it is raised in glory: it is sown in weakness; it is raised in power: it is sown a natural body; it is raised a spiritual body. There is a natural body, and there is a spiritual body." The saints in their bodies then shall be made like to Jesus Christ as well as their souls, at the forty-ninth verse, "And as we have borne the image of the earthly, we shall also bear the image of the heavenly." And that this is a sufficient and abundant compensation for all that is painful or dreadful in death is implied in the fifty-fourth and fifty-fifth verses: "So when this corruptible shall have put on incorruption, and this mortal shall have put on immortality, then shall be brought to pass the saying that is written, Death is swallowed up in victory. O death, where is thy sting? O grave, where is thy victory?" The beauty and brightness, activity and sprightliness of their bodies are not to be described.

which law Christ has delivered us. This threatening is averted by Christ and he has destroyed death, not so that his disciples should not have their souls for a time separated from their bodies, as well as other men, but by making death a servant to them, and then after that entirely destroying of him by the resurrection.[9]

Christ has made death gainful to his disciples, has brought him into bondage and made him servant to bring home his own to glory: has made him a servant to deliver his [own] from affliction, from sin, from temptation, and bring him to heaven, his own abode, and to destroy the corruption of the depraved bodies, that they may rise pure and glorious.

And this is the reason why true Christians die, as well as unbelievers, for as the case stands there is a great deal of mercy in man's mortality, and believers alone are made partakers of the effects of this mercy; for what true Christian upon earth would be willing to live in this world, this loathsome and troublesome place, forever, and be kept from the heavenly happiness? Not one, no, not one true Christian would be willing, though he knew that he should live eternally in as great worldly prosperity as he could desire.

II. Is death gain to a true Christian? Let all be exhorted to strive for true Christianity. Live to Christ and death will be gain to you: this very thing which unbelievers are all their lives' time subject to bondage for fear of is the gain of believers, of all such as have true Christianity in their hearts and act true Christianity in their lives.

We have endeavored briefly to describe the gainfulness of the death of a true Christian to move you to live Christ. In the next place consider [the] death of a wicked man. What a vast difference is there between the death of a child of the devil and a child of God! The one leaves all his troubles and afflictions behind him, never to feel them more; the other, he leaves all his pleasures behind him, all the pleasure that ever he will enjoy while God endures. The one leaves all his temptations forever, but the other instead of that falls into the

---

9. Later inserted here:

What is truly dreadful in death, and therefore only properly could be threatened as a punishment of sin by Christ, is taken away so that it loses its name. Christ promises that those that believe in him shall never die, John 6:49–51: "Your fathers did eat manna in the wilderness and are dead. This is the bread which cometh down from heaven, that a man may eat thereof and not die. I am the living bread which came down from heaven: if any man eat of this bread, he shall live forever; and the bread that I will give is my flesh, which I will give for the life of the world."

hands of the tempter, not to be tempted but to be tormented by him. The one is perfectly delivered from all remainders of corruption; the other, he carries all that vast load of sin, made up of original sin, natural corruption, and actual sins, into hell with him, and there the guilt of them breaks forth in the conscience and burns and scorches him as flames of hell within. The filthiness of sin will then appear and be laid open before the world to his eternal shame.

Death to the true Christian is an entrance into eternal pleasures and unspeakable joys, but the death of a sinner is his entrance [into] never-ending miseries. This world is all the hell that ever a true Christian is to endure, and it is all the heaven that unbelievers shall ever enjoy. 'Tis a heaven in comparison of the misery of the one, and a hell in comparison of the happiness of the other.[1]

The sinner, when he dies, he leaves all his riches and possessions: there is no more money for him to have the pleasure of fingering; there is no more gay apparel for him to be arrayed in, nor proud palace to live in. But the Christian, when he dies, he obtains all his riches, even infinite spiritual, heavenly riches.

At death, the sinner leaves all his honor and enters into eternal disgrace; but the Christian is then invested with his. The one leaves all his friends forever more: when he sees them again at the resurrection, it will be either glorifying God in his justice in damning him, or else like furies ready to tear him. But the other, he goes to his best friends and will again meet his best earthly friends at the resurrection in glory, full of mutual joy and love.

The death of a believer is in order to a more glorious resurrection, but the death of a sinner is but only a faint shadow and preludium of the eternal death the body is to die at the great day and forever more.

So great is the difference between the death of the one and the other, 'tis even as the difference between life and death, between death and a resurrection. Wherefore, now you have both before you—the glorious gainfulness of the death of a Christian, and the dreadfulness of the death of a sinner—or rather you have life and death set before you, to make your choice: wherefore, choose life.[2]

III. To those particularly of whom the doctrine speaks, who are

---

1. This last sentence was later deleted by JE.

2. See the Appendix to this sermon for a major later addition containing five subheads. At this place, JE inserted a brief introduction to the addition: "That you may live to Christ, follow these directions:"

true Christians. If it be so that your death is your gain, be exhorted to wean your hearts more and more from the world. If your gain consists not in staying in the world but in going out of it, how important is it to set your hearts upon it as if it consisted in it. Will you set your hearts upon the things of this life when your gain consists not in this life but in the next? Where your treasure is, there will your heart be also.[3]

IV. Is death gain to you? Be entirely resigned to God's will while living or dying: you are always safe in either of these conditions, for you to live is Christ and to die is gain. Think with yourself, if you are to live long in this world and never with many difficulties and abundance of trouble and affliction, yet therein Christ will be glorified, and if it is appointed by God that you shall thereby have your body and this world, that it will be your gain. And seeing it is so that you are got into such a happy estate and condition that either by life or death you obtain your great end, cast yourself upon God's hands: let his will be your will, knowing that whether you are to die in youth or in old age, this year or next, today or tomorrow, whether a natural or violent death, by sickness or by accident, whether at home or abroad, whether an easy or a painful death; yet let it come when, how, and where it will, it will be your unspeakable gain.[4]

Appendix to Philippians 1:21

First. You must die unto sin. Of this sort of death the Apostle, in Rom. 6:2, "How shall we, that are dead to sin, live any longer

3. The latter portion of this passage, beginning "how important is it," was later deleted in conjunction with the following addition:

> Seeing this world is indeed as loss and dung, let it be so esteemed by us as by the Apostle: Phil. 3:7–8, "But what things were gain to me, those I counted loss for Christ. Yea, doubtless, and I count all things but loss for the excellency of the knowledge of Christ Jesus my Lord, and do count them but dung, that I may win Christ." So far as the things of this world may contribute to our future profit, so far it may be said to be mediately gainful to us; but otherwise, they are our loss. If we may make those things subservient to our main end, it is [MS: "is not"] wisdom; but otherwise, how foolish is it to set our hearts upon that which is our loss. If our treasure be in heaven, surely there is much reason why our hearts should be there too: "For where your treasure is, there will your hearts be also" (Matt. 6:21).

4. Later addition to the original conclusion:

> At the end of all, it will prove your gain. As death is what is most dreaded of all things, so here are [the children of men] most difficultly brought to a resignation, and 'tis what everything else has failed of but the gospel, to bring men to a willingness to die; but Christ Jesus has discovered so much of another world after death, and of the happiness that death brings the godly to, that [it] is sufficient if received by such and well considered, to remove that darkness and horror that usually attends the thought, and especially the immediate prospect, of death.

therein?" and I Pet. 2:24, "Who his own self bore our sins in his own body on the tree, that we being dead to sin, should live unto righteousness." Dying unto sin is the mortification of the habit, power, and activity of sin, of the sinner's inclination to it and his love of it. His relish and taste and the false pleasure he used to experience in it vanishes and dies: as a dead man relishes no food, so the regenerate man is dead to sin.

Second. You must die to the world of this sort of death which is necessary to living to Christ. The Apostle speaks, in Gal. 6:14, when he says the world was crucified unto him, and he to the world. The loosing of the mind from the follies, vanities, pleasures, and glories of the world: 'tis the dying of covetousness and worldly-mindedness. The sinner that is alive to the world suffers worldly thoughts, earthly inclinations, terrestrial pleasures and appetites to live in him and he lives to them. He spends his life in and after those things and looks on them as his life.

But he that is dead to the world, those inclinations, those eager thoughts and earnest desires, die and fade. They were as natural to him before as life itself, and [he] loved them as well because he placed the happiness of his very life in them; but now this worldly nature is dead and this worldly life extinct.

Third. You must die to yourself; that is, you must not set up yourself, mistake yourself, as your main end: not be influenced chiefly by a principle of self-love. In this sense, he that findeth his life shall lose it, and he that hateth not his own life cannot be his disciple.

Fourth. You must live upon Christ. He must be the foundation, he must be the original and principle of that life which you live. It must be faith in him and the derivation of his spirit that must sustain that life; the soul must by faith be united to him and partake of his life so as to live in Christ and Christ in him. Yea, Christ must not only live in him but be his life, be invigorated with Him, with His spirit diffused as new life all over the soul.

Fifth. Let your lives be to his glory and the advancement of his kingdom. Make Christ the end of your living, your principal aim and design which you pursue more earnestly than any other. Keep Christ in your eye in the whole train of the successive actions of your life. Let it be your principal endeavor to do something towards the destruction of the kingdom of Satan, and the setting up the kingdom of Christ in your own soul and in the world.

A declarative forthrightness or outspokenness characterizes this meditation upon the "glorious mysteries of Christ's priesthood, mediation, satisfaction, and sacrifice." As Edwards suggests in framing the statement of doctrine, the sermon's thesis is a paradox, juxtaposing in a single statement two aspects of Christ's function as Mediator. Edwards' pursuit of the implications of his doctrine is characteristically energetic, and given the paradoxical element at the heart of the subject, with its implicit emphasis upon horrific self-immolation, the result is vivid to the point of shock. There is in this sermon, even more remarkably than in the pair on Phil. 1:21, a suggestion of the seventeenth-century metaphysical writer, unabashedly reveling in the bizarre and plangent meditations to be discovered amid platitudes of the Faith.

Yet within the argument there are some essentially practical discussions, such as cautions to the faithful respecting the limitations of all efforts to influence God in the matter of redemption: not only were the ancient ritual sacrifices mere types, Edwards insists, but the efforts of Christians to modify the status of themselves or loved ones through any human device, including that of prayer, are also inefficacious, though not necessarily inappropriate. Edwards argues that all human efforts must be directed through Christ, and therefore made clearly subservient to his wholly efficacious mediation, before the good can be realized in them. As in the case of Protestant Communion, as opposed to the Mass (see p. 596), the human act is at best a pious representation of a divine act long since completed and fulfilled. While men are urged to active appreciation of, and participation in, their redemption, they are not to fall prey to Arminian assumptions about God's need for human—even saintly—propitiation.

But the achievement of the sermon as a whole is more evident in the rhetorical and theological dimensions than the pastoral. Although its argument is somewhat uneven in development, arresting passages occur with impressive frequency. As Edwards passes from the early sacrificial rites to the supreme sacrifice of Christ, the vividness of his language reflects his intention to promote an appropriate astonishment in the hearer. Imagery is normally his most potent resource in such situations and this is no exception, the contemplation of the agony of Christ in the second proposition under the doctrine being a fine example of Edwards' ability to orchestrate the simplest images, as of nails and blood, in order to evoke a much larger and more complex scene. In fact it is not creating a scene so much as expressing the most telling details in a familiar scene, hitherto latent in the conventional conceptions of his auditors, that gives force to the imagery of this sermon. Likewise, on the theological plane, it is the picking out of two well-known aspects of Christ's role in redemption and juxtaposing them that liberates the energy of astonishment implicit within the doctrine of the mediator.

* * *

Unlike the rhetoric it contains, the eight-leaf octavo booklet of the sermon is noteworthy mainly for its lack of distinguishing features. A single infolded quire, the manuscript does not seem to have been significantly revised and it may not have been repreached. Only the addition of a few numbered subheadings within one head suggests evidence for a second preaching, but the ink of these additions is remarkably like the ink of composition save that it is a little thinner. Thus the additions could well have been made after completion of the sermon but before the first preaching. Of course Edwards could have been so impressed with the sermon that he repreached it without modification, though omitting a shorthand record of repreaching would have been uncharacteristic of him during this period. Otherwise, there are two or three relatively small blank spaces which Edwards might have left with the intention of further developing the sermon, and there is one passage of ten lines crossed out at the time of the sermon's composition.

CHRIST'S SACRIFICE

HEBREWS 9:12.

*Neither by the blood of goats and calves, but by his own blood he
entered once into the holy place, having obtained eternal redemption
for us.*

THERE always from the very first was such a thing as sacrificing
in the world. This was not an institution first established by the law
of Moses, but we find sacrificing of beasts and living creatures and
fruits of the earth before the Flood, even as early as Cain and Abel.
We find that the one, he brought of the firstlings of his flock; the
other brought of the fruit of the ground an offering unto the Lord.
Abel's sacrifice we find to be acceptable unto the Lord; wherefore,
we may doubtless conclude that God himself had instituted this manner of worship, to be observed by all men till the coming of the great
sacrifice, thereby signifying the necessity of a sacrifice in order to the
expiation and doing away of sin [Gen. 4:1–5]. By these types and
shadows they were led to true faith and a Mediator, for they must
unavoidably conclude that they are so vile and sinful as to stand in
absolute need of mediation and satisfaction, and that their own good
works would not suffice without a sacrifice, so that they must depend
only on the mere mercy of God in the acceptance of a mediator and
satisfaction.

As this was instituted before the Flood, so it continued to be an
institution in force with Noah and his sons after the Flood, and by
this means without doubt, it came to pass that not only the descendants of Abraham but all nations upon the face of the earth used
this sort of worship, though none but the Jews knew what it was for
or could give any account of it. Yet the heathens everywhere continued and to this day do continue to offer up sacrifices, some human
sacrifices, others sacrifices of beasts and birds, all hoping to appease
their gods by shedding the blood of living creatures, though they

knew not which way in the world God could be pleased or profited by burning of flesh upon an altar.

The Jews, that one nation in the world, had more light. All the manner and different kinds of their sacrifices was instituted by God. They were so ordered as plainly figured forth to them the Messiah. They were also much enlightened by the plain prophecies which they had of Christ. They had prophets all along to instruct them in those things till a little before Christ's coming.

At last all the mystery was unravelled that [had] been in a great measure kept secret from the foundation of the world. The end of these things was clearly known when the church needed no longer to be under tutors and governors but had come to adult years and fit for the more perfect dispensation. Then came the Great Sacrifice himself into the world, the end and antitype of all these things, who was the true sacrifice, the Lamb slain from the foundation of the world; that is, he was the antitype of all these sacrifices that had been slain according to God's institution from the beginning of the world— so some understand that expression in the Revelation.[1]

And now, since he is come, that was the person that had been all along prefigured by those types and had entered in once, which was enough, into the Holy Place with his own blood. He did the business. He finished all there was to do of that kind, and left nothing for men from that time to the end of the world, but only [to] trust in his sacrifice without offering any more of their own.

The design of the Apostle in this chapter is to explain these glorious mysteries of Christ's priesthood, mediation, satisfaction, and sacrifice, and to illustrate them by the types of them in the Mosaical Dispensation, which indeed seems to be the principal design of the whole Epistle. We have here very plainly and clearly set forth to us the excellent gospel scheme, and the sweet harmony of all the parts of the evangelical dispensation, both of the perpetration of redemption by what Christ has done and continually doth, and of the reception of the redemption purchased by Christ by faith.

Our text is a brief summary and comprehension of all the doctrines relating to Christ's sacrifice:

[1.] And here first, this sacrifice is illustrated by its types that were abolished by this, its antitype, not by blood of goats and calves. For

---

1. "That expression" to which JE refers is in Rev. 13:8 where "the Lamb" is identified as being "slain from the foundation of the world."

as the Apostle says, "And almost all things are by the law purged with blood, and without shedding of blood is no remission" (v. 22), but the shedding of blood under the Old Testament was no wise efficacious to the purging any soul from [sin] any otherwise than as they were a means to lead the soul to a trust in the mere mercy of God.

2. Observe who is the priest that offers this sacrifice. It is Christ, the great High Priest after the order of Melchizedek.

3. The sacrifice itself. But by his own blood he entered: he was the sacrifice himself, as well as priest. He offered up himself; 'twas his own blood whereby he wrought our eternal redemption.

4. The place into which he entered to mediate with this sacrifice, into the Holy Place, that which is prefigured by the Holy of Holies under the Law, where God manifested his presence, gave responses, and sometimes appeared by the cloud of glory, and where the high priest used to enter in once a year with the blood of beasts for the sins of himself and the people. It is the highest heavens; here is our Savior entered, and here we are to look unto him and to look for him at the great day of accounts.

5. We may observe how often this sacrifice is offered: but once. He entered once into the Holy Place, whereby we observe and take notice of the ridiculous error of the papists in offering the sacrifice of the mass whereby they hold they do really and truly renewedly offer up the body and blood of Christ continually, for Christ entered but once into the Holy Place, and his sacrifice was never offered but once.

6. Observe the end of this sacrifice: to obtain eternal redemption.

7. For whom this redemption is obtained.

From the words thus considered, various doctrines might be raised, but two especially, which however may very well be contained in one, thus:

DOCTRINE.

Jesus Christ is both the only priest and sacrifice by which eternal redemption is obtained for believers.

He is both sacrifice and sacrificer, offering and offerer. He offered a sacrifice for us and thereby obtained eternal redemption for us, so he is priest. He obtained eternal redemption by offering his own blood, by offering up himself, so he was sacrifice, too, as well as priest.

The priests under the law of Moses used to enter into the Holy of Holies with the blood of goats and calves, but Christ has entered into heaven with his own blood. Here,

I. We shall show how he was the only priest.

II. How he is also the only sacrifice.

III. That by the sacrifice of himself he has obtained eternal redemption.

I. He is the only priest. There are no others but Jesus Christ alone, in heaven or in earth, that has any power to exercise in any of the functions of Christ's priesthood. There is none that can offer any satisfaction but he alone, neither is their salvation in any other, and there is no other name given under heaven amongst men whereby we must be saved. I know this is contrary to the greatest part of the world. Almost all nations have priests offering sacrifices for them. The heathens everywhere have their priests. The Jews yet foolishly and obstinately retain their priests; and the papists have their priests on earth to offer their sacrifice of the mass and to pardon their sins and to satisfy divine justice for their sins, and they have their saints in the other world which they worship as priests and mediators.

But we have better light. We have the light of the gospel which everywhere declares and preaches to us dependence on Christ alone as our Mediator, and not to trust either to the prayers and intercessions of our fellow-creatures that are the friends of God. 'Tis to be feared many trust to their godly parents and relations to be their priests, and to make satisfaction for them, and so neglect [to] do anything themselves, neglect to lay hold on the priesthood of Jesus Christ. But great is their folly and mistake, for although men may and ought to intercede one for another, parents for children, the godly for the wicked, yet they by praying till they are weary and spent won't make amends for one of their sins. If a godly parent sheds an ocean of tears, though they were tears of blood, it would not satisfy God for the least of his sins. Wicked men will not be able to go to heaven hanging on godly relations, wicked children hanging on the skirts of godly fathers or mothers. It will be to no purpose to lay hold on any but Jesus Christ: no other intercessor can make satisfaction. We shall doubtless see many saints glorifying of God in the condemnation of their ungodly children. Saints or angels are but miserable creatures to make mediators of. He only can answer the purpose who is both God and man.

The ministers of the gospel are not priests that can offer any sacrifice to God for others. They can only offer up their bodies a living sacrifice, holy and acceptable to God, which is our reasonable service; and their broken hearts and broken, contrite spirits are their humble thanks to God, in which respects every particular true Christian is a priest and are so called: I Pet. 2:5–9 and Rev. 1:6, and in other places.

But many make priests of themselves in a much worse sense than this. They assume to themselves Christ's priesthood. They take his work upon them; that is, they go to make satisfaction for themselves: they pretend themselves to offer up expiatory offerings to God; they foolishly bring their own righteousness and offer that, and so disannul the office of Jesus Christ. For what purpose is it that Christ has died if our own righteousness will do? We may say as the Apostle did, if righteousness come by the Law then Christ is dead in vain. This Jesus Christ, the Son of God, is the only priest that can work out eternal redemption for us: all the world can do nothing towards it without him.[2]

We cannot now stand to speak particularly to all the parts of Christ's priestly office; wherefore, take them as briefly comprehended under these three things: first, by satisfying; second, by interceding; third, by applying.[3]

First. Jesus Christ has satisfied divine justice; he offered up that that fully satisfied infinite justice. Our glorious Savior descended to the earth and here made a sacrifice of himself that justice might be satisfied. In order to satisfy, it was requisite that he should bear that which justice required. Now justice requires the greatest pain and horror in the soul; this Christ underwent, etc.

Second. He makes intercession in heaven for his people. He is entered into the Holy Place with this blood which he has spilt, and there pleads his torments, his ignominy, his horrors of mind and body, for those whom God has given him. His love to them, his earnest desires that they may behold his glory, etc.

He intercedes not only for eternal, but also for all those temporal

2. For a later preaching of this sermon, JE inserted numbered subheadings to divide this passage at the appropriate points. The headings are: "1. Saints and angels in another world." "2. Godly friends." "3. Ministers." "4. Ourselves." These seem not to be literary subdivisions of the material so much as devices to aid reading the sermon in the pulpit.

3. MS: a ten-line passage initiating a first version of the next subhead was deleted in the ink of the first draft. It suggested "that we may see and admire this contrivance [for man's redemption], let us consider what other way could possibly be thought of but only the salvation of Jesus by his offering up himself to God in sacrifice . . ."

good things they need. Believers in all their difficulties have a person to plead for them and represent their cause before the Governor of the world. He knows how to pity believers, for he himself has felt the same.

Third. He applies his blood and the benefits of his intercession to the souls of his people. The priests of old used to sprinkle the blood of the sacrifices on the people, and almost all things were purged with blood; but this was but typical of the blood of Jesus Christ.

II. As Christ Jesus is the only priest by which eternal redemption is obtained, so also he is the only sacrifice, the only propitiatory sacrifice there is. Nor neither can there be anything else offered up to God that will be of value sufficient to purchase pardon of sin, much less to purchase eternal redemption. All created beings are nothing worth to God in comparison of the least drop of Christ's blood. The blood of Christ is united to the Godhead personally: it is the blood of God, and is so-called in Scripture. Acts 20:28, "Take heed to feed the church of God, which he hath purchased with his own blood." Wherefore, it must needs be a most precious thing; it must be of infinite worth and value, and therefore sufficient to purge away sin which is of infinite demerit. The least drop of Christ's blood is of more worth in God's accounts than all the sacrifices that ever were slain from the beginning of the world till that time.

Let us a little consider this wonderful sacrifice, and let us be astonished of it. It is worthy of our astonishment and of the wonderment of the whole [creation].[4] From the beginning of the world until that time, many thousands of oxen and sheep and goats, birds and beasts, had been slain and their blood spilt; and many among the heathen do sacrifice their fellowmen. But was it ever heard before that divine [blood] was spilt in sacrifice? Was it ever heard of before that the blood of God was falling down to the ground by a bloody sweat and trickling down from a cross, a most tormenting instrument of death? It is divine blood that has been offered up for us. O, what precious blood is this! How much do men esteem their blood; it is more precious to them than all the world. If the blood of mere men be so precious, if the blood of worms be so valued and esteemed, how much may [be] the blood of the dear and well-beloved Son of God!

Now seeing this wonderful sacrifice has been once offered, all other

4. This insertion may not be necessary, although JE rarely uses abstract expressions such as "the whole" in such contexts. The term "creation" of course implies angels as well as earthly created beings, a consideration JE might well have entertained.

sacrifice must cease forever: those that come after do but dishonor it. There is no other blood but this precious blood that will cleanse us, no other sacrifice but this Lamb of God, this spotless, unblemished Lamb who was blameless and perfectly innocent, perfectly holy, perfectly—yea, infinitely—amiable and lovely, who had his body torn with nails and tormented to death with cruel torments, and his soul under such sorrow and horror as caused him to sweat blood.

III. Christ, by the sacrifice of himself and the offering [of] his own blood, has purchased eternal redemption for believers. We may be certain that the redemption that was purchased by so precious a sacrifice must be exceeding beloved of God. The darling of Jehovah did not sweat blood for naught; he did [not] give himself cruelly to be slain and convicted to death for nothing. No, but redemption, eternal redemption, was purchased by it. Eternal redemption runs out of his veins. By this sweet-smelling savor of his sacrifice, he has made all in the nature that he assumed that receive him, acceptable in the sight of his Father.

The smoke of this sacrifice has perfumed the souls of believers and has made them and their prayers and praises sweet in the nostrils of God, so that now he smells a sweet savor in their prayers which were most offensive to him before. The merits of Christ are the incense that ascended out of the angel's hand, accompanied with the prayers of all the saints, whereby they were rendered acceptable to God (Rev. 8:4).

By the pain that this Lamb of God endured when he was slain, all believers are delivered from eternal pain and shall receive eternal pleasure. By the shame that he was the subject of is glory purchased. By dying he conquered death; by entering into the grave he destroyed the power of the grave. By his being tempted by [Satan] he forever disenabled him and crossed him, and has redeemed those that believe in him to God, by his blood, out of every tongue and kindred and nation to be with him, to behold his glory, and to sing hallelujahs to him forever and ever.

APPLICATION.

Thus we have very briefly shown how Jesus Christ is the only priest and only sacrifice by which eternal redemption is obtained for those that believe. Let us now make some improvement. Let us attend diligently to these great mysteries of our religion, for it is our life, our salvation and our eternal redemption, aright to understand them and improve them.

I. Then let us take occasion with admiration to behold the wonderful contrivance of man's redemption. The case is that man once was in such a state that he had no need of a sacrifice to satisfy the justice of God. He never had offended his Maker and so had no need of a Mediator to make peace between them; but after this God had threatened him to inflict temporal, spiritual, and eternal death upon the breach of his commands. But yet he disobeyed and fell and broke the law of God, yea, became a rebel to him. Now God was obliged by his justice to punish the offense, for it is not agreeable to infinite and exact justice for God, who governs the world, to let the sins that are committed in it go unpunished. For God is a God of infinite justice and it is impossible there should be any breach made in it; neither doth God's justice oblige him only to punish sin, but to punish it with an infinite punishment, to punish it eternally or with some other punishment that should be equivalent to an eternal one. Now man had sinned and come short of the glory of God, and the sin must of necessity [be] punished, but how can this be without punishing him that committed the sin? Repentance without satisfaction is to no purpose. If man should shed an ocean of tears, of blood, that is not a repentance answerable to the least of his sins; that will never take away the guilt except satisfaction is made. Or if man should labor in the fire a thousand years to make amends, it is all to no purpose. God has been dishonored and injured, and his laws have been broken. He requires something else to make amends besides the miserable service of a rebellious worm, so that man himself could do nothing at all towards reconciling God.

And supposing his repentance and good works would have been sufficient to make amends for the affront, yet man was so corrupted by sin and his nature was so entirely depraved that he could do nothing of this nature. Love to God is necessary in order to true repentance and good works, but man by sin had lost all this and there was not the least spark of it remaining. If man by his repenting and obeying could have made satisfaction, he was become miserable, wretched, blind, and naked. [He] had lost all his spiritual life and could do nothing without a mediator, so that man was entirely helpless of himself. Neither was there any other creature in heaven or in earth that could help: all the angels in heaven could not purchase any pardon. Here is necessity of a mediator, but where is there a mediator to be found? Where can be found a sacrifice to satisfy divine justice? Where is a sacrifice to satisfy for an infinite offense? The cattle upon a thousand hills will not do; yea, if we could offer up the whole world in sacrifice it would not be sufficient.

But we see that God has contrived; he hath found out a sacrifice. What is it that infinite wisdom cannot do? He has found a sacrifice whereby these sins that deserve eternal punishment may yet be satisfied by a temporal pain and torment, so that this temporal pain shall be equivocal[5] to the eternal, never-ending torments of all mankind; so that justice may be satisfied and yet mercy glorified, the sin may be punished and yet the sinner not punished, God's honor may be fully repaired and yet the sinner honored with everlasting favor and crowned with a crown of glory.

II. Seeing Christ is our only priest and sacrifice, let us offer up all our prayers, petitions, confessions, and praises in his name. He is our Mediator; wherefore, let us always come unto God by him. We are sure that we shall be accepted when we come in his name. Our prayers are loathsome till they are presented by him in his intercession for us, till they ascend up before God with this incense. When we ask mercy, let us hope for receiving only upon the account of an intercessor. Let us plead his blood, for our prayers must be purified thereby before God will receive them. Christ has promised that we shall receive whatever we ask in his name.

Let us also, when we confess our sins, hope[6] for pardon only on his account, for confession and repentance are good for nothing without a satisfactory sacrifice to make way for them. When we offer up our sacrifices of thanksgiving, we must be most wary and careful to do it in the name of Christ, being sensible that he is the medium of all our mercies, and that our thanks and praises are well-pleasing only as they ascend in his name:

> Let the word of Christ dwell in you richly in all wisdom, teaching and admonishing one another in psalms and hymns and spiritual songs, singing with grace in your hearts to the Lord; and whatsoever ye do in word or deed, do all in the name of the Lord Jesus, giving thanks to God and the Father by him (Col. 3:16–17).

5. This unusual locution seems not to be a mere slip of the pen. JE clearly uses the term in the sense of "having an equal voice" or equal weight and influence.
6. MS: "hoping."

III. Let us place our whole trust and reliance in him. His sacrificing himself to satisfy divine justice, his undergoing intolerable torments for sin, his shedding his blood, will all signify nothing to us
except we will trust in him and heartily receive those benefits at his
hand. He has purchased eternal redemption, but for whom? Alone
for those that will receive this eternal redemption at his hands: we
may be sure that none shall ever be the better for Christ but those
only that trust in him.

That you may be moved and persuaded to trust in Christ, consider
especially these two things:

First. Your sin and misery and necessity of him. However great
your aversion is to Jesus Christ, yet hell—one would think—should
be enough [to] overcome it. Certainly, if you were truly sensible of
this—either I must lay hold of Christ or the devil will lay hold of me
and drag me to the pit of misery—your antipathy to Christ would be
conquered and overcome. If you find your heart dead, obstinate, and
listless, place hell-flames before your eyes: you will not be dull and
listless long, except you hide that from your eyes. The consideration
of hell commonly is the first thing that rouses sleeping sinners. By
this means their sins are set in order before them and their conscience
stares them in the face, and they begin to see their need of a priest
and sacrifice to satisfy for them. They then begin to see the insufficiency of their own righteousness and think of seeking out for something else.

Second. Consider how earnestly Jesus Christ invites you to come to
him and trust in him: "Ho, everyone that thirsteth, come ye to the
waters, and he that hath no money; come ye, buy, and eat; yea, come,
buy wine and milk without money and without price." "Whoso is
simple, let him turn in hither: as for him that wanteth understanding,
she saith to him, Come, eat of my bread, and drink of the wine that
I have mingled." "If any man thirst, let him come unto me and
drink." "All ye that are weary and heavy laden, come unto me and I
will give you rest." "He that cometh to me I will in no wise cast out."
"Behold, I stand at the door and knock: if any hear my voice, let him
open the door, and I will come in and sup with him, and he with
me." "My head is wet with the dew, and my locks with the drops of
the night." "The Spirit and the bride say, Come. And let him that
heareth say, Come. Let him that is athirst come. And whosoever will,
let him come and take of the water of life freely."[7] And many more

7. These statements, frequently rather free renderings of the biblical originals, are

such like invitations, but these are enough. Such expressions as these from the Son of God, one would think should be enough to move and overcome the most obstinate heart.

IV. Use may be of consolation to those that do believe in Jesus Christ: who do receive that redemption that is purchased by him, who have had their souls purged by his blood, their sins satisfied for by his sufferings, who have an interest in their Prophet, Priest and King, Jesus Christ. Here is matter of comfort to you believing souls, matter of unspeakable joy and triumph. Your Savior died that he might procure comfort for you, comfort in this life and everlasting glory in the next life. He offered up himself a sacrifice for your sins and transgressions, and has entered into the Holy of Holies and prevailed with God for your pardon and acceptance to glory. He has by his prevalent intercession prevailed to have you loosed from the guilt of Adam's transgressions, from the guilt of your original corruption, and from the guilt of all your personal transgressions, and has obtained eternal redemption for you.

You may judge of the greatness of your deliverance by what it cost your deliverer. Though he was the holy Son of God, yet he could not obtain your redemption without the spilling of his blood in unutterable agonies and torments; whereby you may be sure your deliverance is great, for if the wrath of God for your sins occasioned such torments in the blessed Jesus Christ, what would it have done in you if his wrath had been inflicted on you, who are but a worm? Luke 23:31, "For if they do these things in a green tree, what shall be done in the dry?" If your sins have cost Jesus Christ so much, who is the Son of God, what would they have cost you, if he had not died for you who are less than nothing?

Wherefore, praise your Creator and Redeemer with joy and exultation of soul. Let that be your song of praise to him who is the Lamb that is the sacrifice for your sin: "Unto him that loved us and washed us from our sins in his own blood, and hath made us kings and priests unto God and his Father: to him be glory and dominion forever and ever. Amen" (Rev. 1:5–6).

---

drawn from the following places: Is. 55:1, Prov. 9:4–5, John 7:37, Matt. 11:28, John 6:37, Rev. 3:20, Cant. 5:2, Rev. 22:17, respectively.

FRAGMENT: APPLICATION ON LOVE TO CHRIST

ALTHOUGH it finally provides one of the more remarkable meditations upon the nature of holy love to issue from the pen of Jonathan Edwards, this Application begins with a vehement negation, a denial of the validity of earthly temptations, inferior passions, and even the pursuit of honor, Milton's "last infirmity of Noble mind." Edwards posits the decline of religion and the lack of conviction among even the best upon the commonplace confusion of Christian and secular values. It is not sufficient, he insists, merely to accept the rewards Christ offers—the "crown of life"—but saints must follow their Redeemer in despising "all sublunary honors and greatness [as] . . . unworthy of him who was to be glorified with celestial glory after his resurrection."

But over half of the Application, the exhortation, turns to the positive appeal of holy love, and in a virtually uninterrupted meditative elevation Edwards elaborates the factors which cause the love uniting Christ and the redeemed to be the virtual antitype and fulfillment of all loves upon earth. At once abstract and sensuous, his argument represents an effort to realize in a concrete and profound apprehension the human value of such a "crown of life." Invoking the appeal of a higher aesthetic, a higher rationality, and a higher selfishness (the staple of exhortation), Edwards in course pays tribute to mundane or romantic love while emphasizing the limitations of all loves when compared with that between Christ and his followers. The clear purpose of the final stages of this exhortation is to induce an active or committed involvement on the part of the seeker. While not mentioning the subject of moral conduct and concentrating upon states of mind, Edwards nevertheless discusses his subject in a manner consonant with his introductory emphasis upon practice: the Christian achieves a new relation to the world through his relationship with Christ.

As it stands, this fragment is a complete meditation, though of course it is not a sermon. However, as a result of the recapitulation at the beginning of the fragment, we know the text, the doctrine ("those who love Christ shall receive of him a crown of life"), and have the major heads of the doctrinal development summarized. As a result, we can infer that the distinguishing issue of the sermon is probably the reward of temptation resisted, or heavenly compensations for earthly self-denial. It is within this context of asceticism that the striking sensuous imagery and quasi-erotic emotion of the Application should be viewed. Moreover, beyond certain literary elements such as echoes of Bunyan and variations upon the eroticism of Psalms and Canticles, there seems to be a very personal note of mysticism in the meditation, perhaps most evidently in the concluding sentences.

*　*　*

Although the text is a fragment, the octavo booklet containing it is complete, standard, and in fairly good condition. The explanation of this paradox is that the sermon on Jas. 1:12 was originally a two-booklet sermon such as "The Value of Salvation" above. Consequently, although the first booklet has been destroyed or lost—and with it one half of the sermon text—the second booklet has not apparently been involved in the depredation, although one assumes that the booklets were originally kept together. (In later years, Edwards would usually stitch multiple-preaching-unit sermons together in a single thick booklet so that such separations could not occur without leaving some physical evidence.)

As it exists, the booklet is noteworthy for two physical peculiarities. First, during the composition of the sermon Edwards apparently blocked out sections for development as usual by writing in headings at what seemed appropriate intervals. However, the space left for development of the second head under the exhortation, treating "the excellent effects of love to Christ," turned out to be much too large. In the first draft, Edwards completed the head in a little over a page of writing, leaving two and a half pages blank. Running out of space at the end of the sermon, he used one of these blanks for the final (sixth) subhead which concludes the sermon, and in a subsequent revision of the sermon he added a paragraph of about half a page to the original second head. There are still three blanks remaining which together would amount to about a page. What occasioned such a remarkable misjudgment of space is not apparent, but one cause could have been a change in argumentative strategy after the heads were written in.

The other noteworthy detail is the presence of three pairs of heavy brackets marking off large portions of the text from end to end of the Application. Such brackets were sometimes used by Edwards to mark off passages when he was compressing or abstracting a sermon, although they were also used to mark passages for copying into other manuscripts. Their function in this manuscript is not immediately apparent.

FRAGMENT: APPLICATION ON LOVE TO CHRIST

JAMES 1:12.

Blessed is the man that endureth temptation; for when he is tried, he shall receive the crown of life, which the Lord hath promised to them that love him.

(THE doctrine was that those who love Christ shall receive of him a crown of life. You have heard the explication of this doctrine in the forenoon, wherein we have told you who those are that love Christ and briefly described the crown that they shall receive: it is that eternal life, joy, beauty and glory with which they shall be crowned in the other world. We showed that they should receive this crown, first, as a crown of victory; and second, as a royal crown wherewith they shall be crowned as kings, and here we showed what was to be their kingdom, what their royal robes, what their kingly palace, their glorious throne, their honor, their kingly riches, and their royal dainties upon which they are to feast forever. We are now come to make some application of these things to our practice and improvement in Christianity.)

APPLICATION.

[I.] The first use is of instruction or inference.

First. Hence we may learn: if those that love Christ are to receive a crown of life at the hands of Christ, what a dishonorable thing is it for a true Christian to concern himself much about worldly honor and greatness; what a dishonor is it to Jesus Christ, who has promised you this glorious crown that you might despise worldly honors, as if you were not contented with what he has promised, as if the honor of a celestial crown from the hands of Christ were not enough without worldly honor too.

How do you dishonor yourselves by it! Christ has honored you by making [a gift] more excellent than any earthly thing. He has given you grace in your souls, which is heavenly riches the least grain of which is more worth than mountains of gold and silver. He has honored you by giving of you a right to a crown, not of gold and gems, but of celestial and everlasting glory, and you hope that he will honor you much more yet by actually placing this crown upon your heads and giving to you his own kingdom: placing you upon his own throne, adorning of you with robes of glory, giving you the heavens of heaven as your kingly palace, and himself as your riches, and his eternal love as your royal dainties. And will you now go and dishonor yourself so much as to thirst for silver and gold, or to seek after poor worldly greatness? Will [you] so dishonor your crown that is laid up for you? Will you so much undervalue it as to admit these childish things into your hearts with it; will you do your own crown so much dishonor as to make it so near equal to these things in your affections? Will you regard that honor that Christ is to give you in heaven so little as to seek the honor of men?

Will you who have an immortal crown, in heart thirst for earthly glory? Will you who are to shine with Christ as the sun, follow after poor earthly pomp and show? Will you who have heavenly riches, hug and embrace dirt and dung? Will you who are to be made kings and priests unto God the Father, leave your heavenly kingdom for the baubles of children? You thereby dishonor yourself more than one of the emperors of Rome did, who, although he ruled over the greatest empire in the whole world, yet used to retire constantly by himself, an hour or two every day, to catch flies.[1]

Therefore make not yourself so mean. Leave the thirsting after temporal honor to men of this world who have nothing else; let them take these things and welcome! A thirst after these things is unworthy of you. Remember what a crown you have laid up for [you]; remember what a glorious inheritance you are heir of. When you are actually possessed of your heavenly kingdom, are actually crowned with glory, you will see how despicable these things are.

Let the men of this world know that you value your crown more than that comes to, to desire their foolish, fading glories. Don't dis-

1. The emperor was Domitian as described by Suetonius, an account JE may have received through the medium of Laurence Echard, *The Roman History* (5 vols., London, 1695). Issued in several editions (the fifth in 1713), a mixed set was included in the Dummer collection of books, the early Yale Library of JE's graduate period. It is a work JE cites on the second page of his "Catalogue" of books. In the fifth edition, the reference is II, 233.

honor religion, but honor it by letting the world know that you account all other things as loss and dung in comparison of it. If Christians did so, Christianity would not be a thing so much despised in the world. If Christians did but manifest to all that they did merely scorn and despise and trample upon worldly honors, in comparison of that crown of glory which they were to receive, religion would not be so much fled into corners.

One great thing why it is despised is because the religious themselves hide it, and dare not be so bold as to bring it out before the world and do it open honor before the sun; but they imprudently and dishonorably pursue after worldly greatness too, and show that they are not fully contented with their celestial crown, and this makes other men have a mean opinion of religion when they see the professors of religion value it no more.

Wherefore, follow the example of your Redeemer and Head, Jesus Christ, who although he knew himself to be the Son of God, yet despised all sublunary honors and greatness, for he knew them to be unworthy of him who was to be glorified with celestial glory after his resurrection. He scorned all the fine show of kings and princes because he knew how despicable it was in comparison of the glory that awaited him: "He for the joy that was set before him endured the cross, despising the shame, and is now set down on the right hand of the throne of God."[2]

Second. Hence learn how little reason have those that love Christ to regard reproaches. Seeing they are to be crowned hereafter by Jesus Christ with a crown of immortal honor and glory, consider that although you are reproached by wicked men, that hereafter you will be honored as kings; and what are the reproaches, the greatest reproaches that ever despised saint met with, when compared with that glorious crown that is laid up for you? For what is the despite and scorn of wicked men? 'Tis only the scorn of those that are not worthy of the name of men. 'Tis the scorn of those that God scorns, and that he will scorn forever and will be looked upon by him and all intelligent beings as more hateful and despicable than a toad. And what need you, who are to be crowned as kings in Christ's heavenly kingdom, regard the scorn of such? There are none that are truly excellent and worthy to be regarded that will despise you for your

2. Heb. 12:2.

holiness, but will greatly respect [and] honor you. [You] need not care who despises you as long as God doth not despise, as long as Christ loves you, which will be as long as he himself has a being. If all the world should hate you, how sweetly and with how much pleasure might you retire into the arms of your dear Savior and solace yourself in his spiritual kisses and embraces, knowing that, let who will hate you, Christ loves you and will honor and crown you with glory before all the world.

But [let] all the world hate you and do their worst despite unto you, you have this to solace yourself: that he that made the world and governs it, he who has made those same persons that scorn you and who has their bodies and souls, their life and breath continually in his hands, he loves you and has given himself to you.

When you have once got your crown of glory on your heads, and are placed by Christ on his throne, and shine forthwith in robes of light, and sit down in his eternal royal banquet of love, you shall suffer no more reproaches forever. You will then be advanced too high to be reached by the spite of men or devils. They shall then gnaw their tongues when they see the unspeakable honor and happiness to which you, whom they formerly reproached, are exalted, and into what misery and eternal disgrace they are cast.

Fear not the expressions of their scorn and hatred; for they, except they repent and mourn for it, shall see with their own eyes you sitting with Jesus Christ, arrayed in kingly robes at the last day, judging of them, and shall see you reigning with him forevermore.

Your reproaches cannot be greater than the reproaches of Christ were, but what glory is he advanced to! He is risen from the dead, he is ascended far above all heavens, he has triumphed over his enemies, he has the keys of hell and death, and breaks his enemies with a rod of iron and dashes in pieces as a potter's vessel: in like manner you shall rise from the dead too. Christ is the first fruits and you shall follow. You shall triumph one day over your enemies, too; you shall ascend into heaven, too, and shall be made partakers of Christ's glory.

Third. How little reason have those that love Christ to fear death, since thereby they go to receive their crown of life. And it is this passage to their kingdom, just on this side the heavenly Mount Zion, the city of the living God to which you are traveling, there is a valley: it is the valley of death which, as soon as ever you are passed, you immediately ascend this glorious mountain and enter the gate of the city from whence you may look down with pleasure on this shady vale.

This valley is a dreadful, terribly dark valley for the wicked, and it lets them down to a darker pit of misery; but it is so near the hill of Zion, that bright place, that it is made light unto believers. They may pass through it with joy because as soon as ever they are got through it, they are got through all their miseries and immediately receive their crown, immediately are conducted to their throne.

Wherefore fear not, you souls that love Christ, to pass through this valley because it is dark, because there are many frightful appearances in it; for they are shadows and nothing else, and are not able to hurt you. Look through the shade, keep your eye fixed on that heavenly light that is beyond it, and you will not see the darkness that is in it.

We shall in the

[II.] Second place improve this doctrine by way of exhortation. If all those that love Christ are to receive a crown of life at his hands, what more natural improvement follows from it than to exhort and persuade all to love to Christ? We have endeavored to describe the glory of this crown unto you as far as that which is so glorious may fall under our scanty conceptions, and surely here is motive enough to persuade anyone to strive after love to Christ, if such a glorious and never-fading [crown] shall be bestowed on the lovers of him. But we shall offer some other motives to persuade all to this duty:

First. The first and greatest motive is the loveliness of Christ. As all the loveliness that is to be seen in heaven and earth is only the reflection of the rays of his lovely glory, so there is scarce anything that is glorious, sweet, beautiful and amiable, but what is used to set the beauty of Christ. What is more glorious to look upon among bodies that we behold than the sun, that bright orb that enlightens heaven and earth with its rays? Christ is called the Sun of Righteousness, and he is a sun to whom our sun in the heavens is as darkness; he is called the Bright and the Morning Star; so for his innocency, his sweet condescension, love and mercy, he is called a Lamb, although he is the Lion of the Tribe of Judah.

He is called the Rose of Sharon and the Lily of the Valley. Sharon, being a delightful and pleasant land, bore the sweetest roses, and the lily of the valley excelling all other lilies for beauty, sweetness, and excellent salutary virtue. He is represented thus to flowers because they are pleasant to behold, beautiful to the eye, and pleasing to the smell. He is compared to a rose and lily because they are the chief of flowers for beauty and sweetness; he is compared to the rose of Sharon and lily of the valley because they are the chief and most excellent of all roses and lilies.

What kind of rose and lily is the Son of God, the blessed Jesus; how wonderful and astonishing that God the Son should compare himself to a rose and lily! What kind of rose and lily is here: how sweet, how beautiful, how fragrant! Here is too great a beauty, too divine a loveliness and heavenly fragrancy to belong to any creature. Certainly this lovely rose and lily has divine perfections. Here is all the loveliness in the universe contained in this rose; yea, here are the beauties and glories of Jehovah himself in this lily: this flower is certainly no creature, but the Creator. Here, O believers, O lovers of Christ, is a rose for you, to be ravished with the fragrancy of it, for your eyes to be delighted with the infinite beauty of, for you to be delighted to all eternity in the enjoyment of. This rose and lily is the brightness of God's glory and the express image of his person, which is so amiable and fragrant that it is the eternal and infinite delight of the Father himself.

This infinitely beautiful rose, this spotless and fragrant lily, was once despised with the loathsome spittle of wicked men, and was torn and rent by their rage, and it was for you, O believers, the vials of God's wrath against your sins were poured out upon it.

Here is a sweet bundle of myrrh for you to lie in your bosom forever. He is as the apple tree among the trees of the wood: you may sit down under his shadow with great delight and his fruit will be sweet to your taste.

Second. Consider for motive the excellent effects of love to Christ. It makes the soul to be of an excellent disposition: it is of a transforming nature; it brings on the soul some of the loveliness of the person beloved, and exceedingly to soften and sweeten the mind and to make it meek, humble and charitable, and full of brotherly love. Love to Christ, if it be ardent and lively, transforms the soul very much into love, and destroys envy and malice of every kind, and softens and sweetens every action.

It makes the soul in love with religion and holiness, and sweetens obedience and mortification. Earthly and temporal love makes men glad of an opportunity to labor and spend themselves for the person beloved; they love to deny themselves for them; it takes away the force of pain and turns it into pleasure. So much more doth heavenly love, or love to Christ, make all that they do for Christ pleasant and easy; although they spend and are spent for him, it extracts honey from repentance and mortification.

Of such an excellent nature and tendency is love to Christ. It makes as great a difference in the soul as there is upon the face of the earth in the dead of winter when there are nothing but clouds, cold storms, rain, hail and snow, and in the spring or summer when all things look green and pleasant. Before the soul hated everything that is truly excellent and loved all that is abominable, but now the soul is transformed, is lovely itself, and it is in love with everything else that is truly so. And it not only makes duty easy, and repentance and mortification pleasant, but it sweetens troubles and crosses themselves because the Christian knows that they are ordered to him by the person whom he dearly loves, and who dearly loves him. How easily can we bear things that come from those we love! These are the excellent effects, and this is the usefulness of love to Christ.[3]

Third. Consider the pleasantness of a life of love to Christ. A life of love, if it be from rational principles, is the most pleasant life in the world. Hatred, malice, and revenge are the greatest disturbers of the pleasures of the mind, and fill it with uneasiness; but in the soul where rational love reigns, there is always pleasure and delight, for love is the principle of all delight as hatred is the principle of all sorrow.

But especially must a life of love to Christ be very pleasant, above all other kinds of living. Because as Christ is of all things most excellent, so is the love of him a more excellent kind of love than any other, and the more excellent and refined the love is, the greater and purer is the pleasure of it.

---

3. At this point JE stopped writing in the original draft, leaving over three-quarters of the page blank. For a subsequent preaching, the head was amplified by the following addition:

Afflictions, though sharp in themselves, yet coming to the believer through the Lord Jesus, they contract a sweetness from him. Christ is infinitely sweet in himself, has such an abundance of sweetness, that nothing—however bitter it is in itself—yet it in Christ loses its bitter nature and becomes sweet. The afflictions of believers, though sharp in themselves, are yet dipped in the love of Jesus Christ, and by this means all their venom is lost, and instead of being poison are made of a most health-giving nature. The pills are bitter in themselves, but they are dipped in Jesus' love. This consideration may well render them most sweet and pleasant. If we can but discover the love of Christ in them, this is sufficient to give a pleasure to the mind that shall overcome all the sorrow.

There is no love so reasonable as love to Christ. Some love those things that are not truly lovely, love from false grounds; yea, some love those things that are above all things hateful. Now from such a love as this can arise no true pleasure, inasmuch as it is without a reason or foundation and at last will end in bitterness. But the love of Christ is the love of that which is truly above all things excellent and lovely, and therefore the pleasures that result from it must be solid, real, substantial, and never-fading.

If any godly man's life is unpleasant to him, it must be only because his love to Christ is but small and not vigorous and active enough, because it lies dormant and is not frequently put into exercise; for it [is] utterly impossible but that those [who] live in the lively exercise of love to him should have those sweet meditations, as to make his life far from unpleasant.

Those that have a vehement love to any person can with pleasure spend their time in thinking of that person and of his perfections and actions. So with what great delight may [those] that love Christ with an active[4] love spend their thoughts upon his glories; with what pleasure may they meditate upon those infinite perfections that he is possessed of, and which make him lovely in their eyes. How must it please them to find out continually new beauties and glories which they saw not before, for the excellencies of Christ are infinite and we may make new discoveries to all eternity, and yet not have discovered all. How doth it fill the soul with a kind of rapture when it has discovered something more of excellency in him who is the object of his highest love.

If men have a dear love to any of their fellow creatures, they desire to see them yet more excellent; they delight to see them attain to new perfections. But now those that are the dear lovers of Christ, they have the pleasure of thinking that he has all possible excellency already: there is no room for desiring that he should be yet more excellent, because there is no excellency or beauty, nor any degree of excellency that they can possibly think of, but what he possesses already, so that they have no new beauties to desire for Christ, but only new beauties to discover in him. Now what a pleasure must it raise in those that love Christ to think that he is so perfectly amiable. This is a peculiar delight that is raised from no other love but love to Christ.

With what pleasure may he think of the perfections of his divine

---

4. MS: "Active" has been deleted, as if in revision, but JE supplied no alternative.

nature: of his immense greatness, of his eternity, power and wisdom, etc. With what delight may he think Him he loves with his whole heart and soul is God as well as man, is so great that all the nations of the world are to him as the drop of the bucket and small dust of the balance; so powerful that he weighs the mountains in scales and the hills in a balance, and takes up the isles as a very little thing; so wise that he charges his angels with folly; so holy that the heavens are unclean in his sight. With what pleasure may he think that the object of his highest love has made the world by his power and wisdom, that the sun, moon and stars are the work of his fingers, and he rules all.

How sweet will the thoughts of the perfections of His human nature raise when he thinks of His innocency, condescension, humility, meekness, patience, and charity, the sight of which made the woman so to cry out: "Blessed is the womb that bare thee, and the paps which thou hast sucked" (Luke 11:27).

With what joy may the lovers of Christ think and meditate of what he has done for them. When men dearly love any person, with what joy do they catch at kindnesses and expressions of love from them; with what pleasure will they think it over again. So with what inexpressible joy may those that love Christ think of his bowing the heavens and coming down in the form of a servant: of his lying in a manger, of his suffering the reproach of men, of his agony and bloody sweat, of his dying on the cross for their sakes. How pleasing must it be to read over the history of all those wonderful [things] that their well-beloved has done for them while on earth, as it is recorded in the Scriptures, and to think that Christ has done all this for him: that he was born for his sake and lived for his sake, sweat blood for his sake and died for his sake. This must needs beget an uncommon delight.

With what pleasure may the Christian's soul think on Christ in his exalted state. We love to see those whom we truly love highly honored and exalted; so those that ardently love Christ may sweetly spend their time in meditating on Christ triumphing over his enemies, of his glorious ascending to heaven, of his being made head over all things to the church, of his being crowned with a crown of great glory, of his coming to judge the world at the conflagration.

The love of Christ is far more pleasant than any other love upon these following accounts:

1. Christ is far more amiable than any other object in the world.

2. No other love is of so pure, heavenly and divine a nature as the love of Christ is; and therefore, no other love can raise such a divine and heavenly and exalted pleasure.

3. All that love Christ are certain that they are loved again. Herein is the pleasure of love: to be loved again. If love be not mutual, it is a torment and not a pleasure; but he that knows he loves Christ, knows Christ loves him with a [love] far higher and dearer.

4. There is nothing can deprive those that love Christ either of present communion with, or future enjoyment of, the person loved. Now it is not so in other kinds of love, but they are full of perplexities for fear of being deprived of enjoyment. There are a thousand accidents which may spoil all, and death certainly will separate them; but Christ will be enjoyed to all eternity, and all the world can't hinder it. Christ will receive them into his closest embrace, and in his arms shall they rest forevermore in spite of all the world.

5. The union between Christ and those that love him is more close, and the communion more intimate, than between any other lovers. The believers have the pleasure to think that he whom they love has also loved them so well as to receive [them] so near to himself as to make [them] his bone and his flesh. The believer is joined to Christ and is become one with him. How must this be to those who love him in truth! Love naturally desires a close and inseparable union and intimate communion, but there is no such near or intimate conversation between any other lovers, as between Christ and the Christian.

6. There is no other love so advantageous as love to Christ, and therefore none so pleasant. Love is sweet when the ones loving each other enjoy one another in prosperous circumstances. Now Christ is already crowned with glory, and he will crown those that love him with glory too, so that they shall each other eternally [be] in the greatest glory. So that upon these reasons and many others that might be mentioned, the love of Christ is far the most delightful love in the world.

And in short, to sum up the whole, the love of Christ has a tendency to fill the soul with an inexpressible sweetness. It sweetens every thought and makes every meditation pleasant; it brings a divine calm upon the mind, and spreads a heavenly fragrancy like Mary's box of ointment. It bedews the soul with the dew of heaven, begets a bright sunshine, and diffuses the beginnings of glory and happiness in embryo. All the world smiles upon such a soul as loves Christ: the sun, moon and stars, fields and trees, do seem to salute him. Such a mind is like a little heaven upon earth.

CHRISTIAN LIBERTY

PARADOX and irony are again prominent in this sermon on servitude and liberty, natural and redeemed will. The issue is opened by considering the life of "license" led by headstrong and self-indulgent natural men. Ironically, Edwards insists, the unrestrained life of self-indulgence is wholly governed and confined by sin and Satan. The life of impulse and appetite, or of "lust" in Edwards' vocabulary, is that which restricts, entraps, and ultimately enslaves. In contrast, the life of Christian discipline is that which preserves freedom on earth and leads to the ultimate gratification of all desires in heaven. Thus service, if it is truly in the cause of God, is paradoxically the way of freedom from constraint; the acceptance of Christian obligations relating to spiritual discipline is the way to the most unconfined and unconstrained self-indulgence.

In the course of his argument, Edwards shows a full acquaintance with the mentality of the average person, then as now, as he considers the idea of life on a higher, more disciplined spiritual plane. The humorous empathy with which he evokes the unregenerate's ruminations at the outset of the Improvement proves Edwards was not isolated by his own virtue and high-mindedness from an understanding of less exalted mentalities. Of course, the list of queries at the end of the sermon is calculated to enable ordinary people to ascertain the reality of their mentality and thus to evaluate the validity of their spiritual practice. Coming at the end of this sustained contrast between the slavery of Satan's service and the liberty of God's, the terms of such an assessment are sharply defined.

Although the textual revisions in this sermon are not numerous, particularly in the light of the fact that it seems to have been repreached at least twice, there is one revision of some interest beyond the common level of homiletical considerations. This revision is made in the ink of the sermon's composition and occurs at the outset of the sermon. In the opening sentence, Edwards first wrote that the Messiah "should proclaim a universal liberty to all servants, slaves, captives, vassals, [and] imprisoned [or] condemned persons." However, he immediately deleted with a heavy stroke the word "slaves." Perhaps usage enabled "vassals" to cover the concept of slavery, but Edwards makes explicit use of the term "slave" subsequently, as in this observation a few paragraphs beyond: "Without doubt, when once persons are become the sons of God they are no longer slaves: slaves, prisoners and captives are not consistent with such a relation to God." Clearly, Edwards calls a slave "a slave." On the other hand, the difference between the two passages referred to may explain the revision. The second passage clearly refers to the spiritual condition, and to the fact that those who are spiritually "liberated" cannot really be constrained by gross physical restrictions or even legal bonds from being spiritually "free." However, the first passage presents the image of a Messiah literally freeing slaves as a radical abolitionist; there are no qualifiers. Although Edwards generally ignores the fact of slavery entirely in his writings and is known to have owned at least one slave later in his life, the revision here appears to be a rhetorical tactic which implicitly acknowledges a sticky public issue, though one not yet widely debated. Opening the sermon as it does, the original statement might have given his auditory the impression that Edwards' concern was institutional social reform. He was no John Woolman. The revision is a rare instance of Edwards' acknowledging the secular context of his preaching, although it is apparent that he made many such adjustments before putting pen to paper; moreover, this example clearly defines the locus of Edwards' concern as the liberty of the soul. Reform—personal, social, and political—inevitably begins *within* for Edwards and he ordinarily leaves the secondary social implications to be inferred by his auditory.

* * *

The booklet of this manuscript is a perfect example of the octavo quire, one that has never been tampered with or physically augmented. The revision is not great, though three inks appear in the booklet. The sign for a Bolton repreaching occurs on the front of the booklet, although there is no evidence of a Northampton preaching. Some of the revision for later repreaching involves the sermon's structure, specifically, the combining of the first and second subheads under the first proposition of the Doctrine and the consequent renumbering of the remaining subheads, but little of a material nature was altered. Formally, the piece is not unusual for this period except perhaps in the relative lengths of the Doctrine and Application: here the former is more than twice the length of the latter, an even greater doctrinal emphasis than that common in the early sermons generally. The tone of the sermon does not suggest it functioned as a lecture, though it could have.

CHRISTIAN LIBERTY

JAMES 1:25.

*But whoso looketh into the perfect law of liberty and continueth
therein, he being not a forgetful hearer but a doer of the work, this
man shall be blessed in his deed.*

IT was a great part of the glory of the ancient prophecies of the
Messiah that when he came into the world he should proclaim a
universal liberty to all servants, captives, vassals, [and] imprisoned
[or] condemned persons. In what a pompous, exalted manner are
those glorious prophecies delivered: "I the Lord have called thee in
righteousness, and will hold thine hand, and will keep thee and give
thee for a covenant of the people, for a light of the gentiles to open
the blind eyes, to bring out the prisoners from the prison, and them
that sit in darkness out of the prison house" (Is. 42:6–7); and, "The
spirit of the Lord God is upon me, because the Lord hath anointed
me to preach good tidings unto the meek; he hath sent me to bind
up the broken-hearted, to proclaim liberty to the captives, and the
opening of the prison to them that are bound" (Is. 61:1).

This was typified to the Jews by the Year of Jubilee, wherein all
servants were freed from their masters and an universal liberty was
proclaimed throughout the land of Canaan.

And indeed, one of the great ends of Christ's appearing in the
world was to proclaim liberty to everyone that would accept of it. He
offers a most glorious freedom from the worst of servitudes and
bondages. He opens the doors of the most filthy prisons and draws
out of the most loathsome dungeons, redeems out of the worst captivity to a most cruel enemy, frees from the hardest drudgery and
brings into a perfect and glorious liberty, even the liberty of the sons
of God.

Whoever is bound, without doubt God's own children shall enjoy
freedom; God will never see his sons and his daughters in prison or
captivity. John 1:12, "But to as many as received him, to them gave

he power to become the sons of God." Without doubt, when once persons are become the sons of God they are no longer slaves: slaves, prisoners and captives are not consistent with such a relation to God.

Another reason why they cannot be in bondage is because they are the friends of Jesus Christ: "Henceforth I call you not servants, for the servant knoweth not what the lord doeth; but I have called you friends, for all things that I have heard of the Father I have made known unto you" (John 15:15).

Nor does it hinder our liberty at all that we are bound by a law; for the end of this law is to redeem us from servitude and bondage, and to instate us in a perfect law of liberty, and therefore this law in our text is called the law of liberty.

The Apostle in this place is dehorting from a bare, formal and careless[1] hearing the Word of God without taking care to act according to it and to put it [in] practice. [Those] that are only hearers and not doers of the Word, like a man beholding himself in a glass which goeth away and minds it no more, forgets what manner of man he was.

The things which the Apostle in this place exhorts to, by the world are esteemed the greatest bondage, as acting exactly according to the Word of God, tying ourselves up to self-denying and mortifying gospel rules and precepts, as laying aside "all filthiness and superfluity of naughtiness," as in the twenty-first verse; bridling the tongue and curbing that unruly member, as in the twenty-sixth verse, visiting the fatherless and widows in their affliction, and keeping unspotted from the world (that is, to curb and restrain covetousness, pride, and worldly-mindedness). Those things are accounted by the natural man the greatest bondage, but yet you see the Apostle calls the law by which we are obliged to those things the perfect law of liberty.

Here observe these two properties of this law: first, the tendency of it, that is, liberty; second, the nature or quality, perfection. The perfection here spoken of is a perfection with respect to liberty, with respect to that end of it: to be productive of liberty. Wherefore, it is called a perfect law of liberty, which expression exhibits this doctrine to us:

1. MS: "careless and formal hearing the Word." JE apparently forgot the preceding use of "formal," though a form of awkward rhetorical repetition is possible.

DOCTRINE.

In God's service is a perfect and glorious liberty.

We are never free till we become the servants of God; we are never from under the yoke of bondage till we take Christ's yoke upon us. There is as much difference—yea, more—between a man that ties himself strictly to the laws of God, uses the utmost caution lest he should transgress in any point, and a man that gives himself the liberty to go just as his lusts and the devil drive him, or rather, gives his lusts and the devil liberty to drive him where they will, as there is between a bird at liberty in the open air and shut up in a cage.

When a man first gets into Christ he comes out, as it were, of a stinking, dark dungeon into liberty, and although he loved his dungeon while he was in it because he knew not there was any better place in the world, yet when once he has had experience of perfect liberty he would not return again into it for all the world. John 8:32, "And ye shall know the truth, and the truth shall make you free." Verses 34–36, "Jesus answered them, Verily, verily, I say unto you, whosoever committeth sin is the servant of sin, and the servant abideth not in the house forever, but the Son abideth ever. If the Son therefore shall make you free, ye shall be free indeed."

That you may see how there is perfect liberty in the service of God, we shall:

I. Show what the servants of God have freedom from.
II. What they have liberty for.

I. What have those that serve God freedom from? I answer,

First. They have freedom from the reigning power of sin and Satan. 'Tis enough to raise pity to see how poor sinners are enslaved by sin in a far worse bondage than that of the miserablest caitiffs in the world; to see how they are entirely enslaved to this cruel tyrant, have their souls and bodies given up to him; to see how they are blindfolded, cheated and deluded, unmercifully used by sin, and yet willingly and foolishly submit to all this cruel usage and are very good servants to sin notwithstanding, will be at abundance of pain and undergo many difficulties for nothing, for no wages but death, the wages of sin.

How are poor sinners sometimes driven forward by their lusts to their own ruin: to the ruin of the peace and satisfaction of their minds, to the ruin of their health and very frequently the lives of their bodies, to the ruin of their credit and reputation in the world so that their names do stink as long as they are remembered—"for the memory of the wicked shall rot"[2]—to the ruin of their estates and worldly prosperity. Vice has clothed thousands with rags, to the ruin of their families and relations, to the ruin of their souls and their everlasting misery, yea, to the ruin of their souls and bodies forevermore in hellfire.

What great difficulties are men put to to practice their lusts! How many fears, how many anxieties, how many perplexities, how much labor doth it cost them!

How many are made miserable by covetousness; how many have riches and all the heart can wish, before, and yet through covetousness have not power to enjoy it. How will they spend their strength for the world, and when they have gotten it, had better much be without it for matter of any satisfaction they get by it.

How many thousands have luxury, idleness, drunkenness and lasciviousness ruined! As one says, "Where Christ has had one martyr, sin has had a thousand."[3] What a miserable bondage and slavery is this: how miserable are those that are the subjects of it, and how happy are they that are delivered from it.

Now the servants of God, alone, are the persons that are free from this cruel servitude. They have the victory and triumph over their lusts and will act as those that are free and at liberty: according to reason and not according to the dictates of sin. He is at liberty and consults his own happiness now, and not the pleasure of lust. He is no longer the servant of sin to spend and be spent for sin, but he now acts for his own welfare and for his own profit, as one that is free and not as one in bondage.

Second. Those that serve God enjoy freedom from the chains of the devil. Sinners serve the worst of masters, no better than sin and the devil. The devil has them at his beck. He says to the sinner, "Go," and he goeth, and "Come," and he cometh, "Do this," and he doth it. They don't serve the devil because the devil will ever reward them for this service, for they are to receive nothing for their pains but flames. Though the devil's service is very hard and difficult, yet he

2. This is JE's version of the clause from Prov. 10:7, "but the name of the wicked shall rot."

3. This quotation has not been positively identified, though it could have come from the pens of many preachers.

never intends to reward his servants that do this difficult work with anything but as much torment as he can give them when he gets [them] in his own territories.

But the servants of God enjoy liberty and freedom from this cruel master: he may overcome them now and then with his temptations, but he can't have them at his will as he can wicked men. He gives them over as lost, only endeavors to afflict them as much as he can; but the servants of God know who it is they serve and that He will deliver them from him. They shall at last overcome him and tread him under foot, and gladly triumph over him who is the master and the god of the wicked world.

How glorious and blessed a thing is it thus to be free from Satan, from his shackles and chains and cruel yoke and heavy burden, to act at liberty and as reason directs.

Third. The servants of God are freed from guilt and obligation to punishment. How dreadful is it to be bound over to misery, to be condemned to destruction without end; and what deliverance can be greater than to be delivered from such obligations? The former is the state of wicked men; the latter, the happy condition of the godly. A wicked man is already condemned to burn in hell forever. He is in a damnable estate and condition: if he should die in the state he now is in, he would be forever miserable, forever lost and undone. But what cause of rejoicing have the godly, the servants of God, at the thought of his being forever freed from such obligations. What a glorious liberty is this, to be delivered from such bonds.

Fourth. The servant of God is delivered from the tormenting galls of conscience which wicked men are in bondage under. Such accusations as these are perpetually sounding in the ears of wicked men: "You live in constant rebellion to your Maker and continual enmity to the God that created you, that always sees and beholds you."

But he hears the voice of his Redeemer thus speaking to him: "Thy sins are forgiven thee, they are all put on mine account. I will take care to make intercession for you notwithstanding your sins." The servant of God may lie down and rest in peace, and rise in peace enjoying the peace of God that passeth all understanding, being freed from a guilty, accusing conscience.

Fifth. And lastly, the servant of God enjoys liberty from the slavish fears of death, judgment, and hell. I believe there is no wicked man but what in his own conscience and from his own experience of the bondage of those fears, will own that this is a glorious freedom indeed. What would not some poor miserable creatures give to be delivered from those thoughts about death and hellfire? Every wicked man that enjoys gospel light can't but know the uneasiness of it. How would they leap for joy if they should hear news that hellfire was extinguished and the Day of Judgment was put by and to be omitted! They would doubtless think this to be a glorious thing; they would esteem their freedom from their former fears of hell as a glorious freedom. But yet it is nothing near so glorious as the freedom of the godly, for if the wicked knew they were to be annihilated they would yet be afraid of death. It would be very grievous to them to think that they must live no longer in the world and then be turned to nothing; but the fears of those that serve God are turned into hope. Whereas formerly he used to fear death, he now hopes for it; whereas he used to be dreadfully afraid of the Day of Judgment, it is now become one of the chief objects of his joyful expectations and his soul says, "Even so, come Lord Jesus."

So glorious is the freedom that is enjoyed in God's service: a freedom from the cruel chains of sin and the devil, a perfect freedom from condemnation to eternal punishment, a freedom from the tormenting galls of conscience and twinges of one's own heart—the inward start, dreadful sound, and uneasy internal pain that an accusing conscience gives—a freedom from the restless fears of dying, of being judged and being damned. Thus we have shown what the servants of God enjoy freedom from.

[II.] We are now in the second place come to the positive part of the glorious liberty of those that serve God, to show what they have liberty to do.

True liberty consists in these two things: a liberty to do whatever tends to our own advantage; a liberty to do whatever is for our true pleasure and satisfaction. Now in the service of God, both these kinds of liberty are enjoyed.

First. Those that serve God have the free liberty to do whatever makes for their own profit; by serving of God none are restrained from profiting themselves. While we are busily employed in the service of God, we are not only doing what is well-pleasing to God, but we are doing what is exceeding profiting to ourselves. When a man serves God, he profits not God but himself. That in the twenty-first [chapter] of Job at the fifteenth verse is commonly the language of the hearts of the wicked; 'tis that suggestion of Satan whereby they are kept from the service of God: "What is the Almighty, that we should serve him, and what profit should we have if we pray unto him?" But this is rightly replied to in the next chapter at the second and third verses: "Can a man be profitable unto God as he that is wise may be profitable to himself? Is it any pleasure to the Almighty that thou art righteous, or is it gain to him that thou makest thy ways perfect?"

We can't possibly be so profitable to ourselves any other way as by serving and obeying God. No other exercise in the world is so advantageous, so that the servants of God have the liberty to profit themselves just as much as they please. They are not slaves that are forced to labor only for the advantage of others, but they are the Lord's freemen. The more and the better they serve God, the more they profit themselves, and they may serve God as much as they please: none forbids them. If any man is covetous of profit, let him employ himself very much in heavenly exercises; if any man desires a greater treasure, let him heap up treasure in heaven as fast as he pleases. All the servants of God have this liberty. They have liberty to scrape together as great a heavenly treasure as possibly they can.

There is no service of God, no part of religion, but what is cut out for our own advantage. Self-denial, mortification, prayer, reading and hearing God's Word, meditation, etc. Let no man think that he is in the least restrained from consulting his own profit or advantage because they spend time in those things that otherwise might be improved in getting the world. Alas, do we reckon at this rate? Is that time that is spent for our eternal advantage lost; is the time lost that is spent in laying up treasure in bags that wax not old? How gross and absurd is the mistake of those [who] imagine so. Doubtless more good, more profit may sometimes be gotten by half an hour's exercise in the duties of religion, than in a whole life spent in worldly employments.

We are very apt, when we think we have served God well, to think that he is obliged to us for it, when all the while we have not been doing anything that is of any advantage to him, but only to ourselves. We ought rather at such times humbly to bless and praise God that he has enabled us to serve him so well, and to get so much good thereby to our souls.

Second. In the service of God, there is true liberty to do whatever tends most for our own pleasure. A great and chief argument of Satan to dissuade men from the service of God is that it abridges of all manner of pleasure; it ties one up from seeking our own pleasure, but [we] must be obliged to be mopish and melancholy, and must never more pleasure and divert ourselves.

To this I answer that in the service of God there is full and free liberty to seek as much pleasure as we please, to enjoy the best kind of pleasure in the world, and as much of it as we possibly can obtain with all our might and main. There are no restraints.

Here, perhaps you may object and say how can this be: don't the law of God command us to mortify ourselves and to deny ourselves of sensual pleasures, to take up our cross, to take Christ's yoke upon us; will not allow us the full enjoyment of any worldly pleasure, [and] is not this a restraining of our liberty to?

This I answer. How can that be called an abridging our liberty which only restrains us from those pleasures that in a little time would turn into torments? Only from those that are honey in the mouth but a tormenting poison in the belly. Doth a father or mother abridge the child of liberty because he is not suffered to drink sweet poison? Is the child abridged of liberty because the mother will not suffer it to play with the flame of a candle?

Doth the law of God abridge us of liberty because it will not suffer us to run into hell, because he forbids those lusts that have a seed of hell in them? Are those all the cruel restraints of the service of God, a being restrained from misery? Is it such an unreasonable thing in the law of God that it will not suffer us to be miserable when we desire it? All the liberty that we are denied by God's law is this: he will never grant us liberty by his law to be eternally miserable.

God don't restrain from true pleasure and satisfaction; yea, he obliges us to do that which will bring us to the highest pleasure and the greatest delights. He don't restrain from pleasure in this world; indeed, he restrains us from the beastly pleasure of drunkenness and of fornication: that is, God will not give men liberty to be beasts. But the noblest, the most excellent, the sweetest and most exalted pleasures, we may exercise ourselves in them as much as we please. We may recreate and delight ourselves in those sweet angelical pleasures without any restraint or prohibition. We may refresh ourselves with these delights and none will hinder us: our consciences will not restrain us; God will not hinder us; we may roll ourselves in these pleasures as much as we will. We can never be intemperate in these delights. Other sorts of pleasures have something that checks and hinders them; they affect only the external sense and the mind, the reason, is commonly against them; conscience curbs them so that one can't find an entire satisfaction in them. But in these delights there is no alloy, nothing to restrain, but we have a perfect liberty in the exercise.

Thus we have endeavored briefly to set before you the perfect and glorious liberty of God's service. We proceed to the

IMPROVEMENT.

I. Let sinners take notice that one of their greatest objections against the service of God is taken off: to wit, that it abridges one of his liberty. For we have shown that 'tis the service of Satan wherein is the bondage and servitude, and that there is perfect liberty in the service of God.

Never more make such objections as these:

> If I leave off the ways of sin and enter upon the service of God and become religious, then I must be tied up to strictness and preciseness, must bid adieu to liberty, must see no more good days, shall never more have any such pleasant, merry days and nights as I have had in time past. I must leave my former company that I used to drink and be merry with, and must forever be tied up to self-denial, to chastity and temperance, must deny my senses, must be forced to keep under my body and bring it into subjection, must be forced to fight against my own flesh and blood, must become a melancholy, mopish, dull creature. And instead of drinking, rioting and wantonness, I must be forced to pray and read the Scriptures, and sit sighing and weeping for my sins, and so I must be forced to spend the remainder of my days if I become religious.

Alas, how miserably blind are sinners, to fancy themselves happy when they are serving the devil for the wages of eternal death. They are led like an ox to the slaughter; they are fatted for hell in Satan's pen. They are allured by Satan's bait to be taken by his hook. They think themselves at liberty when they are bondslaves to sin and the devil and are laboring hard, go through many difficulties and dangers. They labor in perpetual fears and stings of conscience, and all to work out their own ruin, all to lay up wrath against the day of wrath; and yet this their miserable state is what they call their liberty, that [which] they so fear being deprived of upon their entrance on a religious course of life. A deliverance from this power of Satan and their lusts, and from the vexatious accusations of conscience and fears of death and hell and condemnation to eternal torments, is the bondage they are afraid of if they enter upon the service of God, although God will give them the liberty of his own children, will give them the glorious freedom, the free exercise of themselves in heavenly, noble and exalted delights and pleasures, the least of which are more eligible than all the satisfactions that are enjoyed in seventy years of a sensual life.

Wherefore, let sinners never more make such foolish objections against the service of God. For you may be assured this day as from God, if you will enter upon his service, he will give the full liberty of doing whatever tends to your own good and advantage, or to your own pleasure. He will [give] you liberty to recreate and delight yourself in the best, the purest and most exquisite pleasures, as much as you please, without any restraint.

II. Let me take occasion from this doctrine to invite all to the service of God. [He] is the best, most kind and gracious master that ever was. To all those that serve him he gives perfect liberty, and more than that, he makes his servants his children: all that serve him, he adopts them and gives them a right to the glorious privileges of the sons of God. He calls them no more servants, but he calls them children; for he manifests himself to them, makes them his intimate friends, his heirs and joint-heirs with his Son. He unbosoms his love to them and embraces them in his arms, and dwells in their souls and makes his abode with them, and gives himself to them to be their father and their portion. They shall not serve him for nothing. In this life he will frequently refresh them with the spiritual dews of heaven, will shine upon them with beams of light and love; but hereafter will make them perfectly happy, and that forevermore. Was there ever so good a master? Is not this better than to serve Satan, to be the devil's drudge, and to be rewarded with nothing but misery at last? Is such a liberty as this far preferable to the devil's dungeon service and slavery? O then, be invited to cast away his chains, throw off his yoke, and resolve to walk at liberty. Arise out of the dark dungeon, shake thyself from the dust, and Christ shall give thee light.

Give me leave here a little to expostulate with you. What do you think of the service of God? What are your intentions about it? Do you intend to serve God or Satan? How do you stand affected to God's service? Speak plainly and fully to your own consciences. If you do not intend to serve God, what are the difficulties you propose to yourself that hinder you from taking Christ's yoke upon you? I suppose they are something of this nature:

First. If you betake yourself to the service of God, you must leave that which you very well love. You love to live as you do now; you love to have the liberty of sinning and of enjoying your sensual appetites sometimes, and it seems very hard to you forever to leave that you love forever. But this is easily answered in one word, by asking again whether you love eternal torments: but except you leave sinning, you cannot avoid misery.

Second. You must betake yourself to that which you hate. You don't find any disposition at all to such employments as those of secret prayer, meditation and the like, but to this I answer: consider whether prayer and meditation would not be easier now than upon a deathbed, when you are under the horrors of immediate misery and ruin.

Third. You don't find strength nor courage enough to set about it; you find a listlessness. Be directed to think frequently of [the] misery of death and eternal judgment, and you will find enough to stir you up.

Let me ask of you a few questions, and let your conscience make the answer.

1. Do you ever intend to serve God at all, or do you intend to serve the devil all your lifetime?

2. When do you intend to serve him: this year or next, in youth or old age? Perhaps you will be in eternity long before that time comes.

3. How do you intend to go about it? Do you intend to break off all your sins by righteousness, or do you intend to retain some and to serve God and mammon both together?

4. Consider how long do you expect to live. Do you depend upon living four-score years in the world or no?

5. Suppose death should overtake you before you are aware: what would you do?

6. Has your mind never changed? Perhaps you intend to begin to serve God the next year, but how do you know your mind will not change by that time?

Thus consider well your ways, and there is no doubt but you will turn your feet into God's testimonies.

TRUE LOVE TO GOD

ONE of the "sweeter" sermons written by Edwards during his New York pastorate is "True Love to God." Now lacking several paragraphs at the opening and conclusion, it is nevertheless a moving and virtually complete meditation upon the nature of Christian love. Edwards' presentation of this love as an experience rather than an abstract principle or theological proposition is probably responsible for much of the seeming mysticism of several passages. Perhaps the heart of the sermon is contained in that passage from the first subhead under the second proposition of the Doctrine which insists that a lively faith "lifts our minds above the earth and carries out the soul to a delightful prospect of the glorious mysteries and wonders of the heavenly world . . . is itself a prospect . . . for faith is the substance of things not seen" (pp. 638–39). The suggestion of a sensuous and immediate apprehension of the divine through faith tinctures the entire discourse and is an essential dimension of that concept of love which Edwards propounds. That persons can have no adequate idea of this concept until they have experienced it is presumed by Edwards, although his discourse is clearly intended at least to *locate* true love to God in relation to the spectrum of normal human experience.

The duties required are essentially acts: mental acts and physical acts. Through them man realizes his faith, his experience of divine things, and achieves both a personal ethical code and an aesthetic taste which in turn predicate all other acts. The result is a new life which is described as essentially "pleasant" or peacefully exalted. Edwards argues throughout the sermon for a willingness to accept the possibility of experiences beyond the ordinary range which can be named, but only suggestively defined. As in his apostrophe to Sarah Pierrepont, the image of the holy life is here one of some isolation and strangeness when defined in contrast to the conventional life; however, Edwards stresses that ordinary human nature nevertheless prospers when guided by the spirit of holy love, and suffers and languishes when driven by lust, guilt, and regret. Here again, as in "Christian Liberty," Edwards insists upon the profound misapprehension of those who assume that the spiritual duties of the Christian are in any way to be associated with melancholy or mere asceticism.

While the language of this sermon is not remarkable for its imagery or brilliance, it is nevertheless interesting for the persistent attempts Edwards makes to render concretely yet comprehensively the most ineffable aspects of man's relation to God. In simple and unpretentious analogies, such as that which defines the Christian life in terms of a series of transcripts, involving both God and the saint in the act of transcription, from divine heart to Word to human heart to deed, Edwards finds rational and sometimes poetic vehicles for his thought. This concreteness may be the most remarkable stylistic dimension of the sermon, and it is this general quality, as well as the presence of some notable parallels in phrase and imagery, that most suggests a relatedness between the sermon and the apostrophe to Sarah Pierrepont.

In the final analysis, Edwards offers in this sermon not merely a defense of the life of Christian love, but a test of the religious life, as he suggests in the last extant paragraph of the original sermon.

*　*　*

The manuscript of this sermon is fairly typical of the octavo quire booklets and has little significant revision. At some point the center stitching was removed from the booklet and the outside double leaf of the manuscript lost. There is no evidence that Edwards was responsible for the cutting of the binding threads, though the discolored outside pages of the extant manuscript indicate that the booklet has been disbound for many years. Whenever it occurred, the removal of the leaves was probably accidental since the two-leaf unit would not have been part of a likely revision of the sermon, involving the first and last leaves of the text and thus unrelated passages. Moreover, there are none of the usual shorthand notes, key signs, or evidences of pins or second stitchings normally present in cases of revision involving page substitution. Thus the six-leaf sermon booklet is technically a fragment, damaged at both ends by the loss of a single sheet, illustrating again the problem of the infolded quire.

Although the manuscript contains no notations concerning repreachings—and they probably would have been recorded on the missing front page in any case—there are three different inks in the manuscript, suggesting that it was repreached at least twice. Certainly it is a carefully wrought sermon with a nice balance of major heads in the Doctrine and Application divisions. It is curious that the final major head, the exhortation, was apparently not written out until the second preaching of the sermon, although the heading itself is original.

TRUE LOVE TO GOD

[I JOHN 5:3.]

[For this is the love of God, that we keep his commandments: and his commandments are not grievous.][1]

THE love of God in our text is described by the two genuine effects of it:

1. The observation of God's commands, "For this is the love of God, that we keep his commandments." This is very frequently given in Scripture as a most certain proof of sincerity, as in the second chapter of this epistle at the third [through] fifth verses: "And hereby we do know that we know him, if we keep his commandments. He that saith, I know him, and keepeth not his commandments is a liar, and the truth is not in him; but whoso keepeth his word, in him verily is the love of God perfected: hereby know we that we are in him." This Christ himself while on earth gave as a certain characteristic of love to him: "He that hath my commandments, and doth them, he it is that loveth me" (John 14:21).

2. The second effect of true love to God is that it makes God's commands not to seem grievous to us. There is a vast difference between that partial obedience of hypocrites and wicked men, and the sincere obedience of true lovers of God. The one goes about his duty as some hard piece of slavery that he is driven to by the twinges of his conscience and the dreadful threatenings of the law, as a thing that is directly against his nature. He acts like one quite out of his element.

But the other sincerely sets about it as what his natural bias inclines him to: of choice and what he delights in, is lively and active therein,

---

1. The missing first leaf of this sermon contained the statement of text and the first portion of textual exegesis. The extant manuscript begins with the following sentence fragment: "-vation of God's commands as an evidence of the second." The edited text immediately follows the fragment as a new paragraph.

is ready at it as one that is taught of God, as this business he chiefly delights in, not so strangely and awkwardly as the wicked but as one that finds that he breathes in an air suitable to his nature. 'Tis this last effect of true love to God that we have chosen to insist upon at this time and to speak from this doctrine implied in the words.

DOCTRINE.

True love to God makes the duties he requires of us easy and delightful.

There is no need of giving any particular description of true love to [God], for this is the very design of the text, is done in the doctrine, and is also our whole business in this discourse from it: to describe the true love of God by the effects of it by which it is best known. Wherefore, we shall explain the doctrine in the three following methods:

I. Why the love of God makes duty easy and pleasant.

II. Show how the particular duties required of God are made easy and pleasant by it.

III. What are those pleasures a true lover of God experiences in the way of his duty.

I. Why the love of God makes duty easy and pleasant. It is for these five reasons:

First. It mortifies that which is the only thing that makes duty uneasy, even our natural depravity and enmity against God. What God requires of us in itself has no manner of difficulty in it but is perfectly easy. If it weren't for our natural enmity to God and aversion to holiness, all the laws of God would be performed as easily as the sun shines or as a river glides down between its banks, with the same ease as we draw our breath when in a sweet sleep.

We should indeed be active, vigorous and lively, and so are the rays of the sun; but it would only be that activeness that would be altogether natural to us. Now indeed we must labor, but what is it we labor at? 'Tis to fight against our corruptions, and that is all, but then we should have no corruptions to fight against.

God don't require of us anything that, of itself,[2] has any pain or labor. 'Tis only to come and take of the water of life freely; 'tis only to be willing—heartily willing—to be made truly happy with a holy and heavenly happiness, merely to rise up and open the doors of our

2. MS: "his self."

souls to Jesus Christ. This is the sum of all that is required of [us]; this is that which seems so exceeding difficult to natural [men]; this is that which millions go to hell rather than perform. Not that there is the least real difficulty in these things as they are in themselves: no more difficulty than it is for a beggar, when he has treasure offered him, to reach out his hand and take it; but yet this beggar if he had a great enmity and hatred to the giver might plead that it is exceeding difficult—with as much reason as the natural man can plead the difficulty of religion.

But now the love of God removes this obstacle, for most certainly the love of God and the hatred of God cannot be predominant in the same heart. Christ Jesus in regeneration gives the body of sin, or the enmity to God, such a blow on the head as he never recovers, but lies dying by degrees till he quite expires.

There are indeed remainders of corruption in the best while in this tabernacle, but the contrary principle predominates and consequently the pleasantness that a godly man experiences must predominate over and be greater than the difficulty.

Second. The true lover of God is supplied with the strength of Christ to enable [him] with ease and pleasure to perform his duty. So weak are we, especially since the Fall, that we can do nothing by our own strength without the strength of Jesus Christ. We should be far from running the Christian race and warring the Christian warfare with ease and delight, if it were not for the strength that he affords. Christ leads them by the hand, and that is the reason they run with such delight; whereas if he should leave them, instead of running they would immediately fall and lie helpless like a weak infant.

Third. The third reason why the love of God makes duty easy and pleasant is because, by obeying God's commands, they do what is well-pleasing to him they love. All the pleasure of love consists in pleasing the person beloved.[3] 'Tis the nature of love to rouse and stir to an earnest desire to please, and certainly it must be a great pleasure to have earnest desires satisfied. Now the love of God causes those in whose heart it is implanted more earnestly to desire to please God than anything in the world, causes them heartily to embrace opportunities of pleasing him and sweetly to reflect on it when he knows they have pleased him.

---

3. At first JE wrote "consists in pleasing and enjoying the person beloved," but he deleted "and enjoying" during the period of the sermon's composition.

Love makes all difficulties vanish and mountains to be made plain when they stand in the way of pleasing or enjoying the person beloved. Thus the love that Jacob had to Rachel made the seven years that he served for her seem but a few days (Gen. 29:20); so the free love of God causes the mortification and self-denial [to] seem easy and pleasant when they stand in [the] way of duty, of pleasing and enjoying God.

Fourth. Because thereby they advance God's honor. Love necessarily causes us to desire the honor of those we love and to delight in honoring them and to rejoice when they are honored, especially when we ourselves are the means of it.[4]

Fifth. The fifth and last reason why love to God makes duty easy and pleasant is because thereby they become like God. This is another effect of love, to cause the lover to delight to see the perfections of the person beloved imitated in himself and in his own actions, and especially is the love of God of this nature. The soul, having had a discovery of the glories of God made to it and being ravished thereby, is transformed into the same image from glory to glory, so that he may see the image of those beloved beauties and excellencies reflected on himself. This must needs be very delighting to the sanctified soul and must cause him to delight to act holily as he acts, and to conform his life to the Word of God and his holy commands which are but a transcript of the holiness of God's nature, and again to transcribe this transcript into his own heart and from his heart into his life. Thus we have given the reasons why the love of God makes duty easy and pleasant. We proceed in the next place to show how.

II. [Second] place, to show how the particular duties required by God are easy to them that love God. Here we cannot stand to insist at large on all the many duties of Christianity, but

First. The internal duties which God requires are easy and pleasant to those that love God. For love to God itself is a fountain from whence flow all the other internal duties and graces, and when this grace is obtained, all the others—repentance, resignation and humiliation, hope, charity, etc., and the exercise of these in meditation— follow naturally and easily of themselves.

How pleasant must a lively faith needs be which lifts our minds

---

4. JE left about a fifth of the next page blank following this point for further development of the head.

above the earth and carries out the soul to a delightful prospect of the glorious mysteries and wonders of the heavenly world; gives one a prospect, or rather is itself a prospect, of the glories of the great Creator of all things, the beauties of his lovely Son, and a view of the glories of the heavenly Jerusalem. It is like that high mountain in the Revelation from whence the angel showed the apostle John that great city, the holy Jerusalem, descending out of heaven from God, having the glory of God and his light like a stone most precious, like a jasper stone clear as crystal. How pleasant must that be which makes the glories of heaven in some measure present, for faith is the substance of things not seen.

How easy must it be to be resigned to the will of God. This duty frees us from all manner of uneasiness: the meaning of resignation is to be free from uneasiness, from the apprehension of God's goodness and faithfulness hoping therein; and so indeed all the internal duties of love, resignation, faith, hope, charity, etc. are nothing but to be easy, calm, serene, pleasant, and happy.

Yea, even the duties of repentance and mortification, as a certain author[5] expresses it, are a very Canaan.[6]

Second. The external duties of religion are made easy and pleasant by true love to God. Duties towards God, such as prayer, singing God's praises, hearing the Word and the like, are his delight. How doth the wicked man hate to come into God's presence, especially in secret, closet prayer, which is so great a duty of a Christian; with how little taste and relish doth he hear the Word of God, and when shall we ever hear them speaking of heavenly things? But it is far otherwise with him that truly loves God; he is never so well pleased as when his heart is engaged in such duties.

He delights also in duties that more immediately respect himself: in external acts of temperance, patience and self-denial; as likewise those that respect his neighbor, such as justice, brotherly kindness, charity, meekness and condescension, beneficence and hospitality. He delights to follow the example of Jesus Christ and to take his yoke upon him, which is easy, and his burden which is light.

---

5. In later ink JE replaced "a certain author" with "one."

6. In a later addition JE illustrated this point: "There is the same sort of pleasure in repentance, only vastly higher and more excellent, as there is in a condemned criminal that confesses and is pardoned, and the same sort of pleasure in mortification as there is in a conqueror after a hot engagement."

III. We are now come in the third place to show what are the particular kinds of pleasure that those that love God experience in doing their duty. Here we shall speak only of the spiritual pleasures, for there are even greater temporal pleasures may be enjoyed in a godly life than in a wicked one. Let sinful pleasures be all killed and removed, and these lawful pleasures that remain give a sweeter relish of life than all the pleasures of those that give themselves up to sense and the enjoyments of it. Satan's yoke is a most cruel, iron yoke. The torments of wickedness, even in this life, are far greater than the pleasures of it, and vastly outweigh the mortification of [the] cutting off of a right hand and plucking out a right eye, which the Gospel requires of us; but however, temporal things are counted as loss and dung in comparison of the excellency of Christ Jesus and the spiritual pleasures they experience, of which I shall speak at this time. Which pleasures are very many as well as exceeding great, but are all implied under these three heads: peace of conscience, and the pleasure of communion with God, and a joyful hope of glory.

First. He that loves God in the way of his commands experiences peace of conscience from the apprehension of the pardon of his sins and the imputation of Christ's righteousness. The mind of a wicked man is bitterly tormented even in this life with the accusations of conscience; he travels in pain all his days, a dreadful sound is in his ears. But he that loves God hears that same person that stilled the winds and sea with his almighty power, crying, "Peace, be still," speaking peace also to his soul. So that that soul which before was as the sea[7] troubled, continually casting forth mire and dirt, is now filled with a divine tranquility and a heavenly calm and serenity, is filled with that peace of God which passes all understanding, [which] is never experienced by wicked men, nor cannot be conceived of by any but those that do experience it.

Second. A true lover of God experiences the pleasures of communion with God. This is the highest kind of pleasure that can possibly be enjoyed by a creature. Angels have no more exalted sort of pleasure than this, and if God should create a sort of beings a thousand times more perfect than they, they would not be capable of a better kind of delight; for what can be more delightful than to converse with the excellent and glorious Creator of all things, to express love to and

---

7. "The sea" is a conjectural reading; "to be" is also a possibility.

mutually to receive expressions of love from, the great Jehovah? But those that love God experience such pleasures as these. The Almighty condescends to maintain a correspondence and intercourse with such as love [him]. They sweetly feel the heavenly influences of his Holy Spirit descending on them like refreshing beams of the sun and like a breeze of wind that causes their spices to flow out, which fill their souls, the garden of Christ, with a sweet fragrancy, sweet to themselves and sweet to God himself.

Third. He that has true love to God experiences in the way of his duty a joyful hope of eternal glory, that sense of a quiet conscience, and the pleasures of society with the King of Kings. [The experiences] that are enjoyed here are only some foretastes in this dry and barren wilderness of those fruits that grow in the greatest plenty and fullness in the heavenly Canaan which they hope for: what they have here are as pledges of what is to come.

God only hereby gives them a taste of what they may expect he of his mercy will bestow on them. God at some seasons calls them up as it were into the mountain, Abarim, to behold and have a distant prospect of the good land they are traveling to.

APPLICATION.

I. Hence we learn the great mistake of those who judge religion to be an exceeding difficult, uneasy and melancholy thing. Multitudes take up a notion that religion is an exceeding hard, difficult thing: if once they embrace religion, they must expect to see no more good days, must depend upon living mournfully, sorrowfully, the remaining part of their days.

But they are those only that have never had experience of religion. They certainly are not fit judges of religion that know nothing about it, that are utter strangers to it, that give their judgments of religion merely at random, without reason or experience. All they that have been acquainted of religion have found the pleasures of it to be greater and better than any sensual delights. They are certainly the fittest judges that have tried both, and never any have declared the contrary but those that have tried but one sort. Never any have accused religion of being bitter but those that have never tasted.

The reason why they take the precepts of religion to be heavy and exceeding burdensome is because they find in themselves a great contrariety and aversion to it; [it] is directly contrary to their sin and corruption; but if ever the love of God, the contrary principle, is infused into their souls by the Spirit of God, their corruption will be mortified and the difficulty ceases with it.

One great reason why religion is judged to be melancholy is because it has no tendency to raise laughter, but rather to remove it; but that is no argument against the pleasantness of religion, for the pleasure that raises laughter is never great, is only flashy and external. This everyone knows by experience. Even the greater sort of worldly pleasures themselves don't raise laughter. The pleasures of religion raise one clear above laughter and rather tend to make the face shine than screw it into a grimace. Indeed, the pleasures of religion when in their height do cause there to be a sweet, inexpressibly joyful smile in the countenance, and the reason why religion is not always attended with such a smile is because we have so many sins to lament and be sorry for, but repentance itself is attended with pleasure as we have shown.

II. Use is of trial. This doctrine gives us occasion and directs us how to examine and try our state. If it be so that it [is] always the effect of love to God that his commands are not grievous, then if we would know whether we truly love God or no, we must examine whether God's commands are pleasant or grievous to us. Do we set about religion as a hard task or as our delight and pleasure? Is corruption so far killed in us that we can obey the commands of God with pleasure? Christ said it was his meat to do the will of his Father. It is our meat too, if we have any true love to God in our hearts. Let everyone ask himself in which doth he place most delight, or which doth he set most by, the pleasures of religion or some sensual sort of pleasure? For if we set more by anything, whether it be eating or drinking, or earthly possessions, or the conversation of friends, or anything else than by religion, by communion, praying, holy meditation, reading or hearing God's Word, we have not the love of God in our hearts. Wherefore, let everyone be critical in examining himself in this matter.

Is it easy and pleasant to you to do the commands of God because thereby you do what is well-pleasing to him? Is it your delight to perform what God has commanded because you thereby honor him, and act like and are conformed to him?

If you truly experience these things in you, verily is the love of

God perfected; but if not, you are in the gall of bitterness and the bond of iniquity.

[III.] Of exhortation.[8]

8. The head was not developed beyond this heading in the original sermon. It may have been preached *extempore* or from a separate paper; however, for a subsequent preaching JE wrote in the head. Since the last leaf of the sermon is missing, we have only a portion of the later exhortation:

> To all to seek after and strive for the love of God. So great are the advantages of it, seek it for your own comfort and ease. Your work that you have to do will be abundantly the easier for it. God has appointed us our work; 'tis to keep all such and such commandments which he has given us. 'Tis a work that must be done or else we shall offend our God and endanger our own souls and make ourselves liable to eternal damnation. And if we would make it easy we must strive for love to God. There is nothing else that will make the yoke of Christ easy and his burden light but this alone.
>
> Indeed, the commands of God to our corrupt nature, they are exceeding heavy and burdensome. What will not men that are destitute of love to God rather do than keep God's commandment? Duties will seem like [. . .]

Sᴇʀᴍᴏɴꜱ are assigned approximate dates of composition. Within period groups, sermons are listed in canonical order; thus sermon numbers do not reflect order of composition within groups.

Fall 1720–Winter 1721
1. (Is. 3:10) Christian Happiness

Summer 1721–Summer 1722
2. (Matt. 16:26) The Value of Salvation
3. (John 8:34) Wicked Men's Slavery to Sin
4. (Heb. 9:27) The Importance of a Future State
5. Fragment: From an Application on Seeking God

Summer 1722
6. (Zech. 4:7) Glorious Grace

Summer 1722–Spring 1723
7. (Job 1:21) The Nakedness of Job
8. (Ps. 89:6) God's Excellencies
9. (Ps. 95:7–8) The Duty of Hearkening to God's Voice
10. (Prov. 29:25) Christian Safety
11. (Is. 35:8) The Way of Holiness
12. (Hag. 1:5) The Duty of Self-Examination
13. (Matt. 5:3 [a]) Poverty of Spirit
14. (Luke 13:5) True Repentance Required
15. (John 6:68) Life through Christ Alone
16. (John 8:12 [a]) Christ, the Light of the World
17. (Rom. 12:1) Dedication to God
18. (Phil. 1:21 [a]) Living to Christ
19. (Phil. 1:21 [b]) Dying to Gain
20. (Heb. 9:12) Christ's Sacrifice
21. (Jas. 1:12 [a]) Fragment: Application on Love to Christ
22. (Jas. 1:25) Christian Liberty
23. (I John 5:3) True Love to God
24. (Matt. 21:5) Fragment (see no. 49 in a later sermon volume)

GENERAL INDEX

Friends: enjoyment of, compared with enjoyment of God, 319, 321, 428–30; seeking for friendship of those with power, 431; loss of, at death, 583–84; of Christ, 622

Funeral sermon for his daughter, Jerusha, 133

Future and eternal state. *See* Eternity; Heaven; Hell; Judgment; Salvation

Future Punishment of the Wicked Unavoidable and Intolerable, The, 168

Ghost, Holy. *See* Holy Spirit

"Glorious Grace": literary techniques in, 237–38, 388–89; themes of, 286–87, 388; Application of, 388, 396–99; commentary on, 388–89; text of, 388–99; revisions of, 389; sermon booklet of, 389; Scripture text of, 390–91; Doctrine of, 391–96; dating of, 645

God: communication of, 6, 7, 326–27; humans' deification through union with, 7; personal perception of, 7–8; and Redemption, 81–83; sun as image of, 222–23; sovereignty in doing whatever He pleases, 238; freedom of, 245; as light, 287 n., 535–36; dealings with humans as reasonable beings, 296; as Judge, 296–97, 358, 364–67, 435, 474–75; as father, 297, 299–300, 435, 462–64, 499; protection of people, 301, 457–60; desire for humans' happiness, 303–04; happiness in, 305, 428–30; place of man as ruler of beasts, 306; Beatific Vision of, in heaven, 324, 331; enjoyment and glorification of, 325, 359, 427; creation of world, 326; value of soul to, 326–28; help needed for salvation, 332; variable providence of, 334; love of, 344, 455–56, 488, 513–14, 632–43 and n.; laughter at and mocking of sinners, 348; creation of humans for higher end, 358–59; on future and eternal state, 360–61; human compared with divine judgment, 364–67; and pardon, 366; lack of thought about, 370–71; and disobedience, 373; as jealous, 373; and deathbed faith and repentance, 373–74; removal of impediments in seeking, 379–80; hatred of sin, 379–80, 426; seeking of, 379–87; making inquiry after, 380–81; ordinances of, 381; prayer as method for seeking, 381; as eternal deliverance from all afflictions, 382–83; motivations in seeking, 382–86; and those who have not found yet, 382–86; goodness of, 383, 424–25; as happiness, 383–84, 417, 554–55; consequences of seeking other things and neglecting, 385–86; reaction to Jews'

offerings and sacrifices, 386–87; having no need for humans, 392–93; grace of, in redemption, 392–95; and Christ, 393–95, 542–43; praise for, 399; as source of all that humans have, 405; divine attributes of, 413, 415–35; incomparable nature of, 416; importance of understanding what is worshipped, 416–17; greatness of, 416–17, 419–20; as ancient of all creatures, 418–19; as having no beginning, 418–19; excellency and loveliness of, 420–21; power of, 421–22; wisdom of, 422–23; holiness of, 423–24, 473–74, 475, 477; anger of, 426–27, 432, 434–35, 439, 442, 447–48, 524; taking upon Himself human form, 427; compared with base and abominable gods, 428; privilege of humans in worship of true, 428; importance of seeking the favor of, 430–34; mercy of, 432–34, 440, 445–46, 455, 464, 514, 556; as terror of wicked, 434–35; as King of Kings, 435; hearkening to voice of, 436–37, 440–43; as rock of salvation, 438–39; as shepherd, 439; contempt for, 442–43; trust in, 451–64, 560–61; false hope in, 454–55; all-sufficiency of, 455; humans' need of, 455; truth and faithfulness of, 455; hope in, 456; holiness as conformity of life and heart to, 471–72; law given to Moses by, 495–96; and the poor of spirit, 497–98, 500–02; fear of, 499; dedication to, 547–62; embracing all of God's commands, 555; resignation to will of, 555, 639; children of, 621–22, 630; profit in service to, 626–27; pleasure in service to, 627–29; invitation to service of, 630–31; keeping commandments of, 635; obedience to, 635–36; duty to, as easy and pleasant, 636–38; peace of, 640; communion with, 640–41. *See also* Christ; Holy Spirit

God Glorified in the Work of Redemption: reputation of, 108; revisions for publication, 108–11, 115; revision for repreaching of, 148–52, 150 n.; delivery in Boston, 152 and n.; compared with "Glorious Grace," 287, 388

Gods, false, 428

"God's Excellencies": theme of, 286, 413; commentary on, 413–14; repreaching of, 413–14; formal structure of, 414; sermon booklet of, 414; Scripture text of, 415–16; text of, 415–35; Doctrine of, 416–25; Application of, 425–35; recapitulation of, 425 n.; dating of, 645

Goliath, 219

Goodness: and happiness, 239–40; of kings, 424; of God, 424–25. *See also* Holiness

Schafer, Thomas A., 43 n., 112 n., 130 n., 266 n., 645
Scriptures: covenant in Gospel, compared with old Hebrew Law, 7–8; Mather on style of, 19–20; use of texts at beginning of sermons, 37, 207–09; substantive notebooks on, 46–51; relation of classical and pagan myth with, 48; translation problems of, 48; JE's priority on reading, 53, 55, 71; JE's favorite sermon texts, 132; JE's stylistic use of biblical text, 207–13; used in fabric or verbal contexture of sermons, 210–13; metaphors in, 224–26; dealings with humans as reasonable beings, 296; availability with, 331, 367; use in proof of eternity, 360–64; questioning of truths of, 368; and making inquiry after God, 380–81; God's voice in, 441; and self-examination, 477; as word of Christ, 477, 526; importance of, in Christian life, 576
Self, death of, 567, 568–69. *See also* Humans
Self-dedication: Scripture text on, 551–52; necessity of, 552–53; and renunciation of flesh, world, and the devil, 553–54; description of, 553–55; and resignation to will of God, 554–55; as embracing all God's commands, 555; reasonableness of, 555–57; motives for, 557–59; directions for, 559–62; negative examples of, 560–62
Self-examination: concerning holiness, 477–78; duty of, 480–92; beasts' lack of, 482; Scripture texts on, 482–84; of what human ways ought to be, 484–89; of thoughts, 486–87; of words, 487; of actions, 487–88; neglect of, 489; and worldly dangers, 489–90; motives for, 489–91; necessary for changes in life, 490–91; directions for, 491–92; frequency of, 491–92; on love of God, 642–43
Self-indulgence, 618
Sermon, formal theory of: studies of the art of preaching, 10; inherited sermon form, 11, 27–36, 121; basic divisions of the sermon, 11, 28–32, 32 n., 36–41, 121; question-answer head, 12–13; Stoddard's style, 12–15; "plain style" of, 12–15, 23 n.; rhetorical repetition, 13–14; Puritan sermon form, 20; structure, 27–36; compared with lecture, 36; JE's sermon form, 36–41; Opening of the Text, 37; Scripture passage as beginning, 37; observations in, 38 and n.; propositions and, 38 and n.; fixed form of sermon, 167–68
Sermon booklets: from Stockbridge ministry, 66 n.; octavo, 91–92, 125–26, 127, 156; formats of, 91–96, 103–04; duode-

cimo, 94, 96, 101, 127; flexibility in format of, 94, 102, 103, 104–05, 130 n.; sample pages, 95; preaching units marked in, 103; "gathering" technique for, 104–05, 120; notes on sermons rather than sermon notes, 123–24, 134; "production record" for each sermon, 139–40, 139 n.; shorthand in, 139–40, 139 n.; signs indicating repreachings, 142; cannibalism of, for repreachings, 160–61; blocked-out sections in, 452, 606–07; brackets in, 607. *See also names of specific sermons*
Sermon canon: dating of, 52 n., 645; number of JE's sermons, 130–31, 130 n.; Schafer index to, 130 n.; cataloging and indexing of, 130 n., 136; Pratt index to, 130 n., 136; chronological periods of, 131; manuscript versus printed sermons, 131–35; favorite texts, 132; diversity of subject matter and stylistic treatment in, 132–34; "mystical" sermons, 134; "occasional" nature of sermons, 134, 138–39, 138 n.; selection of sermons for publication, 134–135, 140 n.; varieties of sermons, 135–40; JE's devices of reference and classification of, 136–40; labeling of, 137–38; repreaching of sermons, 140–63; from sermon to treatise, 163–67; signs used to organize sermons for special purposes, 166–67, 166 n.; literary development in, 167–79. *See also names of specific sermons*
Sermon composition: use of biblical text at beginning of sermons, 37, 207–09; during mastery period (*1727–42*), 41, 93–119; directed by sermon notebooks, 52; origin of sermon in the notebooks, 74–80; apparatus of, 74–90; changing techniques of, 90–129; outlines of sermons, 91–92; during apprenticeship period (*1722–27*), 91–93; aid to pulpit delivery, 96; juxtaposition of opposites in, 96–97, 113–14, 132–33; abbreviations in, 97, 119; syntactical compression in, 97, 119; outlining, 97–99, 102, 121–22, 128–29; subheads and minor heads in, 99; use of colloquialisms in, 99–100; simplicity in, 99–100; revisions during, 99–101, 105–06; avoidance of overuse of alliteration and rhythmic repetition, 100; "keying" passages, 100–01; "blocked out" structure in, 102, 105–06; complexity in, 103–04; "pick up line" marked in, 107; schedule of, 107 n.; preparation of sermons for publication, 108–15; question-and-answer technique, 109–10; JE's involvement in printing of sermons, 115–19; double columns in, 119, 120–21; in Northampton

INDEX OF BIBLICAL PASSAGES

665

NEW TESTAMENT